OPERATIONS STRATEGY:
TEXT AND CASES

David A. Garvin
Harvard Business School

Prentice Hall, Englewood Cliffs, NJ 07632

Library of Congress Cataloging-in-Publication Data

GARVIN, DAVID A.
   Operations strategy : text and cases / David A. Garvin.

   Includes bibliographical references and index.
   ISBN 0-13-638917-1
   1. Production management.   2. Strategic planning.   I. Title.
TS155.G348   1992   91-24116
658.5—dc20   CIP

Acquisition Editor: *Valerie Ashton*
Freelance Coordinator: *Patrick Reynolds*
Production: *Pencil Point Studio*
Designer: *Lorraine Mullaney, Pencil Point Studio*
Cover Designer: *Bruce Kenselaar*
Prepress Buyer: *Trudy Pisciotti*
Manufacturing Buyer: *Robert Anderson*
Supplements Editor: *David Scholder*
Editorial Assistant: *Reneé Pelletier*
Cover Designer: *Bruce Kenselaar*
Cover Art: *OUVERTURE,* © *Studio Walter Benjamin,*
   Turino Italy; courtesy of Silvio Zamorani editor,
   Italy.

 © 1992 by Prentice-Hall, Inc.
A Simon & Schuster Company
Englewood Cliffs, New Jersey 07632

Printed in the United States of America

10 9 8 7 6 5 4 3 2 1

ISBN 0-13-638917-1

Prentice-Hall International (UK) Limited, *London*
Prentice-Hall of Australia Pty. Limited, *Sydney*
Prentice-Hall Canada Inc., *Toronto*
Prentice-Hall Hispanoamericana, S.A., *Mexico*
Prentice-Hall of India Private Limited, *New Delhi*
Prentice-Hall of Japan, Inc., *Tokyo*
Simon & Schuster Asia Pte. Ltd., *Singapore*
Editora Prentice-Hall do Brasil, Ltda., *Rio de Janeiro*

To Lynn, Diana, and Cynthia

Contents

Acknowledgements

A casebook is a bit like a jigsaw puzzle. There are a large number of odd-shaped pieces, and sometimes it is difficult to see how each relates to the whole. But when every piece is finally in place, the resulting picture is clear and complete.

In assembling this particular jigsaw puzzle, I had a great deal of help. My colleagues in Harvard's production and operations management area assisted by providing company contacts, commenting on work in progress, and lending teaching suggestions. Several also contributed cases, notes, and teaching notes. I would like to thank Robert Hayes for permission to use Indalex, Ltd., Chandler Home Products (B), Intercon International (B), The Roles and Responsibilities of the Corporate Manufacturing Staff, Sanyo Manufacturing Corporation: Forrest City, Arkansas, and A Day at Midwest Equipment Corporation; Steven Wheelwright for FMC Crane and Excavator Division and teaching note, Signetics Corporation: Implementing a Quality Improvement Program, and Lehrer McGovern Bovis, Inc. teaching note; Kim Clark for Corning Glass Works: The Z-Glass Project and teaching note; Wickham Skinner for North American Rockwell Draper Division; Richard Olsen for North American Rockwell Draper Division teaching note; and William Abernathy for Project Nantucket and teaching note. I would also like to thank the *Harvard Business Review* for permission to reprint articles written by Robert Hayes, Steven Wheelwright, Kim Clark, Wickham Skinner, Roger Schmenner, and me. All of us owe a special debt to the managers who agreed to allow case studies and articles to be written about their companies and who contributed by providing data, participating in interviews, and reviewing drafts for accuracy.

The bulk of this book was written during a six year span, while my research associates and I were supported by funds from Harvard Business School's Division of Research. I would like to thank my three research directors—E. Raymond Corey, Benson Shapiro, and Warren McFarlan—for their encouragement and support during the book's long gestation period. My research associates also contributed enormously to the project, and deserve special thanks. Artemis March, Janet Simpson, and Norman Klein played many roles. At various times they were writers, editors, proofreaders, interviewers, and researchers. Yet whatever the activity, their work was impressive and of the highest quality.

The cases in this book were originally developed for Operations Strategy, a new second-year MBA elective at Harvard Business School. The course proved to be an invaluable testing ground, largely because my students were so bright, motivated, and insightful. Several cases and notes were revised to reflect their suggestions, and many of the teaching notes contain ideas that first came to light in class discussion. I am grateful to my students for teaching me so much.

My editor, Valerie Ashton, has been a spirited and dedicated champion; she believed in this book from the beginning and contributed to it in countless ways. I have greatly enjoyed working with her on the project. The staff of the Word Processing

Center typed—and retyped—many of the cases and notes with skill and good humor. My secretaries, Betsy Barker and Andrea Truax, handled the balance with equal grace.

Finally, I would like to thank my wife, Lynn, and daughters, Diana and Cynthia, for all they have done to make this book possible. Support on the home front is vital for any long-term project, and *Operations Strategy* was no exception. Lynn, Diana, and Cynthia were a never-ending source of love and enthusiasm; with their help, the pieces of the jigsaw puzzle finally came together. I take great joy in dedicating this book to my three special ladies.

Acknowledgements

Introduction

Operations Strategy (OS) examines the use of manufacturing and operations as competitive weapons. Traditionally, decisions in these areas have been made on narrow, tactical grounds, with little attention to strategy. They have usually been the province of functional specialists. Yet such issues as the choice between large and small plants, the degree of vertical integration, the selection of process technology, and the proper approach to quality and productivity have important strategic implications. All are closely tied to the interests of top managers.

For many years, these strategic impacts were ignored. Few companies regarded manufacturing as a source of competitive advantage. Its usual role was reactive and passive; its usual goals were cost reduction and improved labor utilization. Avoiding problems was a primary concern. In such environments, the prevailing wisdom was best reflected by the phrase, "Everything is going well in manufacturing when we don't hear any complaints about it."

A new perspective began to emerge in the 1970s and 1980s. It was sparked by global competitors who entered and then dominated a wide range of American industries. Japanese firms made especially deep inroads; because their success was frequently attributed to skillful operations and manufacturing, the topic took on increased importance. Quality, productivity, and new product and process development received special attention. To their surprise, American managers frequently found themselves to be far behind. A 1980 study, for example, found vast disparities in the failure rates (reliability) of American and Japanese semiconductors; similar results were later reported for automobiles, air conditioners, and color televisions.[1] In the 1960s and 1970s, Japan's labor productivity increased at a rate three to four times faster than that of the United States[2]. And new product introductions often took considerably less time in Japan, while still avoiding the start-up problems so typical of American manufacturers.[3]

To many observers, these findings were ominous. They suggested that if American companies hoped to remain competitive, they needed a new approach to operations. Manufacturing had to become a competitive asset, linked closely to overall strategy, rather than a corporate millstone. It had to become proactive and responsive. According to one study at the time:

> The industrial landscape in America is littered with the remains of once-successful companies that could not adapt their strategic vision to altered conditions of competition . . . managers must recognize that they have entered a period of competition that requires of them a technology-driven strategy, a mastery of efficient production, and an unprecedented capacity for work force management. They cannot simply copy what others do but must find their own way.[4]

Such themes form the core of Operations Strategy. They suggest a number of questions that are woven throughout the course: How can American managers best respond to global competition? What are the links between manufacturing and competitive success? How does a company ensure superior quality, productivity, and new product and process development? How should operations strategies be modified as environments and competitive conditions change?

To address these questions, OS operates on two levels. It offers both perspective and tools: a way of thinking about manufacturing problems as well as a set of concepts and techniques. Perspective comes from placing manufacturing decisions in a larger context and evaluating them against strategic imperatives. In OS, students are exposed to a wide range of competitive environments; each requires the integration of business and operations strategies and the focus of manufacturing on a narrow set of goals. To assist in the process—and, also, to ensure effective implementation—a number of tools are provided. Some, such as statistical process control and the measurement of total factor productivity, are largely technical, of interest primarily to manufacturing specialists. Most, however, are conceptual and strategic: frameworks such as focused factories and the four stages of manufacturing that provide assistance to general managers planning to compete through superior operations.

These two classes of tools parallel the two audiences that OS is designed to serve: students with a strong interest in operations, who plan a career in the field, and students interested in general management, who want to understand better the connection between operations and business strategy. Because these groups differ in background and training, OS is best taught in the second year of the MBA program or in advanced undergraduate courses. It assumes that students already understand the basics of production and operations management—types of processes, capacity planning, production control, and work force management—as well as the rudiments of strategic and competitive analysis.

The course has also been taught successfully in a wide range of executive education programs. Groups have included general managers as well as manufacturing specialists. In addition, the book can be read profitably on its own, without formal classes, because of its modular design and the introductory materials that put the cases in context.

Course Outline

OS is divided into three parts, and normally covers thirty sessions. It proceeds from broad discussions of operations strategy to assessments of specific strategies (competing on quality, productivity, and new products and processes) to discussions of how those strategies can best be implemented over time. All sections have a strong general management flavor, and almost every case is focused at the vice president level or above. Some cases are accompanied by supplementary materials which are marked with a vertical band on the outside margins of the pages.

Part I, Manufacturing as a Competitive Weapon, develops the concept of an operations strategy and then discusses its basic elements. The need for a close fit between operations and business strategies is emphasized, and students are introduced to the idea of competitive priorities: the few key goals that manufacturing must focus on if it is to contribute to business success. These goals include cost, quality, delivery, and flexibility. Each is itself a complex variable that must be further defined. Moreover, few manufacturing systems can optimize all four goals at once. Tradeoffs are inevitable. An important lesson emerging from this section is that companies are more likely to succeed if they assign to their operations only a limited set of tasks.

These concepts are then applied to a variety of manufacturing decisions. Among the topics reviewed are capacity and facilities, organization and infrastructure, and links with marketing. In each area, major choices are outlined—centralized versus dispersed plants, make versus buy, alternative roles of the manufacturing staff, various ways of organizing the manufacturing department and communicating with other functions—and their implications in differing competitive environments are assessed. Together, these topics help to outline the course, for each involves a different aspect of manufacturing decision-making. The first introduces structural decisions, which involve bricks and mortar; the second introduces infrastructural decisions, which involve people and systems; and the third introduces interfunctional decisions, which involve the cooperation of groups outside of manufacturing and linkages across departments.

Part II, Strategies and Approaches, combines these separate elements into coherent strategies. Three approaches to competition, each requiring careful attention to operations, are discussed: competing on quality, productivity, and new products and processes. Each appears as a self-contained module of four to eight cases. The modules are unified, however, by their insistence on variety and their attention to diverse strategies. Whether the subject is quality, productivity, or new products and processes, OS emphasizes that there is no single best approach. Thus, the segment on quality reviews and contrasts the methods of Deming, Juran, and Crosby, three leading American quality experts; compares American and Japanese approaches to quality management; and explores differences in the quality programs of companies in commodity and specialty markets. The section on productivity takes a similar tack. It too considers a wide range of possible approaches: appointing a productivity "czar," improving yields by stabilizing production processes, investing in automation or factories of the future, and continuously tightening productivity standards through precise measurement and control. As with quality, the emphasis is on identifying the distinguishing features of each approach, its requirements for success, and the fit between approaches and competitive environments. Competing on new products and processes is discussed in the same way, with several cases devoted to such issues as the link between R&D and manufacturing and the proper sequencing, coordination, and integration of product and process development.

Part III, Planning and Implementing Operations Strategies Over Time, shifts the focus to implementation. The preceding sections have been concerned primarily with designing and developing operations strategies; here attention turns to carrying them out. A number of common challenges are discussed, including growth, employee resistance, organizational inertia, and untested technology. All cases in this section therefore contain a strong temporal element. Several, in fact, are multi-part series, with (B) and (C) cases, handed out in the course of discussion, that update events by several months. Through the use of such material, time passes, new problems arise, and students are forced to adapt to strategic decisions they have only recently made. The uncertainties of implementation become quickly apparent. To overcome these uncertainties, operating managers have a number of tools at their disposal, including measurement systems, leadership signals, organizational culture, and personnel rotation. All are discussed at length in Part III.

Most cases in Part III share another important characteristic: They are American success stories. Each represents a profitable, rapidly growing American organization that has succeeded, to some degree, because of excellence in operations. A few of the companies are unquestioned leaders, having long represented "stage 4" manufacturing (in which "manufacturing resources are looked upon as providing major opportunities for enhancing the firm's competitive strength" and such practices as in-house development of capital equipment, proprietary process development, and tight coordination among functions are widespread).[5] Others are in the process of making the transition from lower to higher stages of development, and are thus rethinking and expanding manufacturing's role. To supplement the cases in this section of the course, visitors may be invited to class to share their experiences in manufacturing management. Together, these visitors, plus the cases in Part III, provide an optimistic conclusion to OS, for they convey a seldom-heard message: When it comes to manufacturing excellence, it can happen here.

Major Themes

OS is built around five interrelated themes. They range from the strategic to the tactical, from broad perspectives to the details of implementation. All, however, relate in some way to the use of operations as a competitive weapon and the need to view manufacturing as an integrated system rather than an isolated department or function.

TRADITIONAL VERSUS STRATEGIC APPROACHES TO OPERATIONS

This theme dominates OS, for virtually all cases involve operating decisions that bear heavily on a company's competitive success. Strategic impacts are weighed consciously and carefully. Such thinking bears little relationship to more traditional approaches to operations, which view manufacturing more narrowly. In the traditional approach, operating decisions are often prompted by an immediate need. Rising costs, insufficient capacity, or an impending labor shortage suggest that action must be taken; the need is then addressed in a reactive and ad hoc fashion. Choices are typically based on narrow financial criteria, such as cost savings or return on investment, and manufacturing's competitive contribution is viewed as limited. Linkages between manufacturing and other departments receive little attention; in many cases, they are handicapped by fingerpointing and longstanding disagreements.

The strategic approach to operations differs from the traditional approach on almost every count. Operating decisions are made on the basis of their strategic impact and their contribution to long-run competitive advantage, not on narrow financial criteria. The role of operations is to support and enhance the business strategy, not simply to provide capacity. Companies are assumed to compete in a variety of ways, so low cost is only one of several possible objectives. Manufacturing thus becomes part of a larger system, and tighter integration, on several fronts, becomes a requirement for success. Individual plants become elements of a multi-plant network, rather than isolated entities; manufacturing is seen as intimately linked to marketing, engineering, and other functional groups, rather than an independent fiefdom; and operating decisions become parts of an overall strategy, to be assessed in combination, rather than as discrete, independent events.

MANAGING TRADEOFFS

Tradeoffs are a fact of industrial life, because few systems or organizations can do all things well. Choices must therefore be made, and some goals must be elevated at the expense of others. Without such priorities, managers lack clear direction. Their decision-making is without focus. Unfortunately, the necessary choices are seldom made explicitly; all too often, they come by default.

At the same time, few companies can afford to focus exclusively on a single, desirable goal. A sense of priorities is one thing; an organization that writes off cost, quality, or delivery as unimportant is quite another. Tradeoffs therefore require a delicate balancing act in which organizations set priorities and then struggle to ensure that secondary objectives are not overlooked or dismissed.

That balancing act is a daily event in manufacturing, where managers regularly face conflicting and incompatible demands. They take a variety of forms: Managers are told to meet their short-term numbers while improving long-term performance; urged to be creative and innovative without compromising efficiency or tight control; and required to pursue cost reduction and quality improvement simultaneously. Tradeoffs are rarely acknowledged. Instead, managers are expected to configure their manufacturing operations to meet all demands. The implicit assumption is that most operating systems can be made infinitely flexible and adaptive.

Such reasoning is a prescription for disaster. As the demands on manufacturing increase, its mission becomes more diffuse and its capabilities become less clear. Eventually, the operating system loses its special skills. At best, it becomes an adequate or marginal performer, vulnerable to competitors who have focused their operations on a narrower set of requirements.

The moral here is simple: Tradeoffs in manufacturing must be managed, not ignored. In OS the theme appears in a wide range of cases, and takes several forms. First is the simple recognition of tradeoffs: when they exist in manufacturing and when they do not. Cost and quality, for example, have historically been viewed as competing goals. But recent research on manufacturing conformance suggests that a tradeoff does not always exist. In fact, in most cases fewer defects lead to smoother operations and higher productivity, implying that cost and quality (conformance) move together, not inversely. On the other hand, a broader understanding of quality itself— distinguishing among product performance, features, reliability, conformance, and durability—suggests that tradeoffs may exist *within* the category. Proliferating features, for example, may lead to lower reliability, just as eye-catching designs may interfere with high performance.

Once tradeoffs have been acknowledged, competitive priorities come into play. These require a clear sense of what manufacturing must be especially good at to succeed. Priorities are derived from a company's business strategy, and are then used to evaluate major manufacturing decisions. In OS students gain considerable practice in determining priorities and ranking the relative importance of such goals as cost, quality, delivery, and flexibility.

Finally, OS explores systems and organizational structures that keep conflicting goals in balance. A clear sense of priorities is seldom enough to guide managers. Some goals, like short- and long-term profitability, are almost inevitably at odds; yet both are necessary and desirable ends. To manage such tradeoffs, careful planning is required. For example, companies with tight evaluation and control systems, keyed to standard costs, may still encourage creativity by excluding the costs of process experiments from production managers' budgets. Organizations dominated by design engineers may develop a greater sensitivity to manufacturability by centralizing operations and creating a critical mass of process skills. And purchasing departments that buy heavily on commodities exchanges may become more attuned to suppliers' delivery and service performance by insisting on regular feedback from their own manufacturing plants.

Each of these approaches creates a desirable tension. By keeping a number of competing goals in sight at the same time, each ensures that tradeoffs are actively and consciously managed. The development of such balancing measures, including explicit discussions of the approaches described above, is an important theme of OS.

INTERFUNCTIONAL COORDINATION

Balance is essential in another area as well: between manufacturing and other departments. R&D, marketing, and manufacturing managers must work together if manufacturing is to become an effective competitive weapon. Especially when massive changes are required, narrow efforts, limited to manufacturing alone, are unlikely to succeed. For example, few production managers possess the necessary understanding of customers' requirements; to gain that perspective, marketing input is required. Similarly, product redesign is often the quickest route to solving processing problems; in that case, R&D input is invaluable. Yet such cooperation is surprisingly scarce. Parochialism, with "every tub on its own botton," remains common. As one recent study has observed:

> Part of the problem of U.S. manufacturing is that the common definition of it has been too narrow. Manufacturing is not limited to the material transformations performed in the factory. It is a system encompassing design, engineering, purchasing, quality control, marketing, and customer service as well . . .[6]

Such a systemic view of manufacturing suggests the importance of close interfunctional coordination. Unfortunately, the three core groups—R&D, marketing, and manufacturing—normally respond to different goals and incentives.[7] R&D is primarily concerned with innovation and improved product performance; marketing desires flexibility, responsiveness, and diverse options and features; and manufacturing is interested in producibility, stability, and operating efficiency. A successful operations strategy requires that these differing views be recognized and to the extent possible, brought into balance. Managing such relationships, especially at the boundaries between functions where handoffs are made, is a topic central to OS.

At times the issue is simple communication: how to overcome fingerpointing and get warring departments to talk with one another so that common problems can be resolved. At other times the focus is on teamwork: how to forge effective interfunctional groups that can speedily develop new products. Occasionally, more fundamental issues are involved: how to divide up responsibility for activities, such as market and process development, that lack clear boundaries and overlap several departments. But whatever the issue, the underlying need—addressing operating problems that cannot be resolved by manufacturing managers working in isolation—remains the same. In every case, high levels of cooperation and support are required.

Much the same is true of the relationship between line manufacturing managers and corporate manufacturing staff, another important issue in OS. All too often their division of responsibility is unclear. Frequently, line and staff managers are actively hostile. As with multiple functions, improved communication and coordination are necessary if the groups are to work together effectively, especially on complex systemic problems.

MULTIPLANT NETWORKS

Corporate manufacturing staffs are seldom necessary when manufacturing is confined to a single facility. Then, operating issues can usually be resolved by plant managers and their subordinates alone. Multiple plants, however, create a new set of problems: how to match products with plants, what relationship to establish among facilities, and the proper basis for comparing the performance of dissimilar organizations. Operating decisions become more complex, and a corporate staff is frequently required to coordinate activities across plants. Individual factories can be integrated into a plant network. The creation and management of such networks is an important theme of OS.

When multiple plants are available, managers have considerable discretion in how they organize manufacturing. With one factory, facilities choices are limited; with several factories, the range is enormous.[8] Companies may choose to compete with a few large plants or many small ones; may locate plants close to markets, close to raw materials, close to suppliers, or close to research and development laboratories; and may focus facilities by product lines or production processes. Each of these choices has a large strategic component. For example, large single product plants offer efficiency and economies of scale, but sacrifice responsiveness and flexibility. They are more appropriate in some settings than others. Locating a plant within a market sometimes provides a competitive edge; at other times it does not. Further, deciding how a factory should be focused—the range of products to include, and the variety of production processes—has important links to competitive positioning.

Once a plant network has been established, issues of measurement and control become crucial. They are difficult enough for companies with a single manufacturing plant; when multiple plants are involved, they become especially problematic. How, for example, should the performance of plants with different missions be compared? Does the use of a single measuring system or a single yardstick such as labor productivity unfairly penalize some plants at the expense of others? How should plant managers be evaluated if some factors, such as plant size and scale economies, are outside their control?

Although OS discusses these issues, it provides few firm answers, for there is seldom a single best solution. For example, while some measurement systems can be scaled to adjust for differences in plant size or product mix—yield targets can be set for small, medium, and large facilities, and failure rates can be compared with industry norms rather than other plants in the system—many cannot. Managers must therefore learn to be sensitive to differences in plant mission and strategy when assessing performance. A plant that specializes in prototypes and new product introductions is unlikely to be as productive as one that focuses on a small number of mature, high volume products; for that reason, it should be judged by different criteria. This type of thinking is a recurrent theme in OS. Unfortunately, managers seldom make such distinctions. Most prefer instead to base their evaluations on a small set of yardsticks, geared to cost and efficiency, that are applied uniformly to all plants. According to a recent study of fifteen Canadian manufacturing plants:

> No firm had measures that evaluated production's ability to introduce new products, modify existing products, or adapt to customer needs . . . Instead, [managers] attempt[ed]

to define measures of performance for lines, departments, and plants that [would] be good for all time . . . Productivity and cost were the most frequently used measures . . .[9]

This approach treats plants as independent entities, with little concern for the plant system. Opportunities to share learning, to coordinate activities, and to focus plants on complementary missions are largely ignored. The result is that the performance of individual plants may improve, but the performance of the system as a whole normally lags behind.

TOOLS OF THE OPERATING MANAGER

To accomplish their goals, operating managers have a number of tools at their disposal. They cover a wide sweep, from measurement systems to new technologies to organizational changes. Some, such as automation and corporate manufacturing staffs, are conventional and widely used, part of the fabric of American manufacturing. But others, such as total factor productivity and process experiments, can be considered innovations in manufacturing management. They appear at only a small number of leading edge companies and are only dimly understood.

Much of OS is devoted to exploring the use of such tools, both traditional and innovative. The last segment of the course focuses on them almost exclusively. But the tools arise in early cases as well, because strategic issues are frequently bound up in tactics. A corporate manufacturing staff is unlikely to succeed in introducing a new quality initiative if it lacks the support of line managers, just as a focused factory is unlikely to increase productivity if its mission is diluted by the constant addition of new products. Implementation is very much a part of effective operations strategies.

OS considers tools in six areas:

- Measurement Systems
- Technology
- Organizational Structure
- People
- Leadership Signals
- Culture

These categories overlap, and are without clear boundaries. Each, in fact, can be divided into several additional categories. Measurement systems can be focused on quality, productivity, or ROI; technological advances can be pursued as incremental gains in existing processes or radical improvements in automation; and organizational changes can be centered on focused factories, special purpose divisions, or project teams. As *Exhibit 1* indicates, OS reviews each of these topics, plus a number of others. Cases typically involve the application of several tools. Implementation is thus a recurrent theme of the course, and for the most obvious of reasons: Even the best operations strategy is of little use if it cannot be implemented successfully.

NOTES

1. On semiconductor quality, see The Rosen Electronics Letter, March 31, 1980, pp. 3–5, and Arthur L. Robinson, "Perilous Times for U.S. Microcircuit Makers," *Science*, May 9, 1980, pp. 582–586. On automobile quality, see National Academy of Engineering, *The Competitive Status of the U.S. Auto Industry* (Washington, D.C.: National Academy Press, 1982), p. 90–108. On air conditioner quality, see David A. Garvin, "Quality on the Line," *Harvard Business Review*, September–October 1983, pp. 64–75. On color television quality, see Ira C. Magaziner and Robert B. Reich, *Minding America's Business* (New York: Harcourt Brace Jovanovich, 1982), p. 176, and Michael E. Porter, *Cases in Competitive Strategy* (New York: The Free Press, 1983), p. 511.

2. Manufacturing Studies Board, *Toward a New Era in U.S. Manufacturing* (Washington, D.C.: National Academy Press, 1986), p. 12.

3. W. Earl Sasser and Neil H. Wasserman, "From Design to Market: The New Competitive Pressures," Harvard Business School discussion paper, mimeographed, 1984, and Bro Uttal, "Speeding New Ideas to Market," *Fortune*, March 2, 1987, pp. 62–66.

4. William J. Abernathy, Kim B. Clark, and Alan M. Kantrow, "The New Industrial Competition," *Harvard Business Review*, September–October, 1981, p. 79.

5. Robert H. Hayes and Steven C. Wheelwright, *Restoring Our Competitive Edge* (New York: John Wiley & Sons, 1984), pp. 401–403.

6. Manufacturing Studies Board, *Toward a New Era in U.S. Manufacturing*, p. 50.

7. See Benson P. Shapiro, "Can Marketing and Manufacturing Coexist?", *Harvard Business Review*, September–October 1977, pp. 104–114.

8. For a detailed discussion of these choices, see M. Therese Flaherty, "Coordinating International Manufacturing and Technology," in Michael E. Porter, ed., *Competition in Global Industries* (Boston: Harvard Business School Press, 1986), especially pp. 90–92.

9. Peter R. Richardson and John R.M. Gordon, "Measuring Total Manufacturing Performance," *Sloan Management Review*, Winter 1980, pp. 51, 53, and 55.

EXHIBIT 1 Tools of the Operating Manager

	MEASUREMENT SYSTEMS			TECHNOLOGY				ORGANIZATIONAL STRUCTURE					
	Quality	Productivity	ROI	Product And Process Development	Technology Transfer	Process Experiments	Automation	Multi-plant Networks	Focused Factories	Vertical Integration	Project Teams	Special Purpose Divisions	Plant Managers
I. MANUFACTURING AS A COMPETITIVE WEAPON													
1. Indalex								X	X	X			X
2. Manufacturing-Missing Link in Corporate Strategy							X						
3. Chandler (B)		X						X	X				X
4. Sensormatic										X			
5. Intercon								X					
6. The Roles and Responsibilities of the Corporate Manufacturing Staff				X	X			X					
7. Teradyne				X	X					X	X		
8. How Should you Organize Manufacturing?								X	X				X
9. FMC (A)								X	X				
II. COMPETING ON QUALITY													
10. American Foods	X		X										
11. Quest for the Best													
12. Steinway							X						
13. Sanyo	X									X			X
14. Note on Quality	X										X		
15. Quality on the Line	X						X						
III. COMPETING ON PRODUCTIVITY													
16. Day at Midwest		X						X					X
17. Applichem (A)		X						X					X
18. Why Some Factories		X					X	X					
19. North American Rockwell			X				X						X
20. Allegheny Ludlum		X				X		X			X		X
21. The Case for Managing by the Numbers			X										
22. Note on Aerospace		X	X	X	X								
23. Vought		X		X			X				X	X	
24. Corning Z-Glass	X	X		X	X	X					X	X	X
IV. COMPETING ON NEW PRODUCTS AND PROCESSES													
25. Allstate			X	X	X						X	X	
26. Rogers				X	X			X	X	X	X		X
27. Project Nantucket				X		X	X						
28. Boeing				X	X					X	X		
29. Lehrer McGovern		X		X							X		
30. A Note on Value Analysis				X							X		
V. PLANNING AND IMPLEMENTING OPERATIONS STRATEGIES OVER TIME													
31. Building on the Past	X	X		X	X		X				X		X
32. Digital							X	X			X		X
33. A Note on Manufacturing Resource Planning				X							X		
34. Signetics: Quality Improvement	X						X	X			X		X
35. Signetics: Quality is Free	X										X		
36. Copeland						X	X	X	X		X		X
37. Competing Through Manufacturing				X			X	X			X		

	PEOPLE — Corporate Staff	MANAGEMENT STYLE — Entrepreneurial	MANAGEMENT STYLE — Measurement and Control	MANAGEMENT STYLE — Visionary	LEADERSHIP SIGNALS — Level of Commitment	LEADERSHIP SIGNALS — Risk-Taking	LEADERSHIP SIGNALS — Dominant Values	LEADERSHIP SIGNALS — St. vs. Lt. Thinking	CULTURE — Concern for the Work Force	CULTURE — Pursuit of Incremental Improvements	CULTURE — Manufacturing Excellence	
		X									X	1. Indalex
			X	X	X			X			X	2. Manufacturing-Missing Link in Corporate Strategy
												3. Chandler (B)
		X										4. Sensormatic
	X						X	X	X			5. Intercon
	X										X	6. The Roles and Responsibilities of the Corporate Manufacturing Staff
			X				X				X	7. Teradyne
	X										X	8. How Should you Organize Manufacturing?
						X						9. FMC (A)
	X											10. American Foods
				X	X							11. Quest for the Best
					X		X			X		12. Steinway
					X		X	X		X	X	13. Sanyo
					X		X			X	X	14. Note on Quality
	X				X		X	X	X	X	X	15. Quality on the Line
			X		X							16. Day at Midwest
												17. Applichem (A)
										X		18. Why Some Factories
	X		X		X			X				19. North American Rockwell
			X			X	X				X	20. Allegheny Ludlum
	X		X			X	X	X		X		21. The Case for Managing by the Numbers
			X			X	X	X			X	22. Note on Aerospace
			X	X		X	X	X		X	X	23. Vought
	X		X				X			X	X	24. Corning Z-Glass
	X	X			X	X				X		25. Allstate
		X						X		X		26. Rogers
						X		X			X	27. Project Nantucket
			X			X	X				X	28. Boeing
		X					X				X	29. Lehrer McGovern
										X		30. A Note on Value Analysis
				X	X	X		X	X		X	31. Building on the Past
	X		X	X	X	X		X	X	X	X	32. Digital
			X							X	X	33. A Note on Manufacturing Resource Planning
				X	X	X		X		X	X	34. Signetics: Quality Improvement
					X		X		X	X	X	35. Signetics: Quality is Free
	X		X		X	X		X	X		X	36. Copeland
	X		X		X	X	X	X	X	X	X	37. Competing Through Manufacturing

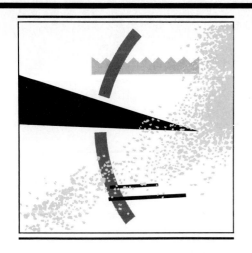

PART ONE

Manufacturing as a Competitive Weapon

Module 1
Manufacturing as a Competitive Weapon*

All too often, top managers regard manufacturing as a necessary evil. In their eyes, it adds little to a company's competitive advantage. Manufacturing, after all, merely "makes stuff"; its primary role is the transformation of parts and materials into finished products. To do so, it follows the dictates of other departments. And since these other departments—notably, marketing and engineering—rule and control, manufacturing is thought to have only limited positive impact.

At the same time, top managers are unusually sensitive to the problems that can be traced to poor manufacturing. Substandard quality, incomplete deliveries, delayed new products, and mushrooming costs are frequently the result of snarls in production. With such difficulties in mind, top managers often conclude that the most effective manufacturing departments are simply those that generate the fewest complaints. In practice, they try to minimize problems by imposing a broad range of demands on manufacturing—superior quality, on-time delivery, responsiveness to new products, and low costs—and then allowing no compromises or tradeoffs among them.

Not surprisingly, manufacturing managers view their activities quite differently. Most are firmly convinced that manufacturing contributes enormously to competitive success. Yet when pressed, they typically frame that contribution in the narrowest of terms. To many manufacturing managers, cost reduction (or, at the very least, cost control) is their group's *raison d'être*, because, they reason, it is primarily through reduced costs that manufacturing is able to enhance margins, profitability, and competitive positioning.

What is one to make of these claims? Each has a superficial appeal, yet each has serious drawbacks. For example, none of the views acknowledges the central role that manufacturing can play in supporting and enhancing a company's overall business strategy. None acknowledges the difficulties that arise when conflicting or inconsistent demands are imposed upon manufacturing. And none acknowledges the limitations of making cost reduction the primary goal of manufacturing managers.

The aim of this module is to explore these weaknesses in detail, through the introduction of a broader, more comprehensive model of manufacturing excellence. In the new model, manufacturing's role is vastly expanded. It is no longer viewed as a secondary activity, but instead becomes an active and equal partner, accorded the same respect as R&D, marketing, and other core functions. In this environment,

* Excerpt from *Operations Strategy: Module Overview: Manufacturing as a Competitive Weapon*, Harvard Business School Teaching Note 5-689-060. Copyright © 1989 by the President and Fellows of Harvard College.

manufacturing managers no longer confine themselves solely to tactical concerns, such as meeting daily production schedules, but focus equal attention on manufacturing's ability to contribute and sustain a long-term competitive edge. The result is normally a small set of focused objectives, pursued relentlessly, and an end to the idea that the most successful manufacturing organization is the one best able to be "all things to all people."

Major Themes

This module is built around three major themes. Together, they provide an introduction to a strategic approach to manufacturing, and thus serve as the foundation for all subsequent cases.

DEFINING THE MANUFACTURING TASK

Manufacturing's traditional role—to produce goods in a timely, cost-effective manner—has long been accepted by managers.[1] Typically, the highest priority has been meeting the production schedule; when improvements have been desired, the goal has invariably been to lower costs. In such settings, the agenda for manufacturing managers has been simple and clear. Unfortunately, it has also often been sorely misplaced.

To serve as a source of competitive advantage, manufacturing must align its goals in support of the company's or division's business strategy. Otherwise, its contributions will remain purely tactical. At times this requires a single-minded devotion to cost reduction; more often it does not. In Indalex, for example, the key competitive variable is service; in Sensormatic it is product availability; and in Teradyne it is speed of new product development and the rapidity of ramp ups to volume production. In all three cases, were manufacturing to focus exclusively on cost reduction, it would add little of strategic value.

Few manufacturing managers, however, recognize their ability to affect competitive performance in such noncost areas. Even those that do often find it difficult to move directly from their company's business strategy to specific manufacturing decisions. Strategies, after all, are usually framed in the most general of terms. Typically, they describe how a company will meet the needs of customers and how it will position itself relative to competitors, without saying much about required activities or skills. These must usually be inferred from broad statements of philosophy or approach. In most cases, the "manufacturing task"—the goals that manufacturing must meet if it is to fully support the business strategy—is left vague and ill-defined.[2]

For this reason, a careful statement of manufacturing's objectives is a crucial first step in developing a manufacturing strategy. Priorities must be established; without them, manufacturing managers are likely to focus on cost reduction, or else will try to be "all things to all people." Most scholars suggest that managers weigh four goals, called competitive priorities, when defining the task of manufacturing: cost, quality, delivery, and flexibility.[3] To provide direction, these goals must be ranked according to their importance in the overall business strategy. This is a surprisingly difficult task, especially when a company has long been successful or the environment is in flux. Indalex, for example, appears to have multiple priorities; it is not clear whether quality, delivery, or flexibility should be ranked first. Chandler presents a related problem. It has historically competed on cost, but now faces larger competitors who make flexibility a more attractive option.

Such choices are further complicated by the fact that each priority can be divided into narrower subcategories. Quality, for example, is a complex concept. It includes such varied elements as performance, features, reliability, durability, and aesthetics.[4] Flexibility is an equally broad term. A flexible organization is responsive to change, but along what dimensions? Flexibility can mean the capacity for rapid volume changes, quick shifts in product mix, speedy rerouting to accommodate equipment breakdowns, or swift adjustments to varying material inputs.[5] Delivery can be similarly decomposed. There, success can be measured by order processing time, shipment speed, dependability, percentage of orders shipped complete, probability of handling damage, or the availability and timeliness of status reports.[6]

These competitive priorities, including many of the major subcategories, are reviewed throughout the module. Cost issues are featured in Chandler and FMC Crane and Excavator; quality issues in Indalex, Intercon, and Teradyne; flexibility issues in Indalex, Chandler, Sensormatic, Teradyne, and FMC Crane and Excavator; and delivery issues in Indalex, Sensormatic, and Intercon. In every case, rankings must be established and priorities set before a specific manufacturing decision can be made. Such rankings provide strategic guidance because they lead to a narrower conception of the manufacturing task. But equally important, they force managers to acknowledge an often overlooked aspect of manufacturing: that no production system is capable of doing all things exceptionally well.

In part, the limits are organizational. Most manufacturing systems depend heavily on people, and people find it difficult to optimize a large number of variables at the same time. Our attention and information processing abilities are limited; faced with too much to juggle, we normally settle for satisfactory solutions rather than optimal ones.[7] A narrower set of goals helps by providing concentration and focus, simplifying the cognitive task.

Technical tradeoffs must also be faced. Few manufacturing policies are so precisely targeted that they impact only one competitive priority. Still fewer are without undesirable side effects. Indalex, for example, has relied heavily on overtime to provide flexibility to meet changing volume requirements, but has found that this results in lower quality as well. Chandler has encouraged long production runs to profit from economies of scale, only to find that its new product flexibility has been compromised in the process. And Teradyne has created a centralized manufacturing organization to allow it to ramp up quickly to volume production, only to find that it is now harder to get the first unit of a product through the system. Such tradeoffs are common in manufacturing. They must be weighed consciously and carefully by managers to ensure that well-intentioned decisions do not, because of unanticipated side-effects, undercut the business strategy.

MANUFACTURING AS A SYSTEM

Factories often convey an air of splendid isolation. Their four walls mark an implicit boundary, the separation of conversion processes from the remainder of the organization. For many years, such rigid separation was considered desirable, because it encouraged efficiency and ensured stability. In fact, in its most extreme form, "the traditional approach to manufacturing [has been] to seal off the core production technology from outside disturbances so that production may be accomplished without disruption."[8] By this reasoning, manufacturing is best managed as a separate, isolated activity, buffered by inventories and geographical distance from direct contact with customers and suppliers. Internal coordination, both among factories and with other departments, is regarded as unimportant, and each factory is managed so that its own efficiency is maximized.

As manufacturing has assumed a more strategic role, such reasoning has come under fire, and a new view has taken its place. According to this view, if manufacturing is to support the business strategy, it must be attentive to and integrated with the rest of the business, not isolated and aloof. Coordination and linkages are critical—across factories, across functions, and across firms. All three are reviewed in the module. Intercon, for example, examines a multi-plant organization and considers the difficulty of melding independent factories into a single, unified network. Chandler, Teradyne, and FMC Crane and Excavator explore interfunctional linkages and the need to coordinate approaches to manufacturing, marketing, and design. Sensormatic and Indalex examine the linkages between manufacturing departments and outside firms, including suppliers that serve the factory and customers that the factory serves.

Such an open, integrated view of manufacturing has several practical implications. Successful manufacturing is no longer simply a matter of efficient conversion processes. Manufacturing managers must now be closely linked to internal and external customers, and must be sensitive to their needs. Constant communication is essential. Moreover, manufacturing managers must become skilled at managing the interfaces between their function and other departments. Some tensions are to be expected, but they must be kept within limits and not allowed to become unhealthy or counterproductive. Such tensions are a central issue in the Teradyne case, where designers and manufacturing experts have long been at odds. Problems of this sort are often further exacerbated by control systems that set incompatible goals, or by cultural differences between departments.[9] Both are important features of the Chandler and FMC cases.

Once factories are viewed as parts of a larger system rather than as isolated entities, manufacturing decisions become more complex. Factories can now serve complementary roles. This is no longer a reason for every facility to produce the same goods, for the same markets, using the same production processes. Specialization becomes possible and, with it, alternative plant strategies.[10] A plant may specialize in new or mature products, a small number of markets or customers, or discrete stages of the production process. Interplant competition may be encouraged by allowing factories to bid for the same business, or discouraged by ensuring that markets and products do not overlap. The sharing of best practice within the plant network can be helped or hindered by training programs, personnel rotation, or evaluation and control systems. Indalex, Chandler, Intercon, and FMC all deal with these issues in the context of large, multi-plant organizations.

SOURCES OF MANUFACTURING EXCELLENCE

In the minds of many managers, superior manufacturing is associated with superior facilities and equipment. And, of course, modern buildings, state-of-the-art technology, and sophisticated tooling do contribute enormously to competitive success. But they are seldom enough by themselves. Without a skilled team of manufacturing managers, trained and enthusiastic employees, and the appropriate systems, organizations, and procedures, little is likely to be accomplished. Three leading manufacturing experts have put the issue bluntly: "We have never seen [a company] able to build a sustainable advantage around superior hardware alone."[11]

For this reason, the module explores both structural and infrastructural decisions. The former involve the "bricks and mortar" of manufacturing: facilities, equipment, production processes, and technology. Critical issues include capacity expansion, plant location, and vertical integration. Infrastructural decisions are softer and more diverse. They include organizational design, measurement and reward systems, and methods of establishing and enforcing schedules, quality policies, and work force rules. The first three cases of the module examine structural decisions, and the next three infrastructural decisions. FMC Crane and Excavator, the last case of the module, is an integrative case that combines elements of both.

Within the manufacturing organization, leadership in these areas is essential. It can come from three possible sources. Two are obvious: line managers and the manufacturing staff. Each group contributes significantly to manufacturing excellence, although their perspectives differ. Line managers have direct control over the shop floor; they are accountable for "meeting the numbers" and, to that end, must find innovative ways of utilizing equipment, upgrading production processes, and motivating the work force. Indalex, Chandler, and FMC provide vivid descriptions of line managers at work. Staff managers, on the other hand, have more diffuse responsibilities. At times they act as internal experts or consultants, pitching in to help solve pressing problems; at other times they serve as communication channels, binding together isolated factories and ensuring that critical learnings are shared. Intercon shows a manufacturing staff at work, and also demonstrates the tensions that arise when line and staff managers do not see a problem in exactly the same light.

A third source of manufacturing excellence is special centers created expressly for the purpose of improving operations. They go by various names: advanced manufacturing groups, manufacturing and engineering divisions, and quality and productivity centers. But whatever the title, their purpose is to provide a critical mass of manufacturing talent and to develop state-of-the-art skills. Such centers often pool line and staff experts, or else serve as training grounds through which managers are circulated to refine their thinking. Teradyne's foundry provides an example of this approach in action, and shows the lengths that companies must occasionally go to improve their manufacturing talents.

NOTES

1. See Wickham Skinner, "The Taming of Lions: How Manufacturing Leadership Evolved, 1780–1984," in Kim B. Clark, Robert H. Hayes, and Christopher Lorenz, eds., *The Uneasy Alliance: Managing the Productivity-Technology Dilemma* (Boston: Harvard Business School Press, 1985), pp. 63–110, for an introduction to manufacturing's traditional ethos.

2. The concept of the "manufacturing task" was first proposed by Wickham Skinner in his article, "Manufacturing—Missing Link in Corporate Strategy," *Harvard Business Review*, May–June 1969, pp. 136–145. It was later expanded by Steven C. Wheelwright and Robert H. Hayes. See Steven C. Wheelwright, "Reflecting Corporate Strategy in Manufacturing Decisions," *Business Horizons*, February 1978, pp. 57–66, and Robert H. Hayes and Steven C. Wheelwright, *Restoring Our Competitive Edge* (New York: John Wiley & Sons, 1984), pp. 40–41.

3. These priorities have shifted over time. In Skinner's original article, the priorities were productivity, service, quality, and return on investment. Most later articles have used the

four priorities cited in the text. See, for example, Wheelwright, "Reflecting Corporate Strategy" p. 61; Hayes and Wheelwright, *Restoring Our Competitive Edge* pp. 40–41; Robert H. Hayes and Roger W. Schmenner, "How Should You Organize Manufacturing?", *Harvard Business Review*, January–February 1978, pp. 107–108; and Paul M. Swamidass, "Manufacturing Strategy: Its Assessment and Practice," *Journal of Operations Management*, August 1986, pp. 471–484.

4. David A. Garvin, "What Does 'Product Quality' Really Mean?", *Sloan Management Review*, Fall 1984, pp. 29–34; David A. Garvin, "Competing on the Eight Dimensions of Quality," *Harvard Business Review*, November–December 1987, pp. 104–108; and David A. Garvin, *Managing Quality*, (New York: Free Press, 1988), ch. 4.

5. Robb Dixon, "Measuring and Managing Manufacturing Flexibility," Research Report, Manufacturing Roundtable, Boston University School of Management, mimeographed, February 1988, and Donald Gerwin, "An Agenda for Research on the Flexibility of Manufacturing Processes," *International Journal of Production Management* 7, 1: 38–49.

6. Peter Gilmour, "Customer Service: Differentiating by Market Segment," *International Journal of Physical Distribution* 7, 3: 141–148, and Myroslow J. Kyj, "Customer Service as a Competitive Tool," *Industrial Marketing Management* 16: 225–230.

7. See, for example, Herbert A. Simon, "A Behavioral Theory of Choice," *Quarterly Journal of Economics* 69: 99–118, and Herbert A. Simon, "Theories of Decision-Making in Economics and Behavioral Science," *American Economic Review*, June 1959, pp. 253–281.

8. Richard B. Chase and Warren J. Erikson, "The Service Factory," *Academy of Management EXECUTIVE*, August 1988, p. 191.

9. For a discussion of the causes of conflict between marketing and manufacturing managers, see Benson P. Shapiro, "Can Marketing and Manufacturing Coexist?" *Harvard Business Review*, September–October 1977, pp. 104–114.

10. See Roger W. Schmenner, "Look Beyond the Obvious in Plant Location," *Harvard Business Review*, January–February 1979, pp. 126–132, and Roger W. Schmenner, *Making Business Location Decisions*, (Englewood Cliffs, NJ: Prentice-Hall, 1982), pp. 11–15, for general discussions of multi-plant strategies.

11. Robert H. Hayes, Steven C. Wheelwright, and Kim B. Clark, *Dynamic Manufacturing,* (New York: The Free Press, 1988), p. 22.

1. Indalex Ltd.

As the year 1977 drew to a close, Mr. Peter McIlwraith, Managing Director of Indalex Ltd., faced some critical decisions that could have a major impact on the future of his company. The previous year had been the best in Indalex's history (see *Exhibit 1*), due largely to the fact that it had been operating at essentially full capacity in a market environment that permitted high margins. Future growth in sales could only be achieved by increasing capacity, but increasing uncertainty was being expressed about the near-term economic prospects for the market area that Indalex served, and McIlwraith wondered if this was really an appropriate time to add to capacity. Moreover, since Indalex's products could go through a sequence of processing steps, each of which was currently operating near to its capacity limit, there were a number of ways by which McIlwraith could "increase capacity". The choice he made could have the effect of changing the balance of his current operation, and might have an effect on Indalex's overall competitive posture.

I. Company Background

In 1961, Mr. James Paterson joined Pillar Holdings Ltd. as Managing Director after 11 years experience with the Alcan (Aluminium Company of Canada) Group. At that time Pillar Holdings was a collection of 6 small private companies having almost no commercial or industrial rationale, and having combined sales of about £1.0 million. Paterson's reason for leaving Alcan was his belief that there were special opportunities, particularly in the U.K., in certain fields of aluminium fabrication and semi-fabrication which were not being properly exploited by the large international al-

This case was prepared by Robert H. Hayes.

uminium companies. He saw Pillar as a vehicle for trying to capitalize on these opportunities.

The extrusion of aluminium, which is one of the most versatile uses of the metal, is essentially a jobbing business, with a different die for every cross-section. It requires relatively little capital compared with smelting or sheet rolling, and in the U.S. in the late 1940's a number of individuals entered the independent extruding business either from scratch or as a form of backward integration from some operation in which they were using extrusions. It was soon evident that relatively small independent extruders (two to three extrusion presses working within a radius of 200–300 miles) could give much better service to customers than the larger facilities and ponderous administrations of Alcoa, Kaiser and Reynolds. As a result, by 1955 some 65% of the aluminium extrusion capacity in the United States was owned by independents.

Surprisingly enough, the situation in the U.K. in 1961 was still similar to that which had existed in the U.S. in 1945: virtually all the extrusion facilities were owned by the four big international companies operating there: Alcan, Kaiser (through James Booth), Reynolds (through British Aluminium) and Alcoa (through Impalco). In 1961 these extrusion facilities were operating on an 8–12 week delivery basis, although only at about 60% of total capacity. Customer service was perfunctory, administration ponderous and expensive, and the actual surface quality of most of the extrusions did not compare with North American standards (surface finish is extremely important where extrusions are going to be used on the outside of buildings).

Indalex (an abbreviation for "Independent Aluminium Extruders") Ltd. was incorporated in

EXHIBIT 1 Profit and Loss Accounts 1975, 1976, and 1977

PROFIT AND LOSS ACCOUNT
FOR THE YEAR ENDED DECEMBER 31st, 1977

Year to 31st December, 1975	Year to 31st December, 1976		Year to 31st December, 1977
£	£		£
5,945,526	9,715,354	SALES	13,296,206
406,777	1,175,115	TRADING PROFIT BEFORE TAXATION	1,429,820
		TAXATION AND AMOUNTS PAYABLE IN RESPECT OF GROUP RELIEF	
158,970	613,817		747,839
247,807	561,298	TRADING PROFIT AFTER TAXATION	681,981
		DIVIDEND (GROSS)	
247,807	561,298	Proposed Final Dividend	681,981
—	—	PROFIT OF THE YEAR UNAPPROPRIATED	—
110	110	RETAINED EARNINGS AT BEGINNING OF YEAR	110
£ 110	£ 110	RETAINED EARNINGS AT END OF YEAR	£ 110

STATEMENT OF SOURCE AND APPLICATION OF FUNDS
FOR THE YEAR ENDED 31st DECEMBER, 1977

Year to 31st December, 1975		Year to 31st December, 1976			Year to 31st December, 1977	
£	£	£	£		£	£
				SOURCE OF FUNDS		
	384,934		1,175,115	Profit Before Tax		1,429,820
				Adjustment for Item not involving the Movement of Funds:		
	99,562		118,460	Depreciation		174,164
	484,496		1,293,575	TOTAL GENERATED FROM OPERATIONS		1,603,984
				FUNDS FROM OTHER SOURCES		
650,000		—		Increase in Long Term Loans	—	
3,730		6,920		Sale of Fixed Assets	12,708	
21,843		957,695		Taxation and Group Relief Received	858,405	
	675,573		964,615			871,113
	1,160,069		2,258,190			2,475,097
				APPLICATION OF FUNDS		
351,936		247,807		Dividends Paid	561,298	
92,665		213,509		Tax and Group Relief Paid	1,618	
831,324	1,275,925	606,649	1,067,965	Purchase of Fixed Assets	592,585	1,155,501
	(115,856)		1,190,225			1,319,596
				INCREASE/DECREASE IN WORKING CAPITAL		
2,216,055		2,455,283		Increase in Stocks	973,541	
172,674		876,993		Increase/(Decrease) in Debtors	(13,184)	
(2,404,807)		(2,098,423)		Decrease/(Increase) in Creditors	229,086	
				Movement in Net Liquid Funds:		
(99,778)		(43,628)		(Increase)/Decrease in Bank Overdraft less cash	130,153	
	£ (115,856)		£1,190,225			£1,319,596
				END OF YEAR:		
		£2,667,866		Accounts Receivable	£2,654,682	
		5,307,222		Stocks and Work in Progress	6,280,763	
		848,852		Other	36,221	
		8,823,940		Total Current Assets	8,971,666	
		2,176,191		Net Fixed Assets	2,581,904	
		(7,858,474)		Total Liabilities	(7,860,798)	
		3,141,657		Total Capital Employed	3,692,772	

1. Indalex Ltd.

June 1961, and it came into production five months later in a rented building in Cheltenham (see map, *Exhibit 2*). Thus it became the first newly created company under the Pillar flag. Indalex set out to offer a 7 day service, highly qualified assistance to customers in designing their sections, and a much better surface finish than was generally available in the U.K. The company broke into the black in June 1962 and enjoyed steadily increasing profits since then. By offering good customer service and high quality products, and by intentionally concentrating on more complicated and difficult sections, Indalex had always been able to achieve prices which were higher than most of its competitors.

In September 1964, Indalex took the next major step in its business plan by installing its own anodising plant, making it the first aluminium extruder in the U.K. able to surface-finish its own extrusions. This capablity made Indalex's

EXHIBIT 2 Location of Indalex and Widness Plants

VIEW OF CHELTENHAM PLANT

MAP OF THE UNITED KINGDOM AND IRELAND

1. Indalex Ltd.

services particularly attractive to companies who utilized aluminium extrusions in building construction (since these parts almost always required protective surface finishes), because they could now deal with a single supplier instead of two or more.

Indalex was particularly proud of its success in constructing and operating this new anodising plant, because it incorporated a couple of major design improvements that had been largely developed by its own personnel. These helped make the new plant one of the most efficient in the U.K.

New extrusion presses were added in 1962 and 1969, but since 1969 anodising capacity had increased much faster than extrusion capacity. By 1977, with four separate anodising plants, Indalex had the largest anodising facilities in the U.K. and anodised about 60% of the output of its 3 extrusion presses.

The Pillar Group of Companies

The foregoing description of Pillar's entry into the independent extrusion market in the U.K. provides an example of the type of special situation in the aluminium industry which the Pillar Group had sought.

Each Pillar operating company (approximately 47 in 1977 in the U.K., of which 6 were distribution companies) fundamentally specialized in one product or operation and was run strictly as a profit center. Worldwide, Pillar operated 10 aluminium extrusion companies who owned a total of 23 extrusion presses. All of these companies bought their own billets, made roughly the same products, had die-making services or capabilities, and faced similar pollution/environmental problems. About one-third of these companies operated anodising plants. The companies all operated completely independently. There was, however, some interchange of techniques, know-how, and personnel between Pillar operations in different countries.

The top management of Pillar had tried to create and maintain an environment which retained and attracted aggressive, dedicated and entrepreneurial managers. For example, it allowed each operating unit to work autonomously, within the guidelines of achieving its budgeted profit for the year and proposing plans to enable

profit growth to continue in the future. Aside from preparing annually a rolling five-year profit plan, submitting monthly interim accounts, maintaining close control of cash, and keeping a fairly close liaison with the divisional chief executive responsible for each specific operating company, the operating management were allowed and encouraged to act independently. There were few service departments or other staff services within Pillar's central management which the operating companies would feel forced to use, or to feel they were subsidising. When specialist services were required, Pillar believed it better to hire the services of specialized third-party firms rather than to undertake such work on an ad hoc basis.

Virtually none of the areas of involvement of Pillar in the aluminium industry were highly capital intensive. The success of its companies, while obviously requiring the most up-to-date equipment, depended more on the skill of a small, highly qualified and motivated top management group, which could master and supervise every aspect of their particular operation so as to provide better service to their customers. Operating companies employing not more than about 400 people, and capable of being managed at the top by 2 to 3 executive directors, had proved to be about the optimum. If the growth of the market for a product reached a point where a larger unit would seem justified, then Pillar preferred to set up a second unit which would compete with the first as well as with outside competitors.

In 1969, in fact, Indalex had faced a major decision when it added its third extrusion press. There had been some sentiment that the new press should be added at a new site, and form the basis for a new company. Instead, a major expansion of the original factory was undertaken to accommodate the press.

In 1977, Peter McIlwraith operated with a total management group of less than 10 people, one of whom was general manager of the fabrication division and so operated relatively autonomously. Another was responsible for the specification and selection of major new pieces of production equipment.

All inter-company trading within the group was done on an "arms length" basis, on the grounds that if an operating management was to be completely profit responsible (and proportionately rewarded) and so in a position to offer the best product, price, and delivery to its own customers, then it could not be saddled with a group requirement to buy its raw materials from within the group except on terms fully competitive with those of third-party suppliers. As a consequence, while there was a certain amount of inter-company trading within the Pillar group, Pillar companies bought substantial quantities of their requirements for semi-fabricated aluminium from third parties. Pillar's view of how an "independent" should operate was in strong contrast to the type of integration which existed within most of the vertically-integrated international aluminium companies.

Pillar did not undertake any fundamental research and development in the aluminium field, since such work was extensively done by the large international aluminium companies and was easily available to customers, at no cost. However, Pillar was always looking for new inventions, processes or techniques which had not been exploited anywhere, or had been developed and exploited in one country but not yet exploited in some other country in which Pillar was engaged in business.

In 1970 Pillar Ltd. joined the RTZ group of companies, whose consolidated assets then exceeded £700 million. This merger had had relatively little impact on Pillar's operating procedures or results.

The preparation of the annual Pillar five-year rolling profit plan was predicated on a targeted real growth in pre-tax profits of 10% per annum. Obviously this could not be achieved in every company, or in each country from year to year, but it was the objective that had been made clear to all the operating managements. If they could not obtain such growth through increases in sales or reductions in the costs of their existing activities, then they were expected to propose ancillary activities which could sensibly be grafted on to their existing management, facilities and technology so as to achieve the target growth rate. The plans were prepared by each operating management, then reviewed and revised by the particular RTZ executive director responsible for each company. They were then reviewed at the Divisional or territorial level and finally by the RTZ executive management as a whole.

II. Process Description

Indalex could perform three separate aluminium processing steps: extrusion (the conversion of an aluminium billet into desired shapes by heating and forcing it through a die); anodising or other finishing processes (in which the surface of the aluminium object was treated to improve its appearance and durability); and fabricating (the machining of finished products to permit the assembly of series of such aluminium parts, together with other materials). A flow diagram of the process is provided in *Exhibit 3*.

Inspection of *Exhibit 3* indicates two aspects of Indalex's operations that are worth commenting on. First, the capacities of the three stages are quite different. The most important processing stage, both in terms of tonnes and sales volume, was its original business—aluminium extrusion. About 40% of its extrusions were sold outside the company in "mill finish" form; the remainder proceeded to the finishing stage, almost all of whose output was sold outside. Only a tiny fraction of the company's total production was fabricated. In 1977 all three production stages were operating essentially at capacity.

Second, a considerable amount of aluminium scrap was produced during the process, particularly in the extrusion stage. This scrap was collected and either sold directly to outside aluminium smelters, or was converted by them back into "secondary" aluminium billet which was reusable by Indalex. This operation, which cost about £110 per tonne including transportation cost, was called "tolling."

Representative manufacturing costs and selling prices per tonne for the various levels of end-product are provided in *Exhibit 4*.

Extrusion

Aluminium extrusion is carried out in hydraulically operated extrusion presses, which heat billets of aluminium to a plastic state and force them through dies. Modern die-making and processing techniques make it possible to produce a wide variety of shapes; a representative sample of Indalex's products is shown in *Exhibit 5*.

A single medium-sized extrusion press produces 2500–3000 metric tonnes of aluminium

EXHIBIT 3 Metal Movements–1977 (Metric Tons)

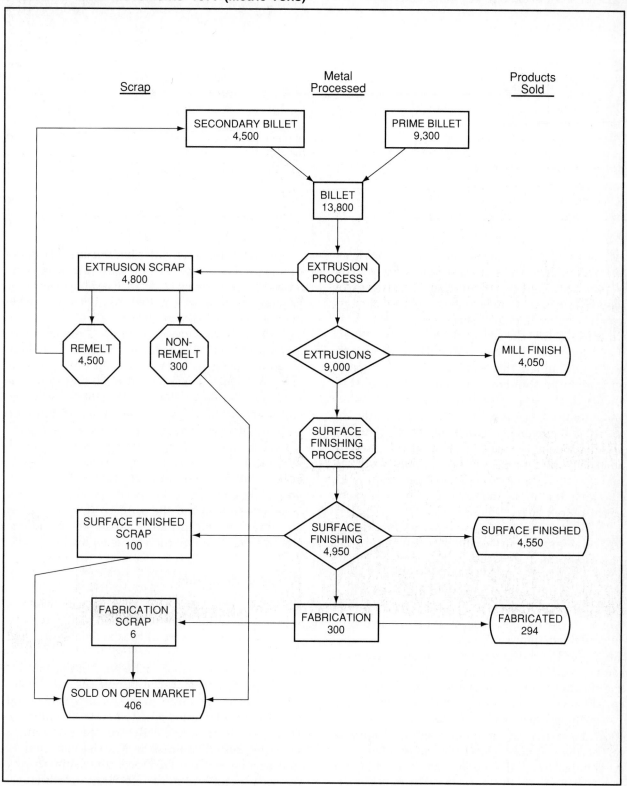

Scrap   Metal Processed   Products Sold

SECONDARY BILLET 4,500

PRIME BILLET 9,300

BILLET 13,800

EXTRUSION SCRAP 4,800

EXTRUSION PROCESS

REMELT 4,500

NON-REMELT 300

EXTRUSIONS 9,000

MILL FINISH 4,050

SURFACE FINISHING PROCESS

SURFACE FINISHED SCRAP 100

SURFACE FINISHING 4,950

SURFACE FINISHED 4,550

FABRICATION SCRAP 6

FABRICATION 300

FABRICATED 294

SOLD ON OPEN MARKET 406

1. Indalex Ltd.

EXHIBIT 4 Representative Costs and Selling Prices by Process Stage

| Stage | Incremental | |
	Mfg. Cost Per Tonne	Selling Price
Extrusion	£1080 (incl. mat'ls)	£1200
Anodising	305 (direct cost only)	410
Fabrication	160 (direct cost only)	200

extrusion per year, depending on the intricacy and difficulty of their cross-sections, on the size of the press, and on the number of changeovers required. In order to reduce the number of change-overs, Indalex had specialized its presses some-what as regards the size of the aluminium billets they could handle: one normally utilized only aluminium billets that were 6 inches in diameter and produced thin cross-sections that were then anodised, the second accepted 7 or 8 inch billets and produced medium cross-sections, while the third could accept 7 or 8 inch diameter billets and produced heavy extrusions, few of which were anodised. Changing a die was a simple matter, taking only a minute or two, compared with changing the input diameter of a press, which might take 2 hours.

Although simple in concept, aluminium ex-trusion required considerable skill and teamwork. The quality of the output was dependent on the quality and characteristics of the input material, the quality of the die, and the skill with which extrusion was carried out. A variety of aluminium alloys was available, each of which affected the surface finish, physical characteristics and overall quality of the output. It was important that the composition of the aluminium be according to specifications, and that the various elements be spread as evenly as possible throughout the metal.

The efficacy and quality of the process was most dependent on the quality and management of the dies. Indalex purchased most of its dies from independent die-makers, all of them located near Cheltenham (by being the first independent aluminium extruder, Indalex had essentially caused the auxiliary services required by extrusion com-panies to locate near it). So as to be able to develop proprietary products, it had also set up its own die-making facilities in 1974.

Once a die was in place, a considerable amount of "art" was required in order to keep it working properly. A die wears out during use; a given die can produce from 3 to 50 tonnes before replacement, depending on the intricacy of its cross-section. Moreover, it wears out at different rates at different places within the die. Therefore, in order to keep it operating properly it must periodically be cleaned and "corrected". Consid-erable skill was required both to do this properly and to decide *when* to do this. Acquiring the skills of the die-maker and the die-corrector, in fact, at one time was the primary barrier to companies who wanted to enter the extrusion business.

Finishing/Anodising

The company's Finishing Division comprised a series of operations whose function was to improve the surface appearance of the extruded parts and to apply a protective coating to them. These operations consisted of "polishing" (a mechanical operation that removed dirt and residual metal fragments using large mechanical brushes and abrasive bands), anodising (whereby the alumin-ium was electro-chemically treated to obtain a corrosion-resistant finish in a variety of colours), and spray-painting. Of these, anodising was by far the biggest and most important operation.

EXHIBIT 5 Examples of Products

First the parts were hand-loaded onto racks, called "jigs," which facilitated their movement through the sequence of electrochemical operations. These took place in a row of long narrow tanks which contained a variety of chemical solutions, and in some of which circulated strong electrical currents.

The jigs containing the extrusions were moved by hand-controlled overhead cranes from one tank to the next, and left for standard periods of time.

First, the extrusions were cleaned, then rinsed, and then etched (etching created the actual final surface appearance of the finished piece). The surfaces were then treated in the anodising tanks to form a tough protective coating of a prespecified thickness of aluminium oxide on them which resisted corrosion and discoloration. After a rinse, the parts were ready for the application, if required, of one of the five color additions that Indalex offered. Next, the aluminium oxide coat-

1. Indalex Ltd.

ing was stabilized with a minute layer of nickel salts. Sealing, rinsing and drying completed the processing.

The quality and efficiency of this process was critically dependent on the skill and speed of the "jiggers" (the men who loaded the racks with extruded parts at the very beginning of the process) and the overhead crane operators. Improper loading of the jigs could affect the uniformity and quality of the cleaning/coating operations, and the crane operators had to exercise considerable judgment in deciding how long to keep the pieces in each tank in order to achieve the desired effect.

Whereas the extrusion presses could be stopped and started relatively easily, anodising was a continuous process which was expensive to start up. Hence, the anodising/finishing operations were most efficient when they were operating at close to 100% capacity and work was scheduled through them smoothly and continously. Each of Indalex's four anodising plants was under the control of its own foreman, who handled the actual scheduling for his plant and was responsible for its overall quality and costs.

Since anodising created large amounts of contaminated water, the company was paying increased attention to (and incurring considerable expenditures for) pollution-control measures. It was proving so difficult to maintain the required degree of control over the out-flow from two of the anodising tanks, in fact, that Peter McIlwraith indicated that they would probably have to be replaced within the next few years.

Fabrication

In this stage of the process finished (anodised) aluminium parts were assembled together with other materials to form completed products. This operation had been set up in 1973, soon after Peter McIlwraith had been made Managing Director of Indalex, but was still relatively small: fourteen men were employed in the fabrication shop, and it accounted for a total sales turnover of less than £1 million. It was managed as a profit center, with finished aluminium extrusions transferred to it at prices that were equivalent to the prices paid for finished parts by Indalex's largest customers. It had proven to be a higher margin business than extrusion or anodising.

The establishment of this operation had represented a natural step in forward integration, permitting Indalex to increase the value it added to its raw materials and giving it more control over the utilization of the capacity of its extrusion presses and anodising plants. It also enabled the company to produce some standard ("off the shelf") and proprietary products. McIlwraith, however, was uneasy about increasing the fabrication business much beyond its current size for several reasons.

First, the market for fabricated products was only growing at 6% per year, and Indalex was competing with two established companies (Alcan Systems and Midland Extruders) who had large resources and offered strong, intelligent competition. Second, in effect, he would be competing directly with his own customers and he did not want to undermine the relationships, based on trust and cooperation, that he had built with them. Finally, he had neither the physical space into which he could expand this business nor the management time required to "grow it" dramatically. In fact, in the previous two years McIlwraith had turned down opportunities to buy out two fabricators, both Indalex customers, who were going bankrupt (due more to lack of capital and management abilities than to lack of market opportunities).

Workforce

Indalex employed just over 100 salaried employees and about 325 hourly workers. The latter received an average wage rate of around £1.50 per hour. Seventy-seven of these people worked in the extrusion operation, 14 in die-correction, 109 in finishing/anodising, 14 in fabricating and the rest in a variety of jobs including packing, shipping, and maintenance. A rather unusual 2-shift schedule, employing a considerable amount of overtime, was used to permit essentially round-the-clock operations five days a week, and half-shift operations on Saturday and Sunday.

Day shift workers worked 5 shifts of 10½ hours each, Monday through Friday, while night shift workers worked 4 shifts of 12 hours each on Monday through Thursday for the same amount of total pay as the day shift workers received for slightly more hours. In addition, the night shift often worked a 12-hour shift on Friday night at an overtime pay rate (a shifting amount, depending on the total number of hours worked during the week, but for Indalex's employees averaging about 1.3 times the standard hourly pay rate). The occasional 5-hour shifts on Saturday and Sunday were covered by volunteers, who also received overtime wages. Workers alternated day and night shifts every two weeks.

This rather unusual work schedule had been instituted early in Indalex's history in order to preserve the flexibility of its response to changes in the volume of work while maintaining a "no lay-off" policy during periods of low business. Fluctuations in workload, caused either by seasonal factors or by general economic conditions, could be handled simply by reducing or increasing the amount of overtime required. It also, in the words of one Indalex executive, probably caused the company to be a more attractive place to work for the more ambitious, "hungry" type of worker who relished the opportunity to earn higher weekly wages than his neighbours.

On the other hand, there was general agreement that the revolving work schedule and the amount of overtime required probably had some detrimental impact on quality and efficiency, and made it more difficult for Indalex to attract new workers. Hence, alternative plans were being considered that would reduce the amount of overtime, while still maintaining an appropriate level of responsiveness with a somewhat larger workforce.

The employees were not represented by a union, which McIlwraith attributed to several factors. One set of reasons was structural in nature. For example, Cheltenham was not in the historical "backbone" of the industrial revolution, which ran through the midlands of England. The workforce also lived close to the plant: 70% within 10 miles and all within 25 miles. This promoted closer identity with the company.

Another set of reasons derived from managerial policies. The company utilized what it called its "updraft" program, which essentially emphasized promoting from within, and hiring new workers on the basis of recommendations from current workers. This policy, together with an informal job rotation program, careful selection and close monitoring of workgroups, and the company's desire to keep the work environment somewhat unstructured and as exciting as possible, cultivated worker support and loyalty. The steady growth of the company provided both a sense of excitement and increased promotion opportunities.

Finally, substantial overtime pay was available to fatten their standard wages, which were average for the area, and the company provided a pension plan which was better than average. In addition, the company made frequent use of one-time bonuses (for example, group outings to London).

Although the workers appeared to be quite satisfied with their situation at Indalex, they were by no means docile. They had subjected the company to a 10-day strike the previous August in attempting to achieve a wage hike.

III. Marketing Strategy

Whereas the annual average world growth in the use of all aluminium products had averaged about 8% since 1960 in most industrial markets, the growth of the sales of extrusions had averaged 15–20% per annum. Japan, for example, has experienced a compound growth rate of over 30% in the past 15 years, while the use of aluminium sheet in Japan only increased at the rate of 14% per annum.

Largely because of its combined extrusion-anodising capability, Indalex's services had been very attractive to the construction industry, since these companies required protective coatings on virtually all of their purchased extrusions. By 1977 about two-thirds of Indalex's total sales were to construction companies, with other major industries like transportation and engineering accounting for less than 10% each. Any change in the percentage of total construction-related work would imply a change in the capacity balance between extrusion and anodising.

Indalex sales were handled by a 10-man outside sales force (who were thought of as "Customer Liaison Engineers"), all of whom had engineering experience and were paid entirely by salary. Its major customer fell into two main groups: suppliers of windows, doors and patio doors to the prime (new construction) building industry, and companies who were in the "home improvement" business.

About 45% of the total sales turnover derived from aluminium extrusions in the U.K. was produced by three companies: Indalex, RTZ Extruders Ltd. (another member of the RTZ-Pillar group), and a subsidiary of Alcan. Indalex and its sister company, which was located in Widnes (about 115 miles from Cheltenham, see Exhibit 2), each owned three extrusion presses, while Alcan owned 12. It was estimated that the total extrusion capacity in the U.K. and Wales was about 160,000 metric tonnes per year, but that industry output was running at a rate of only 120,000 tonnes per year in late 1977.

Indalex, however, was now operating at close to 95% of its capacity, and so its primary current objective was to juggle its capacity to meet its customers' needs as well as possible, while slowly upgrading its sales by culling out low-profit products and poorer customers. The company's salesmen were currently spending a considerable proportion of their time doing two things that few salesmen like to do: rationing customers, and planning ahead. Starting in October the salesmen had contacted the top 20–30% of their customers to determine what their likely requirements would be during the coming year. It appeared in late 1977 that Indalex could increase its sales by 20% during 1978—if it had the capacity. In order to free up capacity for "good" customers, the company had recently reduced the number of customers who did not pay their bills within 30 days beyond their agreed credit period.

Peter McIlwraith attributed Indalex's success, both past and current, to its competitive strategy which, he said, was "based on three words: service, service, service." Indalex competed less on the basis of price than on its quality and flexibility. "We view our factory as being an integral part of our customer's factory. We have very close working relationships with our customers, and try to respond to their needs even when they give us very short notice." For example, customers were allowed to specify die changes up to two days before their order was due to be run and Indalex was willing to accept much smaller orders than did most of its competitors.

When asked how he could continue to re-spond to requests for special service when he was operating so close to capacity, McIlwraith replied that "you have to know who has the slack and who doesn't; we've done enough favors for our customers when they really needed help that when they have some room to spare they don't mind if we shuffle their order around so that somebody else can squeeze in—but to do that properly, we have to know their business almost as well as they do." Despite this special knowledge and cooperation, he admitted that "for 30 weeks of the year our production planning section is stretched to the limit."

IV. Decisions Facing Indalex in Late-1977

Given the current capacity constraint and all forecasts of future demand available to Peter McIlwraith it seemed obvious that Indalex should move quickly to increase its production capacity. But there were several ways in which Indalex could expand, each with its own set of costs and benefits, and it might be unwise to try and do more than one thing at a time. On the other hand, if no additional capacity was provided, the company had no recourse other than to chop off some of its long-time customers. This would not only be painful by itself, but might have disagreeable side effects: the salesmen who handled these accounts might feel slighted, and the remaining customers might decide that Indalex "wasn't willing to grow with us," as Peter McIlwraith put it. Trying to fill the capacity gap through subcontracting out some of his work might be a short term solution, but McIlwraith was also uneasy about the impact on customer relations that too much reliance on subcontractors would have.

The most obvious capacity constraint was in extrusion. The problem with increasing extruder capacity was that the minimum size increment that was available was another press—representing roughly a 33% increase in capacity. Moreover, in order to run this new press efficiently it would have to be specialized for one, or possibly two, billet diameters. Although some shuffling around of orders between machines was possible, this could still have the effect of drastically increasing the capacity for certain sized billets while not serving to relax substantially the capacity constraint on other diameters.

Finally, new presses were very expensive: Peter McIlwraith estimated that the total installed cost would be just over £1,000,000, or nearly 50% of Indalex's net Fixed Assets. Interest rates for long term money were running 9–10% (down from 17% two years earlier), but this cost was balanced by the fact that the cost of capital equipment was rising at a rate of 12–15% per year. The overall rate of inflation for the U.K. was predicted to be in the range of 8–12% through the early 1980's.

If demand grew as expected there promised to be little difficulty in filling the capacity of the new press within a 3 year period, but recently McIlwraith had begun to sense that the growth of the U.K.'s economy might not be as rapid as most people had been predicting a few months earlier. The entire European Economic Community, in fact, appeared to be stagnating, and so he was forced to consider what he would do with the new press if he could not fill it naturally with new demand. He could quickly pull in about 200 tonnes/year that were being subcontracted out, for example, and probably attract another 500 tonnes of small batch size business that he was currently turning down because of his capacity squeeze. In addition he could "buy demand" by submitting a low bid for one or two very high volume orders. In this way he could probably get close to the 1500–2000 tonnes required for a breakeven operation, but at the risk of temporarily compromising his company's long term marketing strategy and reputation.

Complicating the problem was the fact that if he were to maintain his current balance of operations, he should add a new anodising plant, containing a minimum of three new tanks with a combined annual capacity of 2000 tonnes. This would cost another £800,000. Filling this new capacity would present less of a problem, because two of his present anodising tanks were becoming obsolete and would have to be replaced shortly anyway. But the question remained: was this the time to do it?

Over the long term McIlwraith was optimistic that he could fill the capacity of the new press and anodising plant, almost irrespective of the temporary dips and rises in the U.K. economy.

This would require some focused sales planning, of course: beginning by estimating exactly how much of what kind/size capacity would be available at what points in time, then selecting products and customers who were likely vehicles for filling this capacity, and then moving aggressively to get their business. This necessitated some determined long-range thinking, but was essentially how Indalex had built its current business to its present robust state—during most of which time it had been facing comparable over-capacity in the industry, and comparable sluggishness in the overall economy.

Indalex also had the option of expanding in another direction, with less marketing risk. It was currently generating somewhat less than 5000 tonnes of aluminium scrap per year out of its current operations (see Exhibit 3). This scrap was converted back into reusable aluminium billets under a "tolling" arrangement with an outside company. McIlwraith had become intrigued with the possibility of buying his own recycling plant, which would allow Indalex to reprocess its own scrap aluminium.

The equipment that he was looking at was very modern, and would cost about £690,000. It would be housed in a warehouse building that was adjacent to Indalex's plant site. Purchasing and modifying this building would cost an additional £167,000. The plant would conform strictly to the latest pollution-control regulations, and would not release any toxic fumes or smoke to the atmosphere. The estimated operating savings per year are detailed in *Exhibits 6a* and *6b*. In addition to these monetary savings, additional advantages to Indalex included the following:

1. Total capacity of the recycling plant, based on the assumptions of round-the-clock operation 5 days a week, 48 weeks a year, and a 90% efficiency rate, would be approximately 10,500 tonnes per year. This implied that Indalex would be able to handle all of its reprocessing needs through the late 1980's. Another 40% increase in capacity could be provided simply by moving to a 7-day-per-week operation.
2. The proposed plant utilized two separate re-melt furnaces, which permitted Indalex to continue operations at a reduced rate if one of the furnaces went out of operation.

3. It gave Indalex total control over its supply of secondary billet (about one-third of its total aluminium usage), and freed it from having to depend on an outside company. This was expected to become increasingly important as the demand for aluminium increased faster than world production capacity, suggesting the possibility of a world shortage of ingots in the early-to-mid 1980's.

4. In times of billet shortage, Indalex would have the option of buying raw aluminium ingots and converting them to billets itself.

5. Under its current tolling arrangement, Indalex did not transfer ownership of the scrap it produced, so the cost of the capital tied up in scrap inventories would not be affected. In fact, its scrap inventories might even decrease as its scrap "pipeline" contracted and it was able to tailor the billet sizes it produced to its changing extrusion requirements. Other inventories (of various additives) might increase, but only on the order of £50,000 per year.

Once the new plant was working properly, it would be relatively easy to manage. Since Indalex currently purchased 8 grades of alumin-

EXHIBIT 6A New Recycling Plant

ESTIMATED OPERATING COST OF PROPOSED RECYCLING PLANT

	Selected Years			
I. BASE CASE: NO PLANT	1979	1981	1983	1985
Internal Scrap Generated (tons)[1]	5371	5922	6785	7480
Tolling Cost/ton (adj. for infl.)	£ 121	£ 141	£ 165	£ 192
Total Tolling Charge (£000's)	650	835	1120	1436
II. NEW RECYCLING PLANT				
Internal Scrap Generated (tons)	5371	5922	6785	7480
Implied Input[2]	6350	7002	8022	8844
Variable Cost/ton[3]	34.60	37.12	39.82	42.73
(£000's)				
Total Variable Costs	220	260	320	380
Total Annual Costs[3]	112	136	152	171
Total Operating Costs	332	396	472	551
Plus Furnace Reline	—	—	24	—
			496	
Savings	318	439	624	885
Less Capital Allowances (for tax purposes)	822	—	—	—
Additional Taxable Profit From Operation	(504)	439	624	885
Tax Paid (Recovered), at 52%	(262)	228	324	460
After Tax Profit	(242)	211	300	425

Notes:

[1] Scrap tons are estimated from estimated sales tons, according to business plan, and assuming that scrap remains in the same proportion to total sales as is the case currently.

[2] Proper furnace operation requires the addition of about 20% virgin aluminum to the scrap charge, as well as trace amounts of magnesium and silicon. A 2% melt loss is also factored in.

[3] These costs are described in more detail in Exhibit 6b. Inflation has been factored into them, so they represent current best estimates of the costs that will be experienced in each year.

1. Indalex Ltd.

EXHIBIT 6B New Recycling Plant

ESTIMATED VARIABLE COST/TON (1979)[1]

	1979	1981
Consumable materials other than scrap and virgin ingot	£ 8.35	£ 9.71
Energy	19.06	19.57
Other (maintenance, royalties, misc.)	2.68	3.00
Total Variable Costs per Ton	30.09	32.28
Incl. Contingency at 15%[2]	£34.60	£37.12

ESTIMATED ANNUAL FIXED COSTS (£000's)

	1979	1981
Direct labor and employee benefits[3]	61	75
Indirect labor	13	16
Insurance	7	9
Allocated overhead	16	18
	97	118
Incl. Contingency at 15%[2]	112	136

[1] Costs are best estimates, based largely on data provided by the equipment supplier.

[2] This provides a cushion against unforeseen or underestimated costs.

[3] Optimal efficiency is achieved if the furnace is fully crewed for 24 hour operation during the time it is in use. Although it will initially be used only at 50% capacity, the plan is to staff it for continuous operation and then shut it down periodically. During shut down times the 14-man workforce will be assigned to other tasks. Labor cost increases over time, therefore, will arise from wage rate increases rather than from increases in the number of workers employed.

ium, it would have to separate the scrap it produced and process it separately to preserve purity, but this presented no major problems. McIlwraith's superiors in the Pillar Group had already informally agreed to let him buy this new smelter if he decided to recommend it, both on the basis of its own internal economics and the valuable information that would be generated for Pillar's other extrusion companies. But filling the remaining capacity of the remelt plant would present Indalex with new marketing problems,

and it probably did not have the personnel resources to do everything at once.

The question that Peter McIlwraith pondered in late 1977 was: which of the various options in front of him should he choose to do first? Since each of the three alternatives (a new extrusion press, a new anodising plant, or the recycling plant) would require 10–12 months to install, a decision had to be made immediately in order for the new piece of equipment to be available by the beginning of 1979.

1. Indalex Ltd.

2. Manufacturing—Missing Link in Corporate Strategy

The thesis of this article is that manufacturing has too long been dominated by experts and specialists. For many years these were the industrial engineers; now they are the computer experts. As a result, top executives tend to avoid involvement in manufacturing policy making, manufacturing managers are ignorant of corporate strategy, and a function that *could* be a valuable asset and tool of corporate strategy becomes a liability instead. The author shows how top management can correct this situation by systematically linking up manufacturing with corporate strategy.

A company's manufacturing function typically is either a competitive weapon or a corporate millstone. It is seldom neutral. The connection between manufacturing and corporate success is rarely seen as more than the achievement of high efficiency and low costs. In fact, the connection is much more critical and much more sensitive. Few top managers are aware that what appear to be routine manufacturing decisions frequently come to limit the corporation's strategic options, binding it with facilities, equipment, personnel, and basic controls and policies to a noncompetitive posture which may take years to turn around.

Research I have conducted during the past three years reveals that top management unknowingly delegates a surprisingly large portion of basic policy decisions to lower levels in the manufacturing area. Generally, this abdication of responsibility comes about more through a lack of concern than by intention. And it is partly the reason that many manufacturing policies and procedures developed at lower levels reflect assumptions about corporate strategy which are incorrect or misconstrued.

Millstone Effect

When companies fail to recognize the relationship between manufacturing decisions and corporate strategy, they may become saddled with seriously noncompetitive production systems which are expensive and time-consuming to change. Here are several examples:

- Company A entered the combination washer-dryer field after several competitors had failed to achieve successful entries into the field. Company A's executives believed their model would overcome the technical drawbacks which had hurt their competitors and held back the development of any substantial market. The manufacturing managers tooled the new unit on the usual conveyorized assembly line and giant stamping presses used for all company products.

When the washer-dryer failed in the market, the losses amounted to millions. The plant had been "efficient" in the sense that costs were low. But the tooling and production processes did not meet the demands of the marketplace.

- Company B produced five kinds of electronic gear for five different groups of customers; the gear ranged from satellite controls to industrial controls and electronic components. In each market a different task was required of the production function. For instance, in the first market, extremely high reliability was demanded; in the second market, rapid introduction of a stream of new products was demanded; in the third market, low costs were of critical importance for competitive survival.

    In spite of these highly diverse and contrasting tasks, production management elected to centralize manufacturing facilities in one plant in order to achieve "economies of scale." The result was a failure to achieve high reliability, economies of scale, or an ability to introduce new products quickly. What happened, in short, was that the demands placed on manufacturing by a competitive strategy were ignored by the production group in order to achieve economies of scale. This production group was obsessed with developing "a total system, fully computerized." The manufacturing program satisfied no single division, and the serious marketing problems which resulted choked company progress.

- Company C produced plastic molding resins. A new plant under construction was to come on-stream in eight months, doubling production. In the meantime, the company had a much higher volume of orders than it could meet.

    In a strategic sense, manufacturing's task was to maximize output to satisy large, key customers. Yet the plant's production control system was set up—as it had been for years—to minimize costs. As a result, long runs were emphasized. While costs were low, many customers had to wait, and many key buyers were lost. Consequently, when the new plant came on-stream, it was forced to operate at a low volume.

The mistake of considering low costs and high efficiencies as the key manufacturing objective in each of these examples is typical of the oversimplified concept of "a good manufacturing operation." Such criteria frequently get companies into trouble, or at least do not aid in the development of manufacturing into a competitive weapon. Manufacturing affects corporate strategy, and corporate strategy affects manufacturing. Even in an apparently routine operating area such as a production scheduling system, strategic considerations should outweigh technical and conventional industrial engineering factors invoked in the name of "productivity."

Shortsighted Views

The fact is that manufacturing is seen by most top managers as requiring involved technical skills and a morass of petty daily decisions and details. It is seen by many young managers as the gateway to grubby routine, where days are filled with high pressure, packed with details, and limited to low-level decision making—all of which is out of the sight and minds of top-level executives. It is generally taught in graduate schools of business administration as a combination of industrial engineering (time study, plant layout, inventory theory, and so on) and quantitative analysis (linear programming, simulation, queuing theory, and the rest). In total, a manufacturing career is generally perceived as an all-consuming, technically oriented, hectic life that minimizes one's chances of ever reaching the top and maximizes the chances of being buried in minutiae.

In fact, these perceptions are not wholly inaccurate. It is the thesis of this article that the technically oriented concept of manufacturing is all too prevalent; and that it is largely responsible for the typically limited contribution manufacturing makes to a corporation's arsenal of competitive weapons, for manufacturing's failure to attract the top talent it needs and *should* have, and for its failure to attract more young managers with general management interests and broad abilities. In my opinion, manufacturing is generally perceived in the wrong way at the top, managed in the wrong way at the plant level, and taught in the wrong way in the business schools.

These are strong words, but change is needed, and I believe that only a more relevant concept of manufacturing can bring change. I see no sign whatsoever that we have found the means of solving the problems mentioned. The new, mathematically based "total systems" approaches to production management offer the promise of new and valuable concepts and techniques, but I doubt that these approaches will overcome the tendency of top management to remove itself from manufacturing. Ten years of development of quantitative techniques have left us each year with the promise of a "great new age" in production management that lies "just ahead." The promise never seems to be realized. Stories of computer and "total systems" fiascoes are available by the dozen; these failures are always expensive, and in almost every case management had delegated the work to experts.

I do not want to demean the promise—and, indeed, some present contributions—of the systems/computer approach. Two years ago I felt more sanguine about it. But, since then, close observation of the problems in U.S. industry has convinced me that the "answer" promised is inadequate. The approach cannot overcome the problems described until it does a far better job of linking manufacturing and corporate strategy. What is needed is some kind of integrative mechanism.

Pattern of Failure

An examination of top management perceptions of manufacturing has led me to some notions about basic causes of many production problems. In each of six industries I have studied, I have found top executives delegating excessive amounts of manufacturing policy to subordinates, avoiding involvement in most production matters, and

failing to ask the right questions until their companies are in obvious trouble. This pattern seems to be due to a combination of two factors:

1. A sense of personal inadequacy, on the part of top executives, in managing production. (Often the feeling evolves from a tendency to regard the area as a technical or engineering specialty, or a mundane "nuts and bolts" segment of management.)
2. A lack of awareness among top executives that a production system inevitably involves trade-offs and compromises and so must be designed to perform a limited task well, with that task defined by corporate strategic objectives.

The first factor is, of course, dependent in part on the second, for the sense of inadequacy would not be felt if the strategic role of production were clearer. The second factor is the one we shall concentrate on in the remainder of this article.

Like a building, a vehicle, or a boat, a production system can be designed to do some things well, but always at the expense of other abilities. It appears to be the lack of recognition of these trade-offs and their effects on a corporation's ability to compete that leads top management to delegate often-critical decisions to lower, technically oriented staff levels, and to allow policy to be made through apparently unimportant operating decisions.

In the balance of this article I would like to . . .

- sketch out the relationships between production operations and corporate strategy;
- call attention to the existence of specific trade-offs in production system design;
- comment on the inadequacy of computer specialists to deal with these trade-offs;
- suggest a new way of looking at manufacturing which might enable the nontechnical manager to understand and manage the manufacturing area.

Strategic Implications

Frequently the interrelationship between production operations and corporate strategy is not easily grasped. The notion is simple enough—namely, that a company's competitive strategy at a given time places particular demands on its manufacturing function, and, conversely, that the company's manufacturing posture and operations should be specifically designed to fulfill the task demanded by strategic plans. What is more elusive is the set of cause-and-effect factors which determine the linkage between strategy and production operations.

Strategy is a set of plans and policies by which a company aims to gain advantages over its competitors. Generally a strategy includes plans for products and the marketing of these products to a particular set of customers. The marketing plans usually include specific approaches and steps to be followed in identifying potential customers, determining why, where, and when they buy, and learning how they can best be reached and convinced to purchase.

The company must have an advantage, a particular appeal, a special push or pull created by its products, channels of distribution, advertising, price, packaging, availability, warranties, or other factors.

Contrasting Demands

What is not always realized is that different marketing strategies and approaches to gaining a competitive advantage place different demands on the manufacturing arm of the company. For example, a furniture manufacturer's strategy for broad distribution of a limited, low-price line with wide consumer advertising might generally require:

- Decentralized finished-goods storage.
- Readily available merchandise.
- Rock-bottom costs.

The foregoing demands might in turn require:

- Relatively large lot sizes.
- Specialized facilities for woodworking and finishing.
- A large proportion of low- and medium-skilled workers in the work force.
- Concentration of manufacturing in a limited number of large-scale plants.

In contrast, a manufacturer of high-price, high-style furniture with more exclusive distribution would require an entirely different set of manufacturing policies. While higher prices and longer lead times would allow more leeway in the plant, this company would have to contend with the problems implicit in delivering high-quality furniture made of wood (which is a soft, dimensionally unstable material whose surface is expensive to finish and easy to damage), a high setup cost relative to running times in most wood-machining operations, and the need to make a large number of nonstandardized parts. While the first company must work with these problems too, they are more serious to the second company because its marketing strategy forces it to confront the problems head on. The latter's manufacturing policies will probably require:

- Many model and style changes.
- Production to order.
- Extremely reliable high quality.

These demands may in turn require:

- An organziation that can get new models into production quickly.
- A production control group that can coordinate all activities so as to reduce lead times.
- Technically trained supervisors and technicians.

Consequently, the second company ought to have a strong manufacturing-methods engineering staff; simple, flexible tooling; and a well-trained, experienced work force.

In summary, the two manufacturers would need to develop very different policies, personnel, and operations if they were to be equally successful in carrying out their strategies.

Important Choices

In the example described, there are marked contrasts in the two companies. Actually, even small and subtle differences in corporate strategies should be reflected in manufacturing policies. However, my research shows that few companies do in fact carefully and explicitly tailor their production systems to perform the tasks which are vital to corporate success.

Instead of focusing first on strategy, then moving to define the manufacturing task, and next turning to systems design in manufacturing policy, managements tend to employ a concept of production which is much less effective. Most top executives and production managers look at their production systems with the notion of "total productivity" or the equivalent, "efficiency." They seek a kind of blending of low costs, high quality, and acceptable customer service. The view prevails that a plant with reasonably modern equipment, up-to-date methods and procedures, a cooperative work force, a computerized information system, and an enlightened management will be a good plant and will perform efficiently.

But what is "a good plant"? What is "efficient performance"? And what should the computer be programmed to do? Should it minimize lead times or minimize inventories? A company cannot do both. Should the computer minimize direct labor or indirect labor? Again, the company cannot do both. Should investment in equipment be minimized—or should outside purchasing be held to a minimum? One could go on with such choices.

The reader may reply: "What management wants is a combination of both ingredients that results in the lowest *total* cost." But that answer, too, is insufficient. The "lowest total cost" answer leaves out the dimensions of time and customer satisfaction, which must usually be considered too. Because cost *and* time *and* customers are all involved, we have to conclude that what is a "good" plant for Company A may be a poor or mediocre plant for its competitor, Company B, which is in the same industry but pursues a different strategy.

The purpose of manufacturing is to serve the company—to meet its needs for survival, profit, and growth. Manufacturing is part of the strategic concept that relates a company's strengths and resources to opportunities in the market. Each strategy creates a unique manufacturing task. Manufacturing management's ability to meet that task is the key measure of its success.

Trade-Offs in Design

It is curious that most top managements and production people do not state their yardsticks of success more precisely, and instead fall back on such measures as "efficiency," "low cost," and "productivity." My studies suggest that a key reason for this phenomenon is that very few executives realize the existence of trade-offs in designing and operating a production system.

Yet most managers will readily admit that there are compromises or trade-offs to be made in designing an airplane or a truck. In the case of an airplane, trade-offs would involve such matters as cruising speed, takeoff and landing distances, initial cost, maintenance, fuel consumption, passenger comfort, and cargo or passenger capacity. A given stage of technology defines limits as to what can be accomplished in these respects. For instance, no one today can design a 500-passenger plane that can land on a carrier and also break the sonic barrier.

Much the same thing is true of manufacturing. The variables of cost, time, quality, technological constraints, and customer satisfaction place limits on what management can do, force compromises, and demand an explicit recognition of a multitude of trade-offs and choices. Yet everywhere I find plants which have inadvertently emphasized one yardstick at the expense of another, more important one. For example:

- An electronics manufacturer with dissatisfied customers hired a computer expert and placed manufacturing under a successful engineering design chief to make it a "total system."

    A year later its computer was spewing out an inch-thick volume of daily information. "We know the location of every part in the plant on any given day," boasted the production manager and his computer system chief.

Nevertheless, customers were more dissatisfied than ever. Product managers hotly complained that delivery promises were regularly missed—and in almost every case they first heard about failures from their customers. The problem centered on the fact that computer information runs were organized by part numbers and operations. They were designed to facilitate machine scheduling and to aid shop foremen; they were not organized around end products, which would have facilitated customer service.

How had this come about? Largely, it seemed clear, because the manufacturing managers had become absorbed in their own "systems approach"; the fascination of mechanized data handling had become an end in itself. As for top management, it had more or less abdicated responsibility. Because the company's growth and success had been based on engineering and because top management was R&D-oriented, policy-making executives saw production as a routine requiring a lower level of complexity and brainpower. Top management argued further that the company had production experts who were well paid and who should be able to do their jobs without bothering top-level people.

Recognizing Alternatives

To develop the notion of important trade-off decisions in manufacturing, let us consider *Exhibit 1*, which shows some examples.

In each decision area—plant and equipment, production planning and control, and so forth—top management needs to recognize the alternatives and become involved in the design of the production system. It needs to become involved to the extent that the alternative selected is appropriate to the manufacturing task determined by the corporate strategy.

Making such choices, is of course, an ongoing rather than a once-a-year or once-a-decade task; decisions have to be made constantly in these trade-off areas. Indeed, the real crux of the problem seems to be how to ensure that the continuing process of decision making is not isolated from competitive and strategic facts, when many of the trade-off decisions do not at first appear to bear on company strategy. As long as a technical point of view dominates manufacturing decisions, a degree of isolation from the realities of competition is inevitable. Unfortunately, as we shall see, the technical viewpoint is all too likely to prevail.

Technical Dominance

The similarity between today's emphasis on the technical experts—the computer specialist and the engineering-oriented production technician—and yesterday's emphasis on the efficiency expert—time-study man and industrial engineer—

is impossible to escape. For 50 years, U.S. management relied on efficiency experts trained in the techniques of Frederick W. Taylor. Industrial engineers were kings of the factory. Their early approaches and attitudes were often conducive to industrial warfare, strikes, sabotage, and militant unions, but that was not realized then. Also not realized was that their technical emphasis often produced an inward orientation toward cost that ignored the customer, and an engineering point of view that gloried in tools, equipment, and gadgets rather than in markets and service. Most important, the cult of industrial engineering tended to make top executives technically disqualified from involvement in manufacturing decisions.

Since the turn of the century, this efficiency-centered orientation has dogged U.S. manufacturing. It has created that image of "nuts and bolts," of greasy, dirty, detail jobs in manufacturing. It has dominated "production" courses in most graduate schools of business administration. It has alienated young men with broad management educations from manufacturing careers. It has "buffaloed" top managers.

Several months ago I was asked by a group of industrial engineers to offer an opinion as to why so few industrial engineers were moving up to the top of their companies. My answer was that perhaps a technical point of view cut them off from top management, just as the jargon and hocus-pocus of manufacturing often kept top management from understanding the factory. In their isolation, they could gain only a severely limited sense of market needs and of corporate competitive strategy.

Enter the computer expert

Today the industrial engineer is declining in importance in many companies. But a new technical expert, the computer specialist, is taking his place. I use the term "computer specialist" to refer to individuals who specialize in computer systems design and programming.

I do not deny, of course, that computer specialists have a very important job to do. I do object, however, to any notion that computer specialist have more of a top management view than was held by their predecessors, the industrial engineers. In my experience, the typical computer

EXHIBIT 1 Some Important Trade-off Decisions in Manufacturing—or "You Can't Have it Both Ways"

Decision area	Decision	Alternatives
PLANT AND EQUIPMENT	Span of process	Make or buy
	Plant size	One big plant or several smaller ones
	Plant location	Locate near markets or locate near materials
	Investment decisions	Invest mainly in buildings or equipment or inventories or research
	Choice of equipment	General-purpose or special-purpose equipment
	Kind of tooling	Temporary, minimum tooling or "production tooling"
PRODUCTION PLANNING AND CONTROL	Frequency of inventory taking	Few or many breaks in production for buffer stocks
	Inventory size	High inventory or a lower inventory
	Degree of inventory control	Control in great detail or in lesser detail
	What to control	Controls designed to minimize machine downtime or labor cost or time in process, or to maximize output of particular products or material usage
	Quality control	High reliability and quality or low costs
	Use of standards	Formal or informal or none at all
LABOR AND STAFFING	Job specialization	Highly specialized or not highly specialized
	Supervision	Technically trained first-line supervisors or nontechnically trained supervisors
	Wage system	Many job grades or few job grades; incentive wages or hourly wages
	Supervision	Close supervision or loose supervision
	Industrial engineers	Many or few such men
PRODUCT DESIGN/ENGINEERING	Size of product line	Many customer specials or few specials or none at all
	Design stability	Frozen design or many engineering change orders
	Technological risk	Use of new processes unproved by competitors or follow-the-leader policy
	Engineering	Complete packaged design or design-as-you-go approach
	Use of manufacturing engineering	Few or many manufacturing engineers
ORGANIZATION AND MANAGEMENT	Kind of organization	Functional or product focus or geographical or other
	Executive use of time	High involvement in investment or production planning or cost control or quality control or other activities
	Degree of risk assumed	Decisions based on much or little information
	Use of staff	Large or small staff group
	Executive style	Much or little involvement in detail; authoritarian or nondirective style; much or little contact with organization

2. Manufacturing—Missing Link in Corporate Strategy

expert has been forced to master a complex and all-consuming technology, a fact which frequently makes him parochial rather than catholic in his views. Because he is so preoccupied with the detail of a total system, it is necessary for someone in top management to give him objectives and policy guidance. In his choice of trade-offs and compromises for his computer system, he needs to be instructed and not left to his own devices. Or, stated differently, he needs to see the entire corporation as a system, not just one corner of it—i.e, the manufacturing plant.

Too often this is not happening. The computer is a nightmare to many top managers because they have let it and its devotees get out of hand. They have let technical experts continue to dominate; the failure of top management truly to manage production goes on.

How *can* top mangement begin to manage manufacturing instead of turning it over to technicians who, through no fault of their own, are absorbed in their own arts and crafts? How can U.S. production management be helped to cope with the rising pressures of new markets, more rapid product changes, new technologies, larger and riskier equipment decisions, and the swarm of problems we face in industry today? Let us look at some answers.

Better Decision Making

The answers I would like to suggest are not panaceas, nor are they intended to be comprehensive. Indeed, no one can answer all the question and problems described with one nice formula or point of view. But surely we can improve on the notion that production systems need only be "productive and efficient." Top management can manage manufacturing if it will engage in the making of manufacturing policy, rather than considering it a kind of fifth, independent estate beyond the pale of control.

The place to start, I believe, is with the acceptance of a theory of manufacturing which begins with the concept that in any system design there are significant trade-offs (as shown in *Exhibit 1*) which must be explicitly decided on.

Determining policy

Executives will also find it helpful to think of manufacturing policy determination as an orderly process or sequence of steps. *Exhibit 2* is a schematic portrayal of such a process. It shows that manufacturing policy must stem from corporate strategy, and that the process of determining this policy is the means by which top management can actually manage production. Use of this process can end manufacturing isolation and tie top management and manufacturing together. The sequence is simple but vital:

- It begins with an analysis of the competitive situation, of how rival companies are competing in terms of product, markets, policies, and channels of distribution. Management examines the number and kind of competitors and the opportunities open to its company.
- Next comes a critical appraisal of the company's skills and resources and of its present facilities and approaches.
- The third step is the formulation of company strategy: How is the company to compete successfully, combine its strengths with market opportunities, and define niches in the markets where it can gain advantages?
- The fourth step is the point where many top executives cut off their thinking. It is important for them to define the implications or "so what" effects of company strategy in terms of specific manufacturing tasks. For example, they should ask: "If we are to compete with an X product of Y price for Z customers using certain distribution channels and forms of advertising, what will be demanded of manufacturing in terms of costs, deliveries, lead times, quality levels, and reliability?" These demands should be precisely defined.
- The fifth and sixth steps are to study the constraints or limitations imposed by the economics and the technology of the industry. These factors are generally common to all competitors. An explicit recognition of them is a prerequisite to a genuine understanding of the manufacturing problems and opportunities. These are facts that a nontechnical manager can develop, study, understand, and put to work. *Exhibit 3* contains sample lists of topics for the manager to use in doing his homework.
- The seventh and eight steps are the key ones for integrating and synthesizing all the prior ones into a broad manufacturing policy. The question for management is: "Given the facts of

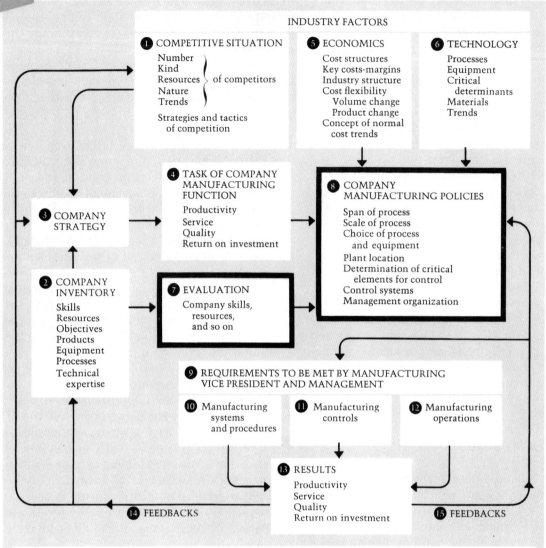

INDUSTRY FACTORS

❶ COMPETITIVE SITUATION

Number ⎫
Kind ⎪
Resources ⎬ of competitors
Nature ⎪
Trends ⎭

Strategies and tactics
of competition

❺ ECONOMICS

Cost structures
Key costs-margins
Industry structure
Cost flexibility
    Volume change
    Product change
Concept of normal
    cost trends

❻ TECHNOLOGY

Processes
Equipment
Critical
    determinants
Materials
Trends

❹ TASK OF COMPANY MANUFACTURING FUNCTION

Productivity
Service
Quality
Return on investment

❸ COMPANY STRATEGY

❷ COMPANY INVENTORY

Skills
Resources
Objectives
Products
Equipment
Processes
Technical
    expertise

❼ EVALUATION

Company skills,
    resources,
    and so on

❽ COMPANY MANUFACTURING POLICIES

Span of process
Scale of process
Choice of process
    and equipment
Plant location
Determination of critical
    elements for control
Control systems
Management organization

❾ REQUIREMENTS TO BE MET BY MANUFACTURING VICE PRESIDENT AND MANAGEMENT

❿ Manufacturing systems and procedures

⓫ Manufacturing controls

⓬ Manufacturing operations

⓭ RESULTS

Productivity
Service
Quality
Return on investment

⓮ FEEDBACKS

⓯ FEEDBACKS

Key

1. What the others are doing

2. What we have got or can get to compete with

3. How we can compete

4. What we must accomplish in manufacturing in order to compete

5. Economic constraints and opportunities common to the industry

6. Constraints and opportunities common to the technology

7. Our resources evaluated

8. How we should set ourselves up to match resources, economics, and technology to meet the tasks required by our competitive strategy

9. The implementation requirements of our manufacturing policies

10. Basic systems in manufacturing (e.g., production planning, use of inventories, use of standards, and wage systems)

11. Controls of cost, quality, flows, inventory, and time

12. Selection of operations or ingredients critical to success (e.g., labor skills, equipment utilization, and yields)

13. How we are performing

14. Changes in what we have got, effects on competitive situation, and review of strategy

15. Analysis and review of manufacturing operations and policies

the economics and the technology of the industry, how do we set ourselves up to meet the specific manufacturing tasks posed by our particular competitive strategy?" Management must decide what it is going to make and what it will buy; how many plants to have, how big they should be, and where to place them; what

EXHIBIT 3 Illustrative Constraints or Limitations Which Should be Studied

A. Economics of the industry
Labor, burden, material, depreciation costs
Flexibility of production to meet changes in volume
Return on investment, prices, margins
Number and location of plants
Critical control variables
Critical functions (e.g., maintenance, production control, personnel)
Typical financial structures
Typical costs and cost relationships
Typical operating problems
Barriers to entry
Pricing practices
"Maturity" of industry products, markets, production practices, and so on
Importance of economies of scale
Importance of integrated capacities of corporations
Importance of having a certain balance of different types of equipment
Ideal balances of equipment capacities
Nature and type of production control
Government influences

B. Technology of the industry
Rate of technological change
Scale of processes
Span of processes
Degree of mechanization
Technological sophistication
Time requirements for making changes

processes and equipment to buy; what the key elements are which need to be controlled and how they can be controlled; and what kind of management organization would be most appropriate.

Next come the steps of working out programs of implementation, controls, performance measures, and review procedures (see Steps 9–15 in *Exhibit 2*).

Conclusion

The process just described is, in my observation, quite different from the usual process of manufacturing management. Conventionally, manufacturing has been managed from the bottom up. The classical process of the age of mass production is to select an operation, break it down into its elements, analyze and improve each element, and put it back together. This approach was contributed years ago by Frederick W. Taylor and other industrial engineers who followed in his footsteps.

What I am suggesting is an entirely different approach, one adapted far better to the current era of more products, shorter runs, vastly accelerated product changes, and increased marketing competition. I am suggesting a kind of "top-down" manufacturing. This approach starts with the company and its competitive strategy; its goal is to define manufacturing policy. Its presumption is that only when basic manufacturing policies are defined can the technical experts, industrial and manufacturing engineers, labor relations specialists, and computer experts have the necessary guidance to do their work.

With its focus on corporate strategy and the manufacturing task, the top-down approach can give top management both its entrée to manufacturing and the concepts it needs to take the initiative and truly manage this function. When this is done, executives previously unfamiliar with manufacturing are likely to find it an exciting activity. The company will have an important addition to its arsenal of competitive weapons.

3. Chandler Home Products (B)

"A few months ago the head of our European organization asked me to recommend whether we should expand my plant again or locate a new production facility somewhere else in Europe. I studied the situation and alternatives for a few weeks and then suggested that this recommendation be made by someone outside my organization. There were simply too many conflicting interests involved, and I think I would have been regarded as being too biased.

"I am very proud of my plant's performance over the past four years. We have been able to maintain our prices and delivery reliability in the face of inflation, exchange rate fluctuations, new products, and political uncertainty. The arguments that led to the construction of this plant over 15 years ago, and the concentration in it of the production for most of our sales in continental Europe, are equally valid today. The plant is not too large, either in comparison with other manufacturing plants in Holland or in comparison with our own U.S. plant in Peoria. We have room to expand, and I am convinced that the costs of expanding here will be less than anywhere else in Europe."

Roland van Zwieten, Manager of Chandler Home Products' Complant ("Common Market Plant") in Nijmegen, Holland, raised his hands expressively and smiled. "You see, I am biased! So my boss agreed with me, and that's the reason a Booz, Allen[1] team is working here now."

[1] Booz, Allen & Hamilton, a U.S.-based multinational management consulting firm.

This case was prepared by Robert H. Hayes.

Chandler Home Products

Chandler Home Products was a privately owned, family-controlled corporation headquartered in Peoria, Illinois. Chandler's lines of household care products were marketed worldwide. Though no company figures were published, industry observers estimated Chandler's 1978 sales at over $1 billion. Approximately 1,500 different products were sold in almost 50 countries. More than half of Chandler's sales were made outside the U.S.A. Of these a majority were recorded in Europe. Van Zwieten's Complant alone produced almost 150 different product formulations. Since most of these were sold in more than one size, the total number of SKUs (stock keeping units) was in excess of 650.

The bulk of the company's business was concentrated in four product areas: floor care products, furniture polish, air fresheners, and insecticides. Although the percentage varied by product line and by country, roughly 60% of Chandler's sales were in the form of aerosols (sold in pressurized cans), a quarter were in liquid form (sold in cans and bottles), and the remainder were solids. Chandler's strategy had been to seek a dominant market position for its products, while maintaining premium prices, through product innovation and the heavy use of advertising. High gross margins (these varied considerably from country to country, but 60% was not unusual) were needed to finance the costs of R&D, advertising and channel support while still providing adequate returns. The company tried to maintain a profit-to-sales ratio of 5% after taxes.

In recent years attempts had been made to diversify into the personal care field with deodorants and shaving gels. Household care products had also been extended into laundry aids and air fresheners. Introducing new lines of products was part of an overall effort to become less dependent upon Chandler's traditional household care products. The markets for these traditional products had matured in the developed countries and promised inadequate future growth. Moreover, the large market shares which Chandler commanded in its traditional product lines were likely to be the target of increasing competitive assault. Competing in new markets, however, frequently pitted Chandler against such international giants as Procter & Gamble, Unilever, and Gillette.

Despite the fact that the markets for many of its products were maturing, and the overall rate of economic growth in the developed countries of the world was predicted to be less than 3% over the foreseeable future, Chandler hoped that the introduction of new products and the growth of markets in developing countries would enable it to maintain a sales growth rate of 15% per year. It intended to finance most of this growth through internally generated funds, so as to maintain its debt/equity ratio at the current level. This would require careful control over costs and investments, since a 15% sales growth could not be maintained if there were any deterioration in either its profit/sales or its sales/assets ratios. As part of its overall program for maintaining, even improving, profitability, the company intended to gradually shift its resources from low-profit, low-growth products to those that promised higher profits and higher growth. Proposed capital investments were expected to promise a return on investment of at least 25% before tax.

Chandler Europe

The decade of the 1960s witnessed a significant expansion of Chandler's European operations. While some European subsidiaries predated World War II, none had represented a major source of revenues until this growth period. Thereafter, existing subsidiaries grew in size and new subsidiaries rapidly blossomed throughout Western Europe.

Although most of the products sold in Europe were based on products developed in Peoria, the mix of sales differed greatly from country to country. Even neighboring European subsidiaries often significantly differed both in size and in the relative popularity of Chandler products in the diverse product categories in which they competed. Products were adapted to local consumers by means of local brand names, and sometimes even their formulations were modified to meet local preferences. Thus, the distribution of the income levels in a country, together with national tastes in home furnishing, greatly influenced the product offerings of the local Chandler subsidiary. Some foreign subsidiaries even sold products which had been developed specifically for their own use and which were unavailable in the U.S.

Country managers had considerable autonomy in determining their individual product lines. They could add, drop, reposition, or emphasize products according to their perception of local market conditions. Major product or marketing decisions (e.g. dropping a product, an unusual pricing strategy, etc.), of course, had to be justified before Mr. Genet, Chandler's Executive Vice President for European Consumer Goods.

In 1978 roughly 85% of Chandler's European consumer goods sales took place on the continent, while the U.K. accounted for the remainder. About a third of the sales in continental Europe came from Chandler's French subsidiary. The next largest subsidiary was Italy, whose sales were about half of France's, followed by Spain and Germany. An organization chart for the activities under Mr. Genet's jurisdiction is contained in *Exhibit 1*.

The Decision to Build the Complant

Before 1962 each subsidiary had been responsible for its own production. Following a major study by Booz, Allen & Hamilton it was decided to consolidate European production into two plants. One would be the existing facility at Buxbridge, England (about 50 miles from London) which would be responsible for the production of all of Chandler's products for the U.K. The other would be a new facility, the Complant, located in Nijme-

EXHIBIT 1 Organization for European Consumer Sales

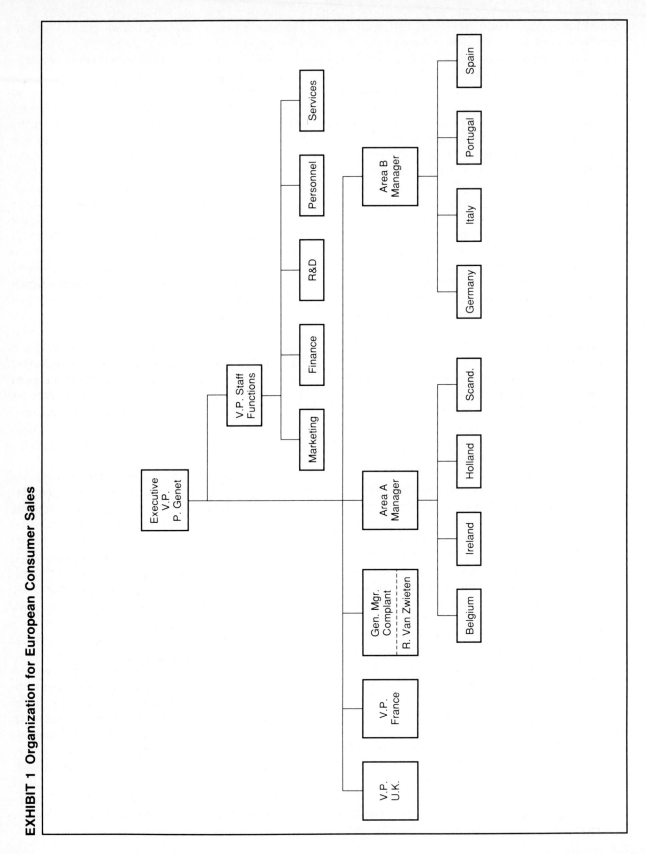

3. Chandler Home Products (B)

gen. This plant would be responsible for the production of the aerosol and liquid products for all of Chandler's EEC subsidiaries (the U.K. was not then a member of the Common Market).

The study which resulted in the decision to build the Complant was triggered by a recognition of two partially related trends in the European environment. First, Chandler's European sales were growing at a rate in excess of 40% per year and therefore would be expected to quadruple (from $6 to $24 million) by 1965 if not before. This forecast sales volume could not be produced in the existing Chandler manufacturing facilities, many of which were inefficient, already operating near capacity, and difficult to expand. Expanding these existing facilities, moreover, was expected to require an investment in additional plant and equipment which was greater than Chandler's total current European investment. Finally, it would be difficult to locate and train adequate managers and staff personnel for all these expansions.

Second, Europe appeared to be progressing smoothly towards its goal of free trade within the group of Common Market countries which accounted for almost all of Chandler's sales on the continent. Tariffs were to be reduced to 40% of their previous levels and quotas abolished by mid-1963. By the end of 1966 it was hoped that all tariffs and other discriminatory practices between member countries would be abolished. This appeared to be a realizable goal in 1962.

As a result, Chandler's management wondered whether the usual risks of centralized manufacturing (for example, supply problems resulting from a plant shutdown or transportation/customs restrictions) in Europe would soon be no greater than they were in the U.S., where Chandler supplied the entire country from a single facility. These risks might even be less in Europe because of the back-up provided by the Buxbridge plant, which was Chandler's largest and most modern manufacturing facility outside the U.S. Unlike most of its European facilities, moreover, Buxbridge had ample room to expand.

The consulting study confirmed Chandler's intuition, and provided additional reasons for moving to consolidated production.

1. Although overall growth in Europe would average over 40% per year, this growth varied widely among countries. Moreover, there was a high degree of uncertainty about the growth rate in several countries. Consolidating production for all countries into one plant was expected to help smooth the total load. It would be easier, that is, to balance production in a single, well-designed and well-managed plant than to balance production simultaneously in several small country-oriented plants.

2. The cost of building a centralized manufacturing plant would be at least $500,000 less than the cost of adding an equivalent amount of capacity to existing facilities. Partly this savings would be due to the economies of scale associated with buying eight modern, highly automated filling lines and auxiliary materials-handling equipment instead of expanding the capacity of older equipment or adding new lines at several locations. Construction costs at a new, carefully chosen site would also be less than at the congested sites where most of Chandler's plants were located. These sites, however, could easily be converted into regional warehouses for Chandler's products.

3. A consolidated plant would be large enough to justify the construction of an on-site polymer plant and large-scale chemical processing and storage facilities. This would enable Chandler to reduce its reliance on outside suppliers and gain more control over its total costs.

4. The annual operating cost of the new plant would also be considerably less than the total cost of operating separate plants. The Booz, Allen study showed that such savings would amount to almost $1.8 million by 1965, or over 20% of total annual costs. A large part of this savings came from the same economies of scale mentioned previously (fewer production workers, a single production control department, etc.), but the major part was expected to come from centralized purchasing of raw materials and containers (the cost of the packaging materials in a typical product was about one-and-a-half times the cost of the chemical ingredients), and from being able to buy in bulk directly from manufacturers as a result of the proposed ability to process these materials in Chandler's own facilities.

5. A centralized plant using modern automated equipment, managed by experts, and utilizing modern testing equipment and a well-equipped laboratory would ensure high and, more important, standardized quality for Chandler's proliferating product line.

6. Finally, a centralized plant would simplify and speed up the development, debugging, and introduction of new products.

After an analysis of several countries the study team decided (somewhat to its surprise, since it had begun with the expectation that either France or Germany would be the most logical location) that Holland would be the best country in which to locate the new plant. Several possible locations in Holland were studied in detail, and Nijmegen was finally recommended for a variety of reasons, including access to raw materials, its proximity to markets via existing rail lines and highways (the distance from Nijmegen to Milan, Italy, for example, was about the same as from Peoria to Philadelphia), labor costs, tax rates, and political and social stability.

As a result the decision was made to buy 70 acres in a newly developed industrial park in Nijmegen, together with options on an adjoining 30 acres. The plant was built and in operation by mid-1964. Since it served the entire regional market, Complant was separated organizationally from the marketing activity in Holland. Its manager reported directly to the Executive V.P. for European Sales.

The transfer price was set equal to Complant's full manufacturing cost plus 10%. Each marketing subsidiary paid for the cost of transporting its goods from the Complant.

At the time of the Booz, Allen study Spain was not a member of the Common Market, and there was no indication that it would become a member in the foreseeable future. Therefore the Complant did not attempt to service the Spanish market, which set up its own filling operations near Madrid. In 1979 this small plant, employing just over 80 production workers, was the only other Chandler production site on the continent. This plant had been modernized and expanded in 1978, a year which also saw Spain make considerable progress towards its goal of joining the EEC in the late 1980s.

History of the Complant since 1964

The performance of the Complant had fully met Chandler's expectations over the period 1964–1978. As Chandler's European sales grew by a factor of 10, to over Dfl. 400 million, the Complant was expanded 5 times. It currently represented a total investment of Dfl. 90 million.[1] With each expansion the additional production space was integrated completely with the existing space, which usually required the shifting around of some equipment and departments to implement the new work flow. In early 1979 the plant was in the shape of a large square containing roughly 400,000 square feet of floor space. Storage tanks containing chemicals and propellants were on one side. These led directly to the chemical mixing and processing department, where the formulas for each product were prepared and stored. At the appropriate time these mixtures were piped to the adjoining area which contained the liquid filling and aerosol filling lines. Following the same flow pattern, filled bottles and cans then were transported to the storage area and then to packing and shipping. Finished products exited the plant on the opposite side from where raw materials entered. Complant's inventory turnover in 1978 was about 7 times for both raw materials and packaging materials. Finished goods turnover was even higher.

The heart of the plant was the 10 bottling lines and the 3 aerosol filling lines. These were operated two 8-hour shifts a day, five days a week. The periods between and after the two shifts were used for cleaning and equipment maintenance. Although it was difficult to put a precise figure on the "capacity" of the plant, since this depended greatly on the production mix (which included the product mix, the size mix, and the mix between aerosol and liquid products), Mr. van Zwieten estimated that under the current production mix the plant was operating at somewhat under 90% of capacity. "We are currently producing about 115 million units per year (where a unit is one can or one bottle of whatever size)", he stated, "and following our current operating procedures we probably could produce as many as 130 million units: 90 million aerosol and 40 million liquids.

[1]Dfl. 1.00 = $.50 in early 1979.

Beyond that point we would have to increase capacity in some manner." The breakeven point for the plant, he estimated, was about 90 million units.

There was ample room to expand the plant, he stated, since the total working space required by current operations only utilized about 17 of the 70 acres that Chandler owned. Any plant expanation, however, could not be incorporated easily into the existing plant, but would probably have to be constructed as a separate adjoining work area. This would present no problems, in his view, because whether or not the expansion took place he was planning to move the chemical storage tanks from the side of the building where they currently were located (which was the side closest to a nearby village which had been gradually expanding towards Chandler's site) to the opposite side of the building for reasons of safety. He was planning to replace some of the storage tanks with bigger tanks during this move, and the production flow in the plant would also have to be redesigned.

The plant currently employed about 420 people (of which about 260 were permanent production personnel), which represented a small portion of the total work force in the area and was smaller than the work forces of several other companies in the region. Chandler's Buxbridge plant employed over 700 people (but only 315 in manufacturing), and its home plant in Peoria currently employed over 2,000 people, working three 8-hour shifts per day.

Complant had been able to build a considerable amount of flexibility into this work force because of van Zwieten's use of students from the nearby university as temporary workers. They usually represented somewhat less than 10% of the total work force (although this could rise to much higher levels). These students were delighted with the opportunity to make extra money and were willing to work on an "as available" basis. Hence they served to increase the job stability of the regular workers. The Buxbridge plant was able to make use of such workers to about the same degree as Complant. In Spain there was even more reliance on such workers. So far there had been no opposition from local authorities or unions to this practice, which allowed Chandler to respond to sales fluctuations

by changing the production level and thereby maintain relatively low inventories of finished goods. This both reduced capital costs and avoided the need for sophisticated control systems.

No radical change in skills or operating procedures would be required by the addition of new filling lines. A manufacturing cost breakdown is provided in *Exhibit 2*.

There had as yet been no attempt at central coordination of Chandler's European plants. Nor was there any standardization of manufacturing cost systems, inventory control techniques, or quality control procedures. This was largely due to the fact that Spain's special status as a standalone plant outside the EEC had restricted the possibility for such coordination to Complant and Buxbridge. Individuals within these two plants had good personal relationships, and such informal contacts appeared to provide a satisfactory degree of communication and coordination.

Evaluating the Complant's Performance

During the period 1970–1977 the Complant had successfully weathered three, almost simultaneous, major crises: the explosion in petrochemical prices in 1974–1975 following the Arab oil boycott in late 1973, a similar explosion in the basic hourly wage in Holland that occurred soon thereafter and which raised the Dutch rate from one of the lowest in Europe to one of the highest, and the European recession of 1974–1975 which reduced Chandler's continental sales (in terms of number of units) by over 20%. Throughout this period the plant had never had a losing year.

Measures of the plant's performance in combatting these cost increases during a period of highly variable but generally rapidly rising sales is contained in *Exhibit 3*, which presents indices of various volume and cost categories for each year since 1970. Mr. van Zwieten particularly emphasized the fact that while the overall cost of living in Holland had risen by 70% during the period 1971–1978, Complant's average price per unit had only increased 36%. Moreover, neither Complant's average cost per unit during this period nor the percentage breakdown of its cost were significantly different from that of Chandler's English plant, despite the considerably lower wage rate in the U.K. (see *Exhibit 4*).

EXHIBIT 2 Cost of Sales Breakdown by Category

	Percentage Base Budget 1978/79
– Materials	63.6
– Direct Labor	6.2
– 25% of Direct Production Overheads	1.7
– 25% of Finished Goods Warehousing	0.4
– Freight Europlant to Marketing Companies	5.0
TOTAL: DIRECT DELIVERED COST	76.9
PLUS:	
– 75% of Direct Production Overheads	5.2
– 75% of Finished Goods Warehousing	1.1
– Environmental Control	0.4
– Production Planning	0.9
– Purchasing	0.8
– Engineering	0.8
– Quality Assurance	1.1
– Management Information Services	1.2
– Finance	1.0
– Administrative Management	0.8
– General Services	1.2
– Interest	0.9
– European Service Charges	0.9
– Profit Sharing	1.2
– European Mark-Up	5.6
TOTAL COST OF SALES TO MARKETING COMPANIES	100.0

EXHIBIT 3 Summary of Complant Sales and Cost Performance Indices

	1971	1972	1973	1974	1975	1976	1977	1978
European Sales (Guilders)	100	125	148	190	195	238	227	226
Number of Units Produced	100	117	127	155	123	157	160	160
Sales/Total Employees	100	124	150	161	169	188	186	190
Units/Production Worker	100	116	137	114	123	123	123	123
Labor Cost/Unit	100	89	85	113	126	137	152	160
Overhead Cost/Unit (Mfg. & Admin.)	100	83	110	113	172	156	176	180
Raw Materials Cost/Unit	100	99	99	132	151	150	147	150
Packaging Materials	100	107	112	123	136	139	130	130
Total Manufacturing Cost/Unit	100	102	106	123	145	145	144	148
Inter-Company Price Index	100	104	106	115	137	134	134	136
Cost of Living Index (Holland)	100	108	116	126	139	152	161	170

Such comparisons between Chandler plants were somewhat suspect, however, because the products produced at each plant were usually quite different in terms of both formula and packaging. Different plants also used different standard costs (whose origins were sometimes hazy), and different methods for breaking down and allocating shared costs. Overhead costs were usually assigned on the basis of a standard percentage of direct manufacturing cost in each plant, but again these percentages varied from plant to plant.

At least part of Complant's ability to insulate itself against inflation was attributable to the fact that it sourced its materials from a number of different countries. Less than 35% of its purchases came from Holland, while the U.K., Belgium and Germany each accounted for about 15% of purchases, and slightly under 10% came from France. This diversity of sources contrasted with the sourcing policies of the English and Spanish plants, where almost all purchases were made within the host country.

Although over 50% of the purchases at Chandler's European plants were from vendors who also supplied at least one of the other plants, there was no formal coordination of purchasing among them (although there was some informal exchange of information). Partly this was due to the fact that a high percentage of purchases were from the large petrochemical multinationals, whose organization and policies tended to preclude any integrated sourcing arrangements.

One of the keys to efficient manufacturing at any of Chandler's plants, according to Mr. van Zwieten, was the avoidance of short production runs. Short runs and frequent changeovers reduced throughput and, therefore, caused average costs to rise. Illustrating this concern, Complant had a policy of offering substantial discounts to its sales subsidiaries on some low-volume products in exchange for their accepting a year's expected sales volume in a single shipment. He also resisted as much as possible any increase in the number of products (and sizes) produced at his plant, because both indirect and direct manufacturing costs appeared to be more dependent on the number of product codes produced than on the total production volume.

The relationship between the Complant and the national marketing organizations had not been entirely without friction. In 1975, for example, the manager of the Italian marketing organization prepared a carefully reasoned argument that the exchange rate between the Dutch guilder and the Italian lira had deteriorated so badly that his product costs were much higher than those of his major Italian competitors. Moreover, his transportation costs were the highest of any Chandler subsidiary in Europe. Therefore, he argued that he no longer could price his products competitively in Italy.[1] The alternatives, he stated, were either to lose market share (in what was then Chandler's fastest growing subsidiary), to utilize the services of local "contract fillers—companies who owned liquid filling lines and would perform the filling function (using ingredients imported in bulk from Complant) for a negotiated price, such as was being done increasingly in England, or to negotiate a new pricing arrangement with Complant. One proposed modification would be to reduce Complant's 10% "profit margin" to 5%; another would be to equalize the unit transportation costs to all subsidiaries (which would have the effect of charging the Northern European subsidiaries more per unit and Italy less). He estimated his total intercompany transportation costs in 1976 at $800,000, or about 6% of his total costs. This was almost twice the percentage at any of Chandler's other subsidiaries.

These arguments had forced Chandler's top management to review carefully both the philosophy behind the Complant and how it was working in practice. After careful consideration, and the recognition that differing transportation costs and exchange rates did put certain subsidiaries at a disadvantage, it was decided to maintain the basic policy of centralized production, although Italy was given more flexibility to use outside fillers under certain circumstances. Partly this decision was based on the fact that the Complant was then operating at less than 60% of capacity and, therefore, a major reduction in the demand from Italy would have an impact on product costs for all of Chandler's subsidiaries on the continent.

[1] See the case, "Chandler Home Products" (9-377-232).

Although there was some concern that the use of contract fillers and multiple production points would lead to a loss of control over product quality, by early 1979 about 15% of Chandler's sales of products on the continent (primarily in Italy) was being handled by outside fillers.

The 1979 Capacity Expansion Decision

In mid-1978 Chandler's European management developed sales projections for the 1980s reflecting its belief that unit sales would grow at an average rate of 6–7% per year during the decade. The annual growth rate was expected to be somewhat higher than this average during the first half of the decade, as several major new products were introduced, and then was expected to slow down. This forecast assumed no major crises in Europe's economic or socio-political environment. Although sales in different countries were expected to grow at somewhat different rates, no major changes were expected in their shares of total European sales by 1990—that is, the sales map of Chandler Europe was expected to look roughly the same in 1990 as it did in 1978, although it would be about twice as big.

Despite this apparent stability, there were expected to be important shifts in the product mix during this period. Liquids and solids were expected to grow somewhat faster than aerosols, which would drop to about half of total sales. New products (products introduced since 1975, that is) were expected to account for over 40% of total sales by 1990, but it was also expected that aerosols, solids and liquids would remain the basic packaging forms for Chandler's products (see *Exhibit 5* for a summary of Chandler's European demand forecasts).

Total European manufacturing capacity in 1979 was about 200 million aerosol units, 80 million liquid units and 20 million solid units, assuming two-shift operations and 100% machine utilization. This represented "peak capacity," however. In order to maintain the flexibility to respond to short-term market shifts and production bottlenecks Chandler preferred to size its plants on the basis of an average capacity utilization of about 85%. In mid-1979 both aerosol and liquid production were nearing 90% utilization at Complant (whereas the production of solids represented only about 50% of capacity). If its sales projections proved accurate, Chandler's manufacturing organization maintained the average output per filling line currently being achieved, and no increase in the reliance on outside fillers was allowed, it was estimated that at least two additional aerosol lines and four additional high-speed liquid filling lines would be required somewhere in Europe by 1990.

Buxbridge (which supplied a number of African and Middle Eastern export markets as well as the U.K. market) currently had annual capacity for 80 million aerosol units, 25 million liquid units and 8 million solid units. Although its sales to domestic markets were growing more slowly than Complant's, export sales were expected to rise rapidly. There was some reluctance, however, given the historic instability of the regions to which it was exporting, for Chandler to justify increased production capacity solely to supply this projected growth in exports.

There was a strong reluctance to move to a three-shift work schedule at Complant, as was used in the Peoria plant, because it was felt that it would be difficult to attract sufficient people of the desired quality to work the third shift. Nor would university students be available for such work. Van Zwieten felt that such an arrangement would also increase the congestion and confusion in the plant to such an extent that efficiency and quality would both suffer. Chandler's top management, he observed, had recently emphasized the importance it placed on the "high quality of the working life" in its plants. He pointed out that even though workers only worked 8 hours in a day, they were actually in the plant for 9 hours or more (because of breaks for lunch, coffee, cleaning up, etc.), and therefore three 8-hour shifts would complicate worker schedules and threaten the cooperative atmosphere he had tried to develop. Also, since equipment maintenance and the cleaning of the plant were being done during the off-shift hours when the plant was idle, removing this idle time would not cause total working hours to increase by the 50% that one might expect.

Since the manufacturing costs at Buxbridge

EXHIBIT 4 Five–Year Comparison of Cost per 100 units in Guilders at Complant and U.K.

		1970/71		1971/72		1972/73		1973/74		1974/75	
		Cost of Production per 100 units	Index 70/71 = 100	Cost of Production per 100 units	Index 70/71 = 100	Cost of Production per 100 units	Index 70/71 = 100	Cost of Production per 100 units	Index 70/71 = 100	Cost of Production per 100 units	Index 70/71 = 100
I.	*U.K. cost in Sterling*										
	Raw material cost	2.27	100	3.02	133	3.22	142	4.38	193	5.97	263
	Component cost	4.21	100	5.41	128	5.94	141	6.95	165	7.62	181
	Direct labor & overhds.	2.20	100	2.76	126	2.53	115	3.41	155	4.16	189
	Total cost of prod. £	8.68	100	11.19	129	11.69	135	14.74	169	17.75	203
II.	*U.K. cost in Guilders:*										
	Average exchange rate £1	8.631	100	8.366	97	7.519	87	6.399	74	5.928	69
	Raw material cost	19.59	100	25.27	129	24.29	124	28.01	143	35.46	181
	Component cost	36.34	100	45.26	125	44.70	123	44.33	122	45.06	124
	Direct labor & overhds.	18.99	100	23.09	122	18.99	100	21.84	115	24.69	130
	Total cost of prod. £	74.92	100	93.62	125	87.98	118	94.18	126	105.21	140
III.	*Complant cost in Guilders:*										
	Raw material cost	22.98	100	22.94	99	22.89	99	30.33	132	34.70	151
	Component cost	37.40	100	40.10	107	41.89	112	46.00	123	50.86	136
	Direct labor & overhds.	16.42	100	16.18	99	16.63	101	18.55	113	25.62	156
	Total Cost of Product.	76.80	100	79.22	103	81.41	106	94.88	124	111.18	145
IV.	*Comparison ot Total Production Cost:*										
	U.K. DF1.	74.92	100	93.62	125	87.98	118	94.18	126	105.21	140
	Complant DF1.	76.80	100	79.22	103	81.41	106	94.88	124	111.18	145

3. Chandler Home Products (B)

and Complant were quite similar (see *Exhibit 4*), there appeared to be little advantage to trans-shipping products between them (the cost of trans-shipment averaged about 10% of Chandler's manufacturing cost). Similarly, the high Spanish import duties precluded shipment into Spain, at least until it achieved full EEC membership. Chandler's European management had also come to the tentative conclusion that the economies of scale involved in the production of aerosol products were such that Complant should continue to be the sole source for these products on the continent (outside of Spain). It was estimated, for example, that a modern aerosol filling line would cost about Dfl. 8 million, and would increase total aerosol capacity by about 40 million units per year. The question was whether additional liquid filling capacity should also be located at Complant. A modern high-speed liquid filling line would cost about Dfl. 3 million and would add about 20 million units per year to liquid capacity.

Some interest had been expressed by various members of Chandler's European organization in locating this new liquid filling capacity either in Italy or Southern France. Their argument was that, apart from avoiding the potential danger of "putting too many eggs in one (Complant) basket," a new plant in Southern Europe would tap a lower cost labor market, reduce transportation costs and offset the growing protectionist sentiment that was being expressed in several European countries—particularly France.

Van Zwieten, however, felt strongly that the most economical location for such an expansion was at Complant. He pointed out that this would minimize the investment required since no land would have to be purchased in Nijmegen, whereas about 10 acres (4 hectares) would be required for a minimum-sized stand-alone plant. The price of good commercial land (in industrial parks or a location similarly conducive to industrial operations) was at least Dfl. 1.5 million per hectare throughout Europe. On the other hand, even if Chandler did have to buy additional land in Nijmegen, under the terms of its option it could purchase an additional 12 hectares (30 acres) adjacent to its present site at a price of Dfl. 300,000 per hectare.

As regards equipment cost, van Zwieten stated that since almost all the equipment was imported from the U.S. or Common Market countries, the cost would be roughly the same no matter where it was located. As a result, he felt that the cost of a 20 million unit expansion in liquid filling capacity would cost at least Dfl. 12 million if a new plant were built, but only require an additional investment of Dfl. 6 million at Complant. An analysis of Complant showed that the synergistic effect of an additional aerosol line was at least 10 MM units higher than if such a line was put in isolation. Synergy of liquid filling was expected to be less severe. Furthermore, Complant now had sufficient liquid capacity to justify a blow-molding facility that would allow it to produce its own plastic bottles. This would give it a cost advantage compared with any other European plant.

Expansion at Complant would also limit the total number of overhead personnal required, for the reasons previously mentioned. Van Zwieten estimated that a minimum-sized new plant, with total annual capacity of at least 20 million units, would require from 50 to 100 total workers of which about 20% would be almost exclusively

EXHIBIT 5 European Demand Forcasts

EUROPEAN SALES FORECASTS (IN MILLION UNITS)			
	1980	1985	1990
Liquids			
• Continental Europe			
−EEC	40	69	90
−Non-EEC	7	14	20
• UK	11	17	25
	58	100	135
Aerosols			
• Continental Europe			
−EEC	90	115	144
−Non-EEC	22	40	45
• UK	33	35	36
	145	190	225

involved in plant administration. Such a plant would not be as automated as Complant, and would have a higher proportion of monotonous jobs. It was also unlikely, in his opinion, that the new plant would have access to university students who were willing to work on a temporary basis, as he did. Finally, a plant in southern Europe would not have the same access to petrochemicals and packaging materials that Complant had because of its proximity to several major ports and refineries.

As a result, despite the lower labor costs in both France and Italy (the labor cost in France, for example, came to just over half of the Dutch cost when fringes and direct supervision were included), the direct manufacturing cost at a French or Italian liquids plant was estimated to be slightly greater (0–2% for liquids, 6–10% for aerosols) than that at Complant. The cost of raw materials and components was generally higher in France and Italy than in Holland (except for plastic containers in Italy because of governmental aid on plastic raw materials). Over time, however, the gap between Italy and Complant was closing.*

Adding distribution costs tended to complicate the issue, of course: the delivered cost to French customers from a French plant, for example, would be slightly less than from Complant, while the delivered cost to German customers would be considerably more. These differences would be affected in the future both by changes in the relative wage rates in France and Holland and the exchange rate between the French franc and the Dutch guilder. There seemed to be no way of predicting whether the differences in total delivered cost would move enough in favor of a French (or an Italian) plant to justify the additional investment required.

Contract Filling

The only realistic alternative to increasing production capacity was to increase drastically Chandler's reliance on outside contract fillers. Currently about 15% of liquid sales on the continent were being filled by outside companies, although less than 1% of aerosol sales were filled outside. The U.K., on the other hand, utilized contract fillers for 30% of sales without apparent problems. There were some who argued, therefore, that at least part of Complant's apparent capacity could be alleviated by increasing its dependence on outside fillers. The cost of this service differed by country and by product type. In the case of liquid products, for example, contract fillers in France typically charged 5–10% less than the Complant price, while Italian fillers often charged 20–30% less.

There were two major arguments against such a move. First, there was concern that the perceived quality of Chandler's products and customer service (which was the cornerstone of its marketing strategy and the justification for its higher prices) might suffer. Second, the costs of inspecting and coordinating outside fillers increased rapidly as their number increased. Van Zwieten argued, in fact, that the cost of contract filling was considerably more than it appeared because of the increase in indirect costs that this caused at Complant. There was particular danger, he felt, in allowing contract fillers to take over 100% of the production of any product because the Complant's ability to solve production crises at a contract filler was heavily dependent on the body of expertise maintained within his plant.

The problem was complicated by the fact that a number of Chandler's products used proprietary formulations. Chandler management was very reluctant to risk the secrecy of these formulations by giving them to contract fillers. This reluctance was particularly strong in the case of Chandler's new "high-technology" products, and weaker in the case of older, low-technology products.

Restricting its attention only to those products which could be contracted out safely, Chandler decided that 14 million units of liquid products would be potential candidates for outside filling by 1980, 10 million of which would be in France and Italy. This number would increase to 42 million by 1990, of which 26 million would be in France and Italy. Although 25 million units of aerosol products were potential candidates for outside filling by 1990, there was less economic

*		Plastic material index	
		Nov. '78	June '79
Outside supplier		100	152
Complant supplier		119	156

justification for doing so. Current quotes from most contract aerosol fillers, even in France and Italy, indicated higher delivered costs than Complant's.

The Booz, Allen & Hamilton Proposal

When the consulting firm of Booz, Allen & Hamilton was asked to make a recommendation about where and how to expand the production of liquid products, it agreed to do so but only within the context of an overall evaluation of Chandler's manufacturing strategy for European production. It suggested an overall planning horizon of 1990, and promised to provide detailed proposals through 1983/84, including recommendations regarding organizational structure and staffing. These proposals would take into consideration a number of guidelines that represented different aspects of Chandler's overall strategy (see *Exhibit 6*).

EXHIBIT 6 Chandler's Competitive Guidelines

1. Meeting well-defined customer needs in niches through creative marketing is the over-ruling factor of success.
2. In coming years, we must be able to develop and introduce *large numbers* of new products in a *timely manner*.
3. We must be able to respond *quickly* to changes in market needs and competitive actions.
4. Our product qualilty, wherever possible, should be clearly distinguishable as superior to the competition in terms of performance, packaging and design finish.
5. Customer service is a critical success factor in the market place. It must be *competitive*—or better. *Exceptional* customer service could be a major success factor, but generally the appropriate level of customer service should be determined by balancing marketing requirements with manufacturing/ distribution/inventory costs.
6. We must develop/maintain expertise in process technology across an important share of our product line. We should maintain state-of-the-art capabilities in some manufacturing areas to ensure a degree of technical pre-eminence in the organization.
7. We want both a very high degree of manufacturing flexibility to respond to changing market conditions, and competitive landed costs with important local competitors.

4. Sensormatic Electronics Corporation

Ron Assaf, president and chairman of the board of Sensormatic Electronics Corporation, once again picked up the memorandum from his desk. The work, dated February 15, 1980, seemed carefully done, and Bill Blakey, his director of planning, had spent weeks checking its accuracy, yet something about the analysis was disturbing. The make-buy decision on plastic parts was an important one, and Assaf was determined to avoid a potentially costly error.

The company's past financial struggles were still a vivid memory. Yet according to Blakey's analysis, in-house fabrication of plastic parts was quite attractive financially, offering considerable savings over the traditional practice of buying from outside vendors. Of the alternatives available, Blakey favored the creation of a fabrication unit within Sensormatic's main plant in Deerfield Beach, Florida, rather than the acquisition of Canon Plastics, a longtime Sensormatic supplier located in Mobile, Alabama, approximately 600 miles away.

Assaf mulled over these options, carefully reviewing the evidence in the memorandum. He wondered if this was the time for the company to be making a move into plastics fabrication. Whatever the decision, it had to be made quickly, for

contracts with Sensormatic's other supplier of plastic parts were coming up for renegotiation within the next two weeks.

The Company

Sensormatic, founded in 1966, pioneered the merchandise security business. Until then, storekeepers had generally protected their goods from shoplifters by keeping a careful eye on customers, often employing closed-circuit television or plainclothes detectives to shadow anyone arousing suspicion. Sensormatic's products, however, took a completely different approach: they watched the goods rather than the customers.

Sensormatic manufactured, marketed, and serviced theft detection devices. These systems, consisting of a transmitter, a receiver, a set of specially designed reusable tags, and a tag remover (See *Exhibits 1* and *2*), all protected by several patents, were sold primarily to department, discount, and other retail stores emphasizing soft goods. Matched transmitter and receiver units were usually placed at all exits from a store, and tags were attached to clothing and other items being sold. These tags could be removed only with the aid of a tag remover kept with the cashier, and were detached only after an item had been purchased.

If an item with its tag still attached was carried out of the store, a diode encased in the tag intercepted the signals being relayed between the transmitter and receiver positioned at the exit, activating an alarm. The principle was similar to radar interference, in which electronic

This case was prepared by David A. Garvin.
Copyright © 1981 by the President and Fellows of Harvard College. Harvard Business School case 681-905.

EXHIBIT 1 Sensormatic's Systems

The System.

No other company in our industry can match the products, performance or professionalism of Sensormatic Electronics.

The flexibility we are able to provide assures that you can get the precise Sensormatic system to match your needs.

As with the tags, the pedestals and overhead units are built with the retailer's needs in mind. It makes no difference whether the store is a small boutique with a small entranceway or a large department store with a wide entranceway. Sensormatic has the scanning units that are specifically designed and priced to meet those needs.

The Mini System—Ideal for the economical protection of entranceways of four feet or less. It can not only protect smaller stores, but this system is also a valuable asset for larger stores in protecting specific departments or employee exits.

The Midi System—This system is designed to protect entranceways of six feet or less. Specifically, it was designed to protect the "double door" store front.

The Escalator System—This system allows multiple floor stores to establish their coverage from floor to floor or, if they wish, from the main floor up. This configuration allows detection of the tag at both the top and the bottom of the escalator.

The Double System—With its twenty foot scanning area, it is ideal for unobtrusive coverage of the spacious storefronts that have been designed for many mall stores.

Source: Company document.

4. Sensormatic Electronics Corporation

EXHIBIT 2 Sensormatic's Tags

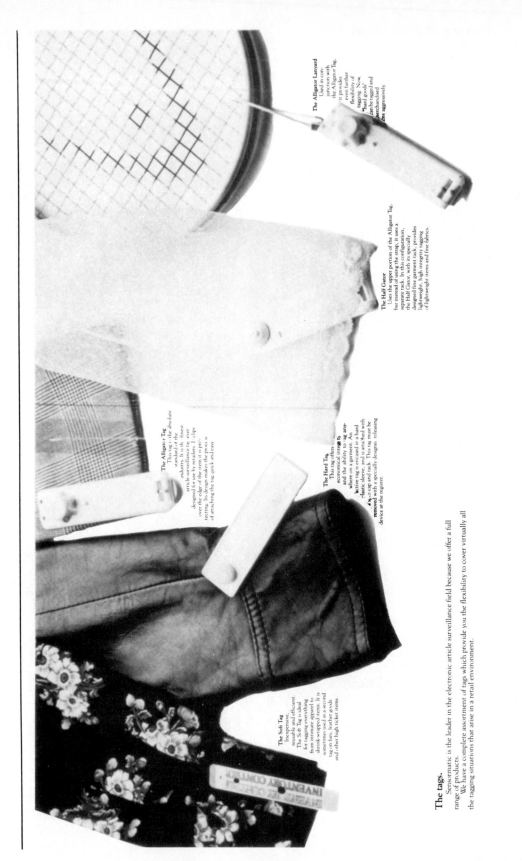

The Alligator Lanyard
Used in conjunction with the Alligator Tag, it provides even further flexibility of tagging. Now, "hard goods" can be tagged and merchandised more aggressively.

The Half Gator
Uses the upper portion of the Alligator Tag, but instead of using the strap, it uses a separate tack. In this configuration, the Half Gator, with its specially designed fine garment tack, provides lightweight, high integrity tagging of lightweight items and fine fabrics.

The Alligator Tag
This tag is the absolute standard of the industry. It is the finest article surveillance tag ever designed for use by retailers. It clips over the edge of the item it is protecting. Its design makes the process of attaching the tag quick and easy.

The Hard Tag
This tag offers economical strength and the ability to tag anywhere on a garment. An active tag is encased in a hard plastic sleeve, and is attached with a cap and tack. This tag must be removed with a specially designed, releasing device at the register.

The Soft Tag
Inexpensive, reusable and efficient. The Soft Tag is ideal for tagging everything from intimate apparel to shrink-wrapped items. It is sometimes used as a second tag on furs, leather goods and other high ticket items.

The tags.
Sensormatic is the leader in the electronic article surveillance field because we offer a full range of products.
We have a complete assortment of tags which provide you the flexibility to cover virtually all the tagging situations that arise in a retail environment.

components sensitive to radar frequencies were dropped from airplanes during World War II in an effort to disrupt defenses.

Initially, this approach received little support from retailers. In its early years, Sensormatic was often unable to sell units and was reduced to offering systems for free trial; occasionally, stores were actually paid to test devices. Convinced of the value of Sensormatic's system, Assaf employed such strategies merely to get units into the field; follow-on sales, he felt, would come once the systems had proved their effectiveness. In 1968, for example, Assaf convinced Stephanie's, a small women's apparel store in Akron, Ohio, to install a Sensormatic system, but only on the condition that the store receive a monthly payment of $200 from Sensormatic for the inconvenience of having to tag its merchandise.

Yet acceptance continued to be elusive. Assaf recalled: "By 1969, when we went public, we had 25 systems installed; 24 were free trials and the other was on lease—but the guy wasn't paying."

Not surprisingly, finances were especially tight during this period. Sensormatic had initially hoped to benefit from its invention of the electronic surveillance system by remaining a profitable middleman. Funds were raised by selling franchises, and Sensormatic expected to buy equipment from an independent manufacturer, market it to franchised dealers, and pocket the additional profits. Between 1966 and 1970, $2.4 millon worth of franchises were sold.

Most franchisees, however, had considerable difficulty overcoming retailers' resistance. Supplies and equipment also proved difficult to obtain. Only stopgap financing—loans from company officers and two banks, as well as a private placement—kept the company solvent during this period.

Because franchised dealers proved to be ineffectual, Sensormatic turned to a direct sales force. In 1968 three salespeople were hired. By 1980 this group had grown considerably, and George Harbin, the company's senior vice president and head of marketing, was responsible for a sales force of 40, backed by a service staff of 63. Management had come to view aggressive sales and service as Sensormatic's major competitive weapon, followed by flexibility, cost, and quality, in order of importance. Salespeople were routinely recruited from companies like Pillsbury, IBM, and Xerox, with Harbin himself boasting 20 years of experience at IBM. The rationale for this approach was straightforward; according to Harbin, "We don't have the time and money to train salesmen, so we like to steal them." In keeping with the importance attached to direct marketing, the company had also reacquired 135 of the 140 franchises originally sold.

Harbin and Assaf worked well together, despite differences in temperament and background. Assaf, an unassuming man who originally wanted to become a college professor, started in business as a management trainee with Kroger Supermarkets. At 21 he had become a store manager. Yet a few years later, restless for more challenging activities, Assaf left Kroger to become a cofounder of Sensormatic. As he remarked later, "After all, you can stack cans only so high." (Sensormatic was founded by three men—Assaf; his cousin, John Welch, who invented the original surveillance system sold by the company; and James Rogers, a personal friend of Assaf's. Rogers retired from the company in 1970 and Welch in 1971. Harbin joined Sensormatic in 1970.) Harbin, however, was more gregarious, yet had spent most of his professional life with a single company. Commenting on their backgrounds, Harbin observed, "People think I'm the wild Irish rose and Ron's the conservative. Actually, it's the other way around." As one example, he cited Assaf's decision to lease $700,000 worth of Sensormatic equipment to Chicago's Community Family Centers, with Sensormatic's only compensation being half of whatever reduction the system made in losses to shoplifters. The gamble was so successful—and so profitable for Sensormatic—that the centers soon asked to switch to a normal lease.

These and other efforts produced a sharp turnaround for the firm. Between 1977 and 1979, for example, Sensormatic's sales and income grew at more than 40% annually. Revenues grew from $8.4 million in 1975 to $27.6 million in 1979, while net income grew from $0.9 million to $4.4 million during the same period (see *Exhibits 3* and *4*). An 85,000-square-foot manufacturing facility was opened in Deerfield Beach in 1979, and construction of a new assembly plant in Puerto Rico was now being considered.

EXHIBIT 3 Consolidated Balance Sheets ($ thousands)

May 31	1979	1978
Assets		
Cash	$1,263	$1,247
Trade and other accounts receivable, less allowance for doubtful accounts of $607 in 1979 and $390 in 1978	6,876	3,274
Trade notes receivable, less allowance for doubtful accounts and unearned interest of $100 and $884 in 1979 and $30 and $237 in 1978 respectively	3,315	1,261
Prepaid insurance and deposits	324	295
Revenue equipment, at cost-net	11,235[a]	7,597[a]
Other property, plant and equipment, at cost-net	5,718	2,875
Other assets		
Cost in excess of net assets acquired, less accumulated amortization of $118 in 1979 and $79 in 1978	1,493	1,510
Debt expense, less accumulated amortization of $235 in 1979 and $162 in 1978	194	199
Cost of certain patents and related rights, less accumulated amortization of $1,081 in 1979 and $939 in 1978	594	736
Prepaid royalties	395	451
Prepaid franchise lease expense	720	—
Total assets	$32,127	$19,445

a. Revenue equipment is summarized as follows ($ thousands):

	1979	1978
On lease		
Revenue producing	$9,110	$6,353
Awaiting installation	850	494
Available for lease or sale		
Systems and accessories	1,694	1,384
Tags	1,807	1,702
Parts inventory	2,485	2,030
Subtotal	15,946	11,963
Less accumulated depreciation	(4,711)	(4,366)
Net book value	$11,235	$7,597

(continued on next page)

4. Sensormatic Electronics Corporation

May 31	1979	1978
Liabilities and Stockholders' Equity		
Accounts payable—trade	$1,691	$1,594
Accrued liabilities		
Franchisees' and dealers' commissions	932	624
Salaries and commissions	634	371
Payroll and other taxes	556	244
Employee stock ownership plan	182	108
Dividends	133	—
Other	904	549
Total accrued liabilities	3,341	1,896
Income taxes payable	1,158	1,350
Deferred income taxes	2,789	447
Notes payable	6,221[b]	2,356
Due on acquisition of European operations	214	332
Total liabilities	15,414	7,975
Commitments and contingencies		
Stockholders' equity		
Preferred stock, 1¢ par value, 500,000 shares authorized, 50 shares 4% cumulative issued and outstanding stated at redemption value	198	500
Common stock, 1¢ par value, 10,000,000 shares authorized 2,658,180 issued and outstanding in 1979 and 2,502,969 in 1978	27	25
Capital in excess of par value	13,229	11,704
Retained earnings (deficit)	3,977	(174)
Stock subscription receivables	(718)	(585)
Total stockholders' equity	16,713	11,470
Total liabilities and stockholders' equity	$32,127	$19,445

b. The increase in notes payable between 1978 and 1979 is due to a modification of an earlier loan agreement resulting in a $600,000 increase in principal and a ¼% reduction in the interest rate, a $2.4 million mortgage note for the facility at Deerfield Beach, a $165,000 note at 11¼% for new equipment, and an increase in unsecured revolving credit notes of $700,000.

Source: Company records.

EXHIBIT 4 Consolidated Statements of Operations ($ thousands, except per share amounts)

	Year Ended May 31				
	1979	1978	1977	1976	1975
Revenues					
Equipment and tag sales	$18,367	$12,158	$7,797	$5,020	$4,306
Equipment and tag rentals and service fees	9,191	6,827	5,888	4,607	4,125
Total revenues	27,558	18,985	13,685	9,627	8,431
Operating costs and expenses					
Costs of equipment and tag sales	6,245	4,756	2,836	1,836	1,632
Depreciation	2,260	1,484	1,877	1,489	1,527
Selling and customer service	5,787	4,087	2,696	1,949	1,882
Administrative	3,467	2,326	1,878	1,388	1,434
Research and product development	548	544	354	203	158
Other operating expenses	850	516	440	394	233
Total operating costs and expenses	19,157	13,713	10,081	7,259	6,866
Operating income	8,401	5,272	3,604	2,368	1,565
Other expenses (income)					
Royalties and fees from licensees	(210)	(168)	(106)	(110)	(68)
Interest expense—net	345	132	340	320	414
Amortization of deferred expenses and cost in excess of net assets acquired	181	199	195	222	275
Sales of franchises and dealerships	—	(171)	—	—	—
Other	97	—	—	—	—
Total other expenses (income)	413	(8)	429	432	621
Income before income taxes and extraordinary credit	7,988	5,280	3,175	1,936	944
Provision for and/or in lieu of income taxes					
Current	1,332	1,549	1,610	958	488
Deferred	2,231	735	—	—	—
	3,563	2,284	1,610	958	488
Income before extraordinary credit	4,425	2,996	1,565	978	456
Extraordinary credit resulting from utilization of a net operating loss carryforward	—	288	1,480	900	450
Net income	$4,425	$3,284	$3,045	$1,878	$906
Primary earnings per common share					
Income before extraordinary credit	$1.52	$1.10	$.63	$.46	$.22
Extraordinary credit	—	.11	.59	.42	.21
Net income	$1.52	$1.21	$1.22	$.88	$.43
Fully diluted earnings per common share					
Income before extraordinary credit	$1.50	$1.05	$.60	$.38	$.19
Extraordinary credit	—	.10	.56	.35	.18
Net income	$1.50	$1.15	$1.16	$.73	$.37

4. Sensormatic Electronics Corporation

The Market and Competition

By 1980 Sensormatic dominated the market for electronic article surveillance systems, accounting for 70% of U.S. sales and over 50% of the European market. In commenting on these figures, Assaf observed, "Our products are near equal in price and equal or superior in quality to those of our competitors." Since the company's creation, nearly 10,700 systems and 80 million tags had been sold to such customers as Federated Department Stores, May Department Stores, R. H. Macy, and Sears, Roebuck. At the end of 1979 the company faced a backlog of 807 systems (for both sale and lease) and approximately 4.5 million tags.

By contrast, Sensormatic's major competitor, the Knogo Corporation, whose technology employed low-frequency radio waves rather than Sensormatic's microwaves, had sold only 4,000 systems, mostly to smaller stores. Knogo had frequently tried to undercut Sensormatic's position by citing the alleged health risks of Sensormatic's microwave system, although tests by the U.S. Department of Health, Education and Welfare had confirmed Sensormatic's claim that emissions from the products fell well below permissible exposure levels.

Knogo earned revenues of $11.2 million in 1979, while Checkpoint Systems, another firm producing surveillance systems (primarily for music stores and supermarkets) had 1978 sales of $5.1 million. Overall, Sensormatic faced relatively little competition, for no major firm had entered the market on a large scale. 3M, however, had been on the periphery of the industry for many years, producing a small number of electronic surveillance systems for bookstores and libraries.

According to industry analysts, the merchandise security business had excellent growth prospects, for only a small proportion of all possible customers had been tapped. Potential candidates for Sensormatic equipment were generally considered to be retail stores emphasizing soft goods with annual sales of at least $500,000. In 1980 there were approximately 30,000 such outlets in the United States and Europe, many of which, because of their large size, were likely to require more than one system. Less than 5% of this potential market had been penetrated.

In addition, Sensormatic had recently developed a new kind of tagging system that could be used for hard goods like records or cassettes, considerably broadening its possible market. It also offered several variations on the basic system, including different-sized transmitters and receivers (some for small stores, others for large shopping malls with wide entranceways), several kinds of tags (ranging from relatively inexpensive soft tags, little more than a thin sheath of material containing a diode, to the top-of-the-line Alligator tags, consisting of molded plastic clips held together by a metal tack and able to withstand up to 200 pounds of pressure without opening), and several tag removers. Tags were reusble, with a life of approximately four years, and Alligator tags were the most important of the varieties sold. A standard security system, which normally included 10,000 Alligator tags, matched transmitter and receiver units, and a tag-removing unit, listed for a sales price of $17,500, or a monthly rental of approximatley $450 for a lease term of 48 months.

Substantial sales growth was predicted, particularly for systems using Alligator tags. Of the Sensormatic systems in the field at the start of 1979, 4,800 alone were devoted to Alligators. (Any reference to Alligator tags in this case is meant to include Half Gator tags, a smaller version of the Alligator, as well. Thus, the 4,800 systems were devoted to either Alligator or Half Gator tags, and the projected tag requirements included the demand for both Alligators and Half Gators.) Eight hundred new Alligator systems were ordered in 1979—implying requirements for 8 million new Alligator tags—with a 30% annual increase in systems demand projected for each of the next five years. Replacement needs had to be met as well, for on average, 25% of all tags in the field at the beginning of the year required replacement within the next 12 months because of losses or damage incurred in use. With 4,800 Alligator systems in place at the start of 1979, and an average of 10,000 tags per system, 1979's replacement demand amounted to 12 million Alligator tags.

Research and Development

New-product development was extremely important at Sensormatic. The company employed 32 people in this area—24 of them engineers or technicians—and in 1979 budgeted $548,000 for research and development. Several new products were then in the development stage, and some, like a new tag code-named Gemini, were scheduled for immediate introduction. Although using the same raw materials as the Alligator Tag, the Gemini tag had the advantage of a more automated production process. The engineering group felt that tags would not change dramatically until the invention of a cheap throw-away tag, which was still several years from commercial development.

Sensormatic was also working on a revolutionary nonmicrowave surveillance system that would lower tag manufacturing costs by at least 30%. That system, code-named "Star Trek," was expected to be compatible with the Gemini tags, while also employing a new disposable soft tag. In 1980 the system was still in the development stage, and was not expected to reach the market for several years.

The Production Process

Manufacturing operations at Sensormatic were divided into two sections. Systems production assembled and tested the transmitters, receivers, and tag removers that were part of all electronic surveillance systems, while tag manufacturing produced the four kinds of tags, as well as the diodes (semiconductors) that were placed inside them. In 1980 all activities were performed at the Deerfield Beach plant, although the two departments were physically separated within the building.

SYSTEMS PRODUCTION. This section operated much like any other organization specializing in light electronics assembly. Items were built only after a firm order had been received, and raw materials arrived on the shop floor kitted in sets of parts. Volume varied from 50 units per month for the floor-mounted transmitters and receivers designed for the European market to 400 units per month for the small, hand-held Double-Checker units that enabled employees to check purchased merchandise to insure that all tags, including any that might have been hidden in the folds of a garment, had been removed (so as to avoid embarrassing a paying customer who might trigger the alarm on leaving the store). Volumes for the

company's other products fell between these two extremes.

Systems production involved three major stages, all of them quite labor-intensive. First, printed circuit (PC) boards had to be assembled, and the following activities peformed: components were mounted on the PC boards; leads were wave-soldered by machine; the boards were inspected, touched up, and inspected again; and the completed boards were tested electronically. In total, 20 kinds of PC boards were employed in Sensormatic's various systems.

Second, subassemblies were formed when the PC boards were mounted in their sheetmetal containers, and additional testing was performed. Third, power packs were added and each system was marked with a serial number to facilitate repair and future parts replacement. After one more testing, the units were ready to ship.

The system production area was clean and quiet, and working conditions were generally considered good. Labor turnover had been limited. Employees, mostly women except for those involved in testing and wave-soldering, were paid from $3.40 to $5.50 per hour. Those responsible for testing received somewhat higher wages, between $5.00 and $8.00 per hour.

TAG PRODUCTION. This section was organized somewhat differently. Two groups were involved, one responsible for the production of the diodes that went into the tags and the other for the tags themselves. The diodes were manufactured in a sterile "clean room" by five white-smocked technicians, while the tags were produced in a larger tag manufacturing room by a group of relatively unskilled workers.

The diode manufacturing operation was one of the smallest in the country, producing 5.5 million units per month at a cost of 0.4 cents each. The figure compared favorably with the 1.2 cents per diode Sensormatic was paying when these parts were purchased from outside vendors. Potential cost savings, however, was not the primary reason for developing an in-house semiconductor facility. Diodes were initially custom-made and purchased in relatively small volumes. As demand grew, Sensormatic approached Texas Instruments and other large semiconductor firms, asking if they would be interested in meeting the company's annual diode requirements. Production volumes, however, were not yet large enough to interest these firms, requiring Sensormatic to develop an alternative source of supply. In 1968 the company hired George Pinneo, an engineer with National Semiconductor Corporation, to set up an in-house semiconductor facility. Pinneo conceived and designed all of the machinery used by Sensormatic to manufacture its diodes, and by March 1969 had established a working semiconductor operation.

Once the diodes had been produced, they were joined to tags in the tag manufacturing room. Again, Sensormatic-designed machinery was employed. Four kinds of tags were produced—soft tags, which could be attached to articles like any other tag or ticket; hard tags, which were little more than soft tags encased in plastic; Alligator tags, which attached securely to articles with a special reusable fastener; and Half Gator tags, which were smaller versions of the Alligator tags (see *Exhibit 2*). (Unlike the Alligator and Half Gator tags, hard tags did not involve the use of injection-molded plastic parts.)

Soft tags, with diodes bonded inside, formed the basis for all other tags. Two tag machines produced soft tags by encasing diodes in mylar, a thin, clear plastic. Precise centering was required (to within $\frac{1}{50,000}$ of an inch), for otherwise the diodes would not respond to the frequency of the transmitter and receiver units. If the soft tags were to be sold in that form, they were custom-printed on Sensormatic's three-color offset press and then boxed.

Alligator and Half Gator tags took the process a step further. Both were formed by first sealing a soft tag between two pieces of polypropylene, a hard plastic. The newly formed piece, called a clip, then became one-half of a complete Alligator or Half Gator. The other half of the Alligator, made of A.B.S., another hard plastic, and called a strap, had a specially-designed tack inserted within it so the tag could be attached to clothing or other merchandise. After these two parts were connected by a hinge, a dome for receiving the pointed end of the tack was added, and all pieces were mechanically and electronically tested. (The Half Gator used a separate tack in place of the strap containing a tack.) The Alligator and Half Gator tags were then ready for shipment. (See *Figure A* for the various parts of an Alligator tag.)

Working conditions in the tag room were considered less desirable than those in systems production. The area was noisy and hot, with a constant buzz of machinery. Few labor skills were required, and workers were brought in at the minimum wage. Although advancement was possible—workers in the tag room could eventually earn as much as $5.50 per hour—turnover had been a continual problem. Management occasionally found it difficult to recruit workers for these jobs from the local labor pool, and had to bus in workers from the neighboring town of Hollywood Beach.

FIGURE A The Alligator III

The Sensormatic Alligator III is the newest addition to our product line. It works in the Sensormatic System the same way as do our other Security Tags.

The Alligator III attaches faster and more easily, and, in the long run, is less expensive to use than our hard Tag.

Sensormatic's Alligator III will prove highly resistant to the unauthorized removal of merchandise from a protected store.

Please note the callouts on the photo below. Familiarize yourself with the parts of the Alligator III. When used correctly the Alligator III will provide fast and reliable service.

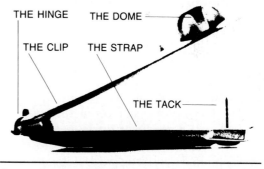

Source: Company document.

The injection-molded plastic parts used for clips and straps had traditionally been supplied to Sensormatic by outside vendors. Although the market for these parts appeared to be quite competitive—firms were typically small, and the industry's median pretax return on assets was between 8% and 10%—backlogs and rising prices had been a persistent problem. In part, this reflected the dependence of the plastics industry on petrochemicals, a basic raw material, and a corresponding sensitivity to oil prices and supplies. Temporary shortages had also arisen because of the limited number of molds—and hence, the limited capacity—of individual vendors. The volatility of raw material supplies had made the materials area a difficult one to manage; in the course of the 1979–1980 year, for example, Sensormatic had employed three different materials control managers. In addition, rapid product change and past uncertainties in the marketing forecast had resulted in large inventories of obsolete parts and raw materials. In 1979 these totaled between $200,000 and $300,000.

For many years, Sensormatic had purchased its polypropylene and A.B.S. parts from two companies, Canon Plastics, of Mobile, Alabama, and Piedmont Plastics, of Asheville, North Carolina. In 1980 both offered clip and strap combinations, together making a single Alligator tag, at the price of $.0576 per unit plus freight (a unit consisting of one clip and one strap). Freight costs were approximately equal from Mobile and Asheville, averaging $.30 per thousand units. Three-quarters of Sensormatic's 1980 demand for plastic parts was met by Canon Plastics and the remainder by Piedmont.

The Decision on Plastic Parts

For several years Sensormatic had been considering integrating backward into the production of plastic parts. Relations with Canon Plastics had always been cordial, and when Assaf broached the subject of a possible merger, he was warmly received. For a purchase price of $500,000, Assaf would acquire 8 molding presses—each equipped with 16 cavity molds (i.e., producing 16 parts on each cycle) and operating with a 30-second cycle time—as well as an on-premises tool and die shop and all other necessary auxiliary equipment (e.g., heaters, chillers, and resin handling equipment). An experienced labor force, including a production coordinator, three foremen, and six machine operators, would also be acquired. Assuming machine up-time of 90%, three shifts per day, and five working days per week, Assaf figured that four machines—two devoted to producing clips, and two to producing straps—could meet Sensormatic's present demand for Alligator tags. The other machines could be employed for outside business—a long-standing contract with Johnson Motors, for example, had traditionally involved the use of one molding press, and the automobile

industy was expected to rely increasingly on plastic parts to help meet more stringent fuel efficiency standards—or otherwise held in reserve.

As an alternative, Assaf wanted to consider the possibility of making plastic parts in-house. Mobile, Alabama, after all, was a 12-hour drive from Deerfield Beach, and Sensormatic needed only four presses to meet its present demand, rather than the eight offered by Canon Plastics. Moreover, an in-house facility would insure that new machinery was involved, operating at faster speeds (a cycle time of 27 seconds with 16 cavity molds) and insuring greater reliability (expected up-time of 95%).

To better compare these options, Assaf had asked Bill Blakey, his director of planning, to prepare a detailed financial review. Blakey's results, presented in a memorandum (see *Exhibit 5*), strongly favored the purchase of new machines and in-house production.

Once again, Assaf pondered Blakey's memorandum. Plastic parts had been a continual headache for Sensormatic, and more direct control over the molding operation seemed like a good idea. Shipments of electronic systems had occasionally been delayed because of an inability to acquire plastic parts and produce tags on schedule. Backward integration into this area would give Sensormatic a distinct advantage over its competitors, for neither Knogo nor Checkpoint had injection-molding facilities. But was this the best time to make the move? The Deerfield Beach plant had been in operation for only a year, while the planned Puerto Rico plant—to operate initially as an assembly facility to relieve the capacity problems in systems production, but later expected to involve tag manufacturing as well—was still on the drawing boards. The new technologies being developed were another concern, although research and development had assured Assaf that any new tag could be accommodated by simply casting a new mold for the injection-molding presses. Still, any acquisition would be just one more thing to worry about.

Assaf still debated which option he favored. He wondered:

> Was integration into plastic parts production in Sensormatic's best long-term interests, or should the idea be dropped completely? And if it was pursued, was the purchase of new machinery for use at Deerfield Beach preferable to the acquisition of Canon Plastics?

EXHIBIT 5 Memorandum for Plastic Parts Production

To: Ronald Assaf
From: Bill Blakey
Date: February 15, 1980
Subject: Comparison of Alternatives for Production of Plastic Parts

In this memorandum I have tried to compare the costs of puchasing plastic parts from outside vendors with two alternatives—the costs of producing the parts in-house, using four new presses installed at Deerfield Beach, and the costs of producing the parts at Canon Plastics, if we were to acquire Canon and to operate it as a wholly owned subsidiary. The calculations show in-house fabrication to be the cheapest alternative available.

COMPARISON OF ANNUAL EXPENSES

Labor	Canon Plastics		In-House Fabrication	
Supervision	$54,700	[Production coordinator & 3 foremen]	$56,000	[Production supervisor & 2 foremen]
Direct/Indirect labor	60,300	[3 materials handlers @ $7,500 ea. & 6 machine operators @ $6,300 ea.]	53,310	[3 materials handlers @ $8,320 ea. & 3 machine operators @ $7,280 ea. plus overtime & night allowances]
Fringe benefits and taxes	42,700	[36% of payroll]	32,800	[30% of payroll]
Total labor	$157,700		$142,110	

Overhead	Canon Plastics		In-House Fabrication	
Rent/Floor space	$59,000	[rental of 15,000 sq. ft., including office space]	$34,200	[allocation of 5,000 sq. ft. at Deerfield Beach]
Depreciation	34,300	[8 presses @ $30,000 ea. plus $35,000 in auxiliary equipment, depreciated over 8 years]	54,300	[4 presses @ $78,200 ea. plus $121,800 in auxiliary equip., install. costs, etc., depreciated over 8 years]
Utilities	63,360	[8 presses @ 50 kw. each plus 80 kw. for auxil. equip. = 480 kw. × 24 hrs. × 5 days × 50 wks. × $.022 per kw. hour]	54,000	[4 presses @ 50 kw. each plus 50 kw. for auxil. equip. = 250 kw. × 24 hrs. × 5 days × 50 wks. × $0.36 per kw. hour]

(continued on next page)

EXHIBIT 5 Memorandum for Plastic Parts Production *(Continued)*

Overhead	Canon Plastics		In-House Fabrication	
Insurance (equipment)	7,200		4,300	
Repair & maintenance	28,000		7,500	
Shop supplies	14,300		6,000	
Variable overhead	57,500	[Controller, billing & sales order clerk, & warehouse mgr.]	—	[All of these functions can be performed by the present staff at Deerfield Beach]
Total overhead	$263,560		$160,300	
Contingency	—		43,200	[Includes allowance for consulting engineer @ $2,000/mo.]
Total operating costs (excluding raw materials)	$421,260		$345,610	

Raw material costs: calculated on the basis of annual Alligator Tag production of 20,000,000 units, with each completed tag requiring one strap and one clip.

	Straps	Clips
Cost per lb. of material, delivered	$.65 per lb. (A.B.S.)	$.40 per lb. (polypropylene)
Yield (parts per lb.)	1,000 straps per 26 lbs.	1,000 clips per 29 lbs.
Lbs. required to meet annual demand	520,000 lbs.	580,000 lbs.
Total cost	$338,000	$232,000

Annual raw material cost: $338,000 + $232,000 = $570,000

COMPARISON OF COSTS PER UNIT

	Canon Plastics	In-House Fabrication
Labor	$157,700	$142,110
Raw materials	570,000	570,000
Overhead	263,560	160,300
Contingency	—	43,200
Total operating costs	$991,260	$915,610
Annual production of Alligator tags (20,000,000)		
Cost per unit	$.0496 plus freight	$.0458

Plastic parts for Alligator tags are now purchased from Canon and Piedmont Plastics at the price of $.0576 per unit (one strap plus one clip) plus freight charges of $.30 per thousand. After learning of our interest in in-house fabrication, Piedmont has quoted new prices of $.0504 per unit plus freight, offering these discounts only if we will agree to longer-term contracts of at least 3 years. Artek Plastics, a relatively new firm in the industry, has been quoting prices of $.0461 per unit plus freight, although no significant quantity has yet been produced at that price.

For purposes of comparison, a price of $.0504 per unit plus freight, or $.0507 per unit delivered, will be used.

EXHIBIT 5 Memorandum for Plastic Parts Production *(Continued)*

	Canon Plastics		In-House Fabrication
Price per unit, delivered:			
Outside purchase	$.0507		$.0507
Produced by			
Sensormatic	.0499	(includes freight)	.0458
Savings per unit	$.0008		$.0049
Annual savings @			
20,00,000 units	$16,000		$98,000

CAPITAL REQUIREMENTS

	Canon Plastics	In-House Fabrication
Acquisition price	$500,000	—
Machinery & equipment	—	$434,600
4 molding machines		
@ $78,200 each		$312,800
Installation cost		
@$5,000 per machine		20,000
Auxiliary equipment		81,100
Contingency (5%)		20,700
Building and building		
equipment	—	$150,000
Total capital		
requirements	$500,000	$584,600
Savings per unit	$.0008	$.0049
Break-even volume	625,000,000 tags	119,300,000 tags
Annual production volume	20,000,000 tags	20,000,000 tags
Payback period	31.3 years	6.0 years

The above analysis shows in-house fabrication to be considerably cheaper than either acquisition of Canon Plastics or outside purchase. Canon Plastics does, however, have some compensating advantages. Because 8 presses are available but only 4 are required for meeting Sensormatic's present production requirements, the remaining 4 presses could be devoted to orders from other customers. Sales to Johnson Motors, for example, a long-standing customer of Canon, are made at approximately the same price per unit and cost roughly the same in operating and raw material expenses as the parts now sold to Sensormatic. These sales, however, are unlikely to outweigh the other financial advantages of in-house fabrication.

Source: Company records.

5. Intercon International (B)

As the big jet bored steadily westward across the Atlantic, Mr. Roy Teeling reviewed the notes he had taken during the three days of meetings he had just completed and felt increasingly frustrated. Mr. Teeling, Manufacturing Coordinator for the International Division of Intercon, Inc., was returning from a visit to Intercon's U.K. factory. The purpose of the visit had been to review the progress that plant's management was making in developing and implementing a new production planning and inventory control (PIC) system. The upshot of three days of discussion was that the PIC program was already six months behind schedule, and no discernible progress had occurred in the past four months. The proposed completion date of July 1, 1981, only nine months away, now appeared to be totally unattainable.

Company Background[1]

Intercon was a U.S.-based producer of electrical connectors and terminals. In the late 1960s, when most of its sales were to the automotive industry, it had developed a new approach for connecting printed circuit boards (PCBs) both to each other and to electrical cables. These proprietary products enabled it to penetrate the commercial electronics industries. During the 1970s the company greatly expanded its technical, manufacturing, and marketing resources as its total sales grew from less than $20 million to more than $135 million (see *Exhibit 1*).

[1] Further information about Intercon, Inc. is contained in the case "Intercon International" (1-680-144).

This case was prepared by Robert H. Hayes.

Copyright © 1982 by the President and Fellows of Harvard College. Harvard Business School case 682-095.

In 1981, although some stock was in outside hands, Intercon was essentially family owned and operated. Ted Davis, grandson of the company's founder, was president and Peter Davis, his younger brother, was in charge of the international activities of the company.

The Domestic and International divisions were managed almost completely independently. Domestic plants still provided slightly under 20% of the items sold by International (down from 100% in 1969), but Domestic purchased very little from International. When a product demanded in Europe was produced only in the U.S. or the Far East, the U.S. was the favored supplier; it was similarly favored as the "second source" for the Far East. Such purchases were made on a "best published price" basis—International almost never received any price favoritism.

Although it had entered the connector industry with a low-price strategy, Intercon had gradually shifted its mode of competition to emphasize quality and new product introduction. About 50% of current sales came from the automotive industry, down from over 70% a few years earlier. Both product design/engineering and process development took place mostly in the U.S. The company spent about 6% of its sales revenue on R&D in 1980.

Because of the relatively rapid production process for most of Intercon's products, their number (the total product line contained over 10,000 items), and the fact that many of these products had a shelf life of only a few months because of potential corrosion of the plated metal surfaces, the company had a firm policy of not holding large finished goods inventories. Most products were produced to order, and small orders

EXHIBIT 1 Financial Summary

INTERCON SIX-YEAR FINANCIAL SUMMARY
(IN THOUSANDS OF DOLLARS)

Operations	1980*	1979	1978	1977	1976	1975
Net sales	$135,400	$115,000	$80,000	$60,000	$48,000	$31,000
Income before taxes	30,031	28,056	19,517	13,733	10,666	5,541
Income taxes	14,352	13,676	9,514	6,978	5,398	2,748
Net income	15,679	14,380	10,003	6,755	5,268	2,793
Earnings per share	4.53	4.17	2.90	1.96	1.52	.81
Net income as a percentage of sales	11.6%	12.5%	12.5%	11.3%	11.0%	9.0%

Financial Position						
Current assets	58,132	49,341	36,218	24,072	19,900	13,464
Current liabilities	25,004	19,494	15,980	9,796	10,849	3,187
Working capital	33,128	29,847	20,238	14,276	9,051	10,277
Current ratio	2.3	2.5	2.3	2.5	1.8	4.2
Property, plant and equipment—net	28,893	22,582	17,865	12,137	9,571	5,969
Total assets	88,025	71,923	55,011	38,438	31,810	19,575
Long-term debt	2,558	2,358	2,018	1,103	213	247
Shareholders' equity	59,463	46,202	34,916	25,975	20,223	15,606
Return on beginning shareholders' equity	33.9	41.2	38.5	33.4	33.7	21.3
Avg. common shares outstanding during the year	3,462,186	3,458,881	3,448,808	2,452,876	3,448,818	3,442,901

*Intercon's fiscal year runs from July 1 to June 30.

were batched together as much as possible so as to reduce changeover costs. The cost of the molds and dies (in some cases as much as $60,000) used for many of the company's products caused the company to attempt to restrict the production of individual products to only one or two locations whenever this was feasible. Rather than build several molds for the same product, molds were often shipped by air freight when a foreign plant needed them. This added, of course, to the production lead time that the International Division had to operate around.

The Electrical Connector Industry

Although still relatively small (total sales in 1981 were estimated at over $3 billion), the electrical connector industry had exhibited a sales growth rate of over 15% per year over the previous decade. This was greater than the growth rate of the electronics industry as a whole. The dominant company in the industry was AMP, Inc., whose estimated sales for 1980 were about $1.2 billion. The "second tier" of companies consisted of five companies which each had sales in the $200–$300 million range. The "third tier," where Intercon and several other companies resided, had sales in the $100–$200 million range. Intercon also faced a number of foreign competitors in its international markets, but most of them were smaller. *Exhibit 2* contains a 1979 market share analysis, by geographic area.

Different companies chose to concentrate on different markets. Intercon, like AMP, tended to focus its attention primarily on OEM markets, while others derived the majority of their business from non-OEM markets. Despite these different strategies, and the competitive struggle for market share in a customer environment that was usually characterized as "cutthroat," most of the companies in the industry exhibited relatively high profitability. Using AMP as the most obvious example, its profit/sales ratio of 11.4% was among the top 30 in *Fortune*'s list of the "500 largest U.S. companies" in 1980.

Most long-range forecasts for the industry were optimistic because of the belief that the advancing state of semiconductor technology would stimulate demand for connectors in the long term. The continual increase in the number of circuits that could be incorporated onto a single LSI chip (which reduced the number of outside connections required for a given circuit module) was not felt to be necessarily damaging because it would also improve the cost and performance of current products, as well as facilitate the development of new products, thus increasing net demand.

But there was considerable belief that competition would become much fiercer, and that profit margins might decline as AMP became more concerned about the competitive inroads being made by some of its smaller competitors. It was also expected that some industry customers, as well as companies in related industries, would eventually become competitors.

Intercon's International Division

By mid-1980 Intercon International's sales were running at a rate of over $60 million per year. It had manufacturing plants in Japan, the U.K., and Hong Kong. A new plant, expected to begin production in mid-1981, was currently being built in Brazil. Sales subsidiaries were also located in all major markets in Europe and the Far East. Approximately 60% of International's total sales came from its Far Eastern operations (see *Exhibit 2*). The Japanese subsidiary had consistently been Intercon's most profitable foreign subsidiary, as well as one of its fastest growing.

The Domestic Division had provided some of the funds required by International's rapid expansion in the past, but by late 1979 the decision had been made that this financing should be discontinued—both because it was drawing too much cash away from U.S. operations, and because it was felt that International had passed its start-up phase and should be able to finance itself in the future. International's budget called for sales growth, in real terms, of over 30% in 1980.

According to Peter Davis:

> Our plan is eventually to make all items which we sell in large quantities, and rely on the domestic company only for relatively low-volume products. This is partly because of the cost of freight and duty, and partly because our domestic

EXHIBIT 2 Market Share by Geographic Area

Market Information			
Connectors (all types)—(from data published by McGraw-Hill)			
Marketing Information 1977–1979			
1) *Total Connector Market ($ mill.)**	1977	1978	1979
Japan	$ 147.5	$ 176.2	$ 184.4
Europe	524.8	581.2	642.1
U.S.	671.5	767.7	834.4
TOTAL	$1,343.8	$1,525.1	$1,660.9

Note: This does not include Latin America, Singapore, Taiwan, Korea, Hong Kong, Canada, Australia, etc.

2) *Intercon Corporate Sales ($ mill.)*			
Intercon corporate sales	$ 60.	$ 80.	$ 115.
Intercon world market share	4.3%	5.2%	6.9%

3) *Intercon Market Share by Area*			
Japan	8.1%	12.2%	15.0%
Europe	2.2%	2.5%	2.8%
U.S.	4.5%	5.3%	6.4%

*These estimates were considered low by Peter Davis.

plants simply can't meet our requirements in terms of cost and delivery time. As a result of this decision, we will have to expand our manufacturing resources rapidly. In the process, we will probably also increase the number of plant locations, because quick delivery and the ability to communicate easily with a plant are probably more important to a customer than whatever cost savings are available from economies of scale.

We certainly need to improve our current organization. We need to give more authority for day-to-day decision making to the local levels. Yet we cannot lose control, or at least visibility, over their operations. For example, each European sales subsidiary operates quite separately, and we are not taking full advantage of the strengths and opportunities that our multinational resources and organization make possible.

International Manufacturing

In an attempt to facilitate coordination among his manufacturing facilities, in early 1979 he appointed Roy Teeling (who had previously been assistant plant manager at Intercon's U.K. plant) to be International Manufacturing Coordinator. "One of your tasks is to define your own job," Davis told Teeling.

But keep in mind the likely evolution in our division's manufacturing capabilities. Currently we are sourcing about half our sales in Europe out of the U.S. As our volume increases, however, we run the risk of being a "second priority" customer if our domestic plants start running up against capacity constraints. So we probably are going to have to make an ever-larger proportion of the products we sell. In Asia, on the other hand, we are already nearly self-sufficient. We have considered shipping products from Hong Kong to Europe, but this adds almost 20% to their cost and can only be a short-term alternative for us.

Over the following year Davis and Teeling had gradually evolved a formal statement of the International Division's manufacturing strategy. Teeling explained:

You have to begin with the understanding that all eight of our major country subsidiaries have considerable autonomy and, in the face of very different market needs and opportunities, they have developed different marketing strategies over time. Even within the European group of companies there is considerable variety.

A problem arises, therefore, when you attempt to supply a number of these subsidiaries out of the same factory, which itself is constrained by the peculiar characteristics of its basic technology. As a result, we are faced with a sort of a balancing act in two dimensions. We want to try to meet the differing needs of our sales subsidiaries, without trying to be all things to all people. Second, we want to be able to transfer the things that are developed or learned in one factory (new equipment, methods, etc.) to our other factories, but we also want factories in different parts of the world to configure themselves to meet the particular needs of their own market area.

For example, in Europe we deal primarily with mature, sophisticated customers. They tend to value delivery dependability and high quality very highly. But they are willing to pay a slightly higher price in return, and they don't demand rapid delivery. Four to six weeks is fine for them. Japanese customers, on the other hand, want quality and rapid delivery (same week) above all else. Dependability of promises is a given but, again, price isn't as critical. Southeast Asia, which we serve out of Hong Kong, is a totally different world. Price, price, price—and how quick can you get it to me; that's all they want to know. Quality isn't as important, *yet*, and business there is so chaotic that nobody's promises can be depended upon. But that's our fastest growing market. Somehow we have to be able to develop manufacturing systems that reflect these different priorities in different regions, while still steadily reducing costs and improving quality everywhere.

Now, let me give you an example of the kind of problem we're facing. We have three major plants in our division. They are different sizes, different ages, serve very different markets and are embedded in different cultures. Each has developed its own order processing and production planning/inventory control systems, and each has chosen a different IBM computer (that's a constraint we did impose on them). As a result, the computer programs that the EDP group in each plant is writing cannot be run on the other plants' computers without modifications. As we speak, all three plants are in the process of updating their production planning systems.

What should I do? Adopt a "let the best plant win" philosophy, and go with home-grown products at each plant? Or should I step in and, as a start, get them all to buy the same computer system (even though they don't all need the same computing horsepower), and start coordinating their system development efforts? Or should we develop a system here at headquarters and install it at each plant? After all, they're all facing the same problems: increasing demand, a higher percentage of smaller orders, increases in both our product delivery times and in the variation of those times, and competitors that appear to be offering better delivery performance.

European Operations

Intercon had entered the Europan market late, and its market penetration was low in all European countries. It was felt that a tremendous sales potential existed in almost all sectors of the European market. Intercon's U.K. facility was presently supplying primarily the U.K., Scandinavian and Italian markets, and Intercon's European managers agreed that if it hoped to supply the large automotive and telecommunications manufacturers in Central Europe, it would have to have a manufacturing presence in either Germany or France. Many continental customers were unwilling to depend on U.K.-supplied products when locally made parts were available.

"Because we came 'late to the table' in Europe we have not achieved the market penetration there that we have in the U.S. and Asia," Davis commented.

> Our profit margins there have been adequate, however, and they should improve to the levels in the rest of the corporation as we increase our penetration. Two problems present themselves, however. First, both facilities costs and operating costs are higher in Europe than anywhere else.
>
> Second, the European market is much more fragmented than those in Asia and South America. There are also many more entrenched competitors in almost every country, with at least one of our competitors being several times our size. We are going to have to fight for every percent increase in market share. On the other hand, excluding North America, Europe is probably the largest potential market for our products.

He justified this latter view by point out that the high wage rates that prevailed in Europe, coupled with the high skill levels among both workers and technicians, made Europe a natural center for the electronics industry in the future. It now surpassed shipbuilding as the main employer there. European governments, recognizing the desirability of this development, were investing heavily in their indigenous electronics companies. Further evidence was provided by a recent article in *Electronic Business* (see *Exhibit 3* for excerpts).

Intercon's European operations had recently gone through a reorganization. Originally all sales and manufacturing facilities had reported directly to Peter Davis. As his organization grew, it became clear that this was no longer feasible. Therefore Davis was moving to develop three "Regional Offices," one each to handle the Americas, Asia and Europe. Each regional director would have profit and loss responsibility for both the marketing and manufacturing operations in his region.

Davis was also expanding his staff, and communicated his expectation that most technical and financial information flows would henceforth occur between the regional offices and appropriate headquarters staff members. His own role would gradually evolve from one of continual "hand holding" to one of general monitoring and crisis management.

The European regional office, located in London, was the second to be set up (after the Americas), and Roger Engles had been appointed to head it up in January 1980. He had worked for one of Intercon's competitors as a regional sales representative (with three years' experience in European sales) until 18 months previously, and had been serving on Intercon's International staff since then. Davis considered him to be technically very proficient, and valued his industry experience highly. Engles was an intense, results-oriented person, and immediately set about getting control of the information flows that linked the various European sales subsidiaries to each other, to the U.K. plant and to International headquarters.

Peter Davis sensed that there was some resentment of Engles by his European subsidiary managers. Much of this resentment, he felt, was natural: Davis had inserted another layer of management between himself and the line organization, and they no longer had as much direct access to him. Moreover, the close personal relationships that he had established with these people (many of whom he had recruited and set up in business) no longer buffered the tensions and conflicts that inevitably strained line-staff and subordinate-superior relationships. This source of resentment could not be helped, in his opinion; it was a cost of "growing up." What bothered him more was what appeared to be a suspicious and unforgiving attitude towards Engles as a person, which Davis felt (from personal knowledge) to be largely unwarranted. He was new, he was tough, and he wanted to accomplish the objectives that Davis had set out for him. Davis felt, with some irritation, that several of his country managers were making an unnecessary amount of resistance to

EXHIBIT 3 Electronic Business in the 1980s—Worldwide Outlook*

. . . [According to Ian Mackintosh, chairman of Mackintosh Consultants] over the next decade Europe's technology will catch up to the U.S. The tremendous advantage that the U.S. had in the 1960s is beginning to wane, because the big growth is no longer in the military and space markets. The entertainment markets are growing fastest, and that's where Europe and Japan have always had something of a lead. Unless the European nations miss a big opportunity, they should have a much larger proportion of world electronics production than ever before. They will capture that margin mostly at the expense of the U.S., but they will also take some of Japan's share.". . ."Europe will register the fastest growth because it's starting from the smallest base," Mackintosh says.

Mackintosh calls the consumer electronics segment the U.S. "soft-underbelly," the weakest link in U.S. electronics production. "How did the U.S. entertainment industry miss that opportunity? It wasn't in the right place at the right time," he says. "The synergistic environment that built the U.S. computer and semiconductor industries just didn't happen for the entertainment industries."

Europe, [he says], will be beset by higher wage levels and labor costs than in Japan and the U.S. To counteract this trend, the region will erect tariff barriers to ward off cheaper imports, creating market distortions and a lag in inflation compared with the U.S. But Japan won't erect such barriers and will try to capitalize on its free market position to penetrate the U.S. and European markets, he notes.

"Since Europe's recognition of the importance of electronics, the countries have heavily invested in the semiconductor industry and studies to ascertain its significance," Mackintosh says. Recently the United Kingdom invested between $400 million and $500 million in its semiconductor industry, and France invested a similar amount on its own. The money doesn't go just to research and development, he notes, but also to developing manufacturing techniques and an industrialist awareness program.

With these large capital investments in industry, manufacturing and education, European electronics production looks to be the rising star of the '80s. [A table accompanying this article contained forecasts that European production of electronic products would more than triple between 1980 and 1990.]

[Excerpts from "Electronic Business in the 1980s—Worldwide Outlook,"* and subtitled "Electronics production to drop in the U.S., gain elsewhere"]
*Electronic Business, December 1979.

---

the coordinating role that Engles had been asked to play.

The U.K. Plant

The U.K. plant had been Intercon's first foreign facility. From bare ground in 1972 it had grown into a 100,000-square-foot facility, employing 150 people (working two shifts) and turning out products worth about $1 million per month in mid-1980.

The plant was similar to Intercon's other plants, in that it produced essentially the same products using basically the same equipment. A typical connector consists of one or more metal terminals (which can range from simple pins to more complicated configurations) mated to a plastic housing (which can either be a single piece or an interlocking combination of two or more pieces). Almost all orders for a specific part, therefore, went through the same four stages of production.

First the terminals were stamped out of metal wire or strip. In most cases the terminals were then plated, in another section of the plant, with one of several coatings. Meanwhile, the housings were produced with plastic molding machines. When both terminals and housings were completed, they were taken to the assembly department to be assembled into finished connectors. Assembly had largely been a manual operation when the plant was young, but machines now assembled over 70% of all products.

Intercon produced over 3,000 different types of connectors in the U.K. plant, utilizing various combinations of about 50 different terminals and 150 different housings. Orders for specific connectors arrived at a rate of about 30 per day, and at any one time over 800 orders were usually being processed somewhere in the plant. The time between the acceptance of an order and the shipment of the completed product was typically on the order of four to eight weeks for most products. About one week was spent in scheduling (to facilitate the batching of small orders), one week in stamping, one week in plating, one week in molding (which could be concurrent), one week undergoing various quality checks, and one to two weeks in assembly. Final inspection and shipping usually took only two to three days.

Except for the plating operation, this production process was not characterized by great economies of scale, since capacity could be increased at each stage of the process simply by purchasing another piece of equipment. The U.K. plant currently had six metal stamping machines in its terminal department, 12 injection molding machines in its housing department, and over 20 different assembly machines (which tended to be specialized for particular families of products) in the assembly department.

Production planning was complicated, however, by the need to process a large number of small orders through these various stages and the many manual operations (sorting, counting, inspecting, and moving) that surrounded them. Moreover, machine and labor capacities were not the only constraints, since neither stamping nor molding could take place without the proper dies, molds and tools (jigs and fixtures). Some of these devices were specific to a particular product, but most could produce a variety of different products after some physical modification (this usually took

an hour or two, and involved changing guidearms and set points). Therefore, a production plan which required a die or mold that was currently unavailable—because it was already in use, was being cleaned or modified, had been sent to another plant, or was simply "lost" somewhere in the plant—was unworkable, and department supervisors had to work around the plan in order to keep workers utilized.

Although he had been away from the U.K. plant for almost two years, during which time its sales had increased by more than 50%, Roy Teeling had been struck during his most recent visit by how little things had changed since he worked there. An air of amiable chaos prevailed: the aisles were clogged with baskets and pushcarts full of parts; unused dies and tools were tucked away into unoccupied niches under the workbenches and on the bookcase-like shelves that lined the walls (there was no central storeroom for dies or tools); and workers and their supervisors were continually poking through the piles looking for things, or running to the production control office to check where an order was and what should be done until it surfaced.

Whereas the injection molding machines appeared to be operating at 70–80% utilization, Teeling's impression was that the metal stamping machines were only being used at about 50% of capacity. Some of this underutilization appeared to be due to the setups that were required, but almost always at least one (and usually two) machines were standing completely idle. Orders often got lost in the plant because there was no formal record-keeping system that tracked their progress through the various stages of production. The fact that an order would miss its scheduled delivery date usually only became apparent when that day arrived, or a customer called to inquire about its status. It had to be tracked down manually when this occurred.

Manual records were being kept of raw materials and finished goods, and semiannual physical stock checks often revealed wide disparities between inventory records and actual amounts. "Work in process" was defined to mean whatever purchased materials had been logged in, but which could not be accounted for in raw material inventory or the finished goods stockroom. On-time delivery performance varied by type of product, but was generally poor and deteriorating. A recent

EXHIBIT 4a On-Time Delivery Performance, U.K. Plant

% of Total Orders	Type of Product	To Original Customer Request Date	To Scheduled* Delivery Date
14%	Pins & terminals	78.8%	87.3%
16	Moldings	70.6	86.6
70	Assemblies	44.3	60.1
100%			

*Customer was informed that requested delivery date was impossible, and given a new delivery date which was accepted.

EXHIBIT 4b Lead Time Distribution Analysis, U.K. Plant

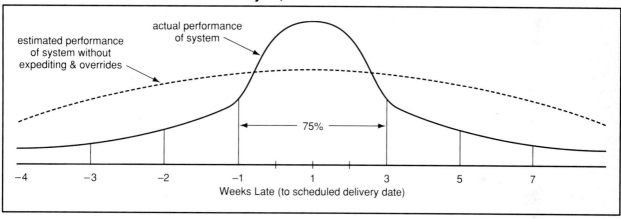

study, commissioned by Roy Teeling, had produced the data summarized in *Exhibit 4*. No reports relating to delivery performance were produced on an ongoing basis.

Althought it was difficult to compare directly the performance of the International Division's three plants because of the many difference between them, there was general agreement that the Japanese plant was by far the most effective. Its costs were less than those in both Hong Kong and the U.K., even though its wage rates were comparable with the U.K.'s and over twice Hong Kong's. Moreover, its quality levels and delivery times were clearly superior to the others'. The performance of the U.K. plant was felt to be about on a par with that of the Hong Kong plant (see *Exhibit 5* for detailed plant comparisons).

Brian Waddell, the U.K. plant manager, was a bluff, good-humored man who had personally hired everyone in the plant and knew them all by name. He was active in community affairs and relished being known around the town as "Mr. Intercon." The result of his outside activities and reputation for integrity, coupled with Intercon's fast growth and continuing hiring, was that the plant was looked upon by the local community as a good place to work. The fact that the plant was one of the few in the region that had not yet been unionized was another tribute to Waddell's "people" skills.

He had been recruited ten years ago into the Intercon organization, from a successful job as a plant manager in another part of the country, by Peter Davis himself. He had worked 15 hours a day to bring the plant into being, and its current size and capabilities were a testament to his sweat and willpower. He and his family still enjoyed a close personal relationship with Peter Davis, a product of the many visits that Davis had made to the plant over the years.

EXHIBIT 5 International Division Plant Comparisons

	United Kingdom		Japan		Hong Kong	
(12 MONTHS ENDING JUNE 30, 1980: ALL FIGURES TRANSLATED TO $MILLIONS AT CURRENT EXCHANGE RATE)						
Sales*	$11.3	100%	$30.7	100%	$6.7	100%
(growth rate over previous 12 months)		(23%)		(30%)		(41%)
Materials		42.4%		39.2%		45.3%
Dir. labor		8.4		4.3		3.9
Var. OH		14.3		8.6		10.9
Fr. & duty		0.6		0.4		1.7
Total var. cost		65.7%		52.5%		61.8%
Period manufacturing		8.3		7.9		7.2
Administration		8.1		7.5		9.9
Total period costs		16.4%		15.4%		17.1%
Profit before tax**	$2.0	17.9%	$10.5	34.1%	$1.4	21.1%
Inventories						
Raw materials	$0.9		$ 0.5		$1.1	
WIP	1.4		1.9		0.9	
Finished goods	1.2		1.6		0.8	
Tools & dies	1.6		2.5		0.7	
Total inventory	5.1		6.5		3.5	
Net fixed assets	3.5		6.2		2.1	
Total assets	9.8		16.3		6.5	
Mfg. employees		153		248		108

*At factory selling prices.

**Plants, which sell to sales subsidiaries at fixed transfer prices and utilize most of the company's fixed assets, typically show lower profitability and ROI values than do sales subsidiaries. Regional profitability and ROI are obtained by combining factory and sales operations (and eliminating internal sales).

Waddell's production manager was Gordon Fellows, who had been one of the first employees at the plant. A skilled machinist, he still personally checked out each new piece of equipment that was installed in the plant, and he was also deeply involved in debugging the new products that were introduced there. Although he and Waddell had once been inseparable, over the years they had gradually divided up the work to be done between them: Waddell managed the human resources in the plant and its relationships with the outside world (including Intercon headquarters and the subsidiary managers), while Fellows managed the plant's internal operation. There was still a strong bond of loyalty between them, however, and Fellows was clearly second in command in the plant even though he had little experience with Waddell's activities. Because he was intimately familiar with both the personnel and the equipment in the plant, many people (including

Waddell) felt that Fellows was the plant's "indispensable man".

The production planning department consisted of three people. They received daily batches of orders from the order processing department and manually scheduled them through the factory using procedures that dated before Roy Teeling's first appearance in the plant (in 1976). When problems arose, they personally tracked down errant orders and walked them through the bottleneck stage. As a result, their days were long and hectic, but they accepted the continual crises (and some telephoned verbal abuse from country managers) with good humor and a "can-do" attitude. Although Larry Ellsworth, the head of the department, recognized that the new computerized PIC system had the potential of vastly simplifying their work, he pleaded that he would not be able to spare much time from his current job in order to participate actively in developing the new system. Nor could he bring much expertise to its design, since he had no background with computers.

Roy Teeling had respect and affection for all these people since he had worked closely with them for almost three years. Yet from his new position he could see the plant's flaws more clearly than he could when he was a part of it. He also knew that his title of assistant plant manager had been something of an exaggeration; in no sense had he been prepared to take over the jobs of either Fellows or Waddell. And lately he was experiencing a gnawing worry: was Waddell, despite his great charm and previous accomplishment, really capable of leading the plant through the next stage of its development?

The PIC Program

Increasing complaints from the country sales subsidiaries about late deliveries, the lack of warning when late deliveries were imminent, and the length of quoted lead times for most products, coupled with complaints from International headquarters about the U.K.'s high inventory levels (including the inventories of tools and dies), brought matters to a head in mid-1979. Roy Teeling had called a meeting, attended by both the U.K. plant management group and headquarters staff personnel (Roger Engles among them, although he

had not yet assumed his current position), to discuss these problems and to begin thinking about ways for dealing with them.

Although Brian Waddell was initially somewhat miffed by Teeling's initiative in calling the meeting (since he felt that most of the U.K.'s delivery problems were due to the rapid growth of sales in Europe, coupled with delays in receiving new equipment and the introduction of two new product lines during the previous 18 months), he and his managers participated in it actively and with good grace. The decision was made to develop a computerized production planning and inventory control system, as well as to make a number of changes in the plant's "housekeeping" systems—relating to mold and die storage, raw material security, etc.—and in its internal management information systems. Additional people having industrial and mechanical engineering skills would be hired, as well as another computer programmer.

Albert Collins was put in overall charge of the project. He had received a master's degree in chemical engineering from the University of Leeds, and worked for 5 years with another company prior to joining the plant several months earlier. He had played an important role during the recent expansion of the plant's plating operation. His vigor, intelligence and desire to get ahead had already impressed Teeling, who felt that he was the ideal project manager for this program. Within three months, working in his spare time (no change had yet been made in his previous responsibilities, so the new task was simply an addition to his usual activities), he had developed an overall plan of action for the project (see *Exhibit 6*). It indicated that most housekeeping items would be completed by the end of 1980, and that the new PIC system would be completed by mid-1981.

After studying the original PIC program schedule, and the comments he had made about its various stages during his recent visit, Teeling began drafting a memo to Peter Davis summarizing his visit (see *Exhibit 7*). After describing and analyzing what he had seen, he wrote the word "Recommendations" and underlined it. Then he mulled the whole situation over again in his mind as he watched the coast of Maine slip by beneath the plane. What should—or could—be done about the situation?

EXHIBIT 6 Status of PIC Project Action Items

Item	Original Completion Date	Current Status (Oct. 1, 1980)
1. Formally establish and staff I.E. section	12/79	One man hired. Another being sought.
2. Expand and improve physical layout in fin. Goods storeroom and shipping area	12/79	Completed.
3. Monthly scrap report	2/80	Program being tested.
4. Materials usage variance: raw materials issues vs. production	4/80	"Almost finished."
5. Establish report on actual delivery time vs. published lead times	5/80	"High priority job": EDP Dept.
6. Report on late delivery by country of destination	6/80	"Preliminary thinking has crystallized"
7. Report of late items for customer liaison department	7/80	On hold until (6) done.
8. Initiate production recording on computer	9/80	No progress.
9. Record work center performance with classification of non-operative time	10/80	No progress.
10. Set up machine/labor/materials standards for each major product	12/80	No plans.
11. Inaugurate weekly production plan detailing desired output by work center	1/81	No plans.
12. Quantify, record and report WIP monthly by line item and location	2/81	No plans.
13. Establish slow/excess reports for components.	4/81	No plans.
14. Introduce and develop two-level computerized production planning package for assembly department	5/81	No plans.
15. Introduce and develop two-level computerized production planning package for molding department	6/81	No plans.
16. Introduce and develop two-level computerized production planning package for stamping department	6/81	No plans.
17. Establish new inventory control system for components	7/81	No plans.

EXHIBIT 7 Status Memorandum

M E M O R A N D U M

TO: Peter Davis

FROM: Roy Teeling

SUBJECT: Status of U.K. PIC Program

I was pleased to see that there had been some progress during the past four months:

1. A new industrial engineer has been hired, and Larry Ellsworth has identified two people who are capable of filling the new position in his PIC department. Both have business degrees and experience with computers. An offer will be made "shortly."
2. The EDP group has written two computer programs that provide additional materials usage information.
3. Initial steps have been taken to seal off the finished goods inventory/shipping section so that access to it is limited and monitored. (I am not yet convinced that the record-keeping in that area has improved; we will have to wait for the newly-initiated rolling physical stock checks before we can verify this.)
4. Improvements have been made in the packaging and shipping department.

On the other hand, it was clear that neither Albert Collins nor Larry Ellsworth are moving ahead as aggressively as they could. For the most part the changes made so far represent relatively simple organizational and housekeeping changes: looking for new people and improving the orderliness of the plant's physical and information flows. Even those obvious changes have taken from three to seven months longer than the completion dates originally promised.

I believe there are four major reasons for this sluggishness:

1. Both Collins and Ellsworth are busy men who have been assigned major new responsibilities without relaxing substantially the load of their previous assignments. Most of their time has been spent trying to do their regular jobs while locating and training new assistants who will take some of the burden off their shoulders in the future.
2. Both are reluctant to go up against the "don't rock the boat; the men won't like this" attitude in the plant. I am becoming convinced that Gordon Fellows is the principal defender of the status quo and appears to exercise what almost amounts to a veto power. At one point, for example, it was mentioned that once before there had been a proposal to institute a job order system like the one we are now proposing, but that "Gordon was against it so we never did it."
3. Both men are also perplexed by the complexity of the production scheduling/inventory control problem they are facing. Neither is familiar with modern inventory control procedures; in fact, Ellsworth appears to be a captive of the simple manual procedures that he inherited when he took over his current job two years ago.
4. Finally, both are keenly aware of the strained relations between Brian Waddell and Roger Engles (who, aside from me, is the most vocal and insistent agent for change in the plant). This adds to their sense of unease and vulnerability to being undercut from either side.

(continued on next page)

EXHIBIT 7 Status Memorandum (*Continued*)

I personally don't know what portion of Brian's inertia is due to this irritation at being pressured to make changes that he didn't initiate himself, to his fear of pushing Gordon beyond his capabilities and limits of patience, or to his own direct contact with the work force that corroborates Gordon's resistance.

Having said this, and keenly appreciating the human dilemma that Albert and Larry face, I still feel that they should be moving ahead faster than they are. Most of the "reasons" given for not proceeding faster only partially hold water, in my opinion. Collins, for example, is unwilling to push Ellsworth because he feels Larry can't devote *any* time to the development of the new PIC system until he is relieved of his current job (which is not scheduled to happen for two months, after the new man is hired and trained). I disagree. The arrival rate of orders has plateaued during the last three months; evidently Europe is poised on the brink of another recession. This kind of lull provides an opportunity to plunge ahead.

Secondly, even if they had not had much time to actually *develop* a new manufacturing control system, I would have expected them to at least have done some preliminary thinking about it. They seem to have done little other than generate revised timetables and reasons for not proceeding faster. No new ideas or other evidence of additional thinking have surfaced since my last visit.

There has not even been any progress on the plan to move the dies and molds to their own storeroom, to which access will be controlled, and where someone will have the responsibility for monitoring their performance, inspecting and repairing them upon their return from a job, and initiating requests for major rework or replacement. They are too critical and expensive a resource to be left lying around, uncovered, unoiled, and untended. Yet Gordon says that the men are used to having them nearby and that formalizing their storage will simply add another bureaucracy in the plant.

The political situation in the plant is highly charged, both because of the deteriorating relationship between Brian and Roger and, relatedly, Gordon's obvious hostility to the changes we are proposing. Albert Collins is still regarded as a newcomer and has to operate very discreetly at the intersection of these pressures. Poor Larry does not appear to be nearly as eager to assume his new role as he indicated a few months ago. Despite all this, and other signs of tension among the management group, I was surprised to see little evidence of a decline in morale among the workers.

Recommendations

6. The Roles and Responsibilities of the Corporate Manufacturing Staff

In most MBA courses one focuses one's attention on the key decisions that various managers have to make. The implicit assumption is that if these decisions are made properly, the company will prosper. But as every experienced manager knows, making the right decisions plays only a relatively small part in making a company ultimately successful. To be effective, decisions must be interpreted and implemented by and through people—people who are often geographically distant from one another, have different skills, job definitions, levels of education, career expectations, and who sometimes speak different languages and have different cultural norms. Somehow the strength, intelligence and allegiance of this mass of diverse individuals must be harnessed and directed toward the common goals. Therefore, the most critical task confronting the manufacturing vice president is not simply to acquire the best resources and make the "right" decisions, but to build—and operate through—a purposeful organization.

This job is particularly difficult and important for the manufacturing vice president because the manufacturing function typically employs the great majority (often from two-thirds to five-sixths) of the people who work for a manufacturing company. As the company's strategy and manufacturing mission change, many (if not all) of these people will have to make some change in their job assignments and behavior if consistent priorities are to be maintained. In this note, we will explore some of he issues that must be addressed when attempting to decide which responsibilities should be undertaken by a company's (or division's) manufacturing staff.

I. The Traditional Organizational Structure

The following organization chart (*Figure 1*) provides one example of the size and complexity of the kind of organization in which these people typically operate, at least in the U.S.

At the top is the manufacturing vice president, who usually has roughly equal authority (but in many companies, not equal influence or remuneration) as the heads of the marketing, finance, control, personnel, and R&D functions. It is interesting to contrast this organizational structure with that of a typical manufacturing company in northern Europe (Holland, say). This is shown in *Figure 2*.[1]

Notice that here all the functions of the company are grouped under two co-equal managers: a "technical director," who is in charge of manufacturing, engineering (including R&D) and usually labor relations, and a "commercial director," who is in charge of marketing, finance, control, and administration (office operations).

This note was prepared by Robert H. Hayes.

Copyright © 1982 by the President and Fellows of Harvard College. Harvard Business School case 682-078.

[1] For a more detailed description of such an organizational structure, see the case "N.V. Philips Gloeilampenfabrieken—The Tessenderlo Plant," (HBS Case Services number 2-679-082).

FIGURE 1 Organization Chart for a Typical Functionally Organized U.S. Manufacturing Company or Division

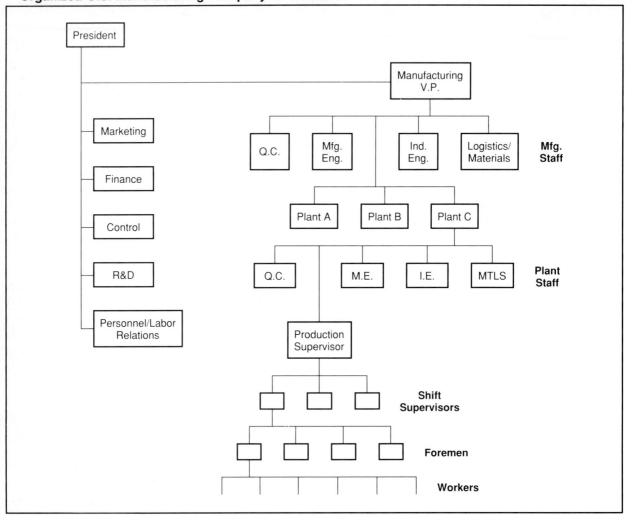

FIGURE 2 Organization Chart for a Typical Northern European Manufacturing Company

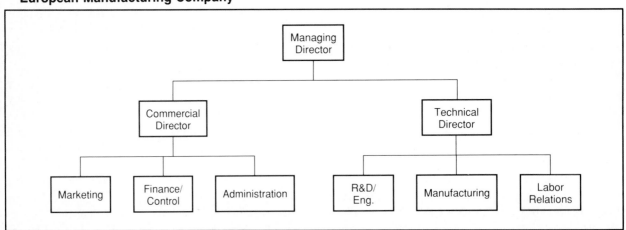

6. The Roles and Responsibilities of the Corporate Manufacturing Staff

The two directors are expected to work together in resolving problems and conflicts, and the managing director (who spends most of his time attending to external affairs) rarely intervenes. This type of organizational structure gives essentially equal power to each group (although the differing competences and personal attributes of various people may cause some shift in this balance of power), and forces coordination between R&D activities, manufacturing, and labor relations. The typical U.S. organization structure, on the other hand, tends to divide responsibilities, thereby increasing the likelihood of uncoordinated activities and raises the possibility that technical issues, specifically those faced on the factory floor, will exercise less influence over the direction of the company as a whole.

Back to *Figure 1*. Normally the manufacturing vice president has a staff group of specialist functions reporting to him or her. These specialist staff groups typically coordinate the activities of the specialists located in each of the company's operating units (which are usually, but not always, in separate facilities), and manage the "plant network": accumulating data about plant performance, evaluating and compensating managers, and coordinating the interlinked activities of groups of plants.

Finally, and most important, we have the "line activities": those that actually involve the production of goods and services in the operating units/plants. Each is usually under the direction of a plant manager, who also has a staff group and his or her own line organization consisting of a factory supervisor (who used to be called, in the European tradition, the "works manager"), one or more shift supervisors, a number of first-level supervisors, and the workers themselves.

In the next section we will focus our attention on the corporate/divisional manufacturing staff. As is generally true for staff organizations, its roles and responsibilities are surrounded by ambiguity.

II. The Corporate Manufacturing Staff

In most manufacturing organizations there is considerable tension, if not always overt hostility, between the line and staff organizations. While the line organization, deep in its heart, usually recognizes the intrinsic value of a corporate staff group (much like the average motorist recognizes the intrinsic value of a radar-equipped police force—as long as it confines its attention to other motorists), it often considers the contribution of such a group to be less than its cost. While line managers often work in remote locations, factories and offices that are at best stark, the staff is pictured as luxuriating in well-appointed air-conditioned offices, and hobnobbing with the "top brass" in plush after-hours watering holes. Yet the line organization feels that *it* is responsible for the actual creation of value in the organization, and the staff is simply (to use the older, more pejorative, term) "burden"—a group of people dedicated to the creation of complex systems which will justify their own existence. *Exhibit 1* contains one recent business school graduate's analysis of the advantages of staff over line jobs.

There are at least ten essential roles that the manufacturing staff can play within a manufacturing organization. Many of these roles are interrelated so any decoupling is, in a sense, artifical. But the following list at least provides a sense of the range of tasks that must be performed if the total organization is to function effectively.

1. *Auditing.* Over time, the company develops standards, goals, and procedures that regulate how various activities ought to be carried out: quality control procedures, personnel management, equipment maintenance, safety measures, "good manufacturing practices" in general, and so on. Part of the responsibility of the manufacturing staff is to oversee the proper carrying out of these activities. This requires regular visits to the plants, and inspections that are similar to the inspections of financial records that are carried out by accounting auditors.

2. *Review and Evaluation of Operating Unit Performance.* As mentioned earlier, one of the key tasks of the manufacturing staff is to collect data relating to the performance of differing operating units, and on the basis of this data to evaluate their effectiveness in carrying out their assigned responsibilities. In some cases, only the performance that results from individual decisions is evaluated; in other organizations the major decisions themselves are scrutinized.

3. *Communications*. In a larger, geographically dispersed organization, communication becomes a problem. Not only must the decisions, inferences and policies that are the product of corporate headquarters be transmitted and explained to line personnel in the field, but also the ideas and approaches that have been developed by and tested out in one operating unit should be communicated to other units so that the organization can learn through shared experience. Finally, relevant information from outside the company—relating to competitors' actions, governmental regulations, and technological developments—should also be disseminated.

4. *Coordination*. Most plants utilize products or services that are produced by other plants within the total organization, and in turn produce products and services for other plants. In order that the total system operate smoothly, these interplant flows must be coordinated by a group which is in possession of the "big picture" and is above the rivalries and self-interest of individual plants. Moreover, this coordination role often makes possible (and therefore includes) centralized services and decisions that are more efficiently done by a headquarters group than by a number of individual plants: purchasing, management recruiting, job assessment, equipment selection, etc. Another function of the corporate staff in many companies is, through careful monitoring of the proposed hiring and layoff plans at different plants, to facilitate the transfer of people or equipment from one plant to another in an attempt to minimize layoffs and bring skills to the points where they are needed most.

5. *Consulting*. Most plants need expert help on various problems from time to time. They cannot always afford to hire such experts on a full-time basis, since they are needed only part time, so one alternative is for them to utilize the services of independent consulting firms. Another alternative is to set up a group within the corporate manufacturing staff which does consulting for the individual plants. Not only can the corporation as a whole achieve a high utilization of the time of these consultants, but also, through repeated exposure, they become intimately familiar with the production processes, equipment and people within the company. Therefore, they may be able to achieve a higher level of specific expertise than is obtainable from a consulting firm which services a broad variety of clients. Finally, the movement of such consultants from plant to plant facilitates the auditing and communication functions described above.

6. *Management Training and Career Development*. Just as new people must be selected, acculturated and trained, so must the skills of the existing people in an organization be enhanced. Usually the manufacturing staff is entrusted with coordinating the training and development of the people in the manufacturing organization as a whole. This might range from simply distributing information about "approved educational programs" provided by outside institutions, and authorizing and monitoring the performance of the individuals who attend them, to designing and staffing instructional programs of its own, to taking an active role in moving individuals from one set of management responsibilities to another as part of a conscious career planning process. Often this training role is integrated with the consulting and coordinating roles described above.

7. *Special Programs*. From time to time, special needs arise that do not fit comfortably into any existing category of responsibilities. Examples include the energy conservation programs that many companies set up after the first oil crisis in 1973–74, special safety programs that arose in response to an increase in the accident rate, and job enrichment programs that sprang up when the "blue collar blues" became endemic in the U.S. in the early 1970s. At the end of the 1970s, this latter program became supplanted in many companies by productivity (and quality) improvement programs motivated by the increasing competition that corporations began to experience from imported products.

8. *Reperesenting Line Management in Corporate Financial Review*. In most companies, major requests for funds (plant expansions, new equipment, etc.) must go through an elaborate review process. The staff organization often

works with the line organization in formulating these requests, reviewing them for accuracy, putting them into the proper format, assembling the necessary supporting data and (assuming it is satisfied with a proposal's viability), shepherding it through the corporate review process and defending it in various corporate forums. These activities often overlap with the performance review, communications and consulting activities described above.

9. *Advanced Process Development.* Line organization managers, especially when they are being evaluated primarily on the basis of financial performance (profit, ROI, etc.), often are reluctant to undertake major process development activities because their cost does not sufficiently outweigh the potential benefits to their organization. Such process development projects include both the development of management systems (production scheduling systems or computer programs, inventory systems, capacity planning systems, etc.) and the development of machinery and ancillary devices.

Profit center managers often see themselves as incurring the risks and expenses of such projects all by themselves, while the rest of the organization shares in the rewards of the ones that are successful. If each waits for another profit center to take the plunge, nothing might get done. Therefore, the corporate staff often feels it must take a lead role in choosing which kinds of projects are pursued, and either carrying them out itself or funding their development in selected operating units.

10. *Guru Wisdom.* The manufacturing staff also becomes the repository of highly skilled senior people, whose experience with the company's technology, products, and personnel is developed over a long period of time. As a result, their knowledge and counsel are sought by a broad range of people, both from within the manufacturing organization and from other corporate functions. They often have titles and responsibilities which appear to be highly specific, but as far as individuals in the organization are concerned, their reputations transcend their particular job descriptions of the moment. They spend much of their time on the telephone, answering questions, giving advice, overseeing the nonprogrammed flow of information through the organization. In some organizations they perform the role of "technological gatekeepers": through their long experience with the technology of their industries, and their wide acquaintanceships with people who work for suppliers, customers and competitors, they are often the first to learn about potentially important new technological developments.

The importance of such gurus should not be underestimated. One company, for example, after requesting a study by a well-known consulting company and conducting a nationwide search, recently created a new position of "manufacturing vice president" and filled it with an extremely able individual. Following the advice contained in the consulting study, this person set up an organization similar to that depicted in *Figure 1*. As he was proceeding with the development and guidance of this organization, he became aware of a certain sense of disappointment among some of the senior corporate officers. Further investigation revealed that the major impetus for the consulting study and the creation of his own position was the loss, through death, of a senior vice president in the company.

This person had been trained as an engineer and had spent many years in the company's manufacturing function. Even though his later career had taken him into general management, and then into the top echelon of corporate management, he remained the "expert" on matters relating to technology or manufacturing. Even thogh the new manufacturing vice president was "doing all the right things," he had not structured himself or his organization to fill the need that was, subliminally at least, the real driving force behind the creation of his position. What the top management in the company really wanted, it turned out, was another guru.

The preceding list provides a brief indication of the variety of functions and roles that have to be performed in a normal manufacturing organization. Notice that they involve very different skills and usually require very different kinds of people. Good auditors and financial analysts are not necessarily good communicators, and good consultants do not necessarily make good managers of special projects or programs. Gurus are gurus, and may not be good for anything else.

Nor do all these functions have to be performed by the corporate manufacturing staff. If the company is highly diversified and decentralized, it may be inappropriate if not impossible for any central group to provide the kind of specialized skill and coordination that would be possible in a more centralized company. Perhaps some of these tasks should be carried out at the division level. Or, if the company utilizes very large, specialized plants, it may make more sense to locate technological expertise at those plants than in some remote location.

It is important to remember that most organizations over time develop informal approaches to all these tasks. Individuals, motivated by their own interests or previous work experiences, undertake some of them as labors of love. Individuals or groups are assigned to perform others on a one-time basis, and then over time find themselves gradually spending more and more of their time on them. Other functional groups within the corporation, because of their own needs, develop the capabilities of performing others. So, recognized or not, coordinated or not, the work usually gets done—somehow, somewhere.

Molding the Manufacturing Organization

The job of the manufacturing vice president is to create order out of this potential chaos. This requires that he or she decide exactly whether and where (at what level and location) in the total organization each of these tasks should be performed, and who should have responsibility for seeing that they are defined and performed properly. Depending on the situation, some of them should probably be the responsibility of individual plants. Others should be the responsibility of divisional management. The remainder become the responsibility of the corporate manufacturing staff.

The subsidiary problem then becomes, given the widely differing personal characteristics required for these tasks, how to attract and manage the people who will be given responsibility for them. This can be a source of considerable concern. The usual idea is to "promote" people from the line organization to fill many of those job positions that require the expertise they have acquired through hands-on experience. But the others (who are asked to fill the roles of auditors, communicators, and program managers, say) might require very different backgrounds and skills. Where do these people come from and, probably more important, where do they go—that is, where are the opportunities for their advancement in the organization?

In making these decisions, and in choosing among alternatives that seem—at least on the surface—to be being equally plausible, there is one central concept that should guide one's decisions: the staff is a *support* group, not the aristocracy of the manufacturing organization. Most organization charts (including the ones depicted in *Figures 1* and *2*) promote this latter impression: the staff is on top and the line organization is on the bottom. But if the role of the staff is really to support line operations, their positions should be reversed: the organization chart should look more like a table than a pyramid. Unfortunately, it is not always easy to maintain this notion of the proper relationship between line and staff because two "laws of organizations" can combine to thwart the best intentions.

The first has to do with the natural tendency of people to want to do a good job, and then to expand their responsibilities:

(1) A strong central staff will find something to do, and will decide that what it wants to do is sufficiently important that it justifies interfering with what somebody else wants to do.

An important corollary to this law is that a weak manager will be glad to let somebody else solve his problems for him, and let that person take responsibility for these decisions. The implication is that if you choose a strong, aggressive person to head a staff function, you should not be surprised to see it grow larger and more powerful over time—a tendency that has been described as "staff infection."

The second law relates to the natural tendency of staff organizations, as they become larger, to become more bureaucratic. Usually managers

EXHIBIT 1 An MBA Compares Line and Staff Positions

'EXCERPTS FROM "HOW TO MAKE LINE POSITIONS MORE ATTRACTIVE FOR MBAs"[2]'

Most graduates of business schools today seek and accept high paying, high powered consulting, investment banking or corporate planning positions rather than first-line production or sales jobs. Only 3% of Harvard Business School's class of 1981 took jobs in production and 8.6% in sales and marketing, while 21.4% went into consulting and 21.6% into finance. An estimated 90% of those who graduated from Wharton in 1981 went into staff areas with no direct responsibility for making or selling a product.

These statistics are alarming to many industry leaders and business professors. Henry Schacht, chairman of Cummins Engine, has said he is "absolutely distressed over the current wave of business school graduates who are going into the consulting business." Harvard Business School professors Robert Hayes and William Abernathy have complained of management's overdependence on "analytical detachment rather than the insight that comes from 'hands-on' experience." Many executives believe management judgment develops slowly as a result of day-to-day dealings with people at the shop, plant and sales office level; they criticize recent MBAs for focusing too much on whiz-bang computer printouts and polished boardroom presentations.

Yet it should be no surprise that so few MBAs seek line positions.

First, the pay isn't as good as it is in staff. Many MBAs have incurred large debts to obtain their degrees and the starting salaries of line jobs ($22,000 to $28,000) cannot compete with those frequently offered by management consultants and investment bankers ($40,000 to $55,000).

Second, the geography isn't the most desirable: Many line jobs are in smaller cities remote from major metropolitan areas. It may sound snobbish, but most MBAs from top schools prefer New York or Los Angeles to Green Bay or Schenectady. It can be lonely working far from peers and friends, and the slow pace of most smaller cities can be frustrating to MBAs who have left school still in overdrive.

Third, the visibility and exposure are lousy. An investment banker or consultant two years out of B-school comes in frequent contact with top executives from a variety of companies. But working in an isolated plant or office focused on specific division goals offers the MBA little or no chance to view or be viewed by even his own company's top management.

Fourth, there is not as much intellectual stimulation in line jobs as in staff: Tracing a lost shipment is less cerebral than analyzing industry ratios. Taking inventory, signing invoices and reviewing production schedules aren't as heady as discussing board business strategies.

Fifth, the pressure is enormous. Responsibility for and risk of making mistakes affecting the bottom line is great. Calling a repairman at 3 a.m. when the machine breaks down, laying off workers when you can't meet your payroll, and accepting back a product a customer claims is bad are lonely decisions which have to be made without two or three days' analysis and a business school group to help.

Finally, starting in a line job often means a slower, more circuitous route to top management. It takes time to get functional breadth of experience. You can't change jobs every six months as a management consultant changes projects without costing both the company and the people who work for you.

Despite all these disadvantages, of course, some MBAs choose line management. They choose it because they like responsibility for people and budgets, because they want to actively implement solutions rather than passively analyze problems and make recommendations and because they believe learning details and practicing daily management will better prepare them to lead companies later.

While MBAs in line positions may miss talking about general business trends and management theories with similarly educated people, they often learn "street smarts" in trying to get a customer to buy excess inventory or dealing with tough, cynical buyers or foremen. They frequently find much greater job satisfaction than in staff: People depend on them to produce; they have decision-making authority, not just influence; they're often on their own, seeing the results of their efforts, having a daily impact on revenues and profits. The feedback is immediate, the orientation very practical and logical. There's nothing like coming home with your first order—and second and third—or like breaking your previous production record again and again.

[2] Written by Anne T. Board, *The Wall Street Journal*, September 7, 1982, page 26. Reprinted by permission of *The Wall Street Journal*. © Dow Jones & Company, Inc. 1982. All rights reserved.

add people to their staff in an attempt to increase their control over the activities for which they are responsible. But often just the opposite occurs. When they increase their staff, they, in effect, insert a screen between themselves and the reality they are entrusted with managing. Hence:

> (2) Large staffs, composed of ambitious and overprotective people determined to justify their existence, make work and make trouble. They cut off the executive from the line organization and the line organization from the executive. The staff becomes a shock absorber around the executive, shielding him from reality.

This statement of the "law of bureaucratic behavior" is paraphrased from Arthur Schlesinger,[3] who went on to describe its operation in government:

> Franklin Roosevelt had three rules about [his] staff: He did not want more special assistants than he could deal with personally; he did not want his assistants to interpose themselves between him and the heads of departments and agencies; and he did not want them to build up staffs of their own. ... He fought the worst depression in American history with fewer high paid officials on the White House payroll than the President's wife has today, and he fought the greatest war in American history with fewer high paid officials than the Vice President has today. The problems he faced were much greater than any faced by his successors, but he was free from the delusion that he could tackle them more effectively if he increased the number of bodies in his immediate entourage.

(Schlesinger then went on to warn how the Bible—Hebrews 11:21—described the manner in which Jacob died: "leaning on the top of his staff".)

[3] Column appearing in *The Wall Street Journal*, January 7, 1981.

6. The Roles and Responsibilities of the Corporate Manufacturing Staff

7. Teradyne: The Foundry

George Chamillard, the first general manager of Teradyne's centralized printed circuit board (PCB) assembly and test operations known as the "foundry," was slated to become a division vice president in January 1985. Before leaving for his new assignment, Chamillard hoped to review what the foundry had accomplished in its 21 months of operation. The foundry had been established initially to keep pace with Teradyne's growing volume of shipments of state-of-the-art automatic test equipment (ATE); over time, it had evolved to become a center of manufacturing excellence. However, such issues as the proper location of the company's test engineers, the best way to lower rejection rates, the responsiveness of the foundry to new products, and the need to reduce the time between product concept and market introduction were still subjects of active debate.

Automatic Test Equipment

ATE Systems

Teradyne designed, manufactured, marketed and serviced a full line of ATE. Such systems were used by electronics component manufacturers to test their semiconductor devices, and by electronics equipment manufacturers to test incoming components as well as PCBs. The typical manufacturing process used by electronics equipment makers was a series of assembly and testing operations that appears in *Figure 1*.

Testing was used to catch errors. It was

FIGURE 1 Typical Manufacturing Process of Electronics Firms

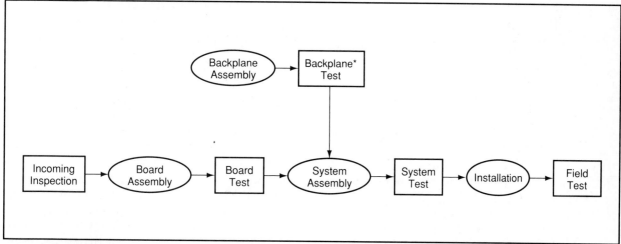

This case was prepared by Artemis March, under the direction of David A. Garvin.

* Several terms, such as backplane, are defined in the glossary. These terms are marked by asterisks (*) in the text.

conducted at several stages because the costs of locating faults increased by an order of magnitude the later they were found. Tests used hardware and software to identify whether performance matched specifications. The simplest tests were in-circuit tests that looked for structural faults (short circuits, assembly errors) and answered the question: Has the board been built properly? Repairs usually involved replacing the component. Functional tests assessed the performance of the entire PCB, and answered the question: Does the board work as it was intended to? Both in-circuit and functional tests were types of board tests. The most complex tests of all were systems tests, which examined the performance of boards after they were plugged into systems. Systems tests operated at much higher speeds than board tests, so some defects could not show up until this point. Moreover, in state-of-the-art systems having 100–180 *types* of boards, boards could interact in ways neither anticipated nor understood. The resulting gap between board and systems test meant that the first pass yield (FPY)—the percentage of boards accepted by the next stage of the production process—would always be less than 100% at systems test.

The ATE Industry

The ATE market doubled between 1979 and 1983 to $1.3 billion, and was estimated at $1.7 billion for 1984. Semiconductor manufacturers, the original ATE market, still bought half of all ATE; their sharp cycles inevitably translated into ATE cyclicality. Advances in semiconductor technology drove changes in ATE architecture, for earlier generation ATE were unable to test later generation semiconductors. ATE vendors had to be ready to catch the front end of customers' product life cycles (which ranged from two to seven years across segments), and to accommodate their ramp-ups to their customers' needs. These technology and market forces exerted tremendous pressure on ATE vendors to get to market with products that were even harder to design, to make and to test.

Teradyne's 55% revenue surge in 1984 may have pushed it into first place against its three major competitors: GenRad, Fairchild and Takeda Riken. GenRad had dominated board test sales for almost a decade, aiming for volume in low-end, in-circuit testers. Fairchild had gained a large installed base of semiconductor testers and locked customers into its software during the 1970s, but its failure to come out with new products was eroding the base. Takeda Riken, an aggressive Japanese company, stressed the high reliability and performance of its equipment, and aimed at the captive semiconductor and mainframe markets.

Teradyne

History, Growth, and Organization

Teradyne was founded by Nick DeWolf and Alexander (Alex) d'Arbeloff in 1960. They located the firm in a downtown Boston loft near South Station, a major railroad and subway terminal, so that they and their employees could walk or take public transportation to work. DeWolf, at 32, already something of a legend in the semiconductor industry for his design work, created all of Teradyne's designs for many years. When he left in 1971, the $15 million company was just emerging from a downslide triggered by an electronics bust. To reduce its dependence on merchant chipmakers, Teradyne began diversifying into backplanes and systems for testing telephone lines, switches, and networks. By 1984, these two product groups were number one in their markets and brought in 30% of the company's revenues.

While this non-ATE diversification proved to be a savvy and stabilizing set of choices, ATE product strategy lagged. Until the middle 1970s, the company made general-purpose equipment that could test many devices. The centralized engineers were not close to customers, and were not developing products with specific applications. The market was also changing dramatically as a result of the breadth and diversity of semiconductor developments. Teradyne lost major market share in several areas in the middle-to-late 1970s.

Once d'Abeloff grasped the magnitude of the change in the market, he redirected product policy. Design engineers were given the green light to create new, high-performance products. The R&D

EXHIBIT 1 Teradyne Financial Data

	1984	1983	1982	1981
Net Sales	$389.3	$251.4	$176.3	$159.9
Expenses				
Cost of sales	193.7	128.2	99.4	90.8
R&D	44.2	30.6	24.3	20.3
Sales and Administrative	79.3	55.9	43.2	39.2
Interest	5.2	6.2	5.6	4.6
	332.4	220.9	172.5	154.9
Income Before Taxes	66.8	30.5	3.9	5.1
Provision for Taxes	23.7	9.2	(.4)	.8
Net Income	43.1	21.4	4.3	4.3
EPS (diluted)	$1.87	$1.01	$ .24	$ .25
ROE	21.4%	15.6%	4.6%	4.9%

Note:

—All $ in millions except for EPS.

—Columns may not add exactly due to rounding.

budget was doubled in 1976, and kept high (12–18% of sales in an industry that averaged 10%) even during recessions. What emerged was a new generation of systems for several segments. Through options and customized configurations, Teradyne could now respond to almost any application its customers wanted. Its revenue growth between 1982 and 1983, and again from 1983 to 1984, was the fastest in the industry. (See *Exhibit 1*.)

During the late 1970s, the company also organized into divisions. Each division focused on developing and manufacturing systems to test a certain set of products. The Semiconductor Test Division (STD), located in California, built systems for digital semiconductor testing, which it marketed to captive and merchant chipmakers. Teradyne's Industrial/Consumer Division (I/CD), located in Boston, built systems to test analog (or linear) devices, the kind found in audio and video equipment, automobiles and many kinds of industrial equipment. Collectively called the Component Test Group (CTG), by 1984 these two divisions accounted for 50% of the company's sales. The Manufacturing Systems Division (MSD), also in Boston, developed systems to test PCBs and backplanes. Its customers were high-volume manufacturers of products containing PCBs, and brought in 20% of Teradyne's revenues (*Exhibit 2*).

Teradyne's Strategy

Teradyne had the broadest product line in the industry, competing in every major segment. It concentrated on key accounts that did high volumes of testing. It had recently emerged as the leader in VLSI logic testing, for example, with a system generally conceded by analysts to offer, at a million dollars, the best price/performance ratio for such applications. By contrast, Takeda and Fairchild were betting on enough growth in state-of-the-art custom chips to support their two-million-dollar systems. Similarly, Teradyne's strategy in the board test market was to provide 95% fault coverage* through its multiple capability L200 system. The volumes needed by a customer to break even with Teradyne equipment had been pinpointed in an algebraic formula that looked at total costs over the system's lifetime relative to its performance. Joseph (Joe) Lassiter, head of MSD, described the implications:

> We are selling performance. The L200 delivers a 10% differential yield* at systems test. When you plug that into the equation, and you are at a high enough volume, the total cost of our system will be lower than the total cost of the competitor's.

The need to deliver performance was summarized by Owen Robbins, vice president for finance and services, as "having the right product at the right time for the customer's product life cycles." He observed that in the early days, Teradyne had followed customers' product life cycles, but could no longer afford to do so. "We had to move to the front end of the product life cycle, because there is no second market." Robbins commented on the pressure on ATE vendors to get new products to market: "If you are within shouting distance [on reliability], and you have tomorrow's product faster, you have a win."

Organization of Operations

Pre-Foundry Organization

Teradyne had become skilled at running the small ($20–50 million) engineering-marketing clusters that marked most of its existence. In the late 1970s, these clusters had been formalized as divisions that did everything needed for the product—engineering, operations, marketing. Chamillard described the thinking behind this choice:

> The prevailing philosophy was to protect engineering from the rest of the company. We [division operations] would say to them, "You get it to work; then we will figure out how to make it." So our operations people became skilled at dealing with other disciplines, but we didn't develop in-depth process skills, such as scheduling or MRP, or rules for component layout to allow automation.

One effort to develop process skills involved putting manufacturing engineers into the divisions, where they were to be concerned with how the product was assembled. This proved unsatisfactory because there were not enough of them in each division to speak to the process issues. For example, no one could focus only on wave soldering, because the scale for specialization was not there.

Another means of trying to develop process skills was to put the test technologists into the divisions (c. 1977–1978), so they could begin working with the design engineers early in the design process to make the board more testable. This required that the technologists stick to their agenda of testability and insist that changes needed to facilitate later testing be made early in the design process. What happened instead was that the technologists got absorbed in the engineers' agenda of getting to market. "Does it work?" replaced "Can we test it?"

There were other operations problems as well. Operations costs had risen from 18% to 22% of sales during the 1979–1981 period. As product mix and life cycles shifted, some divisions had slack while others had trouble meeting demand. Since each division used MSD equipment to test its own work, and used it on one shift only, 10–15% of MSD production was taken out of circu-

EXHIBIT 2 Teradyne Organization Chart (December 1984)

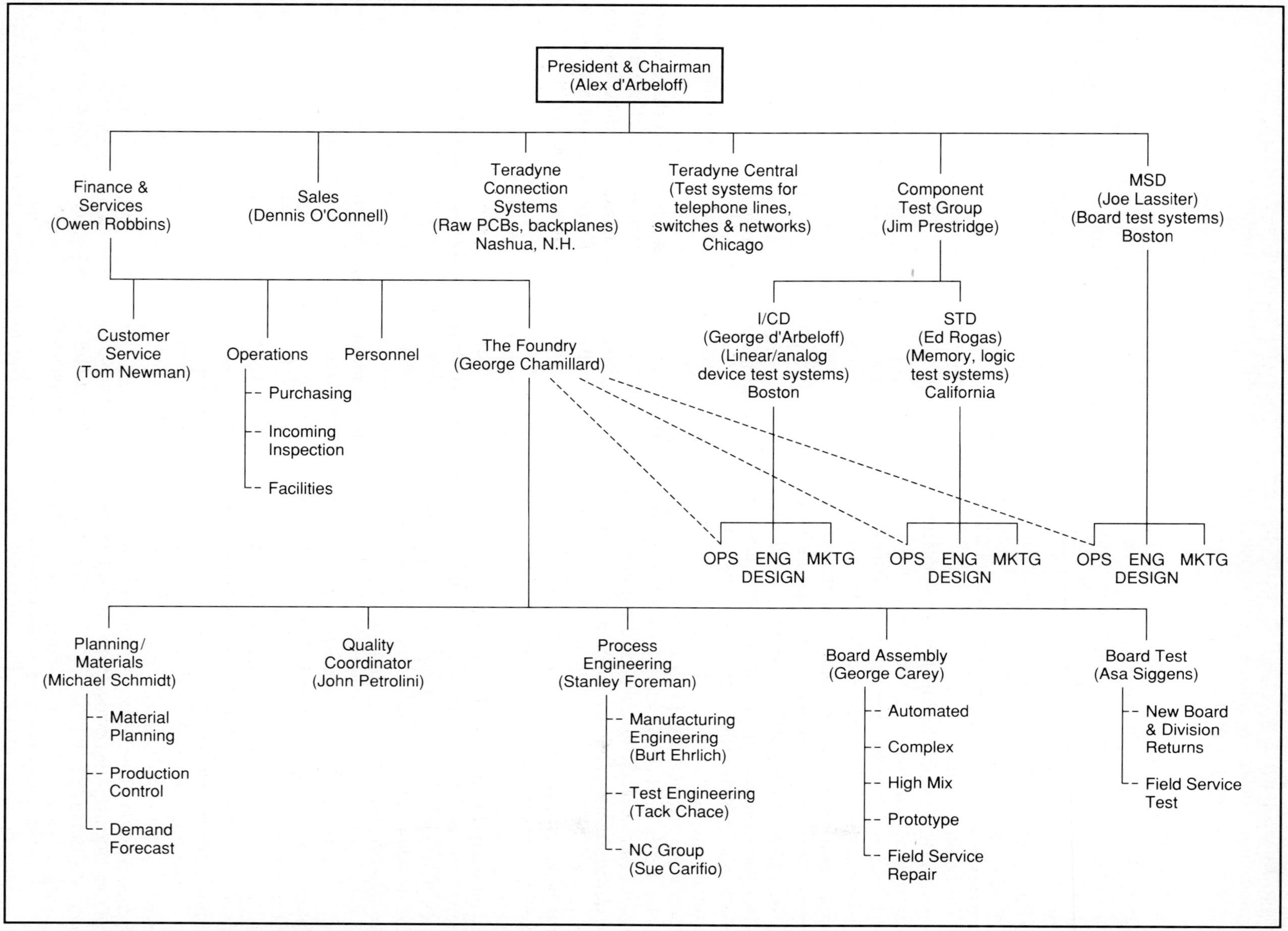

lation. Each division, when a fast ramp-up was needed, had run into problems with device specifications, system performance specifications, soldering, cables and other aspects of new product introductions.

FOUNDRY PRECURSORS. Beginning in 1972, a "core group" had assembled everything that was common to all product lines: backplanes, cables, terminals. Its activities were later dispersed by giving pieces to the divisions (backplanes to I/CD, mechanics to STD, etc.) while PCB assembly became the province of a new group called Central Board Loading (CBL).

CBL was established in January 1982 as an experiment in automating the production of selected boards. Burt Ehrlich, a manufacturing engineer, was brought in to look at how boards were being made with an eye to how to change the process. What he found was a job shop in which boards were assembled manually. To identify automation candidates, his group catalogued the company's 2,000 boards by type and size, and by component type. Over the next 14 months, manufacturing engineering programmed some 100 boards on the basis of automatability* and volume criteria, as well as the divisions' willingness to let CBL take over their production.

FOUNDRY ORIGINS. By the end of the 1970s, there was widespread feeling that the organization of manufacturing needed to change. Discussions went on between Chamillard (then corporate vice president for operations), his boss, Owen Robbins, Alex d'Arbeloff, and the operations managers of the divisions. Top manufacturing management recognized the company's common denominator as being in the board business; the kitting, loading, soldering and testing of boards were so much the same across divisions that they felt manufacturing should be organized around these operations steps. Chamillard proposed the foundry concept to Robbins, and the two became champions of the change.

There was a good deal of support for the move, both because of the perceived need for change and because George Chamillard was behind it. As Jim Prestridge, vice president and head of CTG, put it:

> George decided to do it, and he had a lot of support. My position was this: George had been

my production manager in California, he's a good guy, I trust his judgment, we knew we had a problem and we had talked it over for a long period of time. I thought he knew what he was doing.

But there was also opposition to the foundry. Some design engineers feared diminished ability to bring in rapid product changes. Divisions would lose much of their direct labor and size, and division operations would assume a more integrative role, rather than making the whole product. Lassiter commented:

> MSD operations was against it. I favored it and brought them into the fold. How did I do it? With four billion hours of conversation. Listen, we had $25 million worth of bookings per quarter [for the L200] and were shipping $2 million per quarter. Do you think after seven years of work [heading the L200 project] that I was going to let it die?!

The Charter of the Foundry

The charter of the foundry was to assemble and test PCBs for the divisions. All boards would be transferred to the foundry unless there was good reason not to and their production would be automated if their volume warranted and it was technically possible. Completed boards would then be shipped to the divisions, which would mate them with cabinets, software, display systems and periperhal equipment to produce marketable test systems.

Both Boston divisions did in fact transfer all their boards to the foundry (a necessity because their people and equipment had all been pulled to form the foundry), while STD retained the decision on where its boards were made. Its operations people transferred an increasing percentage of high-volume boards, while keeping the rest. STD also retained control over test activities. Although STD could decline to send its boards to the foundry, Prestridge was asked whether the foundry could decline to make a division's board. He replied:

> I assume that, yes, they can, but that's not how they would handle it. Everything is handled by negotiation at Teradyne. So if they thought a board would be a problem, they'd say, "Let's talk about it."

The foundry's charter was also to change

the dominant manufacturing process by automating the assembly of both new and existing boards. Test procedures were to be improved as well. Chamillard observed:

> During ramp-ups, we had always lost control; we would be short of parts, have quality problems, we couldn't train people fast enough. By automating, we wanted to be able to ramp-up without losing control. We wanted to be in a position to get throughput during a fast ramp-up.

Other objectives behind the automation drive were to gain better control over the production process, thereby increasing consistency and improving product quality; and to improve productivity by reducing the standard hours required to make a board.

The foundry included not only assembly (manufacturing) operations, but, unlike CBL, board testing and the entire process engineering group. This group, under Stanley Forman, included the test technologists who designed the functional board tests, the manufacturing engineers (MEs) who transferred prototypes to volume production and designed and supported the manufacturing process, and the programmers who wrote programs for automated production and designed incircuit tests (the NC group). The foundry created, for the first time, a critical mass of engineers dedicated to improving product manufacturability and the production process.

While there was strong concensus among management that centralization of board assembly as well as of ME was the right direction in which to go, "the debate," as Lassiter noted, "was on test, not on assembly." The argument for locating board test technologists (BTTs) in the foundry was that this would encourage development of breadth and depth in board test design expertise, much as a centralized ME group could develop more process expertise than decentralized MEs. Board tests were more intricate technologically than systems tests, and a BTT did nitty-gritty, complex electronics. A centralized board process also meant that the foundry could deliver to the divisions not merely assembled, but fully tested, boards. Finally, a separate organization with a separate charter—testability—might accomplish what locating TTs near the engineers had not.

There was discussion of locating systems test in the foundry, because the systems test technologists (STTs) would better understand the details of board operations, and the BTTs would better understand what systems test expected of boards. But this approach was not adopted. Because design engineers could not specify and control all board interactions in advance, and because new options (which meant new board subsystems) were continually being added to upgrade or customize systems, virtually everyone felt that it was more important for the STTs and the engineers to be physically and organizationally close together. Both communication and response time would be improved. By contrast, the BTT's and STT's work was less interdependent; the BTT built a model that was as valid for the 500th board of that type as for the 15th.

While there was no support for centralizing systems test, there were arguments for leaving board test in the divisions. These centered around the close communication needed between BTTs and STTs, as well as between them and the engineers, in creating test strategies and procedures. The BTT could do a better job and do it more easily if he or she knew what the systems tests were for. Tack Chace, head of the BTT group, acknowledged, "If we get better definition of what they [STT] want the boards to do, it's easier for us to make sure board test is testing for the same things." Conversely, the STT needed to know what board test would deliver. Fundamentally, both the BTTs and STTs needed to understand what the engineers were trying to do in designing the system, and all three groups needed to communicate to shape the overall test strategy for the system.

The foundry also centralized much of the materials and production planning for the company, and gave a strong boost to the nascent Materials Requirements Planning (MRP) program. After Michael Schmidt conducted an extensive study of how best to handle materials, a $3 million MRP project was funded in 1982. The project created another push toward centralized production, because such centralization would make it easier to get MRP up and running. The foundry needed MRP more than the divisions did, because of the number (over 6,000) and variety of parts it had to handle.

DIVISION OPERATIONS. Although division operations lost many of their people and responsibilities to the foundry, they still had substantial work to do. They worked closely with engineers on new product development and prototyping, developed rough-cut materials and production plans, assembled the boards (together with cables, harnesses, cabinets, backplanes, and the like) into finished systems, and developed and ran options and systems tets. The operations manager also helped to shape the strategic direction of the division, and worked on long-term issues such as capacity planning.

Introduction of the Foundry

The changeover to the foundry did not occur without upheaval. Chamillard called the change "wrenching—400 to 500 people suddenly started working for different bosses." According to Lassiter:

> There was confusion about who had responsibility for what. Design engineers couldn't get changes incorporated. People who had worked together for years were having trouble communicating. We didn't know how to maintain the right inventories because the informal systems that had run the divisions didn't work anymore, and at the same time, vendor lead times skyrocketed. But within six months, the benefits began to show.

Physically, much of the moving of test equipment took place on two successive weekends. The 14 analog testers and 13 digital testers were pulled from MSD and I/CD, as was the labor force. The changeover occurred during the company's biggest growth surge, so there was extensive new hiring and training as well. In five months, board test more than doubled, from 85 to 210 people. A second shift was organized, something the company had never done. As Asa Siggens, manager of board test, noted:

> We were still learning how to manage the second shift when we went to a third. We even developed a "fourth shift" of third-year electrical engineering students who work on Saturday and Sunday nights.

Siggens described some of the early chaos in learning how to develop valid schedules:

> "Are you on schedule?" drove everything else. In the beginning, it was way out of whack.

We had bottlenecks from lead times going way out on parts, manufacturing ramping-up so fast, people on the learning curve, so lots of boards were going back and forth between assembly and test. Fixtures were flimsy, they couldn't take much use, so we had equipment problems. There's also a learning curve in board test.

At first, board test tried to respond to daily "hot lists" from the divisions; since board test was on the receiving end of all the cumulative production delays to that point, the divisions were more than anxious to get particular boards that would complete systems they needed to ship. Although MRP was coming on-line (the first valid run was November 1, 1983), it had no immediate promise for scheduling test. Schmidt recalled:

> The first thing we had to do was to solve the materials-gathering problem. Once we had made headway through MRP on getting the parts to the floor, we began to use MRP for scheduling assembly. There's no reason why you couldn't use MRP to schedule test as well, but we knew a lot more about standard times for assembly, and the routing had fewer choices.

So Siggens and Chamillard had to figure out, without the benefit of MRP, new ways of scheduling test. They began to learn some of the critical variables: Is there a trained operator? Do you have a system configured to do the test? Do you have standard times for the test?

The foundry meant cultural changes as well. Teradyne had been a place in which, as Forman put it, "a couple of bright people in a corner would think up something and we would build it." The foundry, however, was:

> a group with different cultural values. In the divisions, the issue was "Did you ship?" In the foundry, delivery to the divisions was critical, but it could also focus on manufacturing excellence. We couldn't do this when we were being driven by other demands.

The Development Process: From Design to Market

The foundry's contribution came in the middle of the design-to-market cycle, which could be up to three years for a new generation product, and half of that for a major system update (see *Exhibits 3* and *4*).

EXHIBIT 3 Key Activities, Players and Their Location

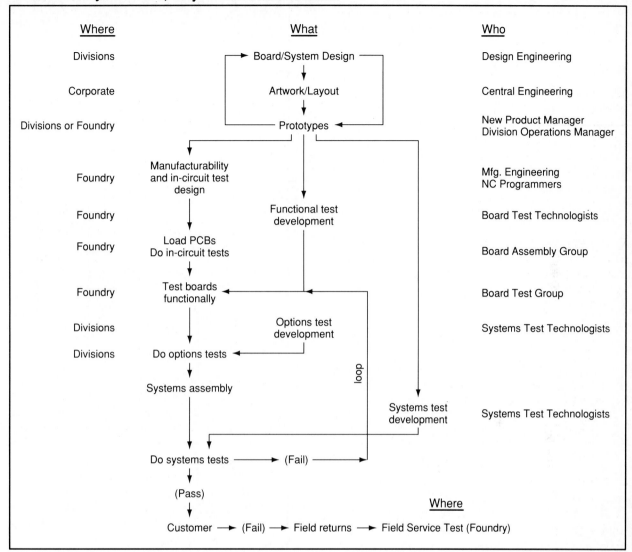

New Product Development

After design engineers developed the system's architecture, sizing and boards, central engineering created the board layout, artwork, and bill of materials and selected "final" components and their locations. Next came prototyping, in which foundry MEs, BTTs, NC programmers, production controllers, and materials planners began working with division engineers, new product planners, operations and STTs on the manufacturability* and testability* of the boards. During this process, a prototype engineer from ME and Sue Carifio, the NC manager, got their first look at the boards,

and worked with the product planner on manufacturability, tooling, and NC programming. Once a loaded board was available, the planner worked with design engineers to debug its functionality. When the engineer declared that his or her board "worked" and the tooling was ready, it was handed off to ME.

Meanwhile, test technologists worked with engineers to develop the test strategy—the best way to verify and test the design—and were then responsible for creating test procedures. For a complex board, these procedures could produce a two-inch thick book of documentation. Because these strategies were based on 95% fault coverage,

EXHIBIT 4 Production Flow: Design to Systems Test

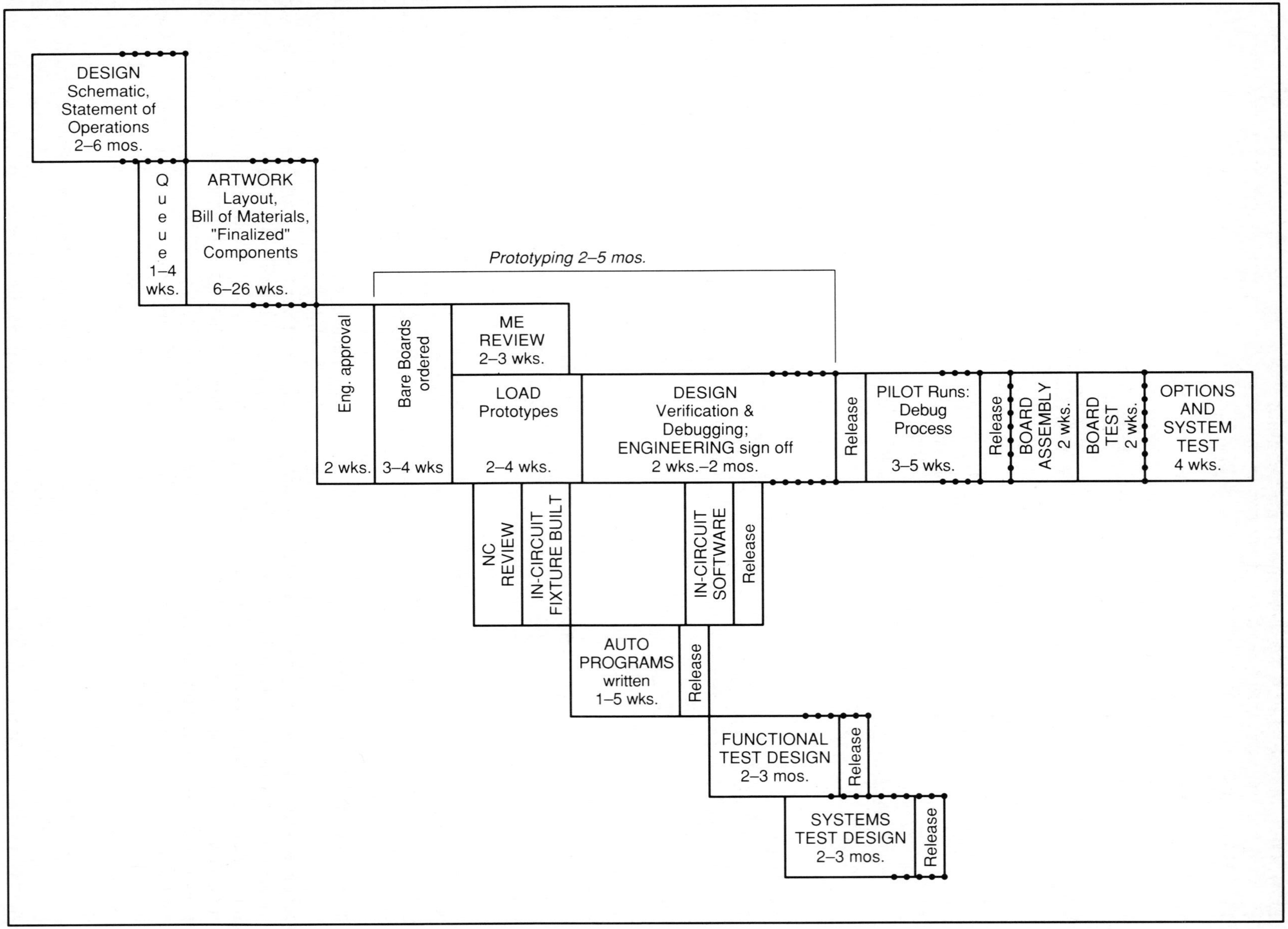

DESIGN
Schematic,
Statement of
Operations
2–6 mos.

ARTWORK
Layout,
Bill of Materials,
"Finalized"
Components
6–26 wks.

Queue
1–4 wks.

Eng. approval
2 wks.

Bare Boards ordered
3–4 wks.

ME REVIEW
2–3 wks.

LOAD Prototypes
2–4 wks.

Prototyping 2–5 mos.

DESIGN
Verification &
Debugging;
ENGINEERING sign off
2 wks.–2 mos.

NC REVIEW

IN-CIRCUIT FIXTURE BUILT

AUTO PROGRAMS written
1–5 wks.

IN-CIRCUIT SOFTWARE

Release

Release

FUNCTIONAL TEST DESIGN
2–3 mos.

Release

SYSTEMS TEST DESIGN
2–3 mos.

Release

PILOT Runs:
Debug Process
3–5 wks.

Release

BOARD ASSEMBLY
2 wks.

BOARD TEST
2 wks.

OPTIONS AND SYSTEM TEST
4 wks.

test design time ran 20 weeks, on average, twice what it would have had Teradyne accepted the 85% coverage of its major rival. Because it was easier to design a test once a good working board was available, BTTs usually began their work about the same time the in-circuit program was being written.

Board test design usually ran ahead of systems test design by several weeks, during which dialogue between the two groups could go on, but systems test work could not yet begin. Systems work absorbed another two to three person-months, which might stretch out over a six month period. Failures of "good" boards to pass systems tests were analyzed, and that knowledge incorporated into revising the board test. When the test-processes were working, they were handed off to the test engineers, who trained floor technicians in their use.

Volume Production

The board assembly group in the foundry assembled both old and new boards. In addition to the automated line, assembly had three manual production groups: complex (boards that required considerable skills to assemble), high mix (low-volume boards), and prototype. On manually-assembled boards, a single technician inserted and hand-soldered all components.

The board test group received physical boards from assembly and the test process from BTTs. After passing board test, boards went to the divisions for options (subsystems) and systems tests. Work could pass or fail at any stage of testing; if it failed, it looped back to a prior stage for rework. If "no fault was found" at the board level after two loops through systems test, STTs and BTTs worked together to figure out the problem. Once a system was installed in the field, responsibility shifted to another group. Boards returned from customers were tested at field servce test and then sent to field service repair. Both were physically part of the foundry, but organizationally part of customer service.

Operating the Foundry

To run the foundry and actually bring these processes into being required decisions about scheduling, equipment, what boards to automate, lot sizes, setups, quality and people.

Production Planning and Control

The foundry was driven by orders from the divisions. On the basis of their forecasts and orders, divisions developed systems-level plans and exploded PCB requirements on their MRP runs. By comparing these with what the foundry was running, foundry planners used MRP to update the master production schedule and develop detailed schedules. Schmidt had not experienced scheduling conflicts between the assembly and test needs of different divisions, but had sometimes run short of materials needed by more than one division, a situation handled by negotiation.

AUTOMATION CRITERIA AND SELECTION. By late 1984, the foundry was producing about 800 board types, and these accounted for 80–90% of all the active board types in the company. Candidates for automation were chosen by manufacturing engineering. All nonautomated boards were ranked by the standard hours needed to make them by hand; this number was multiplied by the total number of those boards to be made in each quarter and the top boards were then chosen for automation. By this process, the most labor-intensive, highest-volume boards had been chosen first. On the basis of a cost-benefit analysis, ME had concluded it made sense to automate board assembly down to a production level of 15 boards per quarter.

LOT SIZES AND SETUPS. ME had worked out optimal lot sizes of 5 for small-volume boards and 15 for large volumes. Setups for these runs were minimal, except for one machine. Manufacturing pushed job lots through in two weeks, but different requirements for scheduling test resulted in a loss of job lot integrity at test. There, technicians intermingled lots, sometimes picking up boards that had just arrived, and sometimes choosing boards that had been around awhile.

Automated and manual boards were scheduled separately so that boards would not exceed machine capacity. Different production managers managed the major steps in automated production, while one manager was accountable from beginning to end on each manual line.

By reducing the direct labor content in automated boards, board assembly had been able to reduce cycle times (the actual time the boards were being worked on) by a factor of between two and four. Throughput time (the elapsed time in board assembly), however, remained at two weeks for automated as well as manual boards. Chamillard explained that a conscious choice had been made to open up the pipeline and increase output before concentrating on cutting throughput time.

Work Force and Teradyne Culture

Teradyne was strongly committed to a policy of avoiding layoffs, and had been forced to deviate from this only once or twice in 24 years. One means for avoiding layoffs was the use of subcontracting during boom times; during a downswing, that work was brought back in-house. George Carey, manager of board assembly, was emphatic that "you *must* have subcontracting as part of your manufacturing strategy because it buffers your work force." The company had maintained its downtown location, drawing on the inner city for assembly workers and professionals who preferred an urban lifestyle, as well as from the suburbs ringing Boston. Workers shuttled between the two downtown Boston buildings in well-used busses that ran continuously between the two locations, which were about a ten-minute walk from each other. The foundry and MSD were located in one building, and I/CD, marketing, sales and finance in the other.

Foundry Relations and Performance

Constituencies and their Needs

As an organization serving the rest of the company, the foundry had several constituencies to satisfy. Among the perspectives were those of George d'Arbeloff, brother of the president and head of I/CD:

> They must deliver what they say they will, and on time. They must develop their test programs in a timely manner. And they must be able to adjust to ramp-ups and ramp-downs; ramp-downs are probably tougher because we want to avoid layoffs.

Joe Lassiter, head of MSD:

> At the new product stage, you want to absorb rapid changes into the product. That means being strongly coupled with engineering. So I want a foundry that is a friendly receptor for new products and processes. With a mature product, I want high quality and timeliness. If they don't manage both, they will die. During the tail-off, they have to undo inventory and reassign people without layoffs.

Jim Prestridge, head of CTG:

> Our business is one of short product life cycles, so we need flexibility to ramp-up quickly. We are very cyclical and we need to be able to respond to that. We have a very high rate of change—200 ECOs a week on a major system are not uncommon. We have short runs, and low volumes for some parts.

Dennis O'Connell, head of sales:

> Reliability. Delivery is important, but not as critical as reliability.

Evaluation of Foundry Performance

There was strong concensus that the foundry had been a successful (and perhaps, necessary) change, even though many issues remained unresolved. Agreement was unanimous that the foundry had kept pace with the enormous surge in volume in 1983 and early 1984, and had held delivery times to competitive levels. Teradyne managers believed this could not have been done with divisionalized operations. They attributed the foundry's success to its multishift setup, and its shared capacity in people and machines, which allowed it to divert resources to where they were needed most. The foundry not only kept pace with growth, but as it went through this build-up, Chamillard noted, "No one lost control."

A second area of progress was automation. Not only had the foundry automated its higher volume boards successfully; its engineers and programmers had even automated products that weren't originally designed to be automated.

Third, the foundry had made headway in increasing the manufacturability of board designs. Most managers felt that, more and more, boards were being designed and laid out with the automatic equipment in mind, although there was still room for improvement.

Assessments of quality changes were mixed. Managers felt it had improved, was better than it would have been had operations remained divisionalized, but was still problematic. At the board level, quality had improved consistently from quarter to quarter, but system return rates were little different from the early months of the foundry.

On the downside, Prestridge commented that:

> The foundry could fail if there is a lack of integration with the rest of the company, if the other guy doesn't really understand what you are doing. The foundry must publicize itself more. Alex and Owen see the measures, but the division managers aren't brought into it: they don't review what the foundry has done. We are a verbal rather than a report culture, so the answer isn't to write reports.

Lassiter found the foundry to be "a hell of an asset for mature products and tail-offs, but a liabilty on the front end. "The fights," he observed, "are about getting new products through the foundry."

MEASUREMENT OF FOUNDRY PERFORMANCE. The foundry tracked several measures of performance, and posted charts in hallways and work areas. Board assembly most often used standard labor hours as the basis for its measures. During the first seven quarters of foundry operation, automatic insertion had substantially reduced the standard hours in most boards; a board that had formerly taken five hours to assemble now took two. Assembly errors had also decreased sharply, according to such measures as faults per standard labor hour at in-circuit test.

The most-used measure of overall board quality was first pass yield (FPY). To get a positive reading on this measure, a board could have no detectable faults and had to work in the system the first time it was tested. In recent years, FPY at systems test had risen from 68% to 83%; this pointed to the increasing rigor of functional board tests, which now caught more problems before boards were sent to systems test.

Despite these improvements, Teradyne had a seemingly intractable "systems return" problem. While the number of faulty boards returned from the divisions was not large (about 10% of the total), returns represented about 20% of all boards when measured by standard assembly hours, and

30% of total test hours. Moreover, these figures had remained virtually flat since the foundry was started. System returns were not simply a foundry problem, however, but reflected the gap between board and systems test. When "returns" had been intradivisional, they were not tracked, so no one had realized the extent of the problem. Today, with better measures, understanding was still limited. Almost half of all returned boards, when retested at the board level, were marked "no fault found" and looped back to the divisions.

To improve quality, Teradyne first tracked faults by category and board type. Faults were then traced back to their origins—which could be in documentation, the stockroom, final assembly, or elsewhere. The top ten problem boards became the focal point of weekly meetings of foundry managers from test, assembly and manufacturing engineering. At these meetings, responsibility was assigned for problem solving; it then became a joint effort of the affected supervisor and shopfloor employees.

The Future of the Foundry

During the foundry's early stages, the emphasis had been on automating existing boards and keeping up with orders. As these matters were brought under control, attention shifted to changing processes, particularly in manufacturing. Board test, as several managers acknowledged, had not gotten the attention it deserved, but this too, was beginning to change. The foundry was now at the point where, to improve its own work further (particularly with new products), it had to push for changes in working relationships that had evolved over many years.

Manufacturability and the Engineering-Manufacturing Handoff

During Teradyne's early years, DeWolf had designed all testers with a limited number of components, thereby facilitating their manufacturability. But this had changed during the 1970s when, as Forman noted:

> We redid the whole product line. Everything was wide open, so the engineers could do whatever they wanted. They had no limits on how to place components—how close to the edge, how tightly

packed. Now we're in a different place, and there has to be a balance. There's been a cultural change; no one used to say, "But can we build it?"

After the foundry was established, ME had provided some general "suggested design guidelines" (based on industry standards) to central engineering. When a conflict arose between the guidelines and the design, however, the engineer had the last word. Since ME did not see the designs until prototyping, its contribution came at a point where major or extensive design changes were costly in time and money. The most popular alternative for incorporating changes was engineering change orders (ECOs).

ECOs had to be issued by engineers, and entered the foundry through production control. Most were mandatory: they made a product work that wasn't working, or made it work to specifications. Some added new features. The changes were then made physically on the board, and the documentation updated. Reworking boards offline added 1–2 weeks to throughput, and increased the probability of human errors. ECOs that affected component numbers or placement, or circuit logic, meant changing test programs and documentation. Because the accounting system absorbed all indirect costs into a single overhead rate and allocated them to divisions in proportion to total sales, the true costs of ECOs were unknown.

There were differing views on what the balance of power between engineering and manufacturing should be. Some felt the balance should be equalized, that ME and technology each had to gain equal status with engineering. A proponent of the opposite view—that the balance must rest with engineering—was Owen Robbins:

> We are not building TV sets by the millions here; this is a very high tech business where technology reigns. The design engineer must make the final choice. Manufacturing *should* complain, but they *must* do it. They have no choice. Only the engineers can decide.

Lassiter summarized this perspective: "Manufacturing's job is to reproduce the engineer's design." Falling between these two views was a third, summarized by George Carey:

> By the time we see it, so much has been invested that it would be a no-no to put a glitch

in the system. We don't have the volume to tell them to rework the design or artwork.

Whatever their feelings about the engineering-manufacturing balance, everyone wanted to see manufacturability continue to improve, and time to market continue to shrink. Ideas on the best ways to achieve those goals differed. Some managers felt more accountability must be demanded of the engineers. As George d'Arbeloff put it:

> They get off too easy. What is their role after they get the prototype to work? Right now, they have no responsibility past that point. It's critical to design it right the first time, but they keep feeding ECO's. We need to give them more responsibility for the success of their product.

Another manager suggested that the design engineer manager act as a project leader throughout the life of the project. Another thought top management could send different signals about the importance of the downstream impact of the engineers' work by asking them questions such as, "How is your board doing in test yield?" Several commented that engineers were not made accountable for the commercial success of their work, rewarded for cost or time savings resulting from the manufacturability or testability of their designs or penalized for their absence; some proposed that such criteria be incorporated into engineers' performance reviews. On the other hand, a few managers felt that engineers *were* responsible (in a broad rather than an accounting sense) for the commercial success of their projects because, "they need to be with successful projects in order to be chosen to work on the more exciting projects in the future."

An often-mentioned means of increasing accountability was to institute a design review* process, something Teradyne had never had. Some felt it was imperative that ME and test engineers get an early look at designs and have an equal say in getting changes incorporated. Others were just as opposed, claiming that:

> Teradyne is a place that hates structure. A design review would be too discordant with the culture: it would create too much resistance from the engineers. They would never go for it.

The need for an accounting system that would track actual as well as standard hours, unbundle overhead, and allow true costs to be known was also viewed as essential by most managers. Ron Dias, head of STD operations who had just been named to succeed Chamillard, observed:

> The divisions make decisions now without recognizing the implications for foundry materials and scheduling. Then the divisions eat it. The foundry must define its products—ECOs, card tests, each thing they do—and set a price so that the divisions know what it really costs and what it will mean for their P&Ls. The foundry needs to operate as a cost center with real chargebacks, not allocations.

Testability and the Test Technology Cycle

George d'Arbeloff spoke for many when he said:

> The toughest problem we face is the link between engineering and test technology. How do we shorten the test technology cycle? How do we shorten the whole time to market?

Several approaches were being considered. The location of test technology was still a live issue. Because of the foundry's early focus on assembly and automation, the value of centralized board test technology was not yet proven. Chamillard commented on the long-term nature of the desired change:

> We've taken the technologists and put them in Stanley's group [process engineering], but we haven't changed how they think or how they work. We've been so involved with a massive build-up, the rush of new products and new tests, there hasn't been time for the tension to develop between engineering and technology to get testability.

Although the foundry's charter had been directed toward all boards being built and tested in the foundry, there were some second thoughts. George d'Arbeloff expressed concern about volume cut-offs, and felt they had perhaps been set too low. Chamillard believed that "we shouldn't let the foundry work on boards that don't count," noting the greater importance of being responsive to ramp-ups.

To shorten the test cycle and time to market, many Teradyne managers wanted to move toward more parallel development. Development had heretofore been largely sequential, with BTTs waiting for a known good prototype board before doing major design work. Systems test often lagged board test design by several weeks, sometimes of necessity. Chace said that the BTTs could start once the schematic was stable and preliminary documentation was available. Indeed, they could start even earlier "if the divisions want to pay for it." Starting before the schematic was stable would entail more rework in test design and NC programming, and possibly increase costs and/or require more professional staff. Such rework time and cost might be justified, however, if fewer downstream problems reduced the total time to market.

To get more parallel development, many of the same proposals were being discussed for test as for manufacturability, such as design reviews and increased engineering accountability. Another means of achieving shorter test time was to use a model being developed by I/CD and the foundry more widely. In mid-1984, a task force (composed of Chace, Siggens, George d'Arbeloff, and two of his design managers) had begun meeting to bring TT into the process sooner. Chace made a series of presentations to I/CD design managers and engineers in which he pointed out:

> If they want the test procedures to be available to do their board in volume, then they need to get the specifications to us early. By doing that, they won't have to spend so much time benchtesting their boards at the prototype and debugging stages. Benchtesting takes time, gives less coverage, and takes them away from what they like to do best—design new things. So, by involving us earlier, we can give them test programs sooner, we get to market sooner, and they get to spend more of their time on designing.

* * * *

As the wintry sun was setting outside Chamillard's window, Forman came in. Chamillard looked up, sat back in his chair, and said, "Stanley, I've been thinking about some of the things we should talk over with Ron. What do you think?"

GLOSSARY

Automatability—how completely and easily components can be inserted automatically or semiautomatically. On automatic equipment, tiny chucks grab the component and place it on the board; if components are too densely packed, the chuck cannot fit between a component's neighbors. Therefore, space between components is a critical specification. Components also need to be placed far enough from the edge of the board so that the feet of the automatic machine can hold them in place.

Backplanes—structures that integrate circuit boards into an electronic assembly. Backplanes provide the complex electrical connections from board to board, and from board to outside world, as well as physical support for racks of PCBs.

Design review—a process used by many companies in which engineers' designs are formally reviewed by manufacturing, marketing and other groups that have varying degrees of authority over the final design. The design review is conducted early (before prototyping) so as to incorporate the input of other disciplines before a heavy investment is made in the design.

Differential yield—as used here, the difference in yield at the next stage of the customer's process gained by using Teradyne rather than GenRad equipment.

Fault coverage—the total percent of errors detected at test compared to the total number of errors on the board.

Manufacturability—as used here, the same as automatability.

Testability—how completely and easily a board or system can be tested. Some elements that affect testability are physical accessibility (Are all the nodes accessible from the solder side during in-circuit test? Do all connections run to the edge connector?); isolability of electrical signals (Does a signal that turns on A also turn off B? If so, it makes it harder for the tester to take superseding control of the signal and get back unambiguous information.); capability for breaking into feedback loops; and initialization (Can everything on the board be put into a known state as a baseline?).

8. How Should You Organize Manufacturing?

Among the characteristics of a company that shape corporate and therefore manufacturing strategy are its dominant orientation (market or product), pattern of diversification (product, market, or process), attitude toward growth (acceptance of low growth rate), and choice between competitive strategies (high profit margins versus high output volumes). Once the basic attitudes or priorities are established, the manufacturing arm of a company must arrange its structure and management so as to reinforce these corporate aims. Examining the extremes of "product-focused" and "process-focused" organizations, the authors illustrate the development of a "manufacturing mission" whereby the organization of manufacturing supports management's needs.

Manufacturing organizations tend to attract the attention of general managers the way airlines do: one only notices them when they're late, when ticket prices rise, or when there's a crash. When they are operating smoothly, they are almost invisible. But manufacturing is getting increasing attention from business managers who, only a few years ago, were preoccupied with marketing or financial matters.

The fact is that in most companies the great bulk of the assets used—the capital invested, the people employed, and management time—are in the operations side of the business. This is true of both manufacturing and service organizations, in both the private and public sectors of our economy. These resources have to be deployed, coordinated, and managed in such a way that they strengthen the institution's purpose; if not, they will almost certainly cripple it.

The problems and pressures facing manufacturing companies ultimately find their way to the factory floor, where managers have to deal with them through some sort of organizational structure. Unfortunately, this structure often is itself part of the problem. Moreover, problems in a corporation's manufacturing organization frequently surface at about the same time as problems in the rest of the company, and they surface in a variety of ways. For example:

- A fast-growing, high-technology company had quadrupled in size in a ten-year period. Its manufacturing organization was essentially the same at the end of that period as before, dominated by a powerful vice president for manufacturing and a strong central staff, despite the fact that its product line had broadened considerably, that the company was beginning to make many more of the components it formerly purchased, and that the number of plants had both increased and spread into four countries. A sluggishness and sense of lost direction began to afflict the manufacturing organization, as overhead and logistics costs soared.

- A conglomerate had put together a group of four major divisions that made sense in terms of their financial and marketing synergy. But these divisions' manufacturing organizations had little in common, little internal direction, and no overall coordination. The parent company was confronted with a series of major capital appropriation requests and had little understanding of either their absolute merits or the priorities that should be attached to them.

- A fast-growing company in a new industry had for a number of years operated in a seller's market, where competition was based on quality and service rather than price. Its manufacturing organization was highly decentralized and adept at new product introduction and fast product mix changes. In the 1970s severe industry overcapacity and price competition caused corporate sales to level off and profit to decline for the first time in its history. Manufacturing efficiency and dependability clearly had to be improved, but there was fear of "upsetting the corporate culture" and "crippling the golden goose."

Why did these companies' manufacturing arms get into trouble? And to what extent were these problems the outgrowth of poorly designed organizational structures? In attempting an answer to these questions, we will begin with a review of the concepts of "manufacturing mission" and "manufacturing focus" that were first defined and explored in a series of articles by Wickham Skinner beginning in 1969.[1] These concepts, and the conclusions that flow logically from them, have since been polished, elaborated, and tested by him and a number of his colleagues in conjunction with various manufacturing companies over the past several years.

After this review we will evaluate the advantages and disadvantages of different approaches to organizing a company's manufacturing function and then apply our concepts to recommending the type of organizational design that is most appropriate for a given company. Finally, we will discuss the various kinds of growth that companies can experience and how these expectations should affect the organization of the manufacturing function.

Basic Elements of Strategy

The concept of manufacturing strategy is a natural extension of the concept of corporate strategy, although the latter need not be as rational and explicit as management theorists usually require.[2] As we use the term, a corporate strategy simply implies a consistency, over time, in the company's preferences for and biases against certain management choices as shown in *Exhibit 1*. We use

[1]See, for example, Wickham Skinner, "Manufacturing—Missing Link in Corporate Strategy," HBR May-June 1969, p. 136, and "The Focused Factory," HBR May-June 1974, p. 113.

[2]Two representative texts are: Kenneth R. Andrews, *The Concept of Corporate Strategy* (Homewood, Ill.: Dow Jones-Irwin, 1971), and H. Igor Ansoff, *Corporate Strategy* (New York: McGraw-Hill, 1965).

EXHIBIT 1 Corporate Attitudes That Imply Strategic Preferences

Dominant orientation
Market
Product or material
Technology

Pattern of diversification
Product
Market (geographic or consumer group)
Process (vertical integration)
Unrelated horizontal (conglomerate)

Corporate attitude toward growth
Growth sought explicitly
Growth viewed as a by-product of successful management of the "core" business

Competitive priorities	
Quality	
Dependability	Volume flexibility
Price	
Product flexibility	

the term company to refer to a business unit that has a relatively homogeneous product line, considerable autonomy, and enough of a history to establish the kind of track record we refer to here. Such a "company" could, of course, be a relatively independent division within a larger enterprise. The following four "attitudes" shape those aspects of a company's corporate strategy that are relevant to manufacturing.

DOMINANT ORIENTATION. Some companies are clearly market oriented. They consider their primary expertise to be the ability to understand and respond effectively to the needs of a particular market or consumer group. In exploiting this market knowledge, they use a variety of products, materials, and technologies. Gillette and Head Ski are examples of such companies. Other companies are clearly oriented to materials or products; they are so-called steel companies, rubber companies, or oil companies (or, more recently, energy companies). They develop multiple uses for their product or material and follow these uses into a variety of markets. Corning Glass, Firestone, DuPont, and Conoco come to mind. Still other companies are technology-oriented—most electronics companies fall into this class—and they follow the lead of their technology into various materials and markets.

A common characteristic of a company with such a dominant orientation is that it seldom ventures outside that orientation, is uncomfortable when doing so, often does not appreciate the differences and complexities associated with operating the new business, and then often fails because it hesitates to commit the resources necessary to succeed. A recent example of a company that ventured, with considerable trauma, outside its dominant orientation was Texas Instruments' entry into consumer marketing of electronic calculators and digital watches.

PATTERN OF DIVERSIFICATION. Diversification can be accomplished in several ways: (1) product diversification within a given market, (2) market diversification (geographic or consumer group) using a given product line, (3) process or vertical diversification (increasing the span of the process so as to gain more control over vendors and/or customers) with a given mix of products and markets, and (4) unrelated (horizontal) diversification, as exemplified by conglomerates. Decisions about diversification are closely interrelated with a company's dominant orientation, of course, but they also reflect its preference for concentrating on a relatively narrow set of activities or, alternatively, its willingness to enter into a wide variety of activities, products, and/or markets—and which ones it will enter.

CORPORATE ATTITUDE TOWARD GROWTH. Does growth represent an input to or an output of the company's planning process? Every company continually confronts a variety of growth opportunities. Its decisions about which to accept and which to reject signal, in a profound way, the kind of company it prefers to be. Some companies, in their concentration on a particular market, geographic area, or material, essentially accept the growth permitted by that market or area or material consumption. A company's acceptance of a low rate of growth reflects a decision, conscious or unconscious, to retain a set of priorities in which a given orientation and pattern of diversification are more highly valued than growth.

Other companies, however, are so structured and managed that a certain rate of growth is required in order for the organization to function properly. If its current set of products and markets will not permit this desired rate of growth, it will seek new ones to "fill the gap." Again, this decision will closely reflect its attitudes regarding dominant orientation and diversification. One obvious indication of a company's relative emphasis on growth is how growth is treated in its planning, budgeting, and performance evaluation cycle, and particularly the importance that is placed on annual growth rate, compared with such other measures as return on sales or return on assets. It is necessary to differentiate between a company's stated goals—words on paper—and what actually moves it to action.

CHOICE OF COMPETITIVE PRIORITIES. In its simplest form this choice is between seeking high profit margins or high output volumes. Some companies consistently prefer high margin products, even when this limits them to relatively low market shares. Others feel more comfortable with a high-volume business, despite the fact that this commits them to severe cost-reduction pressure and often implies low margins. An interesting article describes David Packard's attempts to redirect Hewlett-Packard away from the latter approach, where it was nose-to-nose with Texas Instruments, and back toward the former approach.[3]

This concept can be expanded and enriched, however, since companies can compete in ways other than simply through the prices of their products. Some compete on the basis of superior quality—either by providing higher quality in a standard product (for example, Mercedes-Benz) or by providing a product that has features or performance characteristics unavailable in competing products. We intend here to differentiate between an actual quality differential and a perceived difference, which is much more a function of selling and advertising strategy.

Other companies compete by promising utter dependability; their product may be priced higher and may not have some of the competitive products' features or workmanship. It will, however, work as specified, is delivered on time, and any failures are immediately corrected. IBM has been cited as an example of a company that competes on this basis; in a sense, so do AT&T and Sears, Roebuck.

Still others compete on the basis of product flexibility, their ability to handle difficult, non-standard orders and to lead in new product intro-

[3]"Hewlett-Packard: Where Slower Growth Is Smarter Management," *Business Week*, June 9, 1975, p. 50.

duction. This is a competitive strategy that smaller companies in many industries often adopt. And, finally, others compete through volume flexibility, being able to accelerate or decelerate production quickly. Successful companies in cyclical industries like housing or furniture often exhibit this trait.

In summary, within most industries different companies emphasize one of these five competitive dimensions—price, quality, dependability, product flexibility, and volume flexibility. It is both difficult and potentially dangerous for a company to try to compete by offering superior performance along several competitive dimensions. Instead, a company must attach definite priorities to each that describe how it chooses to position itself relative to its competitors.

Practically every decision a senior manager makes will have a different impact on each of these dimensions, and the organization will thus have to make trade-offs between them. Unless these trade-offs are made consistently over time, the company will slowly lose its competitive distinctiveness.

Without such consistency, it does not matter how much effort a company puts into formulating and expounding on its "strategy"—it essentially does not have one. One test of whether a company has a strategy is that it is clear not only about what it wants to do but also about what it does *not* want to do—what proposals it will consistently say no to.

Toward a Manufacturing Mission

Once such attitudes and competitive priorities are identified, the task for manufacturing is to arrange its structure and management so as to mesh with and reinforce this strategy. Manufacturing should be capable of helping the company do what it wants to do without wasting resources in lesser pursuits. This is what we call the company's "manufacturing mission."

It is surprising that general managers sometimes tend to lose sight of this concept, since the need for priorities permeates all other arenas of management. For example, marketing managers segment markets and focus product design, promotional and pricing efforts around the needs of particular segments, often at the expense of the needs of other segments. And management information systems must be designed to emphasize particular kinds of information at the expense of others.

While it is possible to chalk up to inexperience the belief of many general managers that manufacturing should be capable of doing everything well, it is harder to explain why many manufacturing managers themselves either try to be good at everything at once or focus on the wrong thing. They know that all-purpose tools generally are used only when a specific tool is not available. Perhaps they fall into this trap because of pride, or too little time, or because they are reluctant to say no to their superiors.

All these factors enter into the following scenario. A manufacturing manager has nicely aligned his organization according to corporate priorities when suddenly he is subjected to pressure from marketing because of "customer complaints" about product quality or delivery times. Under duress, and without sufficient time to examine the trade-offs involved, he attempts to shore up performance along these dimensions. Then he is confronted with pressure from finance to reduce costs or investment or both. Again, in the attempt to respond to the "corporate will," or at least to oil the squeaky wheel, he reacts. Step by step, priorities and focus disappear, each lagging dimension being brought into line by some function's self-interest.

Falling into such a trap can be devastating, however, because a manufacturing mission that is inconsistent with corporate strategy is just as dangerous as not having any manufacturing mission at all. The more top management delegates key manufacturing decisions to "manufacturing specialists" (usually engineers), the more likely it is that manufacturing's priorities will be different from corporate priorities. They will reflect engineering priorities, or operating simplicity (often the goal of someone who has worked his way up from the bottom of the organization)—not the needs of the business.

Using Structural Decisions

Translating a set of manufacturing priorities into an appropriate collection of plant, people, and policies requires resources, time, and management perseverance. As we mentioned earlier, the great bulk of most companies' assets (capital, human, and managerial) is found in manufacturing. Moreover, these assets tend to be massive, highly interrelated, and long lived—in comparison with marketing and most financial assets. As a result, it is difficult to redirect them, and "fine-tuning" is almost impossible. Once a change is made, its impact is felt throughout the system and cannot be undone easily.

Such manufacturing inertia is made worse by many manufacturing managers' reluctance to change. And it is further compounded by many top managers' lack of understanding of the kind of changes that are needed, as well as by their unwillingness to commit the resources to effect such changes.

The decisions that implement a set of manufacturing priorities are structural; for a given company or business they are made infrequently and at various intervals. They fall into two broad categories: facilities decisions and infrastructure decisions.

Facilities decisions involve the following considerations:

1. The total amount of manufacturing and logistics capacity to provide for each product line over time.

2. How this capacity is broken up into operating units (plants, warehouses, and so on), their size and form (a few large plants versus many small ones), their location, and the degree or manner of their specialization (for example, according to product, process, and so on).

3. The kind of equipment and production technology used in these plants.

4. The span of the process—that is, the direction of vertical integration (toward control either of markets or of suppliers), its extent (as reflected roughly by value added as a percentage of sales), and the degree of balance among the capacities of the production stages.

Infrastructure decisions involve the following considerations:

1. Policies that control the loading of the factory or factories—raw material purchasing, inventory, and logistics policies.

2. Policies that control the movement of goods through the factory or factories—process design, work-force policies and practices, production scheduling, quality control, logistics policies, inventory control.

3. The manufacturing organizational design that coordinates and directs all of the foregoing.

These two sets of decisions are closely intertwined, of course. A plant's total annual capacity (a facilities decision) depends on whether the production rate is kept as constant as possible over time or, alternatively, changed frequently in an attempt to "chase demand" (an infrastructure decision). Similarly, work-force policies interact with location and process choices, and purchasing policies interact with vertical integration choices. Decisions regarding organizational design also will be highly dependent on vertical integration decisions, as well as on the company's decisions regarding how various plants are located, specialized, and interrelated.

Each of these structural decisions places before the manager a variety of choices, and each choice puts somewhat different weights on the five competitive dimensions. For example, an assembly line is highly interdependent and inflexible but generally promises lower costs and higher predictability than a loosely coupled line or batch-flow operation or a job shop. Similarly, a company that attempts to adjust production rates so as to chase demand will generally have higher costs and lower quality than a company that tries to maintain more level production and absorb demand fluctuations through inventories.

If consistent priorities are to be maintained, as a company's strategy and manufacturing mission change, then change usually becomes necessary in *all* of these structural categories. Again and again the root of a manufacturing crisis is that a company's manufacturing policies and people—workers, supervisors, and managers—become incompatible with its plant and equipment, or both become incompatible with its competitive needs.

Even more subtly, plants may be consistent with policies, but the manufacturing organization that attempts to coordinate them all no longer does its job effectively. For, in a sense, the organization is the glue that keeps manufacturing priorities in place and welds the manufacturing function into a competitive weapon. It also must embody the corporate attitudes and biases already discussed.

In addition, the way manufacturing chooses to organize itself has direct implications for the relative emphasis placed on the five competitive dimensions. Certain types of organizational structures are characterized by high flexibility; others encourage efficiency and tight control; and still others promote dependable promises.

Approaching the Design

How are the appropriate corporate priorities to be maintained in a manufacturing organization that is characterized by a broad mix of products, specifications, process technologies, production volumes, skill levels, and customer demand patterns? To answer this question, we must begin by differentiating between the administrative burden on the managements of individual plants and that on the central manufacturing staff. Each alternative approach for organizing a total manufacturing system will place different demands on each of these groups. In a rough sense, the same amount of "control" must be exercised over the system, no matter how responsibilities are divided between the two.

At one extreme, one could lump all production for all products into a single plant. This makes the job of the central staff relatively easy (in some respects it becomes almost nonexistent), but the job of the plant management becomes horrendous. At the other extreme, one could simplify the job of each plant (or operating unit within a given plant), so that each concentrates on a more restricted set of activities (products, processes, volume levels, and so on), in which case the coordinating job of the central organization becomes much more difficult.

Although many companies adopt the first approach, by either design or default, in our experience it becomes increasingly unworkable as more and more complexity is put under one roof. At some point a single large plant, or a contiguous plant complex, breaks down as more products, processes, skill levels, and market demands are added to it. Skinner has argued against this approach and for the other extreme in an article in which he advocates dividing up the total manufacturing job into a number of *focused* units, each of which is responsible for a limited set of activities and objectives:

"Each [manufacturing unit should have] its own facilities in which it can concentrate on its particular manufacturing task, using its own workforce management approaches, production control, organization structure, and so forth. Quality and volume levels are not mixed; worker training and incentives have a clear focus; and engineering of processes, equipment, and materials handling are specialized as needed. Each [unit] gains experience readily by focusing and concentrating every element of its work on those limited essential objectives which constitute its manufacturing task."[4]

If we adopt this sensible (but radical) approach, we are left with the problem of organizing the central manufacturing staff in such a way that it can effectively manage the resulting diversity of units and tasks. It must somehow maintain the total organization's sense of priorities and manufacturing mission, even though individual units may have quite different tasks

[4]See Wickham Skinner, "The Focused Factory," HBR May-June 1974, p. 121.

EXHIBIT 2 Product-focused and Process-focused Organization

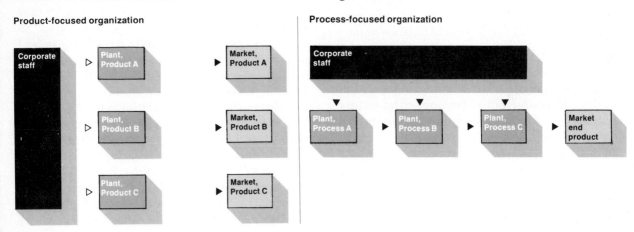

Product-focused organization

Process-focused organization

and focuses. It carries out this responsibility both directly, by establishing and monitoring the structural policies we mentioned earlier (for example, process design, capacity planning, work-force management, inventory control, logistics, purchasing, and the like), and indirectly, by measuring, evaluating, and rewarding individual plants and managers, and through the recruitment and systematic development of those managers.

These basic duties can be performed in a variety of ways, however, and each will communicate a slightly different sense of mission. To illustrate this, let us consider two polar examples—a "product-focused organization" and a "process-focused organization." To clarify this discussion, look at the two highly simplified organizations shown in *Exhibit 2* and think about what the tasks of the corporate manufacturing staff and plant managers would be in each.

The corporate staff clearly must play a much more active role in making the second organization work. Logistics movements have to be carefully coordinated, and a change in any of the plants (or the market) can have repercussions throughout the system.

Only at the last stage (Process C), can the plant manager be measured on a profit-ability basis, and even that measure depends greatly on negotiated transfer prices and the smooth functioning of the rest of the system. He will not have much opportunity to exercise independent decision making, since most variables under his control (capacity, output, specifications, and soon) will affect everybody else. Thus he will probably be regarded as a "cost center" and be measured in large part on his ability to work smoothly within this highly interdependent system.

The distinction between such product-focused and process-focused manufacturing organizations should not be confused with the distinction between traditional functional and divisional corporate organizations. In fact, it is entirely possible that two divisions within a divisionally organized company would choose to organize their manufacturing groups differently. The important distinction has less to do with the organization chart than with the role and responsibilities of the central manufacturing staff and how far authority is pushed down the organization. In a sense, the distinction is more between centralized control and decentralized control.

With this brief overview, let us turn to more realistic product and process organizations.

Product-focused Organization

Basically, the product-focused organization resembles a traditional plant-with-staff organization, which then replicates itself at higher levels to handle groups of plants and then groups of products and product lines. Authority in the product-focused organization is highly decentralized, which contributes to the flexibility of this type of organization in new product introduction. Each product group is essentially an independent small company, and thus it can react quickly to product development considerations.

A product focus tends to be better suited to less complex, less capital-intensive process technologies, where the capital investment required is generally not high, where economies of scale do not demand large common production facilities, and where flexibility and innovation are more important than careful planning and tight control. A product-focused organization is a "clean" one, with responsibilities well delineated, and profit or return on investment the primary measures. Such an organization tends to appeal most to companies that have a high need and tolerance for diversity, and whose dominant orientation is to a market or consumer group, as opposed to a technology or a material.

The responsibility for decisions on capital, technology, and product development are thrust down from the corporate level to lower levels of management. Plant managers become very important people. This places special burdens on the organization. Product focus demands talented, entrepreneurially minded junior managers and thus much concern for recruiting and managerial development. Junior managers must be tracked carefully through the system, and this implies devoting considerable resources to the company's evaluation and reward system.

And, because staff functions are isolated in individual product lines, the corporate staff must coordinate general policies, goals, and personnel across all the product lines. The corporate level central staff is well removed from day-to-day operations, but it is instrumental in communications and coordination across groups regarding such issues as personnel policies, manpower availability, special services (from computer assistance to training programs), capital appropriation requests, and purchasing.

Process-focused Organization

Within a process-focused organization, individual plants are typically dedicated to a variety of different products. Sometimes a product is produced entirely by a single plant in such an organization, but more often the plant is only one of several that add value to the product.

Responsibilities throughout the plant and also throughout the upper management hierarchy are delineated, not by product line, but by segment of the full manufacturing process. Plants tend to be cost centers, not profit centers, and measurement is based on historical or technologically derived standards. An organization with this division of responsibility can properly be called process-focused.

Process focus tends to be better suited to companies with complex (and divisible) processes and with large capital requirements, companies we earlier called material- or technology-oriented companies. Questions of capacity, balance, logistics, and technological change and its impact on the process are critical for such companies and absorb much of top management's energies. A process focus is not conducive to the rapid introduction of new products, since it does not assign authority along product lines. Nor is it flexible in altering the output levels of existing products, because of the "pipeline momentum" in the system. But it can facilitate low-cost production if there are cost advantages deriving from the scale, continuity, and technology of the process.

A process-focused organization demands tremendous attention to coordinating functional responsibilities to ensure smooth changes in the product mix. And, because control is exercised centrally, young managers must ensure a long and generally a more technical apprenticeship with less decision-making responsibility. This places a burden on upper level management to keep junior managers motivated and learning.

Despite the strong centralization of control in a process-focused organization, it may not be more efficient (in terms of total manufacturing costs) than a well-managed product-focused organization. The central overhead and logistics costs required by a process focus can sometimes offset any variable cost reductions because of tight control and economies of scale. A product focus, however, is inherently easier to manage because of its small scale and singlemindedness. This usually results in shorter cycle times, less inventories, lower logistics costs, and, of course, lower overhead.[5]

The plants in a process organization can be expected to undertake one task that the central staff in a product organization cannot adequately perform, however. Since these plants are technologically based, they tend to be staffed with people who are highly expert and up to date in that technology. They will be aware of technological alternatives and trends, current research, and the operating experience of different technologies at other plants. Operating people in such a plant are more likely to transfer to a similar plant of a competitor's than they are to move to one of the other plants in their own company.

In a product organization, each product-plant complex will involve a number of technologies, and there may not be a sufficient mass of technical expertise to keep abreast of the changing state of the art in that technology. This becomes, then, more a responsibility of the corporate staff or, possibly, of a separate research group in the corporation, which may not even be under the aegis of the manufacturing organization. For this reason, businesses that use highly complex and evolving technologies are often forced to gravitate toward process organizations.

A process organization tends to manage purchasing somewhat better than a product organization does. If purchasing becomes too fragmented because of decentralization, the company as a whole tends to lose economies of scale as well as "clout" with suppliers. Conversely, centralized purchasing tends to be more bureaucratic and less responsive to local or market needs. The result is usually a combination of both, where through some decision rule the product organizations are given responsibility for certain purchases and a central purchasing department handles the procurement and distribution of the remainder.

[5]E.F. Schumacher has eloquently argued a similar point in a somewhat different context in his provocative book *Small Is Beautiful* (New York: Harper & Row, 1975).

8. How Should You Organize Manufacturing?

EXHIBIT 3 Differences Between Product-Focused and Process-focused Manufacturing Organizations

	Product focus	Process focus
Profit or cost responsibility: where located	Product groups	Central organization
Size of corporate staff	Relatively small	Relatively large
Major functions of corporate staff	(a) Review capital appropriation requests	(a) Coordination with marketing
	(b) Communicate corporate changes and requests	(b) Facilities decisions
	(c) Act as clearinghouse for	(c) Personnel policies
	personnel information	(d) Purchasing
	management recruiting	(e) Logistics-inventory management
	purchasing	(f) Coordination of production schedules
	used equipment	(g) Make versus buy, vertical integration decisions
	management development programs	
	(d) Evaluate and reward plant managers	(h) Recruit future plant managers
	(e) Select plant managers and manage career paths—possibly across product group lines	(i) Review plant performance, cost center basis
Major responsibilities of plant organizations	(a) Coordination with marketing	(a) Use materials and facilities efficiently
	(b) Facilities decisions (subject to marketing)	
	(c) Purchasing and logistics	(b) Recruit production, clerical and lower management workers
	(d) Production scheduling and inventory control	
	(e) Make versus buy	(c) Training and development of future department and plant managers
	(f) Recruit management	
		(d) Respond to special requests from marketing, within limited ranges

Exhibit 3 gives a summary of the important differences between product-focused and process-focused organizations.

Product or Process Focus?

The polar extremes of manufacturing organization—product and process focus—place fundamentally different demands and opportunities on a company, and the choice of manufacturing organization should essentially be a choice *between* them. That is, manufacturing confronts a very definite either/or choice of organization—either product-focused or process-focused. Just as individual plants must have a clear focus, so must a central manufacturing organization.

Because the demands of a process-focused organization are so different from those of a product-focused organization—as to policies and practices, measurement and control systems, managerial attitudes, kinds of people, and career paths—it is extremely difficult for a mixed manufacturing organization, with a single central staff, to achieve the kind of policy consistency and organizational stability that can both compete effectively in a given market and cope with growth and change.

A mixed or composite production focus will only invite confusion and a weakening of the corporation's ability to maintain consistency among its manufacturing policies, and between them and its various corporate attitudes. If different manufacturing groups within the same company have different focuses, they should be separated as much as possible—each with its own central staff.

To illustrate, we can examine some mixed organizational focuses and the difficulties they might encounter.

- A process-focused factory producing for two distinct product groups would have the organization chart shown in *Exhibit 4*. Here the corporation is trying to serve two different mar-

EXHIBIT 4 Process-focused Factory Serving Two Different Product Markets

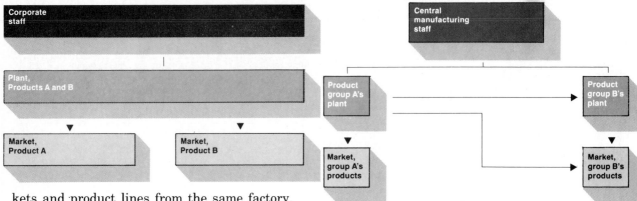

EXHIBIT 5 One Product Group Serving Another Product's Group-Market

kets and product lines from the same factory, whose process technology appears to meet the needs of both (it may, in fact, consist of a series of linked process stages operating under tight central control). This kind of organization invites the now-classic problems of Skinner's unfocused factory. The manufacturing mission required by each market may be vastly different, and a plant that tries to carry out both at the same time is likely to do neither well.

Similarly, an organization that uses the manufacturing facilities of one of its product groups to supply a major portion of the needs of another product group, market would be risking the same kind of confusion—that is, a nominally product-focused organization with an organization chart like the one in *Exhibit 5*.

■ A process-focused factory supplying parts or materials to two distinct product groups would have the organization chart shown in *Exhibit 6*. In this instance a corporate staff oversees two independent product groups, which serve two distinct markets, *and* a process-focused plant that supplies both product groups. The usual argument for an independent supplier plant is that economies of scale are possible from combining the requirements of both product groups. No matter what the reason, the supplier plant is coordinate by the same staff that oversees the product groups. One vice president of manufacturing directs a corporate manufacturing staff with one materials manager, one chief of industrial engineering, one head of purchasing, one personnel director—all supervising the activities of two product-focused organizations and a process-focused organization.

Another variant of this difficulty is for the captive supplier plant for one product group to supply a major portion of the requirements of another product group's plant. Or a plant belonging to a product-focused division might act as a supplier to one of the plants within a process-focused division.

How else can a company organize around such situations? The important notion is that a plant that attaches certain priorities to different competitive dimensions is likely to prefer suppliers who have the same priorities. This suggests that a company should erect managerial dividing lines between its product- and process-focused manufacturing segments. In particular, transfer of products between product- and process-focused plant groups should not be coordinated by a central staff group but handled through arm's-length bargaining, as if, in effect, they had independent "subsidiary" relationships within the parent company.

EXHIBIT 6 Two Product Groups and a Supplier Plant

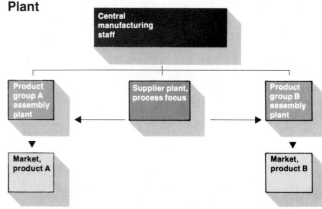

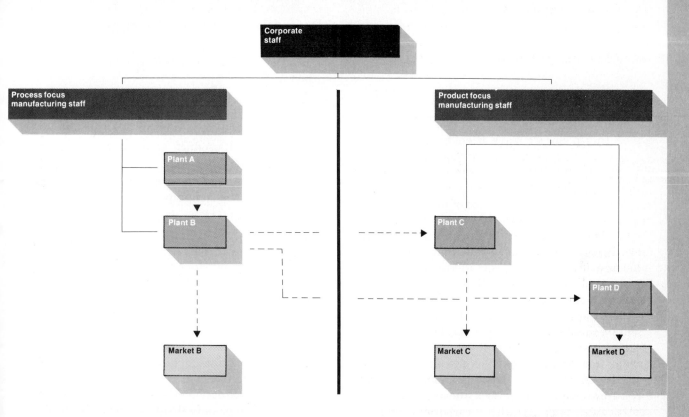

Such an in-house supplier would then be treated like any other supplier, able to resist demands that violate the integrity of its manufacturing mission just as the customer plant is free to select suppliers that are more attuned to its own mission. The organization chart might look something like that shown in *Exhibit 7*.

Such an arrangement may appear to be needlessly complex and add to manufacturing's administrative overhead without clear financial benefits. However, combining two dissimilar activities does not reduce complexity; it simply camouflages it and is likely to destroy the focus and distinctiveness of both. Our position is not that both product and process focus cannot exist within the same company but simply that separating them as much as possible will result in less confusion and less danger that different segments of manufacturing will be working at cross purposes.

Test for Organizational Focus

Many companies, consciously or unconsciously, have moved toward precisely this kind of wide

separation. In some cases it is explicit, with two or more different staff groups operating relatively autonomously; in others, although a single central staff appears on the organization chart, subgroups within this staff operate independently. One way for a company to test the degree of organizational focus in its manufacturing arm, and whether adequate insulation between product- and process-focused plant groups exists, is to contemplate how it would fragment itself if forced to (by the Antitrust Division of the Department of Justice for example). A segmented and focused organization should be able to divide itself up cleanly and naturally, with no substantial organizational changes.

Consider the large auto companies. From the point of view of the marketplace, they are organized by product groups (Oldsmobile, Lincoln, Mercury, Chevrolet, and so on), but this organization is essentially cosmetic. In reality, the auto companies are classic examples of large process-focused organizations. Any effort by the Department of Justice to sever these companies by product group is foolish because it cuts across the grain of their manufacturing organization. If the companies had to divest themselves, it could only be by process segment. But the point is that divestiture could be accomplished readily, and this is the acid test of an effective and focused manufacturing organization.

The Impact of Growth

Up to this point we have been arguing that a company's manufacturing function must structure and organize itself so as to conform to the company's priorities for certain competitive dimensions. Moreover, the choice of manufacturing organizational structure—which provides most of the key linkages between the manufacturing group and the company's other people and functions—must also fit with the basic attitudes, the preferences, and the traditions that shape and drive the remainder of the company.

But companies change and grow over time. Unless a manufacturing organization is designed so that it can grow with the company, it will become increasingly unstable and inappropriate to the company's needs. Therefore, simplicity and focus are not sufficient criteria; the organizational design must somehow also incorporate the possibility of growth.

In fact, growth is an enemy of focus and can subvert a healthy manufacturing operation—not all at once, but bit by bit. For example, growth can move a company up against a different set of competitors at the same time it is acquiring new resources and thus force a change in its competitive strategy.

The strategy change may be aggressive and deliberate or unconscious and barely perceived. In either case, however, success for the company may now require different skills from those already mastered—a different manufacturing mission and focus to complement a new corporate strategy.

Even without a change of strategy, growth can diminish a manufacturing organization's ability to maintain its original focus. Especially if growth is rapid, top-level managers will be pressed continually to decide on capital acquisitions and deployment, and to relinquish some authority over operational issues in existing plants. Slowly, focus disintegrates.

To cope with growth, we believe that first one must identify and understand the type of growth being experienced and the demands it will place on the organization. Growth has four important dimensions:

1. A broadening of the products or product lines being offered.
2. An extended span of the production process for existing products to increase value added (commonly referred to as vertical integration).
3. An increased product acceptance within an existing market area.
4. Expansion of the geographic sales territory serviced by the company.

These types of growth are very different, but it is important to distinguish among them so that the organization design can reflect the *kind* of growth experienced, not simply the fact of growth. This means keeping the organization as stable and focused as possible as growth proceeds.

If growth is predominantly a broadening of product lines, a product-focused organization is probably best suited to the demands for flexibility that such a broadening requires. With such organizations, other aspects of manufacturing, particularly the production of the traditional product lines, need change only little as growth proceeds.

Alternatively, if growth is chiefly toward increasing the span of the process (that is, vertical integration), a process-focused organization can probably best introduce and manage the added segments of the full production process. In this fashion, the separate pieces of the process can be coordinated effectively and confusion can be reduced in the traditional process segments.

Then again, if growth is realized through increased product acceptance, the product becomes more and more a commodity and, as acceptance grows, the company is usually pressed to compete on price. Such pressure generally implies changes in the production process itself: more specialization of equipment and tasks, an increasing ratio of capital to labor expenses, a more standard and rigid flow of the product through the process. The management of such changes in the process is probably best accomplished by an organization that is focused on the process, willing to forsake the flexibilities of a more decentralized product focus.

Growth realized through geographic expansion is more problematic. Sometimes such growth can be met with existing facilities. But frequently, as with many multinational companies, expansion in foreign countries is best met with an entirely separate manufacturing organization that itself can be organized along either a product or a process focus.

Recognizing Common Pitfalls

As we examined a number of manufacturing organizations that had "lost their way"—become unfocused or whose focus was no longer congruent with corporate needs—it became apparent that in most cases the culprit was growth. Problems due to growth often surface with the apparent breakdown of the relationship between the central manufacturing staff and division or plant management. For example, many companies that have had a strong central manufacturing organization find that as their sales and product offerings grow in size and complexity, the central staff simply cannot continue to perform the same functions as well as before. A tenuous mandate for changing the manufacturing organization surfaces.

Sometimes, product divisions are broken out. But the natural inclination is to strengthen the central staff functions instead, which usually diminishes the decision-making capabilities of plant managers.

As the central staff becomes stronger, it begins to siphon authority and people from the plant organization. Thus the strong tend to get stronger and the weak weaker. At some point this vicious cycle breaks down under the strain of increasing complexity, and then a simple executive order cannot accomplish the profound changes—in people, policies, and attitudes—that are necessary to reverse the process and cause decentralization.

We do not mean to imply that decentralizing manufacturing management is always the best path to follow as an organization grows. It may be preferable in some cases to split it apart geographically, with two strong central staffs coordinating the efforts of two independent plant organizations.

However, it is sometimes dangerous to delegate too much responsibility for capacity-expansion decisions to a product-oriented manufacturing manager. To keep his own task as simple as possible, he may tend to "expand in place"—continually expanding current plants or building nearby satellite plants. Over time he may create a set of huge, tightly interconnected plants that exhibit many of the same characteristics as a process organization: tight central control, inflexibility, and constraints on further incremental expansion.

Such a situation could occur in spite of the fact that the corporation as a whole continues to emphasize market flexibility, decentralized responsibility, and technological opportunism. The new managers trained in such a complex will have to be different in personality and skills from those in other parts of the company, and a different motivation and compensation system is required. Such a situation can be remedied either by dismembering and reorganizing this product organization or by decoupling it from the rest of the company so that it has more of an independent, subsidiary status, as described earlier.

Product focus can also encroach on an avowed process focus. For example, a company offering several complex products whose manufacture takes these products through very definite process stages, in which the avowed focus is process-oriented, and with separate divisions for stages of the process all subject to strong central direction, must resist the temptation to alter manufacturing so that it can "get closer to the market." If the various product lines were allowed to make uncoordinated requests for product design changes or new product introductions, the tightly coupled process pipeline could then crumble. Encroaching product focus would subvert it.

Concluding Remarks

Manufacturing functions best when its facilities, technology, and policies are consistent with recognized priorities of corporate strategy. Only then can manufacturing gain efficiency without wasting resources by "improving" operations that do not count.

The manufacturing organization itself must be similarly consistent with corporate priorities. Such organizational focus is aided by simplicity of design. This simplicity in turn requires either a product- or a process-focused form of organization. The proper choice between these two organizational types can smooth a company's growth by lending stability to its operations.

9. FMC, Crane and Excavator Division

In early May 1974 V. L. Martin, the newly appointed manager of the $90 million sales Crane & Excavator (C&E) division of the FMC Corporation, was asked by FMC vice president John F. McKeon to present final recommendations on the best plant expansion strategy for his capacity-constrained division. The C&E division, with headquarters in Cedar Rapids, Iowa, and marketing under the well-known *Link-Belt* brand name, supplied four types of large heavy-duty cranes and excavators to the construction industry: two lines of large wire-rope or cable cranes/excavators (a "crawler" model mounted on bull-dozer-type treads and a truck model mounted on a rubber-tired, truck carrier unit); a line of crawler hydraulic bucket excavators; and a line of hydraulic cranes mounted on truck carrier units. (See product sketches and specifications in *Exhibit 1*.)

Martin and his staff studied expansion alternatives for more than a year. Both he and McKeon knew that the two Cedar Rapids plants (which represented 95 percent of the division's current manufacturing capacity) had been operating near capacity for several years. They believed that this capacity constraint may have cost C&E a reduction in market share in recent months in all of its lines, and they were eager to take advantage of the growing markets for cable and hydraulic equipment in order to help the division meet its long-term objectives.

In late 1973 as a first step in a two-part plan to expand capacity, the division had begun construction on a new $14 million plant in Lexington, Kentucky, that would produce the entire line of hydraulic truck-mounted cranes. That line was expected to be phased out of Cedar Rapids and phased into Lexington after the plant was completed in July 1974. Martin's staff had prepared summaries on three alternatives for the second stage of expansion. Each alternative could provide the capacity needed for all lines through the early 1980s.

Martin now had to decide which of the three alternatives would present the best over-all plan for the division. The first of the alternatives called for a $9.4 million expansion of the Cedar Rapids plants to accommodate the production of all three lines left in Iowa, with a particular emphasis on high-volume production of the soon-to-be-completed redesigned line of hydraulic excavators, the fastest growing product group. The second alternative involved a more limited expansion of Cedar Rapids for the cable products and construction of a new plant in Bowling Green, Kentucky, to produce hydraulic excavators exclusively, leaving all cable products in Cedar Rapids. This alternative would require capital outlays of $16.7 million. The third plan involved construction of a much larger plant in Bowling Green to produce all truck-mounted cable cranes, the C&E division's most profitable product line. Under this alternative, crawler-type cable cranes/excavators and hydraulic excavators would remain in Cedar Rapids. The cost of this third plan would be $16.3 million.

This case was prepared by Steven C. Wheelwright, Paul W. Marshall, and Robert Banks.

EXHIBIT 1 Major Product Lines and Product Specifications, FMC Crane & Excavator Division[a]

Specifications	Cable Crawler Crane/Excavator	Cable Truck Crane	Hydraulic Truck Crane	Hydraulic Excavator
Load capacity in tons	12 to 150	20 to 185	20 to 45	—
Bucket capacity in cubic yards	⅝ to 3	—	—	¾ to 1½
Boom length (min/max)	30 to 250 foot boom[b]	80 to 300 foot boom[b]	28 to 96 feet	—
Configuration				
Upper	crane/bucket	crane	crane	bucket
Lower	Tractor or flat pad crawler	Rubber-tired truck or self-propelled unit	Rubber-tired truck or self-propelled unit	Tractor or flat pad crawler
Number of models available	17	12	8	6

[a]Other C&E products: pedestal cranes, offshore cranes, tower/gantry cranes, diesel pile hammers, lumber handling equipment, repair parts.
[b]A jib extension to the main boom of 20 to 70 feet was also an available option on the cable products.

Martin and his staff spent considerable time investigating these alternatives. Before making a final decision, Martin decided to review all the pertinent information that had been assembled. He had been told that enough investment capital was available to finance any of the three plans, so his job was to weigh the economics of each proposal against their strategic implications for production, marketing, and labor relations.

History of the Crane & Excavator Division

The creation of FMC's Crane & Excavator division had been a result of the 1967 merger between FMC Corporation, then a $1 billion sales producer of machinery, fibers, films, and defense materials, and the Link-Belt Company, a highly respected manufacturer of power transmission and heavy construction equipment whose 1966 sales were $245 million. Link-Belt's operations had been folded into FMC's Machinery Group (50 percent of FMC's 1973 sales of $1.7 billion; the Chemical Group accounted for the remainder) and had been split into two divisions: the Power Transmission division and the Crane & Excavator division. (See organization chart, *Exhibit 2.*)

Certain of Link-Belt's operations were relocated to better fit FMC's existing businesses; however, the C&E division was a new area for FMC and thus was left essentially the same as it was under the old Link-Belt organization. In 1973 the C&E division had three major plants in operation, two large ones in Cedar Rapids (246,000 and 312,000 square feet) for the manufacture of major product lines and a small 69,000-square foot plant in Woodstock, Ontario, which supplied products to the Canadian market. (The division's new 271,000-square foot plant in Lexington was scheduled to begin limited production in July 1974.) In 1973 the C&E division had produced 388 cable crawler cranes/excavators, 294 cable truck cranes, 337 hydraulic excavators, and 205 hydraulic truck cranes. Eleven hundred of these units had been built in Cedar Rapids; the remainder at the Canadian facility.

The Cedar Rapids facilities employed 2400 persons, 1680 of whom were represented by the United Automobile Workers (UAW). The C&E division had recently completed difficult negotiations with the union for a two-year contract. While

both parties had been reasonably satisfied with the settlement, Martin knew that the division had only narrowly averted a strike over an incentive pay issue. That issue had yet to be completely resolved and might precipitate a strike in 1976.

C&E Division Management

Martin had moved to Cedar Rapids from his position as director of planning for FMC in early 1974. He represented a distinct change in management style for the Link-Belt operation. Formerly, the management had been relatively paternalistic and informal. Martin, an MBA from a well-known Eastern business school, had brought with him some younger managers and had attempted to make the operation more systematic. He relied strongly, however, on the advice of the former Link-Belt president, Cal Basile, and vice president of manufacturing, Martin Luber. Both senior executives had been with Link-Belt for over 30 years and were due to retire in 1974 and 1975 respectively.

Link-Belt's traditional management policies had been conservative. In the early 1960s, for example, Link-Belt had desired to maintain its no-debt status and limited its expansion capital to the amount of cash generated internally; the Cedar Rapids facilities, built in the 1930s and 1940s, had not been significantly remodeled since then. The firm restricted most production to Cedar Rapids, because it felt that with its main emphasis on cable equipment—produced on a job shop basis—production economies from split operations were not readily available.

Furthermore, it did not have sufficient management depth to operate separate production facilities. The firm had also shunned backward integration because of the risk and the size of investment it would require.

Prior to the early seventies, FMC had also been fiscally conservative. During the late sixties and early seventies, the Machinery Group had spent only 60 percent or so of its allocated capital budget each year. In 1972 and 1973, however, FMC had raised the Machinery Group allocation to $40 to $45 million and had strongly encouraged investments in new plant and equipment. As a result, 80 percent of those allocations had been invested. Martin expected that the entire Machinery Group allocation of $60 million for 1974

EXHIBIT 2 C&E Division Organization

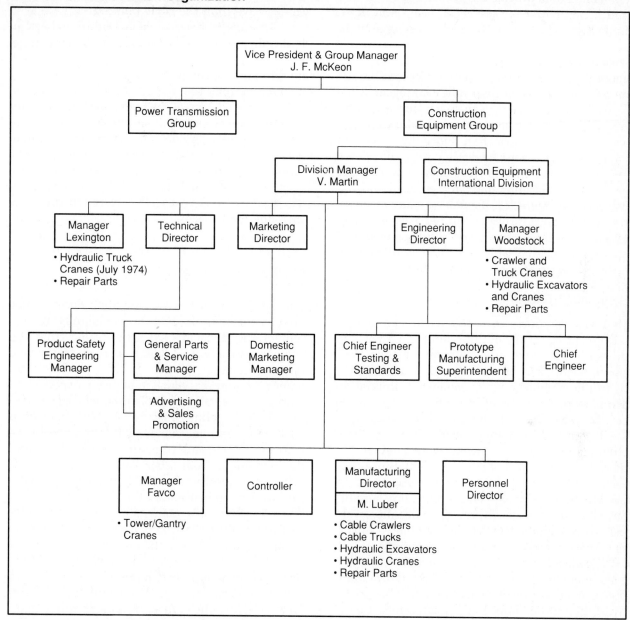

and the projected $70 million for 1975 would be used. (The C&E capital allocation was 25 to 30 percent of the Group's allocation.)

Product Lines

The division manufactured large pieces of heavy equipment for lifting or digging. Approximately 90 percent of C&E's 1973 sales were accounted for by the four major product lines, all marketed

under the Link-Belt trademark. Cable cranes had been the mainstay of the Link-Belt operation since its earliest days. Link-Belt's first hydraulic excavator was introduced in 1967 and the division did not offer a complete line of hydraulic cranes until 1971. The division also offered four models of diesel pile hammers, introduced in 1959.

Cable Products

Cable cranes utilized wire-rope cables attached to large drums and powered through gears and a transmission to provide the necessary movements and lifting power for the crane boom and hoist. Link-Belt, which in 1974 held an estimated 16 percent share of the cable crane market, was a strong name in the business. Cable cranes were generally more custom-tailored pieces of equipment than were their hydraulic counterparts and offered both a longer boom reach and a greater lifting capacity. Cable equipment units were typically more expensive than hydraulic units, but on a cost-per-capacity basis they were considered less expensive. In addition, cable cranes were easier to service and repair in the field. However, cable cranes were less flexible in the variety of their uses; they also often required a day or longer to set up, a larger crew, and a higher degree of operator skill, all of which meant generally higher operating costs for users of cable products.

Hydraulic Products

Hydraulic products achieved boom and bucket movement by means of fluid pumped under high pressure into hydraulic cylinders rather than through the use of cables and drums. While hydraulic products were somewhat limited in terms of reach and load capacities, they offered certain advantages to the user. First, they were smaller and more maneuverable than cable machines and operator controls were simpler, requiring a lower level of operator skill. Since they required less setup time before work could be performed, they were considered more suitable for short-term jobs. However, hydraulics were usually considered less reliable and more difficult to service in the field than cable products.

Hydraulic cranes and excavators first became popular in the 1960s when the Grove Manufacturing Company introduced the first successful hydraulic crane. Link-Belt, a latecomer to the hydraulics field, held only a 6.9 percent share of the hydraulic excavator market and only 4 percent of the hydraulic crane market in 1973. (See *Exhibit 3*.)

The C&E division had entered the hydraulics market because it promised the fastest growth in the next decade. Indeed, the market for hydraulic cranes and excavators had grown 13 to 14 percent for several years. This rapid growth, however, had attracted other larger producers, notably the Caterpillar Corporation, and the hydraulics market had of late become considerably more price competitive than the cable market.

One area that had held Link-Belt back in hydraulics was the line's design. At that time, C&E equipment was large, high priced and high quality and the company was able to capture only a small share of the market. In 1973 C&E began a complete redesign of the hydraulic lines in order to reduce costs and to make the lines more competitive in their product characteristics. The plan was to complete the redesign of the hydraulic crane line in time for the commencement of production at the new Lexington plant in mid-1974. The new hydraulic excavators were scheduled for introduction in 1975.

Marketing Strategy

The C&E division served roughly a dozen major product markets. In 1973 approximately 42 percent of the division's sales had come from the heavy construction market, 20 percent from crane rental companies, 15 percent from pipeline companies (a market which had been expected to increase, especially for cable products, because of the Alaska pipeline construction), 7 percent from offshore oil and gas exploration (also expected to increase), 6 percent from timber handling, and the remainder from other markets. In terms of price and quality the C&E division generally captured the upper end of the market it served.

The division's marketing goals were relatively straightforward in early 1974: by 1980 the company planned to be the number one manufacturer of cable equipment (both crawler and rubber-tired truck units), the number two maker of hydraulic excavators, and the number two producer of hydraulic cranes. In its long-range plan, the division summarized these goals and the general strategy it devised for their accomplishment. (These are presented in *Exhibits 3* and *4*, along with sales forecasts by product line through 1980.)

Martin carefully considered his division's marketing strategy, especially with regard to the planned plant expansion. The C&E goal of achieving a leadership position in the four major product lines was an aggressive one, involving several key steps:

EXHIBIT 3 Current and Projected Market Shares and Rank of Major Industry Competitors

Market	Firms	1973		1980	
		Market Share (in percent)	Rank	Market Share (in percent)	Rank
Cable Crawler Crane	Manitowoc Eng. Co	25.9	1	17.8	3
	American Hoist & Derrick	24.1	2	22.5	2
	FMC Crane & Excavator	19.7	3	26.2	1
Cable Truck Crane	Pawling & Harnischfeger (P&H)	26.4	1	23.7	2
	American Hoist & Derrick	21.1	2	18.2	3
	FMC Crane & Excavator	19.9	3	29.0	1
Hydraulic Excavator	Koehring Company	17.1	1	13.5	3
	Liebherr Company	12.1	2	11.8	4
	FMC Crane & Excavator	6.9	5	17.2	2
	Caterpillar	4.0	7	30.0	1
Hydraulic Truck Cranes	Grove Manufacturing	34.5	1	26.9	1
	Pawling & Harnischfeger	19.2	2	16.1	3
	FMC Crane & Excavator	4.0	8	18.0	2

Brief Characteristics About FMC Competitors Which Could Affect Market Share Forecasts

Cable Crawlers. American Hoist and Derrick: Complete line, auxiliary lifting attachments, good product. Manitowoc Eng. Co.: Complete large machine line, complete attachments, conservative attitude toward capital investment.

Cable Truck Cranes. Pawling and Harnischfeger: Complete product line, good distribution, fair product. American: Good distribution, fair product, heavy concentration on this product line.

Hydraulic Excavators. Caterpillar: Excellent distribution, parts and service, high quality product, capability to mass produce. Koehring Company: Good reputation, acceptable product, obsolete design, fair distribution and service. Liebherr Company: Advanced high quality product, modern manufacturing capability, growth limited by distribution.

Hydraulic Cranes. Grove Mfg.: Currently dominates market, will have distribution problems and lose share of market due to increased competition. P&H: Good hydraulic line, strong distribution due to complete line of products. Petibone Corporation (8 percent of 1973 market): Will phase out of business; poor product line, distribution problems, poor management.

Source: C&E Division long-range planning forecast.

1. Development of a strong independent distributor network by providing the most complete line of cranes and excavators possible.

2. Reorganization of the marketing department into product line groups, with specialists responsible for each business area.

3. Engineering development of competitive models and the improvement of attachments and other features.

4. Increased manufacturing capacity to levels sufficient to permit dominance in a fast growing market.

To achieve this goal, it was important to select the correct distributors and carefully plan research and development expenditures. It was also extremely important to make investments in capital plant and equipment for the fastest growing and most profitable products that would allow the division to increase production volume, lower costs, and bring in-house many items currently purchased from outside sources. These plant expansions also had to be timed to provide protection against labor problems or unforeseen start-up difficulties.

Sales of cranes and excavators historically had been dependent on construction expenditures and on the over-all rate of growth in the GNP. As a result, the sales history of the C&E division had been cyclical, with a long-term growth trend. C&E's planners, while recognizing the cyclical nature of the industry, had tended to develop long-range plans on the basis of long-term industry trends. This had been considered appropriate, because the company's product lines tended to follow different cycles that offset one another, and most products had three- to five-year development lead times. For purposes of sales forecasting through 1980, the division's planners utilized published growth rate predictions from several sources. The most important of the annual growth rates used were: (1) overall construction expenditures, 7.6 percent to 10.4 percent through 1980; (2) heavy construction, 12 percent; (3) sewer and water construction, 15 percent; (4) electricity, gas, and communications construction, 15 percent, and (5) nonresidential building, 6.4 percent.

Competition

In C&E's markets the largest producers typically dominated the market. The Grove Manufacturing Company in hydraulic truck cranes and Manitowoc Engineering Company in cable crawler cranes were the most significant examples. The market share positions of the largest producers in each market are presented in *Exhibit 3*, along with the C&E division's forecast of 1980 market positions and a brief assessment of certain characteristics of each major competitor as they might affect the division's marketing plan.

The Grove Manufacturing Company, a single product producer, had been the first in the market with a good product and as a result had gained a dominant position in hydraulic truck cranes. Pawling & Harnischfeger Company had been a leader in cable truck cranes with strengths in distribution and in product line completeness. The Caterpillar Corporation, a large, high-volume producer of heavy equipment, had only a small share of one of C&E's markets, hydraulic excavators, in 1974. However, Caterpillar had always been considered a formidable competitor in all markets it served, because it combined mass-production techniques with an excellent and extensive distribution network. Caterpillar was expected to dominate the fast-growing hydraulic excavator market by 1980. A rather disturbing indication of the strength of the Caterpillar name in the heavy equipment markets was a 1967 survey in which 8 of 10 respondents had indicated a preference for the hydraulic excavator made by Caterpillar; at the time of the survey, however, Caterpillar did not produce a hydraulic excavator and did not introduce one until 1972.

Distribution

The C&E division distributed its products through a network of 80 dealers throughout North America. The typical distributor sold $3.5 million worth of C&E equipment annually, with a maximum of about $25 million in sales from a single dealer. (C&E distributors tended to be much smaller than typical Caterpillar dealers, who might end up with more than $100 million in sales in a single year.) Over the past decade the typical C&E distributor had grown at an average annual rate of 15 to 20 percent.

Of the company's 80 distributors, only 18 were primarily dependent on the Link-Belt account; the remainder sold substantial amounts of other manufacturers' products. For example, 10 distributors, accounting for 8 percent of C&E sales, were Caterpillar distributors as well, 7 Clark Equipment dealers contributed 5 percent of C&E sales; and 7 dealers representing Grove Manufacturing Company accounted for 8 percent of C&E sales.

EXHIBIT 4 C&E Marketing Goals and Sales Figures

Marketing Goals and Sales Projections (in $ millions)

Product Category	1973 Industry Sales	Projected 1980 Industry Sales			Annual Compound Growth Rate 1973–1980 for Sales Projections		
		High	Likely	Low	High	Likely	Low
Cable Crawler Crane	192	420	320	252	11.8%	7.7%	4.0%
Cable Truck Crane	148	306	230	196	11.8	6.8	4.0
Hydraulic Excavator	217	550	400	362	14.2	9.1	7.6
Hydraulic Truck Crane	234	523	417	380	12.2	8.6	7.2
Total, four product lines	791	1799	1367	1190	—	—	—

C&E Division Domestic Sales (in $ millions)

Product Category	1972 Actual	1973 Actual	1976 Projected	1980 Projected
Cable Crawler Crane	33.8	37.9	57.7	83.8
Cable Truck Crane	24.4	29.4	50.6	66.8
Hydraulic Excavator	15.9	14.9	29.8	69.1
Hydraulic Truck Crane	8.5	9.3	22.1	75.0
Total, four product lines	82.6	91.5	160.2	294.7

Summary of Marketing Goals (1974–1980)

Cable Crawler Crane Market

Objective: To become the dominant manufacturer of cable crawler machines.

Strategy:
1. Expand our large crawler crane line as rapidly as our technical and physical capacities will permit.
2. Offer complete attachments including long booms, auxiliary lifting attachments and tower attachments.
3. Increase our productive capacity to a level sufficient to permit us to aggressively compete in the market place.
4. Strengthen our distributor organization to improve our market penetration.

Cable Truck Crane Market

Objective: To become the dominant manufacturer of cable truck cranes.

Strategy:
1. Expand the large cable truck line.
2. Improve and develop new and more competitive attachments such as long booms, hammerheads and tower mountings.
3. Increase production in these markets to a level sufficient to permit us to achieve dominance.
4. Strengthen the distributor organization and improve and increase market penetration.

Hydraulic Excavator Market

Objectives:
1. Obtain number two market position by 1980.
2. Develop a complete line of hydraulic excavators featuring the most modern technology including second generation ultra high P.S.I. hydrostatics.
3. Lead the industry in the development of 200,000-pound and larger hydraulic excavators.
4. Develop new technology allowing much wider use of hydraulic excavators in boring, piling, material handling, wrecking, timber and pulp wood, and semi-automatic trenching.

(continued on next page)

EXHIBIT 4 C&E Marketing Goals and Sales Figures (Continued)

Strategy:
1. Design and continue updating a complete product line.
2. Strengthen distribution by offering the most complete line of hydraulic excavators in the industry.
3. Adopt manufacturing procedures to the volume concept with capability to mass produce to achieve dominance in a fast growing market.
4. Move completely into the component end of the business allowing in-plant manufacturing of most major piece parts and components.

Hydraulic Crane Market

Objectives:
1. Achieve at least number three position in the market place.
2. Strengthen the distributor network by developing a wider line of products and attracting better distributors.
3. Increase our international position in the crane-excavator industry.

Strategy:
1. Design a quality line of products that are competitive, reliable, and profitable.
2. Achieve mass production economies in our specialized Lexington, Kentucky facility.
3. Minimize as much as possible conflicting accounts within our distributor network.
4. Promote to an extent greater than is currently possible the rental and industrial markets.
5. Develop products that lend themselves to worldwide manufacture.

Source: Data in the first half of this exhibit are from a C&E Division long-range planning forecast; casewriter's estimates include 4 percent annual inflation factor.

Martin considered C&E's strong reputation among dealers one of the company's major strengths. The company had offered several equipment financing plans for dealers that ranged from consignment to full financing loans for each piece of equipment. Because of the rate of inflation in early 1974, the heavy equipment industry adopted a price protection policy that guaranteed prices to dealers for 90 to 120 days. The C&E division, shortly after a price increase in February 1974, also adopted this policy. However, the company's price hike was insufficient to cover rapidly escalating production costs, and C&E found itself in a substantial price squeeze in April. Rather than back down on its commitment to its dealers, C&E chose to swallow more than $1 million in cost increases on units delivered in April and early May.

C&E management felt that the dealer's ability to quickly repair and service the company's products was critical to the success of the division's marketing plans. As Basile, the company's president, had explained:

I've been in this business for 25 years, and I think I have a pretty good overview of it. In my mind, service will be the deciding factor in determining who remains in this business, and who drops out. I see a major shake-out coming, particularly in the hydraulic market, and in order of importance, I have to rate service number one and original design number two. A crane or an excavator is often the most expensive piece of heavy equipment at a construction site; if you are renting, a large crane goes for $1500 a day. Reliability and service are critical to customer satisfaction.

The problem of service is particularly important in the field, where you might be miles from the nearest dealer. Dealers might have to go a long way to help a stuck customer, but it has to be done. And the hydraulics are very vulnerable to the service problem. To service or repair them you really have to understand the scientific principles behind hydraulics. You can't just observe their mechanical operation and fix them, as you can with cable equipment. There's more to hydraulics than just rigging a lot of wire rope.

Manufacturing

In early 1974 the C&E division's fabrication and assembly for all product lines were concentrated in the two Cedar Rapids plants; the exclusive production of hydraulic truck cranes in Lexington was scheduled to begin gradually in July. Crane and excavator production, both cable and hydraulic, were performed on an individual unit basis with final assembly requiring six or seven work stations for each line of product. After the two or three workers (per shift) assigned to each station completed their portion of the assembly operation, a large overhead crane moved the entire unit to the next work station.

Although basically simple in design, cable and hydraulic cranes and excavators required the careful assembly of a large number of parts. A typical unit contained between 20,000 and 30,000 individual items. These were subassembled into parent items that were added to the final assembly at a rate of about 500 per work station. Average cycle time at a work station varied from one to three days, depending on the station. This type of decoupled production assembly system allowed for a certain degree of flexibility. One of the characteristics of the cable product production was that missing parts did not usually stop the entire production process. Instead, work could continue on a partially completed unit until the needed part became available. The production process used for hydraulics was less flexible, since production was performed in a sequential manner and it was necessary to have the appropriate parts on hand at the right time.

The work process flow for all lines was essentially the same. Because of the greater fraction of purchased parts in the production of hydraulic equipment, however, more of a "flow-shop" arrangement was utilized there. (The Lexington plant had been designed with a low-speed moving assembly line.) There were six major steps in the manufacture of both hydraulic and cable cranes: (1) fabrication and machining of parts for both upper and lower portions of the crane; (2) assembly of fabricated parts along with purchased parts into the basic upper and lower portions of the crane; (3) mating of the upper and lower, painting and testing of the crane without the boom; (4) manufacture of the boom assembly; (5) mating of the boom and crane; and (6) final testing and shipment (usually by rail).

Both cable and hydraulic equipment contained a large number of purchased parts. Castings for gears and housings were purchased and machined for the specific product; purchased sheet steel was fabricated into cabs which housed the operator and the machinery; plate steel was purchased and fabricated into the floor plate and mounting for heavy equipment. Many purchased parts went directly into assembly without any additional fabrication; diesel engines were purchased complete from suppliers such as Cummins Engine Company or General Motors. Material purchases averaged approximately 55 to 60 percent of factory selling price for cable products, and 65 to 70 percent for hydraulic cranes and excavators. (See *Exhibit 5* for a cost breakdown of typical products.)

Assembly and Fabrication

The upper assembly of the crane contained the gearing and the power source for the boom and hoist and provided the mounting for the boom and all operator controls. The upper portion of a hydraulic machine differed significantly from that of a cable crane. The cable crane delivered power to the boom by means of wire rope cables on drums, whereas the hydraulic crane delivered power through a closed fluid system requiring pipes, fittings, valves and hoses. There were almost no common parts in the upper portions of hydraulic and cable units.

The lower section of the crawler units was assembled by C&E and consisted of a pad and frame, gearing for driving the treads, and the tread assemblies. The treads and gears were mounted on steel frames and a chain drive was added. On truck-mounted cranes, the truck carrier unit included a truck frame, cab, wheels, and engine. The company manufactured most of its truck lowers in-house. Truck lowers and crawler lowers shared no parts in common. A few parts (less than 10 percent) were common to both cable and hydraulic truck carriers.

The boom for the cable cranes was generally fabricated from steel tubing. The tubing was welded into sections of boom and then these sections were in turn pinned together in varying lengths. In the final product, these sections were carried separately to the field site and assembled there for use on the crane for the larger units. For smaller units the sections were hinged and traveled attached to the crane.

EXHIBIT 5 Product Costs for Typical Products (in Thousands $)

| | Cable Crawlers | | Cable Trucks | | Hydraulic Truck Cranes | | Hydraulic Truck Cranes[a] | | Hydraulic Excavators | |
	Small	Large	Small	Large	Small	Large	Small	Large	Old Design	New Design
Factory price	$49.6	$205.8	$77.8	$155.5	$66.0	$108.6	$43.6	$56.8	$81.5	$79.2
Mfg. cost	32.6	134.9	58.0	97.9	50.9	79.0	35.9	43.3	55.8	51.7
Gross margin	17.0	70.9	19.8	57.6	15.1	29.6	7.7	13.5	25.7	27.5
Gross margin as percentage of factory price	34.1	34.5	25.5	37.0	22.9	27.3	17.6	23.6	31.5	34.7

Manufacturing Costs as Percentage of Total Costs

Purchased Materials

	Small	Large	Small	Large	Small	Large	Small	Large	Old Design	New Design
Castings	27.6	27.4	11.1	9.4	0.7	3.1	4.1	4.5	11.0	17.8
Steel	10.1	13.4	3.7	9.5	4.6	7.8	6.7	8.1	8.4	9.0
Other:										
Purchased stores	12.9	14.4	11.8	33.4	19.2	22.7	55.8	52.2	34.9	25.9
Motor	11.5	7.6	6.5	12.7	—[b]	—[b]	2.4	6.0	8.9	9.6
Carrier truck	—	—	50.9	—[c]	60.1	51.6	—	—	—	—
Pipes & tubes	0.4	1.2	0.2	1.6	0.1	0.2	0.3	0.3	0.4	0.5
Subcontract	1.0	1.0	0.5	0.5	0.1	0.1	0.2	0.1	0.7	0.6
Total other	25.8	24.2	69.9	48.2	79.5	74.6	58.7	58.6	44.9	36.6
Total purchased	63.5	65.0	84.7	67.1	84.8	85.5	69.5	71.2	64.3	63.4
Heat treat	1.0	0.3	0.2	0.1	—	—	—	—	0.5	0.6
Direct labor	10.4	10.2	4.5	9.9	4.6	4.3	9.2	8.7	10.5	10.8
Burden (OH)	25.1	24.5	10.6	22.9	10.6	10.2	21.3	20.1	24.7	25.2
Total	100.0	100.0	100.0	100.0	100.0	100.0	100.0	100.0	100.0	100.0

[a] Self-propelled configuration of rubber-tired hydraulic truck crane.
[b] Motor include in cost of truck carrier.
[c] Truck carrier unit manufactured by C&E Division.

Boom fabrication for hydraulic cranes differed markedly from that of cable cranes/excavators. The hydraulic boom was usually a telescoping one with a rectangular cross section, and was made by C&E from welded plate steel. Most of the hydraulic hoses, pipes, and cylinders that activated the extension of the boom were housed inside the boom itself; lifting cylinders were attached on the outside near the base of the boom.

Labor Relations

Link-Belt had long been a major employer in Cedar Rapids, Iowa's second largest city (population 110,600 in 1970). Relations between the UAW and C&E management had been good for a number of years, and the division had not had a strike since 1970. However, the recently completed round of negotiations on the two-year contract had been tedious and difficult, primarily a result of the issue of incentive pay.

The incentive pay issue had become more important in recent years partly because the piecework rates had not been kept up to date, but primarily because the UAW felt that prior general increases should have been folded into the piecework standards. In early 1974 workers were averaging about 130 percent of standard, and it was clear the union preferred to keep the situation in its favor even though management considered it out of hand. In part because of economic conditions, neither management nor the union desired a strike in 1974 and the two parties settled their differences. Martin, however, surmised that a strike would be a distinct possibility in 1976 as management tried to readjust the standards to bring them into line with rates paid by other heavy equipment manufacturers.

Lexington Plant

Plans for the Lexington plant had been developed and approved in early 1972 when the division adopted its strategy to achieve high volume and penetration in the hydraulic crane market. Cedar Rapids had not been large enough to achieve these goals, and management believed that the manufacture of hydraulics required a different type of process. It was felt that hydraulic production involved more assembly of standard modules in a specific sequence than cables. It was also anticipated that unit volumes on hydraulic products would soon exceed cable unit volumes, making certain economies available through use of a more continuous flow process rather than a job-shop operation.

To achieve the volume of production anticipated for the line over the next five years, the Lexington plant had been intended to function much like an automotive assembly line, though at a relatively slow pace. The plant had a chain-like device installed in the floor to drag the pieces from work station to work station, rather than utilizing an overhead crane as was done at Cedar Rapids. All the control and material planning systems for this plant had been designed to match this new production process. (The company had been developing the systems and testing them by simulation on a computer for several months.) While control of costs had been given a top priority, the firm did not plan to become the low-cost producer, but hoped to continue its reliance on high-quality design and production for its competitive advantage.

The Lexington plant had been expected to cost $14 million, and the pay-back period had been estimated at 6.2 years for invested capital. When requirements for increased working capital ($20 million) were included, the pay-back had been estimated at 10.1 years. The division had predicted a positive cash flow by 1976 and profitable operations by 1977.

Expansion Alternatives

Each of the three alternatives examined by Martin had advantages and disadvantages. The economic projections for each, based on the same market forecasts (see *Exhibit 6*), had been carefully drawn up following the corporate guidelines for Authorizations for Expenditure (AFE). Martin summarized the major pros and cons of each alternative, including the financial results, from each AFE as described in the three alternatives below.

Alternative 1: Expand at Cedar Rapids Only

Martin felt that there were several advantages to expansion right in the division's own backyard. The company had plenty of room for expansion and already possessed a skilled and knowledgeable work force; training would therefore be easy. For another, the firm could use common inventories to a certain extent and attain other economies of scale for cable and hydraulic production. In addition, with the Lexington plant about to go into operation, Martin was concerned about the dilution of the Cedar Rapids management and the trauma of having to open two entirely new plants at the same time. If the expansion took place at Cedar Rapids, however, he was concerned that the problems of modernizing an old plant, and the effects of a possible strike in 1976, might overwhelm the advantages of this alternative.

This expansion would add 182,000 square feet to the Cedar Rapids facilities at an investment

EXHIBIT 6 Projected Manufacturing Space Requirements and Unit Sales[a]

Product Line

Year	Cable Crawlers			Cable Trucks			Hydraulic Excavators			Subtotal	Hydraulic Cranes		Total[b]
	Area	Units	Average Price ($000)	Area	Units	Average Price ($000)	Area	Units	Average Price ($000)		Area	Units	
1973	319,000	388	97.6	205,000	294	100.0	32,000	337	44.2	556,000	48,000	205	604,000
1974	324,000	456	97.1	207,000	314	103.9	32,000	173[c]	47.1	563,000	64,000	244	627,000
1975	375,000	533	96.3	259,000	403	108.1	84,000	259	52.6	718,000	121,000	293	839,000
1976	473,000	619	93.2	306,000	446	113.6	166,000	532	56.0	945,000	156,000	350	1,101,000
1977	466,000	557[d]	118.6	301,000	450	120.5	217,000	714	58.3	984,000	179,000	458	1,163,000
1978	452,000	519	132.4	302,000	429	131.2	247,000	837	61.8	1,001,000	208,000	600	1,209,000
1980	485,000	488	171.7	327,000	440	151.8	319,000	999	69.2	1,131,000	263,000	866	1,394,000

[a] Space requirements (in square feet) for designs not in production were estimated. A computer model was used to calculate floor space using unit sales forecasts.

[b] Present space available in Cedar Rapids is 658,000 square feet. Lexington is scheduled to come on line in 1974–76 and will have excess space until 1978–80.

[c] Sales decline anticipated because of withdrawing old design and introducing new one.

[d] Unit sales decline but dollar sales increase, because the expectation was for the sale of larger units.

9. FMC, Crane and Excavator Division

cost of $9.4 million. The AFE calculations indicated that this option would have a paycheck period of 7.4 years and an internal rate of return of 13 percent.

Alternative 2: Limited Cedar Rapids Expansion Plus a New Hydraulic Excavator Plant in Bowling Green, Kentucky

This possibility intrigued Martin since building a plant in Bowling Green, Kentucky—whether small or large—had several factors in its favor. First, it was close to market and service centers. Second, good quality labor was readily available in the area at a reasonable price: the average wage rate was anticipated at $3.84 per hour against $5.34 per hour in Cedar Rapids.[1] Third, Bowling Green provided excellent educational facilities. Fourth, several of the large employers in the area were not unionized and C&E might be able to maintain a nonunion status in such a plant. Fifth, it was estimated that freight costs would be approximately equal to those of Cedar Rapids (less that one percent of manufacturing cost).

The plan to produce the redesigned and soon-to-be-completed hydraulic excavator line in Bowling Green would allow both cable lines to remain in Cedar Rapids where there would be ample capacity with the shift of the hydraulic truck-mounted line to Lexington. C&E management felt there were also certain advantages to having a new product with a new production process in its own new plant; the same idea had been touted for the Lexington plant. This alternative would also allow some capacity at Cedar Rapids for backward integration into hydraulic component production, with the possibility of moving it all to Kentucky to feed both plants at a later date.

A negative consideration was that hydraulic excavators represented a line largely in the design and development stage. A premature move to a facility dedicated entirely to an experimental venture could compound the problems and risks involved.

Building a 249,000-square-foot-plant at Bowling Green for the manufacture of hydraulic excavators would require $16.7 million capital

outlay. AFE calculations indicated that this alternative would have a payback of 6.6 years and an internal rate of return of 15.2 percent.

Alternative 3: Build a Plant at Bowling Green and Move the Cable Truck Crane Line to the Same Location

The proposal to build a cable truck crane plant at Bowling Green featured all the positive points described above for the hydraulic excavator Bowling Green plant but added a new wrinkle. Martin felt that with the Lexington plant about to come on-stream, the division should be careful about setting up a second completely new plant. In his opinion, producing cable truck cranes in Bowling Green would help mitigate the trauma often associated with beginning operations at a new plant. In the first place, the cable truck line was a relatively stable product (from an engineering standpoint), the company had years of experience with it, and as a result of its stage of development it would require a lower level of over-all work-force training. Second, since the line was the division's most profitable one (37 percent gross margin on the average), there was plenty of room to absorb additional costs and a quick payback was possible. Third, the plan would allow the company to gradually train more of its Cedar Rapids work force in hydraulic assembly techniques and would require minimal investment to automate its current hydraulic production to an acceptable level. Fourth, it would minimize the over-all effect of a strike should one occur in 1976. Fifth, it would allow time for the newly redesigned line of hydraulic excavators to prove itself before the company had to bet an entire new plant on it.

In order to have adequate space to manufacture the division's truck-mounted cable cranes at Bowling Green, construction of a 331,000-square-foot-facility with a total capital outlay of $16.3 million would be required. AFE calculations indicated a 7.1 year payback period and a 14.0 percent internal rate of return for this option.

Other Considerations

Martin realized that staffing was one of the largest problems C&E or any company faced when it

---

[1]These rates did not include piecework incentives which raised the effective hourly rate in Cedar Rapids to approximately $7.

planned a major expansion. Getting people to move from Cedar Rapids would be difficult in his opinion. In addition, he had some misgivings about spreading his management personnel too thin.

> We are a little thin in management here; our bench isn't very deep. We have a lot of "doers" here—people who really know how to work and work well; but many are over forty-five years old. We really don't know what problems we are going to get into trying to get people to move, not only to the Lexington plant, but to any other one we build. Most of the knowledge in this company is in its people, not in formal systems.

Several product considerations also had come to Martin's mind. He mused:

> One of the main arguments for moving hydraulic excavators to Bowling Green is simply to increase productivity and get costs in line with cost structures demanded by the marketplace. Some people here feel that you just can't do everything well if you try and do it all in one place. A logical solution seems to be to dedicate specific facilities to specific product lines, such as a new plant for hydraulic excavators to match the new one for hydraulic cranes.
> On the other hand, if we're going to move something out of Cedar Rapids, we would reduce our over-all level of risk by moving cable trucks rather than hydraulic excavators. We would be dealing with a reliable product with a good margin where we know the production process and have

a clean design. Furthermore, cable trucks in general are a less risky market for us for one simple reason: Caterpillar isn't in it, and Caterpillar is tougher than hell.

Martin knew that equally persuasive arguments had been made by some of his staff to keep all of the cable products in one spot, Cedar Rapids. For one thing, some had wondered whether production of hydraulics would really be much more expensive if kept in Cedar Rapids; Martin, too, had wondered how critical a single location was in the over-all cost of the division's products. For another, it just did not seem right to duplicate a lot of cable parts in two plants in different parts of the country. Finally, Martin was concerned with the possibility of a labor dispute, and whether that factor really was important in making a long-range strategic manufacturing decision:

> Maybe we should simply not worry about the possibility of a strike. Maybe we should do what John Deere did when faced with a similar incentive pay dispute in the late fifties. Deere didn't want to inflate the incentive and so therefore left it out. Deere took it on the nose and got hit with a four-month strike but won out and now has things 90 percent its own way. Besides, even if we move into new plants in Kentucky, what's to stop the union from organizing us down there with matching contract dates. It's a tough problem, let's face it.

9. FMC, Crane and Excavator Division

PART TWO

Strategies and Approaches

Module 2
Competing on Quality*

Quality has suddenly become a hot topic in management circles. The stimulus has frequently been Japanese competition, and the result has been a proliferation of programs and techniques. Today an impressive array of companies cite quality as their chief competitive priority.[1]

Surprisingly, many of these programs have been limited in impact. Few companies have achieved dramatic breakthroughs in performance. Lack of interest has not been the problem, not a lack of resources. Instead, most programs have foundered because of a lack of understanding. All too often, managers have failed to grasp three essentials of quality management: the meaning of quality; its measurement; and its sources in design, purchasing, and production.

Terminology is partly to blame. Quality is an unusually slippery concept, easy to visualize and yet exasperatingly difficult to define. Conflicting definitions are common. Some experts claim that quality is "fitness for use"; others insist that it means "conformance to requirements."[2] Faced with these conflicts, managers have often finessed the issue by saying, "I know it when I see it."[3] While such language offers room for maneuvering, it is of little help to those who must design, manufacture, and market products to exacting specifications.

Measurement has been equally problematic. Traditional quality control departments have normally confined themselves to tracking defect rates, scrap rates, and related measures of manufacturing conformance. These indexes provide a valuable guide to in-plant quality, but they say little or nothing about the quality of products that have reached customers' hands. Moreover, top managers have often found such measures difficult to interpret, because they have seldom been stated in financial terms. For their purposes, more comprehensive indexes are required.

Improvement programs have also suffered from managers' inability to pinpoint the sources of quality. In the absence of such knowledge, generalizations have been the rule. Unfortunately, the suggested behaviors—conservative engineering, demonstrating top management commitment, buying on quality rather than price, and building quality into designs—have seldom been very concrete. One result has been flawed implementation. Similar problems have plagued most attempts to mimic

*Excerpt from *Operations Strategy: Module Overview: Competing on Quality*, Harvard Business School Teaching Note 5-688-044. Copyright © 1987 by the President and Fellows of Harvard College.

Japanese approaches to quality management. Here again, obvious differences in behavior, such as the use of quality control circles, heavy reliance on robots and advanced technology, and placing responsibility for inspection in the hands of production workers, have masked the subtler distinctions in policies and philosophies that truly explain success or failure.

The aim of this module is to address these gaps in understanding. To do so, cases explore both the theory and practice of quality management, using American and Japanese examples. Most cases serve multiple purposes: They provide a precise vocabulary for talking about quality, a range of tools for measuring quality, and a description of the tasks necessary for improving quality. The module conveys a larger message as well, for it documents an important historical shift. At a number of American companies, quality is no longer a problem to be solved, but has become a source of competitive advantage, to be managed carefully by senior executives. This shift, from quality control to quality management, is more than simple semantics. As a report to the 1983 White House Conference on Productivity had observed, the operational implications are immense:

Managing the quality dimension of an organization is not generically different from any other aspect of management. It involves the formulation of strategies, setting goals and objectives, developing action plans, implementing plans, and using control systems for monitoring feedback and taking corrective action. If quality is viewed only as a control system, it will never be substantially improved. Quality is not just a control system; quality is a management function.[4]

Major Themes

This module is built around five major themes. They range from such basic questions as how quality should be defined to broader issues touching on global strategy and competitive positioning.

DEFINING QUALITY

The first task faced by managers wishing to improve quality is often the hardest: deciding what they mean by the term. Three alternatives are explored in the module. The first defines quality as conformance to requirements. According to this view, high quality is synonymous with meeting specifications, and the only acceptable standard is error-free work. Manufacturing experts frequently take this approach, for it is closely linked to their focus on defect and scrap rates. It figures prominently in the American Foods and Sanyo cases, and also in the writings of Deming and Crosby.

A second definition equates quality with fitness for use. This approach is more user-oriented, and has more of an appeal to marketing experts. Stripped to the essentials, it boils down to the claim that quality lies in the eyes of the beholder. By implication, there are few universal standards. Different users have different needs, and to the extent that a product or service meets those needs, it is deemed to be of high quality. In the Steinway case, such reasoning leads students to distinguish between two groups of piano buyers: performing artists, who are able to detect subtle differences in a piano's tone and feel and evaluate instruments on that basis, and less sophisticated consumers, whose judgments of piano quality are based primarily on reputation, recommendations, and appearance. The Neiman-Marcus case segregates buyers in much the same way.

A third approach to quality tackles the definitional problem by breaking it into pieces. Instead of treating quality as a single, uniform concept, it divides the term into eight dimensions or elements: performance, features, reliability, conformance, durability, serviceability, aesthetics, and perceived quality.[5] Each of these dimensions is self-contained and distinct, and each provides an independent basis for ranking products and services. Thus, in some markets consumers equate quality with superior performance, while in others they base their ratings on reliability and up-time. A more precise vocabulary allows students to recognize these differences and see that there is no single route to superior quality. It also highlights a critical distinction between Japanese and American approaches to quality management. Japanese firms have traditionally focused on reliability, conformance, and aesthetics, while American firms have targeted performance and features. Several cases explore this theme, including Steinway, Sanyo, and Quality on the Line.

MEASURING QUALITY

Because quality is so difficult to define, measurement has long been a problem. At many companies, defect and scrap rates remain the only indexes employed. In this module, a number of more comprehensive measures are explored. They can be grouped into three general categories: manufacturing measures, financial measures, and customer measures.

Manufacturing measures are the most traditional. The commonest examples are defect rates, which tally up the proportion of parts, subassemblies, or finished products that fail to meet specifications, and scrap rates, which measure the proportion of parts and materials that have been so damaged by shipment, fabrication, or assembly that rework is impossible or uneconomical. Such measures are discussed in both Sanyo and Quality on the Line.

Manufacturing measures, however, are not always this conventional. Broader indexes can be developed to track additional aspects of manufacturing quality. Such measures might, for example, capture the impact of incoming materials on processing times and test procedures, or aspects of service, such as how frequently raw materials arrived in the promised quantities and on schedule, that rarely appear in simple defect counts. Several of these innovative approaches are discussed in the American Foods case.

A second group of quality measures is financially oriented. Such measures quantify the costs of poor quality and the benefits of improvement. Both Juran and Crosby, for example, argue that the costs of quality should be computed and then carefully communicated to senior managers, in order to secure their interest and commitment. They define quality costs as any expenditures on manufacturing or service in excess of those that would have been incurred if the product had been built or the service had been performed exactly right the first time. These costs are usually divided into four categories: prevention costs, appraisal costs, internal failure costs, and external failure costs. Prevention costs include expenditures on supplier education, training, and other efforts to keep mistakes from happening in the first place; appraisal costs include expenditures on inspection, testing, and other activities to ferret out mistakes once they have occurred; internal failure costs include expenditures on rework, scrap, and other errors found within the factory; and external failure costs include expenditures on warranty claims, product liability suits, and other problems that arise after a product has reached the customer.[6]

Typically, these measures serve two purposes: They demonstrate that quality problems are more serious than managers first assumed, and they provide a rationale for increased spending on prevention. Managers are often surprised by their companies' costs of quality. Frequently, they are as high as 10 to 20 percent of sales. The largest proportion of these costs is usually due to internal and external failures. And because prevention is normally cheaper, on a per unit basis, than correcting failures after the fact, both Juran and Crosby maintain that a company's total costs of quality will fall as it devotes more resources to prevention. (The two experts differ, however, on whether this is always true or whether, at some low level of defects, spending on prevention becomes uneconomical because of diminishing returns.)

A third group of quality measures is customer-oriented. Such measures are more outward-looking than manufacturing or financial measures, and more closely tied to strategic quality management. Because they define quality from the customer's point of view, they suggest that quality improvements can be linked directly to higher margins and gains in market share. Not surprisingly, customer measures require a broader framework than either manufacturing or financial measures. Quality is no longer confined to defect rates or manufacturing conformance, but expands to include reliability, durability, aesthetics, and the other dimensions of quality. Moreover, in this approach customers are not limited to the buyers and final consumers of a product or service, but also include internal customers (i.e., any department or functional group that receives products, parts, or services from others within the company).

Customer-related measures take a variety of forms. Some, such as consumer satisfaction surveys and service call rates, are quite conventional; others, such as intracompany ratings of departmental performance and estimates of product obsolescence, are innovative and comparatively rare. These and other customer measures are discussed in several cases, including American Foods, Neiman-Marcus, Steinway, A Note on Quality, and Quality on the Line.

THE SOURCES OF QUALITY

There is no secret to superior quality, no magical formula awaiting discovery. The building blocks are common knowledge, and have been for years. They include such basics as top management commitment, detailed quality information, close links between R&D and manufacturing departments, careful selection and monitoring of vendors, work force training, and tools such as statistical quality control.

Implementation has often been flawed, however, because of a failure to link these building blocks with day-to-day events. It is one thing for managers to profess a commitment to improving quality or to pursue new methods by taking courses on statistical quality control; quite another thing for them to communicate their commitment or to manage with statistical methods over time. Frequently, the difference between successful and unsuccessful quality programs has been the management of these daily details, rather than underlying principles or philosophies.

Every class in the module examines the sources of quality from some vantage point. In some cases the focus is on companies like Steinway that have long had superior quality; in others the focus is on companies like Sanyo and American Foods that have recently upgraded their operations. Cases differ in the degree to which they emphasize particular tools or approaches. American Foods focuses on data collection and quality information systems; Steinway focuses on raw material selection, craft skills, and product testing; Sanyo focuses on supplier management, design for manufacturability, and top management commitment; and Neiman-Marcus focuses on customer contact, buyer behavior, and a responsive sales force. In every case, however, the sources of quality are explored at the micro-level and in fine detail, in order to identify the specific practices that support successful programs.

JAPANESE QUALITY MANAGEMENT

Surprisingly, a great mythology still surrounds Japanese manufacturers, despite the publicity they have received. Few analysts question the Japanese success in global markets or their superior product quality. The source of that superiority, however, remains a subject of heated debate. Is the explanation culture and national character? A distinctive manufacturing philosophy? A particular set of design, purchasing, and production practices? Or have the Japanese succeeded simply because they adopted long-established American quality control techniques that U.S. firms ignored?

There are partisans in each camp. And in fact, all four views contain elements of truth. Japanese culture is indeed distinctive; so is the Japanese approach to manufacturing. Morever, Japanese managers have frequently pursued continuous improvement and enforced "quality first" philosophies with a dedication unmatched by managers in other countries. A variety of innovative practices have also been used, including foolproofing to prevent assembly errors, early warning systems to distinguish routine quality problems from emergencies, and internal consumer review boards to ensure that new designs are sensitive to the consumer's point of view.[7] Yet at the same time, such fundamentals of Japanese quality management as process control charts and reliability engineering have clear American roots.

Several cases explore the sources of Japan's superior quality and the possible explanations for it. The issue first arises in the Steinway case, where Yamaha and Kawai, two Japanese manufacturers, have begun to cut into Steinway's market by offering high quality pianos at much lower prices. How have they managed to do so? In Sanyo, the issue is a bit different. Sanyo has managed to cut defect rates substantially at the color television factory it recently purchased from an American manufacturer, while keeping the work force virtually intact. What, if anything, was Japanese about its approach? Which steps were innovative, and which were simply sound manufacturing practices that had been ignored by prior managers? Quality on the Line completes the Japanese story by reviewing a range of design, purchasing, and production practices that have contributed to superior Japanese quality in a single industry, room air conditioning.

STRATEGIC QUALITY MANAGEMENT

In recent years, countless American companies have sought to upgrade their quality, adopting such traditional methods as statistical quality control, cost of quality calculations, and zero defects. Few, however, have learned to *compete* on quality. For the most part, their approaches have been defensive and reactive. Quality has remained a problem to be solved, and success has been measured by the absence of defects or product failures.

Such approaches are quite different from the strategic quality management practiced by Japanese manufacturers and a small number of leading U.S. firms. To them, quality is an opportunity to please customers, not simply the avoidance of problems. Quality improvement is therefore linked to basic business objectives, rather than being pursued in a vacuum. This approach, which goes by the name of company-wide quality control or strategic quality management, has five basic tenets: (1) quality is defined from the customer's point of view, (2) quality is linked with profitability on both the market and cost sides, (3) quality is viewed as a competitive weapon, (4) quality is built into the strategic planning process, and (5) quality requires an organization-wide commitment.

Strategic quality management thus involves a sharp change in philosophy, a shift from the traditional production and cost-based view of quality to a marketing and customer-based view. It is also more comprehensive than its predecessors, which assigned responsibility for quality to engineering and manufacturing personnel. In the strategic approach, the entire organization—all levels and all functional groups—is active in quality improvement. Senior managers provide the leadership and are personally involved in program design and implementation. These distinctions between strategic quality management and its predecessors, quality control and quality assurance, are discussed in the final two classes of the module. They provide a fitting conclusion to the unit, for they show how far quality management has come in the sixty years that it has been a distinct discipline.

NOTES

1. See, for example, Jeffrey Miller, Jinchiro Nakane, and Thomas Vollman, *The 1983 Global Manufacturing Futures Survey: Summary of Survey Responses & Preliminary Report* (Boston: School of Management, Boston University, April 1983), pp. 7–8, and Kasra Ferdows *et al*, *Evolving Manufacturing Strategies in Europe, Japan, and North America* (Fontainebleau, France: INSEAD, 1985), pp. 2–4, 9.

2. The first definition is Joseph Juran's; the second is Philip Crosby's. See, respectively, J.M. Juran, *Quality Control Handbook*, Third Edition (New York: McGraw-Hill, 1974), pp. 2–2—2–11, and Philip B. Crosby, *Quality Is Free* (New York: New American Library, 1979), pp. 14–15.

3. For a splendid discussion of the pitfalls of this approach, see John Guaspari, *I Know It When I See It* (New York: AMACOM, 1985).

4. *Final Report of the American Productivity Center Conference on Quality and Productivity* (Washington, D.C.: September 22–23, 1983, mimeographed), p. 10.

5. For more on the dimensions of quality, see David A. Garvin, "Product Quality: An Important Strategic Weapon," *Business Horizons*, March/April 1984, pp. 40–43; David A. Garvin, "What Does 'Product Quality' Really Mean?," *Sloan Management Review*, Fall 1984, pp 25–43; David A. Garvin, "Competing on the Eight Dimensions of Quality," *Harvard Busines Review*, November–December 1987, pp. 101–109; and David A. Garvin, *Managing Quality* (New York: Free Press, 1987), ch. 4.

6. See Jack Campanella and Frank J. Corcoran, "Principles of Quality Costs," *Quality Progress*, April 1983, pp. 16–22, for a more detailed discussion of quality costs.

7. For descriptions of a number of these practices, see David A. Garvin, "Japanese Quality Management," *Columbia Journal of World Business*, Fall 1984, pp. 3–12, and Richard J. Schonberger, *Japanese Manufacturing Techniques* (New York: Free Press, 1982), ch. 3.

10. American Food and Grains: Commodity and Ingredient Procurement

On the afternoon of December 27, 1983, Leah King, director of Commodity and Ingredient Procurement for the Consumer Foods Group of the American Food and Grains Company, was planning a meeting with her boss, Stuart Erikson, vice president for Procurement. The two had been moving the department in new directions for some time, and three of their quality initiatives had reached critical stages. The vendor analysis program, for example, had hit a temporary roadblock. Procurement had begun formally evaluating its vendors nearly a year ago, but so far had been unable to involve American's own plants. Its survey of buyer team performance, on the other hand, had received 100% response from plant personnel. But King had done nothing with the data yet, because she still had not decided how to interpret and use the results. Finally, King and her colleagues were considering accepting the quality tests provided by American's top-rated vendors rather than performing the tests in-house.

In addition to these initiatives, King was wrestling with the problem of a sole-source supplier whose performance had deteriorated badly.

King thought that the price of continuing to do business with this company had become too high, but recognized that severing the relationship immediately entailed considerable risk. Yet wouldn't allowing the problems to continue undermine Procurement's other quality efforts?

The American Food and Grains Company

American Food and Grains was founded in 1869 as a flour milling company. In the 1950s, the company expanded into flour-based products such as dry cake and cookie mixes. It diversified next into refrigerated and frozen foods for the consumer market; bulk mixes sold to organizations such as schools, prisons and hospitals as well as to wholesale bakeries; and restaurant chains.

American's businesses were organized into three major groups: Consumer Foods, Agricultural Foods, and Restaurants. (See *Exhibit 1.*) Consumer Foods consisted of three major businesses: Dry (or grocery), Frozen and Refrigerated. These were distinguished by the technologies involved in preparing and packaging the food. Dry, for example, encompassed anything that could go in a truck without temperature controls. Each Consumer Foods group had profit and loss responsibility for its own products, as did the general managers of constituent business units.

Between 1980 and 1983, Consumer Foods

This case was prepared by Artemis March, under the direction of David A. Garvin.

Copyright © 1985 by the President and Fellows of Harvard College. Harvard Business School case 685-095.

EXHIBIT 1 Partial Organizational Chart, December 1983

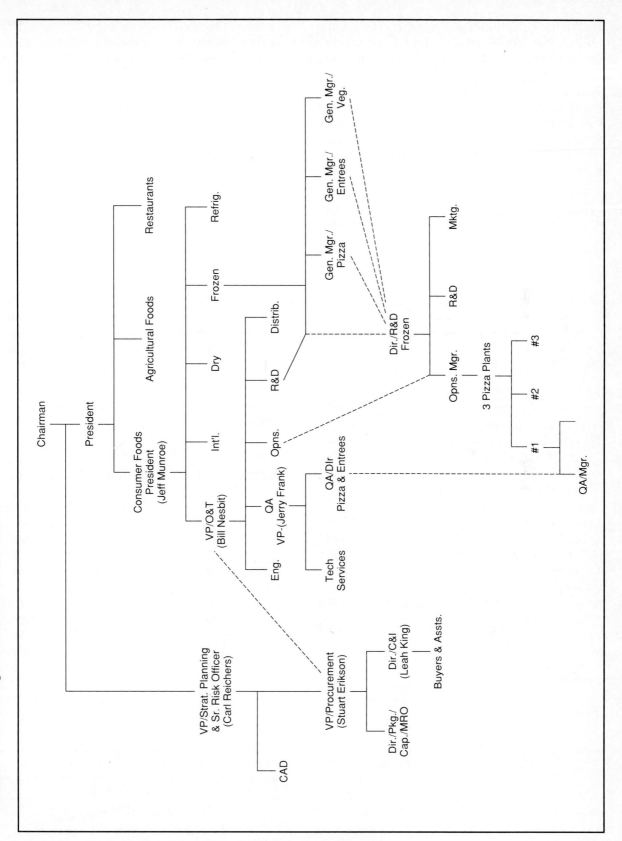

contributed about half of American's sales dollars and profits. (See *Exhibit 2*.) Total company sales for fiscal 1983 (June 1, 1982–May 31, 1983) were over $3 billion, marking the twelfth consecutive year of increases in net sales, net income and dividends. Top management showed its pride in this accomplishment by leading off reports and speeches to stockholders, as well as its annual report, with this information. American's commitment to earnings was also reflected in its executive compensation plans, which were tied to various measures of financial performance.

If financial growth was American's key measure of performance, the bedrock of corporate culture was food safety. Company managers generally believed that American Foods had "written the book" on the subject in the 1960s. Primary responsibility for seeing that materials complied with food safety standards rested with Quality Assurance (QA).

EXHIBIT 2 Selected Financial Data, 1980–1983

	FY 83	FY 82	FY 81	FY 80
	(in millions)			
Net Sales				
Consumer Foods	$1,652.1	$1,635.7	$1,599.8	$1,490.5
Agricultural Foods	627.5	568.6	586.8	544.2
Restaurants	1,494.6	1,279.3	1,207.2	1,080.5
(Less Intersegment Sales)	(88.3)	(98.5)	(92.1)	(83.2)
Total	3,685.9	3,385.1	3,301.7	3,032.0
Operating Profit (= PBIT)				
Consumer Foods	139.4	134.8	127.8	88.2
Agricultural Foods	16.4	28.6	47.7	71.8
Restaurants	135.3	116.3	108.3	99.3
Total	291.1	279.7	283.8	259.3
Net Earnings	138.9	136.3	119.6	104.7
Earnings Per Share	$ 3.20	$ 3.14	$ 2.98	$ 2.61

Source: Company annual reports.

Quality at American Food and Grains

More recently, the company had been emphasizing a broader concept of quality. Quality of "people, products, and performance" was becoming something of a corporate campaign, stimulated in part by the best-selling book *In Search of Excellence,* which pinpointed an obsession with quality and service as one of eight principles of excellent management. The book served as the focal point for an off-site meeting of American Foods top management in February 1982, and led to further discussion about quality. Jeff Munroe, then president of Consumer Foods (he would become president of the company a year later), took the lead in articulating American's position on the subject through a follow-up memo in which he stated, "We need to make product quality a fetish." Discussion of the subject rippled throughout the company.

Even before the February meeting, Jerry Frank, vice president for Quality Assurance, and his staff had developed a quality awareness program that included audiovisual materials, posters, and brochures, along with an informal structure that any plant could use. Frank observed, "Ultimately, it is the consumer who determines quality. It's our job to translate the consumer's views into physical tests that can be measured and monitored."

One of Frank's directors observed how QA had changed during his career at American Foods:

> Twenty-four years ago, we were policemen; it was a no-thanks job. Fourteen years ago, when I came up to Des Moines, quality was an idea, but it's only gotten teeth in the last three years. You have to have top management support—people like Jeff Munroe and Bill Nesbit—to make an impact. We're not pushing quality because we've been told to, but because we believe in it.

Erikson and King had been preoccupied with quality since they joined the company. Erikson commented on what quality meant to him:

> Quality is more than specs, it's more than the materials that go into a product—it's the whole package we get from a vendor. It includes on-time delivery, and flexibility—can they get something to us on three days' notice if need be? It means that when something of less than perfect quality comes in, we can sit down and talk to one another and not get mad; it means responsiveness.

Procurement at American Food and Grains

Since 1981, procurement at American Foods had embraced five areas: commodities, ingredients, capital goods, packaging and MRO (maintenance, repairs and operating parts). Leah King's buyers and buyer assistants were in charge of the first two areas, which King referred to as "anything you can chew." Commodities were "major chews," meaning that they were traded on commodity exchanges in Chicago or New York, that buy-and-sell positions involved considerable risk, and that American Foods spent tens of millions of dollars on them annually. Major commodities included flour, sugar, meat, edible oils, cheese, cocoa and eggs; total yearly volume for these purchases was a quarter of a billion dollars. Ingredients were "minor chews." Their prices were less volatile and involved less risk, and their dollar volume was lower than that for commodities. Ingredients included nuts, fruits, spices, flavor, yeast and salt; their dollar volume was over $100 million. At the end of 1983, King had 14 people—7 teams of two each—specializing in these areas. Commodities and Ingredients (C&I) bought raw materials for all consumer products; 90% of its buying was on behalf of the business units in Consumer Foods, while the rest was nonflour ingredients for Bakery Mix.

Buying commodities at American Foods involved two distinct sets of activities. One was hedging in the commodities markets—buying and selling futures contracts on the commodities exchanges. Buyers' work as traders was supported by research on primary agricultural commodities done by the Commodity Analysis Department (CAD). Buyer recommendations were aimed at helping business units manage their (profit) margins. This involved both market savvy and knowledge of the business for which the commodities were being bought. As King put it:

> We blend business decisions with market [trading] decisions. We help the business unit managers manage their margins, which means giving them the lowest *predictable* cost. You don't surprise them with these costs because their margins are driven by the price of raw materials.

Technically, once American Foods bought a commodities contract it owned the goods at the stated price. Most contracts, however, were paper transactions, sold without ever taking physical possession. What hedging provided was an opportunity to reduce the risk of significant price changes and, if possible, to earn additional revenue from trading. American Foods prided itself on maintaining an excellent balance of business and market opportunity; King claimed, "We take more risk and do a better job with markets than most other food companies that we know of."

The second part of a buyer's job involved working with the suppliers who provided the materials American Foods plants actually used. A critical task was negotiating and then "locking in" the refining margin—what the supplier charged to process the raw materials for American Foods. Hedging and buying from vendors intersected only in this way: when American needed a commodity such as refined oil, the oil buyer called the Chicago Board of Trade, and asked that it turn over one or two contracts to a particular oil refiner, who then took physical possession of the oil. The gain or loss on the contract was applied to American's account (specifically, the account of the business unit for which it had been bought), and was separate from the refining margin paid to the vendor.

Negotiations with vendors took place in the broader context of developing long-term relationships with suppliers, being responsive to the plants' needs, and developing purchasing strategies that fit with each business unit's strategy and market positions. King commented on the difficulty of finding people who could master this range of activities: "We need people who can follow up on a truck delivery and who can develop hedging strategies; it's hard to get both in one person."

PROCUREMENT BEFORE 1972. Such across-the-board skills had not always been sought. Before 1972, purchasing's mission had been to get the best price for purchased materials and not to let a plant shut down because of a missing ingredient. Quality was left to QA. The price orientation of purchasing often drove it to short-run, adversarial relationships with vendors in which each party was trying to outdo the other in getting a deal. During this period, commodity prices were stable and shortages were few; a buyer could quote a price a year ahead and still be close to the mark. Commodity charting and analysis were virtually unheard of. In this environment, one manager observed, buyers were people who "would not have made it in other parts of the organization."

PROCUREMENT, 1974–1978. Things changed dramatically between 1972 and 1974. Poor world crops, the oil crisis, soaring interest rates, and a new Soviet willingness to buy huge U.S. grain surpluses altered the rules of the game. It became evident that purchasing involved risk, and that if not well managed, could hurt the company badly. Senior management asked, "Who's managing risk?" and, finding the answer was "no one," hired Carl Reichers, an economist, as senior risk officer. Between 1974 and 1978, Procurement was run as a corporate function reporting to Reichers; he, in turn, reported directly to the chairman.

Reichers quickly added a Commodity Analysis Department to analyze and predict market trends. To build the department further, Reichers began looking for "intellectual horsepower" as well as people who understood the market. In January 1978, Leah King was hired as the buyer for meat and cocoa. She was the first of a new breed of buyers with a commodities or trading background. (King had previously traded for a major grain trading company.) Although Reichers was looking for people with master's degrees in agricultural economics, King convinced him to hire her on the basis of her market knowledge, her relative cheapness, and her (self-attributed) aggressiveness.

Reichers was regarded by many as technically brilliant. His focus on risk management was reinforced by daily meetings at which his buyers were asked, "What is your position?" In a world in which cocoa prices jumped 500% between 1978 and 1980, the concern was to limit the company's exposure to extreme price volatility.

PROCUREMENT, 1978–1983. The change from Procurement's low cost and risk management orientations to a broader focus on supplier relationships, quality, and total value was associated with the arrival of Stuart Erikson in July 1978. According to one manager:

> When Erikson arrived, he became the champion of quality, redirecting purchasing to include

the whole value package. He is known for his motto: "The true cost is never equal to the stated price." Today, Procurement doesn't always buy from the lowest [stated] cost vendor.

Reichers had searched for 18 months for a director of the new, combined Commodities and Ingredients Department before hiring Erikson. Erikson had worked in commodity analysis and in purchasing after completing his MBA at Harvard. Previously, he had worked at an advertising agency for two years, and as a marketing assistant at another food giant.

Erikson outlined his personal philosophy and how it affected his approach to procurement and vendors:

> Vendors are really nice people. You don't have to believe you're always paying them more than you have to. Before, the attitude was that when you go for a deal, you don't trust anyone. But you have to start trusting your suppliers more, and trying to get them on your side. The buyers saw that it was okay to do this, and they got excited about developing long-term relationships. We believed that building these relationships would affect quality over the long run.

Carl Reichers didn't always agree. There were times when he felt that Erikson was getting "too close to the suppliers and buyers." But the buyers and managers from other departments felt differently. They commented on the increased professionalism of the department, the quality of its people, its orientation to total value rather than to price alone, and the greater confidence it engendered.

Erikson cultivated relationships not only with vendors and buyers, but also with marketing and R&D. Procurement had previously known little about new products until very late in the development process, and so had little say in the initial selection of vendors. As marketing began to share its information earlier, Procurement could better anticipate what was coming, and became more involved in the choice of suppliers.

Procurement also began forging links with R&D through monthly "R&D updates" provided by vendor liaison Tom Hill. Hill was housed with R&D, funded by QA, and worked closely with both departments as well as Procurement. For the updates, he gathered information from R&D section heads on the 65–75 funded projects and then

presented a status report on each as well as a description of new products and issues. Hill even got formulas from R&D, blocking out percentages where that made scientists more comfortable, and gave them to purchasing.

R&D, too, benefited from Procurement's earlier involvement. It could estimate costs for new products more accurately, and avoid embarrassments like the one it had suffered when the volume of American's buttermilk purchases for a "super pancake" had upset a delicate market balance, driving prices out of sight.

Bill Nesbit, corporate vice president for R&D, took information sharing a step further by proposing sharing with suppliers as well as with buyers. Hill described his own work in this area by saying, "Suppliers have to know what we are doing. I'll write a secrecy agreement rather than withhold information."

THE VANWYCK ACQUISITION. In March 1979, American Foods acquired VanWyck, a packer of frozen and canned vegetables. The purchase resulted in a companywide reorganization. Top management was strongly split about what to do with the purchasing department. Some executives wanted procurement to report to the business units. Reichers, however, believed purchasing should remain with corporate, so that the company's total risk could be known.

The result was a compromise. In June 1979, purchasing was split into two departments on the basis of price volatility. Corporate Procurement was made responsible for major commodities, where risk management was central. Erikson chose to stay with this group. Consumer Procurement, now including MRO and capital buying as well as ingredients and packaging, reported to the new head of marketing. Buyers who had been with VanWyck were in this second group. The organizational split sharpened the distinction—and tension—between those commodity buyers who took risks in volatile areas and those who did not.

Relations remained strained until June 1981, when the two departments were merged. At that time, everything that touched the flow of the product—R&D, engineering, manufacturing, quality assurance, product safety, and distribution—was put under a new Office of Operations and Technology, headed by Bill Nesbit. Erikson was made vice president, procurement, still reporting directly to Reichers, but now with a dotted line responsibility to Nesbit. A year later, Leah King took up Erikson's old position as director of C&I.

EVALUATION OF PROCUREMENT STAFF. The evolution of procurement was also reflected in how the department, and particularly its buyers, were evaluated. A monthly "report card" summarized how the department had performed relative to plan and relative to the markets, comparing trading results with what the department would have paid if it bought only on the spot market as materials were needed. The report card was broken down by business unit, and showed comparisons for each major commodity used by the unit. The director of C&I was also evaluated on how well she had performed relative to market, and on her subjective impact upon the company. In Reichers' view, the latter was a direct reflection of the former. In Erikson's view, the latter also included people development and the quality initiatives introduced by King.

Individual buyers were also rated on their performance in the markets. They could earn bonuses up to 20% of their base salary with favorable market performance. They were not penalized, however, if they did less well than the markets, because Erikson and King were also pushing them on their handling of suppliers and plant issues and other nonmarket performance measures.

Procurement's Relationships with Other Groups

Procurement interacted with four major groups: R&D, QA, the business units and vendors. Under Erikson and then King, the quality of these relationships had changed, and was continuing to evolve.

R&D

R&D worked for the business units. Its role was to keep the businesses strong; this meant maintaining volume, since unit managers were under pressure for short-term PBIT results. As a practical matter, this translated into programs for line extensions and product proliferation, profit-improvement projects (PIPs), and quality maintenance. R&D also saw itself as having a second mission: identifying opportunities for "real growth." Such opportunities, as one of its directors put it, "will be risky, require investment, and are not always easy to sell." He estimated that about 60% of R&D resources went into maintaining existing businesses, and 40% into innovations that could generate new businesses.

All 450 engineers, scientists and technicians in R&D were housed in a single laboratory about a mile from American's Des Moines headquarters. Project assignments were decided upon through meetings of the business units and R&D directors, who together identified opportunities, established priorities and set timetables.

New products usually involved working closely with a supplier who was handpicked by R&D scientists. If and when the product went into volume production, the supplier usually got a good share of the new business. However, most of R&D's work with suppliers depended less on their expertise in developing new ingredients than on the selection of ingredients they already had available.

American Foods scientists knew vendors primarily through the vendors' scientists, and secondarily through sales and technical representatives. They tended to choose vendors with whom they had had satisfying research experiences in the past. R&D had little way of knowing how a vendor performed in nontechnical areas—whether its product passed quality tests at the plants, whether deliveries were on time, and whether the product worked well on the line. Buyers, on the other hand, received complaints from the plants about just such issues, and might or might not be aware of the work the vendor had put into developing the new product. From his vantage point as vendor liaison, Tom Hill believed R&D was now getting information from Procurement far earlier and that cooperation was much better than it had been.

Hill was formally responsible for furthering contact between vendors and R&D. When a sales or technical representative was coming to American Foods, Hill posted an announcement so that interested R&D people could sign up for a meeting. He received and responded to countless phone calls from scientists along the lines of, "I need a starch that will do thus and so; whom should I talk to?"

Hill also coordinated all supplier and alternate supplier approvals. To be on the approved list, a vendor first had to meet American's specifications, and to have passed a QA inspection of its plants. Procurement, which made up the list, normally wanted alternative sources approved, but this competed for R&D and QA time and resources.

R&D worked closely with QA. Their mutual dependence was described by one R&D manager:

> It's very close, it has to be. QA relies heavily on our output for products and specs, and they need specs to operate. QA Tech Services works closely with our development teams and I work closely with the QA directors because so much of what we do affects quality.

Quality Assurance

QA was responsible for a number of activities. QA's Technical Services group coordinated the writing of specifications, inspected vendor plants, audited American's plants, had charge of materials compliance, and had budget responsibility for vendor liaison. Plant QA teams had day-to-day responsibility for the quality of product produced, while plant QA managers were responsible for examining raw materials, in-process and finished goods, maintaining sanitation, and leadership on food safety.

When members of the procurement group referred to "the plants," they almost always meant the plant QA people—typically a manager, several supervisors, and a number of technicians who performed the actual tests. Each buying team had contact with 10 to 20 plants, and dealt with them nearly every day, mostly by phone. Few buyers, however, had visited the plants. Buyer assistants generally talked with the "ordering people," or requisitioners (who reported to production control), when ordering and expediting materials; they talked with QA managers or supervisors about problems with materials once they had arrived at the plants. Whatever the buyer assistants couldn't handle was passed on to the buyers; this meant that when a buyer and a QA manager talked, the problem was already serious.

Procurement tried to tailor its buying strategies to the risk profile and market position of each business. Although the businesses preferred their ingredients to be purchased at less than market prices, it was equally, and sometimes more, important that those prices be predictable; otherwise, planned profit margins could disappear. They also looked for good forecasting that kept them on top of trends that could affect future prices.

Complaints at the plants ranged from broken or dirty boxes to food safety problems. QA filled out a complaint form for each; copies went to the buyer, QA/Tech Services, QA/headquarters, inventory and the plant QA manager. Whom QA called was more variable. According to one supervisor:

> I do different things depending on the situation, but I have three options. I can call Tech Services, the buyer, or talk to the vendor directly.

In the event of a quality problem, King expected her buyers to act as neutral liaisons between the vendor and plant QA. She felt in these circumstances the best thing that one could say about her people was, "You can never tell whom the buyer works for [the vendor or American Foods] when there's a quality problem."

Specifications provided the standards against which raw materials and work-in-process were tested and measured. Until 1980, the responsible scientist in new product development had written the specifications, sometimes so tightly that only one vendor could meet them, and in other cases so broadly that anyone could comply. Now the process was coordinated by spec writers in QA. Once the R&D work on a new product was finished, the appropriate spec writer worked with R&D, Tech Services, the Product Safety Office, and packaging to create the finished specification. This process (see *Exhibit 3*) drew heavily on pre-existing ingredient specifications, material specifications, and testing procedures. Even after specifications were approved and published, they could be revised. If, for example, someone in the plant observed that an ingredient was not working well on the production line, he or she could contact Tech Services and the specifications would be changed accordingly.

In general, what plant QA wanted from Procurement was consistency of ingredients and

EXHIBIT 3 Specification-Development Process

Support Documents
(pull out and plug in
for specific product)

Product Specification
(6–30 pp. bound booklet on finished product)

	What it is	*Who does it*
	INDEX = table of contents	
INGREDIENT SPECS ⟶ written by QA/Tech Services working with R&D	FORMULA = what's in the product	R&D
	CRITICAL PROCESS = how do you put the product together?	R&D
TESTING PROCEDURES ⟶ for packaging— written by packaging R&D for ingredients— written by R&D/ Analytical for products— written by R&D product develop- ment scientist	ACCEPTANCE TEST CRITERIA = tests to use during processing and after put together to make sure it's right	QA & R&D
	LABEL INFORMATION = regulatory and legal information for label	Consumer Service and Product Safety Office (Corporate groups which assign individuals to business units)
PACKAGING MATERIAL ⟶ SPECS Packaging R&D	PACKAGING INFORMATION = formula for materials, how to assemble	Packaging R&D
PHYSICAL SYSTEMS ⟶ CONTROL (= information base for FSA on plant systems such as metal detectors, etc.)	FOOD SAFETY ANALYSIS = checklist that ingredients are approved and ok, processing system approved and safety devices in place, and final product is safe	Product Safety Office

↓

BUSINESS UNIT APPROVALS

↓

PRODUCT SAFETY OFFICE APPROVALS

↓

PUBLISH

supplies. This was important even for such seemingly minor items as box size. One vendor, for example, had changed the size of its onion box without formally notifying American Foods. People on the plant floor, unaware of the change, continued to mix boxes of onions and peppers in the same ratio used in the past. The plant soon shut down because it ran out of onions, even though peppers were still available.

Business Units

Each business unit was a profit center, focused on a group of products—for example, canned vegetables or boxed cake mixes—sharing a common technology. General managers came up through marketing, and were evaluated on their sales and operating profitability. Their objectives were to gain market leadership for their products, and to achieve acceptable and predictable returns on invested capital. The target was 25%.

Corporate Procurement had been forging links with the business units since Erikson had joined the company in 1978. One joint activity was the monthly procurement strategy meeting, at which CAD and buyers made presentations to the business units on topics such as recent market activity and price forecasts. Procurement also made coverage recommendations for the units' key ingredients, recommendation which the units usually accepted. These meetings were attended by the business's general manager and his key marketing people, Erikson, King, the head buyer for the unit's primary ingredient, and sometimes other members of the business unit. Both Procurement and the businesses considered the meetings to be extremely important.

Procurement and Quality

Since becoming commodities director, King, with her buyers, had initiated three programs to improve their own and their suppliers' performance. These were vendor analysis, the plant performance survey, and the seal of approval program. King was also concerned about continuing deterioration in the performance of Squier, a major supplier of oils.

Vendor Analysis Program

Through 1982, there had been no uniform method for evaluating overall vendor performance. Corporate QA, for example, focused on food safety, while plant QA was more interested in the match between raw materials and specifications.

King had been thinking about how to bring suppliers in line with Procurement's "best value" orientation. In particular, she and Erikson had talked about developing a formal method to evaluate vendors. In November she wrote a memo that said, in effect, "Let's do it"; the buyers and buyer assistants then developed the project, and ran it. The group decided the first step was to develop an instrument for rating vendors on a number of key criteria. The form was kept deliberately simple so people would fill it out. The group tried out its first form during the quarter ending February 1983, met with Tom Hill for R&D input in March, put a slightly revised survey into effect for the next three quarters (*Exhibit 4*), and began soliciting plant input in the fall.

The buyers gave equal weight to four areas of performance—technical assistance, pricing, logistics and quality—with each section of the form counting for 25% of the total rating. Ratings were not meant to be compared across vendor groups, but only within similar categories.

After each quarter, buying teams rated those vendors for whom they had buying responsibility. This involved getting out files on the vendor, checking on complaints, and discussing possible ratings for the pricing, logistics and quality sections of the form. Forms were then sent to Tom Hill, who evaluated the vendors on technical assistance. If he was not familiar with a vendor's recent work with R&D, he checked with the most knowledgeable section head or scientist.

Procurement's first attempt to involve the plants was a letter to the ordering people, asking for written comments on vendors. No written responses, and only a handful of phone calls, were received.

RESULTS AND USE OF VENDOR ANALYSIS. After the forms were filled out, buyers tallied the scores for each vendor. These were then plotted on simple charts, one for each ingredient. The overall aim of the program was to drive suppliers to the upper

EXHIBIT 4 Vendor Analysis Form

SUPPLIER: _____

DATE: _____

VENDOR ANALYSIS

RATING:
(1 = low, 5 = high)

	1	2	3	4	5
1. Technical Assistance and Research & Development:					
A. Development activity with R&D	1	2	3	4	5
B. P.I.P. projects and product improvement	1	2	3	4	5
C. Quality of representation to R&D	1	2	3	4	5
2. Innovative Pricing:					
A. Competitive	1	2	3	4	5
B. Knowledge of market environment	1	2	3	4	5
3. Logistics:					
A. Follow-up on problems	1	2	3	4	5
B. Accessibility	1	2	3	4	5
C. Flexibility	1	2	3	4	5
D. Timely shipments	1	2	3	4	5
4. Quality:					
A. Number of complaints/orders placed	1	2	3	4	5
B. Severity of complaints	1	2	3	4	5

TOTAL: _____

COMMENTS:

FIX-IT PLANS:

QUARTERLY VOLUME:

$ _____

Cwt. _____

right-hand corner of the chart—that is, the highest quality vendor would ideally get the highest volume of business. (See *Exhibit 5.*) If a vendor were in the lower right, buyers worked to bring it up on quality; if it were in the upper left, they worked to expand its volume.

The forms provided a focus for meetings with sales representatives and served as a stimulus for change. When a sales representative called to say that he or she would be in on a certain day, the buyer would respond: "Fine, but while you're here, we'd like to go over the results of our vendor analysis with you." Very often the sales representative brought along people two or more levels up, including vice presidents and presidents, to see the results. At these meetings, buyers displayed the charts (with competitors' names blocked out) and also gave specific feedback about where

EXHIBIT 5 Vendor Analysis

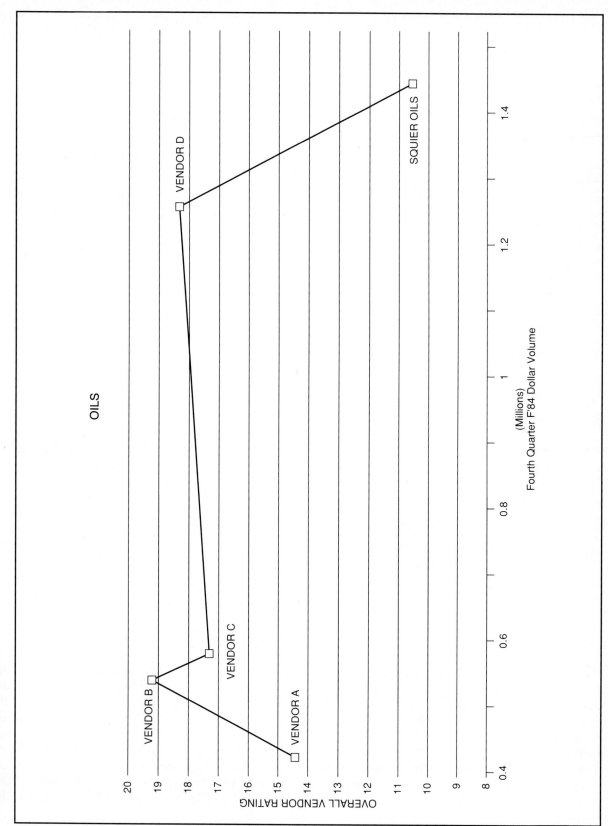

OILS

the vendor was falling down. In many cases, they began to work out "fix-it plans" with vendors to correct those shortcomings.

Communication between vendors and buyers had improved as a result of the program, and buyers were also becoming better acquainted with R&D, although Tom Hill estimated that only 10–20% of the R&D staff was actually aware of the rating scheme. By having both R&D and the buying teams rate the same vendor, and by making each aware of the other's ratings, the program had reduced the tendency among some vendors to try to play the two groups off against one another.

King thought the time had come to reassess the program. The survey form had met the early goal of simplicity; was it sophisticated enough to carry the project through its next stages? Although suppliers' attention had been gained, and many had shown a strong interest in moving to the upper right corner of their charts, fix-it plans were still ad hoc and individual. Procurement had as yet no program to reward progress or to reduce buying from vendors who remained in the lower right. How formal or standardized did this need to be?

This concern was echoed by Jerry Frank, who commented:

> Once you have evaluated a vendor, what do you do with the ones that are clearly performing less acceptably? How do you get them up to standards or get them out? It was and probably still is the perception that price plays too big a role in a buying decision. Procurement is now after quality and service. But the internal perception carries over, especially at the operating end—at the plant, QA and manufacturing see that a vendor doesn't perform and still has the business.

Getting plant involvement was therefore critical. How could it be obtained? And to whom should requests be directed? A more structured instrument was necessary, but what should it be?

Perhaps it was asking too much of the requisitioners to expect them to coordinate the plant responses: Should QA be asked instead? In addition, King considered going to a higher level of authority, rather than approaching the plants directly. If plant people heard from corporate QA or operations, they might be more inclined to respond.

King was similarly concerned that contact with R&D needed to be broadened. How, she wondered, could more people in that area be made aware of the vendor analysis program?

Plant Performance Survey

The meeting that launched the vendor analysis program also generated the idea of asking the plants what they thought of the purchasing department; they were, after all, one of its primary "customers." A survey focused on ordering and communication was sent, with a covering letter, to the requisitioners, asking for their assessment of the buying teams with whom they dealt. (See *Exhibit 6*.) Shorter letters and copies of the survey were sent to plant managers and to corporate operations directors, letting them know what Procurement was doing and why. In exchange for their time, respondents were promised feedback, as well as Procurement's best efforts to improve where problems were uncovered.

Response to the first survey was 100%. King worked with a senior buyer to compile and sort the data. Profiles were developed for each plant and each buying team; separately for C/I, packaging, and MRO; and for the entire department. (See *Exhibit 7* for sample ratings of two buying teams.) The biggest problem that emerged was that the plants did not see enough of the buying teams.

King gave individual feedback to each buying team, summarizing what the plants had said, and using the survey as a tool to improve performance. She also gave feedback on the overall results to all buyers and assistants. Nothing, however, had yet been sent to the plants, although King was considering several options.

Her goals were clear: to give the plants information that would be useful to them, but that would neither cause new problems nor violate her promise of confidentiality. Certainly, plants would want a profile of their own operations, but circulating profiles of all the plants could create problems. Similarly, aggregating buyer ratings could obscure important differences between buying teams, but sending separate scores would violate prior assurances of confidentiality. King also had to decide how to handle situations where

EXHIBIT 6 Survey Sheet

Team: Responsibilities:

ORDER AREA	U	M	G	S	O
		TEAM PERFORMANCE IS:			
1. Orders are placed on a timely basis.	1	2	3	4	5
2. There is sufficient information on delivery requirements given to suppliers by the Procurement Department.	1	2	3	4	5
3. Problems are communicated to the plant as soon as they are known in Des Moines.	1	2	3	4	5
4. The best alternatives are chosen when a supplier problem exists.	1	2	3	4	5
5. Plant opinions are considered in developing the alternatives when a supplier problem exists.	1	2	3	4	5
6. Responses to "rush" orders are done in a favorable way.	1	2	3	4	5
7. Expedited shipments are handled as positively and reasonably as possible.	1	2	3	4	5
8. Problems are solved as soon as possible with the supplier, QA, and the Transportation people involved.	1	2	3	4	5
9. Products are replaced from the nearest supplier as soon as possible *or* transferred from another plant when a problem exists.	1	2	3	4	5
10. Procurement responds quickly to pricing differences and handles billing problems with suppliers.	1	2	3	4	5

COMMUNICATIONS

	U	M	G	S	O
1. It is easy to deal with Buyer and Buyer Assistant.	1	2	3	4	5
2. Buyer and Buyer Assistant communicate with you on all orders when your production may be in jeopardy, and it is imperative that you are informed quickly.	1	2	3	4	5
3. Plants are able to contact people in Procurement when a problem exists.	1	2	3	4	5
4. All communications from Procurement to the plant are handled in a polite and professional way.	1	2	3	4	5
5. Buyer maintains a visible presence at plant locations.	1	2	3	4	5

COMMENTS:

U = Unacceptable; M = Marginal; G = Good; S = Superior; O = Outstanding.

EXHIBIT 7 Sample Scores for Two Buying Teams

		SCORES PER TEAM			
Team 1	N	Mean	Standard Deviation	Minimum Value	Maximum Value
Timely orders	20	3.90	0.85	3.00	5.00
Delivery info. given to suppliers	20	3.85	0.81	2.00	5.00
Problems communicated to plants	20	3.90	0.91	2.00	5.00
Best alternatives chosen	20	3.90	0.79	3.00	5.00
Plant opinions considered	19	3.74	0.87	2.00	5.00
Responses to rush orders	20	3.70	0.98	2.00	5.00
Expedited shipments	20	3.75	0.79	3.00	5.00
Problems solved ASAP	20	3.50	0.76	2.00	5.00
Products replaced ASAP	20	3.50	0.76	2.00	5.00
Response to pricing/billing problems	18	3.56	0.86	2.00	5.00
Easiness to deal with	20	3.90	0.91	2.00	5.00
Communication on production orders	20	3.80	1.06	2.00	5.00
Easy to contact team	20	3.50	0.83	2.00	5.00
Polite and professional	20	3.90	0.91	2.00	5.00
Visible presence	16	3.00	0.92	1.00	4.00
Team 2					
Timely orders	17	4.24	0.75	3.00	5.00
Delivery info. given to suppliers	17	4.06	0.56	3.00	5.00
Problems communicated to plants	17	4.12	0.60	3.00	5.00
Best alternatives chosen	17	4.00	0.71	3.00	5.00
Plant opinions considered	16	4.13	0.62	3.00	5.00
Responses to rush orders	17	4.41	0.62	3.00	5.00
Expedited shipments	17	4.18	0.81	3.00	5.00
Problems solved ASAP	17	3.88	0.70	2.00	5.00
Products replaced ASAP	17	4.06	0.66	3.00	5.00
Response to pricing/billing problems	15	3.93	0.59	3.00	5.00
Easiness to deal with	17	4.24	0.66	2.00	5.00
Communication on production orders	17	4.12	0.70	3.00	5.00
Easy to contact team	17	3.94	0.75	3.00	5.00
Polite and professional	17	4.35	0.49	4.00	5.00
Visible presence	14	3.14	1.29	1.00	5.00

10. American Food and Grains: Commodity and Ingredient Procurement

scores were particularly low. Did Procurement need to develop a standard approach to handling these scores? If so, should the plants be involved? (Other than providing later ratings to indicate whether improvement had been made?) So far, the survey had been limited to the ordering people; at what point should the survey be broadened, and opened to QA for its assessments?

King recognized that in setting up the survey, the assumption had been that buyers would not be penalized by the results. On the other hand, if they were not rewarded for good performance, where was the incentive? She wondered if plant assessments of buyers should be incorporated formally into their performance evaluations.

Seal of Approval Program

In October 1983, King was invited by QA to speak to a meeting of quality personnel in St. Louis. She cleared her schedule to fly down and make a 20-minute speech. A casual conversation between King, Tom Hill and a QA director uncovered agreement that it made little sense for American Foods to spend as much time testing products from good suppliers as products from weaker ones. Wouldn't it be nice to devise a goal that suppliers could aim for, and a way of giving top performers more business? It could even be tied to vendor analysis. Borrowing from Good Housekeeping, the group came up with the idea of a "Seal of Approval" program.

King then discusssed the idea with Erikson, Hill, and Frank. Seal of Approval would mean that for select vendors, American Foods would not repeat the tests the supplier had already done. Both parties would have to agree on the tests to be performed by the vendor, who would then be responsible for delivering only goods that met all test criteria. The idea was expected to meet heavy resistance, for it was contrary to the food-safety consciousness and testing orientation that had long dominated American Foods. Hill observed:

> When we first talked about the idea, it sounded just great. Then as I got thinking about it the day after, I thought, "Oh, boy! Problems!" R&D has pride of authorship in their tests; I could just hear them saying: "What do you mean, you don't need them!?" And I could just imagine

QA's reaction: "Do you realize how many cases it [an uncaught safety or quality problem] could affect? Everyone [in QA] but Jerry had some reservations.

Such a program would ultimately lead to less work for QA at the plants. For the vendors chosen, the program would be a powerful sales tool, giving them leverage in securing other business. The program would improve the exchange of technical data, continuing the trend toward more open communications. Yet even with those advantages, the idea would have to be sold.

King considered how to proceed. First, she wondered what purchasing's role should be. Although Frank seemed to think that vendor relations was an area in which purchasing should lead, might it not be better to hand this program off to QA or R&D?

There were a number of other questions as well. Should the program be sold as a cost-reducing effort, or on the basis of quality's being better if testing were done at the vendor's plant? Should it be sold from the top down, or from the bottom up? The plants, after all, would be the first to experience the program's benefits. But the program also signified a major shift in American's approach to suppliers. Should there ever be a problem, the company's image could be jeopardized. This suggested the need for top-level support.

King wondered how much control QA and R&D would willingly relinquish. She thought QA might willingly give up some tests, or that it might argue for testing every second or third batch, but that the department would find it difficult to accept no functional tests whatsoever. Basic safety checks—for example, whether the product smelled, tasted, and looked like edible oil and not fuel oil—would probably be retained.

Assuming these problems could be solved, the team still had to pick a vendor to kick off the program. What selection criteria should be used? Should they go with a high-visibility ingredient that was used extensively year-round? Should it be a test-intensive ingredient, so that the impact would be felt immediately by QA at the plants? Or should it be something that tied up storage space and required extensive handling while waiting to be tested? King knew that the entire concept was likely to rise or fall on the performance of the first company chosen.

Squier Oils

A critical ingredient for American's products was edible oil. Oils and emulsifiers blend ingredients to give smoothness to taste, carry flavor to different parts of the tongue, prolong shelf life, and even make pizza crust crispy. To obtain specific blends of oils that perform these functions, crude soybean oil must first be separated (or "fractionated") into its components, and then refined and custom-blended. In the early 1970s, Squire Oils discovered how to fractionate oil and it quickly captured the market. Squier provided good service—it was the only oil supplier that assigned both a technical person and a salesperson to each account—and charged a premium price. The company worked closely with R&D at American Foods; according to Erikson, that group "loved Squier" and consistently favored it for new products.

After four or five years, other companies began to fractionate oil, and began to cut into Squier's business. Squier's performance had also deteriorated over the period of its monopoly. It was unwilling to negotiate prices, and its limited order entry system gave it little flexibility on deliveries. Squier increased some margins, and wanted longer lead times. It often failed to notify American Foods about late arrivals. Its arrival temperatures were often wrong. But because other vendors were still not able to duplicate the quality and features of some of Squier's offerings, it remained a sole-source supplier for several products.

American's efforts to get Squier's attention had produced little change. In the summer of 1983, R&D and Procurement had joined forces to speak at Squier; they found its top management more interested in displaying its new technology than in rectifying problems. King and her oil buyer had each tried repeatedly to get through to the company. Tougher measures now had to be considered.

King knew that one option was simply to keep talking to Squier about its service and delivery problems. Experience suggested this would produce few changes. It might be possible to gain the company's attention, however, if communication came from higher levels.

At the other extreme was the option of whittling away Squier's business. Where there was no second supplier, however, an immediate cut-off of business was not possible. One could never project with certainty whether, and how quickly, a supplier could come up with a new oil. Moreover, even when substitutes were available, they were often not as good as Squier's. As an R&D manager observed, sometimes Squier's oils were the only ones that could "make the product dance."

R&D could work with other suppliers to see if they could meet the specifications on critical oils that only Squier had been able to provide. It might also be possible to loosen the specifications on some oils, although doing so would probably undercut other quality efforts. R&D, for example, might say that Procurement was talking out of both sides of its mouth: on the one hand, requesting tight specifications; on the other, asking for enough room that it could find a second source.

An alternative approach would be finding process changes that allowed the use of another supplier's oil. Pizza production, for example, required one of Squier's premium oils because of its high stability, which was unmatched by competitors. With less stable oils, free fatty acids formed during frying, leading to rancidness. R&D was working on several process changes that might overcome this problem: decreasing the time the oil was in the fryers, filtering out particles that acted as catalysts for the breakdown of fatty acids, and reducing the amount of oil in the fryer at any given time. Just when breakthroughs would be achieved, however, and whether they would allow the use of less stable oils, was unknown.

Procurement could also discuss the need to change oil suppliers with the business units, emphasizing the cost savings that might be possible. They, in turn, could put pressure on R&D to qualify additional suppliers.

As King prepared for her meeting with Erikson, she examined her options for each program, and their likely interaction. Keeping a vendor like Squier, for example, would probably dilute the impact of both the vendor analysis and the plant performance surveys. If American Foods were serious about matching purchasing volume with overall vendor performance, systematic efforts in a single direction had to be visible to the plants and to R&D. King wondered: Just how far could her group move such programs by itself, and what degree of commitment was needed from other departments and other levels of the organization?

11. Quest for the Best[1]

The Death of Elegance

Funeral services for eighteenth-century ELEGANCE were held in the mid-twentieth century without fanfare or even any general cognizance of its occurrence by admirers. Death was attributed to a variety of causes, including the replacement of hand labor by machine production, the establishment of the minimum wage, high taxation, the overthrow of monarchical government, and inevitability. Most of the friends of ELEGANCE were unaware of the long illness that had preceded its death.

So might an obituary have read, if the press took the same notice of the decease of eras as it does of people. I know, because I was there.

Elegance, to me, is a summary word denoting the ultimate in beauty, craftsmanship, and quality—all put together with taste. Elegance suggests selectivity, fitness, and authority—whether in decoration, personal adornment, or manners. It is an achievement of an elite society which had sufficient leisure, wealth, and interest to devote its attention to living in tasteful luxury.

The great craftsmen and merchants of the Renaissance were challenged by the same requirements as their counterparts are today. They had to possess a discerning eye for the best, an ability to detect the slightest flaw, and a consuming desire for perfection.... Fine quality manufacturers, workers, and merchants understand that good things don't happen by accident; they are

made to happen by an unwillingness to accept second best.

* * * *

Good, Better, Best

It was a mixed blessing to have a father who had no uncertainty about his taste or standards of quality. As far as Herbert Marcus, Sr., was concerned, the best was none too good and he had unshakable confidence in his own taste. Learning about the retail business under his direction was both rewarding and frustrating: he was a difficult man to satisfy, for he always knew how anything could be done better.... Although a realist, he was reluctant to admit the demise of elegance.

My education in the subject of quality was later completed by Neiman-Marcus's first buyer, Moira Cullen, a remarkable woman, who gave me experience in the buying field. She trained my eye to see and to search for those things that were the best: the finest methods of merchandise construction, the ultimate in quality, the simplest design. When I completed my five-year training period under the two of them, I had the equivalent of a Ph.D in merchandise that no business school could have given me. I learned to differentiate, not between good and bad but between better and best, and to pursue the best, regardless of cost or effort. The difference in cost to achieve the best may be negligible, but overcoming the inertia of the status quo and the willingness of most people

[1]From QUEST FOR THE BEST by Stanley Marcus. Copyright © 1979 by Stanley Marcus. Used by permission of Viking Penguin, a division of Penguin Books USA Inc.

to settle for less than perfection always takes greater effort.

When buying ready-to-wear in the manufacturer's showroom, it is customary to put an X after a style number if any change is being specified. Miss Cullen was so discerning, so demanding, that almost every style she purchased was X'd.... Many times I squirmed with impatience as she held up the buying process to criticize the fit of a garment, the quality of the fabric, the design of the buttons, or the shape of the belt. She would call for the designer and point out that the waistline needed to be dropped three-eighths of an inch; she would summon the factory's piece-goods buyer to demand the substitution of a more desirable fabric; she would insist that the findings buyer submit samples of less ornate, but usually more expensive, buttons. It often took as long as a half hour to complete the purchase of a single style, during which time the normal showroom activities were disrupted.

Many buyers are suppressed designers and invoke changes as an ego demonstration; but not so with Miss Cullen, who had no illusions about her designing capability. She was not grandstanding by making her incessant demands; she was simply trying to get as perfect a garment for her customers as possible, and while manufacturers disliked the ordeal of a buying session with her, they invariably followed her requests, having learned from prior experience that she was usually right. Since she rarely had to pay a bonus for her changes, the customer was rewarded with a better product at no extra charge.

Miss Cullen was the last of a breed of apparel buyers who knew enough to make constructive changes. The current crop of buyers, recruited from college graduates who have gone through stores' executive-training programs, simply don't have the merchandise knowledge to function in a similar manner. They have been trained to read computer printouts essential for multiple stores, to balance their stocks by price lines and color, and to latch onto the newest fashion trends, but few of them know or care enough to demand adequate hems, "under pressing," or bound seams.

Today, most stores follow a personnel-promotion program dictated by both their own internal requirements and the pressure of young buyers for quick advancement and new assignments. Too many able trainees are opting for rapid job changes in the mistaken belief that the largest number of job experiences in the shortest period of time is the best qualification for the first management job available. Barely has a shoe buyer learned the difference between calf and kidskin when he is promoted to buy men's clothing.

Merchandise deterioration occurs because many buyers don't know what is best, much less where to look for it or how to get it. "Market average" replaces best as a standard without management's recognition of the change. Too often, management has its eyes focused on the comparison with the previous year's profits, not on the quality barometer.

However, in fairness to this generation of buyers, market conditions have changed radically since Miss Cullen's time. Manufacturers have become more inflexible as they have grown larger and are less willing to make changes; fabrics are more standardized, and cost pressures have become greater. Smaller domestic makers and the foreign markets provide the only opportunities for the buyer to exercise quality improvement.

*   *   *   *

In the field of apparel manufacturing, the actual labor is performed by outside contractors; the manufacturer contributes design, selling and delivery functions and has limited control on the quality of the merchandise produced under his name. If he is dissatisfied with the quality, he can change contractors. The contractors, being profit-motivated, also try to squeeze the maximum number of garments out of the yardage allocated to them.... In past years, when a manufacturer produced his own garments, he knew what was going on in his own factory and could insist on the maintenance of his quality standards. He could also respond more affirmatively to his customers' demands.

The drop in apparel quality should not be blamed entirely on the contracting system alone, for many manufacturers do their own kind of cheating. After they have approved the designs and taken orders from their store customers, they call in their production managers, or "take-out" men, as I call them, to determine what they can take out of the garments by the simplification of design, or by the substitution of a less expensive fabric for the original, or by the elimination of a skirt lining. If the garment still proves to be too expensive to make, it is simply withdrawn from the line and the buyers are notified that it won't be made because of late fabric delivery. Not all makers follow these practices, but the next time you experience or hear of a skimpy garment, you will know the reason why.

The unions must bear a share of the responsibility for the decline in quality, for they have been concerned more with lifting average wages than in rewarding the exceptionally talented workers. By doing so, they are satisfying the majority of their constituents, but quality suffers as a result.

With few exceptions, retailers do little to examine the goods that come into their stocks. Only a few have inspection departments to check on fit and construction, leaving it to their salespeople or customers to discover any defective merchandise. Large stores usually receive merchandise at a remotely located warehouse which the buyers visit only at infrequent intervals, so it is not easy for them to examine their receipts to determine if the goods were received as bought, if the fabric is the same as originally shown or if there was a substitution, or if the shipment comes up to the maker's normal standards.

A formal inspection system, conducted by trained technicians, in which merchandise is spot-checked at the time of arrival or at the factory before delivery, is an expensive process but the only way that large organizations can exercise any quality control over what they sell. Otherwise they merely give lip service to quality.

I made it a practice to capitalize on my acquaintanceship with top manufacturers by requesting that they share their knowledge with me, and I was never turned down. Once I went to the foremost neckwearmaker and took with me a half dozen neckties, all in the same relative price range. I laid them before him and asked him to criticize them for me. He examined the unlabeled ties and very quickly pointed out the techniques by which yardage had been skimped in three out of the six.

Manufacturers in other fields will respond readily if approached by a young buyer eager to add to his fund of knowledge. The only caveat is to select a maker who is the best in his field and who has the reputation for honesty. Usually, *best*

makers have that quality, for "best" and "honesty" are clearly interrelated.

* * * *

As a retail merchant I've had the opportunity to observe those who knew the best, and those who watched those who knew and followed their lead. Quality to many is an approach *to* or a way *of* life. They have learned from either parents or experience to buy the best they can afford, even if it means buying fewer or less frequently. Obviously, everyone cannot buy the finest diamond or fur, but everyone can buy the best he can *afford*.

My favorite complaint came from a customer who wrote that her coat purchased seven years previously wouldn't wear out, but that it was now too short. I replied:

> *Dear Mrs. Carstairs:*
>
> *We can either shorten your coat to a three-quarter length for twenty-five dollars or we can add a fox border for two hundred dollars. I would recommend the first solution.*
>
> *Sincerely,*
> *Stanley Marcus*

She took my advice and wrote me seven years later that she had just given her coat to a less fortunate neighbor and that she fully subscribed to the doctrine of "buying the best."

* * * *

The elephantine growth of stores has forced the managements to devote a large portion of their working hours to budgeting and the solution of operational problems; expansion programs demand attention for reviews with the architects and interior planners. The result is that there is an inadequate amount of time left over to devote to the two most important elements of a retail business: merchandise and customers. Under these conditions, it is inevitable that the quality of both goods and services will deteriorate sharply.

As a test, I telephoned twenty retail-executive friends in various cities between nine-thirty and eleven o'clock in the morning. I was able to reach only one person on the first call; the others were in "closed door" meetings. When I did talk to the others subsequently, I asked them to describe the general nature of the meetings. Without exception, the meetings were on the subject of expense control, new store development, or sales budgeting for the next season. Not a single meeting was held on the subject of store service or merchandise quality. I seriously doubt if there has been a merchandise meeting of top executives devoted to the subject of a handbag: how to improve it by making it larger or smaller, by using a better quality of leather or lining, by strengthening the construction for greater longevity, or by sewing it with smaller stitches. True, this responsibility has been delegated down the line to the buyer and the divisional merchandise manager, but when the buyers feel that senior management is not as much interested in merchandise quality as in the sales gain over the last year, then they cannot be expected to have a dedication to quality improvement. The missing ingredient in most stores is the enthusiastic encouragement from the boss to attain and improve quality standards of merchandise and service. When the boss gets excited, so does everyone else in a retail organization.

* * * *

Service Goes Down the Drain

Specialty-store retailing is a business of minutiae, things which may not be of monetary significance, but of great importance, to the customer. Early in the game I learned to carry a notebook so that I could jot down observations and clues customers dropped by chance. If I overheard a woman mention at a party that she had been unable to find a particular article, I would locate it the next morning and have a salesperson call her to tell her we had found what she was looking for. One night, during intermission at a symphony performance, a man I knew approached me to mention that he had bitten through the stem of the pipe he had bought and had been advised there would be a three-month delay for its replacement. The following day I called the buyer and told him the story. "That's ridiculous," he said. "We have just received a new shipment of stems. The salesman must not have known of their arrival. Give me the customer's name and I'll call him." By the time the man had arrived at his office, there was a message on his desk that Neiman-Marcus was delivering the replacement before noon.

Obviously the customer was flattered and pleased. He called me to thank me and to say that he didn't realize that service of this type still was in existence. A month later, he came to the store and made a purchase of a $50,000 diamond ring. Perhaps the two incidents had no relationship. I like to think they did.

Contrary to popular opinion, customers like to be sold, if, and when, they get in the hands of an authoritative salesperson who knows the stocks and shows an understanding of their needs. I'm not referring to high-pressure selling, for that involves selling something the customer doesn't want or need. Admittedly, customers in a Neiman-Marcus store are apt to have more discretionary income than those in other stores, but every store sells its customers only a small percentage of what they are capable of buying.

I witnessed one of the finest demonstrations of creative selling in the Neiman-Marcus men's store one day by a young buyer, Dean Ferguson, whom I had originally employed a few years previously because he had the temerity to ask if there was any reason he couldn't become president of the company in fifteen years.... We were visiting one of the out-of-town stores and he was showing me some newly arrived neckties. A saleswoman approached him and asked if he could help her out by writing up a sales check so she could wait on another person. She handed him the $15 tie and introduced him to the lady customer. As he started to write the check, he looked up and said, "This is a beautiful tie you have selected. What is he going to wear it with?" The woman reached into her purse and pulled out a swatch of fabric. Dean looked at it a moment and said, "There's an ancient madder pattern which comes in two color combinations that would go very well with this suit." He pulled out the two ties as he was talking to her. She readily agreed and took both of them—at $22.50 each.

Dean asked, "Doesn't he need some new shirts to go with his new suit?" The customer replied, "I'm glad you asked; he does need some, but I haven't been able to find any white ones with French cuffs. Do you have any size fifteen-thirty-three?" He showed her two qualities, pointing out the difference in the cloths. She selected three of the more expensive shirts at $40 each. "Doesn't he ever wear colored shirts?" Dean inquired. "Yes, if you have this same shirt in blue I'll take two."

I was watching the progress of the sale with great interest, wondering what his next ploy would be, or whether he was going to stop while he was ahead. He didn't disappoint me; he was in command, and the customer obviously liked the professional attention she was receiving. He reached into the case and took out a pair of cuff links to show her. "Here's an interesting new cuff link that a lot of our customers have liked much better than the ones they've been using. They are gold-filled and with this Florentine finish, they won't show any scratch marks. They are fifty dollars," he said as he inserted one of the links into his own cuff. She couldn't resist them, and he added them to the sales check.

"Since you liked the ancient madder ties, you might be interested in a travel robe with a matching ascot that we had made in England out of the same fabric." He took one off the rack and tried it on to show it to best advantage. "It is a hundred and sixty-five dollars including the ascot." "That's great," she said, "I'll give it to him for his birthday." By this time, Dean had already pulled out two $45 pairs of pajamas in colors harmonizing with the robe, and asked if she didn't think the gift would be more complete with them and a pair of $50 Italian soft calf lounging slippers. She took them all, and Dean assured her that the robe, pajamas, and slippers would be specially gift-wrapped in a birthday package and marked for delivery the day before the birthday. The woman was grateful and vowed she would never think of shopping elsewhere in the future.

By this time the original saleswoman was free and Dean turned over a sale of $615 which was built on the $15 tie the saleswoman had sold and was willing to settle for—an increase of 4000 percent. What was of even more importance, he had made a firm new customer for the department. When it was all over, I congratulated him on one of the greatest examples of good selling I'd ever seen but that, being a perfectionist, I had detected one flaw. I asked him why he hadn't sold her socks to go with her husband's new suit. He hit his forehead with his hand in disgust. "That's what I like about working for you. You won't settle for less than a hundred-percent performance. I'll call her this afternoon and ask if she'll let me

select a couple of pairs." He did; she acquiesced with pleasure; I was satisfied.

* * * *

Many large sales present problems and sometimes dilemmas. I have experienced many problems, but maintaining a steadfast standard of a single-price policy has prevented me from getting into many dilemmas. The other rule I've lived by is the principle upheld by the father, who stated: "No sale is a good sale for Neiman-Marcus unless it is a good buy for the customer." These principles have answered both problems and dilemmas.

* * * *

Taste

It is reported that Renoir once said to Cézanne, "How can you wear that cravat? Can't you see it's in bad taste?" To which Cézanne replied, "If it were in bad taste I wouldn't be wearing it."

At best, taste is a matter of opinion, subject to changing times and fluctuating evaluations. Each person is entitled to his own taste opinions, but some more so than others. There is bad taste, good taste, and superb taste; there is insecure taste and sure taste; there is conservative taste and garish taste. Many tend to overrate the quality of their own taste, and they take great umbrage when it is questioned. Others, who are unsure of their taste, mask their insecurity by purchasing articles with designer labels or "as seen in *Vogue*" tags.

Good taste, I am convinced, can be acquired through environment and education; the eye can be disciplined to differentiate between good and bad by a constant looking process, and any person with a normal IQ can develop good taste. The achievement of superb taste is as difficult as the attainment of perfection in any endeavor.

Who are the tastemakers? The Beautiful People reported in *Women's Wear Daily?* The fashion magazines? Designers? Stores? When the history of taste of the twentieth century is written, I anticipate that the department and specialty stores of Europe and the United States will be credited with having made the single largest contribution to the formation and, at times, the improvement of mass taste. The public has more frequent experiences with stores than with any other types of business or cultural institutions. Admission is free and, with the exception of a few of the old-time formidable saleswomen, there is nothing inhibiting or forbidding about wandering from floor to floor to see the wonders of the world—brass from the Turkish bazaars, foods from the Middle East, porcelains from the Orient, fashions from the best designers of both continents. It's the greatest free show on earth.

The shopper or looker might witness a fashion show and be able to observe the manner in which the clothes have been accessorized and how the designers have used fresh color combinations, or see a new group of model rooms inspired by Brazil or a collection of Vasarely paintings. Forty years ago, I borrowed twenty canvasses by Gauguin from private collectors and commissioned a series of ball gowns by leading designers in the colors of the painter's Tahitian series. It proved to be a tremendous success, with a sellout of the clothes and the arousal of a vast amount of public interest. The large part of the Dallas public had never before seen an original Gauguin, much less twenty. Art lovers from all over the state came especially to see the pictures; schoolteachers brought their entire classes to view the exhibition. Most important of all was the fact that thousands who didn't know anything about Gauguin were exposed to his paintings unwittingly and went away enriched, at no cost.

*   *   *   *

There are some who exaggerate the importance of taste, who make it a shrine at which they worship. That, of course, is pure nonsense. A person with bad or indifferent taste can live a perfectly happy and normal life, have a loving family, and be financially successful. Good taste, like education, simply opens new opportunities for the enjoyment of life.

I know about this firsthand, for I spent my business life in the operation of a business dedicated to the distribution of quality merchandise in good taste. I found it both profitable and pleasurable to supervise the quality and taste of the merchandise we sold and, thereby, to earn the loyalty of customers who appreciated our standards. They bought from us because they got their money's worth, because the surroundings pleased them, because they liked our taste. They phoned us to find out the correct length of gloves to wear for a particular social occasion; they came to us for counsel on what to wear with what. Our objective was to send them out properly attired, correctly accessorized—always in good taste, so that they could wear their clothes with assurance.

As the head of Neiman-Marcus, I directed the efforts of a merchandising and buying staff in the procurement of the finest-quality merchandise in the world, as well as serving as its final taste arbiter. I covered the international markets myself in search of the best, the rare, the esoteric—in part because I relished the excitement of the hunt, and in part to maintain the kind of familiarity with world production that enabled me to give our buyers proper guidance and moral support. We always found a market for the best.

*   *   *   *

The Building and Preservation of a Mystique

. . . [A] mystique is formally defined by Webster as a "complex of quasi-mystical attitudes and feelings surrounding some person, institution, or activity."

PR people can raise a lot of ballyhoo about . . . an institution, but all they accomplish is to turn on the spotlight; it will take time and repeated demonstrations of ability, performance, integrity, and consistency before the mystique emerges. . . . The core of mystique is an idea—widely and fondly held by a large number of people—that has been built on "remembrances of things past": acts of kindness and thoughtfulness, deeds of courage and conviction, repeated demonstrations of leadership and reliability, proofs of devotion to the public welfare as well as to profits, all tied together by the qualities of humor, talent, and integrity.

I had no idea I was helping to build a mystique when I entered Neiman-Marcus to start my business career. It was a small, family business with a good local reputation for integrity, fashion leadership, and quality, and I proceeded to build on those solid assets to attain national recognition.

I owe much of what I learned about advertising to my father, but an understanding of the nature and use of publicity was something I picked up from friends in public relations and journalism and which I applied to Neiman-Marcus. I recognized the value of a newspaper story, so I attended the fur auctions held at the Fromm silver-fox ranch and in New York, and paid the highest prices for top bundles of skins. These purchases merited local news stories with a picture of me holding up my prize skins, adding to the store's reputation of buying the best wherever it was sold.

Unlike politicians whose main concern is the number of letters for or against a proposition, my major interest has always been in the identity and qualifications of the writer. As a goal, I wanted the text in a Neiman-Marcus advertisement to pass the scrutiny of the grammarians among our readers, and the fashion illustrations to please the art critics. All complaints were answered within forty-eight hours, but those coming from persons with special qualifications to complain were given particular management consideration, on the theory that if we could satisfy the most critical of our customers it would be easy to please the balance. Conversely, we believed that if we didn't satisfy the "bell ringers," they would drift away from us and would lead the flock of less discriminating customers with them.

There is no question that our expeditious handling of complaints solidified our reputation for reliability and satisfaction. I am convinced that the speed of reaction to customer dissatisfaction is as important as the final settlement. Establishing a policy of speedy answers and adjustments is easy, but enforcing it requires a hard-nosed management which checks constantly for compliance and refuses to accept excuses for failure to live up to the forty-eight-hour rule.

We were rigorous in maintaining our standards of taste, be it in merchandise, advertising, or other activities in which the store was a participant. This required a certain presumptuousness on my part in setting standards with which some of my associates disagreed at times. I recall an incident in which I criticized our candy buyer for having too large a proportion of her stock in milk chocolate rather than in the dark bittersweet. Her merchandise manager came to her defense arguing, "This is what the public wants. What right do we have to tell them to eat dark choco-

late?" I replied, "Milk chocolate is a yokel taste. Chocolate-educated customers will be turned off by seeing so much milk chocolate and we will lose their trade. I'd rather satisfy them than the yokels, if it comes to choosing up sides, but I think we can please both by simply reversing the percentages between two kinds of chocolate. It's our job to educate our customers as well as to sell them." My directive was followed and eventually our customers switched to the dark chocolate. What the buyer and the merchandise manager had not understood was that our reputation would be endangered when our customers sent Christmas gifts of milk chocolate to sophisticated friends around the country. Both the sender and the store would be blamed; so, in the long run, we did a service for the customers as well as the store.

Our advertising department was always given great creative latitude, but I was adamant that the copy and the art in our advertising be free of vulgarity, either in words or offensive poses. I was critical of hyperbole and extravagant claims that taxed the credibility of our advertising, for I always wanted our readers to believe everything we stated and never to be offended by anything our artists drew.

Not only did we try to keep our reputation in good condition but we made efforts to enhance it constantly. Store life is full of valid, human-interest news stories, but most stores don't capitalize on them. When we opened the store on a Sunday some years ago to outfit a bride and groom who had flown a great distance to shop with us, we tipped off the press (with the customers' consent); . . . when American Airlines had a strike some years ago, stranding fifty stewardesses in Dallas, we gave them temporary jobs and reaped thousands of lines of free publicity.

Our public-relations department was trained to be alert for news happenings outside the store and to capitalize on any story that might have some value for Neiman-Marcus. When Anthony Eden, then British foreign secretary, was visiting the United States in 1952, he lost his homburg hat at a reception. We heard of the loss and wired him that the store was "taking the liberty" of replacing the hat. United Press reported that the new hat arrived by air in time for Eden to wear it to hear the president's State of the Union message, and that Eden had wired me, "Duly touched by your generous gesture and greatly impressed by this typical example of American courtesy. The hat fits as a hat should, and will be a further and constant reminder of my stay in your country." Not only was it a great story for the store and the hat department but I'm confident that our customers who read it were proud that their store had made such favorable news.

Many who visit Dallas for the first time, and having heard so much about Neiman-Marcus, are disappointed when they see several undistinguished, cream-colored buildings of mixed styles of architecture. Publicity had conjured a miniature Taj Mahal in their minds. But, once they go through the doors, their spirits are lifted by the feeling of warmth and welcome, by the wide uncluttered aisles and high ceilings, by the quality and design of the fixtures, by the incorporation of paintings and sculpture in the decor.... It has been our long-standing conviction that fine merchandise needed to be housed and displayed against a background of fine materials, so we used imported marbles, beautiful wood, and top-quality carpets to create an atmosphere of beauty, not of sumptuousness. These materials, together with the spaciousness we have maintained, create an environment our customers have appreciated.

Publicity and beautiful stores are fine, but are not sufficient to build an enduring reputation in the field of merchandising. The goods must represent honest value, the best available at the various price ranges carried, and the customer service must be superior. Neither of these objectives is accomplished by broad executive directives, but, rather, by painstaking attention to the thousands of details involving both. Retailing ... is truly a business of minutiae. A buyer who goes to New York to attend the seasonal apparel showing must visit twenty to thirty showrooms, see three thousand models, select some twenty-five styles from each manufacturer, determine the colors and sizes for each one, write her orders and get home within two weeks, all with the objective of assembling the most authoritative stocks in the land. How wise her judgment was won't be known till the end of the following season, for commitments have to be made from four to six months before the selling period. In addition, he must remember ... that a Fort Worth debu-

tante wants a special glamorous dress in pale blue embroidered with delicate silver beading, that she must get expedited delivery on four styles to cover two forthcoming newspaper advertisements, that she must cajole a shipping clerk to give her preferential delivery on two current styles for which her salespeople are clamoring.

Even while the buying is in progress, and in recent years it has become a twelve-month affair, business must go on. Customers must be served, displays arranged, fashion shows staged, adjustments made, new salespeople trained, recent merchandise arrivals explained, sales enthusiasm maintained. Obviously, there are department heads who oversee these activities, but management must be able to spend an adequate amount of time on the selling floors to detect flaws in the execution of these many jobs, to be the watchful eye that the rank and file of any organization needs and wants.

From the very beginning of the store, management was successful in developing an extraordinary standard of customer service—unsurpassed by any store in the world.... New salespeople are taught how to greet customers in a warm, friendly manner; how to find out what the customer is looking for; how to bring the sale to a successful conclusion. They are instructed that "May I help you?" is not the sentence to use when approaching a customer. They are encouraged to start talking about a piece of merchandise that may have stopped the shopper, or to say, "Hello, I'm Dottie Jones. I'll be happy to assist you."

Like no other store I know, the members of the Neiman-Marcus staff have a great feeling of proprietorship, a keen interest in doing things the "Neiman-Marcus way," a genuine devotion to the interest of the customer as well as the store, a deep respect and pride in the organization of which they are a part. I am more proud of this spirit than any other accomplishment we may have made.

The building of any corporate mystique presupposes a competent management that has a clear understanding of its direction and the public which it is serving; the perpetuation of such a mystique requires similar competence.

*   *   *   *

The Future for Fine Quality

Barring a proletarian dictatorship which reduces everything to a standard of uniformity for one and all, I find it difficult to conceive of a time when there won't be a premium for the best. As long as there are different sizes of oranges, there will be customers willing to pay more for the largest and juiciest.

I have watched men and women buy a wide variety of products for many years, and I have frequently heard them ask: "Is this the finest?" or, "Is this the best?" I've studied their motives for wanting the finest or the best, and I have found them varied. To some, it's a matter of prudence, for they have found the best may last longer; to others, it's a point of pride, of leadership, of self-distinction. Another group gets sensual and aesthetic satisfaction from the actual handling and ownership of the best. And, of, course, there are those who are trying to "keep up with the Joneses" and buy the best because it's the snobbish thing to do.

The success of the fine-quality specialty store was built on the foundation of superior selections, the ability to create certain merchandise specialties of the house, fashion leadership, personalized service to the customers by well-informed and trained salespeople, and an authoritative owner-customer relationship. As a business expands into multi-units in widely separated cities, all of these qualities become diluted to the point of ineffectiveness.

Conditions which made it possible to run personalized, high-service stores in the past are no longer prevalent, and never will be again. This calls for a new scenario, in which stores must find fresh solutions to satisfying the customers; stores must recognize that profits can be permanent only if satisfaction is rendered, and must be aware that the demand for quality is not only still alive but growing. Customers, in turn, should not be bashful in their insistence on the best, for, as Somerset Maugham wrote in *The Mixture as Before*: "It is a funny thing about life, if you refuse to accept anything but the best you very often get it."

12. Steinway & Sons

Gents: I have decided to keep your grand piano. For some reason unknown to me it gives better results than any so far tried. Please send bill with lowest price.

Yours,
Thomas Alva Edison
June 2, 1890

Peter M. Perez, president of Steinway & Sons, piano makers, looked up as William T. "Bill" Steinway, director of research and development, walked in for their ten o'clock meeting on July 16, 1981. The meeting was an important one, scheduled to discuss the company's plans to reintroduce the Model K. This upright, or vertical, piano (so called because its strings and sounding board were mounted vertically, rather than horizontally, as was true of grand pianos) was last produced by the firm during the 1920s. The Model K was being considered to meet competitive threats posed by Yamaha and Kawai, the leading Japanese piano makers, whose success in the American market, particularly in sales of high-quality verticals, had been considerable.

Perez knew Steinway's R&D group had already invested $200,000 in working up the Model K, and Bill Steinway had personally devoted nearly two years to the project. Still, he could not help wondering whether the reintroduction of a long-discontinued product line was the appropriate way to meet the Japanese challenge. Would it stand up to the competition of the 1980s? Would

This case was prepared by David A. Garvin.

Copyright © 1981 by the President and Fellows of Harvard College. Harvard Business School case 682-025.

extensive modifications of the production process be required? More important, would the Model K distract Steinway from its traditional focus on grand pianos? Perez hoped his meeting with Bill Steinway would provide answers to these questions.

Company Background

Steinway & Sons had long been recognized as a leader in the market for high-quality pianos. Established in New York City in 1853 by Henry Engelhard Steinway, a German immigrant, the firm had prospered from the very first, largely because of its technical excellence. A year after its founding, the company won a gold medal at the Metropolitan Fair in Washington, D.C., for one of its square pianos; a year later, it introduced the cross-stringing technique in a piano with a cast-iron frame and won another first prize at a New York industrial exhibition. Orders grew rapidly, and in 1860, a new and larger factory was constructed on Fourth (now Park) Avenue in New York, a site chosen, according to Steinway family lore, because "the Harlem and New Haven Railroad cars passed directly in front, making thousands of people acquainted with the name of Steinway."

This promotional flair continued with the opening in 1866 of Steinway Hall, which served as New York City's major concert facility for many years. The firm also dabbled in artist management, bringing to the United States such piano virtuosos as Anton Rubinstein and Ignacy Jan Paderewski for their first American performances.

Henry Steinway died in 1871, leaving the leadership of the firm to his son, William. William continued many of his father's practices, meanwhile consolidating and expanding operations. A London sales branch opened in 1875, while a new factory, to service the international trade, was built in Hamburg in 1880. Today, both remain important elements of the firm. In the spring of 1871, William embarked on his grandest venture, purchasing a 400-acre tract of farmland on Long Island to serve as the company's domestic headquarters and sole U.S. manufacturing plant. Over the years, the surrounding area would be developed as Steinway Village, a largely self-contained company town complete with its own kindergarten, public bath, park, library, ferryboat, and streetcar line. Few vestiges of the village remain, although the factory can be found at the same location.

Succeeding generations of Steinways guided the company into the 1900s, still following the advice of its founder to "build the best piano possible. Sell it at the lowest price consistent with quality." Technical excellence continued to be emphasized, with members of the firm taking out over 100 patents in piano making. Notable milestones in the company's more recent history include the construction of the specially designed 100,000th Steinway piano, presented to the White House in 1903; the presentation of a second grand piano, the 300,000th Steinway, to the White House in 1938; the firm's survival during World War II, when piano making was deemed unessential to the war effort, through a combination of precision wooden parts manufacturing for troop-carrying gliders and the construction of over 2,500 40-inch vertical pianos, the famous fatigue-green "GI pianos" shipped to combat zones throughout the world; and Steinway's rapid postwar recovery and return to piano-making eminence.

In April 1972 the company made its most dramatic shift, giving up its independent status to become a member of the CBS Musical Instruments Division, which then included Fender guitars and amplifiers, Leslie speakers, Rhodes electric pianos, Rogers drums, and Squier strings. The Musical Instruments Division later acquired Gulbransen, a maker of electric organs, the Gemeinhardt Corporation, a maker of flutes and piccolos, and Lyon & Healy, a manufacturer of harps. All were considered to be among the quality leaders in their fields.

Commenting on the merger with CBS, John H. Steinway, a fourth-generation family member who was vice president at the time, observed:

> Certainly there was a tug at the heart strings, but this was more than counterbalanced in being assured of the continuity of the firm. As a medium-sized family-owned business we were facing the classic problems of estate and inheritance taxation, in addition to increasing government regulations, growing legal requirements, and all of the other problems facing business today. There was also the situation, found in many family-owned businesses, where ownership was spread out among members of the family who were not interested in providing capital for development and expansion.[1]

Capital spending at Steinway did increase substantially after the company was acquired by CBS, from premerger levels of $100,000 annually to $1–2 million per year. Otherwise, there was little apparent change. A Steinway remained as company chairman—first Henry Z. Steinway, who was president at the time of the merger, and later John H. Steinway—although day-to-day operating responsibilities shifted to a CBS-appointed president.

In mid-1977 CBS appointed the first nonfamily president of Steinway. His tenure was relatively brief, lasting only until late 1978. Executives close to CBS's decision to remove him midway through his three-year contract observed that the individual in question was not well received by existing Steinway management. One longtime Steinway executive commented, "He imposed his own way of doing things, without any consideration for the more than a century's worth of experience at his fingertips."[2]

CBS then appointed Peter Perez, an executive with extensive experience in the music industry, as Steinway president. A graduate of Yale with an MBA from Indiana University, Perez had risen, at the age of 34, to the presidency of C. G. Conn, Ltd., a competing musical instruments manufacturer. In 1977 he joined the CBS Musical Instruments Division as an executive vice president with responsibilities for long-range planning and business development. His preference for operating issues over planning, however, soon became apparent, leading to his appointment as president of Steinway.

[1] "Pianomaker Henry Steinway and Family," *Town & Country*, December, 1977.

[2] "The Steinway Tradition," *New York Times*, August 24, 1980.

Perez spent considerable time in his first two years with the firm touring the factory, chatting with employees, and taking notes and responding to what he saw. One result of these tours was the purchase of new grinding tools for one department and the installation of a new router in another. According to Perez, he became much more "people-oriented" as a result of this experience. He observed, "It's important for our people to know that there are no barriers between them and management."[3]

Perez hoped eventually to expand Steinway's output, although he considered his first challenge to be improving existing operations. Perez commented on his plans for the future:

> I don't view my role here as being simply a conservator at all. But quality will remain paramount. What has been accomplished here is the result of unstinting attention to detail and standards. It would be foolish to jeopardize that franchise. There'll be no headlong rushing. That's not the way things are done at Steinway.[4]

Under CBS, manufacturing and marketing practices had continued in much the same way as before, leading John Steinway to observe:

> I'm sure if we suddenly became unprofitable we'd hear a loud noise about it. But I think they know that what they bought was 120 years of reputation and quality, and that it would be suicidal for them to mess with it.[5]

The Steinway Tradition

For many years, Steinway pianos had been received enthusiastically by knowledgeable musicians. In the late 1970s fully 95% of all classical music concerts featuring a piano soloist were performed on a Steinway grand. Major music schools and conservatories showed a similar fondness for Steinways; in 1979, Juilliard alone had 220, Oberlin 160, and Indiana University 100.

The reasons for this attachment had changed little over time, for the company had followed the same basic principles throughout its history. All Steinways were still assembled by craft methods, with little use of assembly-line techniques. Volumes remained small—the Long Island plant turned out 3,500 instruments in 1980, 2,000 grand pianos and 1,500 verticals, while the Hamburg plant produced 2,000 pianos, 1,400 grands and the remainder verticals. Skilled labor was employed throughout the process, and many employees, often continuing an association begun by their parents and grandparents, had been with the firm for 20 or 30 years. Only the finest materials were used—Steinway relied on its own wood technologist, for example, to aid in the purchase of millions of dollars worth of wood annually, including rosewood from Brazil, mahogany from Africa, and Sitka spruce from Alaska—yet after the wood was weathered, the firm still discarded half or more of some kinds of lumber because standards had not been met. Even so, few materials were perfectly uniform, and workers often had to accommodate parts to one another during fabrication and assembly to insure proper fits.

Research and development were also important at Steinway. New methods of construction, new materials, and new design features often originated with the firm. In 1980, for example, urea resin adhesives, bonded by ultrasonic heat, were being used to hold Steinways together, replacing the cabinetmakers' glue used for generations. Similarly, plastic keys, which lasted much longer, had replaced ivory in the mid-1950s, again after extensive testing by the firm. No single innovation or patented process, however, accounted for the Steinway sound; according to John Steinway, "It isn't as much a matter of innovation as of intelligent synthesis, using the best of everyone's previous experience with pianos."[6] Continuing this tradition, Steinway in 1980 was experimenting with electronic actions (which would transmit the pianist's pressure on a key to a hammer striking the strings by electronic, rather than purely mechanical, means). The research and development group had a budget that year of $250,000 and employed 10 engineers; it also collaborated with scientists at the CBS Technology Center on several other projects.

All of these projects sought to improve fur-

---

[3]*The Music Trades*, August, 1980, p. 74.
[4]"The Steinway Tradition," *New York Times*, August 24, 1980.
[5]"Steinway Key: In Tune with All Times," *Washington Post*, August 31, 1975.

[6]Ibid.

ther the already legendary sound and durability of a Steinway. Concert pianists generally cited the instrument's even voicing (the evenness of character and timbre in each of the 88 notes of the keyboard), the duration of its tone, and the sweetness of its registers (the roundness and softness of tone throughout the piano's entire range, without any sacrifice in volume) as especially significant. Steinways were also renowned for their extremely long lives; Peter Perez once remarked, only half in jest, that the most serious competition he faced in the piano market came from used Steinways.

Much of this reputation rested on the Steinway grands, and particularly on the Concert D, the nine-foot-long grands used in performing halls (see *Exhibit 1* for pictures of the Concert D, a medium-sized Steinway grand, and a Steinway vertical). Fewer than 300 of these concert grands were produced in 1980. Each sold for $25,500.

Their widespread use by performing artists was assisted by the Steinway Concert Service, which maintained a "bank" of pianos in cities across the United States for the use of Steinway-approved artists. Some 300 pianos and 160 cities were involved. Once a performer had achieved sufficient stature to be considered eligible by the company, he or she was offered the opportunity to use Steinways for all performances, the only expense being the cost of hauling the piano to the recital hall. A performer could visit dealers in any of the cities involved, try out the concert grands available there—ranging from one piano in out-of-the-way places to over 40 in New York—and request that a particular piano be made available on a particular date. Steinway would then handle the logistics.

Sometimes the firm went to great lengths to accommodate musicians. The great pianist Arthur Rubinstein once found himself in Buenos Aires without his own piano (a Steinway), which was on board a ship unable to dock because of a strike. After requesting help from Steinway's concert artist manager in New York, Rubinstein received, by air, another instrument that the concert manager knew from past experience he would like.

Because of the concert bank, long-standing relationships often developed between performers and particular pianos. Artists considered each piano subtly different in tone and feel. Moreover, pianos were specially adjusted and tuned to suit the individual performer's temperament and style, and Steinway provided master piano technicians to insure that the concert grands were well maintained.

In return for these services, Steinway was granted exclusive use of participating artists' names for publicity purposes. In addition, concert pianists served as informal testers of the company's pianos. According to John Steinway:

> We use the concert pianist as a proving ground. They know it. Part of this association with performing artists is the fact that we say, "Look, we are trying to make a better piano for you guys, will you try this one?" And a Gary Graffman or a Grant Johannesen or a Rudolph Serkin or one of today's fine performing artists say, "Sure." They'll try it and come back and say, "Johnny, you know that dog—I just couldn't get what I wanted out of it," and *that's* what I want to know. That's the help they give us. There's no real scientific laboratory way you could take an experimental action, put it in a piano and test it, and say, "This is 89.27 percent better than the other" or something. I want Gary Graffman to *try* the thing.[7]

Concert grands were only one model in the company's product line. In 1980 grand pianos were offered in five sizes and vertical pianos in three. Including variations in cabinet styling and types of wood, 27 product types were available, ranging in price from $4,340 for an ebony, 40-inch contemporary-styled vertical to $25,500 for the concert grand. In 1975 the prices of these models had been $2,465 and $12,450, compared to $1,445 and $7,500 in 1957.

Steinway was far better represented in the market for grand pianos than in the market for verticals. Despite its small production—in 1980, less than 2% of all pianos sold in the United States were Steinways—fully one-quarter of all grand pianos sold were produced by the firm. Its position as a manufacturer of vertical pianos was less established, a fact often reflected in its advertisements. Because of limited production volumes, backlogs were common, especially for grands. In the late 1970s a wait of six to eight months was typical. Company management, however, did

[7]"Conversation with John Steinway," *The Boston Monthly,* April, 1980.

not see this as a major concern, arguing that the lengthy backlog only heightened the mystique associated with buying a Steinway.

Since its acquisition by CBS, Steinway had not publicly reported either revenues or earnings. Industry analysts, however, estimated that the company's 1980 revenues were approximately $50 million, compared with the piano industry's total

EXHIBIT 1 The Concert D, a Medium-sized Grand, and a Steinway Vertical

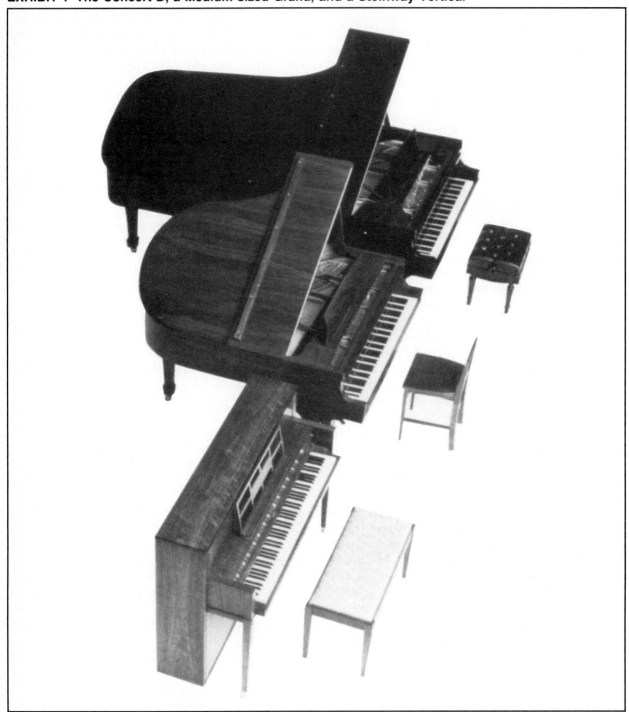

12. Steinway & Sons

sales of $424 million. As a percentage of sales, Steinway's pretax profits were thought to be nearly 15%.

The Market and Competition

The piano industry had changed dramatically since 1900, although the instruments themselves had not. Peak U.S. piano production was achieved in 1909, during the years of the player piano, when 364,545 units were produced. Production remained high during the 1920s, only to decline to a low of 34,305 units in 1933, during the Great Depression. From then on, unit sales, including a rising share of imports, grew reasonably steadily, reaching 136,332 in 1940, 172,531 in 1950, 198,200 in 1960, 193,814 in 1970, and approximately 223,000 in 1980.

After 1920, the number of piano manufacturers declined sharply, dropping from about 250 to about 30 by 1935, and then to 18 by 1961. According to the most recent *U.S. Census of Manufacturers*, in 1977 there were 16 establishments whose primary business was the production of pianos. They employed a total of 4,700 people (4,100 of them production workers), paid wages of $32.9 million, contributed a value added in manufacturing of $72 million, incurred materials costs of $100.1 million and capital expenditures of $1.8 million, and produced shipments valued at $175.3 million.

Pianos represented a large and expensive purchase for most buyers, and like other consumer durables, were expected to last for long periods. They served not only as musical instruments, but also as pieces of furniture; according to a 1961 market study, some 70% of all families kept their pianos in the living room.[8] In fact, the same study observed that nearly 10% of all piano owners did not even play the instrument.[9]

Most consumers found buying a piano very difficult. After polling a sample of piano buyers, the 1961 market study concluded that:

> The piano, as a musical instrument, is extremely difficult to evaluate. Most potential

customers are not able to perceive differences in the musical qualities of various instruments. Thus, they are afraid to trust their evaluation of "good tone." Moreover, they do not know what to look for in buying a piano. Thus, the differences between instruments go unnoticed or, if presented by the dealer, merely raise doubts and create new fears. Finally, some quality features relate to the durability rather than the immediate performance of the instrument. The consumer is forced to take the value of such features on faith. Thus, to many consumers buying a piano is a psychological hazard. Although it is an important decision and contains real risks, they are reluctant to admit to dealers their ignorance of the product and their inability to evaluate it.[10]

These difficulties were often compounded by the limited selection offered by most dealers (because of high inventory carrying costs) and their consequently limited knowledge of the differences between various makes and product lines.

The two major segments of the piano market were grands and verticals. Grand pianos were larger and more expensive than verticals, and generally possessed a louder and more resonant tone. The market for grands was much smaller than that for verticals, and fewer firms were involved. (See *Exhibits 2, 3,* and *4* for more detailed data on the U.S. piano industry.) Some companies specialized in vertical pianos alone, while others produced grands as well. In recent years, many of the small, independent firms had been absorbed by large conglomerates, as had happened in other segments of the musical instruments trade.

DOMESTIC COMPETITION. The two largest domestic piano makers were Baldwin Piano and Organ Company, a subsidiary of the Baldwin-United Company, and Kimball International, which also manufactured Bosendorfer pianos through its Austrian subsidiary. Baldwin, founded in 1862, had over the years developed a broad line of pianos that it sold through an extensive dealer network. Approximately 800 dealers were involved domestically (compared with 140 for Steinway), and each was given strong marketing and financial support. Because Baldwin-United was also involved in various financial services, the company had a policy of financing finished goods and installment contracts for its dealers, often on

[8]Milton P. Brown, John B. Stewart, and Walter J. Salmon, *A Study of the Piano Industry* (National Piano Manufacturers Association, 1961), p. 20.

[9]Ibid., p. 25.

[10]Ibid., p. 75.

EXHIBIT 2 Sales of U.S. Piano Manufacturers by Product Type

Product Type	No. of Companies with Shipments Greater Than $100,000[a] (1977)	No. of Units Shipped (thousands) (1977)	Value of Shipments ($ millions) (1977)	No. of Units Shipped (thousands) (1972)	Value of Shipments ($ millions) (1972)
Verticals, uprights, or consoles					
37″ or less in height	8	[b]	$54.6	90.3	$37.3
Greater than 37″ in height	15	155.3	104.1	109.1	56.2
Grand pianos	6	7.5	20.7	6.5	13.9

Source: U.S. Bureau of the Census, *1977 Census of Manufacturers*, Preliminary Industry Statistics.

a. Figures for the number and value of units shipped are reported for all producers in the industry, not just for those with shipments valued at greater than $100,000.

b. Data in this category were not reported by the Census Bureau because too high a proportion of the data was estimated to insure reliability.

EXHIBIT 3 U.S. Piano Industry Shipments, Domestic Sales Only

Category	No. of Units (1980)	Percent (1980)	No. of Units (1979)	Percent (1979)	No. of Units (1978)	Percent (1978)
Vertical pianos						
Short scale	689	—	1,075	—	1,418	—
Spinet (38″ and lower)	49,660	25	68,982	29	80,932	34
Console (38″ to 44″)	106,019	53	118,806	51	115,171	48
Studio (over 44″)	29,337	15	30,869	13	27,852	12
Subtotal	185,705	93%	219,732	93%	225,373	94%
Grand pianos	9,648	5	10,864	5	10,254	4
Player pianos	4,283	2	4,514	2	5,220	2
Total	199,636	100%	235,110	100%	240,847	100%

Source: Steinway & Sons.

Note: Data include shipments from Yamaha's fully owned Everett Piano Company in the United States, but do not include shipments from Yamaha's Japanese manufacturing plants.

EXHIBIT 4 Sales of Vertical Pianos over 44 Inches by Wholesale Prices

	1980		1979		1978	
	Industry	Steinway	Industry	Steinway	Industry	Steinway
Under $400	1					
$401–450	—					
$451–500	—					
$501–550	—					
$551–600	—					
$601–650	—					
$651–700	—		4		1	
$701–800	18		441		1,640	
$801–900	700		5,389		10,437	
$901–1,000	3,361		12,215		10,795	
$1,001–1,100	12,852		7,746			
$1,101–1,200	3,194		703		} 3,390 {	
Over $1,200	6,599	918	1,586	740		935
Domestic total	26,725	918	28,084	740	26,263	935
Export	2,612		2,785		1,589	
Total	29,337	918	30,869	740	27,852	935

Source: Steinway & Sons.

terms that could not be obtained from more conventional financial institutions.

Baldwin offered a full line of pianos and organs, ranging from high-quality grand pianos, well respected by trained musicians, to relatively inexpensive verticals, assembled in a highly automated plant completed in Truman, Arkansas, in 1980. Overall, the company maintained a reputation for high quality. The sales of its music division, which included guitars, drums, cymbals, and other band instruments as well as pianos and organs, were $112 million in 1980.

Kimball International was also involved in several major product lines, including pianos and organs, furniture and contract cabinets, and processed wood products. The firm displayed a high degree of vertical integration, employing its own processed wood products (such as lumber, plywood, and veneer) in its piano, organ, furniture, and contract cabinet lines, as well as manufacturing its own piano keys, actions, and metal components. All together, 35 manufacturing facilities were involved, primarily in the South and Midwest.

All of Kimball's domestic piano manufacturing had been consolidated in a single plant in West Baden, Indiana, with the exception of its recently acquired Krakaner subsidiary, which produced hand-crafted vertical pianos competing at the high end of the quality/price spectrum. In addition, Kimball continued to produce a limited number of concert grands through its Bosendorfer subsidiary. Bosendorfer, acknowledged as a quality leader by performing artists throughout the world, had recently introduced three new vertical pianos, including a 52-inch upright designed for the institutional market. The total sales of Kimball's piano and organ lines amounted to $105 million in 1980, and were supported by an extensive dealer network.

FOREIGN COMPETITION. Japanese firms were a growing force in the U.S. piano market, with Yamaha and Kawai being particularly strong. In

EXHIBIT 5 Assembly Line in the Yamaha Plant

Source: "On Yamaha's Assembly Line," *New York Times*, February 22, 1981.

1980 over 23,000 pianos were imported into the United States; of these, 21,700 were Japanese. Yamaha alone, a diversified multinational with $1.5 billion in sales, produced nearly 250,000 pianos in 1980, most of them verticals and baby grands. Assembly-line techniques were used whenever possible, even for grand pianos, which were produced at the rate of 90 per day. (See *Exhibit 5* for one of the company's main assembly lines.) Yamaha's concert grands, however, were produced by traditional craft methods in a workshop closed to visitors as a precaution against industrial espionage. In 1980 the firm produced between 250 and 300 concert grands.

Yamaha made no secret of its interest in emulating, and eventually surpassing, Steinway. Company managers commented:

> We are chasing hard, we want to catch up with Steinway. Oh, but it's unfair to compare the two, like comparing Rolls Royces with Toyotas. That makes us nervous; Steinway too, no doubt.[11]

There were several elements to the Yamaha strategy. The firm sought the finest raw materials, often claiming that its lumber came from the same mills supplying Steinway. Its engineers

[11]"On Yamaha's Assembly Line," *New York Times*, February 22, 1981.

carefully followed Steinway's research and development efforts, regularly purchasing and disassembling its competitor's pianos. (Perez once remarked, "If a quiz on Steinway pianos were given to Yamaha and Steinway engineers, I'm not sure who would score higher.") Yamaha's production process was highly automated—the lumber yard, for example, made extensive use of automated materials handling equipment, while partially completed pianos were transported throughout the factory on moving assembly lines—and also displayed a high degree of vertical integration. Yamaha was the only piano maker in the world to cast its own metal frames (the inner core of the piano, to which the strings were attached), drawing on its experience in casting moving parts for the motorcycles that it also manufactured. Worker discretion was kept to a minimum, and the entire operation was designed to insure that automation produced a consistent product. In this respect, Yamaha was not alone, for several U.S. piano manufacturers were following a similar strategy. According to David Campbell, vice president of manufacturing at Currier Piano Company:

> It has been our goal to reduce the amount of individual value judgments in the piano manufacturing process, so that we can produce a more consistent product. Skilled labor is getting more and more difficult to find and train, so the future of quality pianos really depends on improved tooling and automation. Automation will not necessarily reduce our costs; however, it will allow us to continue to manufacture a consistent, value-packed product in the face of rising costs and a lack of skilled labor.[12]

The prices of Japanese pianos were quite low, with an average landed value in 1980 of $1,215. Yamaha's vertical pianos sold for between $2,155 and $4,485 in the United States, with grands beginning at $4,900. In 1980 a Yamaha medium grand sold for $6,300, while a comparably-sized Steinway was priced at $10,500.

Both Yamaha and Kawai hoped to overcome Steinway's dominance in the grand piano market by inducing trading up among their customers. By devoting special attention to their top-of-the-line vertical pianos, designed for music schools and other institutional buyers, both firms hoped

[12]*The Music Trades*, June 1981, pp. 94, 99.

to secure the loyalty of budding performers who would eventually be in the market for grand pianos. It was precisely this strategy that Steinway's Model K professional upright was designed to combat.

Steinway's Production Process

Manufacturing operations at Steinway could be divided into two parts—traditional woodworking operations related to furniture making, and manufacturing and assembly activities peculiar to piano making. All were carried out at the firm's 440,000-square-foot factory on Long Island, a series of linked buildings that had evolved over 87 years. Within the factory, roughly 40% of the direct labor force and 50% of the floor space were allocated to furniture-making operations, with the balance of both devoted to piano making.

Two years were required to manufacture a Steinway grand—one year to dry the lumber and one year for the actual manufacturing. At any one time, the firm normally held a lumber inventory worth about $2 million. On an annual basis, this was the firm's largest raw materials expense, amounting to approximately 7.5% of the cost of goods sold. Total materials costs were between 1.5 and 1.6 times direct labor costs for grand pianos, and about 2.5 times direct labor costs for uprights.

FURNITURE-MAKING OPERATIONS. Lumber came from various sources, weathered outdoors, and then dried in large kilns with recently installed computer controls. Time was a critical element in the process, for Steinway believed that natural aging was necessary to insure the woods' best sound-producing qualities. After drying, the furniture-making operations began. These included cutting the piano's case and sounding board (a specially tapered board placed inside the case to reflect the sound made when a string was struck), building the rim for grand pianos (the curved sideboard giving grand pianos their shape, formed of multiple-ply maple that was forced into shape manually, held in molds for several hours, bombarded by high-frequency radio waves to boil out moisture, and then seasoned for 10 weeks before being matched to other wooden parts, see *Exhibit 6*); and the fabrication of piano actions (the intri-

EXHIBIT 6 Rim-bending Operation at Steinway

cate mechanical assemblies, made almost completely of wood, that transmitted pressure on the keys to hammers that struck the strings).

In these operations, the company's approach was first to find the tasks for which handcrafting was relatively unimportant, and then to provide automatic machinery for those operations. In the action department, for example, Steinway was experimenting in 1981 with a Belgian-made wood-turning machine that performed 12 operations. If adopted, it would consolidate the activities of several employees now working on separate machines, each dating back to the 1920s, that performed one or two operations apiece.

The action was a particularly important part of pianos, for it was this mechanical linkage that gave Steinways their distinctive feel. Actions were constructed of a large number of small, mostly wooden parts. Although the firm had experimented with plastic parts and considered them to be more accurate than those made of wood, consumer resistance—the perception that Steinway employed only traditional materials—had prevented their widespread adoption.

In the action department, each operator was responsible for inspecting his or her own work, with all assembled actions further subject to 100% inspection. Because component parts were coded by number, defects were easy to trace. Overall, the reject rate in the action department was 20%–30%. Only grand piano actions were manufactured by the firm; those destined for Steinway uprights were purchased from Pratt & Read, the only independent action manufacturer in the United States. Purchased actions, like all other important incoming parts, were subject to 100% inspection.

PIANO-MAKING OPERATIONS. Bellying—so called because workers both concentrated on the heart of the piano (the marriage of piano plate, soundboard, and rim) and also performed many of these tasks while leaning their stomachs against the rim of the piano—was generally considered to be the first of the piano-making operations. At this stage, tight fits were extremely important for tonal quality. Because of individual variations in the material, bellying often took considerable skill and required several hours per piano. The fitting of metal frames generally required 1.5 hours per instrument, while the fitting of sounding boards required between 3 and 4 hours.

Following the bellying operations, pianos were strung. Steinway usually purchased its strings. Stringing was extremely tedious work, involving the attachment of strings to pins and the hammering down of those pins, an operation requiring approximately two hours per piano. In 1981 the company investigated the possibility of mechanizing this operation, employing hydraulic equipment to hammer down the pins.

After stringing, pianos moved to the finishing stage, where grand and vertical pianos were physically separated (by being placed on different floors of the factory) for the first time. Up to this point, both types of pianos followed roughly similar paths, segregated only by being in separate production lots. Verticals were processed in lot sizes of approximately 42 (depending on the model and type of wood), while grands were processed in minimum lots sizes of 12.

At the finishing stage—roughly akin to final assembly—the various components of the piano were assembled into a working instrument. Actions and keyboards were fitted individually to each instrument to accommodate differences in materials and tolerances. This fitting normally took 2 or 3 hours, but occasionally took as long as 26 hours.

Pianos were also "broken in" in the finishing department. Keys were weighted for touch, the piano underwent its first rough tuning, and a piano banger (an electrically driven testing machine with plungers that struck all 88 keys at the rate of 10,000 cycles per hour) then went to work, exercising each instrument so that tuners and tone regulators would be able to work with aged pianos not subject to drifting off-key. Piano bangers were also used occasionally for

destructive testing to determine an instrument's durability.

Finally, the instruments moved to the polishing, tone regulating, and rubbing departments. There, woods were polished and shined, keys were cleaned, and most important, pianos were voiced. Unlike tuning, which involved the loosening and tightening of strings, voicing required the softening of the felt surrounding the hammers that struck the strings, an operation of extreme delicacy. Ten tone regulators were employed by the firm, two for uprights and eight for grands. They were widely considered to be among the most skilled artisans at Steinway. The voicing of a concert grand required nearly perfect pitch, and took as much as 20 to 30 hours. All tone regulators at Steinway had worked for the company in various positions before reaching their present posts, and several had more than 20 years with the firm.[13] After tone regulation, all pianos were inspected a final time and were then sent off for shipment.

In total, Steinway grands were thought to include 12,000 parts, according to an estimate made by John Steinway in the 1950s. Four hundred thirty people worked at the firm's Long Island plant, all but 100 of them in production. They were represented by Local 102 of the United Furniture Workers, a small, two-company local that had been bargaining with Steinway management for many years. Their last strike had been in 1970. Wages averaged approximately $7.00 per hour ($10 including fringes), with the lowest hiring-in rate being $4.05 per hour. Seventy-five percent of all workers were paid on a stright-time basis; the remainder, primarily skilled artisans, were paid piece rates. Total direct labor costs for a grand piano averaged between $900 and $1,500. For vertical pianos, the average was between $400 and $500.

Steinway's major labor concern was insuring a stable supply of skilled workers. In particular, young people were needed to replace older artisans when they retired. Various apprenticeship programs had been established to meet this need. Yet according to Joseph J. Pramberger, director of manufacturing operations at Steinway:

[13]Finding qualified tone regulators had been a particular problem for Yamaha. In 1980 the company created a Piano Technical Academy to train them for products already in the field; in April 1981, it planned to start training tone regulators for manufacturing.

My biggest problem is getting and keeping skilled people. After several years with Steinway, our employees become highly marketable, and often leave to start firms of their own specializing in the rebuilding of old pianos. The apprenticeship programs haven't helped all that much, for they simply result in more people having transferable skills.

Steinway had traditionally followed a policy of no layoffs. During the tenure of the first CBS-appointed president, however, workers had briefly been placed on short and alternating work weeks to combat quality problems. One result of this move, according to Perez, had been the existing workforce's discovery of its marketability. At the time, several employees had left Steinway for jobs elsewhere.

The Model K

The original version of the Model K, a 50-inch vertical piano, had been produced by Steinway in the United States from 1903 until the late 1920s. At the firm's Hamburg plant, production had continued into the 1960s, although in ever-decreasing numbers. There were differences of opinion within Steinway about why the original line had been phased out, for it had been extremely popular, and many knowledgeable piano technicians considered the Model K the best vertical piano the firm had ever built. Some company insiders cited the trend toward smaller vertical pianos and the shift away from 50-inch uprights as the reason for the model's demise, while others considered the rapid growth in demand for grand pianos and the resulting reduction in the volume of verticals the cause.

Steinway's interest in reintroducing a 50-inch vertical piano was triggered by the actions of others. According to Bill Steinway:

> I wish we could claim originality, but several of our competitors got there first. In the late 1960s Mason & Hamlin, an American piano maker [now a division of the Aeolian Corporation, a diversified musical instruments manufacturer], introduced a 50-inch upright. At about the same time, several Japanese firms entered the market with comparable models.
>
> We began to think seriously about introducing a 50-inch upright of our own, and our thoughts turned immediately to the Model K. But

things move slowly here at Steinway. The possibility of reintroducing the Model K was kicked around for 10 or 15 years with little real progress. It was only in 1977 or 1978 that we began active work on the project, for it was only then that we had a large enough R&D staff to pursue the matter without diverting attention from other activities.

The early phases of the project involved dismantling old Model Ks and working up parts specifications and engineering drawings, for none had survived from the earlier production period. At the time, there was some disagreement about how closely the new model should duplicate the old. Bill Steinway argued that the two should be as much alike as possible. That, he claimed, would enable the firm to capitalize on its image of traditional craftsmanship. This view eventually prevailed, and a tentative advertising slogan, "An Old Friend Returns," was designed to build on the theme.

Occasional difficulties appeared in working up the new Model K, for certain production practices had changed since the model was first produced. In the early 1900s, for example, Steinway had manufactured all of its actions, while in the 1970s and 1980s, it produced actions only for grand pianos. Arrangements were therefore made with Pratt & Read to produce the necessary parts for the Model K. Only after close consultation between the two firms and one or two unsuccessful efforts, however, were Steinway engineers satisfied with the actions Pratt & Read provided.

Once parts specifications had been drawn up, a year was spent building prototypes. Twelve prototypes were built in all. Unanticipated problems were ironed out at this time, and once the sixth or seventh prototype had been completed, Steinway's engineers felt that few bugs remained. As an example of the changes made during this stage of development, Bill Steinway cited the discovery that the Model K's larger-than-normal size had resulted in pedals that were too high off the ground to be played comfortably. Subsequent prototypes therefore incorporated "drop pedals" that were easier to reach. All prototypes were constructed on the shop floor, rather than in a separate pattern shop. At each of the piano-making operations the best worker had been singled out, and that stage of the Model K's production had been assigned to him or her.

Employee reactions appeared to be favorable, a result that Bill Steinway attributed to the rarity of major new-product introductions at Steinway and the excitement employees felt when working on anything new.

Annual production of 200 to 250 units was anticipated for the Model K. Prices were expected to be between $7,000 and $7,700, depending on the wood employed. A comparable 50-inch upright manufactured by the Aeolian Corporation sold for approximately $5,000 in 1981, while one produced by the Japanese sold for a bit less.

Bill Steinway had worked on the Model K project from its inception. He began his July 16 meeting with Perez with the following comments:

> I don't think there's any doubt that we will benefit from the Model K. It's certain to do no damage to our sales of grand pianos, and can only help. Remember, Peter, that once a vertical piano reaches 50 inches in height, the sound it produces comes closer and closer to that of a grand. String length and soundboard size increase significantly. This way, we should be able to attract customers who wouldn't buy Steinway grands because they are either too expensive or too large.
>
> Furthermore, introducing the Model K should have little impact on our existing production process. Because grands and uprights are separated at the piano-making operations, the Model K should have no effect at all on our ability to produce grands. And since we presently have excess capacity in the upright departments, we should have no trouble there either.

Perez replied:

> Bill, I understand your feelings, but I'm still concerned about the Model K's impact. Is it the best way to repel Yamaha and Kawai? Or will it simply cannibalize sales from our 45-inch upright? We really haven't done enough market research to determine its ultimate impact.
>
> Besides, I still wonder if this is the best way to spend our limited time and resources. Aren't we diverting our attention from grand pianos, where we're strongest? And won't a new product introduction at this time merely create delays and confusion? Maybe we should sit down and rethink our plans for the future.

13. Sanyo Manufacturing Corporation— Forrest City, Arkansas

On January 1, 1977, the ownership of Warwick Electronics Corporation's television operations formally shifted to Sanyo Electric Co. of Japan. A rapidly growing, diversified multinational company whose worldwide sales in 1976 were about $2.2 billion, Sanyo had agreed in May 1976 to buy Whirlpool Corporation's 57% ownership of Warwick's television business for $11 million. The company subsequently purchased an additional 16% of Warwick's outstanding shares for a little over $3 million through a tender offer. A separate U.S. corporation, Sanyo Manufacturing Corporation (SMC), was set up to operate Warwick's former plant in Forrest City, Arkansas, a small city of about 13,000 inhabitants that was located 40 miles west of Memphis, Tennessee.

Warwick's television business had originally been established in 1964 as a joint venture with Sears, Roebuck and Co. In 1966 the Whirlpool Corporation purchased Warwick. The television business then became a joint venture between Whirlpool and Sears and was expected to serve primarily as a captive supplier of color television receivers to Sears, which owned 25% of its common stock. During the 1960s the Forrest City plant's output grew rapidly, and employment rose to over 2,500 people. However, in the 1970s it became increasingly difficult to meet competitive prices, quality, and technology, and Sears began to purchase more and more sets from Sanyo for sale under the Sears name. In 1976 Warwick's television sales to Sears fell to $71 million from $160 million in 1974, and Warwick incurred a loss of over $9 million on those sales. Warwick's officials

noted that Sears had increased its purchases from offshore suppliers by 50% during that year, and blamed "intensified competition from foreign manufacturers . . . and low consumer demand" for the company's declining sales. Because of its increasingly precarious financial situation, Warwick discontinued the production of portable and table model color television sets in late 1976 and closed down four of the five assembly lines in the Forrest City plant. Employment there had dropped to about 500 people when Sanyo took it over. A survivor of that era recalled those days:

> This was really a desolate place then. The plant was clearly going downhill. We knew that Sears was supplanting us with Japanese suppliers, even though they owned a big piece of the company. People were continually being laid off, and the handwriting was on the wall for everyone to see. There was no money, so we were letting the equipment run down. We were having terrible quality problems and spending nights and weekends reworking sets so that we could keep up with our delivery schedules. The management group was working as hard as it could, and yet things kept getting worse. It was really demoralizing.

The quality problems seemed to stem largely from a series of major design changes that the company had made over the previous six years. Warwick had been very proud of its technological capabilities in the early 1960s (for example, one old-timer boasted that the plant had been 14 months early in starting up the production of television receivers in 1964, when they were widely acknowledged to be one of the most difficult-to-produce consumer products that had ever been created). By the late 1960s, however, the company

This case was prepared by Robert H. Hayes and Kim B. Clark.

Copyright © 1981 by the President and Fellows of Harvard College. Harvard Business School case 682-045.

fell behind technologically when most of its competitors introduced new designs incorporating solid-state components.[1] Warwick countered with a crash program that resulted in the "Ultra I," a hybrid design (incorporating both solid-state devices and vacuum tubes) that turned out to be almost impossible to manufacture.

One manager recounted:

> The "infant mortality rate" on those sets was awesome. We would consider it a triumph if, by the time a completed set arrived at the end of the assembly line, it simply lit up when we pushed the ON button. Sears was frantic. We kept shipping them sets that either wouldn't work in their showrooms or, worse, in their customers' living rooms. We were always rushing up to their corporate offices to explain to them what we were doing to improve quality. But, to be truthful, basically there was very little we could do with that design. It might have been makeable in the designers' laboratory, but it wasn't makeable on a mass production assembly line.

> Once we realized this, we started another crash program to develop a new design, and simply tried to hang on until it was ready. Three years after the Ultra I appeared we introduced the Ultra II, which was a completely solid-state design. It was a tremendous improvement, both in terms of final quality and manufacturability. But it was too late. Sears had lost confidence in us.

When Sears decided that Forrest City was unlikely to rebuild its position as a major supplier under Warwick management, it approached Sanyo Electric, which was Sears's major foreign supplier of television sets, to see if Sanyo would be interested in taking over the plant. Although Sanyo had misgivings about this proposal, it finally decided to accept for various reasons. According to Hajime Nakai, the president of SMC in 1981:

> The name Sanyo means "three oceans." That means we want to expand to the world, not merely grow in Japan. Our founder . . . had the desire to establish facilities in different countries, and today we have 30 overseas plants [television sets were produced in 13 countries]. Our move to the United States was spurred by the restrictions on color television imports.[2]

[1] See the case "Zenith Radio Corporation (A)" HBS No. 9-674-026 for another perspective on this period.

[2] Quoted from an interview on page 98 in the June 15, 1981, issue of *Fortune* magazine. At the time of the acquisition negotiations (1976), the restrictions referred to were not yet in place but were under discussion. In July 1977 the governments of the United States and Japan agreed to limit Japanese exports through an "Orderly Market Agreement."

Other informed observers speculated that Sanyo saw the acquisition as another way to lock in its business with Sears. At the same time, moreover, Sanyo could acquire relatively cheaply the equipment and trained workers that would enable it to expand its penetration of the U.S. market and learn how to manage in the U.S. environment. They pointed out that Sanyo Electric had been founded only in 1947, and its incredible growth since then was largely attributable to its intense competitiveness. When Sanyo's Japanese archrival, Matsushita, acquired Quasar (Motorola's television subsidiary) in 1974, it was only a matter of time before Sanyo followed. Sears made the deal even more attractive by agreeing to loan Sanyo $9 million under an unsecured 6% term loan agreement due in four annual installments of $500,000 each, beginning December 31, 1978, with the balance due on December 31, 1982.

The Turnaround at Forrest City

SMC commenced operations on January 4, 1977, with one color television production line that produced console models. A second production line for console color receivers was added in February. Tabletop color receivers were added in midyear, necessitating the addition of three more production lines during the balance of 1977. One survivor of that period marveled at the rapidity with which the turnaround occurred:

> Within two or three months the mood in the plant changed from apprehension to a feeling that we were going to make it. There was a sense of confidence and purpose. The company was increasing production, adding equipment, and hiring people back. It was clearly here to stay.

In 1979 SMC entered into a new five-year agreement with Sears, to commence on January 1, 1980. Sears agreed to purchase at least 70% of its annual requirements of color television receivers for sale in the United States from SMC (at prices to be determined by periodic negotiations). During 1980 about 82% of the company's production went to Sears; the remainder was sold through SMC's parent company.

In mid-1981 the Forrest City plant hummed with activity. About 1,750 workers were employed in its television operations, turning out roughly 800,000 sets per year. Another 350 people worked in the plant's furniture shop (which produced wooden cabinets for television sets, sewing machine cabinets, and hotel/motel furniture), and an additional 250 people produced microwave ovens—an activity that SMC had entered into in early 1980. Most of the hourly employees had worked for Warwick previously, as had most of the 420 salaried employees. Although five of the top nine officers in the company (including the president and senior vice president) were Japanese, only 16 other Japanese worked at the plant. A summary of SMC's operating results and financial positions for the years 1977 to 1980 is contained in *Exhibit 1.*

The industry's competitiveness had, if anything, grown more fierce over that four-year period. There were approximately 18 domestic and international manufacturers that had substantial sales in the United States in 1981, several of which were subsidiaries of such giant multinationals as RCA, GE, Philips (of Holland, through its acquisition of Magnavox), Matsushita, Toshiba, and Hitachi. In terms of unit sales, SMC estimated that it was one of the seven-largest suppliers during 1980, with a market share of 7% to 8%. SMC characterized its industry as "intensely competitive in terms of price, service, warranties, and product performance."

Interviews with managers who had participated in the turnaround at SMC offered various explanations for the achievement. According to one person:

> The first thing Sanyo did when they took over was [that]· they retained essentially all the employees and managers who were there. You really have to respect the fact that they defined their task as one of changing the organization's effectiveness without changing the people. They did move some people around, though. For example, they took the former manager of Quality Control—who really had been taking a lot of heat from everybody during the previous two years, because of the quality problems we were having—and made him the plant manager. That, by the way, was just one of the signals they gave that the number-one priority for the plant was improving quality. All they talked about was quality.

The quality problem was attacked through various measures. One of the new management's first actions was to clear out the plant over a weekend, clean it, and polyurethane the floors.

Not only did this make the whole plant look cleaner and brighter, but it also reduced the dust in the air that sometimes caused equipment to gum up or interfered with the connections of electronic parts. "Also, when a floor is clean like that, anything that falls on it is more visible, so you automatically pick it up. It seems like a silly little thing, but it made a noticeable improvement in morale," remembered one employee.

Another employee mentioned that Sanyo had separated Quality Control from Quality Assurance, instituted new assembly procedures (the assembly cycle time per worker was reduced substantially), and put expanded resources into preventing quality problems before they arose.

> In the Warwick days, volume and cost were all-important. If we had a quality problem and I wanted to put some additional people on the line, the line managers would fight me. They were under orders to keep their costs down. If a snag develops on the line today, we put more people on it right away and don't worry about the cost. I don't think [one of the senior Japanese managers] even knows what a labor utilization sheet is!

Higher quality standards were announced (many workers and managers felt that they were unrealistically high), and new equipment and procedures were instituted to assist workers in meeting them. For example, one new piece of equipment reduced the time required to pinpoint and correct problems in the convergence of the electron beam onto the television screen from as much as two days to one hour. Production flows were speeded up through the addition of conveyor belts and other materials-handling equipment.

Most important, perhaps, was the plant's shift from producing Warwick's old Ultra II model to Sanyo models; the PC boards and major components for these sets were imported from Sanyo's Osaka (W4) plant. The quality of these imported boards awed the inspectors of incoming goods at Forrest City. "We started off testing them with our usual sampling procedures, and after two weeks realized it was just a waste of time. Not only were they all within the tolerance ranges, they were right in the *middle* of the ranges."

The company also began making several parts that it had formerly purchased from outside suppliers. For example, SMC purchased four modern, high-volume foam-molding machines and began producing all of its own plastic inserts for use in packing finished sets in their cardboard boxes. In 1981 SMC was still using only a portion of the total capacity of these machines and was seeking work from other manufacturers in the area. The company manufactured all of its wooden cabinets for television sets. Metal-stamping equipment had also been added, which allowed SMC to produce all the metal work for its microwave ovens. Several managers commented on Sanyo's belief in vertical integration.

In connection with all the improvements that SMC made internally, the company also emphasized improving the quality of purchased items. A new supervisor of incoming inspection, Jim Steinmetz, was hired and asked to increase the standards for purchased parts. He instituted a system of 100% inspection for all parts, but he

EXHIBIT 1 Financial Results ($ in millions)

Year Ending November 30	1977	1978	1979	1980
Gross sales	$94.9	$159.0	$146.4	$257.3
Cost of goods sold	88.1	150.4	141.7	239.1
Purchases from parent company	43.8	87.9	78.1	118.2
General and administrative expenses	2.2	3.5	4.4	6.5
Interest expenses	0.9	1.0	4.4	5.6
Income (loss) before taxes	3.8	3.1	(4.1)	6.3
Provision (credit) for income taxes	1.9	1.5	(2.0)	2.6
Net income (loss)	1.8	1.5	(2.1)	3.7
Retained earnings, end of year	1.8	3.4	1.3	5.0
Net additions to				
Buildings and improvements	1.8	1.9	0.5	2.3
Machinery, equipment, and tools	1.8	2.2	1.1	5.4
Elimination of fully depreciated assets from accounts	0.2	0.3	1.1	1.8
Inventories	12.5	33.0	28.7	53.9
Raw materials	8.9	9.4	24.8	19.8
Work in process	1.0	1.0	2.1	2.6
Finished goods	2.5	22.5	1.8	31.5
Other current assets	16.5	14.1	36.4	28.9
Buildings and improvements	7.5	7.5	7.9	10.3
Machinery, equipment and tools	3.3	3.9	4.9	10.4
Less: allowance for depreciation and amortization	(3.6)	(4.1)	(4.3)	(4.8)
Construction in progress	N/A	N/A	0.5	4.1
Current liabilities	16.2	13.5	50.7	67.8
Long-term debt	12.2	31.5	19.6	19.9
Stockholders' equity	7.8	9.4	7.3	11.0
Total assets	$36.3	$54.5	$77.7	$99.1
Unit production:				
TV (sets)	317,000	625,000	420,000	840,000
Microwave	—	—	—	142,000
Adapter[a]	—	—	—	38,000

Note: N/A means not available.

a. In 1980 Sanyo began producing an adapter that provided video captions for the deaf.

hoped eventually to reduce the need for this by working with SMC's suppliers to improve the quality and uniformity of their products. For example, Steinmetz recounted one of his early experiences with the supplier that produced the corrugated cardboard boxes that the finished sets were shipped in:

> The Japanese managers were shocked by the quality of those cardboard boxes. There were imperfections in the cardboard; the letters printed on them were often uneven, and the color [all the printing is done in "Sanyo blue"] wasn't uniform. "You must get that supplier to produce better boxes," I was told. Now remember, those boxes take a lot of abuse. They are stacked, unstacked, and shipped around three or four times before they arrive at a customer's house, and then they're usually torn open without even a look. But I went to that company and said, "I want perfect boxes: no flaws in the corrugation, perfect letters, and uniform color." They said, "You have to be kidding. You don't need perfect boxes; we can't produce them, and even if we could, it would cost more than it's worth." I said, "Okay, if you can't produce perfect boxes, I'll go find someone who can." "Hey, wait a minute," they said, "at least give us a chance."
>
> So I worked with them for over a year, and by the end of that time they were producing boxes that met our specifications. Recently Sharp and Toshiba [two major Japanese companies] set up plants in Memphis and Lebanon, Tennessee, respectively, and this company went to them and said, "We can make perfect boxes. Sanyo buys all their boxes from us. Why don't you?" They got the business and now they're telling me, "Thanks for showing us that we can make boxes to Japanese standards."

Difficulties along the Way

By 1981 SMC's management team felt that it had developed a strong competitive base from which to expand. Since the acquisition, unit production had increased almost by a factor of 10, and the incidence of defects caught at final inspection had dropped to one-fourth of its preacquisition figure. The company was solidly profitable, and its biggest customer was indicating its satisfaction by increasing its purchases. This satisfaction was tempered, however, by the realization that the road to success had not been entirely smooth and that there were still problems that had to be overcome.

Organization

As might be expected, there were difficulties in developing an organizational approach for handling the necessary coordination between SMC and Sanyo, its parent, which supplied approximately half of SMC's purchased parts and bought almost 20% of its total output. This parent, moreover, was 12,000 miles away, and few of its managers had any experience working in the United States.

Immediately after the acquisition, Sanyo tried to manage the plant using a committee approach. The committee consisted of six vice presidents: three Americans (all of whom had been with Warwick before the acquisition) and three Japanese living in the United States. Over time it became apparent that this approach was not satisfactory. Decision making was slow, and production personnel had difficulty obtaining answers to basic questions within a reasonable amount of time. In general, Americans were awaiting guidance from the Japanese (who, after all, were the new owners of the plant), and the Japanese were expecting the Americans to make the changes that were inferentially being suggested. A communications gap clearly existed. After roughly two years, a senior executive vice president at Sanyo moved from Japan to Forrest City, and a more traditional organization was established. *Exhibit 2* shows the organization chart in mid-1981.

Worker-Management Relations

Most of the hourly workers in the plant were organized by the IUE (International Union of Electrical Workers), whose attitude toward the acquisition and turnaround had generally been supportive. In 1979, however, the union went out on strike for eight weeks during August and September in the course of an attempt to negotiate a new three-year contract. SMC blamed this strike for the loss in profits incurred during 1979, and a residue of disappointment and animosity on both sides resulted from this incident. As 1982 approached, management was uneasy over the prospect of renegotiating the union contract.

Managers had different explanations for the strike. One described it as "an exercise in reality testing": the union was somewhat uneasy about

EXHIBIT 2 Organization Chart as of Mid-1981

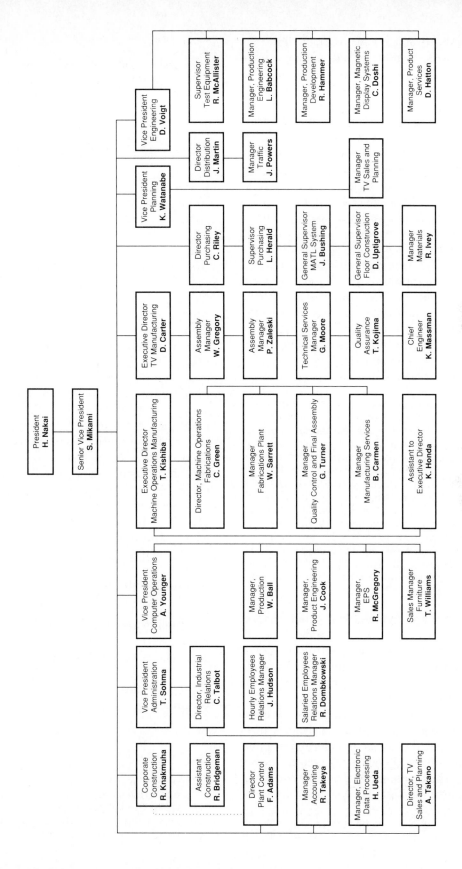

a possible erosion of its power under Japanese management and wanted to find out how tough the Japanese really were. Another explanation was that the strike was simply an attempt by the union to share in the increased profitability of the company. Another manager argued that the problem mostly arose from the workers' hostility toward their first-level supervisors, who were essentially the same people operating in the same way as before the acquisition. "What we have here is a Japanese philosophy at the top, but it's being implemented on the plant floor by a lot of 'theory X' hardnoses." Another manager offered this perspective, "To see [the strike] simply as a consequence of differing Japanese and American management philosophies is a little too neat; what you have here is a tension that results from a variety of cultural differences: black versus white, Yankee versus Rebel, and Japanese versus American. The fact that the union is primarily black complicates the issue even more."

According to Nakai:

> American workers maintain a much looser relationship toward their company compared with Japanese. . . . However, we learned some lessons from [the strike] and are now trying to improve the situation. In Japan, the union lives with the company and never pulls the trigger unless it finds itself in an extremely serious situation. It tries as much as possible to work with us on the same ground, because its members' future and prosperity are directly linked with ours. The important question for us right now is how to instill this concept in our American workers . . . [they] must be aware that their own standard of living is very much related to the prosperity of their company.

An American manager commented further, "The Japanese regarded the strike almost as self-destructive, particularly since we are the biggest employer in Forrest City, had only recently moved out of red ink, and the whole economy of the area depended on us."

Workers and managers both pointed to some positive development in workers' attitudes, however. For example, there was considerable support for SMC's attempts to level production rather than try to chase demand through the year. According to Hajime Nakai:

> Given different American conditions, we haven't been totally able to transplant the Jap-

anese way [a strict no-layoff policy] to America. . . . Heavy sales [are] focused in November and December for the Christmas season. We've naturally had to adjust our production schedule and lay off some workers, as do other American manufacturers.

The extent of these January layoffs, however, was not nearly as severe as they had been under Warwick management, when from 700 to 900 people were laid off every year for several weeks. Nor, under SMC, did workers have to contend with unexpected short-term "quality layoffs." As one manager explained, "If they were having a quality problem somewhere that caused the line to stop, Warwick would just lay off the workers for a day or two until the problem was solved. None of these layoffs lasted very long, but they probably totaled a couple of weeks every year."

The Japanese had also been working to break down the barriers between "management" and hourly employees. They encouraged periodic meetings between the two groups and were "thinking about instituting Quality Circles into the organization." Most of these attempts were rather small and tentative, but managers detected a clear change in emphasis. "Warwick didn't think the plant people knew anything," was one comment. Some Americans, however, perceived the Japanese as hardheaded. "They never really *demand* anything, but they are very persistent in *asking* you to do it until it's done," was how one employee described their tenacity.

Vendor Relations

SMC had retained most of the vendors who had supplied it under the previous Warwick management. As mentioned earlier, SMC was working with these vendors to help them improve their quality. This did not always proceed smoothly. Steinmetz described two problems he had encountered.

> We have a little supplier of plastic parts which is located a couple of hundred miles north of here. Their quality is okay, but it hasn't improved over the past couple of years, despite our encouragement and pressure. Finally, I went up there to visit the plant to see if there was any way I could help. They were very friendly and cooperative, but their operation was a mess. It

was dirty and poorly laid out. Worse, they couldn't even see the imperfections in the parts they were sending us because the lighting at the inspection station wasn't good enough. They have a long, long way to go, and I'm not sure they have the capability to do it.

Another supplier is just the opposite: a big sophisticated company that supplies us with one of our major components. The quality of those components has always been excellent, to the point where we didn't even bother to conduct incoming inspections of their shipments anymore. But a few weeks ago we noticed an abnormally high rate of failure [3 to 4 times the usual rate] in that component during our final testing process. We went to the company, and they told us, "Oh, yes, we were having some problems with our process and were trying to get it straightened out." But they never *informed* us. I nearly hit the roof.

Now I have to decide whether to keep either or both of these suppliers, and write them both letters explaining my decision and describing the changes that I want made.

Looking at Forrest City from the Japanese Perspective

Many Japanese naturally viewed Forrest City as a foreign and perplexing environment. Reflecting this uneasiness, several of them had left their families in Japan and were living together in a "bachelors' house." Beyond the obvious differences in language, culture, racial mix, and population density (most of Sanyo's plants in Japan were in crowded urban settings), there were basic differences in business philosophy and practice. Examples abounded, and at the heart of many of them was the absence in America of the concept of "teamwork," as the Japanese understood it. As Nakai stated:

> The key element [for productivity improvement] is teamwork, with the responsibility resting squarely on management to motivate its workers. The reason there are workmanship problems in the United States, I believe, is the different

concept of teamwork. In a Japanese plant there is much more dialogue between blue-collar and white-collar workers; in fact, the rapport is so natural, we take it for granted. Such, however, is not the case in the United States. In this respect we may even be more advanced in the concept of democracy than Americans.

Another Japanese manager described the frustration of getting U.S. workers to inspect the work done by other workers further up the assembly line:

> They feel that it is wrong to say that a fellow worker has made an error, or even to correct the errors they see. But surely this is essential if the company is to turn out good products. If we make defective products, who will buy them? And where will these people work if nobody buys them?

A third manager, who coordinated shipments between Japan and the United States, mentioned that the managers with whom he was dealing in Japan found it very difficult to understand the different attitudes toward the production schedule that existed in the two countries. He explained:

> In Japan, if the production schedule for the week is 1,000, exactly 1,000 will be produced. If, at the end of the normal work week, the workers have only produced 950, they will then stay on and work until the 1,000 sets have been produced. But in the United States they go home when their workday is over—irrespective of how many sets they have completed.
>
> And the absenteeism of the American worker is incomprehensible at home. Almost every day as many as 5% of our workers do not come to work. Think of the cost and waste caused by this. The American managers accept this as "normal," but we can never accept it.

Another manager, when asked if colleagues in Japan were beginning to understand U.S. practices better as they gained more familiarity with them, replied with an ironic smile: "No, they do not understand. They do not *want* to understand!"

14. A Note on Quality: The Views of Deming, Juran, and Crosby

During the 1980s concerns about American competitiveness steered many U.S. companies to a new interest in quality. The three leading "quality gurus" were W. Edwards Deming, Joseph Juran, and Philip Crosby. Each was an active consultant, lecturer, and author, with years of experience. Deming and Juran were in their eighties and had been enormously influential in Japan; Crosby was in his sixties and had worked previously at ITT as vice president of quality. Each had developed his own distinctive approach to quality management.

Deming

W. Edwards Deming was widely credited with leading the Japanese quality revolution. The Japanese began to heed his advice on statistical process control (SPC) and problem-solving techniques in 1950, but 30 years passed before American businesses began to respond. By then, Deming's message to managers was blunt: "The basic cause of sickness in American industry and resulting unemployment is failure of top management to manage."[1] Known to dismiss client companies that did not change, he stated, "I give 'em three years. I've got to see a lot happen."[2] Best efforts were not enough; a program was needed, and it had to be adopted wholeheartedly:

> Everyone doing his best is not the answer. It is necessary that people know what to do. Drastic changes are required. The responsibility for change rests on management. The first step is to learn how to change.[3]

What Deming then expected from his clients was summarized in a 14-point program (see *Exhibit 1*).

To begin, managers had to put aside their preoccupation with today to make sure there was a tomorrow. They had to orient themselves to continuous improvement of products and services to meet customers' needs and stay ahead of the competition. They had to innovate constantly and commit resources to support innovation and continuous quality improvement. They had to build quality in. They had to break down department and worker-supervisor barriers. They had to rid themselves of numerical targets and quotas and instead had to concentrate on improving processes, giving workers clear standards for acceptable work, as well as the tools needed to achieve it. Finally, they had to create a climate free of finger pointing and fear, which block cooperative identification and solution of problems.

If management committed itself to this new order, Deming argued, productivity as well as

---

[1] W. Edwards Deming, *Quality, Productivity, and Competitive Position* (Cambridge, MA: Massachusetts Institute of Technology, Center for Advanced Engineering Study, 1982), p. i.

This case was prepared by Artemis March under the direction of David A. Garvin.

[2] Jeremy Main, "The Curmudgeon Who Talks Tough on Quality," *Fortune*, June 25, 1984, p. 122.

[3] Deming, *Quality*, p. ii.

EXHIBIT 1 Deming's 14 Points

1. **Create constancy of purpose for improvements of product and service.**[a] Management must change from a preoccupation with the short run to building for the long run. This requires dedication to innovation in all areas to best meet the needs of customers.

2. **Adopt the new philosophy.** Shoddy materials, poor workmanship, defective products, and lax service must become unacceptable.

3. **Cease dependence on mass inspection.** Inspection is equivalent to planning for defects; it comes too late and is ineffective and costly. Instead, processes must be improved.

4. **End the practice of awarding business on price tag alone.** Price has no meaning without a measure of the quality being purchased. Therefore, the job of purchasing will change only after management establishes new guidelines. Companies must develop long-term relationships and work with fewer suppliers. Purchasing must be given statistical tools to judge the quality of vendors and purchased parts. Both purchasing and vendors must understand specifications, but they must also know how the material is to be used in production and by the final customer.

5. **Constantly and forever improve the system of production and service.** Waste must be reduced and quality improved in every activity: procurement, transportation, engineering, methods, maintenance, sales, distribution, accounting, payroll, customer service, and manufacturing. Improvement, however, does not come from studying the defects produced by a process that is in control but from studying the process itself. Most of the responsibility for process improvement rests with management.

6. **Institute modern methods of training on the job.** Training must be restructured and centered on clearly defined concepts of acceptable work. Statistical methods must be used for deciding when training has been completed successfully.

7. **Institute modern methods of supervising.** Supervisors must be empowered to inform upper management about conditions that need correction; once informed, management must take action. Barriers that prevent hourly workers from doing their jobs with pride must be removed.

8. **Drive out fear.** Because of the tremendous economic losses caused by fear on the job, people must not be afraid to ask questions, to report problems, or to express ideas.

9. **Break down barriers between departments.** Members of the research, design, procurement, sales, and receiving departments must learn about problems with raw materials and specifications in production and assembly. Each discipline must stop optimizing its own work and instead work together as a team for the company as a whole. Multidisciplinary quality-control circles can help improve design, service, quality, and costs.

10. **Eliminate numerical goals for the work force.** Targets, slogans, pictures, and posters urging people to increase productivity must be eliminated. Most of the necessary changes are out of workers' control, so such exhortations merely cause resentment. Although workers should not be given numerical goals, the company itself must have a goal: never-ending improvement.

11. **Eliminate work standards and numerical quotas.** Quotas focus on quantity, no quality. Therefore, work standards practically guarantee poor quality and high costs. Work standards that state percentage-defective or scrap goals normally reach those targets but never exceed them. Piecework is even worse, for it pays people for building defective units. But if someone's pay is docked for defective units, that is unfair, for the worker did not create the defects.

12. **Remove barriers that hinder the hourly workers.** Any barrier that hinders pride in work must be removed, including not knowing what good work is, supervisors motivated by quotas, off-gauge parts and material, and no response to reports of out-of-order machines.

13. **Institute a vigorous program of education and training.** Because quality and productivity improvements change the number of people needed in some areas and the jobs required, people must be continually trained and retrained. All training must include basic statistical techniques.

14. **Create a structure in top management that will push every day on the above 13 points.**

a. Deming's words are in bold heading. The remainder of each paragraph paraphrases the discussions in *Quality, Productivity, and Competitive Position*, pp. 17–50.

---

quality would improve. Contrary to conventional wisdom in the United States, quality and productivity were not to be traded off against each other. Rather, productivity was a by-product of quality and of doing the job right the first time:

> Improvement of the process increases uniformity of product, reduces rework and mistakes, reduces waste of manpower, machine-time, and materials, and thus increases output with less

effort. Other benefits of improved quality are lower costs, . . . happier people on the job, and more jobs, through better competitive position of the company.[4]

Because management was responsible, in Deming's view, for 85% of all quality problems, management had to take the lead in changing the

[4]Ibid., p. 1.

systems and processes that created those problems. For example, consistent quality of incoming materials and components could not be expected when buyers were told to shop for price or were not given the tools for assessing a supplier's quality. Management had to develop long-term relationships with vendors, work with vendors to improve and maintain quality, train its own purchasing department in statistical quality control, require statistical evidence of quality from vendors, and insist that specifications be complete, including an understanding of how the material actually worked in manufacturing. Once management had changed purchasing systems and procedures, buyers could then not only be expected but also able to do their job in a new way. When top management had seriously committed to quality, lower-level personnel would be more likely to take action on problems that were within their control.

Accordingly, Deming delineated two means of process improvement: changing the "common causes" that were systemic (and were thus shared by numerous operators, machines, or products) and removing the "special causes" that produced nonrandom variation within systems (and were usually confined to individual employees or activities). Common causes included poor product design, incoming materials unsuited to their use, machines out of order, improper bills of materials, machinery that would not hold tolerances, poor physical conditions, and so on. Special causes included lack of knowledge or skill, worker inattention, or a poor lot of incoming materials. Management was responsible for common causes, and operators were responsible for special causes:

> The discovery of a special cause of variation and its removal are usually the responsibility of someone who is connected directly with some operation. . . . In contrast, there are common causes of defectives, of errors, of low rates of production, of low sales, of accidents. These are the responsibility of management. . . . The worker at a machine can do nothing about causes common to all machines. . . . He cannot do anything about the light; he does not purchase raw materials; the training, supervision, and the company's policies are not his.[5]

[5]Deming, *Quality*, p. 116.

The key tool that Deming advocated to distinguish between systemic and special causes—and indeed, the key to quality management in general—was statistical process control (SPC). Developed by Walter Shewart while at Bell Labs in the 1930s and later refined by Deming in a well-known paper, "On the Statistical Theory of Errors," SPC was required because variation was an inevitable fact of industrial life. It was unlikely that two parts, even when produced by the same operator at the same machine, would ever be identical. The issue, therefore, was distinguishing acceptable variation from variation that could indicate problems. The rules of statistical probability provided a method for making this distinction.

Probability rules could determine whether variation was random or not, that is, whether it was due to chance. Random variation occurred within statistically determined limits. If variation remained within those limits, the process was a stable one and in control. As long as nothing changed the process, future variation could be predicted easily, for it would remain indefinitely within the same statistical limits.

Data of this sort were normally collected and plotted on control charts kept by the operators themselves. Such charts graphically plotted actual performance readings (e.g., the outside diameters of pistons) on graphs that also depicted the upper and lower control limits for that characteristic, which were statistically determined (see *Figure A*).

As long as the readings, taken on a small sample of units at predetermined intervals (such as every half hour), fell between limits or did not show a trend or "run," the process was in control and no intervention was required, despite the obvious variation in readings. Readings that either fell outside the limits or produced a run indicated a problem to be investigated.

The practical value of distinguishing random from nonrandom variation was enormous. Operators now knew when to intervene in a process and when to leave it alone. Further, because readings were taken during the production process itself, unacceptable variation showed up early enough for corrective action, rather than after the fact.

FIGURE A A Typical Control Chart

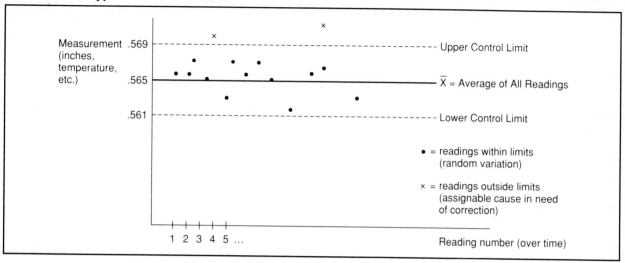

Once a process was in control, readings that fell outside the limits indicated a special cause. When the cause of such nonrandom variation was found and removed, the system returned to its stable state. For example, if a particular lot of goods showed yields that were below control limits, further analysis might determine that raw materials peculiar to that lot were the cause. The removal of such special causes, however, did not improve the system (i.e., raise yield levels), but simply brought it back under control at the preexisting yield.

To improve the system itself, common causes had to be removed. Simply because a system was in statistical control did not mean it was as good as it could be. Indeed, a process in control could produce a high proportion of defects. Control limits indicated what the process was, not what it should or could be. To move the average (yield, sales, defects, returns, etc.) up or down—and thus also move the control limits up or down—typically required the concerted efforts of engineering, research, sales, manufacturing, and other departments. To narrow the range of variation around the target point could consume even more effort. In both instances, control charts would readily document the improvements in the process.

Deming viewed training in the use of control charts as essential if workers were to know what constituted acceptable work. He was adamant that quotas, piecework, and numerical goals be eliminated. Instead, workers had to be shown good work and given the tools to do it. Such tools would also allow them to monitor their own work and correct it in real time, rather than find out about problems days or weeks later.

Control charts were but one part of the statistical approach to quality. Because 100% testing was inefficient, sampling techniques had been developed to provide a scientific basis on which to accept or reject production lots based on a limited number of units. Although sampling and control charts could indicate problems, they could not by themselves identify their causes. For that purpose, other statistical techniques were needed, such as Pareto analysis, Ishikawa or "fishbone" cause-and-effect diagrams, histograms, flow charts, and scatter diagrams.

By 1986 Deming's lectures concentrated more on management than SPC, but SPC remained at the core of his approach. Many U.S. firms sought him out, and some, such as the Ford Motor Company, adopted his approach throughout the company with great success. Deming, who still worked out of the basement of his home with his secretary of 30 years, was hardly sanguine about the prospects for American business. He believed that it would take 30 years for Americans to match the progress of the Japanese and that the

United States was still falling behind. With the specter of a lower U.S. standard of living, he concluded, "We should be pretty scared."[6]

Juran

Joseph M. Juran's impact on Japanese quality was usually considered second only to Deming's. At 82, he had enjoyed a varied and distinguished career that included stints as a business executive, government administrator, lecturer, writer, and consultant. After years of independent activity, he established the Juran Institute in 1979 to serve as a base for the seminars, consulting, conferences, and videotapes long associated with his name. His clientele included Texas Instruments, Du Pont, Monsanto, and Xerox.

Juran defined quality as "fitness for use," meaning that the users of a product or service should be able to count on it for what they needed or wanted to do with it. For example, a manufacturer should be able to process a purchased material or component to meet the demands of its customers while achieving high yields and minimal downtime in production; a wholesaler should receive a correctly labeled product, free from damage during shipment and easy to handle and display; and a consumer should receive a product that performed as claimed and did not break down—or, if it did, receive prompt and courteous adjustment of the claim.

Fitness for use had five major dimensions: quality of design, quality of conformance, availability, safety, and field use.[7] Quality of design was what distinguished a Rolls Royce from a Chevrolet and involved the design concept and its specification. Quality of conformance reflected the match between actual product and design intent and was affected by process choices, ability to hold tolerances, workforce training and supervision,

and adherence to test programs. Availability referred to a product's freedom from disruptive problems and reflected both reliability (the frequency or probability of failure) and maintainability (the speed or ease of repair). Safety could be assessed by calculating the risk of injury due to product hazards. Field use referred to a product's conformance and condition after it reached customers' hands and was affected by packaging, transportation, storage, and field-service competence and promptness.

To achieve fitness for use, Juran developed a comprehensive approach to quality that spanned a product's entire life—from design through vendor relations, process development, manufacturing control, inspection and test, distribution, customer relations, and field service. Each area was carefully dissected, and approaches were proposed to specify and quantify its impact on the various elements of fitness for use. A broad range of statistical techniques was included to assist in the analysis.

Juran's approach to reliability provides a representative example. His reliability program began by establishing reliability goals. It then apportioned these among product components; identified critical components; identified possible modes, effects, and causes of failures; and developed solutions for those most critical to successful product operation and safety. Juran also discussed the setting of realistic tolerances, design reviews, vendor selection, and testing of designs. Statistical methods for improving reliability included analysis of various types of failure rates, analysis of relationships between component and system reliability, and setting of tolerance limits for interacting dimensions. The aims of these activities were quantified reliability goals, a systematic guide for achieving them, and a measurement and monitoring system for knowing when they had been achieved.

Although Juran's analytical methods could identify areas needing improvement and could help make and track changes, they were in the language of the shop floor: defect rates, failure modes, not within specification, and the like. Juran recognized that such measures were not likely to attract top management attention; for this reason, he advocated a cost-of-quality (COQ) accounting system. Such a system spoke top man-

---

[6]Main, "The Curmudgeon Who Talks Tough on Quality," p. 122.

[7]The key parameters of fitness for use, as well as their dimensions, vary somewhat in Juran's writings over a 35-year period. Their comprehensiveness and their spanning the entire product life cycle, however, are constants. The present discussion draws most heavily on Joseph M. Juran and Frank M. Gryna, Jr., *Quality Planning and Analysis* (New York: McGraw-Hill, 1980).

agement's language—money. Quality costs were costs "associated solely with defective product—the costs of making, finding, repairing, or avoiding defects."[8] They were of four types: internal failure costs (from defects discovered before shipment); external failure costs (from defects discovered after shipment); appraisal costs (for assessing the condition of materials and product); and prevention costs (for keeping defects from occurring in the first place). (See *Exhibit 2*.) In most companies, external and internal failure costs together accounted for 50% to 80% of COQ. When these were converted to dollars or presented as a percentage of sales or profits, top management usually took notice.

COQ not only provided management with a dollar cost for defective products, it also established the goal of quality programs: to keep improving quality until there was no longer a positive economic return. This occurred when the total costs of quality were minimized (see *Exhibit 3*). Two assumptions were built into this analysis: that failure costs approached zero as defects became fewer and fewer, and that prevention and appraisal costs together approached infinity as defects were reduced to lower and lower levels. COQ minimization therefore occurred at the point where additional spending on prevention and appraisal was no longer justified because it produced smaller savings in failure costs.

This approach had important practical implications. It implied that zero defects was not a practical goal, for to reach that level prevention and appraisal costs would have to rise so substantially that total costs of quality would not be minimized. As long as prevention and appraisal costs were cheaper (on a per-unit basis) than failure costs, Juran argued, resources should continue to go to prevention and testing. When prevention activities started to pull COQ unit costs up rather than down, however, it was time to maintain quality rather than attempt to improve it further.

To reach and maintain this minimum cost of quality, Juran proposed a three-pronged approach: breakthrough projects, the control sequence, and annual quality programs. In the early stages, when a firm's failure costs greatly exceeded

its prevention and appraisal costs, there were significant opportunities for breakthrough projects, aimed at chronic problems. Problems, such as the need to revise tolerances, were ignored because they were neither dramatic nor thought to be solvable. The "breakthrough sequence" involved identifying the "vital few" projects, selling them to management, organizing to analyze the issues and to involve the key people who were needed for implementation, and overcoming resistance to change (see *Exhibit 4*). Juran claimed that most breakthrough analyses found that over 80% of the problems (e.g., defect rates, scrap rates) were under management control and fewer than 20% were caused by operators.

After successive breakthrough projects, a firm reached the point of optimal quality—in Juran's formulation, the bottom of the COQ curve. The organization then needed to employ the control sequence to preserve its gains. This sequence was actually a large feedback loop. The first step was to choose an objective to control, then to define a unit of measure, set a numerical standard or goal, create a means of measuring performance, and mobilize the organization to report the measurements. After these preparatory steps, an action cycle was repeated over and over: actual performance was compared with standard, and action was taken (if needed) to close the gap.[9]

The control sequence was also used to attack sporadic problems—sudden, usually dramatic changes in the status quo, such as a worn cutting tool. Eliminating sporadic problems only returned processes to their historical levels; to improve them to optimum levels, breakthrough teams were needed because chronic problems were involved. Juran's contrast between these two types of problems is illustrated in *Figure B*.

Both the control and breakthrough processes demanded sophisticated analysis and statistics. The comprehensiveness of Juran's program (it ran from vendor relations through customer service and covered all the functions in between) required high-level planning and coordination as well. For this reason, Juran argued that a new group of professionals—quality control engineers—was needed. This department would be involved in

[8]Juran and Gryna, *Quality Planning*, p. 13.

[9]This description of the control sequence is based on Joseph M. Juran, *Managerial Breakthrough* (New York: McGraw-Hill, 1964), pp. 183–187.

EXHIBIT 2 Juran's Categories of Quality Costs

Internal failure costs = costs from product defects before shipment to the customer. They include the following:

- *Scrap*–net losses in labor and material resulting from defective goods that cannot economically be repaired or used.
- *Rework*–costs of correcting defective products to make them usable.
- *Retest*–costs of reinspection and retesting of products that have been reworked.
- *Downtime*–costs of idle facilities, equipment, and labor due to defective products.
- *Yield losses*–costs of process yields lower than could be attained through improved process control.
- *Disposition*–the time of those involved in determining whether noncomforming products are usable and what should be done with them.

External failure costs = costs associated with defects found after shipment to customer. They include the following:

- *Complaint adjustment*–costs of investigating and responding to complaints due to defective products, faulty installation, or improper instructions to users.
- *Returned material*–costs associated with receiving and replacing defective products returned from the field.
- *Warranty charges*–costs of services and repairs performed under warranty contracts.
- *Allowances*–income losses due to downgrading products for sale as seconds and to concessions made to customers who accept substandard products as is.

Appraisal costs = costs associated with discovering the condition of products and raw materials. They include the following:

- *Incoming materials inspection*–costs associated with determining the quality of vendors' products.

- *Inspection and test*–costs of checking product conformance throughout design and manufacture, including tests done on customers' premises.
- *Maintaining accuracy of test equipment*–costs of operating and maintaining measuring instruments.
- *Materials and services consumed*–costs of products consumed in destructive tests; also materials and services (e.g., electric power) consumed in testing.
- *Evaluation of stocks*–costs of testing products in storage to assess their condition.

Prevention costs = costs associated with preventing defects and limiting failure and appraisal costs. They include the following:

- *Quality planning*–costs of creating and communicating plans and data systems for quality, inspection, reliability, and related activities—includes the costs of preparing all necessary manuals and procedures.
- *New products review*–costs of preparing bid proposals, evaluating new designs, preparing test and experimentation programs, and related quality activities associated with launching new products.
- *Training*–costs of developing and conducting training programs aimed at improving quality performance.
- *Process control*–costs of process control aimed at achieving fitness for use, as distinguished from productivity (a difficult distinction to make in practice).
- *Quality data acquisition and analysis*–costs of operating the quality data system to get continuing data on quality performance.
- *Quality reporting*–costs of bringing together and presenting quality data to upper management.
- *Improvement projects*–costs of building and implementing breakthrough projects.

Note: This is a summary and rewording of Joseph M. Juran and Frank M. Gryna, Jr., *Quality Planning and Analysis*, 2nd edition (New York: McGraw-Hill, 1980), pp. 14–16. Reproduced with permission of McGraw-Hill, Inc.

EXHIBIT 3 Minimizing the Costs of Quality

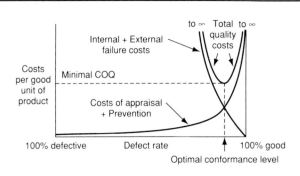

Note: This figure is adapted from Joseph M. Juran and Frank M. Gryna, Jr., *Quality Planning and Analysis*, 2nd edition (New York: McGraw-Hill, 1980), p. 27. Reproduced with permission of McGraw-Hill, Inc.

EXHIBIT 4 Juran's Breakthrough Sequence

1. **Breakthrough in attitudes.** Managers must first prove that a breakthrough is needed and then create a climate conducive to change. To demonstrate need, data must be collected to show the extent of the problem; the data most convincing to top management are usually cost-of-quality figures. To get the resources required for improvement, expected benefits can be monetized and presented in terms of return on investment.

2. **Identify the vital few projects.** Pareto analysis is used to distinguish the vital few projects from the trivial many and to set priorities based on problem frequency.

3. **Organize for breakthrough in knowledge.** Two organizational entities should be established—a steering group and a diagnostic group. The steering group, composed of people from several departments, defines the program, suggests possible problem causes, gives the authority to experiment, helps overcome resistance to change, and implements the solution. The diagnostic group, composed of quality professionals and sometimes line managers, is responsible for analyzing the problem.

4. **Conduct the analysis.** The diagnostic group studies symptoms, develops hypotheses, and experiments to find the problem's true causes. It also tries to determine whether defects are primarily operator controllable or management controllable. (A defect is operator controllable only if it meets three criteria: operators know what they are supposed to do, have the data to understand what they are actually doing, and are able to regulate their own performance.) Theories can be tested by using past data and current production data and by conducting experiments. With this information, the diagnostic group then proposes solutions to the problem.

5. **Determine how to overcome resistance to change.** The need for change must be established in terms that are important to the key people involved. Logical arguments alone are insufficient. Participation is therefore required in both the technical and social aspects of change.

6. **Institute the change.** Departments that must take corrective action must be convinced to cooperate. Presentations to these departments should include the size of the problem, alternative solutions, the cost of recommended changes, expected benefits, and efforts taken to anticipate the change's impact on employees. Time for reflection may be needed, and adequate training is essential.

7. **Institute controls.** Controls must be set up to monitor the solution and see that it works and to keep abreast of unforeseen developments. Formal follow-up is provided by the control sequence used to monitor and correct sporadic problems.

Note: This summary is adapted from Joseph M. Juran and Frank M. Gryna, Jr., *Quality Planning and Analysis*, 2nd edition (New York: McGraw-Hill, 1980), pp. 100–129, and Joseph M. Juran, *Managerial Breakthrough* (New York: McGraw-Hill, 1964), pp. 15–17. Reproduced with permission of McGraw-Hill, Inc.

high-level quality planning, coordinating the activities of other departments, setting quality standards, and providing quality measurements. Juran also believed that top management had to give overall leadership and support to quality improvement for it to succeed.

Juran's major vehicle for top management involvement was the annual quality program. Akin to long-range financial planning and the annual budget process, this program gave top management quality objectives and was especially important for internalizing the habit of quality

FIGURE B Juran's Sporadic and Chronic Problems

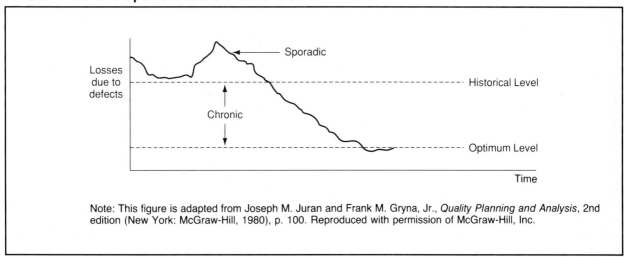

Note: This figure is adapted from Joseph M. Juran and Frank M. Gryna, Jr., *Quality Planning and Analysis*, 2nd edition (New York: McGraw-Hill, 1980), p. 100. Reproduced with permission of McGraw-Hill, Inc.

improvement to ensure that complacency did not set in.

Crosby

Philip B. Crosby started in industry as an inspector. He eventually rose through the ranks at several companies to become vice president of quality at ITT. In 1979 he left ITT to found Philip Crosby Associates, Inc., along with the Crosby Quality College, which by 1986 approximately 35,000 executives and managers had attended. General Motors owned over 10% of Crosby stock and had set up its own Crosby school, as had IBM, Johnson & Johnson, and Chrysler.

Crosby directed his message to top managers. He sought to change their perceptions and attitudes about quality. Typically, top managers viewed quality as intangible or else to be found only in high-end products. Crosby, however, spoke of quality as "conformance to requirements" and believed that any product that consistently reproduced its design specifications was of high quality. In this sense, a Pinto that met Pinto requirements was as much a quality product as a Cadillac that conformed to Cadillac requirements.

American managers must pursue quality to help them compete, Crosby argued. In fact, he believed that if quality were improved, total costs would inevitably fall, allowing companies to increase profitability. This reasoning led to Crosby's most famous claim—that quality was "free."[10]

Ultimately, the goal of quality improvement was zero defects, to be achieved through prevention rather than after-the-fact inspection. Crosby had popularized the zero defects movement, but it had actually originated in the United States at the Martin Company in the 1960s, where Crosby was employed. The company had promised and delivered a perfect missile, with limited inspection and rework, and its managers had concluded that perfection was possible if, in fact, it was expected. The company then developed a philosophy and program to support that goal.

Crosby elaborated on this approach. He believed that the key to quality improvement was changing top management's thinking. If management expected imperfection and defects, it would

get them, for workers would bring similar expectations to their jobs. But if management established a higher standard of performance and communicated it thoroughly to all levels of the company, zero defects was possible. Thus, according to Crosby, zero defects was a management standard and not simply a motivational program for employees.

To help managers understand the seriousness of their quality problems, Crosby provided two primary tools: cost of quality measures and the management maturity grid (see *Exhibit 5*). Costs of quality, which Crosby estimated to be between 15% and 20% of sales at most companies, were useful for showing top management the size of its quality problem and the opportunities for profitable improvement. The management maturity grid was used for self-assessment. It identified five states of quality awareness: uncertainty (the company failed to recognize quality as a management tool); awakening (quality was recognized as important, but management put off taking action); enlightenment (management openly faced and addressed quality problems by establishing a formal quality program); wisdom (prevention was working well, problems were identified early, and corrective action was routinely pursued); and certainty (quality management was an essential part of the company, and problems occurred only infrequently). For each of these five stages, Crosby also examined the status of the quality organization, problem-handling procedures, reported and actual costs of quality as percentages of sales, and quality improvement actions.

Once companies had positioned themselves on the management maturity grid, Crosby offered a 14-point program for quality improvement (see *Exhibit 6*). It emphasized prevention over detection, and focused on changing corporate culture rather than on analytical or statistical tools. The program was designed as a guide for securing management commitment and gaining employees' involvement through actions such as Zero Defects Day. Crosby believed every company should tailor its own defect-prevention program; nevertheless, the goal should always be zero defects. In this process top management played a leadership role; quality professionals played a modest but important role as facilitators, coordinators, trainers, and technical assistants; and hourly workers were secondary.

[10]Philip B. Crosby, *Quality Is Free* (New York: McGraw-Hill, 1979).

EXHIBIT 5 Crosby's Quality Management Maturity Grid

Measurement Categories	Stage I: Uncertainty	Stage II: Awakening	Stage III: Enlightenment	Stage IV: Wisdom	Stage V: Certainty
Management understanding and attitude	Fails to see quality as a management tool.	Supports quality management in theory but is unwilling to provide the necessary money or time.	Learns about quality management and becomes supportive.	Participates personally in quality activities.	Regards quality management as essential to the company's success.
Quality organization status	Quality activities are limited to the manufacturing or engineering department and are largely appraisal and sorting.	A strong quality leader has been appointed, but quality activities remain focused on appraisal and sorting and are still limited to manufacturing and engineering.	Quality department reports to top management, and its leader is active in company management.	Quality manager is an officer of the company. Prevention activities have become important.	Quality manager is on the board of directors. Prevention is the main quality activity.
Problem handling	Problems are fought as they occur and are seldom fully resolved; "fire-fighting" dominates.	Teams are established to attack major problems, but the approach remains short term.	Problems are resolved in an orderly fashion, and corrective action is a regular event.	Problems are identified early in their development.	Except in the most unusual cases, problems are prevented.
Cost of quality as percentage of sales	Reported: unknown Actual: 20%	Reported: 5% Actual: 18%	Reported: 8% Actual: 12%	Reported: 6.5% Actual: 8%	Reported: 2.5% Actual: 2.5%
Quality improvement actions	No organized activities.	Activities are motivational and short term.	Implements the 14-step program with full understanding.	Continues the 14-step program and starts Make Certain.	Quality improvement is a regular and continuing activity.
Summation of company quality posture	"We don't know why we have quality problems."	"Must we always have quality problems?"	"Because of management commitment and quality improvement programs, we are identifying and resolving our quality problems."	"We routinely prevent defects from occurring."	"We know why we don't have quality problems."

Note: This chart is adapted from Philip B. Crosby, *Quality Is Free*, (New York: McGraw-Hill, 1979), pp. 32–33. Reproduced with permission of McGraw-Hill, Inc.

EXHIBIT 6 Crosby's 14-Point Program

1. **Management commitment.** Top management must become convinced of the need for quality improvement and must make its commitment clear to the entire company. This should be accompanied by a written quality policy, stating that each person is expected to "perform exactly like the requirement, or cause the requirement to be officially changed to what we and the customers really need."

2. **Quality improvement team.** Management must form a team of department heads (or those who can speak for their departments) to oversee quality improvement. The team's role is to see that needed actions take place in its departments and in the company as a whole.

3. **Quality measurement.** Quality measures that are appropriate to every activity must be established to identify areas needing improvement. In accounting, for example, one measure might be the percentage of late reports; in engineering, the accuracy of drawings; in purchasing, rejections due to incomplete descriptions; and in plant engineering, time lost because of equipment failures.

4. **Cost of quality evaluation.** The controller's office should make an estimate of the costs of quality to identify areas where quality improvements would be profitable.

5. **Quality awareness.** Quality awareness must be raised among employees. They must understand the importance of product conformance and the costs of nonconformance. These messages should be carried by supervisors (after they have been trained) and through such media as films, booklets, and posters.

6. **Corrective action.** Opportunities for correction are generated by Steps 3 and 4, as well as by discussion among employees. These ideas should be brought to the supervisory level and resolved there, if possible. They should be pushed up further if that is necessary to get action.

7. **Zero defects planning.** An ad hoc zero defects committee should be formed from members of the quality improvement team. This committee should start planning a zero defects program appropriate to the company and its culture.

8. **Supervisor training.** Early in the process, all levels of management must be trained to implement their part of the quality improvement program.

9. **Zero Defects Day.** A Zero Defects Day should be scheduled to signal to employees that the company has a new performance standard.

10. **Goal setting.** To turn commitments into action, individuals must establish improvement goals for themselves and their groups. Supervisors should meet with their people and ask them to set goals that are specific and measurable. Goal lines should be posted in each area and meetings held to discuss progress.

11. **Error cause removal.** Employees should be encouraged to inform management of any problems that prevent them from performing error-free work. Employees need not do anything about these problems themselves; they should simply report them. Reported problems must then be acknowledged by management within 24 hours.

12. **Recognition.** Public, nonfinancial appreciation must be given to those who meet their quality goals or perform outstandingly.

13. **Quality councils.** Quality professionals and team chairpersons should meet regularly to share experiences, problems, and ideas.

14. **Do it all over again.** To emphasize the never-ending process of quality improvement, the program (Steps 1–13) must be repeated. This renews the commitment of old employees and brings new ones into the process.

Note: This summary is adapted from Philip B. Crosby, *Quality Is Free*, (New York: McGraw-Hill, 1979), pp. 132–139 and 175–259. Reproduced with permission of McGraw-Hill, Inc.

15. Quality on the Line

Analyses of what has gone wrong with American industry have returned, time and again, to the poor quality of American-made products and to the management philosophy responsible for that quality. To date, most of the available evidence has been largely impressionistic, and few managers have felt the need to question familiar, long-established approaches to the work of manufacturing. We no longer have that excuse.

When it comes to product quality, American managers still think the competitive problem much less serious than it really is. Because defining the term accurately within a company is so difficult (is quality a measure of performance, for example, or reliability or durability), managers often claim they cannot know how their product quality stacks up against that of their competitors, who may well have chosen an entirely different quality "mix." And since any comparisons are likely to wind up as comparisons of apples with oranges, even a troubling variation in results may reflect only a legitimate variation in strategy. Is there, then, a competitive problem worth worrying about?

I have recently completed a multiyear study of production operations at all but one of the manufacturers of room air conditioners in both the United States and Japan (details of the study are given in the insert, *Research methods*). Each manufacturer uses a simple assembly-line process; each uses much the same manufacturing equipment; each makes an essentially standard-

ized product. No apples versus oranges here: the comparison is firmly grounded. And although my data come from a single industry, both that industry's manufacturing process and its managers' range of approaches to product quality give these findings a more general applicability.

The shocking news, for which nothing had prepared me, is that the failure rates of products from the highest-quality producers were between *500* and *1,000* times less than those of products from the lowest. The "between 500 and 1,000" is not a typographical error but an inescapable fact. There is indeed a competitive problem worth worrying about.

Measuring Quality

Exhibit 1 presents a composite picture of the quality performance of U.S. and Japanese manufacturers of room air conditioners. I have measured quality in two ways: by the incidence of "internal" and of "external" failures. Internal failures include all defects observed (either during fabrication or along the assembly line) before the product leaves the factory; external failures include all problems incurred in the field after the unit has been installed. As a proxy for the latter, I have used the number of service calls recorded during the product's first year of warranty coverage because that was the only period for which U.S. and Japanese manufacturers offered comparable warranties.

Measured by either criterion, Japanese companies were far superior to their U.S. counterparts: their average assembly-line defect rate was

EXHIBIT 1 Quality in the Room Air Conditioning Industry 1981–1982*

		Internal failures			External failures			
	Fabrication: coil leaks per 100 units	Assembly-line defects per 100 units			Service call rate per 100 units under first-year warranty coverage			
		Total	Leaks	Electrical	Total	Compressors	Thermostats	Fan motors
Median								
United States	4.4	63.5	3.1	3.3	10.5†	1.0	1.4	.5
Japan	<.1	.95	.12	.12	.6	.05	.002	.028
Range								
United States	.1-9.0	7-165	1.3-34	.9-34	5.3-26.5	.5-3.4	.4-3.6	.2-2.6
Japan	.03-.4	.15-3.0	.0015-.5	.0015-1.0	.04-2.0	.002-.1	0-.03	.001-.2

* Although most companies reported total failure rates for 1981 or 1982, complete data on component failure rates were often available only for earlier years. For some U.S. companies, 1979 or 1980 figures were employed. Because there was little change in U.S. failure rates during this period, the mixing of data from different years should have little effect.

† Service call rates in the United States normally include calls where no product problems were found ("customer instruction" calls); those in Japan do not. I have adjusted the U.S. median to exclude these calls; without the adjustments, the median U.S. service call rate would be 11.4 per 100 units. Figures for the range should be adjusted similarly, although the necessary data were not available from the U.S. companies with the highest and lowest service call rates.

almost 70 times lower and their average first-year service call rate nearly 17 times better. Nor can this variation in performance be attributed simply to differences in the number of minor, appearance-related defects. Classifying failures by major functional problems (leaks, electrical) or by component failure rates (compressors, thermostats, fan motors) does not change the results.

More startling, on both internal and external measures, the poorest Japanese company typically had a failure rate less than half that of the best U.S. manufacturer. Even among the U.S. companies themselves, there was considerable variation. Assembly-line defects ranged from 7 to 165 per 100 units—a factor of 20 separating the best performer from the worst—and service call rates varied by a factor of 5.

For ease of analysis, I have grouped the companies studied according to their quality performance (see the *Appendix*). These groupings illustrate an important point: quality pays. *Exhibit 2,* for example, presents information on assembly-line productivity for each of these categories and shows that the highest-quality producers were also those with the highest output per man-hour. On the basis of the number of

direct labor hours actually worked on the assembly line, productivity at the best U.S. companies was five times higher than at the worst.

Measuring productivity by "standard output" (see *Exhibit 2*) blurs the picture somewhat. Although the Japanese plants maintain a slight edge over the best U.S. plants, categories of performance tend to overlap. The figures based on standard output, however, are rather imperfect indicators of productivity—for example, they fail to include overtime or rework hours and so overstate productivity levels, particularly at the poorer companies, which devote more of their time to correcting defects. Thus, these figures have less significance than do those based on the number of hours actually worked.

Note carefully that the strong association between productivity and quality is not explained by differences in technology or capital intensity, for most of the plants employed similar manufacturing techniques. This was especially true of final assembly, where manual operations, such as hand brazing and the insertion of color-coded wires, were the norm. Japanese plants did use some automated transfer lines and packaging equipment, but only in compressor manufacturing

EXHIBIT 2 Quality and Productivity

Grouping of companies by quality performance	Units produced per assembly-line direct labor man-hour actual hours*		Units produced per assembly-line direct labor man-hour standard output†	
	Median	Range	Median	Range
Japanese manufacturers	NA‡	NA	1.8	1.4-3.1
Best U.S. plants	1.7	1.7§	1.7	1.4-1.9
Better U.S. plants	.9	.7-1.0	1.1	.8-1.2
Average U.S. plants	1.0	.6-1.2	1.1	1.1-1.7
Poorest U.S. plants	.35	.35§	1.3	.8-1.6

* Direct labor hours have been adjusted to include only those workers involved in assembly (i.e., where inspectors and repairmen were classified as direct labor, they have been excluded from the totals).

† Computed by using the average cycle time to derive a figure for hourly output, and then dividing by the number of assembly-line direct laborers (excluding inspectors and repairmen) to determine output per man-hour.

‡ NA = not available.

§ In this quality grouping, man-hour data were only available from a single company.

and case welding was the difference in automation significant.

The association between cost and quality is equally strong. Reducing field failures means lower warranty costs, and reducing factory defects cuts expenditures on rework and scrap. As *Exhibit 3* shows, the Japanese manufacturers incurred warranty costs averaging 0.6% of sales; at the best American companies, the figure was 1.8%; at the worst 5.2%.

In theory, low warranty costs might be offset by high expenditures on defect prevention: a company could spend enough on product pretesting or on inspecting assembled units before shipment to wipe out any gains from improved warranty costs. Figures on the total costs of quality, however, which include expenditures on prevention and inspection as well as the usual failure costs of rework, scrap, and warranties, lead to the opposite conclusion. In fact, the total costs of quality incurred by Japanese producers were less than one-half the failure costs incurred by the best U.S. companies.

The reason is clear: failures are much more expensive to fix after a unit has been assembled than before. The cost of the extra hours spent pretesting a design is cheap compared with the cost of a product recall; similarly, field service costs are much higher than those of incoming inspection. Among manufacturers of room air conditioners, the Japanese—even with their strong commitment to design review, vendor selection and management, and in-process inspection—still have the lowest overall quality costs.

Nor are the opportunities for reduction in quality costs confined to this industry alone. A recent survey[1] of U.S. companies in ten manufacturing sectors found that total quality costs averaged 5.8% of sales—for a $1 billion corporation, some $58 million per year primarily in scrap, rework, and warranty expenses. Shaving even a tenth of a percentage point off these costs would result in an annual saving of $1 million.

Other studies, which use the PIMS data base, have demonstrated a further connection among quality, market share, and return on investment.[2] Not only does good quality yield a higher ROI for any given market share (among businesses with less than 12% of the market, those with inferior product quality averaged an ROI of 4.5%, those with average product quality an ROI of 10.4%, and those with superior product quality an ROI of 17.4%); it also leads directly to market share gains. Those businesses in the PIMS

[1]"Quality Cost Survey," *Quality,* June 1977, p. 20.

[2]Sidney Schoeffler, Robert D. Buzzell, and Donald F. Heany, "Impact of Strategic Planning on Profit Performance," HBR March–April 1974, p. 137; and Robert D. Buzzell and Frederik D. Wiersema, "Successful Share-Building Strategies," HBR January–February 1981, p. 135.

EXHIBIT 3 Quality and Costs

Grouping of companies by quality performance	Warranty costs as a percentage of sales*		Total cost of quality (Japanese companies) and total failure costs (U.S. companies) as a percentage of sales†	
	Median	Range	Median	Range
Japanese manufacturers	.6%	.2-1.0%	1.3%	.7-2.0%
Best U.S. plants	1.8	1.1-2.4	2.8	2.7-2.8
Better U.S. plants	2.4	1.7-3.1	3.4	3.3-3.5
Average U.S. plants	2.2	1.7-4.3	3.9	2.3-5.6
Poorest U.S. plants	5.2%	3.3-7.0%	>5.8%	4.4->7.2%

* Because most Japanese air conditioners are covered by a three-year warranty while most U.S. units are covered by a warranty of five years, these figures somewhat overstate the Japanese advantage. The bias is unlikely to be serious, however, because second- to fifth-year coverage in the United States and second- to third-year coverage in Japan are much less inclusive—and therefore, less expensive—than first-year coverage. For example, at U.S. companies second- to fifth-year warranty costs average less than one-fifth of first-year expenses.

† Total cost of quality is the sum of all quality-related expenditures, including the costs of prevention, inspection, rework, scrap, and warranties. The Japanese figures include expenditures in all of these categories, while the U.S. figures, because of limited data, include only the costs of rework, scrap, and warranties (failure costs). As a result, these figures understate total U.S. quality costs relative to those of the Japanese .

study that improved in quality during the 1970s increased their market share five to six times faster than those that declined—and three times faster than those whose quality remained unchanged.

The conclusion is inescapable: improving product quality is a profitable activity. For managers, therefore, the central question must be: What makes for successful quality management?

Sources of Quality

Evidence from the room air conditioning industry points directly to the practices that the quality leaders, both Japanese and American, have employed. Each of these areas of effort—quality programs, policies, and attitudes; information systems; product design; production and work force policies; and vendor management—has helped in some way to reduce defects and lower field failures.

Programs, Policies & Attitudes

The importance a company attaches to product quality often shows up in the standing of its quality department. At the poorest performing plants in the industry, the quality control (QC) manager invariably reported to the director of manufacturing or engineering. Access to top management came, if at all, through these go-betweens, who often had very different priorities from those of the QC manager. At the best U.S. companies, especially those with low service call rates, the quality department had more visibility. Several companies had vice presidents of quality; at the factory level each head of QC reported directly to the plant manager. Japanese QC managers also reported directly to their plant managers.

Of course, reporting relationships alone do not explain the observed differences in quality performance. They do indicate, however, the seriousness that management attaches to quality problems. It's one thing to say you believe in defect-free products, but quite another to take time from a busy schedule to act on that belief and stay informed. At the U.S. company with the lowest service call rate, the president met weekly with all corporate vice presidents to review the latest service call statistics. Nobody at that company needed to ask whether quality was a priority of upper management.

How often these meetings occurred was as important as their cast of characters. Mistakes do not fix themselves; they have to be identified, diagnosed, and then resolved through corrective action. The greater the frequency of meetings to review quality performance, the fewer undetected errors. The U.S. plants with the lowest assembly-line defect rates averaged ten such meetings per month; at all other U.S. plants, the average was four. The Japanese companies reviewed defect rates daily.

Meetings and corrective action programs will succeed, however, only if they are backed by genuine top-level commitment. In Japan, this commitment was deeply ingrained and clearly communicated. At four of the six companies surveyed, first-line supervisors believed product quality—not producing at low cost, meeting the production schedule, or improving worker productivity—was management's top manufacturing priority. At the other two, quality ranked a close second.

The depth of this commitment became evident in the Japanese practice of creating internal consumer review boards. Each of the Japanese producers had assembled a group of employees whose primary function was to act as typical consumers and test and evaluate products. Sometimes the products came randomly from the day's production; more frequently, they represented new designs. In each case, the group had final authority over product release. The message here was unmistakable: the customer—not the design staff, the marketing team, or the production group—had to be satisfied with a product's quality before it was considered acceptable for shipment.

By contrast, U.S. companies showed a much weaker commitment to product quality. At 9 of the 11 U.S. plants, first-line supervisors told me that their managers attached far more importance to meeting the production schedule than to any other manufacturing objective. Even the best performers showed no consistent relationship between failure rates and supervisors' perceptions of manufacturing priorities.

What commitment there was stemmed from the inclusion (or absence) of quality in systems of performance appraisal. Two of the three companies with the highest rates of assembly-line defects paid their workers on the basis of total output, not defect-free output. Is it any wonder these employees viewed defects as being of little

consequence? Not surprisingly, domestic producers with low failure rates evaluated both supervisors and managers on the quality of output—supervisors, in terms of defect rates, scrap rates, and the amount of rework attributable to their operations; managers, in terms of service call rates and their plants' total costs of quality.

These distinctions make good sense. First-line supervisors play a pivotal role in managing the production process, which is responsible for internal failures, but have little control over product design, the quality of incoming materials, or other factors that affect field performance. These require the attention of higher level managers, who can legitimately be held responsible for coordinating the activities of design, purchasing, and other functional groups in pursuit of fewer service calls or reduced warranty expenses.

To obtain consistent improvement, a formal system of goal setting is necessary.[3] Only three U.S. plants set annual targets for reducing field failures. Between 1978 and 1981, these three were the only ones to cut their service call rates by more than 25%; most of the other U.S. plants showed little or no change. All the Japanese companies, however, consistently improved their quality—in several cases, by as much as 50%—and all had elaborate companywide systems of goal setting.

From the corporate level at these companies came vague policy pronouncements ("this year, let the customer determine our quality"), which were further defined by division heads ("reduced service call rates are necessary if we are to lower costs") and by middle managers ("compressor failures are an especially serious problem that must be addressed"). Actual quantitative goals ("improve compressor reliability by 10%") were often set by foremen or workers operating through quality control circles. The collaborative nature of this goal-setting process helped these targets earn wide support.

At the final—or first—level of goal setting, specificity matters. Establishing an overall target for an assembly-line defect rate without specifying more detailed goals by problem category, such as

---

[3]For a summary of evidence on this point, see Edwin A. Locke et al., "Goal Setting and Task Performance: 1969–1980," *Psychological Bulletin*, vol. 90, no. 1, p. 125.

leaks or electrical problems, is unlikely to produce much improvement. A number of U.S. plants have tried this approach and failed. Domestic producers with the lowest defect rates set their overall goals last. Each inspection point along the assembly line had a target of its own, which was agreed on by representatives of the quality and manufacturing departments. The sum of these individual targets established the overall goal for the assembly line. As a result, responsibility for quality became easier to assign and progress easier to monitor.

Information Systems

Successful monitoring of quality assumes that the necessary data are available, which is not always true. Without specific and timely information on defects and field failures, improvements in quality are seldom possible. Not surprisingly, at the poorest U.S. companies information on defects and field failures was virtually nonexistent. Assembly-line defects and service call rates were seldom reported. "Epidemic" failures (problems that a large proportion of all units had in common) were widespread. Design flaws remained undetected. At one domestic producer, nearly a quarter of all 1979–1981 warranty expenses came from problems with a single type of compressor.

Other companies reported more extensive quality information—daily and weekly defect rates as well as quarterly and, occasionally, monthly service call rates. These variations in the level of reporting detail correlated closely with differences in quality performance. Among average U.S. performers, for example, quality reports were quite general. Data on assembly line defects gave no breakdowns by inspection point; data on field failures were for entire product lines, not for separate models. Without further refinement, such data cannot isolate quality problems.

A 10% failure rate for a product line can mean a number of things: that all models in the line fail to perform 10% of the time, with no single problem standing out; that several models have a 5% failure rate and one a 30% rate, which suggests a single problem of epidemic proportions; or anything in between. There is no way of distinguishing these cases on the basis of aggregate data alone. What is true of goal setting is equally true of reporting systems: success requires mastering the details.

The best U.S. companies reported defect rates for each inspection point on the assembly line and field failure rates by individual model. The Japanese not only collected information that their U.S. counterparts ignored, such as failure rates in the later years of a product's life; they also insisted on extreme precision in reporting. At one company, repairmen had to submit reports on every defective unit they fixed. In general, it was not unusual for Japanese managers to be able to identify the 30 different ways in which Switch X had failed on Model Y during the last several years. Nor did they have to wait for such information.

Service call statistics in the United States took anywhere from one month to one year to make the trip from the field to the factory; in Japan, the elapsed time averaged between one week and one month. Differences in attitude are part of the explanation. As the director of quality at one Japanese company observed, field information reached his company's U.S. subsidiaries much more slowly than it did operations in Japan—even though both employed the same system for collecting and reporting data.

Product Design

Room air conditioners are relatively standardized products. Although basic designs in the United States have changed little in recent years, pressures to improve energy efficiency and to reduce costs have resulted in a stream of minor changes. On the whole, these changes have followed a common pattern: the initiative came from marketing; engineering determined the actual changes to be made and then pretested the new design; quality control, manufacturing, purchasing, and other affected departments signed off; and, where necessary, prototypes and pilot production units were built.

What did differ among companies was the degree of design and production stability. As *Exhibit 4* indicates, the U.S. plants with the lowest failure rates made far fewer design changes than did their competitors.

Exhibit 4 conveys an important message. Variety, at least in America, is often the enemy of quality. Product proliferation and constant design change may keep the marketing department happy, but failure rates tend to rise as well. By contrast, a limited product line ensures that workers are more familiar with each model and less likely to make mistakes. Reducing the number of design changes allows workers to devote more attention to each one. Keeping production level means less reliance on a second shift staffed by inexperienced employees.

The Japanese, however, have achieved low failure rates even with relatively broad product lines and rapidly changing designs. In the room air conditioning industry, new designs account for nearly a third of all models offered each year, far more than in the United States. The secret: an emphasis on reliability engineering and on careful shakedowns of new designs before they are released.

Reliability engineering is nothing new; it has been practiced by the aerospace industry in this country for at least 20 years. In practice, it involves building up designs from their basic components, determining the failure probabilities of individual systems and subsystems, and then trying to strengthen the weak links in the chain by product redesign or by incorporating more reliable parts. Much of the effort is focused up front, when a product is still in blueprint or prototype form. Managers use statistical techniques to predict reliability over the product's life and subject preliminary designs to exhaustive stress and life testing to collect information on potential failure modes. These data form the basis for continual product improvement.

Only one American maker of room air conditioners practiced reliability engineering, and its failure rates were among the lowest observed. All of the Japanese companies, however, placed considerable emphasis on these techniques. Their designers were, for example, under tremendous pressure to reduce the number of parts per unit; for a basic principle of reliability engineering is that, everything else being equal, the fewer the parts, the lower the failure rate.

Japanese companies worked just as hard to increase reliability through changes in components. They were aided by the Industrial Engineering Bureau of Japan's Ministry of International Trade and Industry (MITI), which required that

RESEARCH METHODS

This article is based mainly on data collected in 1981 and 1982 from U.S. and Japanese manufacturers of room air conditioners. I selected that industry for study for a number of reasons: it contains companies of varying size and character, which implies a wide range of quality policies and performance; its products are standardized, which facilitates inter-company comparisons; and it employs a simple assembly-line process, which is representative of many other mass production industries.

Nine of the ten U.S. companies in the industry and all seven of the Japanese companies participated in the study. They range in size from small air conditioning specialists with total sales of under $50 million to large home appliance manufacturers with annual sales of more than $200 million in this product line alone. Taken together, they account for approximately 90% of U.S. industry shipments and 90% of Japanese industry shipments. I have collected data separately for each plant (two of the American companies operate two plants apiece; otherwise, each company employs only a single plant). Of the 18 plants studied, 11 are American and 7 Japanese.

Once U.S. companies had agreed to participate in the study, I sent them a questionnaire requesting background information on their product line, production practices, vendor management practices, quality policies, and quality performance. I then visited them all in order to review the questionnaire results, collect additional data, tour the factories, and conduct interviews with key personnel. The interviews were open-ended and unstructured, although I posed similar questions at each company. A typical visit included interviews with managers in the quality, manufacturing, purchasing, engineering, and service departments, as well as several hours spent walking the production floor.

Preliminary analysis of the interviews and questionnaires showed that companies neither employed the same conventions in reporting data nor answered questions in the same degree of detail. I therefore sent each company its own set of follow-up questions to fill in these gaps and to make the data more comparable across companies. In addition, I requested each company to administer a brief questionnaire on quality attitudes to each of its first-line production supervisors.

I followed a similar approach with the Japanese manufacturers, although time constraints limited the amount of information that I could collect. All questionnaires were first translated into Japanese and mailed to the participating companies. Six of the seven companies completed the same basic quality questionnaire as did their American counterparts; the same companies also administered the survey on quality attitudes to a small number of their first-line supervisors. With the aid of a translator, I conducted on-site interviews at all the companies and toured six of the plants.

EXHIBIT 4 Quality and Product Stability

Grouping of companies by quality performance	Median number of design changes per year	Median number of models	Median number of design changes per model*	Median percentage that peak production exceeded low production†
Japanese manufacturers	NA‡	80	NA	170%
Best U.S. plants	43	56	.8	27
Better U.S. plants	150	81	1.9	63
Average U.S. plants	400	126	3.2	50
Poorest U.S. plants	133	41	3.2	100%

* Column 1 divided by column 2.
† The figures in this column were derived by dividing each plant's largest daily output for the year by its smallest (non-zero) output for the year.
‡ NA = not available.

all electric and electronic components sold in the country be tested for reliability and have their ratings on file at the bureau. Because this information was publicly available, designers no longer needed to test components themselves in order to establish reliability ratings.

An emphasis on reliability engineering is also closely tied to a more thorough review of new designs before units reach production. American manufacturers usually built and tested a single prototype before moving to pilot production; the Japanese often repeated the process three or four times.

Moreover, all affected departments—quality control, purchasing, manufacturing, service, and design engineering—played an active role at each stage of the review process. American practice gave over the early stages of the design process almost entirely to engineering. By the time other groups got their say, the process had gained momentum, schedules had been established, and changes had become difficult to make. As a result, many a product that performed well in the laboratory created grave problems on the assembly line or in the field.

Production & Work Force Policies

The key to defect-free production is a manufacturing process that is "in control"—machinery and equipment well maintained, workplaces clean and orderly, workers well trained, and inspection procedures suited to the rapid detection of deviations. In each of these areas, the Japanese were noticeably ahead of their American competitors.

Training of the labor force, for example, was extensive, even for employees engaged in simple jobs. At most of the Japanese companies, preparing new assembly-line workers took approximately six months, for they were first trained for all jobs on the line. American workers received far less instruction (from several hours to several days) and were usually trained for a single task. Not surprisingly, Japanese workers were much more adept at tracking down quality problems originating at other work stations and far better equipped to propose remedial action.

Instruction in statistical quality control techniques supplemented the other training offered Japanese workers. Every Japanese plant relied heavily on these techniques for controlling its production process. Process control charts, showing the acceptable quality standards of various fabrication and assembly-line operations, were everywhere in general use. Only one U.S. plant—the one with the lowest defect rate—had made a comparable effort to determine the capabilities of its production process and to chart the results.

Still, deviations will occur, and thorough and timely inspection is necessary to ferret them out quickly. Japanese companies therefore employed an inspector for every 7.1 assembly-line workers (in the United States the ratio was 1:9.5). The primary role of these inspectors was to monitor the production process for stability; they were less "gatekeepers," weeding out defective units before shipment, than providers of information. Their tasks were considered especially important where manual operations were common and where inspection required sophisticated testing of a unit's operating characteristics.

On balance, then, the Japanese advantage in production came less from revolutionary technology than from close attention to basic skills and to the reduction of all unwanted variations in the manufacturing process. In practice, this approach can produce dramatic results. Although new model introductions and assembly-line changeovers at American companies boosted defect rates, at least until workers became familiar with their new assignments, Japanese companies experienced no such problems.

Before every new model introduction, Japanese assembly-line workers were thoroughly trained in their new tasks. After-hours seminars explained the product to the work force, and trial runs were common. During changeovers, managers kept workers informed of the models slated for production each day, either through announcements at early morning meetings or by sending assembled versions of the new model down the line 30 minutes before the change was to take place, together with a big sign saying "this model comes next." American workers generally received much less information about changeovers. At the plant with the highest defect rate in the industry, communication about changeovers was limited to a single small chalkboard, listing the models to be produced each day, placed at one end of the assembly line.

The Japanese system of permanent employment also helped to improve quality. Before they are fully trained, new workers often commit unintentional errors. Several American companies observed that their workers' inexperience and lack of familiarity with the product line contributed to their high defect rates. The Japanese, with low absenteeism and turnover, faced fewer problems of this sort. Japanese plants had a median turnover of 3.1%; the comparable figure for U.S. plants was two times higher. Even more startling were the figures on absenteeism: a median of 3.1% for American companies and *zero* for the Japanese.

In addition, because several of the U.S. plants were part of larger manufacturing complexes linked by a single union, they suffered greatly from "bumping." A layoff in one part of the complex would result in multiple job changes as workers shifted among plants to protect seniority rights. Employees whose previous experience was with another product would suddenly find themselves assembling room air conditioners. Sharp increases in defects were the inevitable result.

Vendor Management

Without acceptable components and materials, no manufacturer can produce high-quality products. As computer experts have long recognized, "garbage in" means "garbage out." Careful selection and monitoring of vendors is therefore a necessary first step toward ensuring reliable and defect-free production.

At the better U.S. companies, the quality department played a major role in vendor selection by tempering the views of the engineering ("do their samples meet our technical specifications") and purchasing ("is that the best we can do on price") departments. At the very best companies, however, purchasing departments independently ranked quality as their primary objective. Buyers received instruction in the concepts of quality control; at least one person had special responsibility for vendor quality management; goals were set for the quality of incoming components and materials; and vendors' shipments were carefully monitored.

Purchasing departments at the worst U.S. companies viewed their mission more narrowly: to obtain the lowest possible price for technically acceptable components. Site visits to new vendors were rarely made, and members of the purchasing department seldom got involved in the design review process. Because incoming inspection was grossly understaffed (at one plant, two workers were responsible for reviewing 14,000 incoming shipments per year), production pressures often allowed entire lots to come to the assembly line uninspected. Identification of defective components came, if at all, only after they had been incorporated into completed units. Inevitably, scrap and rework costs soared.

In several Japanese companies incoming materials arrived directly at the assembly line without inspection. New vendors, however, first had to pass rigorous tests: their products initially received 100% inspection. Once all problems were corrected, sampling inspection became the norm. Only after an extended period without a rejection were vendors allowed to send their products directly to the assembly line. At the first sign of deterioration in vendor performance, more intensive inspection resumed.

In this environment, inspection was less an end in itself than a means to an end. Receiving inspectors acted less as policemen than as quality consultants to the vendor. Site visits, for example, were mandatory when managers were assessing potential suppliers and continued for as long as the companies did business together. Even more revealing, the selection of vendors depended as much on management philosophy, manufacturing capability, and depth of commitment to quality as on price and delivery performance.

Closing the Gap

What, then, is to be done? Are American companies hopelessly behind in the battle for superior quality? Or is an effective counterattack possible?

Although the evidence is still fragmentary, there are a number of encouraging signs. In 1980, when Hewlett-Packard tested 300,000 semiconductors from three U.S. and three Japanese suppliers, the Japanese chips had a failure rate one-sixth that of the American chips. When the test was repeated two years later, the U.S. companies had virtually closed the gap. Similar progress is evident in automobiles. Ford's Ranger trucks, built in Louisville, Kentucky, offer an especially dramatic example. In just three years, the number of "concerns" registered by the Louisville plant (the automaker's measure of quality deficiencies as recorded at monthly audits) dropped to less than one-third its previous high. Today, the Ranger's quality is nearly equal that of Toyota's SR5, its chief Japanese rival.

But in these industries, as with room air conditioners, quality improvement takes time. The "quick fix" provides few lasting gains. What is needed is a long-term commitment to the fundamentals—working with vendors to improve their performance, educating and training the work force, developing an accurate and responsive quality information system, setting targets for quality improvement, and demonstrating interest and commitment at the very highest levels of management. With their companies' futures on the line, managers can do no less.

Appendix   Classifying Plants by Quality Performance

To identify patterns of behavior, I first grouped U.S. plants into categories according to their quality performance on two dimensions—internal quality (defect rates in the factory) and external quality (failure rates in the field).

Table A presents the basic data on external quality. I measured field performance in two ways: by the service call rate for units under first-year warranty coverage (the total number of service calls recorded in 1981 divided by the number of units in the field with active first-year warranties) and by the service call rate for units under first-year warranty coverage less "customer instruction calls" (only those service calls that resulted from a faulty unit, not from a customer who was using the unit improperly or had failed to install it correctly).

The second measure was necessary because companies differed in their policies toward customer instruction calls. Some reimbursed repairmen for these calls with-

out argument; others did their best to eliminate such calls completely. An accurate assessment of product performance required the separation of these calls from problems that reflect genuinely defective units.

I classified plants on the basis of their rankings on the second of the two measures in *Table A*, and then grouped them according to their actual levels of field failures. In most cases, the dividing lines were clear, although there were some borderline cases. Plant 8, for example, had a total service call rate well above the industry median, yet after subtracting customer instruction calls, its failure rate differed little from the other average performers. Because this second figure more accurately reflects the rate of product malfunction, I treated Plant 8 has having average, rather than poor, external quality. A number of companies with high failure rates did not break out customer instruction calls. I have treated them as having poor external quality because their customer instruction calls would have to have been two or three times as frequent as the highest rate recorded in 1981 for them to have warranted an average ranking.

I followed a similar procedure in classifyng plants on internal quality. Because companies differed in how they defined and recorded defects (some noted every single product flaw; others were interested only in major malfunctions), I employed several indexes to ensure consistency. The results are displayed in *Table B*. I ranked companies first by their total assembly-line defect rates (every defect recorded at every station along the assembly line divided by the number of units produced) and then by the number of defects requiring off-line repair. The second index compensates for the different definitions just noted, for it more accurately reflects the incidence of serious problems. Minor adjustments and touch-ups can generally be made wihtout pulling a unit off the line; more serious problems normally require off-line repair. Measured on this basis,

the high total defect rates of Plants 1 and 9 appear to be much less of a problem.

Because several companies had to estimate the off-line repair rate, I used a third index, the number of repairmen per assembly-line direct laborer, to measure defect seriousness. The proportion of the work force engaged in repair activities, including workers assigned to separate rework lines and to rework activities in the warehouse, is likely to correlate well with the incidence of serious defects, for more serious problems usually require more time to correct and necessitate a larger repair staff. This measure provides important additional information, confirmng the conclusions about Plant 1 (its high total defect rate appears to include a large number of minor problems) but contradicting those about Plant 9 (its large number of repairmen suggests that defects are, in fact, a serious problem, despite the small proportion of units requiring off-line repair).

TABLE A Field Performance for U.S. Plants in 1981

Plant	Service call rate, first year warranty coverage		Service call rate less "customer instruction" calls	
	Percentage	Rank	Percentage	Rank
1	5.3%	1	< 5.3%	1
2	8.7	2	< 8.7	2,3
3	9.2	3	5.6	2,3
4	10.5	4	9.8	5
5	11.1	5	9.3	4
6	11.4	6	10.5	6
7	12.6	7	10.5	6
8	16.2	8	11.8	8
9	17.5	9	13.8	9
10	22.9	10	<22.9	10
11	26.5%	11	<26.5%	11

	Ranking of plants on field performance external quality		
	Good	Average	Poor
Plant number	1,2,3	4,5,6,7,8	9,10,11

TABLE B Internal Quality for U.S. Plants in 1981

Plant	Assembly-line defects per 100 units		Assembly-line defects per 100 units requiring off-line repair		Repairmen per assembly-line direct laborer	
	Number	Rank	Number	Rank	Number	Rank
1	150	9	34	5,6	.06	3
2	7	1	7	1	.05	2
3	10	2	10	3	.04	1
4	NA*	NA	NA	NA	.09	8
5	57	5	47	7	.13	9
6	70	6	67	8	.06	3
7	26	4	7	1	.08	6
8	18	3	11	4	.08	6
9	>100	7	> 30	5,6	.16	11
10	165	10	165	10	.13	9
11	135	8	> 68	9	.07	5

* NA = not available.

	Ranking of plants on internal quality		
	Good	Average	Poor
Plant number	2,3,7,8	1,4(?),5,6	9,10,11

TABLE C Classification of Plants on Internal and External Quality

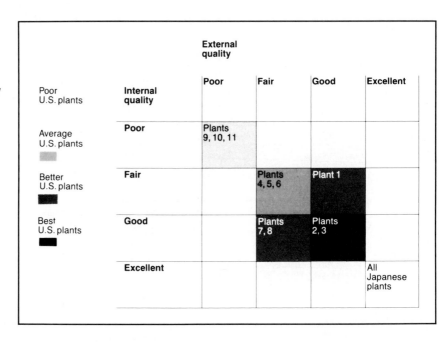

Poor
U.S. plants

Average
U.S. plants

Better
U.S. plants

Best
U.S. plants

Internal quality	External quality			
	Poor	Fair	Good	Excellent
Poor	Plants 9, 10, 11			
Fair		Plants 4, 5, 6	Plant 1	
Good		Plants 7, 8	Plants 2, 3	
Excellent				All Japanese plants

15. Quality on the Line

I assigned plants to groups using much the same procedure as before. I first computed a composite ranking for each plant by averaging together the three rankings of *Table B*. Dividing lines between groups followed the absolute levels of the indexes for each plant. Once again, some judgment was involved, particularly for Plants 4, 5, and 9. Plants 5 and 9 were borderline cases, candidates for ranking as either average or poor internal quality. I classified the former as average, even though its overall rank was low, because its absolute scores on the first two measures were quite close to the median. I classified the latter as poor because its absolute scores on both the first and the third measures were so high. Plant 4 presented a different problem, for it provided no information at all on assembly-line defects. Rather than classifying the plant on the basis of the third index alone, I employed supplementary data. Based on its defect rate at the end-of-the-line quality audit and its rework and scrap costs as a percentage of sales, both of which were quite close to figures reported by other companies with average internal quality, Plant 4 showed up as an average performer.

Table C combines the results of the previous two tables. Overall quality rankings appear for each plant. In most cases, success on internal quality implied success on external measures, although the correlation is not perfect, as Plants 1, 7, and 8 demonstrate. The Japanese plants are in a category of their own, for on both internal and external measures they are at least twice as good as the best U.S. plant.

Module 3
Competing on Productivity*

America's productivity problem is by now common knowledge. For many years, U.S. productivity grew steadily if unspectacularly; then, in the early 1970s, growth suddenly tapered off. The figures for labor productivity are representative. Between 1960 and 1973, output per labor hour in manufacturing grew at 3.4 percent annually. Between 1973 and 1983, growth slowed to 1.8 percent per year.[1]

International comparisons show an equally disturbing trend. Although America has long been the productivity leader in absolute terms, its advantage is rapidly eroding. Japan's labor productivity has, for two decades, been growing at a rate three or four times that of the U.S. In most European countries, labor productivity has been growing at twice the U.S. rate.[2] The long-term implications of these trends are ominous. According to William Batten, former chairman of the New York Stock Exchange:

> In 1960, the typical American worker in manufacturing annually produced as much as four Japanese workers or two French or German workers. Today [in 1979], the American's output is matched by $1\frac{1}{2}$ Japanese and by $1\frac{1}{4}$ Germans or Frenchman. If the trend continues, all three will be outproducing us by the end of the next decade.[3]

For such reasons, productivity growth has become a closely watched index of the nation's economic health. Rapidly growing productivity leads to higher standards of living, holds inflation in check, and enhances international competitiveness. These relationships are not new; most, in fact, have been recognized for decades. As far back as 1911, Frederick W. Taylor, the father of scientific management, was arguing that "maximum prosperity can exist only as the result of maximum productivity." His entire analysis of factory procedures was motivated by "the larger question of national efficiency" and a desire to find ways to improve it.[4]

Economists have been researching the sources of productivity growth for an equally long time. Typically, they have used a growth accounting framework which attempts, at the macroeconomic level, to isolate the relative contributions to productivity of labor, capital, and technological progress.[5] Most economists have tackled the recent productivity slowdown in a similar fashion. Among their explanations for the decline are falling R&D spending; reduced capital per worker; the influx of women and young people, with few skills, into the work force; and environmental and safety regulations, which have diverted resources from other, more productive activities.[6]

These explanations, while helpful, have two serious deficiencies: (1) They fail to account fully for the productivity slowdown, leaving as much as fifty percent of the decline unexplained, and (2) They provide little or no insight into the sources of productivity at the factory level. To accommodate the first concern, a number of competing theories have emerged. They pin America's declining productivity on such factors as a growing defense sector, which relies heavily on cost-plus pricing and other practices that promote inefficiency, and modern management methods, such as portfolio analysis and capital budgeting techniques, which discourage long-term investment and shift attention away from manufacturing needs and toward purely financial goals.[7]

Even the new theories, however, are of little help in explaining intraindustry or intrafirm variations in productivity. A growing body of evidence now shows that productivity levels are not uniform within industries. The most and least productive firms differ by as much as a factor of 10.[8] Manufacturing managers have long noted the same phenomenon within their companies. Despite common products and technologies, some factories are consistently more productive than others.

Such wide and persistent gaps require further explanation. The traditional economic approach cannot be invoked; it assumes that the productivity of a firm is fully determined by available technology and market conditions. Yet differences in capital equipment and prices seldom account fully for the observed differences in productivity. Instead, they must frequently be traced to organizational and managerial variables. Factories differ in their production and control systems, reward and promotion practices, and levels of employee motivation and commitment. Each is related in an important way to productivity and plant performance.

The aim of this module is to explore such sources of productivity and productivity improvement. Most cases are focused at the factory level, and most deal explicitly with the links between management behavior, employee attitudes, and productivity. The cases also examine traditional sources of productivity improvement, such as capital investment and R&D spending, that have long appeared in the economics literature, as well as several of the newer theories that purport to explain the productivity slowdown, such as cost-plus pricing and an inefficient defense sector. Together, they provide a composite picture of America's productivity problem and a description of programs and activities that have met with great success at the factory level.

Major Themes

This module is built around five major themes. They range from measurement to management, and from operational matters, such as the best way to organize for productivity improvement, to strategic concerns, such as how best to integrate productivity goals with the strategic planning process.

PRODUCTIVITY MEASUREMENT

Few companies are without some measure of productivity. Yet surprisingly, despite the volumes that have been written on the subject, managers frequently employ measures with known deficiencies. According to one recent survey, over fifty percent of the indicators companies were using to track manufacturing productivity were either nonstandard or misleading.[9]

For this reason, the module examines a broad range of productivity measures. They can be grouped into three general categories, moving from simple to more complex: utilization and efficiency measures, partial factor productivity measures, and total factor productivity measures. Each has distinctive strengths and weaknesses; together, they cover the needs of most companies.

Utilization and efficiency measures are the easiest to collect and interpret. They reflect the intensity with which machinery and equipment are used and typically appear as percentages: productive hours divided by available hours multiplied by 100. Such measures are narrowly drawn—they fail to establish a clear connection between inputs and outputs—but are still valuable, especially in capital-intensive industries where efficient equipment usage is a key to success. They appear in several cases. Allegheny Ludlum, for example, tracks contact time (for every piece of equipment, the percentage of time that unfinished steel is "in contact" with equipment and being worked), while Vought monitors spindle utilization (the percentage of time that the spindle of a cutting tool is actually cutting metal, rather than waiting for parts to be delivered).

Partial factor productivity measures go a step further by formally comparing inputs and outputs. But they too are limited, because they track only a single input at a time. Substitution effects, with one input traded off against another, are not captured. The most popular partial measures involve labor, because it has traditionally been such a large component of costs. At the macroeconomic level, this has resulted in measures such as output per labor hour; and at the company or factory level, it has led to measures such as sales or units per employee. These measures are discussed in A Day at Midwest Equipment Corporation, Applichem, and Why Some Factories Are More Productive than Others. As direct labor has become a smaller proportion of total manufacturing costs—current estimates put the figure at ten to fifteen percent—partial measures have begun to focus more heavily on other inputs. Measures of materials usage and process yield are typical examples. They appear in several cases, including Applichem, Allegheny Ludlum, and Corning Z-Glass.

Finally, a few companies have begun to track productivity in its most comprehensive form: total factor productivity, or the ratio of output to all inputs consumed. Such indexes combine labor, materials, capital, and energy into a single aggregate input, which is then matched against output. Measurement problems are formidable, and the recommended procedures are often complex and difficult. But total factor productivity has an important advantage over partial measures: It accounts simultaneously for all inputs and thus captures tradeoffs, such as reductions in direct labor that are due solely to new capital investment, that might otherwise be overlooked. Total factor productivity measures appear in both Applichem and Why Some Factories Are More Productive than Others.

Choosing a productivity measure, however, is only the first step toward effective measurement. Absolute productivity scores are of little use by themselves; there must also be a basis for comparison. Comparisons may be either temporal (the same plant, reviewed every year) or cross-sectional (plant-by-plant comparisons within a company or one plant contrasted with others in the industry). Real improvements in productivity must also be distinguished from shifts due to inflation or fluctuating exchange rates. Both A Day at Midwest Equipment Corporation and Applichem involve comparisons of this sort.

Both cases also underline the importance of matching productivity measures with their intended use. No measurement system is perfect. Some measures are simple to interpret but incomplete; others are complex but comprehensive. A central lesson for students is that there is no one best system. Productivity measures serve multiple purposes and must be selected with particular goals in mind. For example, a system designed to track internal improvement is likely to call for different data than one that compares plants with industry averages, if only because the desired industry data are seldom available. Similarly, a system designed to evaluate plant manager performance is best limited to factors under their control, while a system that determines the least-cost combination of products and plants normally includes a larger set of variables. Such distinctions are discussed in Applichem, Why Some Factories Are More Productive than Others, and Allegheny Ludlum Steel.

BARRIERS TO PRODUCTIVITY IMPROVEMENT

Productivity improvement is a slow, painstaking process. It is as much a matter of culture and attitude as a matter of capital investment and advanced technology. Most gains are incremental, the result of a series of small steps rather than a single big leap. Even when large, highly visible projects are involved, success or failure often hinges on the care that has been taken in implementation.

A variety of barriers may disrupt or impede this process. One has already been discussed: flawed measurements. If productivity measures signal that all is well or otherwise create a false sense of security, managers will have little incentive to change. The problem appears in several guises, including internal comparisons of productivity performance that fail to capture the improvements of competitors (as in Allegheny Ludlum Steel); interindustry comparisons that are based on narrow partial measures (as in A Day at Midwest); international comparisons that fail to net out currency fluctuations and other purely financial effects (as in Applichem); and productivity trends that make no adjustment for changes in product mix (as in Corning).

Flawed measurements are but one example of a larger, more pervasive problem: incentives that fail to encourage productivity improvement. Here, reward and promotion systems play a pivotal role. If managers focus primarily on short-term objectives—either because they are evaluated on quarterly earnings, must meet a targeted return-on-investment, or are judged solely by their most recent productivity performance—they will have little incentive to invest today's resources for future payoffs. Eventually, short-term opportunities will be exhausted; then, productivity growth will tail off. The evidence on this point is not encouraging. In one recent survey, seventy-five percent of executives said that their companies' productivity programs had time horizons of less than a year.[10] Both A Day at Midwest Equipment Corporation and North American Rockwell: Draper Division provide vivid examples of such a short-term perspective.

Incentives to improve productivity may be lacking for other reasons as well. In the aerospace industry, for example, contracting procedures have been a major deterrent to capital investment. The Department of Defense has developed several programs to overcome the problem and change the incentives facing firms; they are discussed in A Note on the Aerospace Industry and Vought Aero Products. In other settings, the primary barrier to productivity improvement has often been inertia. Without a crisis, employees see little reason to alter the status quo. A Day at Midwest

Equipment Corporation presents a telling example. Because the company's "new" productivity program is staffed largely by industrial engineers who were transferred, as a group, from their old department, there has been no mandate for change. Most employees have therefore continued to operate according to the old rules.

At times, resistance to change becomes more severe. Old, accepted forms of behavior tend to develop a life and constituency of their own. When productivity improvement demands new approaches, employees may resist cooperating; in extreme cases, they may engage in acts of defiance. Either way, productivity improvement is likely to stall. The module examines several versions of this problem. At Applichem, plant managers have been unwilling to adopt innovative policies or procedures that were pioneered by other plants; at Vought manufacturing and engineering managers initially resisted the close cooperation required to design and implement the flexible machining cell; and at Corning the plant staff has strongly opposed the switch from loose, ad hoc process controls to formal documentation and specified procedures. Each of these incidents is representative, and each shows the difficulty of initiating change. In fact, according to a recent survey, work force and supervisory resistance to change was the single biggest barrier to productivity that managers faced.[11]

Managers, however, are not without blame. They too are part of the problem. A number of experts have concluded that productivity programs often fail because managers have not developed or communicated a clear, consistent productivity strategy.[12] Projects have been piecemeal and unconnected; funding decisions have been motivated purely by cost reduction; and programs have failed to include explicit links to business unit and corporate strategies. Such deficiencies present formidable barriers to productivity improvement, as both A Day at Midwest Equipment Corporation and North American Rockwell demonstrate. Allegheny Ludlum and Vought provide an instructive contrast. Each involves a company that has planned carefully for productivity improvement and has successfully meshed productivity goals with its business strategy and competitive needs.

ORGANIZING FOR PRODUCTIVITY IMPROVEMENT

The burning organizational issue in productivity management replays an old theme: How should responsibility be divided among line and staff managers? Productivity improvement, after all, has long been a line function. Is there any justification for an independent productivity staff? If so, what is its role?

This module explores three alternatives, which together cover the spectrum: (1) no productivity staff; (2) a supportive productivity staff that follows the lead of line managers; and (3) a strong productivity staff that, on occasion, dictates to line managers. Each approach has strengths and weaknesses. As with measurement systems, the lesson is that there is no single, best model. For example, Allegheny Ludlum, with a culture that encourages productivity improvement and a program that is tightly linked to corporate strategic goals, has enjoyed great success without a productivity staff. But North American Rockwell, also without a productivity staff, has been far less successful, and has undercut a productive and competitive division by inadequate investment and strategic mistakes. Midwest Equipment Corporation, with its director of corporate productivity, productivity coordinators, and productivity councils, follows a model frequently recommended by experts: an extensive but supportive productivity network.[13] Yet its productivity program has been weak and ineffective.

By contrast, Vought and Corning show productivity staffs exercising strong leadership. Vought's Industrial Modernization group has played a pivotal role in designing and developing the company's flexible machining cell. Because of top management support, careful planning, and attentiveness to implementation, it has produced an innovative and workable system. Corning's Manufacturing and Engineering division has been equally successful with technology transfer, but has struggled in its efforts to impose process documentation and disciplined procedures. There, it has met great resistance from line managers, who have been unwilling to accept recommendations that might undercut the prevailing plant culture.

Together, these cases show that organization alone does not determine the success or failure of productivity improvement programs. Different arrangements are likely to be beneficial, depending on the circumstances. In environments where productivity improvement has been integrated into the culture and planning process, an independent productivity staff is often unnecessary. In environments where line managers are moving aggressively to improve productivity but still lack the skills, information, or measurements necessary for further progress, a supportive productivity staff may be helpful. And in environments where radically new approaches are required and line managers are resistant, companies may have no other alternative than to rely, at least initially, on an aggressive and proactive productivity staff.

PRODUCTIVITY PORTFOLIOS

For all its diversity, this module has a single, dominant theme: There is no one, best route to superior productivity. A wide range of approaches have proven to be successful. The task for managers is therefore to recognize the alternatives that are available and then to choose the approaches that best match their company's culture, capabilities, and competitive needs.

Alternatives for improving productivity fall into three broad categories: investments in facilities and equipment, programs and systems, and people. Each category can, in turn, be further subdivided. Facilities and equipment include retrofitting and upgrading existing plants with new equipment, building new plants and equipping them with conventional technology but an improved layout or production flow, and building new plants and equipping them with state-of-the-art technology. Programs and systems include productivity measurement, the development of productivity goals and standards and their monitoring over time, and the conversion of new production processes from "art" to "science." People includes education and training, incentives that encourage productivity improvement, techniques that stimulate work force participation, and work redesign. Every case in this module examines at least one of these alternatives; together, the cases cover the entire spectrum.

These alternatives are not mutually exclusive. Companies can, and do, pursue several approaches simultaneously. But because each approach places different demands on a firm—for example, state-of-the-art technology requires engineering excellence and close collaboration between manufacturing managers and engineers, while goal setting and tight standards require precise information systems and rapid, real-time feedback—companies tend to choose a dominant orientation for their productivity improvement programs. Thus, Allegheny Ludlum has focused on standards and monitoring, because of its management culture and comprehensive information system; Vought has focused on factories of the future, because of its interest and expertise in advanced technology; and Corning has focused on yield improvement and process control, because of its heavy reliance on new products and its experience with statistical techniques, troubleshooting, and handoffs from the laboratory to manufacturing.

Unfortunately, companies do not always think systematically about such choices when they launch improvement programs. The idea of a "productivity portfolio"—the menu of productivity alternatives that is available, given the company's resources and skills—is seldom articulated. Nor do most companies approach the choice of a dominant orientation with much care. All too often, managers fall into a pattern of productivity decisions without first assessing their appropriateness or likely competitive contribution. Both A Day at Midwest Equipment Corporation and North American Rockwell present examples of companies that failed to make such assessments.

STRATEGIC APPROACHES TO PRODUCTIVITY

Like quality, productivity has long been viewed in narrow, tactical terms. Traditional programs share several features. They have normally been confined to manufacturing; have focused primarily on reductions in direct labor; have pursued quick cost savings by attacking symptoms of problems rather than causes; and have consisted largely of unrelated but easy-to-justify investments. A Day at Midwest Equipment Corporation, Applichem, and North American Rockwell: Draper Division all exemplify the traditional approach to productivity.

In recent years, a more expansive, strategic approach to productivity has emerged. It has a number of distinguishing features. Programs are not limited to manufacturing but include multiple functions and departments; do not focus solely on direct labor but devote attention to the entire cost structure; do not seek out quick cost reductions but aim to enhance skills and capabilities; and do not throw together unconnected projects but screen proposals to ensure consistency and a common direction. Most important, such programs are linked explicitly to business needs, usually through the strategic planning process. This linkage ensures that managers pursue goals of impact and competitive significance and that, as one expert puts it, "questions are . . . raised about whether the *right* things are being worked on—not just how the work can be done more efficiently."[14] Otherwise, the resulting programs are likely to be misdirected. For example, a company that chooses to improve productivity by equipping its factories with the latest in labor-saving equipment has made a sensible choice if labor is thirty percent of total costs, but a much poorer decision if labor is only five percent of total costs. By placing productivity decisions in context, strategic approaches ensure that programs are tailored to competitive needs. Allegheny Ludlum, Vought, and Corning all illustrate strategic approaches to productivity and the programs and policies that support them.

NOTES

1. Manufacturing Studies Board, *Toward a New Era in Manufacturing* (Washington, D.C.: National Academy Press, 1986), p. 12. The slowdown is also evident in more comprehensive measures of total factor productivity. See Solomon Fabricant, "Issues in Productivity Measurement and Analysis," in Ali Dogramaci, ed., *Productivity Analysis* (Boston: Martinus Nijhoff, 1981), p. 26.

2. Patricia Capdevielle and Donato Alvarez, "International Comparisons of Trends in Productivity and Labor Costs," *Monthly Labor Review*, December 1981, p. 15.

3. Ali Dogramaci, "Perspectives on Productivity," in Dogramaci, *Productivity Analysis*, p. 1. The quotation originally appeared in the *Wall Street Journal*, December 31, 1979.

4. Frederick Winslow Taylor, *The Principles of Scientific Management* (New York: W.W. Norton & Company, 1947), pp. 5, 12.

5. For a summary of the growth accounting framework and the neoclassical model on which it is based, see Richard R. Nelson, "Research on Productivity Growth and Productivity Differences: Dead Ends and New Departures," *Journal of Economic Literature*, September 1981, pp. 1030–1033.

6. Campbell R. McConnell, "Why Is U.S. Productivity Slowing Down?", *Harvard Business Review*, March–April 1979, p. 37.

7. For discussions of the links between a growing defense sector and falling productivity, see Seymour Melman, *The War Economy of the United States* (New York: St. Martin's Press, 1971); Seymour Melman, *The Permanent War Economy* (New York: Simon and Schuster, 1974); and Seymour Melman, "Productivity Change as a Function of Variation in Microeconomy," in Dogramaci, *Productivity Analysis*, pp. 71–85. For discussions of the links between modern management methods and falling productivity, see Robert H. Hayes and William J. Abernathy, "Managing Our Way to Economic Decline," *Harvard Business Review*, July–August 1980, pp. 67–77, and Robert H. Hayes and David A. Garvin, "Managing as if Tomorrow Mattered," *Harvard Business Review*, May–June 1982, pp. 70–79.

8. See, for example, John W. Kendrick and the American Productivity Center, *Improving Company Productivity* (Baltimore: Johns Hopkins University Press, 1984), pp. 65–74, and Nelson, "Research on Productivity Growth," pp. 1040–1044.

9. David J. Sumanth, "Productivity Indicators Used by Major U.S. Manufacturing Companies: The Results of a Survey," *Industrial Engineering*, May 1981, p. 71.

10. Arnold S. Judson, "The Awkward Truth about Productivity," *Harvard Business Review*, September–October 1982, p. 94.

11. Robert B. McKersie and Janice A. Klein, "Productivity: The Industrial Relations Connection," *National Productivity Review*, Winter 1983–84, p. 27.

12. For representative surveys supporting this conclusion, see Judson, "The Awkward Truth about Productivity," p. 94, and Kendrick and American Productivity Center, *Improving Company Productivity*, p. 114. For more detailed discussions of the importance of strategic planning for productivity, see Arnold S. Judson, "Productivity Strategy and Business Strategy: Two Sides of the Same Coin," *Interfaces*, January–February 1984, pp. 103–115, and D. Scott Sink, "Strategic Planning: A Crucial Step toward a Successful Productivity Management Program," *Industrial Engineering*, January 1985, pp. 52–60.

13. See, for example, William A. Ruch and William B. Werther, Jr., "Productivity Strategies at TRW," *National Productivity Review*, Spring 1983, pp. 115–116, 125, and Kendrick and American Productivity Center, *Improving Company Productivity*, pp. 115–116.

14. Judson, "Productivity Strategy and Business Strategy," p. 111.

16. A Day at Midwest Equipment Corporation

James Pritchard welcomed the casewriter into his office with a friendly wave. William Dearden, Director of Corporate Productivity for Midwest Equipment Corporation, had recommended that the casewriter talk to Pritchard, who coordinated the productivity improvement efforts for Midwest's Machine Tool Division. "He is positioned so that he can flow-down the specific productivity goals and policies emanating from the very top levels of our corporation to the different Product Groups in his division. You should discuss how he controls this flow-down," Dearden had told the casewriter.

Pritchard expressed appreciation for the casewriter's interest in the work of his group and, under some prodding, briefly described his background. He had spent most of his professional career—over 20 years—with Midwest, primarily in various engineering functions. About 18 months previously he had been transferred from another Midwest division to his current position. The core of his job was the Chairmanship of the Productivity Council for the Machine Tool Division. This Council included representatives from six functional groups other than his own: Production, Engineering, Marketing, Finance, Procurement and Control. His own group encompassed what had been formerly the Industrial Engineering group.

Pritchard had been one of the first people assigned to Dearden's group. When asked how he had prepared himself for the job of Productivity

Coordinator, for which he had no previous formal background and which had not existed prior to his appointment, he laughed and stated, "That was a problem! I did what anybody else in my position would have done, probably—I went to the library and tried to find the best books on the subject. I soon found out that there weren't very many, and the ones that were available were generally not very current. But I read them and went to a lot of meetings (largely attended by people like myself who had recently been asked to head up Productivity Improvement efforts that hadn't previously existed at their companies). Mostly I learned on the job. Anytime you have to carve out a new set of responsibilities you have to walk a fine line, needless to say. But I was pleased to find that by and large people were very cooperative and supportive of my efforts.

"One of the things that I found out early in my managerial career is that few things happen of their own accord. They have to be made to happen, and productivity improvement is no exception. It has to be managed. Our division is probably the most advanced in promoting productivity efforts within Midwest, and the reason is that we decided early on that it was important, that it required resources (primarily in the form of people), and that specific plans had to be developed, based on agreed-on goals and means. Our council only meets formally four times a year now, but most of the work is done outside these meetings. Bill Dearden sort of rides herd on us from afar, providing information and keeping track of what we're doing, but he doesn't get involved in the actual development of plans for our division or the implementation of these plans. That's our job, and that's why I report to the division manager."

This case was prepared by Robert R. Hayes.
Copyright © 1980 by the President and Fellows of Harvard College. Harvard Business School case 681-041.

Industrial Engineering (IE)

After their conversation, Pritchard introduced the casewriter to his colleague, Hank Brown. Brown, an industrial engineer, had been with Midwest for 30 years. He had been assigned to Pritchard's group soon after its formation, and brought his on-going cost reduction projects with him.

He described three of these projects to the casewriter, all of which were concerned with improving the efficiency of various overhead functions. When asked why he had concentrated so much of his effort of these overhead activities, Brown responded, "Because they're important. We have almost 3,000 people who fall into the 'overhead' category in this division, against less than 2,000 people classified as 'direct labor'. However, most of the industrial engineering attention in the past has focused on the direct labor category."

One of these projects was an analysis of the Maintenance Department at one of the Division's plants, which had resulted in a 50% reduction in the ratio of maintenance workers to hourly workers over a five year period. Another had enabled the Technical Publications Department to increase its sales per person by over 50% between 1978 and 1979, while almost doubling its on-time delivery percentage. This had involved a series of interrelated activities including improving the estimating of the time required to develop a new publication, redesigning the workflow pattern through the department, establishing a production control department and developing a tracking system to monitor the flow of material through the process, and establishing a disciplined and detailed reporting system to check actual job times against estimated times.

The third had involved a series of activities with the Stores Department, which was responsible for the physical receipt and storing of purchased parts and tools, and the record-keeping and report generation associated with these stores. These activities had resulted in a reduction in the inventory-to-worker ratio of about 3%, which saved approximately $900,000 in inventory investment.

The case writer expressed interest in learning more about this last project, and Brown offered to introduce him to the head of the Stores Department. As they walked down to Stores, the casewriter asked Brown whether his transfer to

Jim Pritchard's group had had any major impact on the scope or nature of this activities. "Not really," he stated. "A lot of productivity improvement is simply due to old-fashioned cost reduction projects that used to be in the domain of the Industrial Engineering group. We shouldn't stop these projects simply because we've expanded the definition of productivity improvement efforts."

Stores Department

Brown introduced the casewriter to Phil Reif, a robust, smiling white-haired gentleman who pushed aside the work on his desk and motioned for them to sit down. When asked about his experience with Hank Brown's IE group, he brightened and admitted that Brown had made a very important contribution to his Department. He had originally invited Brown to do a study of the Stores Department in mid-1978, at least partly out of frustration. It had been both difficult to measure the performance of his Department and to provide convincing evidence to his boss to support his request for additional personnel. An IE study appeared to be a way of obtaining objective performance measures.

Brown's people had done some work sampling which enabled them to reduce the number of people in one area of the Department by 12%. In another area they had combined a similar study with a series of other changes: the walls were painted bright colors, new furnishings and some simple equipment were added, and a new supervisor was put in charge of the group.

The result had been remarkable. Within a year the number of people had decreased somewhat, even though the number of transactions had increased by over 50%. The transactions/person ratio had almost doubled as a result, and the group's morale had also shot up as they received recognition for their superior performance.

The casewriter asked if there had been any resistance to either of these studies, or had any problems arisen in trying to implement their recommendations. "Not really," answered Reif, "but it's important to understand that today's generation of workers is motivated by very different things than was true for Hank and my generation. We used to look forward to the opportunity for overtime, for example; and if we were asked to sacrifice our outside activities because of problems at the plant, we did so automatically. 'The company' was important to us and to our families as well.

"Now it's different. Young people today regard their 'private time'—that is, their time away from their job—as the most important thing in their lives. They'll work like hell the eight hours they're here, but then it's 'goodbye, don't bother me'. If you ask them to work overtime, they're likely to refuse. Or, if they do help you out by coming in on a Saturday, they're likely to take the following Monday off. They want those two days of freedom.

"And they don't believe in deferring pleasure. Why save for a rainy day, when it may never come? Tomorrow will take care of itself, they say. My generation considers that frivolous, but who's to say who's right? They're fine, hard working young people—most of them, that is. And they don't like to see anyone goofing off and spoiling things for the others who do want to work. But they have different values, and you can't 'manage' them very easily."

When asked whether he had ever attempted to explore these new attitudes and values in a more organized fashion, through attitude surveys, for example, he responded. "Sure I have, but I'm not sure whether I know much more afterwards than I did before I started. You see, before I can conduct such a survey, or even ask a group of workers to sit down and discuss their attitudes towards their work and the company (over coffee and doughnuts, say) I have to get the union's O.K. They say, 'Sure, go ahead', but then they go around and tell the workers, 'Enjoy the coffee and doughnuts. And say whatever you want, with two exceptions: don't say anything that will hurt or make life more difficult for a brother worker, and don't say anything that will reduce your paycheck or anybody else's.' So you can imagine what kind of discussions we end up having over coffee and doughnuts!"

In response to another question about his awareness of the Division's recent emphasis on productivity improvement, and Jim Pritchard's new role, he replied affirmatively. "I think it's a very healthy thing," he said, although he admitted that he was not exactly sure how Pritchard's group would interact with his department. He indicated that he might, however, call in Hank Brown's people to do another study at some point, in which case he would probably be interacting with Pritchard indirectly.

As the casewriter prepared to leave, he asked Reif what he was going to do for an encore—after effecting such a remarkable improvement in the performance of his department over the previous two years, what was he going to do next? Reif smiled appreciatively and admitted he didn't know. He had visited a sister plant in Florida recently and looked at a new computerized conveyor system the Stores Department there had recently installed, but he doubted whether he would request a similar system for his own department. "Partly it's just my natural tendency to discount exaggerated praise," he admitted. "Anyone who invests $250,000 in some new equipment is going to tell you afterwards it was a great idea and he is glad he did it. If you ask if he's experienced many problems, he'll probably say, 'No, not many.'

"But you have to be careful. The situation there is different; for one thing, they don't have a union. So you want to go there and look the situation over very carefully. One thing I noticed is this ladder lying on its side against the wall. 'What's that for?' I ask. 'Well,' they tell me, 'if that conveyorized hoist starts to malfunction, they lean the ladder against the wall and the foreman or his department supervisor climbs up and fixes it'. If the same thing happened here, because of the union we'd have to wait for a steeplejack *and* an electrician to come and fix it. And while we're waiting, everything grinds to a halt. No, we'll probably do something much more modest here. Besides, the division doesn't have much money to spend on cost-reducing investments. We're growing 20% a year, and most of what we earn goes back into financing that growth."

The Employee Suggestion Program

The next stop on the casewriter's agenda was the office of Fred Miller, who was Director of Employee Relations at one of the Machine Tool Division's plants. A former salesman, Miller emphasized that his sales background had been very helpful in his job, as it often involved getting people's agreement to try something new. "You have to sell them on the concept, and then after you've sold them, you have to make sure that it's working properly. You want *satisfied* customers, not just one-time customers. And, just as in selling, you not only have to sell your customers but sometimes you have to sell your bosses as well."

A major part of Miller's activity revolved around the employee suggestion system used in the plant. Miller felt that not only was this program one of the most advanced of its kind within Midwest (and, in fact, advanced compared with other companies all over the country), but that it was a major factor in Midwest's relatively high productivity improvement over the previous half-dozen years. He indicated that he held senior positions in several regional and national productivity associations, and expressed the view that he and Jim Pritchard were both attacking the same problem from somewhat different directions.

"There are three secrets to making an employee suggestion system successful," he observed. "First, you have to get employees to submit suggestions. Second, you have to evaluate those suggestions promptly and fairly. If your employees ever lose their faith in the fairness and quality of the screening system, they quickly become cynical about the program. And if they have to wait too long between the submission of their suggestion and the response, you lose some of the enthusiasm that keeps them thinking of new suggestions. Third, you have to reward them adequately for their suggestions. We publish their awards in the in-house magazine. Some of them are very substantial—several years' wages, in a few cases. People see that and they say to themselves, 'Hey, this company is serious!' "

Most of the rewards were much more modest, of course, and came in the form of "points." Workers accumulated these points (much like green stamps) until they had enough to exchange for one of a number of products (radios, hair driers, coffee makers, etc.) that were on display in little showcases around the plant. As another indication of the psychology that he used in administering this program, Miller mentioned that a number of companies had very similar points-for-gifts systems in their plants, and that as a result a couple of entrepreneurs had started up businesses which undertook the job of purchasing and inventorying the suggestion plan products for these companies. The company with the suggestion plan would send these subcontractors the names and addresses of the employees who were entitled to each gift, and the subcontractor would mail the gifts to the employee. "That would simplify our job considerably, of course, and probably reduce our costs," said Miller, "but we don't use these outside people. We want our department supervisors and managers to hand the product to the employee personally. We never want to lose that connection with the company and with its management. 'You have done a good job; it has benefitted the company and you have helped me and everyone else in this department.' *That's* the message that I want our employees to receive."

Saying Goodbye

On the way back to Jim Pritchard's office the casewriter noticed a large, brightly colored chart on the wall in one of the corridors. Labeled "Assembly Department Productivity Improvement," it showed work efficiency (as measured by standard hours divided by actual hours) increasing steadily from under 85% to over 90% during a four-month period.

As he was saying goodbye to Pritchard, the casewriter mentioned the chart and asked if it was another example of his efforts. "No," Pritchard replied, "I don't know the specific chart you're talking about, since there are lots of them around. It was probably a departmental chart put together by the department manager to inform and motivate his or her people. That's just another aspect of their regular managerial job, and we don't try to coordinate these individual efforts. Something like that is awfully hard to interpret, you see, because you don't know any of the circumstances behind it. It might be a new product that's just in its initial production run, or it might be a group of new workers who are going through a training phase, or the production job might have recently been re-engineered and retooled. So that performance improvement is likely to level off after a while. Productivity growth, on the other hand, is a long-term phenomenon. It shouldn't ever level off."

He thought for a moment, then added, "But that kind of chart is completely in keeping with our efforts. You can't really manage productivity growth from 'on high.' What you have to do is develop measurements and get people to establish goals for themselves that will ultimately lead to productivity improvement. We call that 'goaling,' and if you can do that well, almost everything else falls into place."

After his visit the casewriter studied the transparencies that William Dearden had used in a recent talk on productivity improvement that he had given to the Productivity Council at the Machine Tool Division. Some of these transparencies are reproduced in *Exhibits 1–8*.

EXHIBIT 1 Sales Per Employee Midwest Equipment Corporation

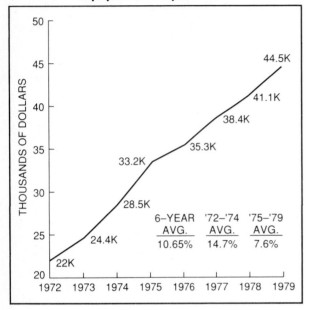

EXHIBIT 2 Sales Per Employee at Other Well-known, Well-managed Companies

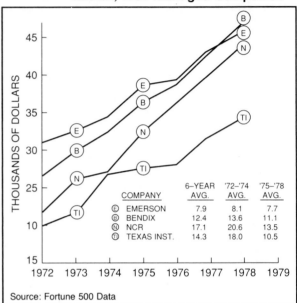

EXHIBIT 3 Sales Dollars Divided By Salaries and Wages

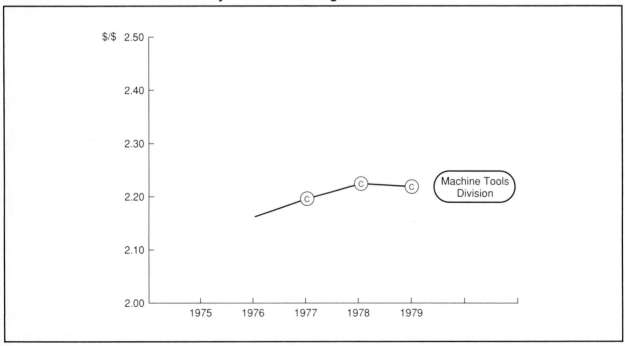

EXHIBIT 4 Major Factors Affecting Employee Productivity

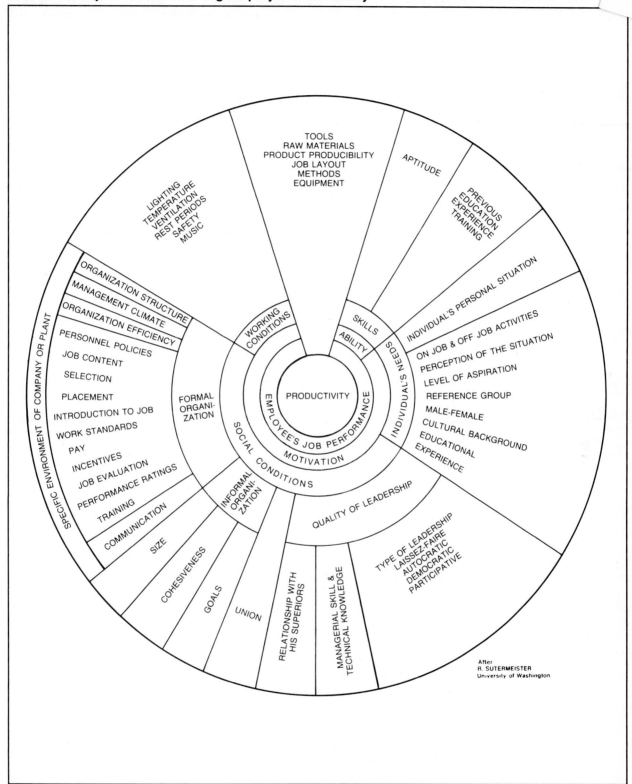

After
R. SUTERMEISTER
University of Washington

EXHIBIT 5 Productivity Improvement Tools

PRODUCTIVITY IMPROVEMENT TOOLS

- Effective supervision
- Automation
- Work simplification
- Work measurement
- Job enlargement, job redesign
- Systems analysis and design
- Manpower Management
  (Recruiting, staffing, training, upgrading, marginal)
- Incentives
- Training—JIT

EXHIBIT 6 Training?

TRAINING?

Except for factory managers & supervisors, most managers
have not been trained in productivity tools

- Manloading
- Work simplification
- Work measurement
- Job redesign
- Motivation, incentives

16. A Day at Midwest Equipment Corporation

EXHIBIT 7 Percent of Total Workforce Employed in Factory vs. Non-factory Jobs at Midwest

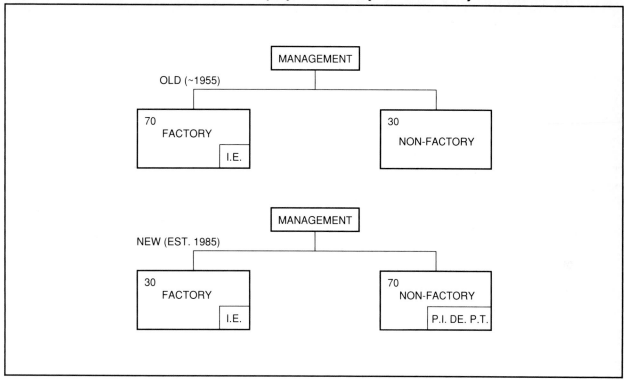

EXHIBIT 8 What Next?

WHAT NEXT?

1. Collect productivity data
2. Decide what to measure
3. Set goals
4. Build plans
5. Implement productivity improvements
6. Monitor progress

17. Applichem (A)

The Gary [Indiana] plant had had obvious problems for years. It was an ineffective operation. It had a fiefdom type of management. The people had grown complacent and inefficient. They had lost their technical curiosity. And the state-of-the-art technology was in Frankfurt. In the late 70's, when I was business manager, I tried to get them to invite Ari (the Frankfurt manufacturing and technology expert) to Gary. After months of talking, they finally invited him to get me off their backs.

In the Fall of 1981, we [top management] had a meeting reviewing our 10 year plan. After my part, I said that I was going to shift production of Release-ease and another product from Gary to Frankfurt as fast as possible. I almost got punched in the mouth for that. We had been working on it [the Gary plant] for years. But we were not doing anything! At Gary there were still 1300 people putting out 300 million pounds of material a year. At Frankfurt, 600 people put out about 10 percent less material.

J. S. (Joe) Spadaro, Vice President and Director of the Plastics Business, was discussing the conditions in Release-ease manufacturing which led him to request a study comparing productivity at six Release-ease plants. He had requested the study in June 1982, and it had been finished in September 1982.

Spadaro had joined Applichem in 1956 when he was 27. His bachelor's degree was in mechanical engineering, and he had held several jobs before that, including managing a machine shop, but not including anything related to the chemical industry. His first assignment had been in Italy where he spent 10 years; then he had spent 5 years in the U.K. before returning to work at corporate headquarters in Chicago.

Business Background

Release-ease was a specialty chemical. Applichem developed it in 1952 in response to a customer's request for help in formulating a plastic molding compound which released easily from metal molds after compression molding. It was sold as a dry powder.

Making molded plastic parts is much like making molded jello. Both jello and the plastic molding compound are hot and liquid when put in the mold; both harden as they cool. Both tend to leave residue on the mold after they are unmolded. Washing a jello mold is easy, and the mold is rarely needed again immediately. But molds for plastic parts are precision stainless steel; they can be difficult to clean; and they are used repeatedly, with unmolding and cleaning being the bottleneck.

When a customer requested help in cleaning molds quickly, Applichem applications engineers came up with "Release-ease." It was a chemical to be added in low concentration to the plastic molding compound during its manufacture so that the molded parts would be easier to separate from the mold and would leave the mold cleaner. Release-ease was widely used in molding plastic parts.

Applichem had held the patent, and the product family had been a steady sales and profit generator for the company through 1982. Applichem had done no research on the Release-ease product or process after about 1953. What product and process changes there had been were made

This case was prepared by Therese Flaherty

Copyright © 1985 by the President and Fellows of Harvard College. Harvard Business School case 685-051.

by manufacturing people in the plants. And most of those had been made by Aristotle (Ari) Pappas, Manager of Release-ease manufacturing at the Frankfurt plant.

The specifications of Release-ease varied slightly among regions. Over the years as customers encountered problems in their molding processes, Applichem's applications engineers had worked with them to identify aspects of Release-ease or other aspects of the customer's process which could relieve the symptoms. The process was one of trial-and-error. Customers were also continually finding ways to use lower concentrations of Release-ease to achieve the same results. In 1982 Applichem's market research group expected little net increase in demand for Release-ease during the next five years.

In Europe suspendability of the particles in liquid came to be an important property, and most promotional literature stressed this property. Competition was fiercer in Europe than in the U.S.; quality and product specifications were more closely monitored there. Several managers told the casewriter that they were convinced that Release-ease made in the Frankfurt plant met specifications better than that made in other plants. There were two other important differences in customers' uses in Europe and the rest of the world. First, European customers used their Release-ease within one year of purchase, whereas some final customers in the U.S. would use it as long as 3 years after manufacture, and customers in other regions varied between the two extremes. Second, European customers purchased Release-ease in 50-kilo bags, but customers in the U.S. and Japan used packages in many sizes from $\frac{1}{2}$-kilo on up.

Release-ease sold at an average price of $1.01 a pound. Applichem's Release-ease sales by region, production by each of the six plants, as well as exports and imports by region (all in millions of pounds) were as shown in the table below.

Applichem's strongest competitor was a large U.S.-based chemical company whose only plant for making a close substitute for Release-ease was located in Luxembourg. Its sales in Europe were strong and it made some export sales to the U.S. and Latin America. But Applichem had by far the largest market share and the mystique associated with having patented the earliest available form of the product. A third U.S.-based company provided some competition in the U.S. but J. (John) Benfield, who was Operations Manager for the Plastic North American Business Team in 1982, said that he thought that the latter company was not seriously committed to the business for the long-run. They had a plant with some excess capacity, and in 1982 they were using it to produce another close substitute for Release-ease.

In Japan Applichem was the only company whose product had been approved by the regulators. Joe Spadaro said that eventually there would be some other products sold in Japan, even if only exports from Europe. And the Plastics Operations Manager of the Pacific Area told the casewriter that he had heard that someone in the Japanese government had been approached with the idea of approving a Release-ease-type product.

	Sales	Plant	Actual 1982 Production	Exports by Region	Imports by Region
North America (incl. Mexico and Canada)	32	Gary Canada Mexico	14.0 2.6 17.2	14.2	12.4
Western Europe (incl. Middle East and Africa)	20	Frankfurt	38.0	18.0	0
Latin America	16	Venezuela	4.1	0	11.9
Pacific and Rest of World	11.9	Sunchem	4.0	0	7.9
Total	79.9		79.9	32.2	32.2

Company Background

Applichem was a manufacturer of specialty chemicals founded in Chicago just before World War II. Most of its products were devised by Applichem's applications engineers as solutions to a specific customer's problems. Applichem's Research department subsequently refined the product and process—in successful cases—to arrive at a product with broader application.

Applichem had a strong functional orientation, even though some matrixing had been introduced to the organization during the mid-1970's. There is evidence of matrixing in the June 1982 organization chart presented in *Exhibit 1*. There were Business Managers for two businesses reporting to a Group Vice President and four Area

Vice Presidents reporting to the Chief Operating Officer. Each Business Manager led four business teams, one for each of the four Areas. Each Area business team was headed by one full-time manager. On each team were a financial manager, a marketing manager, an R&D manager (who usually focused on new product introductions) and an operations manager. The functional managers also held line jobs in their respective Area organizations. The operations and marketing managers, like employees in the manufacturing plants and sales and marketing organizations, reported up through the Area organizations. Finance and R&D reported up through the functional organizations. For example, John Benfield, Operations Manager for the Plastics North America Business Team in 1982, reported through two boxes on the

EXHIBIT 1 Organization Chart, June 1982

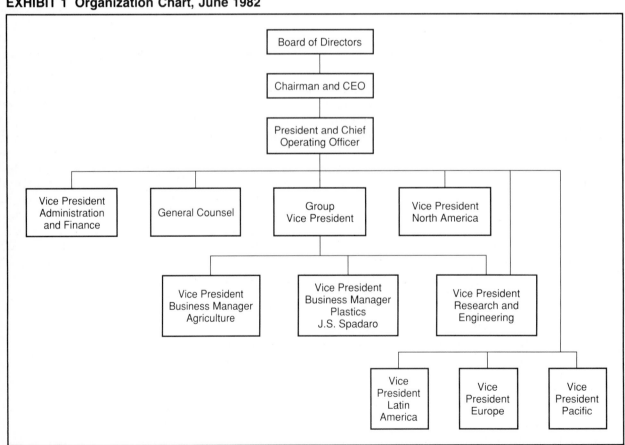

organization chart in *Exhibit 1*: directly to Joe Spadaro and through several people to the Vice President of the North American area.

Technology

Release-ease was manufactured by a 4-step process. In the reaction step the raw materials (several of which were hazardous, flammable, and therefore not transportable internationally) were combined in a precise sequence under pressure and heat to form the Release-ease. The Release-ease was then precipitated out to form a slurry. The timing of introducing materials into the pressurized vessel (or kettle)—as well as the temperature and pressure which prevailed, the feedrates, heat removal, and agitation—affected the size and composition of the forming Release-ease particles. The quality of the Release-ease, the amount of raw materials, and the characteristics of the process were unaffected by the source of energy used in the plant. So steam, natural gas, oil and electricity were combined differently at different plants to minimize local cost.

The second step was to clean, or isolate, the Release-ease particles from the slurry. This was done by moving the slurry on a conveyor belt made of mesh so that the liquid fell through the belt to the trough below, leaving wet Release-ease particles on the belt. In the third step, Release-ease particles were dried; and in the fourth step the Release-ease powder was packaged in bags on an automated filler line.

Laboratory samples were taken for analysis at the end of the reaction, cleaning and drying steps. It usually took four hours for operators to get the laboratory results. Since waiting between the cleaning and drying steps impaired product properties, Release-ease particles moved continuously between cleaning and drying. The information was used to classify the material after it was processed. Material that was off-spec was reworked in some plants; in other plants some of it was reclassified as QC-3 (QC-1 was the category for product which conformed to specs) and sold for a lower price.

Throughout the process there were possibilities for yield loss. For example, in the reaction step some of the raw materials were added in powder form, and they could be lost as dust on the floor and in the air. In the cleaning step, particles might be filtered out with the liquid and impurities. Recapturing waste materials was an important source of yield increases; the manufacturing people typically improved recapture gradually over years of work. Waste could also be an important health and safety measure.

The average yield of Release-ease on raw material A was a key indicator of the overall performance of the Release-ease manufacturing processes at different plants. The yield was defined by dividing the actual number of pounds of active ingredient in the final product by the number of pounds of active ingredient which would be in the Release-ease if all the key raw material A were converted to active ingredient. Yields were usually expressed in percentages. Benfield explained, "Plants designed for larger volumes of output generally have higher yields. Raw material A might not wind up in the final product for one or both of two reasons: (1) There might be physical losses (waste) during the process. For example, raw material A per pound of Release-ease left in a drum container (used in low volume processes) would be greater than that left in a railroad tank car (used in high volume processes). (2) The available raw material A might not be converted during the process. Larger scale processes would have less waste than smaller scale processes. But the proportion of available raw material A converted to Release-ease would be determined by how well the process was run, regardless of scale. A well-run, low- volume (around 5 million pounds a year) process would have an average yield on A of 91 or 92 percent; a well-run, medium volume plant would have an average yield on A of 94-95 percent; a well-run, high volume plant would have an average yield on A of 98-99 percent."

Usually, the manufacturing process was run 24 hours a day, 7 days a week. This was because shutting down the process required expensive cleaning of the reaction kettles and the driers where Release-ease particles stuck. Similarly, changing the size of bag in the packaging line frequently took a day.

One of the main quality measures for the final product performance was the percent of active ingredient in the powder since high active ingredient correlated well with good application properties, especially for U.S. markets.

The Plastics North America Business Team estimated that in 1982 it would cost about $20-25 million to build another plant like that in Gary, Indiana. And they expected that the plant would have a useful technical life of about 20 years if properly maintained.

The Manufacturing Plants

The *Gary* plant was managed by the North American Area. It supplied Release-ease to customers located in that Area. The plant was located in Gary, Indiana (just outside Chicago) and in a neighborhood where immigrants from Eastern Europe had settled during the early twentieth century. The plant was founded in 1905 and purchased in 1951 by Applichem as the company's first large manufacturing facility. Many people who worked in the Gary plant in 1982 had followed 6 to 10 other members of their families who had worked there over the generations. They were loyal to the plant and to the plant manager, who had grown up in the neighborhood and called himself the "Gary kid."

Release-ease was the first product Applichem manufactured there, and the process had changed incrementally with the market for Release-ease. Most equipment for the process used in 1982 had been installed between 1959 and 1964. It was designed to run a wide range of product formulation and package types. In 1982 Gary ran 8 formulations of Release-ease and about 80 package sizes, while the Frankfurt plant, for example, ran only 2 formulations of Release-ease and one 50-kilo package.

The plant manufactured 19 product families in addition to Release-ease. It had a total of 1000 non-union employees, down from about 2,000 during the mid-1960's. It had a Release-ease design capacity of 18.5 million pounds a year, and around 60 people manufactured 14 million pounds of Release-ease in 1982.

The *Canadian* plant, located in Southern Ontario, had been started up in 1955. It was managed by Canadian nationals who reported to the North American Area. It had a non-union work force. And in 1982 it supplied four products in addition to Release-ease.

The plant was generally well-regarded within Applichem for its efficiency and the quality of its product. It had a "no- frills" design and had been well-maintained since its inception. It had a rated annual capacity of 3.7 million pounds of Release-ease and it manufactured 2.6 million pounds of Release-ease in 1982. It supplied Release-ease only in 50-kilo packages.

The *Frankfurt* plant was managed by German nationals who reported through the European Area, and it supplied customers located in Europe, the Middle East, and Africa as well as other Applichem plants. It made 12 product families in addition to Release-ease. The plant had 600 employees in 1982. It made about 38 million pounds of Release-ease a year in 1982, and its design capacity was 47 million pounds a year. It had two processes for manufacturing Release-ease: one installed between 1971 and 1974 and one installed in about 1961, with later major modifications to increase capacity. The processes featured computer control of the first process step and extensive solids recovery and waste treatment. Frankfurt bulk-shipped Release-ease to other company plants which then packaged it and shipped it to customers.

Release-ease manufacturing was managed by Ari Pappas. He was a Greek national who had headed Release-ease manufacturing at Frankfurt since the mid-1960's. He had gotten to know Joe Spadaro and several other members of Applichem's top management team when they had worked in Europe during the sixties. Pappas had a technical bent; and he had worked with customers, the Applichem Technical Center in Europe, and his own employees to improve the yields and reliability of the Release-ease he made.

The *Mexican* plant was part of a wholly owned subsidiary of Applichem. It was managed by Mexican nationals, who reported to the vice president of the Latin American Area. It supplied the Mexican market and in early 1980s the Far East. The plant processed about 17.2 million pounds of Release-ease during 1982, and had a design capacity of 22 million pounds a year. All its Release-ease was packaged in 50-kilo bags. The process had been installed in 1968 with extra drying capacity introduced in 1978. It was similar in design to the Gary plant, and manufactured 6 product families in addition to Release-ease.

The *Venezuelan* plant was started up in 1964. It had a "no frills" design, and no improvements had been made between 1964 and 1982. Its rated annual capacity was 4.5 million pounds, and it produced 4.1 million pounds of Release-ease in 1982. Its Release-ease was packaged only in 50 kilo bags. The plant had old equipment and the only dryer was in poor repair. It was managed by Venezuelan nationals, who reported to the vice president of the Latin American Area. And it manufactured one product family in addition to Release-ease.

The educational levels of the Mexican and Venezuelan operators were significantly below those of operators in the other plants. John Benfield explained that the Mexican operators had some technical depth and were able to maintain process improvements suggested by Ari, while the Venezuelans were not. The Venezuelans had not improved process yield or capacity.

Sunchem was Applichem's 50% Japanese joint venture in Japan which owned and operated a manufacturing plant for Release-ease and one other product for the plastics industry. It was managed by Japanese nationals and reported to Applichem's Pacific Area. It was founded in 1957 and had supplied the Release-ease requirements of Japanese customers after that. The process had been redesigned in 1969. Some automation and waste recovery had been introduced. Its volume was constrained by low dryer capacity in 1982. The Japanese plant processed many $\frac{1}{2}$- kilo and 1-kilo packages. The plant had a rated capacity of 5 million pounds a year, and it produced 4 million pounds in 1982. Within Applichem the Japanese plant was generally thought to be technically excellent. Employees there did more development work than the other plants: they had a product test laboratory, a plastics engineering lab and a workers' dormitory for single men. Japanese managers said that they required more environmental protection measures than the other plants. Theirs was, for example, the only plant with scrubbers for processing gaseous wastes.

There was no union at this plant although there generally were industry—as opposed to company—unions in the Japanese chemical industry. In 1979 the plant manager wrote to U.S. management to explain why an unusually large number of employees was needed in Japan relative to similar Applichem plants elsewhere. He wrote:

> Work rules and regulations seem to be more severe than those in other countries. For example, the Japanese Fire Prevention Law prescribes that the work of handling flammable raw materials must be performed by those having a license for doing such work. Among the works requiring similar licenses—there are those of wide variety in which we handle high-pressure gas as in refrigerators, toxic substances, organic solvents, and drying works being performed where oxygen is not sufficient. A number of plant operators will have to attend training courses to acquire such licenses. . . .
>
> We know that one operator has been taking care of running several kettles at the Gary plant. Only one operator would not be enough to handle all kettles here because our workers do more work with the kettles. . . .
>
> In accordance with a strong recommendation by the Shift Work Committee of the Japan Industrial Hygiene Institute, manufacturers are required to allow a temporary sleeping time for two hours a day to all who are engaged in midnight works.

The Cross-Plant Productivity Study

John Benfield had managed the study comparing productivity at different plants. Talking in retrospect about it, he said:

> The report got things on an even keel. It set the agenda. Until then our report managers at one plant rarely encountered managers from sister plants. And they never gave much attention to improving their process on the basis of what other plants had done.
>
> While the standard costs and volumes of Release-ease were easily available for each plant, the technical information needed for the Study was not available. Allocating indirect labor over products was a major problem. The Japanese and Gary employees, for example, complained throughout that they simply had low volumes which caused their overhead to be too high. Yield information was available, but only the technical people in the plants had it. The Study was able to identify precise labor productivity differences among plants and to set an agenda for improvement.
>
> It was important that financial and technical people in all the plants worked together developing the numbers. We argued back and

forth during the process, trying to ensure that everyone in the plants agreed with the numbers. For example, to satisfy some concerns at Gary, where a lot of time was spent packaging Release-ease in small packages, packaging was studied separately for all plants. And the Japanese over-estimated their material usage in their standards because they did not want to be caught short. So we took their usage numbers from their actual experience year-to-date.

Over the 4 months that we worked on the report before it was published in September 1982, probably 4 man-months went into it. The individual plants were not interested in repeating the comparison project. In fact, some said that they hoped it was never done again. It was a pain.

Exhibit 2 presents the breakdown and comparison of manufacturing costs for Release-ease at Applichem's six plants in 1982 as it appeared in the Study. *Exhibits 3* through *6* present some of the data which Benfield's group used in defining and computing the cost figures presented in *Exhibit 2*. The costs in *Exhibit 2* are manufacturing, as opposed to delivered, costs. Annual volume of Release-ease was a plant's forecast volume of Release-ease in 1982. Indirect costs were allocated over all the products in each plant; the standard cost of Release-ease included the allocated indirect costs. The operating costs were derived by dividing a plant's annual budget for the corresponding

EXHIBIT 2 Comparison of Worldwide Release-ease Manufacturing Cost

(U.S. DOLLARS PER HUNDRED POUNDS OF RELEASE-EASE)						
	Plants					
Expense	Mexico	Canada	Venezuela	Frankfurt	Gary	Sunchem
Raw Materials						
A	27.00	28.32	24.67	24.02	27.96	29.62
B	14.57	15.26	26.82	11.69	13.52	20.41
C	16.39	11.19	19.18	9.03	6.92	24.68
D	5.89	7.45	9.52	3.75	6.48	5.50
Other	11.20	6.48	7.10	4.51	5.95	11.65
Subtotal	75.05	68.70	87.29	53.00	60.83	91.86
Raw Material						
Overhead	—	—	—	—	2.65	—
Operating Costs						
Direct Labor, Salary & Fringes	2.38	7.03	4.68	5.78	8.46	12.82
Depreciation	.95	.97	.94	1.05	1.60	3.23
Utilities	5.08	5.50	5.96	5.54	5.45	10.49
Maintenance	1.60	2.75	2.17	1.34	3.71	3.77
Quality Control	.64	1.30	1.81	.57	1.54	2.77
Waste Treatment	1.37	.96	—	.64	1.02	10.61
Plant Administration	1.11	3.62	4.58	2.91	1.22	4.07
Development	—	—	—	.38	.97	2.48
Supplies	2.25	.98	3.65	—	.77	.56
Building Expense	—	—	—	1.12	.64	.36
Other	2.20	1.44	1.23	1.01	.29	6.22
Subtotal	17.58	24.55	25.02	20.34	25.67	57.38
Subtotal: Cost Before Packaging	92.63	93.25	112.31	73.34	89.15	149.24
Package, Load, & Ship	2.38	4.10	4.03	3.35	13.78	4.56
Total Cost	95.01	97.35	116.34	76.69	102.93	153.80

Notes:

[1] Operating costs include indirect labor and associated material costs other than raw materials.

[2] Raw material overhead in the Gary plant included incoming inspection, handling, and inventory carrying costs related to raw materials. For other plants those costs were included in Operating Costs.

17. Applichem (A)

EXHIBIT 3 Number of People at Each Operation at Each Plant

Plants

	Mexico	Canada	Venezuela	Frankfurt	Gary	Sunchem
Direct Labor						
Reaction	5.5	3.1	3.4	13.9	6.3	50
Clean	1.8	2.0	1.7	11.8	2.5	34
Dry	1.8	2.0	1.7	5.6	3.6	34
Package	10.4	5.0	6.2	14.6	11.3	27
Subtotal	19.5	12.1	12.9	45.9	23.7	144
Indirect Labor						
Maintenance	5.6	2.0	1.5	14.6	6.4	3
Quality Control	1.8	2.1	1.8	4.9	3.2	24
Production Supervision	2.1	1.6	.6	7.3	3.4	25
Plant Administration	3.1	3.7	4.3	NA	1.5	34
Development	.6	—	—	1.7	2.2	32
Waste Treatment	1.8	1.4	—	.8	.1	25
Utilities	1.3	1.0	1.3	2.8	1.1	8
Raw Materials Handling	—	.6	—	2.4	4.1	—
Shipping	3.1	1.9	1.5	5.7	9.2	—
Miscellaneous	5.5	1.3	—	NA	3.4	15
Subtotal	24.9	15.6	11.0	40.2	34.6	166
Total	44.4	27.7	23.9	86.1	58.3	310

EXHIBIT 4 Miscellaneous Information

	Plants					
	Mexico	Canada	Venezuela	Frankfurt	Gary	Sunchem
Utility Usage *(per million pounds product)*						
Steam (metric ton)	2.09	3.06	NA	3.18	2.74	NA
Natural Gas (cubic meter)	—	84.31	277.20	—	78.40	—
Oil (liter)	98.00	—	—	74.20	—	214.20
Electricity (kilowatt hours)	298.20	360.12	387.8	245.00	344.40	463.40
Utility Costs, *($ per unit purchased)*						
Steam (metric ton)	25.00	19.50	5.21	20.56	23.43	NA
Natural Gas (cubic meter)	—	.12	.05	—	.18	—
Oil (liter)	.32	—	—	.35	—	.31
Electricity (1000 kilowatt hours)	40	40.	71	45	56	79
Raw Material Usage *(lb/hundred pounds of Release-ease)*						
A	20.04	19.53	19.27	18.9	20.75	19.14
B	51.21	51.15	50.60	47.82	53.8	48.23
C	55.97	50.96	52.00	50.28	53.6	49.49
D	26.40	26.09	26.00	24.21	28.77	25.07
% Active Ingredient (A.I.) in Product as Shipped Average A.I.	85.6	84.7	NA	84.4	84.6	85.4
Average Yield on Raw Material A (Percent) $\left(\dfrac{\text{Actual pounds A.I.}}{\text{Theoretical pounds A.I.}} \times 100 \right)$	94.7	91.1	91.7	98.9	90.4	988
Volume (million pounds)						
Annual Production Volume in 1982	17.2	2.6	4.1	38.0	14.0	4.0
Annual Design Capacity	22.0	3.7	4.5	47	18.5	5.0

EXHIBIT 5 Transportation Costs Among Plants (¢/Pound)

Plants

FROM/TO	Mexico	Canada	Venezuela	Frankfurt	Gary	Sunchem
Mexico	0.0	11.4	7.0	11.0	11.0	14.0
Canada	11.0	0.0	9.0	11.5	6.0	13.0
Venezuela	7.0	10.0	0.0	13.0	10.4	14.3
Frankfurt	10.0	11.5	12.5	0.0	11.2	13.3
Gary	10.0	6.0	11.0	10.0	0.0	12.5
Sunchem	14.0	13.0	12.5	14.2	13.0	0.0

Notes:

1. It cost 11¢ to transport a pound of Release-ease from Canada to Mexico and 11.4¢ to transport a pound of Release-ease from Mexico to Canada. The price of transport depended on distance, type of transport and the volume transported. Where there were differences in transport costs between two locations, they were due to differences in the volumes Applichem had historically shipped in each direction between the locations.

2. These costs exclude duty into each country. In 1982 the duty into each country was the following percent of the value of Release-ease imported:

Mexico	Canada	Venezuela	Germany	U.S.	Japan
60%	0%	50%	9.5%	4.5%	6%

EXHIBIT 6 History of Exchange, Inflation, and Wage Rates

	Mexico	Canada	Venezuela	Germany	U.S.	Japan
			Country			

Average Annual Exchange Rates: (currency/$1 U.S.)

	Mexico	Canada	Venezuela	Germany	U.S.	Japan
1982	96.5	1.23	4.3	2.38	1.0	235.0
1981	26.2	1.18	4.3	2.25	1.0	219.9
1980	23.2	1.19	4.3	1.96	1.0	203.0
1979	22.8	1.17	4.3	1.73	1.0	239.7
1978	22.7	1.19	4.3	1.83	1.0	194.6
1977	22.7	1.09	4.3	2.10	1.0	240.0
	(Pesos)	(Canadian Dollar)	(Bolivares)	(Deutsche Mark)	(Dollar)	(Yen)

Average Annual Price Indices (1980 = 100)

	Mexico	Canada	Venezuela	Germany	U.S.	Japan
1982	194.2[a]	116.8	123.0[c]	114.1[b]	113.7[b]	103.2[a]
1981	124.4	110.2	113.8	107.8	110.6	101.4
1980	100.0	100.0	100.0	100.0	100.0	100.0
1979	80.3	88.1	83.3	93.0	86.1	84.9
1978	67.9	77.0	76.3	88.7	76.3	79.1
1977	58.6	70.5	71.0	87.7	71.0	81.2

[a] Wholesale prices

[b] Industrial prices

[c] Home and imported goods

Source: *International Financial Statistics*, International Monetary Fund.

Average Gross Money Wages (Before Income Taxes, Social Security Contributions, and Benefits) (local currency per hour)

	Mexico	Canada	Venezuela	Germany	U.S.	Japan
1982	99.42	10.25	14.37	14.64	8.50	1424.86
1981	63.46	9.17	13.08	13.92	7.99	1372.77
1980	48.11	8.19	11.26	13.18	7.27	1292.66
1979	39.91	7.44	10.42	12.36	6.69	1203.80
1978	34.17	6.84	9.88	11.73	6.17	1134.00
1977	29.70	6.38	8.74	11.14	5.68	1061.00

Source: Business International Corporation, *Worldwide Economic Indicators*, One Dag Hammarskjold Plaza, NY, NY. The values for Venezuela were estimated by John Benfield using Applichem sources because the complete series was unavailable in *Worldwide Economic Indicators*.

element of expense for all Release-ease production by the annual volume. Raw material prices and exchange rates were those used in the plants' 1982 business plans. Benfield said,

> Although exchange rate changes have a significant impact on comparative raw materials costs stated in dollars, the impact is lessened due to the fact that more than half of the raw materials are available in competitive international markets. We estimate that over the long haul only 30 to 40 per cent of the raw material cost is directly influenced by exchange rate changes. A variety of energy sources are used by the plants depending on local price and availability. We expect the overall utility costs per pound of Release-ease to continue to be roughly equivalent for all plants except Sunchem, where high local electricity costs reflect Japan's generally high energy cost.

Two employees from the Gary plant spoke with the casewriter about the study. T. E. (Tom) Schultz was a project manager in development engineering at the Gary plant when John Benfield was assembling the productivity study. He had joined Applichem in 1978 just after completing his Bachelor's degree in Chemical Engineering. And in the period before Applichem's U.S. Controller took over, Schultz and Gary's Production Manager for Release-ease began work to improve productivity in the Release-ease area. By the time John Benfield requested information for the Productivity Study, they had it close to ready. The entire process of getting the data ready for the Study took about 2 man-years. But Schultz had been enthusiastic about the study because he had believed that corporate managers were seeking to identify the best process ideas from all the plants and to implement them wherever they were relevant throughout the Applichem manufacturing network. Tom Schultz said:

> There were several difficulties in comparing cost, usage and yield statistics across plants—even data assembled as carefully as Benfield did. For example, the Gary plant was designed to manufacture prototype samples for customers, and most products in the Release-ease family had first been manufactured in Gary. Also, being an old product, Release-ease has folklore in Gary. There was also a body of opinion to the effect that older product [greater than two years] suffered some degradation in applications performance. As it was not unusual for product in the U.S. to be in the distribution channel for two years, Gary placed great emphasis on achieving high A.I. at time of manufacture. We were also very leery about implementing some of the changes that the Frankfurt plant had made because we were afraid that our product shelf life might be adversely affected. As Frankfurt's product stayed in the distribution channel for at most one year, their emphasis on high A.I. product was less than ours and they were more adventuresome in adopting process changes.
>
> You know, when I joined the Gary plant it seemed that we had the lowest costs of any plant. But then the exchange rates changed a lot. And the productivity study came along just when we looked bad . . . I wonder when the exchange rates will swing back and make Gary look good again.

W. C. (Wanda) Tannenbaum was Financial Analyst at the Gary plant during the Productivity Study. She had joined Applichem in 1981, after completing an undergraduate degree in business from the University of Illinois. She noted that the study was very technically oriented, that she was involved only to "look it over." She explained:

> At Applichem we use fully allocated standard costs for operations management. For sourcing we used out-of-pocket costs. The data needed for the Study were available, but not in accessible form. For example, we had many monthly reports, but no data was cumulative. And standard costs were redefined only once or twice a year, so it was just about impossible to get actual costs for Release-ease by month.
>
> In Finance we did a lot of computer work to get the reports we wanted. In fact, we installed an Apple III in 1982, the first PC [personal computer] in Applichem.
>
> The allocation of indirect costs was a big problem for the Study—especially for a plant like Gary. It was not designed to be a real streamlined operation. It was designed to be a batch operation for research and specialty products. Its equipment is unique. It is spread out all over the place. You just can't compare it with plants that make commodities.

18. Why Some Factories Are More Productive Than Others

The battle for attention is over. The time for banging drums is long past. Everyone now understands that manufacturing provides an essential source of competitive leverage. No longer does anyone seriously think that domestic producers can outdo their competitors by clever marketing only—"selling the sizzle" while cheating on quality or letting deliveries slip. It is now time for concrete action on a practical level: action to change facilities, update processing technologies, adjust workforce practices, and perfect information and management systems.

But when managers turn to these tasks, they quickly run up against a stumbling block. Namely, they do not have adequate measures for judging factory-level performance or for comparing overall performance from one facility to the next. Of course, they can use the traditional cost-accounting figures, but these figures often do not tell them what they really need to know. Worse, even the best numbers do not sufficiently reflect the important contributions that managers can make by reducing confusion in the system and promoting organizational learning.

Consider the experience of a U.S. auto manufacturer that discovered itself with a big cost disadvantage. The company put together a group to study its principal competitor's manufacturing operations. The study generated reams of data, but the senior executive in charge of the activity still felt uneasy. He feared that the group was getting mired in details and that things other than managerial practices—like the age of facilities and their location—might be the primary drivers of performance. How to tell?

Similarly, a vice president of manufacturing for a specialty chemical producer had misgivings about the emphasis his company's system for evaluating plant managers placed on variances from standard costs. Differences in these standards made comparisons across plants difficult. What was more troubling, the system did not easily capture the trade-offs among factors of production or consider the role played by capital equipment or materials. What to do?

Another manufacturer—this time of paper products—found quite different patterns of learning in the same departments of five of its plants scattered across the United States. Although each department made much the same products using similar equipment and materials, they varied widely in performance over a period of years. Why such differences?

Our point is simple: before managers can pinpoint what's needed to boost manufacturing performance, they must have a reliable way of ascertaining why some factories are more productive than others. They also need a dependable metric for identifying and measuring such differences and a framework for thinking about how to improve their performance—and keep it improving. This is no easy order.

These issues led us to embark on a continuing, multiyear study of 12 factories in 3 companies (see the appendix for details on research methodology). The study's purpose is to clarify the variables that influence productivity growth at the micro level.

The first company we looked at, which employs a highly connected and automated manufacturing process, we refer to as the Process Company. Another, which employs a batch approach based on a disconnected line-flow organization of work, we refer to as the Fab (fabrication-assembly) Company. The third, which uses several different batch processes to make components for sophisticated electronic systems, is characterized by very rapid changes in both product and process. We refer to it as the Hi-Tech Company. All five factories of the Process Company and three of the four factories of the Fab Company are in the United States (the fourth is just across the border in Canada). Of the three factories belonging to the Hi-Tech Company, one is in the United States, one in Europe, and one in Asia.

In none of these companies did the usual profit-and-loss statements—or the familiar monthly operating reports—provide adequate, up-to-date information about factory performance. Certainly, managers routinely evaluated such performance, but the metrics they used made their task like that of watching a distant activity through a thick, fogged window. Indeed, the measurement systems in place at many factories obscure and even alter the details of their performance.

A Fogged Window

Every plant we studied employed a traditional standard cost system: the controller collected and reported data each month on the actual costs incurred during the period for labor, materials, energy, and depreciation, as well as on the costs that would have been incurred had workers and equipment performed at predetermined "standard" levels. The variances from these standard costs became the basis for problem identification and performance evaluation. Other departments in the plants kept track of head counts, work-in-process inventory, engineering changes, the value of newly installed equipment, reject rates, and so forth.

In theory, this kind of measurement system should take a diverse range of activities and summarize them in a way that clarifies what is going on. It should act like a lens that brings a blurry picture into sharp focus. Yet, time and again, we found that these systems often masked critical developments in the factories and, worse, often distorted management's perspective.

Each month, most of the managers we worked with received a blizzard of variance reports but no overall measure of efficiency. Yet this measure is not hard to calculate. In our study, we took the same data generated by plant managers and combined them into a measure of the total factor productivity (TFP)—the ratio of total output to total input (see the appendix for more details on TFP).

This approach helps dissipate some of the fog—especially because our TFP data are presented in constant dollars instead of the usual current dollars. Doing so cuts through the distortions produced by periods of high inflation. Consider the situation at Fab's Plant 1, where from 1974 to 1982 output fluctuated between $45 million and $70 million—in nominal (current dollar) terms. In real terms, however, there was a steep and significant decline in unit output. Several executives initially expressed disbelief at the magnitude of this decline because they had come to think of the plant as a "$50 million plant." Their traditional accounting measures had masked the fundamental changes taking place.

Another advantage of the TFP approach is that it integrates the contributions of all the factors of production into a single measure of total input. Traditional systems offer no such integration. Moreover, they often overlook important factors. One of the plant managers at the Process Company gauged performance in a key department by improvements in labor hours and wage costs. Our data showed that these "improvements" came largely from the substitution of capital for labor. Conscientious efforts to prune labor content by installing equipment—without developing the management skills and systems needed to realize its full potential—proved shortsighted. The plant's TFP (which, remember, takes into account both labor and capital costs) improved very little.

This preoccupation with labor costs, particularly direct labor costs, is quite common—even though direct labor now accounts for less than 15% of total costs in most manufacturing companies. The managers we studied focused heavily on these costs; indeed, their systems for measuring direct labor were generally more detailed and extensive than those for measuring other inputs that were several times more costly. Using sophisticated bar-code scanners, Hi-Tech's managers tracked line operators by the minute but had difficulty identifying the number of manufacturing engineers in the same department. Yet these engineers accounted for 20% to 25% of total cost—compared with 5% for line operators.

Just as surprising, the companies we studied paid little attention to the effect of materials consumption or productivity. Early on, we asked managers at one of the Fab plants for data on materials consumed in production during each of a series of months. Using these data to estimate materials productivity gave us highly erratic values.

Investigation showed that this plant, like many others, kept careful records of materials purchased but not of the direct or indirect materials actually consumed in a month. (The latter, which includes things like paper forms, showed up only in a catchall manufacturing overhead account.) Further, most of the factories recorded materials transactions only in dollar, rather than in physical, terms and did not readily adjust their standard costs figures when inflation or substitution altered materials prices.

What managers at Fab plants called "materials consumed" was simply an estimate derived by multiplying a product's standard materials cost—which itself assumes a constant usage of materials—by its unit output and adding an adjustment based on the current variation from standard materials prices. Every year or half-year, managers would reconcile this estimated consumption with actual materials usage, based on a physical count. As a result, data on actual materials consumption in any one period were lost.

Finally, the TFP approach makes clear the difference between the data that managers see and what those data actually measure. In one plant, the controller argued that our numbers on engineering changes were way off base. "We don't have anything like this level of changes," he claimed. "My office signs off on all changes that go through this place, and I can tell you that the number you have here is wrong." After a brief silence, the engineering manager spoke up. He said that the controller reviewed only very large (in dollar terms) engineering changes and that

our data were quite accurate. He was right. The plant had been tracking all engineering changes, not just the major changes reported to the controller.

A Clear View

With the foglike distortions of poor measurement systems cleared away, we were able to identify the real levers for improving factory performance. Some, of course, were structural—that is, they involve things like plant location or plant size, which lie outside the control of a plant's managers. But a handful of managerial policies and practices consistently turned up as significant. Across industries, companies, and plants, they regularly exerted a powerful influence on productivity. In short, these are the managerial actions that make a difference.

Invest Capital

Our data show unequivocally that capital investment in new equipment is essential to sustaining growth in TFP over a long time (that is, a decade or more). But they also show that capital investment all too often reduces TFP for up to a year. Simply investing money in new technology or systems guarantees nothing. What matters is how their introduction is managed, as well as the extent to which they support and reinforce continual improvement throughout a factory. Managed right, new investment supports cumulative, long-term productivity improvement and process understanding—what we refer to as "learning."

The Process Company committed itself to providing new, internally designed equipment to meet the needs of a rapidly growing product. Over time, as the company's engineers and operating managers gained experience, they made many small changes in product design, machinery, and operating practices. These incremental adjustments added up to major growth in TFP.

Seeking new business, the Fab company redesigned an established product and purchased the equipment needed to make it. This new equipment was similar to the plant's existing machinery, but its introduction allowed for TFP-enhancing changes in work flows. Plant managers discovered how the new configuration could accommodate expanded production without a proportional increase in the work force. These benefits spilled over: even the older machinery was made to run more efficiently.

In both cases, the real boost in TFP came not just from the equipment itself but also from the opportunities it provided to search for and apply new knowledge to the overall production process. Again, managed right, investment unfreezes old assumptions, generates more efficient concepts and designs for a production system, and expands a factory's skills and capabilities.

Exhibit 1 shows the importance of such learning for long-term TFP growth at one of Fab's plants between 1973 and 1982. TFP rose by 96%. Part of this increase, of course, reflected changes in utilization rates and the introduction of new technology. Even so, roughly two-thirds (65%) of TFP growth was learning-based, and fully three-fourths of that learning effect (or 49% of TFP growth) was related to capital investment. Without capital investment, TFP would have increased, but at a much slower rate.

Such long-term benefits incur costs; in fact, the indirect costs associated with introducing new equipment can be staggering. In Fab's Plant 1, for example, a $1 million investment in new equipment imposed *$1.75 million* of additional costs on the plant during its first year of operation! Had the plant cut these indirect costs by half, TFP would have grown an additional 5% during that year.

Everyone knows that putting in new equipment usually causes problems. Everyone expects a temporary drop in efficiency as equipment is installed and workers learn to use it. But managers often underestimate the costly ripple effects of new equipment on inventory, quality, equipment utilization, reject rates, downtime, and material waste. Indeed, these indirect costs often exceed the direct cost of the new equipment and can persist for more than a year after the equipment is installed.

Here, then, is the paradox of capital investment. It is essential to long-term productivity growth, yet in the short run, if poorly managed, it can play havoc with TFP. It is risky indeed for a company to try to "invest its way" out of a productivity problem. Putting in new equipment is just as likely to create confusion and make things worse for a number of months. Unless the

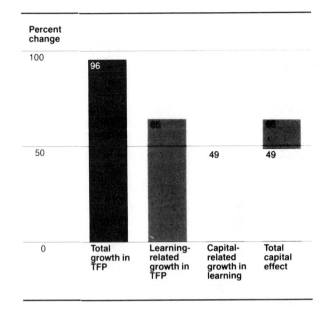

EXHIBIT 1 Capital Investment, Learning, and Productivity Growth in Fab Company's Plant 2
1973–1982

These estimates are based on a regression analysis of TFP growth. We estimated learning-related changes by using both a time trend and cumulative output. The capital-related learning effect represents the difference between the total learning effect and the effect that remained once capital was introduced into the regression. The total capital effect is composed of a learning component and a component reflecting technical advance.

investment is made with a commitment to continual learning—and unless performance measures are chosen carefully—the benefits that finally emerge will be small and slow in coming. Still, many companies today are trying to meet their competitive problems by throwing money at them—new equipment and new plants. Our findings suggest that there are other things they ought to do first, things that take less time to show results and are much less expensive.

Reduce Waste

We were not surprised to find a negative correlation between waste rates (or the percentage of rejects) and TFP, but we were amazed by its magnitude. In the Process plants, changes in the waste rate (measured by the ratio of waste material to total cost, expressed as a percentage) led to dramatic operating improvements. As *Exhibit 2* shows, reducing the percentage of waste in Plant 4's Department C by only one-tenth led to

EXHIBIT 2 Impact of Waste on TFP in Process Company Plants

Plant/department	Average waste rate	Effect on TFP of a 10% reduction in waste rate	Degree of uncertainty*
1-C	11.2%	+1.2%	.009
2-C	12.4	+1.8	.000
3-C	12.7	+2.0	.000
4-C	9.3	+3.1	.002
5-C	8.2	+0.8	.006

*The probability that waste rate reductions have a zero or negative impact on TFP.

EXHIBIT 3 Impact of Work-in-Process Reductions on TFP

Company	Plant/department	Effect on TFP of a 10% reduction in WIP	Degree of uncertainty*
Hi-Tech	1-A	+1.15%	.238
	1-B	+1.18	.306
	1-C	+3.73	.103
	1-D	+9.11	.003
Process	1-H	+1.63%	.001
	2-H	+4.01	.000
	3-H	+4.65	.000
	4-H	+3.52	.000
	5-H	+3.84	.000
Fab	1	+2.86%	.000
	2	+1.14	.000
	3	+3.59	.002

* The probability that work-in-process reductions have a zero or negative impact of TFP.

a 3% improvement in TFP, conservatively estimated.

The strength of this relationship is more surprising when we remember that a decision to boost the production throughput rate (which ought to raise TFP because of the large fixed components in labor and capital costs) also causes waste ratios to increase. In theory, therefore, TFP and waste percent should increase together. The fact that they do not indicates the truly powerful impact that waste reduction has on productivity.

Get WIP Out

The positive effect on TFP of cutting work-in-process (WIP) inventories for a given level of output was much greater than we could explain by reductions in working capital. *Exhibit 3* documents the relationship between WIP reductions and TFP in the three companies. Although there are important plant-to-plant variations, all reductions in WIP are associated with increases in TFP. In some plants, the effect is quite powerful; in Department D of Hi-Tech's Plant 1, reducing WIP by one-tenth produced a 9% rise in TFP.

These data support the growing body of empirical evidence about the benefits of reducing WIP. From studies of both Japanese and American companies, we know that cutting WIP leads to faster, more reliable delivery times, lowers reject rates (faster production cycle times reduce inventory obsolescence and make possible rapid feedback when a process starts to misfunction), and cuts overhead costs. We now know it also drives up TFP.

The trouble is, simply pulling work-in-process inventory out of a factory will not, by itself, lead to such improvements. More likely, it will lead to disaster. WIP is there for a reason, usually for many reasons; it is a symptom, not the disease itself. A long-term program for reducing WIP must attack the reasons for its being there in the first place: erratic process yields, unreliable equipment, long production changeover and set-up times, ever-changing production schedules, and suppliers who do not deliver on time. Without a cure for these deeper problems, a factory's cushion of WIP is often all that stands between it and chaos.

Reducing Confusion

Defective products, mismanaged equipment, and excess work-in-process inventory are not only problems in themselves. They are also sources of confusion. Many things that managers do can confuse or disrupt a factory's operation: erratically varying the rate of production, changing a production schedule at the last minute, overriding the schedule by expediting orders, changing the

18. Why Some Factories Are More Productive Than Others

crews (or the workers on a specific crew) assigned to a given machine, haphazardly adding new products, altering the specifications of an existing product through an engineering change order (ECO), or monkeying with the process itself by adding to or altering the equipment used.

Managers may be tempted to ask, "Doesn't what you call confusion—changing production schedules, expediting orders, shifting work crews, adding or overhauling equipment and changing product specifications—reflect what companies inevitably have to do to respond to changing customer demands and technological opportunities?"

Our answer to this question is an emphatic, No! Responding to new demands and new opportunities requires change, but it does not require the confusion it usually creates. Much of our evidence on confusion comes from factories that belong to the same company and face the same external pressures. Some plant managers are better than others at keeping these pressures at bay. The good ones limit the number of changes introduced at any one time and carefully handle their implementation. Less able managers always seem caught by surprise, operate haphazardly, and leapfrog from one crisis to the next. Much of the confusion in their plants is internally generated.

While confusion is not the same thing as complexity, complexity in a factory's operation usually produces confusion. In general, a factory's mission becomes more complex—and its focus looser—as it becomes larger, as it adds different technologies and products, and as the number and variety of production orders it must accommodate grow. Although the evidence suggests that complexity harms performance, each company's factories were too similar for us to analyze the effects of complexity on TFP. But we could see that what managers did to mitigate or fuel confusion within factories at a given level of complexity had a profound impact on TFP.

Of the sources of confusion we examined, none better illustrated this relationship with TFP than engineering change orders. ECOs require a change in the materials used to make a product, the manufacturing process employed, or the specifications of the product itself. We expected ECOs to lower productivity in the short run but lead to higher TFP over time.

Exhibit 4 , which presents data on ECO activity in three Fab plants, shows its effects to be sizable. In Plant 2, for example, increasing ECOs by just ten per month reduced TFP by almost 5%. Moreover, the debilitating effects of ECOs persisted for up to a year.

Our data suggest that the average level of ECOs implemented in a given month, as well as the variation in this level, is detrimental to TFP. Many companies would therefore be wise to reduce the number of ECOs to which their plants must respond. This notion suggests, in turn, that more pressure should be placed on engineering and marketing departments to focus attention on only the most important changes—as well as to design things right the first time.

Essential ECOs should be released in a controlled, steady fashion rather than in bunches. In the one plant that divided ECOs into categories reflecting their cost, low-cost ECOs were most harmful to TFP. More expensive ECOs actually had a positive effect. The reason: plant managers usually had warning of major changes and, recognizing that they were potentially disruptive, carefully prepared the ground by warning supervisors, training workers, and bringing in engineers. By contrast, minor ECOs were simply dumped on the factory out of the blue.

Value of Learning

If setting up adequate measures of performance is the first step toward getting full competitive leverage out of manufacturing, identifying factory-level goals like waste or WIP reduction is the second. But without making a commitment to ongoing learning, a factory will gain no more from these first two steps than a one-time boost

EXHIBIT 4 Impact of Engineering Change Orders on TFP in Three Fab Company Plants

Plant	Mean level of ECOs per month	Number of ECOs in lowest month	Number of ECOs in highest month	Effect on TFP of increasing number of ECOs from 5 to 15 per month
1	16.5	1	41	−2.8%
2	12.2	2	43	−4.6
3	7.0	1	19	−16.6

in performance. To sustain the leverage of plant-level operations, managers must pay close attention to—and actively plan for—learning.

We are convinced that a factory's learning rate—the rate at which its managers and operators learn to make it run better—is at least of equal importance as its current level of productivity. A factory whose TFP is lower than another's, but whose rate of learning is higher, will eventually surpass the leader. Confusion, as we have seen, is especially harmful to TFP. Thus the two essential tasks of factory management are to create clarity and order (that is, to prevent confusion) and to facilitate learning.

But doesn't learning always involve a good deal of experimentation and confusion? Isn't there an inherent conflict between creating clarity and order and facilitating learning? Not at all.

Confusion, like noise or static in an audio system, makes it hard to pick up the underlying message or figure out the source of the problem. It impedes learning, which requires controlled experimentation, good data, and careful analysis. It chews up time, resources, and energy in efforts to deal with issues whose solution adds little to a factory's performance. Worse, engineers, supervisors, operators, and managers easily become discouraged by the futility of piecemeal efforts. In such environments, TFP lags or falls.

Reducing confusion and enhancing learning do not conflict. They make for a powerful combination—and a powerful lever on competitiveness. A factory that manages change poorly, that does not have its processes under control, and that is distracted by the noise in its systems learns too slowly, if at all, or learns the wrong things.

In such a factory, new equipment will only create more confusion, not more productivity. Equally troubling, both managers and workers in such a factory will be slow to believe reports that a sister plant—or a competitor's plant—can do things better than they can. If the evidence is overwhelming, they will simply argue, "It can't work here. We're different." Indeed they are—and less productive too.

'Where the Money Is'

Many companies have tried to solve their data-processing problems by bringing in computers. They soon learned that computerizing a poorly organized and error-ridden information system simply creates more problems: garbage in, garbage out. That lesson, learned so long ago, has been largely forgotten by today's managers, who are trying to improve manufacturing performance by bringing in sophisticated new equipment without first reducing the complexity and confusion of their operations.

Spending big money on hardware fixes will not help if managers have not taken the time to simplify and clarify their factories' operations, eliminate sources of error and confusion, and boost the rate of learning. Of course, advanced technology is important, often essential. But there are many things that managers must do first to prepare their organizations for these new technologies.

When plant managers are stuck with poor measures of how they are doing and when a rigid, by-the-book emphasis on standards, budgets, and exception reports discourages the kind of experimentation that leads to learning, the real levers on factory performance remain hidden. No amount of capital investment can buy heightened competitiveness. There is no way around the importance of building clarity into the system, eliminating unnecessary disruptions and distractions, ensuring careful process control, and nurturing in-depth technical competence. The reason for understanding why some factories perform better than others is the same reason that Willie Sutton robbed banks: "That's where the money is."

APPENDIX   Research Methods

There are three basic approaches for identifying the effects of management actions and policies on factory-level productivity: first, a longitudinal analysis, which looks at a single factory over a long time; second, a cross-sectional analysis, which compares the performance (at the same time) of two or more factories that make similar products and have similar manufacturing processes; and third, a combined approach, which collects several years' worth of data for factories having a variety of structural characteristics and uses statis-

FIGURE
Productivity at Process Company Plants

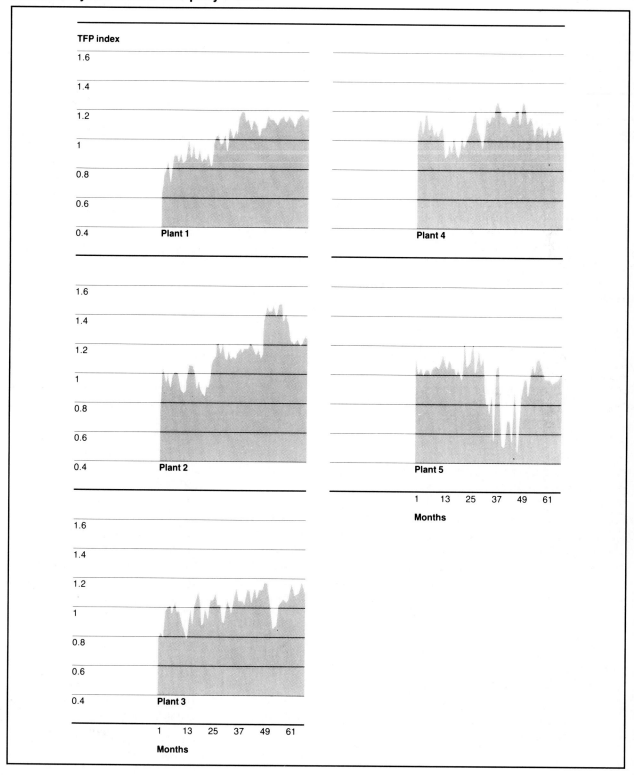

tical analysis to identify the effects of what managers do. We have used all three methods.

For each factory, we gathered data on a monthly basis for at least one-and-a-half years and usually for more than five. In several cases, we were able to track performance over a nine-year period; in more than half the cases, our data go back to the factory's start-up. To our knowledge, this is the first attempt to explore in such depth the sources of productivity growth at the factory level in the United States, and our data base is the most comprehensive yet compiled.

We developed our central performance measure, total factor productivity, by first calculating each factory's monthly partial factor productivities—that is, by dividing its output in turn by labor, materials, capital, and energy (for both outputs and inputs, we used 1982 dollars to eliminate the impact of inflation). To calculate a factory's total monthly output, we multiplied the quantity of each of the products it made in any month by that product's 1982 standard cost. To estimate labor input, we relied on total hours of work in each major employee classification (direct labor, indirect labor, and so forth); to estimate capital input, we used the book value of assets adjusted for inflation; and to estimate materials input, we deflated the dollar values of materials consumption by a materials price index based on 1982 dollars.

We then combined these partial measures into an index of overall total factor productivity (TFP). Because of the large fixed component in capital as well as labor cost, each factory's TFP is quite sensitive to changes in production volume and to the timing of major capital investments. To separate the movements in TFP linked to changes in production capacity from those linked to changes in operating efficiency, we included an estimate of capacity utilization in all regression analyses.

The *Figure* shows the quite different productivity experience at the Process Company's five plants. Hi-Tech's plants enjoyed rapid growth in output and productivity, but some of the Process and Fab plants had declining productivity and (in one case) declining output. All the Hi-Tech plants learned at a very high rate, although productivity growth in the early months was anything but fast or smooth, and some plants seemed to learn faster than others. Moderate growth and learning characterized the Fab Company's plants 2, 3, and 4; at Plant 1, however, volume declined, and TFP growth was flat or negative during much of the time we studied it.

This disparity in performance is not limited to comparisons across companies. Even within a company, productivity growth differed significantly across plants—even where each produced identical products and faced the same market and technological conditions. We cannot explain these differences by reference to technology, product variety, or market demands—they have to do with management.

Once we developed the data on TFP, we discussed each factory's results with its management. Some of the anomalies we found resulted from errors in the data provided us; others were caused by certain events (the advent of the deer-hunting season, for example, or a year-end peak in purchased materials). We made no attempt to relate monthly TFP figures to managerial variables until each factory's managers understood our method of calculating TFP and agreed that the patterns we found fairly represented their factory's behavior.

After developing credible TFP estimates, we had to identify and measure those managerial policies that might have an impact on TFP. The *Table* lists these policies and describes the measures we used to capture them.

TABLE Managerial Policies

Policy category	Indicators
Equipment	Average age of equipment
	Average maintenance expense as a percentage of equipment book value
Quality	Process waste; yield as a percentage of total input materials
	Intermediate and final reject rates
	Customer return rates
Inventory	Work-in-process as a percentage of total materials or production cost
Work force	Average age and education of workers
	Hours of overtime per week
	Absenteeism rate
	Hiring and layoff rates
	Average hours of training per employee
Policies affecting confusion	Fluctuations in production volume
	Number of product types produced
	Number of production orders scheduled
	Number of schedule changes as a percentage of number of production orders scheduled
	Number and type of engineering change orders
	Introduction of new processing equipment

Using multiple linear regression analysis, we first examined the effect of these policy variables on TFP in the same factory over time. Early findings, coupled with discussions with a number of managers, suggested that the simple ratios and averages we were using did not adequately capture the phenomena we were trying to understand. Actions like overhauling older equipment, training workers, and implementing an engineering change order are similar in nature to investments—that is, they will likely cause short-term inefficiencies. To test the long-term effects of such actions, we included lagged variables, which allowed us to estimate the effect on TFP of management actions taken in previous months.

Other management activities may have little effect on productivity unless they are held at a certain level for several months. Boosting the amount spent on maintaining equipment, for example, does not do much if sustained for only one month. In these cases, we looked at the relationship between TFP and a five-month moving average of relevant management variables. For still other activities—a profound change, say, in production rates—it matters greatly if the change is highly unusual or is part of a pattern of widely fluctuating rates. For each of these variables, we examined the relationship between TFP and the variable's average absolute deviation (using the five-month moving average as the estimated mean value for the variable).

A last, brief note about the importance of combining statistical analysis with ongoing field research. We found immense value in discussing our findings with the managers involved. We expected, for example, that equipment maintenance and workforce training would share a positive relationship to productivity growth. Our plant data, however, revealed a consistently negative relationship: high expenditures on maintenance and training, even in lagged forms, generally were associated with *low* TFP. When we talked about this with plant managers in all three companies, we discovered that they used maintenance and training as *corrective* measures. That is, they boosted maintenance in response to equipment problems; when the problems were solved, they reduced it. By themselves, the data would not allow us to separate corrective from preventive maintenance, or even from the costs of modifying or rebuilding equipment.

19. North American Rockwell Draper Division

In October 1971, the Draper Division of North American Rockwell (NR) was cited for emitting from its North Foundry gaseous and particle pollutants in quantities exceeding permissible levels under Massachusetts law. Draper responded by promising to eliminate the pollution at its source within two years and to report on its specific plans for action by May 15, 1972. The sources of the pollution were the cupolas used for melting iron in one of its three foundries.

Mr. Robert Mace, President of the Draper Division since January 1970, was being forced to deal with the North Foundry pollution problem at a time when the sales of Draper looms were at their lowest level in many years (3308 looms in fiscal '71 vs. 18,500 in 1965). Sales of repair parts represented about two-thirds of dollar volume in 1971. In pursuing a course of action on the pollution problem, he was concerned with the possibility of improving the overall foundry operations of the Division as well as eliminating the pollution problem. Between October and the following April the problem was discussed, alternatives studied, and their implications considered with a view toward reaching a final decision by May 15.

The Company

The Draper Corporation was founded in 1816 in Hopedale, Massachusetts, as a manufacturer of loom parts. Over the years the company had become one of the world's largest producers of looms for the weaving of textiles. In 1966 Draper was acquired by the Rockwell Standard Corporation which merged shortly thereafter with North American Aviation to become North American

This case was prepared by C. Wickham Skinner.

Rockwell Corporation. The Draper Division along with the Knitting Machinery Division and two smaller divisions made up the Textile Machinery Division, which in turn was included in the Industrial Products Group of the parent company.

Because Draper's sales had traditionally been largely confined to the United States, erosion of the American textile industry by increased competition from foreign imports was having a serious impact on Draper's performance. Competition was particularly acute in Draper's market segment—single-color cloth. In addition, one foreign manufacturer of textile equipment had made substantial inroads into the U.S. market by competing on the basis of product innovation. This company had introduced new looms which offered U.S. textile manufacturers substantially different features from those offered by Draper, namely, more flexible looms and multi-color weaving capability.

Draper's manufacturing operation involved the casting and machining of metal parts, machining of wood parts, and the assembly of these parts into looms and spare parts. Draper operated several plants in the fall of 1971, as shown in *Exhibit 1*. An organization chart of the manufacturing operation is shown in *Exhibit 2*.

The Hopedale plant was the oldest and by far the largest of Draper's seven manufacturing facilities. The plant floor-space of this facility was allocated as follows:

North Foundry	430,000 sq. ft
West Foundry	70,000
Machine Shop	500,000
Assembly	180,000
Storage	320,000
Offices	200,000
Other	130,000

EXHIBIT 1 Plants in Operation, Fall 1971

Location	Principal Products and Operations	Number of Employees	Size in Square Feet
Hopedale	Looms, spare parts, accessories, subcontracting, foundries, machine shop and assembly, warehouse, wood parts	1,693	1,826,000
East Spartanburg, South Carolina	Foundry, gray iron machining, spare parts, warehouse	612	320,000
Marion, South Carolina	Steel machining, wood parts, shuttles, picker sticks	256	119,000
Beebe River, N.H.	Bobbins	209	222,000
Tupper Lake, N.Y.	Wood loom parts, bobbin blanks	62	47,000
Limerick, Ireland	Small loom accessories	50	15,000
Mexico City, Mexico	Shuttles, bobbins, picker sticks, warehouse	80	35,000

EXHIBIT 2 Manufacturing Organization

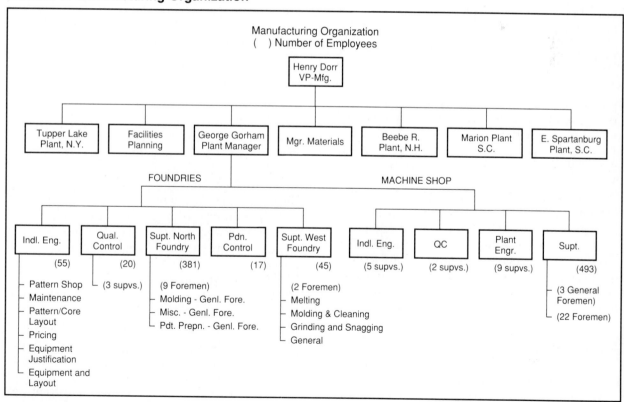

In 1971 total division sales were over $50 million. Most of this volume involved products which used castings. The net book value of Draper's Hopedale buildings and equipment was approximately $20 million of which $2.0 million represented foundry equipment. The plant was operating at a level estimated to be approximately 30% of full three-shift capacity in the fall of 1971. Both the melting and molding operations of Hopedale could meet the required production output by using only one shift. Layoffs had been made reluctantly, considering the age and seniority of many employees and the economic dependence of the area on Draper. Termination benefits were considered liberal, costing Draper about $1000 per employee.

Foundry Operations

Draper operated the largest foundry in New England at its facilities in Hopedale, Massachusetts. Foundry operations at Hopedale were located in two areas, the North Foundry and the West Foundry, which were approximately one-quarter of a mile apart. The two foundries differed greatly in appearance, operations, capacities, working conditions, and technologies, with the West Foundry being the newer, cleaner, and more modern of the two. The Hopedale facility and a view of the West Foundry are pictured in *Exhibit 3. Exhibit 4* shows the floor plans of the foundries, and *Exhibit 5* contains sales, cost, capacity, output and employment data. *Exhibit 6* shows employment by departments and *Exhibit 7* the 1972 cost plan based on the present operating pattern.

Foundry operations at Draper comprised the following steps: melting a mix of pig iron and scrap metal, pouring the molten iron into sand molds, allowing the iron to cool and solidify, breaking the mold, cleaning the castings by sand blasting, removing the burrs and excess metal (caused by the pour hole and mold crease) by grinding operations, and painting the castings. The manner in which these operations were performed differed radically between the North and West Foundries.

Melting Operations

The North Foundry melting operation involved the use of a cupola, a heavily constructed vertical cylinder into which a charge of coke and iron was placed to produce molten iron. The foundry contained two large cupolas with a capacity of 22 tons per hour each, and a small cupola with a capacity of 12 tons per hour. The melt process, based upon a technology which was hundreds of years old, involved the burning of coke in a stream of forced air (much like the hearth and bellows of a nineteenth century blacksmith), and allowing the iron in the charge to melt and trickle downward through the coke. The molten iron collected at the bottom of the cupola and drained off into a collecting tank. The molten iron was poured from the collecting tank into ladles (which could hold about 200 lbs. of iron). These ladles, traveling on overhead rails, were pushed to the molding areas where the iron was poured off into sand molds.

The production of the molten iron in the cupola was a continuous eight-hour process. Throughout the cycle, carefully measured charges of coke and metallics were loaded into the cupola at regulated intervals. After eight hours of operation, it was necessary to clean out and reline the cupola with a cement-like refractory material. The relining process involved a three-man crew working a total of 21-man hours. Normally one cupola was in use while the second large cupola was being relined. In this way, the effective capacity of the melting operation could be adjusted to a one-, two-, or three-shift basis by varying the size of the workforce.

The melt process could be speeded up or slowed down by regulating the rate of air flow and the quantities of coke and metallics added; however, there was a minimum and maximum operating rate. The maximum rate was determined by the temperature decline of the charge which resulted if metallics were added too rapidly. The minimum rate resulted from the deterioration of the metallurgical properties which occurred if the metallics were added too slowly. The minimum output of each cupola was about 60% of its capacity.

Because the operation of the cupolas was, in effect, a carbon-burning process, the process produced an undesirable amount of smoke in the form of noxious carbon oxides, ash particles and iron oxides. In contrast, melting with an arc furnace, as was done in the West Foundry, was virtually a pollution-free process.

The West Foundry melting operation involved the use of an arc furnace in which heat was supplied to a charge of pig iron and scrap iron by an arc between two electrodes. Although the West Foundry contained only one arc furnace, it had been sized to accommodate two. The cycle time to produce a 15-ton batch of molten iron (the capacity of the arc furnace) was two hours. Once melted, the molten iron was poured into a ladle with a capacity of 20 tons. This ladle was carried by overhead crane and poured into one of three, 20 ton insulated, induction heated "holding furnaces," which could hold the iron indefinitely until molds were ready to receive the melt. When ready the molds were filled by the use of buckets (which had a capacity of 1000 lbs.). The buckets were transported from the holding furnace by a fork lift truck which set them into the pouring equipment, one on each side of the track conveying molds.

Molding Operations

Similarly there was a wide difference in the process technologies used in sand casting at the North and West foundries. To produce a mold for sand casting, sand is packed around a pattern. The pattern is a duplicate of the part to be cast. It is slightly oversized to allow for shrinkage when the molten iron cools and solidifies. The container which holds the sand and pattern is called a flask. The flask is usually divided into two equal halves, the upper half called the cope and the lower half called the drag. After the sand is firmly packed, the pattern is removed leaving a cavity of the desired shape. A new mold has to be prepared for each part produced (see *Exhibit 8*).

Draper made use of both split pattern and matchplate molding techniques in its foundry operations. In split pattern molding the pattern is divided into two halves. Molds of the upper and lower halves of the part are prepared separately and then joined to form the desired mold cavity. Split pattern molding was primarily used by Draper to produce larger-sized castings.

In matchplate molding the upper and lower halves of the pattern are attached to a metal plate called the matchplate. After the sand is packed firmly around the entire matchplate pattern, the mold is broken exactly in half and the matchplate pattern removed. In closing the mold, both halves will always be in proper alignment. Matchplate molding is a more flexible process and was primarily used by Draper to make smaller castings.

Molding in the North Foundry consisted of both matchplate and split pattern work. Approximately 70% of the tonnage and 95% of the annual molds were produced using matchplate techniques. The molds were prepared manually by the molders who worked at individual work stations and were compensated by a piecework incentive system. A train conveyor material handling system was used to assist the movement of the finished molds to the pouring area. A conveyorized line process consisting of similar equipment was also used in the pour area. The equipment for these processes was 20 to 25 years old with the last major mechanization having taken place in 1945.

The West Foundry had been completed in 1966 around a highly mechanized molding system—the Taccone process. The Taccone unit had been purchased at a cost of $3 million. During that period, Draper was producing 15,000 to 18,000 looms per year and wished to set up a mechanized foundry to more economically produce the large, heavy parts in their looms. Presently, the Taccone process was used exclusively for split pattern molding. The integrated system automatically prepared the molds, removed the completed castings, prepared the sand and flask for reuse and cleaned the completed parts by sand blasting. The only operations which required any labor input were the removal of the pattern and the pouring of the molten iron. A standard crew of 24 was required regardless of the operating volume.

In order to achieve the high degree of mechanization, it was necessary that the Taccone process be restricted to the use of one standard-size flask. This imposed a limit on the depth of a casting to 8 inches. The process also required the use of relatively expensive special patterns to withstand the 1500 pound sand packing pressures (manual molding pressures were about 80 pounds). Taccone patterns cost $2000-$4000 while normal matchplate patterns cost only $300. It was considered uneconomic to use the machine for parts which weighed less than 5 to 10 pounds and which had an annual volume of 4000 pieces or less. Based on reworking only those patterns which met the size limitations of the process, it was estimated that it would cost $1,300,000 to convert the North Foundry matchplates so they would be

EXHIBIT 3a Hopedale Facilities—West Foundry in Foreground

EXHIBIT 3b West Foundry

19. North American Rockwell Draper Division

EXHIBIT 4 Layout of Foundries

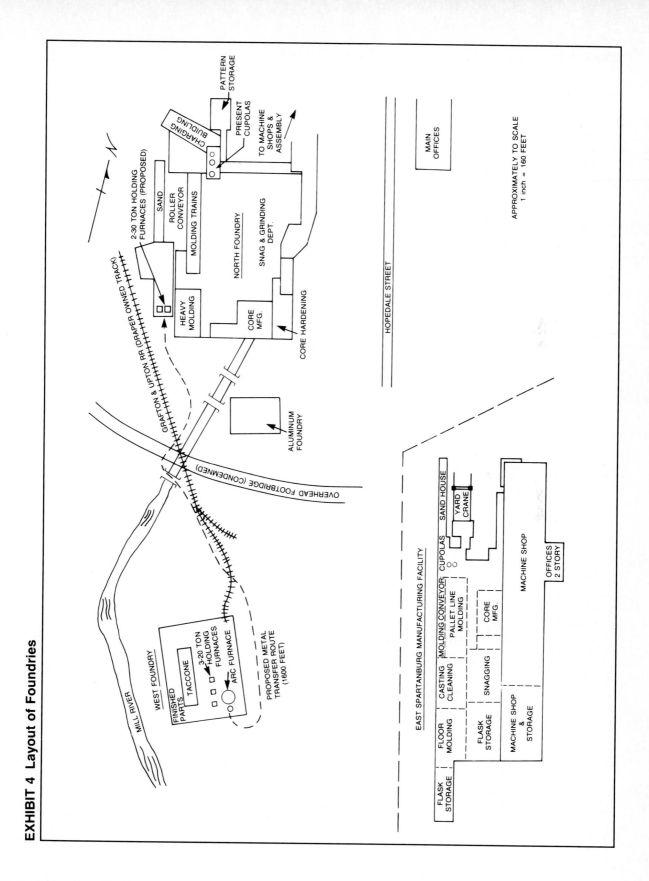

EXHIBIT 5 Sales, Cost, Capacity, Output, and Employment Data

	North	West	East Spartanburg
1972 Sales Forecast[1]	$5,890,000	$2,177,000	$5,144,000
Price Per Ton[2]	$490	$420	$373
Ratio Draper Work/Outside Work	55/45	62/38	75/25
Variable Cost as a % of Sales			
Direct Labor[3]	13%	8%	12%
Material[3]	13%	11%	13%
Overhead[3]	38%	21%	21%
Fixed Costs	$344,000	$766,000	$1,175,000
Melt Capacity	150 tons/shift	60 tons/shift	80 tons/shift
Present Melt Rate	100 tons/day	45 tons/day	120 tons/day
Molding Capacity[4]	6,670 molds/shift	800 molds/shift	6,000 molds/shift
Present Molding Rate	7,000 molds/day	550 molds/day	15,000 molds/day
Yield lbs shipped/lbs melted	48%	46%	46%
Book Value-buildings & equipment	$673,000	$2,423,000	$761,000
patterns & tools	$605,000	$203,000	$186,000
Number of Employees		[See Exhibit 6]	336
Molding Furnaces for hot metal	None	3-20 ton	N/A

Source: Cost estimated by casewriter. Other data from company sources.

[1] Transfer pricing: Foundry work was priced at 1.15 times full standard cost for both Draper and outside jobs.

[2] Based on 250 days/year

[3] In addition to these costs, there were $2,267,000 in joint costs for the Hopedale Foundry (see Exhibit 7 for details).

[4] A West Foundry mold is equivalent to about four North Foundry molds. The pouring of a West Foundry mold produced on the average four parts.

EXHIBIT 6 Employment by Department

	Number of Employees October 1971		
Department	North Foundry	West Foundry	Services[1]
Melt Shop	16	5	
Floor Molding	25		
Conveyor Molding	124	24	
Cleaning	15		
Snag and Grind[2]	73	13	
Paint	5		
Aluminum Foundry	10		
Slinger Molding	23		
Flask Storage	8		
General		3	42
Pattern Shop			33
Quality Control			20
Core Room			35
Production Control			17
Maintenance			17
Industrial Engineering			5
Shipping			5
Totals	299	45	174

[1] Employees listed under "Services" served both foundries. Organizationally, the structure under which they reported is shown in Exhibit 2.

[2] Snagging involved removing gates and risers and other excess metal. Grinding involved removing the parting line, i.e., a slight ridge caused by the junction of the two mold halves.

19. North American Rockwell Draper Division

EXHIBIT 7 1972 Cost Plan

(Assumes No Change in Operations)
$000

North Foundry	Direct Labor	Variable Overhead	Fixed Overhead	Total
Melt Shop	0	392	142	534
Floor Molding	120	239	21	380
Conveyor Molding	263	723	34	1,020
Cleaning	0	164	4	168
Snag and Grind	242	477	37	756
Paint	16	53	0	69
Aluminum Foundry	31	52	34	117
Slinger Molding	119	153	5	277
Flask Storage	0	0	68	68
Total	791	2,253	345	3,389

West Foundry				
Melt	0	176	271	447
Mold	138	181	210	529
General	0	12	286	298
Snagging	42	100	2	144
Total	180	469	769	1,418

Services				
General	0 ⎫	432 ⎫	730 ⎫	1,162 ⎫
Pattern Shop	0	383	27	410
Core Room	126 ⎬ 126	262 ⎬ 1163	19 ⎬ 978	407 ⎬ 2267
Maintenance	0	3	202	205
Shipping	0 ⎭	83 ⎭	0 ⎭	83 ⎭
Total of all three	$1,090	$3,887	$2,091	$7,074

Source: Company data.

19. North American Rockwell Draper Division

EXHIBIT 8 Illustration of Pattern and Matchplate Mold Making

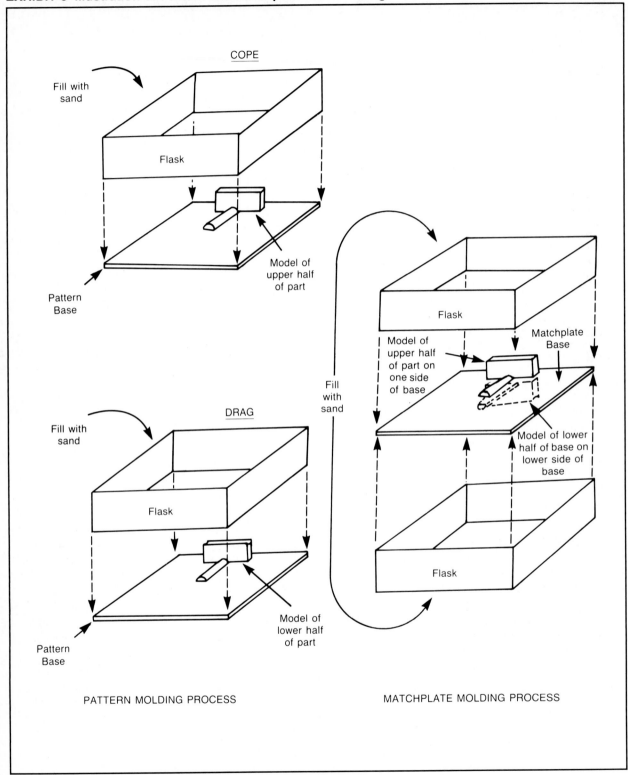

PATTERN MOLDING PROCESS

MATCHPLATE MOLDING PROCESS

usable in the West Foundry. These patterns represented about 36 tons per day of finished parts at current production volumes.

The Taccone process was criticized by Mr. George Gorham, Plant Manager, on several counts:

> First, there are a number of shortcomings to the Taccone system. The process was a good choice when they bought it but when the bottom dropped out of the market, it proved to be costly at low production volumes.
>
> Second, it is inflexible in terms of the standard size flask, the limited casting depth combined with minimum weight castings, and the special patterns required.
>
> Third, the pouring system is a problem. The two operators (one on each side of the stool) cannot get a smooth enough, accurate enough, or fast enough action due to its inherent mechanical, electrical and hydraulic design.[1] We feel a better pour-off system—which would cost about $68,000— would cut our scrap from 18% now to 13% and save 40 minutes delay each day. We're now pouring 110 flasks per hour and with a better pour system that could be raised to 120.
>
> Finally, it takes as much manpower to handle 100 tons per day as 200.

The equipment and process technology of the East Spartanburg foundry, built in 1955, was generally similar to that of the North Foundry. Cupolas were used for melting and the bulk of the molding was performed as described for the North Foundry, using mostly matchplates and a conveyorized mold moving setup. A company spokesman described the foundry as follows: "Its strengths are in flexible molding processes, proximity to a good outside market, and high margin outside jobs. Its weaknesses are in marginal working conditions, no pattern making, a tight labor market, limited space for expansion, and pollution complaints are a future threat. It costs about $250 to hire and train a man, but four out of five recently hired quit after a short time." Presently the foundry was operating both the melting and molding operations on a three-shift basis.

Work Force Management

The Hopedale plant was located in a town of 4,000 population about 45 miles southwest of Boston. The town impressed the case writer as unusually

[1]The conveyor moved intermittently, moving the molds forward to a different station every 33 seconds.

attractive. It was neat, laid out with considerable open space, green grass, old trees, and town parks, beautifully wooded, and through it passed a modest stream which had been dammed in the 1800's to form a scenic lake just above the plant site where many in the town swam in the summer and skated in the winter.

Hopedale had been for years a "company town" in the traditional sense. The company had owned a number of houses, a company store, and put in the town sewer system in the early 1900's at its own expense. The Draper family had donated the land and built the clubhouse for a nine-hole golf course, with membership open only to company employees and town residents. Mr. George Draper had built a library and a gymnasium and he and others in his family had, over the years, made dozens of improvements and additions to the town and its facilities. The town had in fact been established in the early 1800's as a Utopian religious community and the several Draper brothers had started the company as one means of providing a living for the members of the religious sect. Thus the relationships between company owners and employees and town residents had, therefore, from the beginning been a most unusual one, largely paternal and certainly highly humane according to the tenets and values of those times.

In the early 1960's after the Draper Corporation "went public," all of the company–owned houses were sold, the company store closed down, and operations of the country club and other Draper dominated external facilities were turned over to townspeople. In 1971, of the 1,700 employees, about 400 lived in the town of Hopedale itself. Many more lived in Milford, about two miles from the plant beyond Hopedale.

Foundry employees had been unionized under the AFL (International Molders and Allied Workers) since the 1940's but shop employees had not been unionized until 1965, by an AFL-CIO Union. Many NLRB elections had been held in the shop. Until 1965, the Union had always been defeated. In 1965, placing a major emphasis on improving worker productivity, the company brought in a large industrial engineering firm to expand its use of standards to include most of its direct labor work including set-up and machine changeovers. In 1971, the plant manager, George Gorham, felt that this program had been effective in reducing costs but that it was largely responsible for the vote to authorize collective bargaining through the Union. Union-management relations were entirely cordial and the company had never had a strike. Mr. Gorham, who had been with Draper since 1945 when he started in as a pattern maker, stated that "our people here average about 54 years old. They work. They like to work and they work happily. Morale only goes down when the work load goes down."

An incentive wage plan was used in most production operations throughout the plant. In the foundry, for example, about 140 employees were paid on incentives. There were approximately 65 job classifications in the foundry and some jobs were divided into as many as 6 grades with grading based on seniority. No limits were set on piece rate earnings, and employees were able to produce at up to 150% of standard. A sample of average wages is shown below; wages at East Spartanburg were approximately 85% of those at Hopedale.

Hopedale Plant Average Hourly Rate Earned	
Molder	$4.50
Molding line laborer	3.17
Grinding and snagging machinist	4.45
Grinding and snagging laborer	2.98
Patternmaker	4.30

Foundry workers were difficult to obtain and laborers in the melt and molding operations were hired at the maximum ($3.17) of the job classification in order to attract them. Turnover of these lower grade jobs was high and recruiting difficult in spite of the high unemployment levels (7%-8%) in Massachusetts in 1971. The apparent causes of this problem are described in an interoffice memo *(Exhibit 9)*.

Future Demand for Castings

In October 1971, loom demand was expected to move back up in the years ahead and Draper sales were forecast to grow at a rate of 6% per year over the next five years. The outside market for castings was a mixed picture. Foundry production in New England had been dropping at 6% per year from 1966 to 1969, and 15% in 1970. Since 1968, 21 foundries out of about 100 had closed. Substantial excess foundry capacity was in existence in the New England area. Some work was being obtained in New York and New Jersey, and some work was being done for other NR divisions and, in particular, for the knitting division where billings for castings were running at about $100,000 per month.

The forecast for future foundry work at Hopedale in 1975 is shown in *Exhibit 10*.

Alternatives Being Considered

Six alternatives had been proposed and were being considered in April, 1972 to alleviate the pollution problem and improve operating costs. Excerpts from a company report concerning these alternatives are as follows:

A. *Install scrubbers on cupolas*

A wet scrubber is a mechanical device which cleans exhaust gases by forcing them to impinge on and/or pass through water on their way from a cupola to the atmosphere. Scrubbers require high horsepower blowers, create noise (sometimes at nuisance levels), have inherent maintenance problems, and yield a wet sludge which cannot be discharged into normal sewage channels.

Scrubbers for the North Foundry cupolas have been studied in considerable depth by the Foundry Industrial Engineering Department. They report the following cost/benefit picture based on installing one scrubber, sufficient to allow a maximum melt capacity of 220 tons per day.

One-Time Costs:

New equipment cost	$215,000
Installation and building changes	322,000
New Capital Investment	$537,000

Start-up Costs:

North Foundry production would be interrupted for at least 3 months.

Continuing Effects:

Annual scrubber operating cost	$85,000
Annual depreciation added	36,000
Annual profit impact	$(121,000)

B. *Close the North Foundry and Transfer Work*

The concept is to utilize more fully our existing melt and molding capacity at East Spartanburg and in the West Foundry, allowing us to close down all melting and molding in the North Foundry. In operational terms, this alternative implies:

(a) Moving all North Foundry matchpiece molding jobs to East Spartanburg; 33,000 patterns would be transferred at a freight

EXHIBIT 9 **Interoffice Memo**

INTERNAL LETTER

Date: January 14, 1972   No.:

TO: Mr. James A. Harvey   FROM: Mr. Anthony E. Fasano
Address: Main Office   Address: Personnel

                                    Phone:

Subject: Foundry Personnel

For some time we have been aware of the difficulty in securing foundry help.
Athough we have been successful in meeting our personnel needs we are now experiencing problems that seriously affect the efficiency of the foundry operations.

Not too many years ago the popular flask sizes were 10'' x 15'', 12'' x 15'', 10'' x
17'', etc. These were of moderate weight and people could work comfortably without
excessive strain. Molding was the best paying and the prestige job in the foundry.
There was a waiting list of people who had requested such work. To supplement our
loom work we turned to outside casting work. In order to become competitive, we
were compelled to increase the size of our molds. Weight became an issue and the
Union attempted to restrict the size of the flask that a man was required to handle.
They were partially successful and the Company established certain limits. However,
the so-called ''one man jobs'' were heavier than previously and men were not so anxious to become molders. The waiting list for molding gradually began to diminish. At
present we have no one seeking these positions. Molders are attempting to transfer to
other jobs and are willing to accept less wages.

Foundry supervision has been aware of this problem and has expressed great concern. Our younger employees are not interested and are unwilling to train. Our present group is getting older and productivity will undoubtedly suffer. We are experiencing an above normal number of back strains and in many instances must provide
adjusted work for these men. This, of course, affects our production schedules and
our direct labor dollars. Workmen's Compensation costs are also increasing. Though
an employee may return from sick leave, in the case of a back condition, we are faced
with the prospect of a recurrence of the injury.

We have been able to hire foundry laborers in sufficient numbers to meet our present
level of business. If we cannot induce men to become molders, hiring people would be
of no avail. I would seriously question our ability to increase our production if future
business levels dictated such an increase.

Many foundries have been forced to suspend operations because of their inability to
overcome these very problems. We must look to new and improved methods of making castings or be confronted with a similar decision.

Anthony E. Fasano
Personnel Manager

AEF/dj

EXHIBIT 10 Forecasts for 1975

	Outside	Outside	Draper	Total Tons
		Tons and Thousands of Dollars		
		(Outside)	(Draper)	(Total Tons)
North Foundry				
Matchplates	$2,182	5,400 tons	4,900 tons	10,300
Floor and rollover	766	2,000	1,900	3,900
Total	$2,948	7,400	6,800	14,200
West Foundry	1,235	3,500	4,000	7,500
Total Hopedale	$4,183	10,900 tons	10,800 tons	21,700

Maximum capacity based on present yields 36,000 tons North - 2 shift
21,000 tons West - 3 shift

Note: Tonnage data represents weight of finished parts

	Outside	Draper	Total	Capacity
		Thousands of Molds		
North				
Matchplates	970	964	1,934	4,560
Floor and rollover	45	51	96	240
Total	1,015	1,015	2,030	4,800
West	87	138	225	576

Source: Company data.

cost of $6,000. Dispose of North Foundry equipment (Net book value $66,000).

(b) Moving rollover and floor molding to the West Foundry. Cost estimated at $41,000.

(c) Shipping castings from East Spartanburg to Hopedale for machining. Transportation costs estimated at $80,000 per year.

(d) Constructing some new areas in the building at East Spartanburg. Cost estimated at $89,000.

C. *Close the North Foundry and Buy Castings Outside*

The best information available to date, based on quotations received from outside foundries and from other NR sources, is that Draper work bought outside would cost 1.5 times the present (full absorption) North Foundry Cost.

D. *Transfer Molten Iron from West Foundry*

By transferring molten metal between foundries, we can maintain our foundry capability in both locations.

Dubbed the "Thermos Bottle Approach," this alternative has been studied and found to have cost advantages. The arc furnace melts more economically than do the cupolas, because it eliminates the need for coke and pig iron and substitutes electricity and scrap metal. A $65,000 per year saving is available in the difference between coke costs and electric melt energy and supply costs. Adding some new operating costs, net savings are expected to be between $20,000 and $30,000 per year. The investment required would be $560,000 for purchase and installation of truck mounted vessels and handling equipment for transferring molten metal. This would include $400,000 for two 30–ton induction holding furnaces.

E. *Install Electric Melt in the North Foundry*

Arc melting and induction melting were considered. Of the two, arc melting is the more efficient at North Foundry volumes.

(a) One-time costs:

New Equipment Costs, including installation:

Arc furnace similar to present West Foundry furnace	460,000
3 induction holding furnaces	600,000

19. North American Rockwell Draper Division

(1) 30T bridge crane	73,000
Building changes	270,000
Move ductile iron operation	40,000
Electric substation	50,000
New Capital Investment	$1,493,000

(b) Continuing Effects:

Annual labor savings	$ 100,000
Annual material savings—pig iron & coke	530,000
Arc power and electrodes	(280,000)
Electric power for receivers	(177,000)
Relining and ladle maintenance	(48,000)
Straight line depreciation	(100,000)
ANNUAL PROFIT IMPACT	+$ 25,000

F. *Expand and Improve West Foundry Molding Capacity to do all Hopedale Foundry Work*

The West Foundry Expansion was studied in detail in July of 1971. To make the Taccone Machine versatile enough to be reasonably marketable would require a $1 million investment in pouroff, bottom boards, and molding line modifications. To carry out the full expansion program, including the Taccone modifications, would require a total investment of $11.7 million.[1] This proposal would allow complete razing of the present North Foundry building, and would allow a 16% reduction in labor costs, or $700,000 per year at present volume.

In April 1972, Mr. Mace faced the necessity of responding to the state government by May 15 with a statement of the company's plans for meeting air pollution regulations. He reviewed these six alternatives and compared their implications to Draper's future operations. In making his final decision he was aware that these six alternatives had been selected from a wider variety of possibilities. He realized that he need not necessarily limit his selection to one of these six but should attempt to develop a plan which would make the best sense for the future of the Division.

[1] In addition to the $1 million investment this alternative would require major modifications of the Taccone machinery and molds to allow it to produce the entire line, two additional furnaces and major building expansions to accommodate core, finishing, and rollover operations.

EXHIBIT 11 Pictorial Supplement

1. *General view of Taccone process, West Foundry*

2. *Patterns for Taccone process*

3. *Patterns about to enter molding cycle*

4. *Pouring molds in the Taccone process*

5. *Shakeout station in Taccone process*

6. *Cleaned castings are off-loaded from conveyor at this end of machine.*

7. Cope flask with matchplate in place. North Foundry.

8. Drag flask and mold with matchplate removed.

9. Cope flask and mold being placed over drag flask and mold. Note cores (light pieces) in mold.

10. Completed molds after flasks have been removed, but before pouring.

19. North American Rockwell Draper Division

11. *Molten iron being received from cupola. North Foundry.*

12. *Pouring ladle being refilled at cupola. North Foundry.*

13 & 14. *Pouring molds on train conveyor. North Foundry.*

19. North American Rockwell Draper Division

15. *Shaking out casting from mold after cooling.*

16. *Completed casting.*

17. *Grinding casting.*

18. *"Snagging" (removing burrs) on large casting.*

19. North American Rockwell Draper Division

20. Allegheny Ludlum Steel Corporation

Richard (Dick) P. Simmons, CEO of Allegheny Ludlum Steel Corporation, summarized his business philosophy:

> Running a business is like life: it's a series of screw-ups. If you can identify them, prioritize them, and attack them quickly, you can then go on and be creative and innovative. That way, you are not devoting a massive portion of the company's efforts to just fixing things—generally, long after they should have been fixed.

Between 1980 and 1984, despite a prolonged recession, heavy increases in imports, and a very strong dollar, Allegheny averaged an annual return on investment of over 15%, making it the most consistently profitable domestic competitor in the specialty steel industry.

Even though Allegheny's stainless business had grown 4-5% annually while many competitors went bankrupt or ran large losses, it was rapidly losing share in its other business, silicon steel. Silicon imports had risen 400% during 1984; today they accounted for 30% of the market. Because silicon steels were less protected by tariffs and quotas than other steel products, foreign producers were expected to shift further attention to this area. Now, in June 1985, Allegheny had to make a choice. It could milk silicon as a cash cow, meet the Japanese threat head-on, or get out of the silicon business altogether. The context was dynamic: Allegheny might or might not achieve the needed breakthrough in its own silicon research; Armco, its major domestic competitor in silicon,

This case was prepared by Artemis March under the direction of David A. Garvin.

Copyright © 1985 by the President and Fellows of Harvard College. Harvard Business School case 686-087.

was in serious financial trouble; and import quotas were under discussion. At the same time, Allegheny needed more stainless steel capacity. It soon had to choose between expanding its facilities or making a major acquisition. The first option would require converting some silicon capacity to stainless. Simmons recognized that the timing of the decision was as critical as the decision itself:

> What we're trying to do is keep our options open as long as possible. So you start with Simmons's management rule number one: don't make a decision before you have to make it, but then don't make it after you should have made it. There is an appropriate time at which a strategic decision has to be made, and that's what people like me get paid to do.

The Steel Industry

In the 1980s domestic producers of carbon steel, which accounted for 98% of U.S. steel tonnage and 90% of sales dollars, were besieged by imports and fighting for survival. Specialty steel producers were not in such dire straits, although they too were being hurt by imports. Specialty steels included stainless, grain-oriented silicon, and tool steels, as well as special alloys used in high technology applications. Stainless steels, which accounted for 90% of the specialty market (exclusive of silicon), were growing at 4% per year. Total domestic production of stainless steel was around 1.2 million tons, and the average selling price per ton was approximately $2,500, compared with $350-400 for carbon steel. High-end silicon steels, which were used in electrical applications where minimizing energy loss was essential, competed in a market that had shrunk 40%—to 260,000 tons—in the last 10 years.

The Company

Background

In 1980 Dick Simmons and George Tippins, a Pittsburgh industrialist, headed a group of 17 managers that bought Allegheny Ludlum from Allegheny International for $195 million plus the assumption of $28 million in debt. Tippins, who bought 80% of the stock, became chairman, while Simmons remained as president and became CEO. In the spring of 1985, Robert (Bob) Bozzone, then executive vice president and chief operating officer, became president. (See *Exhibit 1*.)

EXHIBIT 1 Organization Chart

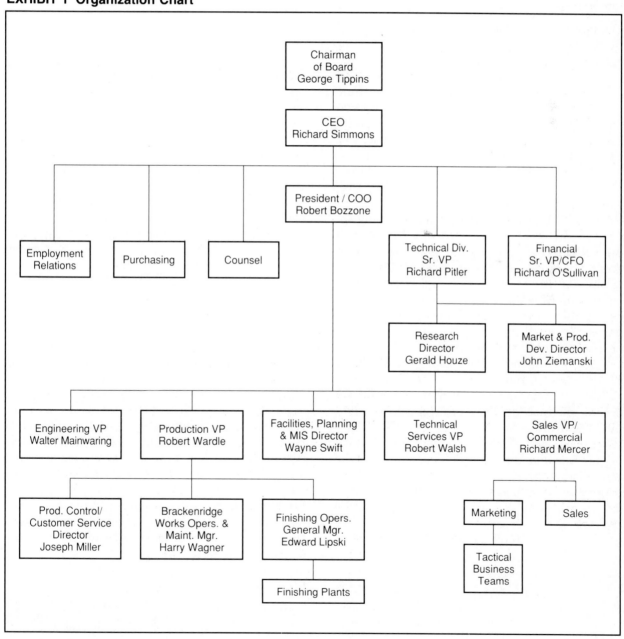

Allegheny was the largest specialty steel producer in the country. Two-thirds of its 1984 sales of $764 million came from stainless and other high-tech alloys, the rest from silicon. All of its products were flat-rolled into coils. It considered two-thirds of its stainless tonnage to be commodity products: steels produced in standard grades, widths, and thicknesses, sold primarily on price to multiple customers.[1]

Customized versus Standard Products

Standard products lacked differentiation; many vendors had to meet identical specifications, or multiple customers bought the same product. Standard products were usually produced and sold in high volume, faced numerous competitors, and increasingly were sold through distribution centers at a price set by the market. Typical products included sheet used for milk trucks or strip used for consumer appliances.

Customized products, by contrast, were tailored for direct customers by alloy, grade, size, finish, or other required property. Applications were specific and demanding, such as drawing 10″ deep to form a cooking pot or drawing to .002 inch to form a hypodermic needle. Customers often received extensive technical assistance from Allegheny on how to make the steel work well on their equipment. Profit margins on these products were higher than for standard products, either because the products were proprietary or because there were only one or two competitors.

Much of the time, customized and commodity products went through the melting, casting, and hot rolling processes no differently, and only took on their distinct identities later during the cold rolling and finishing operations (see *Exhibit 2*). The number and types of finishing steps—which rolling mills and annealing and pickling lines the steel passed through—took products down to a certain thickness or gauge, imparted certain properties critical to the application, or gave the products a certain edge or finish. Commodity grade 304, for example, required six steps after

the hot strip mill; a more customized grade, 921, required 35 steps. In some cases, a product began to be customized as early as the Melt Shop. For example, grade 201 piston rings had a limit on the number of oxygen blows that could be used to correct temperatures during the melt. If the melter violated this limit, Technical Services downgraded the heat and it would be used for some other, less demanding application. Melters did more planning for such heats, making sure nothing would cause a delay and make the heat go cold.

Competition

Allegheny's domestic competitors were of three types: specialty steel divisions of larger carbon steel companies that made standard products, usually in a limited number of grades; smaller, free-standing companies that made either custom or standard products, but rarely both; and rerollers, who imparted finishing steps to semifinished steel. The larger, integrated producers were not well suited to making custom products; they did little R&D, and none was set up to offer extensive technical support. Unlike Allegheny, they were prone to initiating price cuts. The smaller, non-integrated producers—whether of standard or custom products—had to buy their slabs or hot-roll bands (the semifinished coils of steel that came off the hot strip mill). That increased costs, as did finishing equipment that was less economically sized than Allegheny's. Small size was an advantage, however, in providing prompt delivery and reliable customer service.

The ability to react quickly to customers and/or to fill small orders was also a strength of rerollers; they inventoried certain grades and sizes that they could then finish, slit and ship, sometimes converting commodity to custom products. The need for quick responsiveness and also for technical support had so far kept foreign producers out of most customized products (except for silicon steel). Imports were sold primarily to steel service centers which competed on price and delivery responsiveness.

Strategy

Allegheny's strategy was to be the low-cost producer of stainless steel commodities, and at the same time to pursue new niches for customized

---

[1]Allegheny Ludlum distinguished its two major product groups by the terms "commodity" and "specialty." To avoid the confusion of discussing "specialty specialty steel" and "commodity specialty steel," the word "customized" is used here to indicate those specialty products tailored to customers' needs, and "standard" to indicate generic products bought by multiple customers and/or for multiple applications.

EXHIBIT 2 Major Processing Operations

PRIMARY END:

MELTING AND REFINING steel involved one of two routes at Allegheny:

most stainless was melted in an ELECTRIC ARC FURNACE (EAF) and then refined in an ARGON OXYGEN FURNACE (AOD);

all silicon was melted in a CORELESS INDUCTION FURNACE and then refined in a BASIC OXYGEN FURNACE (BOF).

STAINLESS:

From the AOD, over 90% of the melts went directly to the CONTINUOUS CASTER, which cast SLABS directly from the molten metal. Slabs were 8 inches thick, and weighed 10–15 tons. The concaster eliminated many of these steps associated with ingots, and had much lower yield losses. The surfaces of some directly cast slabs were so good they did not have to be conditioned on grinders.

Some stainless melts were teemed into INGOT molds, cooled, stripped from the molds, heated in a soaking pit furnace, shaped by the blooming mill into large rectangular slabs, and their outer surface removed in slab conditioning. The ingot route was used for those melts that could not be concast, or when Brackenridge melting or casting was full.

Whether concast or ingot, a slab had to be reheated up to 2300°F and prepared for the HOT STRIP MILL where powerful electronically controlled rollers reduced the thickness of the metal while improving its properties. The Universal Mill took the slab to 1 inch thickness in five passes, while the Tandem Mill took it to a gauge of .080 to .300 inches. The slab had now become a HOT-ROLL BAND, a flat coil of steel up to 50" wide, weighing 25,000 pounds. It was rolled into a coil by the downcoiler.

SILICON:

From the BOF, all silicon melts were teemed into ingots, and followed the same steps as stainless ingots except that the surface did not have to be conditioned, nor the slab reheated.

STAINLESS FINISHING:

Allegheny then FINISHED its bands into SHEET, STRIP, or PLATE. Sheets were flat-rolled into coils 24 inches or wider, strip less than 24 inches, while plate was at least 3/16" thick. To make better use of equipment and reduce yield losses, COILS could be BUILT-UP or welded together to form a 50,000 pound coil.

Before being finished, coils had to be softened and prepared. ANNEALING, SHOT BLAST, and PICKLING processes were used, the choice depending on the product's chemistry and intended use. The various COLD-ROLLING MILLS reduced the thickness of the coils through a series of rolling operations to thicknesses as thin as .005 inches thick.

Finishing operations might also include BRIGHT ANNEAL lines that protected the steel from oxidation, and other annealing and pickling steps. SLITTERS cut the steel into narrower widths; much strip, for example, was sold in 1.5 to 2-inch widths. Finished tonnage yield was about 83% of the melt tonnage.

SILICON FINISHING:

Silicon finishing included many steps similar to those for stainless, and special steps to improve its magnetic properties. These included MAGNESIUM OXIDE COATING, a TUNNEL FURNACE in which grain growth was controlled, and several NORMALIZING processes. Finished tonnage yield was about 50% of the melt tonnage.

EXHIBIT 2 (continued)

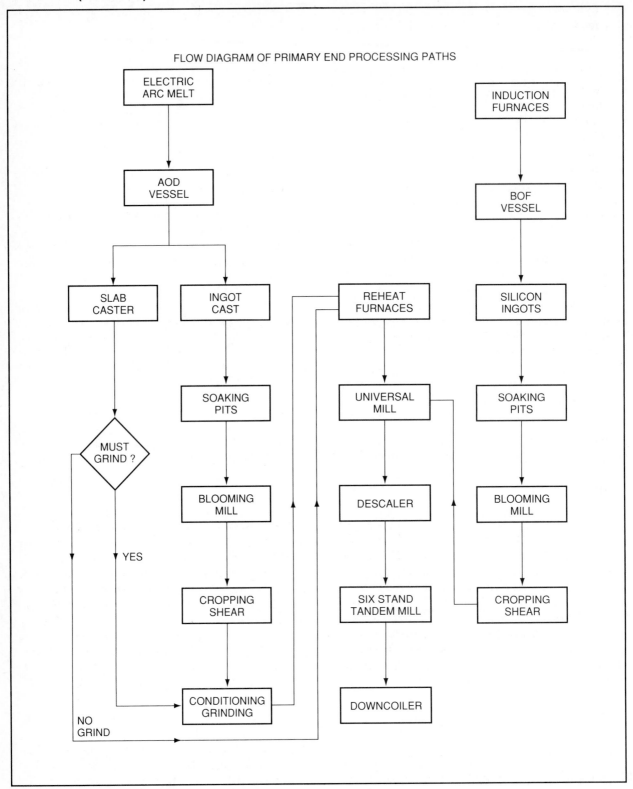

FLOW DIAGRAM OF PRIMARY END PROCESSING PATHS

20. Allegheny Ludlum Steel Corporation

products. The links between the two were multiple and dynamic. Commodities carried part of the overhead of the company's high-volume facilities, allowing Allegheny to make custom steels in larger volume and at lower cost than its competitors. This meant that Allegheny's primary end delivered a low-cost, hot-roll band—whether then finished as a standard or custom product—at a cost no small competitor could match. The price premium commanded by Allegheny's custom products also supported the company's extensive research, market development and technical services. These activities in turn developed new products and processes and reduced manufacturing costs through continued process improvements.

SUPPORT OF LOW-COST PRODUCTION. Because raw materials accounted for up to 80% of variable costs for commodities, low-cost production required good contracts on alloys and other materials. Such savings benefited customized products as well. Low-cost production was also supported by an extremely rigorous standard cost accounting system, a low-cost routing system, and a system of objectives established annually by the managers themselves. Such efforts had increased net tons of steel per employee by almost 40% between 1979 and mid-1985.

SUPPORT OF CUSTOMIZED PRODUCTION. Customized production was supported by extensive customer interchange and the broadest technical development effort in the industry. Allegheny spent 2% of its sales dollars on research (about 10 times what its stainless competitors spent), and another 2% on technology, including equipment computerization, software programs, and process control. Its market development group obtained market intelligence; competitors either did not do this at all, or did it much less deliberately. And its technical services group worked closely with customers to create a match between their manufacturing processes and Allegheny's steels, while also providing metallurgical assistance to Allegheny's own line operators.

Organization

The Plant System

Most stainless was melted at the Brackenridge plant, and all silicon at nearby Natrona (see *Exhibit 3*). Brackenridge housed the continuous caster and the hot strip mill, which meant that silicon went to Brackenridge for hot rolling before being finished at Bagdad. Brackenridge produced hot-roll stainless bands for the four stainless finishing plants. Products were normally assigned to particular plants, although there was frequent overlap. Because the routing system aimed to maximize margins by minimizing costs, different capacity and product mix conditions led to different assignments.

Functions

Direct reporting to Simmons and Bozzone was divided by function (see *Exhibit 1*). In addition to the usual functions and activities, such as sales, engineering, and operations, the Technical Division, Technical Services, and the tactical business teams were of particular note.

The Technical Division

Headed by Richard (Dick) Pitler, the Technical Division encompassed both Research and Market and Product Development.

RESEARCH. About 20% of Research's work supported sales or manufacturing, 60% went toward new products or process improvements, and 20% was high-risk experiments. The division had its own melt shop where it could make small melts of new alloys; it also took steel off the plant floor to cut apart and examine. Multiple laboratories carried out work in heat treating, magnetic testing, electron optics, x-ray diffraction, corrosion testing, mechanical testing, and other areas.

Process improvements were often sought through physical and/or mathematical models. A model of the continuous caster, for example, used water, whose viscosity was similar to that of molten steel, to understand flow rates, eddies, traps and patterns in the caster's internal currents created by the submerged entry nozzle. As a result, several new nozzle designs were developed, each tailored to a particular grade of specialty steel, to get the right temperature distribution and flow.

MARKET AND PRODUCT DEVELOPMENT. This group of five men had spent their working lives in the company; each combined a background in engineering, research, and some other functional

EXHIBIT 3 Allegheny's Plant System

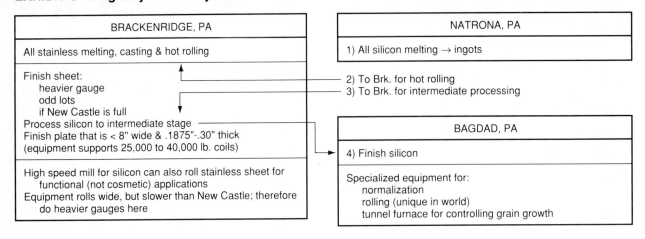

BRACKENRIDGE, PA

All stainless melting, casting & hot rolling

Finish sheet:
- heavier gauge
- odd lots
- if New Castle is full

Process silicon to intermediate stage
Finish plate that is < 8" wide & .1875"-.30" thick
(equipment supports 25,000 to 40,000 lb. coils)

High speed mill for silicon can also roll stainless sheet for functional (not cosmetic) applications
Equipment rolls wide, but slower than New Castle; therefore do heavier gauges here

NATRONA, PA

1) All silicon melting → ingots

2) To Brk. for hot rolling
3) To Brk. for intermediate processing

BAGDAD, PA

4) Finish silicon

Specialized equipment for:
- normalization
- rolling (unique in world)
- tunnel furnace for controlling grain growth

NEW CASTLE, IND.

Finish sheet: 48" wide, lighter gauges, higher volume
Finish wide standard strip: roll 48" & then slit to 23–24"; higher volume

Equipment supports 2x weight that Brackenridge does, so roll double coils (50,000 lb.)
Equipment reduces steel quickly so roll to lighter gauges

LEECHBURG, PA

Finish standard strip — higher volume
Finish specialty strip — less value-added than Wallingford

Most equipment supports 1 1/2 coils (37,500 lbs.)

WALLINGFORD, CT

Finish specialty strip — much more value added than Leechburg

Equipment supports single 25,000 lb. coils

WESTWOOD, PA

Finish plate > 48" wide

Heavy equipment for shearing, cutting, handling

CLAREMORE, OKLA

Form tubing from strip

20. Allegheny Ludlum Steel Corporation

field. Organized along major customer-industry lines, members spent 60% of their time on the road, introducing new Allegheny materials and making sure they were used properly. The group's director, John Ziemanski, noted: "Our ability to get in and talk to engineers early on gives us a leg up in anticipating market needs."

Technical Services

Headed by Robert (Bob) Walsh, and with a dotted line relationship to Pitler, Technical Services defined and coordinated the steelmaking process, decided whether a product met customer specifications and whether it would be shipped, and helped customers use existing products. It consisted of three subgroups: product services, metallurgical engineering, and quality assurance.

PRODUCT SERVICES. Trained as metallurgists or as tool and die makers, members of this group tried to insure that Allegheny understood exactly what the customer needed, helped customers' operating personnel work with Allegheny materials, and suggested changes either in the customers' equipment and fabrication processes and/or in Allegheny's materials. Charles (Charlie) Rietdyke, a section manager for Technical Services, described the group's role:

> Everything starts with the customer: we must meet his requirements. Our metallurgists can determine if the material is within specifications, but that in itself says nothing about whether the customer can make the part with it. Our tool and die people help close that gap.

METALLURGICAL ENGINEERING. These plant metallurgists defined the production process that orders would follow, monitored the process in operation, and provided technical assistance to operators on the floor. The parameters established by this group included the chemistry of the process, the number and types of annealing and rolling cycles the steel would go through, the temperatures and pressures at which operations would be run, and sometimes the specific pieces of equipment that could be used, or had to be used, for certain steps. Process definition was dynamic; as Leonard (Len) Greco, formerly of Tech Services and recently named operations manager at Wallingford, put it, "First we make it right, then we learn how to make it cheaply." The customer's

intended use of the product was the starting point for defining the alloy and the kind of reductions that would be needed—without restrictions on cost. But because the number of passes in cold rolling affected the properties of the final product, subsequent experimentation included efforts to change the alloy to allow reductions in the number of passes needed, or to reach the same end point with the same alloy with fewer passes. Each was aimed at getting costs out of the product.

The assistance offered by plant metallurgists to line operators took many forms. Victor (Vic) Ardito, general manager of the Melt Shop, described their role:

> If you put somebody in a job where he has to make a decision that can't wait—like our melters, who always have another heat behind them—then he has to do something. If you leave him alone, he will play it safe, and you are always going to lose when he does that. But when our melters have a problem, they not only have round-the-clock telephone numbers to call, they also have the metallurgist there. So our melters end up making intelligent decisions—yes, with a certain amount of risk in them.

QUALITY ASSURANCE. The third group in Tech Services had ultimate responsibility for deciding what did or did not meet customer requirements, and final say over whether or not a product would be shipped. It also decided which operating unit would be charged for defects. In making such decisions, Reno Giapponi, general supervisor of inspection and physical test at Wallingford (but better known to his colleagues as "God"), noted that: "The key thing is end use: will it make the product?" Deciding what to do in gray areas was often handled by direct customer contact: "This is what we have—can you use it?" QA also coordinated the company's response to customers' orders—within 48 hours for repeat orders, and from three days to three weeks for new orders. When asked whether the competition could respond as quickly, Pitler replied:

> They could be as fast, but they won't be as accurate. Or they'll say they can make anything. Although it sometimes feels as though customers have a memory span of five minutes, we think they come to us because we can do more for them. And, we think it helps our credibility to say, "We cannot give you a reasonable answer within too short a time" or, "No, we can't make this."

Exhaust Alloys

A recent example of the role played by the technical staff was their response to information that Market Development and Technical Services engineers had picked up from their engineering contacts in the auto industry. Domestic automakers wanted to switch to stainless steel for exhaust manifolds, but 30-50% of conventional 409 grade stainless (used successfully for catalytic converters for a decade) cracked when bent into these pretzel-like forms. Allegheny's engineers sensed a large potential market if a more malleable alloy could be developed. Their informal conversations spurred Bob Walsh to call a meeting of all the key players; in one day, the group pounded out the chemical, metallurgical and process steps they would use for a high-performance exhaust alloy, called 409HP. Walsh and Pitler skipped the laboratory stage, and went directly to mill experiments on the shop floor, melting five full-scale (100-ton) heats in a week. Walsh recalled, "We got some out to customers for evaluation, and they confirmed our expectations. Now that we knew what 409HP could do, the question was cost and repeatability." By substituting 409HP for a whole week's 409 production, Allegheny got larger volumes out to customers. Thus, within six weeks, the company developed the new alloy, made 2,000 tons, got it out to customers where reject rates dropped to 1-3%, learned its costs, and defined a repeatable manufacturing process. These efforts were facilitated by Bozzone's and Simmons' familiarity with market and metallurgical issues. Gerald (Gerry) Houze, director of Research, noted:

> Simmons and Bozzone had already seen Market Development's presentation, engine by engine, on the potential of this market. They also knew what we were trying to do technically and could make their own assessments. Technical literacy runs throughout the company, and makes it easy to sell a project like this.

Tactical Business Teams (TBTs)

Allegheny divided its products into six groups, and delegated operating responsibility for managing these businesses to six tactical business teams. From most commodity-like to most customized, the six were stainless plate, stainless sheet, stainless standard strip, stainless customized strip, silicon, and high-tech alloys. The teams were headed by Marketing, and included the appropriate plant manager and representatives from Technical Services and Production Control. The TBT was held accountable for sales, conversion costs, variances, and the use of working capital and equipment—all measures under its direct control. Objectives were to meet the targeted variable margin dollars (revenues minus variable standard costs plus or minus variances) for the business, gain a good return on controllable assets, and achieve the "critical issues" for the year.

These teams worked on the middle ground between daily operating decisions and larger decisions with strategic impact. Although TBTs were, in Simmons's view, expected "to be the point dog on strategic issues affecting their businesses," members had to go to their functional bosses (or higher, if necessary) on such questions. The same recourse was available if a team member disagreed with the direction his or her team was taking. But this route was rarely taken, for as Reitdyke put it, "We would have to go up one level to resolve it, and that's ridiculous. If we can't settle it when we are so close to it, who else can?" Len Greco concurred:

> Having the team prevents someone from making a decision that doesn't take everything into account. Say Marketing wants to change the coil size for a customer, but that affects our equipment; as a team, we talk about it and see how our choices affect other people, and whether or not we can do it. Or maybe we are running into bottlenecks, so then Production Control can give us another route.

The system of plural management at Allegheny went beyond the TBT structure, however. Bob Walsh described how he viewed his job and that of his colleagues:

> Bob Wardle's [vice president for Operations] job is to make a product at the lowest cost that meets customer standards and our objectives in the market. My job is to meet customer standards and our objectives in the market at the lowest cost. I cannot escape responsibility for costs; he cannot escape responsibility for quality and reliability. That's what Dick Simmons wants, and that's what trickles down. In this company's culture, there's no such thing as "*you* failed." Either *we* survive or *we* fail.

Control Systems

Evolution of the Systems

Allegheny's control system and plural management were Dick Simmons' response to the parochialism he had experienced in his first 15 years in the steel industry. Simmons believed functionally organized companies created department- and plant-focused thinking, as well as adversarial relationships so tangible "you could see them, you could taste them, you could smell them—almost like a religious war." When he returned to Allegheny in 1969 as vice president of manufacturing, he found each plant to be "an empire," and a profit center with its own cost system, making it impossible even to compare the costs of making the same product in different plants directly.

Simmons's first step was to turn plants into cost centers, a move that was perceived as being a staff reduction. He recalled: "We didn't just eliminate managers; we designed them out of the system." Next, Simmons instructed the controller to develop a standard direct cost system that allowed the costing of each coil. Some 100,000 standards were built into the database. (A standard was the variable conversion cost of performing an operation on a particular grade, size, and thickness of steel using a particular piece of equipment.) With this information, one could identify and compare the cost of producing the same grade, size, and thickness of steel on different equipment, or the cost of producing different grades, sizes, or thicknesses on the same equipment. This system became the foundation for choosing alternate routes in production scheduling, and for generating weekly (and now daily) variance reports in which variances were converted to dollars. The system reflected Simmons's philosophy:

> If you can measure it, you can manage it. But traditionally, the steel industry has thought in terms of tons. We converted everything to dollars because people bank dollars, live on dollars, and buy food with dollars; I wanted them to run their businesses on dollars too.

Simmons's third major step was to create the tactical business teams to push responsibility for profits below the level of president.

The Cost Accounting System

Standards were developed, and actual costs tracked, for every department, machine, process, grade, width and gauge of steel. Work was actually tracked to the individual coil level. By dividing the number of coils produced from a given batch of work, the variance per coil could be obtained and applied to the standard cost to give the actual cost of the coil. This database could be exploded in any way: by grade, by product, by customer, by thickness, in any fashion the TBT believed of value. To Allegheny's knowledge, no other competitor could track its coil costs so precisely.

Standard costs for purchased materials were based on historical experience and expectations of price changes. Standards for productivity and efficiency, by contrast, were based on best past performance, generally referred to as the "Olympic standard." These standards were renegotiated annually between Operations and Accounting. Each year, the company strove to take away most of the favorability by tightening standards; for example, in 1984, $11 million was taken out of the standards. Wardle commented, "If the variance is unfavorable, we ask, 'what are we doing wrong?' If it's favorable, we ask, 'what's wrong with the standard?'" As Allegheny's controller Charles (Chuck) May noted, "To loosen a standard, there has to be a very good reason."

Managing Day-to-Day Production

Managers used reports issued daily, weekly, or monthly to keep close tabs on production, costs, and profit margins. These reports, in turn, provided a barometer of the managers' effectiveness, and were the foundation of the incentive pay system.

PRODUCTION REPORTS, OR "WHAT HAPPENED YESTERDAY?". Production managers received daily reports on yesterday's orders, production, and shipments (both planned and actual). Bob Wardle, who had grown up in Maintenance and then Engineering and who knew every piece of equipment by heart, commented on his use of these reports:

> Because of experience, I can usually go through this 17-page report on seven plants in 15 minutes, and know where to ask questions. When

I see something unusual, I ask, "why" and I'm on the phone. By 9:15, no matter what plant I'm at, I've talked to Joe Miller, to Harry Wagner and to Eddie Lipski. By 9:30, I've talked to Bob Bozzone about what my problems are. Then he talks to Dick [Simmons] who demands to know every morning what happened yesterday. What makes this system work is the accuracy of the data and the speed with which we get it. That allows us to make decisions on the basis of facts—immediately.

Ardito also described how his morning began:

We start with "what happened yesterday." I review the morning report and talk to my supervisors. We put together a story and I talk to Harry by 9 o'clock. Every day he wants to know, "Were there any delays? Why? What are the costs?" It takes time, and sometimes the fellows grumble about having to spend the first hour of their day like this. But the key to keeping variances low is real-time responsiveness.

EFFICIENCY REPORTS. The cost system was also the basis for weekly efficiency reports that converted the four key variances of productivity, utilization, yield, and rejects to dollar values (see *Exhibit 4A*). These variances were calculated in the following way:

- *productivity:* net tons per hour compared with standard tons per hour
- *utilization:* contact time (amount of time equipment was in contact with the work) divided by turn time (an 8-hour shift)
- *yield:* tons of material coming off equipment divided by tons going on
- *rejects:* coils scrapped and heats aborted compared with total coils and total heats

Every department head had to comment each week in writing on the variance report for his or her area. These comments were circulated to all

EXHIBIT 4a An Efficiency Report—Weekly Summary

Location & Department	Tons Produced	Productivity Variance $	Utilization Variance $	Yield Variance $	Total Prod. and Yield Var. $ Week	Total Prod. and Yield Var. $ MTD	Quality Cost Variance MTD
BRACKENRIDGE							
#8–3 Melting & slab casting	8,764	17,000	0	79,000	96,000	87,000	0
#8–7 Natrona—Induction furnace	5,647	3,000	5,000	(25,000)			
—BOF	6,988	0	8,000	0	(9,000)	(9,000)	0
#8–2 Blooking & hot strip mill	16,515	6,000	36,000	42,000	84,000	117,000	11,000
#8–2 Coil build-up	5,454	3,451	(140)	(1,605)	1,706	1,706	0
#10 Conditioning	4,491	6,000	0	12,000	18,000	61,000	0
#3 Alloy finishing	16,126	2,584	(4,679)	24,906	22,811	59,775	15,000
#7–3 Silicon finishing	13,110	(16,635)	(28,826)	(42,360)	(87,821)	(104,115)	0
Primary operations	0	0	0	0	0	0	63,000
Quality costs in hot roll band variance	0	0	0	0	0	0	62,000
Total Brackenridge	77,095	21,400	15,355	88,941	125,696	213,366	151,000
#7 New Castle	14,852	43,279	(5,378)	(9,609)	28,292	58,049	10,000

20. Allegheny Ludlum Steel Corporation

other managers, including Simmons, and were one of the topics at Simmons's weekly meeting with officers. Once a month, TBT leaders joined the group to discuss their products, problems, and opportunities.

SALES AND NET MARGIN REPORTS. Issued monthly, these reports showed the net contribution margin for each major product category (e.g., chrome nickel) within major product lines (e.g., sheet). (See Exhibit 4B). They quickly revealed how each product line, and thus each TBT, was doing financially, and identified problems and opportunities. Marketing people took these slender reports on the road and were able to quote prices on the spot.

MARGINS, ROCI, AND INCENTIVE PAY. These net margin reports, together with a monthly report showing return on capital invested (ROCI), made up the "report card" for each TBT. ROCI indicated how well managers were using the company's working capital and equipment. (A Typical ROCI calculation is shown in Exhibit 5.) Robert (Bob) Rutherford, head of the TBTs for both standard and specialty strip, commented on his use of the ROCI report: "I'm looking for trends. The key measures for being out of control are days out for receivables and excess inventory weeks."

Margin dollars also counted heavily in calculating incentive pay for the 105 eligible managers. Seventy-five percent of their bonus was based on the company's operating profits and cash

EXHIBIT 4b A Sales and Net Margin Report (Monthly)

Product & Grade	Pounds	Sales Dollars	Per #	Net Margin Dollars	Per #	%	Plan N.M. Per #
Sheets: C.R.—CR NI	197,306	202,265	1.025	85,418	0.433	42	0.304
CR NI+	10,002	14,272	1.427	5,749	0.575	40	0.408
CR MN	1,882	1,990	1.057	1,099	0.584	55	0.460
ST CR	7,172	7,118	0.992	1,974	0.275	28	0.292
Low CR	12,544	8,778	0.700	3,410	0.272	39	0.190
Emission control	55,078	34,819	0.632	16,710	0.303	48	0.234
Hot rolled	14,702	9,658	0.657	3,001	0.204	31	0.131
Excess primes	6	4	0.714	0			
Commodity	17,698	16,131	0.911	6,490	0.367	40	0.196
Total Stainless Sheets	316,390	295,033	0.932	123,850	0.391	42	0.279

```
CR = Chrome      MN = Manganese
NI = Nickel      ST CR = Straight Chrome
```

Note: These two reports are abbreviated, and are included only to show the kind of information Allegheny collects; they are not intended as the basis of any analysis.

EXHIBIT 5 A Typical ROCI Calculation

RETURN ON CONTROLLABLE CAPITAL INVESTED, 1984
(units in thousands)
(sheet only)

	Plan		Actual	
	$	Non $	$	Non $
SALES				
TONS		152,988T.		158,195T.
DOLLARS	$258,744		$295,033	
NET MARGIN				
DOLLARS	79,592		123,850	
AS % OF SALES		30.8%		42.0%
OPERATING PROFIT [= net margin				
—period costs]				
DOLLARS			71,154	
AS % OF SALES				24.1%
ASSET USE				
INVENTORY DOLLARS [= raw			45,800	
materials + WIP]				
[Raw materials allocated by forecasted				
sales for 3 mos.]				
[WIP: each order @ standard cost]				
INVENTORY TONS [= raw materials + WIP]				60,782T.
TOTAL INVENTORY WEEKS				14 wks.
REQUIRED WEEKS [# weeks				7 wks.
required to produce				
projected sales volume]				
AUTHORIZED WEEKS [# weeks of				7 wks.
inventory above required				
weeks, to increase sales				
via quick delivery]				
EXCESS INVENTORY [# weeks of				0 wks.
inventory above authorized				
weeks]				
ACCOUNTS RECEIVABLE				
DOLLARS [actual amount			31,329	
outstanding]				
# DAYS OUTSTANDING				46.1 days
NET PLANT & EQUIPMENT [% of net book			42,174	
value of each piece of equipment				
on which products were processed;				
% based on projected volume sheet				
will generate]				
TOTAL CONTROLLABLE INVESTMENT			$119,303	
ASSET TURNOVER [sales ÷ controllable				2.47
investment]				
OPERATING PROFIT [asset turnover x % operating				59.6%
profit; or, operating profit ÷ controllable				
investment]				

flow, the other 25% on individual and TBT achievements. This 25% was in turn divided between meeting margin dollar targets for the product line and achieving critical issues.

Planning and Critical Issues Program

Whereas the cost system reacted to problems, the critical issues program was designed to find opportunities and set priorities for the following year. The program had three levels—goals, critical success factors (CSFs), and critical issues (CIs)—that were redeveloped annually through a process coordinated by Wayne Swift, director of Facilities, Planning and MIS. Input was also provided by a strategic planning process that identified major threats and opportunities that had to be addressed. Simmons commented: "This process does not spit out financials. We only want to know from our CFO: Can we finance it? We look only at the best, the worst, and the most probable scenarios."

Simmons, Bozzone, Pitler and Richard O'Sullivan, the chief financial officer, developed broad annual goals that meshed with the business plan and budget. Within this framework, a broader tier of management, including directors and plant managers, developed critical success factors. These were top priorities for the coming year, specific enough to assign to functions, but leaving open how particular people and departments would work toward realizing an objective; that was the role of critical issues.

Critical issues were task-oriented programs that supported CSFs. They were committed to individually by each of Allegheny's top 105 managers but included hundreds more below them. Because they included quantified objectives and timetables, critical issues were targets against which managers could be measured. Three times a year, at a meeting with the other participants in the program, managers spoke for about two minutes on what they had accomplished. As Swift pointed out, "In front of 104 peers, you don't get up and say you haven't done anything. You don't want to flop or be embarrassed."

Critical issues were developed by the people who would be held responsible for meeting them. Simmons described the process:

> We all get our chance. We argue and haggle, for an issue is not just accepted—unless someone says, "I want to do this." When we finally disseminate the plan at the end of the year, we will have agreed on a rather detailed list of problems and opportunities that everybody has signed onto.

An Example: Increasing Melt Capacity

Increasing Melt Shop had been Vic Ardito's major critical issue for several years. Improvement had been steady: since 1977 capacity had doubled, but without any physical capacity being added (see *Exhibit 6*). Ardito described the improvement process:

> We began working with the melters and general foremen, the people that run the show on each turn. They began to understand what was needed and they applied their creativity and began to make it happen. Many of the great ideas have come off the floor from the foremen.

The Melt Shop spent up to $650,000 a day on materials, so it began by asking, "What can we do to make the furnace accept cruddy materials?" Although it meant putting up with broken electrodes, strong fumes and surging flames, the additional 1/4¢ per pound conversion cost was more than offset by the 4¢ picked up on materials bought.

To make better use of the 120-ton AOD—a $100 a minute operation—and the continuous caster, and to solve shifting bottlenecks, the melters developed new methods. These included combining heats from two EAFs (which had smaller capacity than the AOD) in the AOD, losing less time between emptying one AOD heat and refilling it with another, and having a chemically identical heat ready to be cast at the moment the first heat was all the way through the caster.

To help the Melt Shop reach its tonnage goals, other departments had related critical issues. Research, for example, had to develop computer programs that would increase control over melt parameters while decreasing total melt time. Heretofore, bringing a heat to the desired end point meant testing it at several points and making ad hoc adjustments. This process was not only time-consuming but often compounded the original problem (much as a cook might compensate for too much thyme by adding too much basil). By contrast, Research's computer program, which operated in real time, told melters how much

EXHIBIT 6 AOD and Caster Productivities

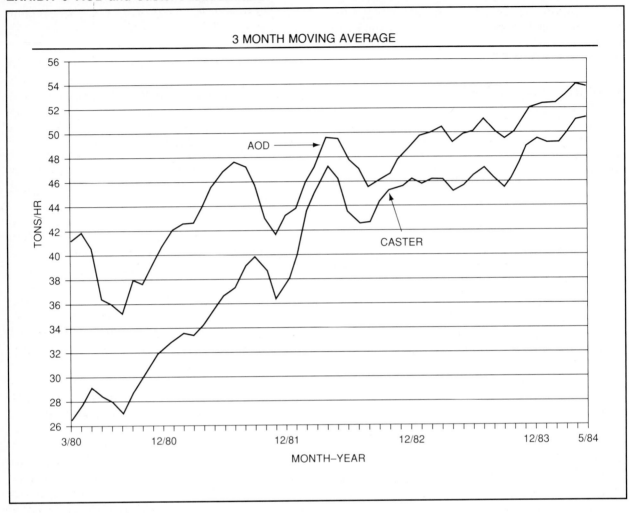

oxygen to blow right now, or what materials to add in what quantities.

Tools and Techniques

Allegheny had developed other mechanisms to support the basic building blocks of the standard cost system, the critical issues program, and plural management. Among the most important were laboratory and production experiments and the low-cost routing system.

Experiments

Most of Research's work was written up as experiments, which were of three types: laboratory experiments, mill experiments, and 710s. Labo-

ratory experiments were forerunners of full-scale trials in the mill. Mill experiments and 710s, on the other hand, had to be scheduled around regular production. The difference between mill experiments and 710s lay in the degree of risk, and in how costs were accounted for.

The 710s were high-risk experiments. To encourage this kind of experimentation, 710s did not show up in production costs; they therefore did not detract from variable margins. They required sign-offs from four vice presidents (Pitler, Walsh, Wardle, and Richard Mercer, vice president of Commercial) who had to agree that the process was reasonable, that it would not damage the equipment, and that it was worthwhile commercially.

While the dividing line between 710s and

other mill experiments was not always clear, the latter typically aimed at modifying and improving something that was already known. This might be the simplification of an existing operation, a change in equipment use, or a metallurgical change. At least 100 mill experiments were performed yearly, compared with the usual one 710 per month. Costs of mill experiments were included in operating departments' budgets. When asked why he agreed to mill experiments, since they made his costs go up, Harry Wagner, works manager at Brackenridge and Natrona, replied:

> I'll do it if it sounds like a smart thing to do; we're not after mosquitoes with cannons here, so we don't want to spend a dollar to save a dime. Yes, it may mess up my operation temporarily, and give me a negative variance or at least raise costs. But it may also lower my long-run costs or improve my quality. If an experiment messes you up, they change the yardsticks. It's the bottom line that drives us.

Bob Walsh added, "You have to put your money where your mouth is. If you encourage people to innovate, then you don't penalize them when it results in a negative variance."

Experiments got started for several reasons. Research had developed something in its own labs that it wanted to test in the mill; a customer had a new material that it wanted to try in full production; or the company wanted to experiment with variations of current production practices, such as new chemistry or new process techniques, to improve quality or reduce costs. An additional important use of experiments was to open the door to new business, but on a small enough scale that the risks were minimized.

Low-Cost Routing

Allegheny's routing system provided options for routing products over different pieces of equipment. Most of the routing choices involved cold rolling and stainless finishing operations. In general, the greatest latitude was in breaking down coils to intermediate gauges; the least, in the final rolling of thin gauges and other finishing steps.

Routing options that were ultimately chosen on an economic basis were first screened and constrained by certain equipment, metallurgical limitations, and customer needs. These considerations included coil size (every piece of equip-

ment had a maximum coil size, measured in weight, that it could support); the 24-hour rolling requirement (all silicon and 40% of stainless had to be rolled within 24 hours of being cast); and necessary end-product qualities that could be obtained only by using a particular piece of equipment. Within such constraints, Production Control identified all alternative equipment over which a product could, from a technical standpoint, be routed; it then tallied the costs associated with each step and ranked the routes by cost.

An invaluable tool for making these choices was Allegheny's proprietary computer program, ROUTE COST, developed by Wayne Swift to follow certain decision rules. Production Control used the program to schedule production, and Accounting used it to develop expected conversion costs for new products. No competitor had a similar program because none had the detailed standard cost accounting system needed to support it.

ROUTE COST was essential in helping Allegheny meet its overall objective of maximizing margins. Once equipment capacity limits were reached, however, its decision rules were overridden to avoid temporary bottlenecks that could lengthen delivery times. Then, critical units were scheduled first for high margin, specialty products, and less efficient equipment was brought on-stream as necessary. The potential conflict between Production Control's need to look at capacity, equipment use, and scheduling for all product lines and the TBTs' desires to maximize their own margins was resolved by Marketing, or, if necessary by Bozzone and Simmons. In making such a decision, they relied heavily on margin reports.

Low-cost routing could also be overridden by customer service. Marketing put five or six items out of 4,000 monthly invoices on a hot list; Production Control then did whatever it had to to get the order out.

Stainless and Silicon Decisions

In the near future, Allegheny faced decisions about both its stainless and silicon steel facilities. The market for stainless, as well as Allegheny's share, was expected to continue to increase. The company's melting and casting capacities, however, were approaching their limits. At the same time, there was no longer enough silicon volume to keep the Natrona melt shop running at anything close to capacity. Because Natrona could be adapted to melt stainless, the two capacity decisions were closely interlinked.

Silicon Markets and Products

Although Allegheny participated in the full range of silicon markets, its concerns focused on the high end. Competition for high-end power and distribution transformer markets centered on energy efficiency; the more energy efficient the steel, the lower the utility's operating costs. A competitor with a less efficient product could offer a more attractive initial price, or responsiveness to the unique design needs of each utility. A maturing utility infrastructure and more efficient steels had greatly shrunk tonnage demands.

Improving the magnetic quality of silicon was difficult to do; even more difficult was getting a process with 80–90% repeatability. Orienting the grains increased magnetic quality; getting the grains lined up and controlling their growth was at the heart of this difficult process. Indeed, only four companies in the world could make high-quality, grain-oriented silicon. Historically, Allegheny and Armco had shared the domestic market. But in 1984, Kawasaki Steel and Nippon Steel grabbed 30% of the U.S. market with their "high B" product that was 10% more efficient than the steel the Americans were making. At the low end, the Europeans, Brazilians, and Canadians were aggressively gaining share on the basis of price.

Allegheny had designated the achievement of a silicon product competitive with high B as a CSF, and was spending half its research dollars on this effort. Simmons also lobbied actively for silicon quotas—not tariffs, because, as he was quick to point out, foreign subsidies could be used to offset American tariffs. Yet even if quotas were achieved, the company would face competitive threats. Bozzone pointed out:

> The transformer people could go to Mexico or somewhere else and have their cores wound there, using Japanese steel. The product would then come into the country as a transformer rather than as steel. Or the Japanese could sell to the Swedes, without profit, to get around our quotas. I was meeting with some of the transformer people just a few weeks ago, and they are already looking at the Swedish option.

Silicon Options

Allegheny had several options for its silicon business.

1. *Meet the Japanese head on.* Under this option, the company would intensify its efforts to develop a product capable of competing with the Japanese in the high end of the market. Research and experimentation had raised magnetic quality 2-4%, bringing Allegheny's product to parity with Armco's; another 10% was a tall order. Bozzone acknowledged the company had a long way to go in achieving a repeatable process: "We try to understand the reaction of the metal, while the Japanese understand *why* things happen. We could accelerate the pace of R&D, but can we get close enough?" Even if Allegheny could improve the product's quality and process repeatability, pricing it to recoup the investment might be difficult. The Japanese had a history of accepting low returns or even selling below costs for long periods in markets they had targeted.

2. *Joint venture with the Japanese.* Allegheny could possibly get a license with Kawasaki Steel to produce some of its recipes. This would give Allegheny the opportunity to regain its competitiveness in the high end, and perhaps enhance low-end sales. Allegheny would still require a major silicon research effort, but it would be focused on finishing operations.

3. *Adapt some silicon facilities for making stainless.* Allegheny had over $100 million invested in silicon equipment, most of it depreciated. Some of the excellent finishing equipment was dedicated and could not be adapted for stainless use. Some equipment, such as a highly computerized, high-speed rolling mill and seven slitting lines, could be changed over permanently, at modest cost, or used alternatively for silicon and stainless, with minor modifications such as in the lubrication system.

4. *Run Silicon as a cash cow, and get out of the business.* This option would stretch out the time horizon for getting out of the business, while continuing to support 20-35% of the company's overhead. Allegheny would sharply reduce its research and technical support, and continue to cut prices. Bozzone, however, noted:

Most businesses in which you could pull back on management attention and technical support are commodity businesses. But if you took away the support in this highly technical business, you might lose share even in the conventional end of the business. So we are not sure the cash cow approach would work.

Given the uncertainties of running silicon as a cash cow, Allegheny could instead take an immediate write-off of nonadaptable equipment, and get out of silicon quickly.

Stainless Markets and Capacity

Allegheny had increased its stainless sales 4%-5% per year (in tons) for the last several years, and had incrementally raised its Brackenridge melt capacity to over 400,000 tons per year. While the hot end was in balance, it was reaching its limits for squeezing out more tonnage. Management estimated that it would need 150,000 tons by 1990. They anticipated two major sources of that increase: exhaust alloys, and supplying competitors that had closed their melt shops with hot-roll bands.

Natrona, by contrast, had melt capacity of 600,000 tons for silicon steel, but was currently producing no more than 40% of that. Allegheny had experimented with modifying one of the two BOFs at Natrona so it could refine some grades of stainless there. The potential capacity of the modified BOF would be a little more than half its silicon capacity, because a silicon heat was almost twice as fast as a stainless heat. While the quality of these heats were comparable to those from Brackenridge, the modified BOF could accommodate only some grades of stainless, and entailed a cost penalty. Currently, that penalty came in two parts: a 3¢ premium for refining in the BOF rather than in the AOD, and a 5¢ premium for using ingots rather than the caster.

Stainless Options

Several steps could be taken, either singly or in combination, to deal with the stainless situation:

1. *Do nothing.* If any of several events transpired (a competitor cancelled its contract for bands, the domestic auto industry suffered a major reversal, big carbon steel companies moved into exhaust alloys), Allegheny might be unable to recoup a major investment in expanded capacity. Standing pat was one response to such uncertainty.

2. *Expand Natrona Facilities for Making Stainless.* This option would involve buying or modifying one or more major pieces of equipment. Three independent alternatives were being considered.

   2A. *BOF Modification.* The company had spent a bit less than $1 million already to modify one of the two BOFs at Natrona so it could make some grades of stainless. Further modification would expand the number of grades that could be made there. The commercial viability of the method had not yet been established, and process control needed improvement. Some cost penalty relative to AOD steelmaking would always remain; management believed, however, that the current 3¢ penalty would eventually be brought to under 1¢ per pound. Moreover, the unified management structure of the Natrona and Brackenridge Melt Shops would ease technology transfer and training.

   2B. *Replace the BOF with a second AOD.* It was also possible to tear out one BOF and replace it with an AOD for about $3 million. Such a process change would require new pollution controls and re-certification, an additional investment of $5 million. Unlike the BOF, the AOD could refine every stainless alloy.

   2C. *Design and build a second continuous caster.* Given the sizable cost penalty of ingots, Allegheny was considering building a second continuous caster, this time at Natrona. Initially, it would be used to cast stainless; over time, the company would try to learn how to cast silicon continuously as well, assuming it stayed in that business. It could be fed by either a modified BOF or a second AOD. Such a caster could potentially double production; for this reason, it entailed considerable risks. Bozzone asked:

   > How do we play the game when there is overcapacity in the world? Do we freeze or grow? Can we put in another caster and get our money back before

the situation changes again? This kind of move would definitely send a message to the industry that no one else should, or could, make a major move in the hot end of the business for the next five to seven years.

The caster decision was complicated by the fact that two competitors had just announced increases in planned finishing capacity totaling 140,000 tons. If Allegheny lost share to them in finished products, utilization of the caster, which would cost around $35 million installed, would be less than projected. These competitive moves raised additional questions. Should Allegheny sell its bands to these firms? If it did, would it be displacing its own finished products? If it did not, wouldn't other companies sell bands?

3. *Buy an outside company.* Another alternative was to buy Adamson, a competitor whose net worth had been deteriorating rapidly. Adamson had EAFs, an AOD, and a caster; its yearly capacity was 120,000 tons. Because of Adamson's inefficiencies, conversion costs (including freight to and from Brackenridge's ample hot rolling mill) were expected to run 5–7¢ a pound higher in the first year than Allegheny's costs. Allegheny believed it could reduce part of this penalty through management, systems and work force changes, but inherent equipment inefficiencies would always leave a 2-4¢ penalty. Folding Adamson's manual data collection into Allegheny's would require work, but was considered doable by Simmons. If Allegheny decided to buy Adamson, it preferred to wait until the company went bankrupt, so it would not incur some $50 million in liabilities.

*　*　*　*

Allegheny had to decide among these many options, and decide rather soon. Simmons summarized the outcomes of those choices:

> In the next couple of years we're going to know, number one, are we in the silicon business? Or, number two, are we going to be in a phaseout of silicon? Number three, to what level of stainless capacity have we committed? And number four, are we going to continue to maintain a strategy of being undiversified and concentrate in specialty steel?

21. The Case for Managing by the Numbers

MANAGEMENT must manage! Management MUST manage! Management must MANAGE!

It is a very simple credo, probably the closest thing to the secret of success in business. The strange thing is that everybody knows it, but somehow managers forget it all the time.

To want to achieve certain year-end results is not enough. Managing means that once you set your business plan and budget for the year, you *must* achieve the sales, the market share, and the earnings to which you committed yourself. If you don't manage to achieve those results, you're not a manager.

Managers in all too many American companies do not achieve the desired results because nobody makes them do it. Explanations and rationalizations are all too readily accepted. You get what you expect to get. Seldom, if ever, do you get more.

A manager must set standards for production, sales, market share, earnings, whatever, and anything short of those standards should be unacceptable to him. Recently I met a man who operates the jewelry concession in a number of department stores. He told me: "I don't think I'm doing my job unless I get 4% of the store's traffic." "How do you know it's 4% you need?" I asked. "I don't," he replied, "it just works out that way." "Why not 5%?" I asked. "No, just 4%," he insisted, explaining that 4% was more than any other counter in the department store got. Without sophisticated controls, this man had set his own standards. He couldn't sleep if he did not get that 4%. He would feel guilty if he did not get it. He would work through the night, he would do anything he had to, but he would get that 4%. I don't know precisely what he did to achieve the 4%, and perhaps 5% or even 8% would have been possible, but it makes little difference: he was managing.

The efficacy of management is quantifiable. It can be measured by the profit and loss statement. In an established company, you can measure performance by the quarter. I used to tell my management team at ITT that making the first quarter's quotas was the most important challenge of the year. If you don't make your budget quota that first quarter, then you probably won't be able to catch up in subsequent quarters. Worrying about the quarterly numbers is not short-term management: careful study of them will alert you to potential long-term problems in time to take appropriate action.

What do you do if your company or your division or your department has not made its quota for the quarter? First of all you locate the problem. Then you find the cause. Then you fix it. That is why we had the controllers of every ITT company sending us in headquarters the figures of their companies every week. Less than satisfactory results showed up in those reports very clearly. That's why our line managers "red-flagged" their major problems for immediate attention. That's why we held monthly managers' meetings. We wanted to pinpoint the causes of the problems and find the best possible solutions as quickly as possible.

Management must manage became our credo at ITT. It meant that we would do everything we had to that was honest and legal to bring in the results we desired. If one solution to a problem did not work, we tried another. And another. Our red-flag items remained on the first page of each division's monthly report, updated for changes, every single month until they were solved. A red-flag item was like a thorn in an ITT manager's side. He had to solve it. He could not merely walk into one of our meetings and announce that he still had the problem, that nothing had changed. He had to tell me and our headquarters management team and his peers what he was doing and what he proposed to do about that problem. If he was stumped, we would send him help. Together we would manage.

But we *would* manage. I brought this point home at a general managers' meeting early in my reign at ITT when the man in charge of our Latin America operations reported that he had failed to sell our newest, multimillion-dollar telephone switching system to the government of Brazil. I probed for quite a while into the efforts that had been made. He told me of all the avenues he had explored.

"Who makes the final decision there on whether or not they buy our system?" I asked.

"President Kubitchek."

"Did you see him?"

"No."

"Why not?"

"Because —— really makes the decision and he recommends the decision and the president follows his advice," he explained, adding, "Besides, I don't think I can get in to see Kubitchek."

"Well, why don't you try? You have everything to gain and nothing to lose."

The following month he returned with a sheepish grin on his face to announce that he had seen the president of Brazil and had sold the ITT system. The men in the room applauded him.

At a succession of general managers' meetings in Europe we were all stumped over a serious problem of inventory control. Our European inventory of supplies, which usually ran between two and three billion dollars, had risen some $500 million above desired levels, and we were paying interest every month on those idle supplies. Task force after task force had investigated, and month after month those inventories seemed to be rising. Finally, at one meeting, one manager suggested that he had solved his own inventory problem by placing a man at the receiving dock of each of his factories with instructions to turn back any supplies that were not ordered or needed. It was such a simple solution. And it worked. We put a staff man at the receiving dock of every one of our factories to check supplies being unloaded, often in advance of our orders.

At ITT we used everything available to us to get results. We used everything we had learned at school, everything we had learned from our own experience in business, everything we could learn from one another. We used our intuition. We used our brains. And we always used the numbers.

No business could run without them. Numbers serve as a thermometer that measures the health and well-being of the enterprise. They serve as the first line of communication to inform management what is going on. The more precise the numbers are, the more they are based upon unshakable facts, the clearer the line of communication.

When a manager makes up a budget for the coming year, he is putting down on paper a series of expectations, expressed in numbers. They include the whole gamut of costs of his division's product—design, engineering, supplies, labor, plants, marketing, sales, distribution—and also anticipated income from sales, based on market share projections and back orders. These figures had better not be pulled out of the air. They must be based on the best facts available. When all the figures are pulled together for one company or one division, you have its budget. At ITT we had 250 of these profit centers. Their annual budgets, when lined up side by side, occupied 30-odd feet of shelf space.

For numbers to tell their whole story, they have to be compared to other numbers. As the budget year proceeds, the numbers reflecting actual operations pour into headquarters. Actual costs, sales, profit margins, and earnings can be compared to the budget forecasts. Does one set of numbers match the other? Is the actuality above or below the company's expectations? If it is either, what are you going to do about it?

Any significant variation is a signal for action. The sooner you see the numbers, the sooner you can take action if needed. If one of your products is selling above expectations, you may want to increase production immediately. If, as happens more often, one or more of your products is not selling as well as expected, then you may have to find some way to get those sales up or begin to reduce the costs and expenses involved, and the sooner the better. However—and this is most important—the numbers themselves will not tell you what to do. The key issue in business is to find out what is happening behind those numbers.

Once you start digging into the areas that the numbers represent, then you get into the guts of your business. If sales are off, is it because of the design of your product? Its cost? Marketing? Distribution?

When you find the source of the problem, you insist that management must manage to solve that problem. You don't want them to manage the numbers—pushing sales or receivables from one quarter to another. That is like treating the thermometer instead of the patient.

The difference between well-managed companies and not-so-well-managed companies is the degree of attention they pay to numbers, the temperature chart of their business. How often are the numbers reported up the chain of command? How accurate are those numbers? How much variation is tolerated between budget fore-

Listen to the numbers.

casts and actual results? How deep does management dig for its answers?

At ITT we took our numbers very seriously indeed. Our budget planning, which begins as early as February and March and continued through the year, was negotiated very carefully. The final budget was considered a solid commitment for performance expected the following year. Our monthly managers' meetings focused on the variations, if any, between budget forecasts and the results for that given month.

We wanted no surprises. As soon as we discovered something amiss, or going amiss, we threw every means and every effort into solving our problems. As a result, we felt that we were

Red-flag problems should elicit an immediate response.

in control. The unexpected shocks and surprises that accost everyone in life became manageable for us.

Numbers can be accurate or not so accurate, precise or rounded off, detailed or averaged and vague. Their quality, as reported, usually depends upon the chief executive of the company and what he expects from the men reporting to him. If he does not give much personal attention to the detailed figures beyond ascertaining the earnings per share, no one else in his company is going to worry about them. They will round off their figures, averaging the odd numbers, perhaps shaving off a few points from the costs, adding something to boost profit margins. As the practice spreads from division to division, the accumulation of inexact, fuzzy, and then plain incorrect figures can cause havoc with managerial decisions.

If an executive begins to look closely at all the figures that come in from the divisions of his company and insists that they be timely, accurate, and detailed, things will happen in that company that change it ever so imperceptibly into a well-managed enterprise. He will have to keep at it constantly, or else things will begin to slip again. Managing a company is like writing in the snow: you have to go over and over the same words as the snow falls if you want your writing to remain legible. The reward, however, is that you get better and better at it as you repeat the same process.

Sometimes, however, outside events beyond the control of any individual company overtake even the early warning system that good numbers provide. A sudden rise in the cost of energy, a significant international event, a plunge into recession of a whole national economy can make a shambles of the best-laid plans.

Consider, for example, one company with $40 million in annual sales, reaping a handsome profit. It expands to $60 million in annual sales, earning even more money. It builds its sales volume to $80 million a year, and profits rise proportionally. Then the economy slumps, customers suddenly stop buying, annual sales slide back down to the old level of $40 million a year. But now the company is losing money on that volume. What happened? What can you do about it?

At ITT, when outside events overtook us and there was nothing else we could do, we restructured the business so that it could cope with its new environment. We went over every relevant figure of every operation and scaled the business back down to the size it was when it was making money on annual sales of $40 million. It is simply amazing how many expenses once deemed necessary become luxuries when your company is operating at a loss.

At the same time, we made it a practice that while restructuring we put on a tremendous effort to try to increase sales a little bit, even 5% or 10%. We cut the company back to the $40-million structure and then tried to do $42 million or $44 million in business. We called it our one-two punch.

There is a price to pay for all this analysis, of course: paying attention to the numbers is a dull, tiresome routine—it's drudgery. The more you want to know about your business, the more numbers there will be. They cannot be skimmed. They must be read, understood, and compared to other sets of numbers that you have read that day, that week, or earlier that year. And you have to do it alone, all by yourself, even when you know that it would be far more stimulating to be doing almost anything else.

If you are running a well-managed company, most of the numbers will be those you expect. That makes them even more mundane and dull. But you cannot skip over them; you dare not allow your concentration to flag. Those numbers are your controls, and you read them until your mind reels or until you come upon one number or set of numbers that stand out from all the rest, demanding your attention, and getting it.

What you are seeking is *comprehension* of the numbers: what they mean. That will come only with constant exposure, constant repetition, retention of what you read in the past, and a familiarity with the actual activities that the numbers represent. You cannot speed up the process. Comprehension seeps into your brain by a process of osmosis and gradually you find yourself at ease with numbers and what they really represent.

The truth is that the drudgery of the numbers will make you free. The confidence that you are in control, that you are aware of the significant variations from the expected, gives you the freedom to do things that you would have been unable to do otherwise. You can build a new plant, or finance risk-laden research, or go out and buy a company, and you can do it with assurance because you are able to sit down and figure out what that new venture will do to the balance sheet. You will be able, in short, to manage.

22. Note on the Aerospace Industry and Industrial Modernization

Industry Structure

Aerospace companies designed and built aircraft and missile systems, including the increasingly sophisticated electronics systems with which airframes were equipped. Several major aerospace firms had been building planes since the 1920s; a few, such as Boeing, Lockheed, and McDonnell Douglas, later became active in missile and space technology. By acquisition or internal development, they also added electronics capabilities. This enabled them to compete with, as well as subcontract to, large electronics firms such as General Electric, Raytheon, and Hughes Aircraft, in addition to smaller, specialized firms. Today, the value of electronics in aircraft and missiles was nearly 20% of total defense procurement, and military aircraft were viewed as "weapons systems": complex electronic systems that guided weapons to a designated target by means of the aerostructures that housed them.

PRIMES AND SUBCONTRACTORS. Major aircraft systems contracts were let to one of a shrinking handful of "prime" aircraft contractors. (See *Exhibit 1*.) By 1984, only eight such primes remained: United Technologies, McDonnell Douglas, Lockheed, Boeing, General Dynamics, Rockwell International, Grumman, and Northrup. Many industry observers expected the number of primes to drop still further, leveling off at five or six within a decade. Some, in fact, thought Northrup and

Grumman were even now subcontractors, rather than full-fledged primes.

The role of primes had shifted during the 1950s. Previously, they had designed and built airframes themselves, and then assembled them with all other parts and subassemblies. But their responsibility stopped with the parts and subassemblies they made themselves: the military assumed responsibility for the performance of other systems. As aircraft gave way to weapons systems, however, responsibility for the integration and performance of all systems shifted to primes, along with the responsibility for managing these gigantic programs. The military dropped back to an oversight role but, to simplify its job, insisted that primes use program management and specified accounting procedures. This prompted the wise use of matrix management techniques and also determined how primes kept records and collected cost data.

Although primes now carried responsibility for entire weapons systems, they actually built fewer and fewer of the system parts themselves. By the 1970s, primes were subcontracting between 30% and 70% of components and subassemblies, and some detail design work as well. Several factors contributed to the greater use of subcontractors. Aerospace programs had become so complex that no one company could design and build everything. The McDonnell Douglas F-15 fighter, for example, had 585,000 parts; these had been designed, fabricated, assembled, and tested by over 22,000 people. The fighter contained 4,200 feet of tubing, 20 miles of wiring, 475 castings, and 437 forgings. The sophistication of such products made it impossible for primes to know everything about their design and manufacture. No one company could build up the required resources—plant, equipment, engineering and manufacturing skills, people, teamwork, and management tal-

This note was prepared by Artemis March under the direction of David A. Garvin.

Copyright © 1985 by the President and Fellows of Harvard College. Harvard Business School case 686-087.

EXHIBIT 1 U.S. Aircraft Primes (Excluding General Aviation)

1942	1952	1984
Boeing Consolidated Curtiss-Wright Douglas Fairchild Goodyear Grumman Lockheed Martin McDonnell North American Northrop Republic Ryan Vought-Sikorsky Vultee	Boeing Chance Vought Convair Douglas Fairchild Grumman Lockheed McDonnell North American Northrop Republic	Boeing Fairchild General Dynamics Grumman Lockheed McDonnell Douglas Northrop Rockwell
⑯	⑪	⑧

ent—quickly enough, or keep them occupied through the "bridge" to the next contract—if, indeed, another major program followed. The risk of cancellation, or, more likely, of programs being stretched out, also made such build-ups precarious. Finally, the Department of Defense (DoD) and Congress wanted technology shared among companies so that a rapid build-up would be easier in a prolonged crisis or war. Congress also wanted as many states as possible to receive defense contracts.

The world inhabited by primes was very different from the world of subcontractors. Most of a prime's R&D and working capital, all of its production costs, and some of its capital costs were paid by the federal government. For example, many primes leased parts of their plants from the government, thereby reducing their capital requirements. Subcontractors, by contrast, funded their own plants, equipment, and working capital, and ordinarily had to run close to 90% capacity utilization simply to survive. And although some retained design skills, most had only limited engineering support and simply built according to the specifications primes gave them. A few held monopolies on components and charged accordingly; the majority, however, competed on cost in what many observers described as a dog-eat-dog world.

COMPETITION AMONG PRIMES. Military performance, requirements, rather than price sensitivity, had historically driven defense procurement. Competition therefore centered on design, and on which proposals best met the mass of specifications established by the military. Cost, producibility, and manufacturing capabilities were not given major consideration in awarding engineering and development contracts. Once a prime won the contract for full-scale development of its design, it was virtually assured a follow-on production contract. Thus the route to all contracts, whether engineering or production, came through design.

The only significant exception occurred when DoD chose a second production source. This was an increasingly popular practice, for second-sourcing freed the government from the constraints of a single contractor. It also transferred technology among first-tier firms. Though second-sourcing was favored by the government for strategic reasons, primes did not like to share their technical knowledge with direct competitors or give their engineering away. The benefits of second-sourcing also had to be traded off against the higher costs of tooling two producers, neither of which would get as far down the learning curve as a single manufacturer.

Although industry critics complained about

the lack of competition among aerospace primes, design competition was fierce before development contracts were awarded. In fact, it had grown more intense as the number of new program starts dwindled in the 1970s and 1980s—a decline expected to continue in the 1990s. Failure to win a major contract could devastate a prime, as thousands of skilled employees were laid off and migrated to the winner. Eventually, continued failure to win new program starts might force a company out of the first tier of prime contractors.

PHASES OF WEAPONS SYSTEMS DEVELOPMENT. The intensity of competition varied with the phases that all programs followed. Initially, many primes competed for research contracts to explore new weapons concepts; most, however, were winnowed out during the subsequent development process. (See *Exhibit 2*.) Concept research asked, Will this idea work in principle? Should it be developed further? Engineering contracts were then awarded to between two and five companies to demonstrate the feasibility of their ideas. Usually only one prime received a contract for the third and critical phase of full-scale engineering development (FSED), especially if development costs were high or production lots fairly small. FSED involved the development of detailed specifications, limited production of prototypes, and testing. For example, in response to DoD specifications for weight, range, and payload, contractors would develop detailed plans for wing structures, incorporating trade-offs among range, speed, and weight. These first three phases of systems development now averaged about eight years, and were gradually getting longer. Preproduction costs totaled hundreds of millions, and sometimes billions of dollars.

Once prototype testing had established that a weapons system performed as required, a production contract for the first lot of planes was awarded. The winner of the FSED competition was virtually assured of this production contract. Typically, early lot sizes were small, and involved further production and testing. The winner of the FSED competition then received a full-scale production contract; it might subsequently remain the sole source for the life of the program, or else share production with a second contractor. In the final stage of development, deployment, DoD was especially likely to develop second sources to repair, maintain, upgrade, and provide spare parts for weapons systems.

Defense Procurement

Just as the degree of competition varied over the life cycle of programs, so the balance of power between primes and DoD shifted over the 10-12 years from concept to full production. No other industry depended as heavily on government contracts as aerospace. But once the military awarded a sole-source contract, it was locked in. The dependency ran both ways, however. The Department of Defense was not only the industry's primary customer, specifier, regulator, auditor, and banker, it also relied heavily on major contractors for research, testing, and evaluation of new weapons concepts and systems.

Although this interdependence had increased in recent years, military procurement practices had always shaped the industry. During the 1930s, for example, the military began favoring firms with large financial backing when awarding contracts. This had the predictable effect of allowing "preferred suppliers" to survive while others went bankrupt. The preferred suppliers soon clustered around either the Army or the Navy, from which they repeatedly received contracts and for whose needs they developed special expertise. For example, the Army Air Corps' preference for long-range strategic bombing fostered an association with firms that built long-range transports, such as Boeing and Consolidated, whereas the Navy, which wanted carrier-based fighters, turned to Curtiss, Grumman, and Chance Vought. Such contracts gave an edge to those companies that chose to apply their design and production expertise to the emerging commercial markets; in this way, Boeing, Douglas, and Lockheed come to dominate commercial aviation.

Military procurement patterns have had an equally powerful impact in recent years. During the 1970s and '80s, there have been fewer new program starts, but each new program has been increasingly complex and sophisticated. This has lengthened development cycles and imposed greater demands for coordinating and integrating subsystems. As a result, fewer companies have been

EXHIBIT 2 Major Weapon Systems Acquisition Process

	Concept Exploration	Advanced Development	Full-Scale Engineering Development	Production	Deployment
Technical & Cost Uncertainty	Very Large	Very Large	Large/Medium	Medium/Small	Small
Contract Type	None	Cost Plus	Cost Plus Fixed Fee Cost Plus Incentive Fee Fixed Price Incentive Fee	Fixed Price Incentive Fee Firm Fixed Price	Firm Fixed Price
Time	Continuing	1–2 Years	2–5 Years	3–15 Years	Up to 25 Years
Relative Cost	Small	Small	Medium	Large	Large
Number of Competitors	Many	2–5	1–2	1	1+
Competition	Yes	Yes	Maybe	Sometimes	Yes

Source: Defense Financial and Investment Review, DoD, June 1983.

able to sustain the full array of state-of-the-art engineering disciplines required to design and integrate systems, leading to the decrease in the number of primes discussed earlier.

THE ACQUISITION PROCESS. Weapons systems procurement was a complex process occupying thousands of people at each prime, and thousands more at the Department of Defense. Officially, contractors bid on Request for Proposals (RFPs) issued by agencies such as DoD and NASA; the company whose designs best met performance requirements at a competitive cost was then awarded the contract. In practice, any contractor that waited to become involved until an RFP was issued stood virtually no chance of winning a contract. Firms therefore sought to participate in defining the program's mission, and in writing the RFP that outlined required specifications.

Detailed specifications and agency oversight were substitutes for the discipline of the marketplace. But, as DoD pursued its oversight role, it became more and more involved with "micromanagement"—telling contractors how to do their work, rather than simply demanding that they meet specifications. At a typical prime, this led to tens of thousands of visiting days annually, by representatives of up to 12 federal agencies, plus staggering amounts of paperwork. The Tomahawk

missile, for example, was accompanied by over 300,000 drawings and 4 million pages of documentation. And the F-16 fighter, which weighed 32,000 pounds when fueled, was supported by documentation weighing nearly five times as much—approximately 150,000 pounds. Efforts to streamline this process (which some contractors called "oversight overkill") had met with only limited success.

TYPES OF CONTRACTS AND THEIR EFFECTS. Most aerospace contracts were of two basic types: cost-plus[1] or fixed-price. On *cost-plus* contracts, the government paid the actual costs plus either a fixed fee (CPFF) or an incentive fee (CPIF); in both cases the fee (or profit) was based on a percentage of the original target costs. If, for example, a $12 million markup had been negotiated on a target cost of $180 million but actual allowable costs ran $235 million, the contractor would be reimbursed for the full $235 million, and would still collect $12 million in profit. Incentive fees played a minor role: they were characterized by industry observers as small in relation to the size of contracts, easy to manipulate, and of little significance.

[1]DoD referred to these as "cost-type" contracts, but virtually everyone else used "cost-plus" when speaking of them.

On *fixed-price* contracts,[2] a contractor agreed in advance to complete all work for a certain price that included the markup. Such contracts were normally used for routine production, when technology and design were already demonstrated, performance requirements were well-established, and costs could be reasonably estimated. On firm fixed-price (FFP) contracts, the government paid only the prenegotiated price, whereas on fixed-price-incentive (FPI) contracts, an additional small incentive could be earned. In both types of contracts, the markup was based primarily on costs, with risk and difficulty factored in. For example, if a $100 million FFP contract included a $10 million fee and actual costs ran $95 million, the contractor—at least in theory—absorbed the higher costs. In practice, however, the "fixed" price was normally renegotiated several times to accommodate a constant stream of design changes. Cost overruns were often buried in this stream of engineering and product changes. By contrast, if actual costs ran $80 million, the contractor would, in effect, make an immediate $20 million profit—$10 million more than anticipated. Underruns, however, were immediately negotiated away in the following year's contract; the contractor's cost base was lowered, and yielded a smaller profit when multiplied by the same markup factor. In this example, the second year's price (for the same number of planes) would drop to $90 million, and the 10% markup would produce only $9 million profit.

For both cost-plus and fixed-price contracts, then, profits were based on costs. Industry observers agreed unanimously that such contracts gave companies little or no incentive to control costs. Such distortions were most visible in cost-plus contracts. Obviously, a contractor had little, if any, incentive to control costs if all would be reimbursed. But, even though fixed-price contracts appeared to shift more risk to contractors, their ability to bury overruns in design changes also worked against effective cost control. Nego-

tiating away cost savings further reduced incentives to cut costs.

IMPACT OF GOVERNMENT PROCUREMENT POLICIES ON MODERNIZATION. For similar reasons, other procurement policies had an enormous impact on contractors' willingness to make capital investments (reinvestment rates were quite low, except for firms involved in commercial as well as military aviation. See *Exhibit 3*). Four factors were chiefly responsible.

1. *Cost-based markups.* Since lower costs resulted in lower profits, modern plants and equipment that decreased manufacturing costs could actually lower the contractor's profits. Contractor interest in productivity-improving investments was also diminished by the DoD practice of taking away the savings generated by cost underruns. Together, these practices had the effect of limiting the return on investment in a very risky industry.

2. *Plant and equipment leasing.* Because of massive plant shutdowns following World War I, contractors were reluctant to make huge plant investments during World War II. To remedy the problem, DoD began leasing plants and equipment to contractors, a policy that has continued to the present. Both plants and equipment, however, had become inefficient and out-of-date. Nevertheless, their mere existence, coupled with severe industry overcapacity, discouraged major new investments. When contractors did improve their leased facilities, improvements such as new foundations, floors, or wiring then belonged to the government.

3. *Industry and funding volatility.* The instability of the aerospace business also worked against large investments. Both Congress and DoD could cancel or stretch out contracts at any time. Even without stretch-outs, the practice of year-to-year funding created much uncertainty about how many planes would actually be built, at what price, and, more recently, who would build them. In this environment, contractors found long-range planning difficult. They were leery of committing large sums of money to production equipment whose amor-

---

[2]Fixed-price contracts were routinely renegotiated each year, for Congress funded most programs a year at a time. This meant that it contracted to buy only a certain lot of planes each year; the number often differed from earlier projections. The cost implications of such instability had drawn sharp criticism in recent years and prompted more multiyear funding.

tization might exceed the length of the program.

4. *Accounting practices.* Some of the accounting practices required by DoD discouraged investment or induced other biases in behavior. For example, the use of progress payments for partially completed work aimed to provide contractors with much-needed working capital; yet it also encouraged high levels of work-in-progress inventories, for there was little incentive to minimize WIP carrying costs. Similarly, the use of overhead rates that allocated overhead to direct labor discouraged investments, such as computer-based manufacturing equipment, that reduced the denominator used to calculate these rates, even though manufacturing efficiency would increase as a result.

New Modernization Incentives

During the past ten years, DoD had taken several steps to encourage greater capital investment by contractors. First, it had modified its method of calculating profits to include facilities capital as well as equipment. Second, it had begun various initiatives, such as multiyear funding, to provide greater program stability. Third, it had initiated manufacturing technology programs aimed at developing new technologies for the factory floor. These included Manufacturing Technology (ManTech), Technology Modernization (TechMod), and the Industrial Modernization Incentive Program (IMIP). All three focused on designing and developing process technologies; in this respect, they differed from prior development contracts, which had always been geared to products. The programs were similar in approach in that they all provided seed money or other financial incentives to bring investment risks within acceptable limits.

MANTECH. The ManTech program supported laboratory development of generic process technologies. Contracts were awarded to promising proposals for advancing manufacturing technologies. Projects were selected by government laboratories; they had included nondestructive inspection techniques; methods for improving production of electronic components and advanced materials; and the development of other, often highly specific fabrication and assembly methods.

By demonstrating the workability of these new technologies, ManTech hoped to encourage the private sector to apply them and expand their use. It also aimed to increase technology transfer by building a network of technical experts. And as a focal point for technology development, it hoped to reduce duplication of effort while supporting projects that were beyond the reach of a single company.

TECHMOD. The TechMod program was developed by the Air Force to support the application of new or existing technologies on the factory floor. Contracts were awarded for the design, development, and implementation of technologies—in short, for transferring technologies from the laboratory to the shop floor. The program did not, however, pay for capital investments. Most efforts had focused on the integration of computer-aided design and manufacturing (CAD/CAM).

IMIP. In 1982, the Department of Defense expanded TechMod into a departmentwide effort, renaming it the Industrial Modernization Incentive Program. Its objective was to stimulate additional capital investment and productivity improvement by defense contractors, thereby reducing DoD acquisition costs. IMIP incentives were not to be used for investments that contractors needed to make to meet base-line program targets or to remain competitive. Rather, they were intended for investments that contractors would not otherwise make, usually because they would not provide an acceptable return on investment (ROI) or because program instability created large risks. Most IMIP investments were aimed at reducing program costs or making companies more responsive to defense needs.

The two most significant IMIP incentives were productivity savings rewards (PSRs) and contractor investment protection (or indemnification). Without IMIP, a contractor that lowered its production costs through capital investments profited only in the year in which the investment was made. In future years, the company's lower costs would be reflected in lower prices, renegotiated by DoD. This discouraged investment in projects whose payback exceeded one year. But with IMIP, the savings were shared by the government and the contractor. Productivity savings were calculated as the difference between what

EXHIBIT 3 Aerospace Capital Spending as Percentage of Sales, 1973–83 ($ in millions)

		1973	1974	1975	1976	1977	1978	1979	1980	1981	1982	1983
Boeing	-Sales	3,335	3,731	3,719	3,919	4,019	5,463	8,131	9,426	9,788	9,035	11,308
	-Cap. Exp.	33	84	71	67	99	269	569	668	545	331	200
	-Percent	0.99	2.25	1.90	1.71	2.47	4.92	7.00	7.09	5.57	3.66	2.00
Fairchild	-Sales	237	252	219	264	399	544	702	906	1,339	1,093	892
	-Cap. Exp.	2	15	11	11	14	21	18	24	29	30	23
	-Percent	0.84	6.10	4.99	4.21	3.58	3.82	2.56	2.63	2.19	2.74	2.55
General Dynamics	-Sales	1,642	1,626	1,861	2,222	2,598	2,892	3,642	4,383	4,759	6,155	7,146
	-Cap. Exp.	54	89	157	130	77	135	194	197	139	134	215
	-Percent	3.26	5.47	8.44	5.85	2.96	4.67	5.33	4.49	2.92	2.18	3.01
Grumman	-Sales	1,083	1,053	1,243	1,393	1,410	1,386	1,373	1,559	1,788	2,057	2,255
	-Cap. Exp.	10	18	23	21	24	29	26	34	50	53	88
	-Percent	0.88	1.67	1.83	1.52	1.71	2.12	1.89	2.20	2.78	2.56	3.91
Lockheed	-Sales	2,757	3,279	3,387	3,203	2,999	3,191	3,531	4,445	5,176	5,613	6,490
	-Cap. Exp.	62	23	39	33	51	54	136	155	209	220	258
	-Percent	2.26	0.70	1.16	1.03	1.71	1.68	3.85	3.49	4.04	3.92	3.98
McDonnell Douglas	-Sales	3,003	3,075	3,256	3,544	3,545	4,130	5,279	6,066	7,385	7,331	8,111
	-Cap. Exp.	33	35	33	41	55	142	157	266	234	262	352
	-Percent	1.10	1.14	1.02	1.14	1.55	3.44	2.97	4.38	3.17	3.57	4.33
Martin Marietta	-Sales	1,140	1,221	1,053	1,213	1,440	1,758	2,061	2,619	3,294	3,527	3,899
	-Cap. Exp.	71	NA	NA	72	87	156	231	353	489	391	212
	-Percent	6.21	NA	NA	5.97	6.06	8.89	11.21	13.48	14.84	11.09	5.44
Northrop	-Sales	699	853	988	1,265	1,601	1,832	1,583	1,655	1,991	2,473	3,261
	-Cap. Exp.	13	32	25	26	24	97	70	121	190	377	293
	-Percent	1.82	3.75	2.54	2.05	1.47	5.27	4.45	7.32	9.53	15.24	8.99
Raytheon	-Sales	1,590	2,185	2,529	2,826	3,263	3,787	4,354	5,002	5,636	5,513	5,937
	-Cap. Exp.	41	76	100	91	129	180	248	289	297	303	305
	-Percent	2.58	3.46	3.95	3.23	3.95	4.75	5.70	5.79	5.27	5.50	5.14
Rockwell	-Sales	3,179	3,998	4,301	4,691	5,391	5,309	6,176	6,907	7,040	7,395	8,098
	-Cap. Exp	122	217	169	144	196	219	276	281	317	539	479
	-Percent	3.83	5.44	3.94	3.06	3.63	4.12	4.47	4.07	4.50	7.29	5.92
LTV Aerospace and Defense	-Sales	535	489	540	465	426	491	555	652	797	777	1,142
	-Cap. Exp.	15	11	11	11	8	5	12	12	34	14	17
	-Percent	2.86	2.15	2.02	2.39	1.81	1.08	2.16	1.89	4.29	1.85	1.48

Source: Annual Reports.

the government would have paid had the contractor used its existing equipment, and what it would pay with the new, more efficient equipment. A new price was negotiated in advance; it was designed to give the contractor a sufficient ROI, usually 18-25%, to justify the investment. The contractor then paid for the capital investment from its own funds. It later received payments from DoD as it generated productivity savings until the prenegotiated ROI was reached. After that, DoD received all additional savings.

Under IMIP, the government could also indemnify a program to cover possible cancellation. It did so by agreeing to acquire the relevant capital equipment (at its unamortized value) if a planned weapons system was not purchased. This provision was designed to combat the disincentives caused by program instability. It was not often used, however, because Congressional approval was required in every case.

IMIP projects were usually conducted in three phases. Phase I consisted of a structured analysis of the existing manufacturing operation, development of IMIP projects, and a plan for their integration. In Phase II, these ideas were further refined and validated and implementation plans were developed. Phase III was implementation. Together, these steps encouraged a systems engineering approach to IMIP projects.

Despite their appeal, these technology initiatives were not without risk. Should projected cost savings fail to materialize, a contractor would be locked into a new and lower fixed-price contract. It would then have to absorb the higher costs. This made it important to gauge the savings correctly, and to get new equipment and systems in place precisely on schedule.

*   *   *   *

Conversations with the following people aided the development of this note: Carolyn Castore, of the National Research Council's Manufacturing Studies Board; Wolfgang Demisch, of First Boston Corporation; Richard Stimson, Director of the Industrial Productivity Office in the Office of the Undersecretary of Defense (Research and Engineering).

Sources consulted include:

1. Adams, Gordon, *The Iron Triangle: The Politics of Defense Contracting* (New York: Council on Economic Priorities, 1981).
2. Bluestone, Barry; Jordan, Peter; Sullivan, Mark; *Aircraft Industry Dynamics* (Boston: Auburn House Publishing Co., 1981).
3. *Defense Financial and Investment Review.* Department of Defense. June 1985.
4. Department of Defense, "Federal Acquisition Regulation Supplement: Industrial Modernization Incentives Program (IMIP)," *Federal Register,* 28 May 1986.
5. Department of the Navy, "Navy Manufacturing Technology Program."
6. Gansler, Jacques. *The Defense Industry* (Cambridge, MA: MIT Press, 1980).
7. *Industrial Modernization Incentives Program (IMIP).* Formal Coordination Draft, DoD Guide 5000.XX-G, August 1985.
8. John Kerr, "Military Electronics; the Heat is on." *Electronic Business,* January 15, 1986.
9. Kucera, Randolph. *The Aerospace Industry and the Military: Structural and Political Relationships.*
10. Joyce Kufel and Lloyd Lehn, "Manufacturing Technology Program," Office of Deputy Assistant Secretary of Defense (Production Support), September 30, 1985.
11. "Making Arms Makers do it Right," *New York Times,* June 15, 1986.
12. Rowland Moriarty and Benson Shapiro, "The Airframe Industry," Harvard Business School case #9-579-057.
13. Richard Stimson and A. Douglas Reeves, "Tri-Service DoD Program Provides Incentives for Factory Modernization," *Industrial Engineering,* vol. 16, no. 2, February 1984.

23. Vought Aero Products: Factory of the Future

In April 1986, Frederick (Fred) Cooper, vice president of Manufacturing Development and Support at the Vought Aero Products Division (VAPD) of LTV Aerospace & Defense, recommended that the division approve investment for its proposed Flexible Composites Center (FCC). (See *Exhibit 1*.) In doing so, he accepted most of the recommendations of IMOD (Industrial Modernization), the group that had worked on the design and development of the FCC for the past two years. The FCC would give Vought the ability to make complex, contoured composites in a computer-controlled environment. Total costs, expected to run around $150 million, included a new plant.

Cooper also needed to make recommendations to senior management on another IMOD proposal: an Integrated Machining System (IMS) that would allow Vought to machine large titanium parts at extremely high metal removal rates. He viewed the FCC, the IMS, and other modernization proposals as the means toward an end: ". . . a cohesive manufacturing capability that will allow us to make aerostructures of unique complexity." Choosing among such projects was part of the newly created position that Cooper had occupied for seven months. His boss, Paul Lofton, senior vice president of operations, described the job succinctly: "Fred's primary responsibility is to manage our future competitive position."

Cooper had more reservations about the IMS than the FCC. While increased titanium machining capability was essential for producing the next generation of aerostructures, an IMS was not required. The use of subcontractors, the modification of existing equipment, and the purchase of stand-alone machining centers were all alternatives. Any decision, however, had to be evaluated against Vought's long-term goal of computer-integrated manufacturing (CIM). Lofton observed:

> These projects are a way to get to CIM. We can't get there all at once. IMOD designs the projects, and we have to ask: "Does it fit the scheme? And, if so, is it affordable? Where do we get the most bang for the buck?"

Vought's Changing Situation

The aerospace division had built military airplanes since World War I, primarily for the Navy. In the 1960s it was bought by the conglomerate now known as LTV (formerly Ling-Temco-Vought). The division's fortunes changed sharply in the late 1970s after production on its bread-and-butter contract—the A-7 fighter (known within the division as the "iron lung")—had peaked, and it did not receive any new large contracts. Most engineers and managers thought Vought was a "lead pipe cinch" to win the Navy version of the Air Force's F-16; they were deeply shocked when it did not. Vought thus became the only prime (major aerospace contractor) without a new program start.[1]

This case was prepared by Artemis March under the direction of David A. Garvin.

[1] "Vought," "VAPD," and "the division" are used interchangeably throughout the case.

EXHIBIT 1 Organization Chart

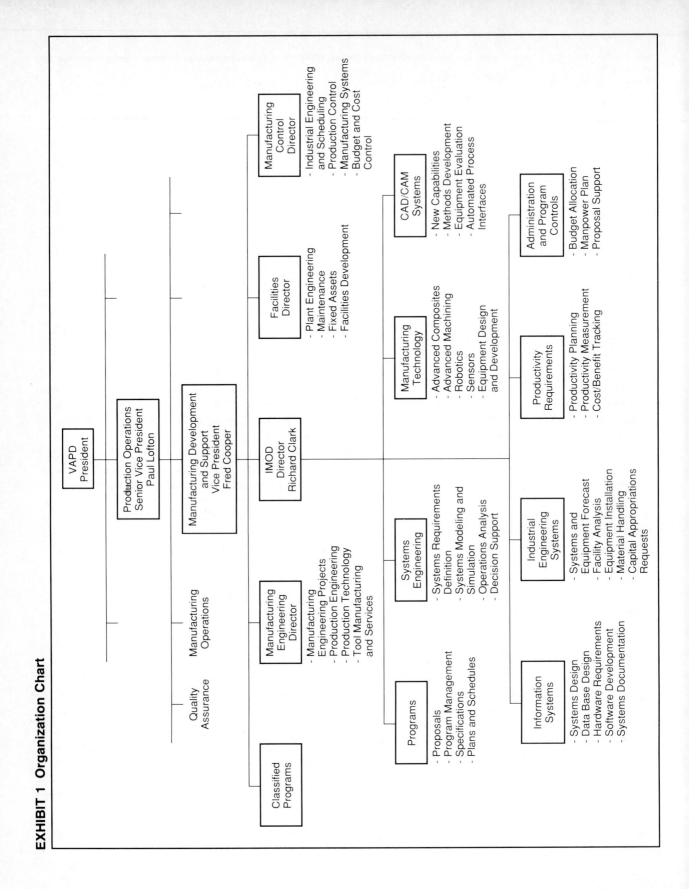

23. Vought Aero Products: Factory of the Future

Vought next tried an unfriendly takeover of Grumman, its chief competitor in Navy fighters. Failing this, the company turned to more commercial aerospace work. For over a decade, VAPD had produced commercial aerostructures for other primes, building a track record of on-time delivery within cost. Key products included complete tail sections and horizontal stabilizers for Boeing 747s.

Near-Prime Strategy

These setbacks led to intense discussions about the division's future direction. In the early 1980s, senior management developed the idea of a "near-prime" strategy. As a near-prime, Vought would no longer compete directly with primes for contracts to design, build, and integrate entire weapons systems. Instead, it would market itself to primes, seeking subcontracts to build substantial portions of airplanes. It would also provide the detailed design work on airplane sections that had already been broadly designed by primes. As a near-prime, VAPD would no longer support the 50 or more state-of-the-art engineering capabilities needed to design an overall weapons system, nor have to integrate all the hydraulics, guidance systems, radar detection, and other systems with the aerostructures to form a single unit. But in comparison with build-to-print subcontractors who competed on cost alone, Vought would have vastly greater engineering design, test, and support capabilities, as well as far greater fabrication capabilities. Managers summarized the differences between being a prime, a near-prime, and a subcontractor with an automotive analogy:

prime	system	automobile
near-prime	subsystem	engine
subcontractor	component	piston

The decision to stop competing as a prime was not received enthusiastically by employees. The heaviest resistance came from the engineers. Some of them transferred to the missile division; others—mostly "airplane people"—left the company. But because a big contract was lacking, senior managers saw no alternative.

Vought could, however, market its ability to build high-quality aerostructures cost effectively and on time. As Richard Clark, IMOD's second director, pointed out:

The primes are on pins and needles until their subcontractors' parts come in. We can give them reassurance because they know we're able to manage a big chunk of their planes and that we have very sophisticated project management systems. And they know our track record on both military and commercial programs.

Senior managers were confident that the primes would be interested in buying this package. Political pressure to share defense work among as many states as possible was increasing, and the Department of Defense (DoD) wanted to disperse technology because this would expand the industrial base for military production. And while primes would seldom share technology with direct competitors, Vought no longer fell into that category so it became a more acceptable partner. The increased scope and complexity of programs also created strong pressures for greater subcontracting; the alternative would have been the periodic building and dismantling of huge organizations, and a return of the wild, volative swings in employment that had marked the industry for decades.[2]

Although Vought initially possessed few unique skills, primes could not develop depth in all areas. They had to focus on winning huge contracts and integrating production programs. Vought therefore believed that many of them would rather buy selected expertise than duplicate the investment in time, people, and equipment.

Building a Competitive Edge

While Vought would no longer compete as a prime, it did not want to build conventional sheet metal airplanes either. To carve out a distinctive competitive edge, senior managers held a series of planning meetings between 1982 and 1984. Lofton recalled:

We consciously took a positive approach and asked, "What do we need?" We couldn't be all things, so we concentrated on what we thought

[2] See the "Note on Aerospace Industry Modernization" (HBS #9-687-009) that accompanies this case for a discussion of industry structure, primes and subcontractors, competition among primes, the military procurement process, factors that retard modernization, types of contracts, and new DoD incentives such as ManTech, TechMod, and IMIP.

it would take to build the big sections of advanced aircraft that we wanted to make. If you start with planes that fly very high, very fast, and in very high temperature environments, you require advanced materials, new structural geometries, and the manufacturing equipment and skills to make them. These were all extensions of what we were already good at.

Vought identified its core skill as the design and building of aerostructures. It had developed manufacturing innovations such as semiautomated systems for fastening together metal fuselage skins and substructures; because a fuselage required hundreds of thousands of fasteners, the system's sevenfold cost savings were significant. Vought also had considerable expertise in the development and fabrication of advanced materials. It had developed carbon carbon, a material used on the leading edge of shuttle wings to withstand extreme reentry temperatures. Vought was also a leader in vibroacoustics, creating structures which did not suffer fatigue under the noise blasts of powerful new jet engines; and for over 20 years it had worked with advanced composites, such as epoxy resins impregnated with graphite fibers and other materials. It had developed software for laying down composite tape in complex contours; when used with Vought's single, semiautomated tape layer, the tape could be laid at very high speeds with a tenfold productivity gain over more labor-intensive methods. (See *Exhibit 2*.)

In order to become a desirable partner in advanced weapons systems production, Vought felt it had to deepen its skills in selected technological niches. According to Jack Flaherty, vice president of engineering:

EXHIBIT 2 Vought's Automated Tape Laying Machine

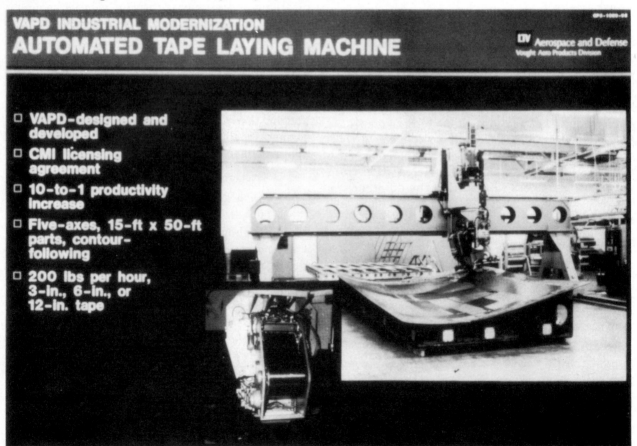

Reprinted with permission of company.

When it became obvious we were going to be a subcontractor, we had to do two things. We had to develop leadership in technological niches so that primes would not only want us on their teams, but would give us entry even before there was a request for bids. Second, we had to become very competitive in cost and quality because the lowest bid would win. That meant we had to improve our productivity faster than the industry. We were going to have to learn how to work differently, not harder.

Or, as Clark summarized the strategy, "Technology gets you in the door, but cost sells your product."

Modernization

Although top management considered manufacturing to be one of Vought's strengths, for decades the company had done little to modernize its technological and manufacturing base. The average age of equipment was over 30 years, and capital investment was below the industry average. But, during the early 1980s, five key events began to move Vought toward modernization: the Factory of the Future (FoF) study, the hiring of Pete Gresh, the Flexible Machining Center (FMC) project, the B-1B bomber contract, and the Industrial Modernization Incentive Program (IMIP).

FOF CONTRACT. Between 1979 and 1981, Vought actively sought and won an Air Force study contract to head a consortium of 28 companies, universities, and consultants in the development of a conceptual framework for the factory of the future. Although the Air Force had previously funded several projects to identify and apply new manufacturing technologies, these projects had not broken through conventional thinking. The FoF project was intended to do just that. It looked not just at the shop floor but at everything that was needed to produce an aerospace product, and then created a framework to integrate these activities. Vought personnel later drew on this framework and their experience with the project to guide the division's modernization activities.

HIRING OF GRESH. Around the same time, discussions between Jack Flaherty and Dan Clayton, then senior vice president of operations (and later

president of the division), led to the formation of a group to develop computer-aided manufacturing (CAM). In August 1980, Pete Gresh was hired to head the group, reporting directly to Clayton. The new group's charter was to consolidate and coordinate computer-aided design (CAD) and computer-aided manufacturing devices throughout Vought. Initially, however, it had no real authority. But with Clayton's approval Gresh soon gained control of the CAD/CAM budget. Gresh (variously described by Vought managers as "brilliant," "creative," "aggressive," and "flamboyant") started meeting with forward-looking people, trying, as Lofton put it, "to wrap his arms around all the systems and computer requirements needed to tie modernization efforts together."

EMERGENCE OF THE FMC. In fact several modernization projects were already under discussion. David Lyons, then superintendent of the machine shop, recalled:

> I had been thinking about modernization for years because of the lack of craftsmen. Others were thinking about ways to expand CAM or to improve energy management. Steve Booth in manufacturing engineering had been dreaming about a flexible machining cell for ages. A lot of the FMC ideas came from him. Then along comes Pete who could sell it to the tower [LTV's corporate headquarters in Dallas]. He agreed to do a study in January [1982].

B-1B CONTRACT. In the same month Vought won its first major military subcontract: an award from Rockwell International for two fuselage sections of 100 B-1B bombers. The companies negotiated a fixed-price contract for the first lot of two planes, and Vought submitted a proposal for the second lot of six. The B-1B contract sharply accelerated Vought's need for additional machining capacity and gave a strong boost to the FMC.

IMIP. At about the same time, DoD began to develop the Industrial Modernization Incentive Program (IMIP) to encourage contractors to modernize. Through IMIP, DoD agreed to share with contractors the cost savings gained from certain capital investments; a company would now share in the savings from production improvements for several years, rather than seeing them disappear

EXHIBIT 3 Flexible Machining Cell (FMC)

B-1B Program Need:

The B-1B business contract would require Vought to perform 900,000 machine hours more than it could perform in-house on existing equipment. These 900,000 hours would be applied to the last 92 shipsets (completed fuselage sections)—or lots 3, 4, and 5. The baseline cost for this work was the cost if all 900,000 hours were subcontracted.

Voght asked: How much of this work can we bring back in-house, and at what cost?

Existing Equipment Base:

Current "conventional" capacity included some stand-alone NC equipment. Average utilization was 45%—due to breakdowns, improper use, tool changes, etc. Typically, an aluminum blank crossed four machines in the process of being turned into a part.

Alternative #1: Buy additional conventional equipment (manufacturing's proposal)

202,000 machine hours could be brought in-house through purchasing 24 conventional machine tools and using them on 3 shifts. This option would employ 81 people to make the same number of parts as an FMC.

Alternative #2: Flexible Machining Cell (IMOD's proposal)

An FMC was estimated to give a 3:1 productivity gain in machine hours over conventional machining; therefore, only 70,000 hours of machining time would be needed. This amount of work could be done by 8 machining centers.

An FMC could make 541 parts for the B-1B, employ 19 people, be used on 3 shifts, 6 days a week. Estimated utilization was 85%, with the remaining 15% reserved for preventive maintenance, software enhancement, and setups.

Estimated ROI for the FMC was approximately twice that of conventional equipment.

The estimated saving in nonrecurring expenses on lots 4 and 5 (i.e., the last 82 shipsets) was $21 million. (There was no way an FMC could be installed and made operational while Vought was cutting parts for the 10 planes in lot 3.) The $21 million was subtracted from the baseline cost to become the new fixed price at which Vought agreed to deliver the last 82 shipsets. Vought and the Air Force agreed to split the savings equally and the Air Force began making payments as soon as the new contract was signed.

FMC Configuration:

The cell consisted of 8 machining centers, 4 robocarriers, 1 wash station, 2 coordinate measuring machines (for quality control), and 1 chip removal and flume system. The FMC schedule was downloaded from the main computer and told operators what cutters and materials were needed. They manually changed cutters, and put the aluminum or steel blanks on fixtures, the fixtures on risers, and the risers on pallets that went on the robocarriers, guided by wires in the floor. The rest of the operation was automated until the finished part was unloaded. One machining center performed all operations necessary to complete the part; some parts had to be refixtured (to machine the back as well as front), bringing the average number of passes per part to 2.3.

IMOD selected a 4-axis machine with a work envelope of 32″ × 36″ × 32″ to make prismatic parts. The spindle of a 4-axis machine moved in the x, y, and z axes, and the workpiece rotated around a vertical axis through 360 degrees. The work envelope was the size of the cube in which parts could be made. Prismatic parts were held in a fixed position while the spindle and cutters moved, turning a rectangular blank into a finished part. The machine choice was made after analysis showed that a larger work envelope and/or a 5-axis machine (which added rotation of the spindle head) would make only a few more B-1 parts.

FMC Operator:

The key objective of cell operation was to maximize spindle utilization—the percentage of time the spindle was actually cutting metal. The design of the cell supported this objective in many ways, such as parallel loading, 2-part fixtures, 4-face risers, rotating tables, and other features which minimized setup and maximized cutting time.

Initially, it was estimated that 541 parts would fully load the cell. In fact, more parts had to be added to keep the spindles utilized. By the spring of 1986, the FMC was producing 568 parts for the B-1, and was three months ahead of schedule on these parts.

The FMC was run as a cost center separate from the rest of manufacturing; everything affecting the FMC was collected separately in order to establish costs.

FMC Results:

After 10 months of operation, utilization had reached 85% and remained there. Productivity increased 3:1 as anticipated. The FMC operated 24 hours a day, 6 days a week.

A key measurement used by Vought was realization: the ratio of cutting time to auxiliary or support time. For example, if it took 1 hour to load, unload, travel, wash, and inspect, and it also took 1 hour of tape time (the length of time the program ran and the machine tool worked), realization would be 100%. If 1 hour of cutting time required 40 minutes of support work, realization was 150%.

The FMC had achieved 150% realization rates (and higher) by spring 1986; the rest of manufacturing ran at around 45% realization.

into lower prices the year after the investment was made.

Twin Births: IMOD and the FMC

These five factors provided an economic rationale for the FMC. (See *Exhibit 3*.) It won out over other modernization projects and also over the alternative of conventional machine tools plus subcontracting. George Starr, who would later head the Integrated Machining System project, described the process:

> The FMC bubbled to the surface once we found it had the highest yield of the projects we were looking at. Companies who had tried machining cells had had only limited success, but there were enough examples for us to think we could make it work. The FMC was also saleable to Rockwell and the Air Force, and it gave validity to the expansion of CAD/CAM. CAD/CAM was searching for a vehicle; the FMC was that vehicle. But it meant we needed a new organization because the CAD/CAM group was too limited to undertake a project of this magnitude.

In addition, the project could not be implemented by the existing line organization. Under existing arrangements, the FMC computers would belong to the computer department, its robocarriers to materials handling, the machining centers to the machine shop, and the measuring machines to quality control. To meet the need for integration, IMOD was created with Pete Gresh as its first director.

IMOD had a broad charter. Its role, according to Clark, was "to look across functions at our total operations requirements for tomorrow's business, rather than at stand-alone department needs." The driving force was to improve productivity. Several key groups were necessary for an integrated systems approach: systems engineering to design and develop systems; information systems to develop software; industrial engineering to design and specify equipment and facilities; and program management to coordinate and run the projects. (Later, IMOD would also incorporate the development-oriented part of manufacturing technology to insure that design requirements, which sometimes included new processes, were met.)

IMOD became a reality in July 1982 when Gresh began pulling the development people and their projects from other functions. Most existing groups strongly resisted the change, although Gresh agreed that the engineers would continue to work on their previous projects. But as the FMC began to require more and more people, he removed engineers from these earlier projects, assigning them where needed. Clark, who succeeded Gresh in 1985 when he left to head a $1.5 billion modernization effort at a prime, commented:

> IMOD would not have lasted long if it had just continued with the projects we pulled. Pete had to make something happen. He had to prove the concepts would work, and the FMC was his showpiece. He even used the IMOD logo—not LTV's—on everything he sent out, and that offended public relations. But he created credibility with professional groups and customers and leveraged that internally.

IMOD reported to Flaherty, who added various operations development responsibilities, such as manufacturing engineering and facilities, to his engineering responsibilities. Flaherty had moved back and forth between manufacturing and engineering for years and was considered "the right person" to oversee IMOD even though his engineering base was "the wrong function." As one manager pointed out: "It's very hard to implement anything from the engineering side of the house." Flaherty agreed: "IMOD did not belong with me; I said, 'When we find the right guy for IMOD to report to, we will put it back in manufacturing because that's where it belongs.' "

The Flexible Machining Call

The financing and selling of the FMC were tied to the B-1B program. It was sold to LTV headquarters on the basis of indemnification, cash flow, and a projected ROI double that of an investment in conventional machine tools. For example, it was essential to LTV management that the Air Force indemnify the investment in case the B-1 was again cancelled, and that 50% of the $21 million IMIP savings be provided up front to improve cash flow. Both were secured.

A machining cell, though very complex, was only a Level 5 undertaking in the hierarchy of computer control that had been developed for the

Air Force FoF study project. (See *Exhibit 4.*) A cell had to mediate several machines and/or functions (e.g., materials handling plus machining), providing control of both information flow and physical activity. But the cell envisioned by IMOD was more complex than anything Cincinnati Milacron, the primary vendor, had ever built, and more complex than any American-built cell at-

EXHIBIT 4a Factory of the Future: Hierarchical Architecture

Developed for the Air Force FoF study, this hierarchy of computer control began with shop floor control of individual machines, moved above the shop floor to computer control of the entire factory, and eventually rose to the level of the integration of the factory with the business. (See accompanying diagram.) Each of the six levels controlled both information and physical activity, but the span of control, and thus the complexity of the software, increased geometrically (or even exponentially) as the number of constraints and the number of tasks to be integrated increased.

FoF Levels (see diagram)

EQUIPMENT—LEVEL 6:	Control of individual module or machine, e.g., a numerically controlled (NC) machine tool; Also referred to as shop floor control, or stand-alone mode.
CELL—LEVEL 5:	Control of 2+ lower level devices or functions; e.g., 2+ machining centers, or machining center + materials handling
SYSTEM—LEVEL 4:	Control of 2+ cells (whether like or unlike), e.g., FMC_1 + FMC_2, or IMS = FMC_1 + FMC_2 + ASRS + cutter & grinder cell
CENTER—LEVEL 3:	Control of multiple systems that together perform all the operations of a particular process, such as machining or flexible composites; e.g., FCC will integrate systems performing composite lamination, core fabrication, stiffener fabrication, part buildup, water jet trimming, and quality inspection through ultrasound and coordinate measuring. Each of these systems, in turn, will be composed of multiple cells or functions.
FACTORY—LEVEL 2:	Control of multiple centers that operate an entire factory; organizational analogy would be vice president of manufacturing.
BUSINESS—LEVEL 1:	Integration of factory with rest of business; organizational analogy would be president of company.

EXHIBIT 4b Functional Hierarchy for Flexible Machining Systems

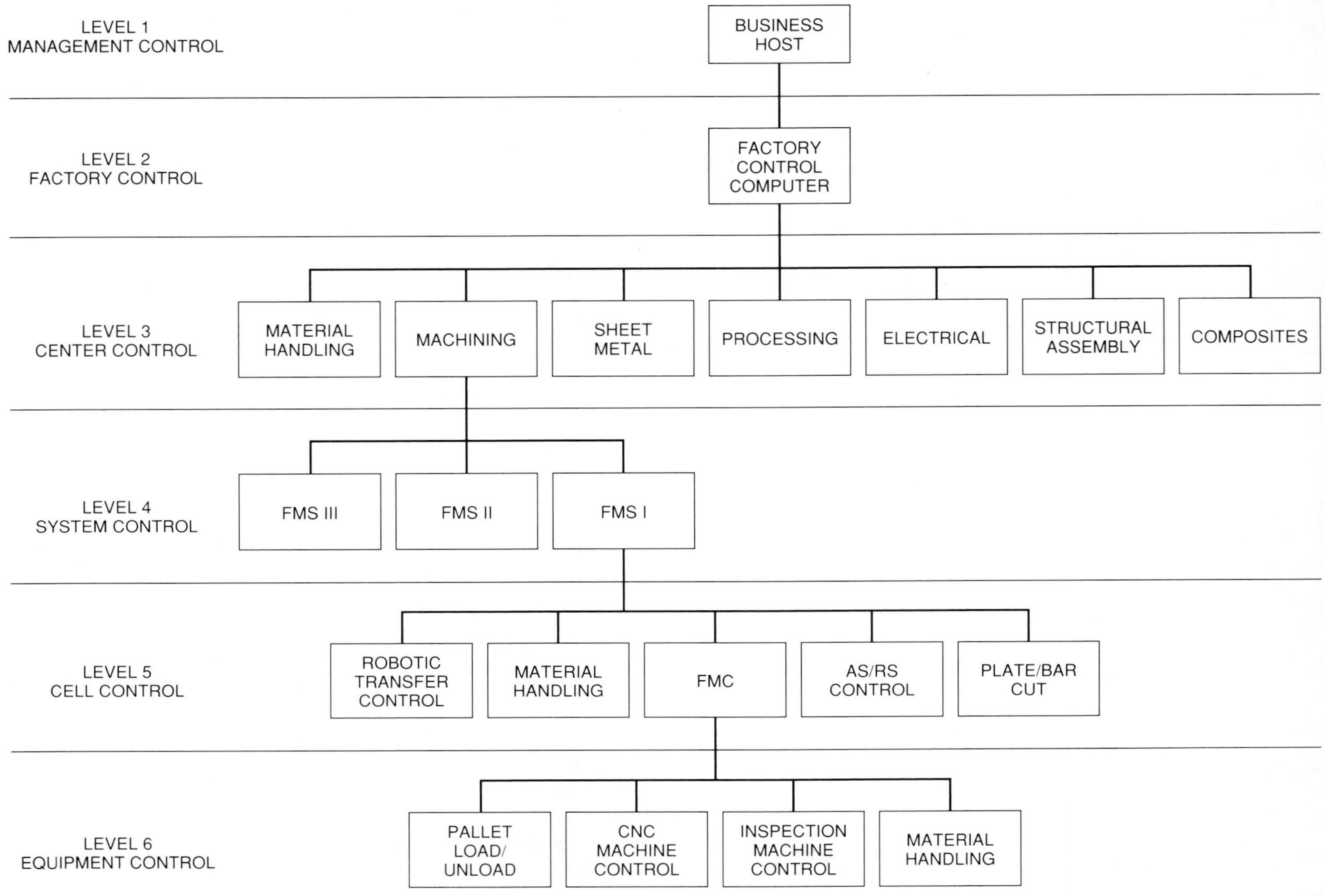
LEVEL 1
MANAGEMENT CONTROL
BUSINESS HOST
LEVEL 2
FACTORY CONTROL
FACTORY CONTROL COMPUTER
LEVEL 3
CENTER CONTROL
MATERIAL HANDLING
MACHINING
SHEET METAL
PROCESSING
ELECTRICAL
STRUCTURAL ASSEMBLY
COMPOSITES
LEVEL 4
SYSTEM CONTROL
FMS III
FMS II
FMS I
LEVEL 5
CELL CONTROL
ROBOTIC TRANSFER CONTROL
MATERIAL HANDLING
FMC
AS/RS CONTROL
PLATE/BAR CUT
LEVEL 6
EQUIPMENT CONTROL
PALLET LOAD/ UNLOAD
CNC MACHINE CONTROL
INSPECTION MACHINE CONTROL
MATERIAL HANDLING

Reprinted with permission from company.

tempted before 1983. Vought not only had to make the FMC work, it also had to get it operational by July 1, 1984 when work was scheduled to begin on the last 82 B-1 planes. If Vought was not ready to use the FMC at that time, it would still be locked into its fixed-price contract and would have to absorb the higher costs of subcontracting to stay on schedule.

IMOD's design of the FMC had several key elements. The goal of the system was an unmanned operation in which computer controls anticipated every contingency. In order to avoid any single-point failure in the system, every key point would have a manual backup. Cincinnati Milacron was selected as a turnkey vendor, using proven hardware. Unique features would be the system's custom software and a cell design which maximized spindle utilization (the percentage of time the machines actually cut metal).

IMPLEMENTATION AND RESISTANCE. Even after the project was approved, considerable resistance remained. David Lyons, who eventually became the FMC manager, recalled:

> A lot of people would like to have seen it fail. They said, "This is not the way we've done it for the last 30 years." Industrial engineering was not happy because it had no control over the project and feared we would need fewer IE's if we automated; it was the same with other groups. And manufacturing was unhappy because it would not be able to identify its own needs, or buy its own equipment.

The accompanying $21 million reduction in delivered costs came from reductions in many operating budgets. Lyons noted: "We were asking people to give up part of their budget for an untried thing, something that was still all theory." Countless meetings and explanations, and pressure from top management brought about the acquiescence, if not always the full acceptance, of the various departments. Flaherty told IMOD and the functions, "Work out problems among yourselves, but if you can't, come see me."

Some of the division's best maintenance workers were brought into the project early. They were trained for and then dedicated to the FMC. The facilities group began writing specifications for floors and power systems, and industrial engineers began figuring loading and parts. Pro-

grammers began writing tapes; they, too, became dedicated to FMC work. New job codes, created outside of the existing union contract, kept FMC and non-FMC workers separate. Control room operators were selected and trained both at Cincinnati Milacron and on the job.

Defining the cell's hardware was easier than developing its software. IMOD had to determine each component's function and software requirements, each computer's responsibility, and the language for communication among the computers. It also had to convince the vendor to provide customized software. When Cincinnati Milacron had problems developing the software on schedule, IMOD sent a team of six engineers to the company for six months. This group became the core of the FMC support staff, troubleshooting problems, enhancing the cell, and, later, working on specifications for the IMS and the FCC.

IMOD got the system up and running by its target date of July 1, 1984. When the first parts were cut, the cell was turned over to manufacturing. Many managers, including Lyons, thought this was too soon, at least from a technical standpoint. One IMOD manager commented:

> IMOD should design, develop, implement, and bring a system to a mature state before handing it off. By mature, I mean debugged and meeting system requirements, including the utilization level. You design a system to run a certain way to get certain savings, so if you let it go too soon, you may not get it working that way.

It took almost a year before the FMC reached its target of 85% utilization. (Research shows that most Japanese companies also take a year to reach this degree of utilization, and that most American companies achieve only 50–60% utilization.)

Predictably, implementing the FMC was difficult. But as Lofton pointed out:

> Putting David Lyons in as manufacturing superintendent was key. With 35 years of manufacturing experience, he gave IMOD reality—until then, operations people viewed IMOD as "blue sky." David was our one-man transition team. He brought practical knowledge that engineers would not think of, little things that make the difference in whether something worked or not. He would say, "If you do that, what about X?" And he made important contributions to tooling.

Other managers also gave considerable credit to Lyons for making the FMC a reality. Lyons himself, however, credited Clayton:

> It worked because Dan was behind it. He was the driving force; it couldn't have happened without him. He created IMOD, gave it the necessary people, and isolated it from the rest of the organization. If the project had been handled any other way, it would have failed.

FMC Lessons. Vought managers felt they had learned a great deal about user involvement, partnership with vendors, and managing the process of designing, developing, and implementing an automated cell. For example, they now knew that responsibility for systems design could not be delegated to a turnkey vendor. Instead, Vought had to define its own needs, develop complete specifications, and hold design reviews from the earliest stages of development. Specifications for the first FMC had only totaled 80 pages; by contrast, the IMS required 1500 pages and the FCC 2200 pages. Vought had also learned software development management. Initially, Cincinnati Milacron had sent programmers off to develop parts of the code and then had difficulty integrating the pieces. Vought recommended that a better approach was to plan system architecture first; code could then be written so that it was uniform and readily integrated. Finally, Vought learned about the complexity of scheduling; many more resources had to be tracked in an automated cell than expected. Cincinnati Milacron had developed a scheduling algorithm on the assumption that an infinite supply of cutters, fixtures, risers, and blanks were available; but in the manufacturing world, a finite number existed. Thus, scheduling algorithms had to be based on finite resources, and tracking these resources in real time made scheduling far more difficult.

Organizational Changes

IMOD. Although implementation of the FMC had improved relations between IMOD and the rest of the organization, barriers were still there. Conversations on this topic between Clayton and Lofton produced several changes. Most significantly, IMOD was placed under operations in

August 1985; the result was immediate improvement. As Clark noted, "Once we became part of the 'gun club,' they started thinking of ways to help us." Moreover, a few months earlier, Gresh had left and was succeeded by Clark as director of IMOD. Clark recalled:

> We couldn't go any further with things as they were. We had to change our image to get anywhere within the company. Pete was moving towards that, but it was easier for me being new.

Manufacturing development and support. Both Lofton and Clayton shared a desire for further manufacturing integration. For that purpose, they formed a new group, consisting of about 4,000 employees, called manufacturing development and support (MD&S). There were four functions within MD&S: IMOD, which designed advanced projects based on new technologies; manufacturing engineering, which shaped the vision, broke projects into chunks, and created tooling; facilities, which brought the project into the plant, laid it out, and "made it happen"; and manufacturing control, which directed everything on the shop floor. Except for IMOD, the groups supported daily production as well as future plans. Flaherty summarized MD&S as the "interface between engineering and the shop floor." Fred Cooper was recruited from General Dynamics to run the new organization. He described his new position:

> My job is to look at manufacturing from a global standpoint, and to develop manufacturing capabilities for the future. IMOD looks at advanced systems technologies using customer funding, while I look at how we integrate them into the business. MD&S is there for coordination. Once I added advanced programs and additional facilities people to those I inherited, we had everything necessary to get from design to market.

Lofton distinguished between Cooper's and Clark's jobs:

> Richard looks at what exists and at where we want to be, and then tells us what it takes to get there. He's supposed to work with blinders on. Fred has the whole thing, today and tomorrow—all the projects. He needs to look at our capital requirements, what we can afford to do,

the best way to get there, and then make investment recommendations to us.

Managing Vought's Competitive Position

FUTURE WEAPONS SYSTEMS REQUIREMENTS. Weapons systems of the 1990s were expected to cost more, be fewer in number, lower in volume, and of increased complexity and sophistication. Strategic requirements for future planes called for low visibility to radar, the ability to withstand extreme temperatures, and light weight. Meeting such requirements required fundamental changes in aerostructure geometries and materials. In particular, Vought expected a massive changeover from aluminum to advanced fiber composites for the skin of airplanes, and from aluminum to titanium for their substructures.

Aluminum melts at 3000°F., but future planes would have to withstand reentry temperatures twice as high. Composites could not only withstand the temperatures, but weighed about one-third as much, were as strong or stronger than metals, carried a lower signature for radar detection, and eliminated the problem of metal fatigue. At their current price, however—$300 per pound versus $14 for aluminum—commercial applications were a long way off. Titanium offered similar advantages over aluminum: it was lighter, could withstand extreme temperatures, and could bear heavier loads and greater dynamic stress on airfoils. Cooper commented on what these changes meant for Vought:

> The complexity of new weapons systems, together with our near-prime strategy, means that manufacturing rather than engineering will require heavy technological investments. We need the ability to manufacture flat and curved composites, to machine titanium, to hot form titanium, and to fasten together unlike materials. The FCC and the IMS are just two of the projects we are considering.

CHOOSING TECHNOLOGICAL NICHES. Because only a few materials (such as epoxy resins, titanium, and carbon composites) met the performance demands of advanced weapons systems, potential areas of specialization were limited. From this list, Vought had chosen two niches: the fabrication of large, complex-contour, advanced fiber composite parts, and high-throughput titanium machining of large, complex geometric parts.

Composites formed unitary, lightweight parts when a large number of plies, reinforced by built-in stiffners, were cured together in an autoclave (a large oven). The only other composite fabricators were primes; most were investing in composite fabrication, but in areas complementary to, rather than directly competitive with, Vought's niche. Vought's pursuit of a totally integrated center was also unique.

Titanium was enormously difficult to machine; it required very stiff spindles, wore out tools in 10–15 minutes, and involved metal removal rates 30 times slower than aluminum. No prime or subcontractor had yet developed the cutter technology, spindle engineering, materials handling technology, or computer controls necessary for significant advances in this area, as Vought was considering with its IMS.

Flexible Composites Center

Lofton, Cooper, and Clark agreed that Vought had to expand its composites capabilities; advanced programs demanded it and there was no one to whom to subcontract the work. The only question was the form the project would take: how much of the process would Vought automate, and at what level would there be computerized controls? Vought decided on a composites center that would automate most, but not all, aspects of computer fabrication, and that would be controlled and integrated at the center level (or Level 3 in the FoF hierarchy; see *Exhibit 4*).

FCC DESIGN. The FCC would automate ply fabrication, core milling, materials handling, and information flows, but not assembly or bagging. The autoclaves were already automated as a stand-alone operation once the doors were shut; now they would be integrated and scheduled as part of the center. The key elements distinguishing the center from stand-alone equipment were materials handling and computer coordination. An automatic storage and retrieval system (ASRS) and robocarriers would replace forklift trucks and drivers, and computer control would extend from the shop floor to the entire center. Lofton and Cooper had imposed only two requirements on the FCC's design: that Vought not build islands of automation that could not be integrated later, and that the FCC be expandable. One IMOD manager elaborated:

> We are designing it as a system, from the top down, not bottom up. It will be modular and flexible, so we can later expand our capacity and the technology. And it will be a microcosm of our factory of the future, automating almost the entire process from raw materials receiving to finished parts.

CHOICE OF A CENTER. Vought managers were heavily committed to the FCC for its potential strategic value, despite the $150 million price tag. Cooper summarized this view:

> The FCC is critical for the placement of the company. It's the right thing to do, and it's smart because we can create new business through it. Timing is key here, because if we do it now, we can get the jump on other people and create an edge. Others may go this road, but we hope they will team with us rather than reinvent the wheel.

While the risks of a center were acknowledged to be enormous, a manual composites operation would simply not be fast enough. A stand-alone operation, with automated equipment but no computer integration, would mitigate much of the risk, but would also double the price. Because scheduling could not be as tightly controlled, equipment usage would be much less efficient; more equipment would therefore be needed to do the same amount of work. For example, the stand-alone operation would require 22 rather than 13 tape layers, several additional autoclaves (at $5 million each), 35–40% more floor space, and 40% more people—yet would still result in 20–25% higher rejection rates. This option would also require 14 acres for tooling storage, and numerous forklift trucks and operators. (By contrast, the ASRS would automatically pick and deliver tools from a 150′ × 300′ building, 14 stories high.) The additional equipment and facilities would bring the price for stand-alone automation to $300 million. Finally, and most critically, the nature of the materials did not favor a stand-alone operation, as Clark explained:

> It's the time-critical nature of the materials that drives you to a center. You must schedule all operations before the autoclave as a single entity. Once they are taken out of the freezer, these materials have only 168 hours before they have to be thrown away—if they haven't been cured.

CENTER RISKS. Yet the financial and technological risks were almost as great as the forces favoring a composites center. Although Vought had $12 million in customer funding to design, develop, and implement the center, it would have to bear the investment costs itself. LTV's steel business was deeply depressed, and the recent plunge in oil prices had hurt its drilling equipment and energy products business as well. Even so, Clark was confident that headquarters would approve the FCC investment and the IMS if it were proposed.

> Our CEO says he has never turned down an Aerospace & Defense capital request that made sense. If one of your three companies is making money, you make sure you keep it going—but you need sound justification to do the project.

Technological risks were equally formidable. For example, there was the possibility of alternative materials technologies, such as thermoplastics or metal matrices, displacing thermoset epoxy resins, the basis for the FCC. Thermoplastics would make autoclaves redundant and would require significant adaptations of other FCC equipment and software. Vought was betting that the immaturity of these technologies left a 10–20 year window for epoxy resins.

There were two more immediate types of technological risks. First, many of the elements of the center were neither mature nor fully understood. These included composite fabrication operations, the support technologies needed to make automated operations work, and the management data system. Second, the inherent difficulty of integrating all the equipment and technologies (mature or not) into center-level computerized control was staggering.

IMMATURE TECHNOLOGIES. The FCC would be attempting to automate processes that were not completely understood, including the very nature of composites themselves. Mike Webber, head of the FCC project, explained:

With metal, you present the work to the tool, manipulating one or the other; but, in composites, there is no inherent rigidity, and they're dimensionally unstable. We are still trying to understand the physical science of composites.

Except for the autoclaves and some ply lay-up, current composite operations at Vought and elsewhere were largely manual; automating the operations meant simultaneous mechanization of many parts of the process.

Automated operations would require the addition of sensors and intelligence to many pieces of equipment, and opinions varied concerning the state of development of these and other support technologies. Ply fabrication, for example, would require a second vision system to recognize tool locations and align the tools used to lay tape; yet no existing vision system could compensate the way a person could. Nonetheless, such a support system would allow automated tool loading, saving considerable labor time and allowing much more efficient utilization of the tape layer. Although some concern was expressed about the development of automated materials handling technology for transferring tools (which weighed up to 8000 pounds and were up to 22 feet long), Webber and Cooper did not see this as an issue. They noted the auto industry's use of such technology to move equipment of similar size.

Of greater concern to Webber than the state of development of these support technologies was a third element: the FCC would attempt to automate processes at the same time that it changed over to an electronic data system. Until now, Vought's composite operation had been scheduled, routed, forecast, and tracked manually.

INTEGRATION RISKS. While the need to obtain maximum efficiency convinced Vought to choose a composites center over separate pieces of automated equipment, there was universal agreement about the great risks of the required software. A center was two levels up from a cell in the FoF hierarchy. The difficulty of coordination increased geometrically (some said exponentially) as one moved up levels. Vought had never developed software, interfaces, and computer controls for operations this extensive. Neither had any prime or subcontractors attempted a center, in composites or any other area. Computer language was one dimension of this complexity. Each of the 30 pieces of equipment from 20 different vendors would have its own computer controller in its own language, requiring a translator at every interface. Instructions also had to arrive at the machines in their proper sequence; this, in turn, depended on the correctness of the scheduling algorithm. And no one had yet developed a real-time scheduling algorithm for batch manufacturing of materials having time limitations on use—the 168 hours available before curing.

Integrated Machining System

Advanced weapons systems requirements suggested that titanium substructures would be critical to Vought's future business base. Moreover, Vought's current advanced programs already demanded extensive titanium machining. The question, as with composites, was how to fabricate the parts. But, unlike composites, titanium machining could either be subcontracted, or done in-house—on conventional machine tools, or on specially designed stand-alone profilers, or on identical profilers integrated into a machining system. (See *Exhibit 5*.)

TITANIUM MACHINING ISSUES. Conventional machine tools could machine titanium, but not efficiently; metal removal rates were only 1.5 cubic inches per minute compared with 40–50 cubic inches per minute for aluminum. Titanium required a much tougher, stiffer spindle. Titanium also chewed up cutters in 10–15 minutes because of its toughness, and because it did not absorb heat but sent much of it back into the cutting tool. Productivity requirements in titanium machining would require technological advances to get more efficient spindles and longer-lived cutters. A spindle that cut more deeply would be the foundation of high-throughput machining (HTM).

IMS DESIGN REQUIREMENTS. Like the FCC, the IMS would have to be modular and expandable, with all of its elements integrated or interchangeable. In addition, it had to be flexible enough to accommodate changes in materials. For this reason, the specially designed profilers would have to accommodate interchangeable spindles for high-

EXHIBIT 5 Integrated Machining System

Advanced Program Need:

Advanced programs created a need for extensive titanium machining. The 300+ parts that fit the IMS work envelope would require 7,000 machining hours per shipset (completed airframe sections) if done on conventional equipment. All options used this 7,000 hours as the baseline condition.

Alternative #1: Subcontract 4,900 hours per shipset:

By upgrading, refurbishing, and investing in new conventional equipment, Vought could machine 2,100 hours per shipset, subcontracting the remaining 4,900 machine hours to outside machine shops. In-house investment would run about $37 million. The recurring costs of the subcontracted work would be higher than for in-house work, but these costs would be passed through. Although quality was usually good, it was harder to control and required more of Vought's attention to oversee than if done in-house. Delivery was more apt to be a problem, as subcontractors fell behind schedule.

Alternative #2: Invest in additional conventional machine tools:

The same 7,000 hours per shipset would require 93 spindles (or 42 machines) if conventional machine tools were chosen for doing all the machining in-house. The equipment alone would require over 350,000 square feet of floor space, probably necessitating a new plant. Equipment and facilities costs would exceed $100 million. Recurring costs were estimated at twice that of an IMS, an utilization to be around 45%.

Alternative #3: Develop specialized profilers for in-house machining in stand-alone mode:

As in option #4, Vought would work with outside vendors to improve spindle efficiency and develop large profilers—machine tools whose spindles operated in axes and created complex contours. Because development costs for the machine would be high, they had to be spread over the purchase of several machines. The 7,000 hours would require 14 dual-spindle profilers that would cost $2.5 million each. The improved spindle of these profilers was estimated to give a 3:1 productivity improvement over conventional machines. This equipment would require over 100,000 square feet of floor space. Additional support equipment (such as more wash stations) would require another 30,000 square feet. Materials handling would add another 50,000 square feet; without an automated storage and retrieval system (ASRS), material would have to be staged around the machines. Recurring costs were estimated to be twice that of an IMS, and utilization to be around 45%. Estimated costs were:

```
$35  million—profilers (14 @ $2.5 million)
 30  million—support equipment
 15  million—facilities changes and additions
 10  million—materials handling (racks, trucks, etc.)
 ─────
$90  million total
```

Alternative #4: Develop specialized profilers for in-house machining and software to create an integrated system (IMS):

The 7,000 hours would require 7 dual-spindle, 5-axis profilers that cost $2.5 million each. This equipment would require 62,000 square feet of floor space, including a cutter cell, and would be supported by an ASRS requiring 19,000 square feet. Utilization was estimated at 85%. Estimated costs were:

```
$18  million—profilers (7 @ $2.5 million)
 18  million—system equipment (pallet shuttles, inspection
             machines, washer, load/unload equipment, chip
             coolant system, turnkey installation, shop floor
             control systems, and program management
  6  million—facilities changes and additions (Foundations,
             demolition and clearing, utilities)
  8  million—materials handling (ASRS, automatic guided
             vehicle, cutter cell, tool assembly, computerized
             control)
  6  million—other computer hardware, software, and com-
             munications network
 ─────────
 60  million total
```

IMS Configuration

The system would consist of 7 dual-spindle, 5-axis profilers; an ASRS; a tool and grinder cell; 2 material transport systems on separate tracks (the small system to carry tools and small parts and a large shuttle car system to carry large parts); a coordinate measuring machine, a wash station, a chip/coolant recovery system, and a deburr unit.

The system would begin operation as soon as the part number was scheduled by the host computer. It would pull the right blank, take it by overhead conveyor and load it onto a fixture and pallet, take it by shuttle car to the front of the machine, and wait until the machine was ready to work on it. This process would be coordinated with an automated tool cell. Whereas in the FMC the cutter operation was manual once the operator was told by computer what tools were needed, the IMS would identify the needed tool and get it from the cutter inventory; the robocarrier would bring it to the machine, and a robit arm would insert in the machine. The cutter cell would also maintain cutter inventory, reorder cutter stock, and grind the tools.

IMOD selected a 5-axis profiler with a work envelope of 7' x 11' x 4 ' to make large prismatic parts. The spindle would have the flexibility to do either high-speed machining (HSM), removing aluminum at a rate up to 200 cu. in. per minute, or high throughput machining (HTM), removing titanium at a rate of 10–15 cu. in per minute.

speed machining (HSM) of aluminum as well as HTM of titanium. Such flexible profilers would cost more than one that could accommodate only one type of spindle.

IMS DESIGN OBJECTIVES. As with the FMC, the key operating objective of the IMS would be productivity improvement through maximum spindle utilization. The target was again 85% utilization, with the remaining 15% reserved for preventive maintenance, system enhancements, tool changes, and shuttling pallets in and out of the machine. Unlike the FMC, the achievement of such high utilization would be supported by two key cells: an automated storage and retrieval system (ASRS) and a cutter and grinder cell. Because of short tool life and the expectation that the IMS would consume 27,000 cutters per month, automated cutter management would be key to realizing the full productivity gains of the system. The ASRS would store and distribute both materials and fixtures, reducing the manufacturing time lost from late deliveries to the floor, and reducing inventory requirements through improved logistics.

SUBCONTRACTING OPTIONS AND ARGUMENTS. Vought could subcontract its titanium machining needs to various machine shops. The major disadvantages were lack of control over delivery and quality, and high recurring costs. (Recurring costs were those that were repeated every time a part was built, including setups, operator costs, cutter costs and execution of numerical control programs.) These costs had two components: the subcontractors' rates, and the opportunity cost to Vought from not gaining a steeper learning curve for its own work. On the other hand, should business shift away from titanium, or should Vought not receive a large share of future titanium business, it would not have committed itself to an IMS. Cooper asked:

> Can I use the IMS on the next program? Will there be follow-on contracts? Will we get some of them? If there is no follow-on to our current classified programs, we would have this huge thing we couldn't use; it would be overkill just for aluminum.

STAND-ALONE OPTIONS AND ARGUMENTS. Theoretically, Vought had two stand-alone options: to invest in conventional equipment (non-high-speed machine tools), or to invest in 5-axis profilers computerized only at the shop floor level. The enormous equipment and facilities requirements of the former virtually eliminated it from serious consideration. (See *Exhibit 5.*) Stand-alone profilers, however, could provide an order of magnitude productivity gain while greatly reducing the risks of developing software integration associated with an IMS.

Dramatic productivity gains in titanium machining would derive from two sources: more efficient spindles for HTM, and higher utilization of the spindle. More efficient spindles would provide equal gains, whether used in stand-alone profilers or integrated into an IMS. Starr estimated these gains would give a threefold productivity increase relative to conventional machines. Used in a stand-alone mode, however, the profilers' spindles would not be leveraged for maximum use, and their utilization would be no higher than that of conventional machines (which ran about 45%). Nonetheless, the 3:1 gain in machining hours, coupled with the minimal software and implementation risks, made this option attractive.

Because the cost of additional profilers and facilities would exceed the cost of an IMS, arguments for the stand-alone option were based on risk management, not on cost savings. Both the inherent risks of developing an integrated system and the need for an accelerated timetable raised questions about whether Vought had enough people to do an IMS at the same time as the FCC.

IMS OPTION AND ARGUMENTS. Arguments for the IMS centered on its strategic value and the high throughput and productivity gains that a system could provide. Maximizing spindle use would almost double the gains from stand-alone equipment, according to Starr. These gains would come from such things as parallel loading, improved resource tracking, automated cutter management, and scheduling. Further, recurring costs would be half those of a conventional shop or stand-alone operation.

Three risks weighed against an IMS: machining technologies, software integration, and future contracts. Both spindle and cutter technology needed further development. Starr observed:

> The cutter technology does not yet exist for doing either HSM or HTM, so we have to work with tool vendors to push the state of the art. The spindles for HSM are just starting to come along, and we need a lot of engineering work to get the trade-offs in spindle design to do both HSM and HTM. The IMS aims to remove metal at rates greater than any so far demonstrated in a production environment, and, except for very brief periods, in a research environment. There are very real questions about whether machines can in fact achieve these rates. And, if they can, will they also be able to protect themselves, the parts, and the fixtures?

Cooper, however, was less concerned about the maturity of cutter technology than with its overall cost effectiveness.

Agreement was virtually unanimous that the most difficult and riskiest aspect of the IMS was software integration. Not only would the IMS have to schedule machining; it would also have to integrate that cell with an automated storage and retrieval system and a cutter cell. An IMS would entail changing computer hardware as well, which meant the operating systems would also be different. Cooper pointed out:

> We are talking about a huge database that has to be refreshed constantly, and we cannot afford a supercomputer. The closest analogy to what we would be doing are flight simulators which also have vast databases and operate in real time. We don't know if the controllers can communicate fast enough with each other; if not, huge parts could crash into each other. Doing this simultaneously with the FCC, and making

it perfect in two-and-a-half years, is a gigantic undertaking.

Clark added:

> There are very few people with hands-on experience with factory-of-the-future automation. Our people are constantly being approached by other companies, and we try to attract and keep the best and the brighest by pursuing the kind of state-of-the-art projects they find so exciting to work on. It's even harder to find leadership in this new field; you have young people who may be outstanding technically, but who don't yet have the maturity and skills to manage a project.

The IMS was designed on the basis of a 70/30 titanium/aluminum product mix. Clark was cautiously optimistic about Vought's future business base:

> We think there will be a market for large titanium parts, and that we are creating a unique niche for ourselves. We can go to the primes—who have to keep making huge capital investments—and say, "Let us do this work for you, and you won't need to make this investment yourselves."

Yet the future was so uncertain and the environment so dynamic that the spectre of a possible $60 million white elephant haunted Cooper. Competition in aerospace for fewer program starts might squeeze Vought's business base:

> Two years ago, no one ever though General Dynamics and McDonnell Douglas would team up, but that may happen. There are fewer contracts coming up for the ATF [Advanced Tactical Fighter]—you have seven primes bidding for two contracts. If the primes do it all among themselves, where will that leave us?

24. Corning Glass Works: The Z-Glass Project

After several highly successful years, 1977 had been difficult at Corning Glass Work's Harrisburg plant. In July 1977 the yields and productivity of the Z-Glass process began a long decline, and the entire plant organization was working overtime trying to correct the problem. Morale plummeted as yields continued to decline throughout the summer and fall. In December 1977 a team of engineers from the corporate manufacturing and engineering (M&E) staff were assigned to the plant; the group's charter was to focus on long-term process improvement while the line organization concentrated on day-to-day operations.

On the morning of March 24, 1978, Eric Davidson, leader of the M&E project team at Harrisburg, sat in his office and reflected on the group's first three months at the plant. The project had not gone well, and Davidson knew that his team members were discouraged. The technical problems they faced were difficult enough, but apparently the line organization had resisted almost everything the M&E team had attempted. In addition to conflicts over responsibility and authority, deep disagreements arose concerning the sources of the problems and how best to solve them. Cooperation was almost nonexistent, and tense relationships developed in some departments between team and line personnel. Davidson favored an immediate change in the project's direction.

Sifting through the comments and memos from his team, he recalled David Leibson, vice president of manufacturing and engineering, say-

ing to him shortly after he accepted the Harrisburg assignment: "Eric, this is the M&E group's first major turnaround project, and the first real project of any kind in the Industrial Products Division. I picked you for this job, because you're the kind of guy who gets things done. This is a key one for our group and I think a big one for the company. In situations like this, you either win big, or you lose big. There's very little middle ground."

Corning Glass Works in the 1970s

During the late 1960s and early 1970s Corning Glass Works was a corporation in transition. Long a leader in the development of glass and ceramic products for industrial and commercial uses, Corning had entered several consumer goods markets during the 1960s. Under the direction of Lee Waterman, president from 1962–1971, Corning developed a strong marketing emphasis to accompany several new consumer products.

Although the public's perception of Corning in the 1960s was no doubt dominated by its well-known Pyrex and Ovenware cooking products and Pyroceram dinnerware, its most successful consumer product was actually TV tube casings. Utilizing an innovative glass-forming process, Corning entered the market for TV tube funnels and front plates in 1958 and soon attained a strong market position. Throughout the mid-to-late 1960s growth in TV at Corning was rapid, and the profits at the TV division constituted the backbone of the income statement.

During the heydey of TV, Corning's organization was decentralized. The operating divisions had considerable control over marketing and manufacturing decisions, and corporate staffs in these areas were relatively small. Only in research and development did corporate staff personnel influence the company's direction. The Technical Staff Division was responsible for all research and development activities, as well as for manufacturing engineering. New products were regarded as the lifeblood of the corporation, and the director of new product development, Harvey Blackburn, had built a creative and energetic staff. This staff developed the glass-forming process that made TV tube production possible, and the corporation looked to this group when growth in the TV division and other consumer products began to slow in the late 1960s.

Changes in TV and Corporate Reorganization

The critical year for the TV division was 1968. Until then sales and profits had grown rapidly, and Corning had carved out a substantial share of the market. In 1968, however, RCA (a major Corning customer) opened a plant in Ohio to produce glass funnels and front plates. Several of the engineering and management personnel at the new RCA plant were former Corning employees. RCA's decision to integrate backward into glass production had a noticeable effect on the performance of Corning's TV division. Although the business remained profitable, over the next three years growth slowed and Corning's market share declined.

Slower growth in TV in the 1969–1972 period coincided with reduced profitability in other consumer products as costs for labor and basic materials escalated sharply. These developments resulted in weaker corporate financial performance and prompted a reevaluation of the company's basic direction.

These deliberations created a reemphasis of the technical competence of the company in new product development and a focus on process excellence and productivity. A major step in the new approach to operations and production was the establishment of M&E at the corporate level. This reorganization brought together staff specialists in processes, systems, and equipment under the direction of Leibson, who was promoted from director of manufacturing at the TV division to a corporate vice president.

Shortly after the M&E Division was formed, Thomas MacAvoy, the general manager of the Electronics Division and the former director of Physical Research on Corning's technical staff, was named president of the company. MacAvoy was the first Corning president in recent times with a technical background; he had a Ph.D. in chemistry and a strong record in research and development. An internal staff memorandum summed up the issues facing Corning under MacAvoy:

> Our analysis of productivity growth at Corning from 1960–1970 shows that we performed no better than the average for other glass products manufacturers (2%–4% per year) and in the last two years have actually been below average. With prices on the increase, improved productivity growth is imperative. At the same time, we have to improve our ability to exploit new products. It appears that research output has, if anything, increased in the last few years (Z-Glass is a prime example), but we have to do a much better job of transferring products from the lab into production.

Manufacturing and Engineering Division

Much of the responsibility for improved productivity and the transfer of technology (either product or process) from research to production fell to the new and untried M&E Division. Because of the company's historical preference for a small, relatively inactive manufacturing staff, building the M&E group into a strong and effective organization was a considerable challenge. Remembering the early days, Leibson reflected on his approach:

> I tried to do two things in the first year: (1) attract people with very strong technical skills in the basic processes and disciplines in use at Corning; and (2) establish a working relationship with the manufacturing people in the operating divisions. I think the thing that made the difference in that first year was the solid support we got from Tom MacAvoy. It was made clear to all of the division general managers that productivity growth and cost reduction were top priorities.

From 1972 to 1977 engineers from the M&E Division participated in numerous projects throughout Corning involving the installation of new equipment and process changes. A typical project might require 4 or 5 M&E engineers to work with a plant organization to install an innovative conveyor system, possibly designed by the M&E Division. The installation project might last 3 to 4 months and the M&E team would normally serve as consultants thereafter.

In addition to equipment projects and internal consulting, the M&E group participated in the transfer of products from R&D to production. After laboratory development and prototype testing, new products were assigned to an M&E product team that designed any new equipment required, and engineered and implemented the new process. Leibson believed that successful transfer required people who appreciated both the development process and the problems of production. In many respects M&E product teams served as mediators and translators; especially in the first few projects, their primary task was to establish credibility with the R&D group and with the manufacturing people in the operating divisions.

By 1976 M&E had conducted projects and helped to transfer new products in most of Corning's divisions, although its role in Industrial Products remained limited. The manufacturing organization in that division had been relatively strong and independent, but Leibson felt that the reputation and expertise of his staff was increasing and that opportunities for collaboration were not far off. He also felt that M&E was ready to take on a completely new responsibility—a turnaround project. Occasionally parts of a production process, even whole plants, would experience a deterioration in performance, sometimes lasting for several months with serious competitive consequences. Leibson maintained that a concentrated application of engineering expertise could significantly shorten the turnaround time and could have a measurable impact on overall corporate productivity.

The Z-Glass Project

The opportunity for M&E involvement in a major turnaround effort, and for collaboration with the Industrial Products Division came in late 1977.

FIGURE A Overall Yield, 1973–1977

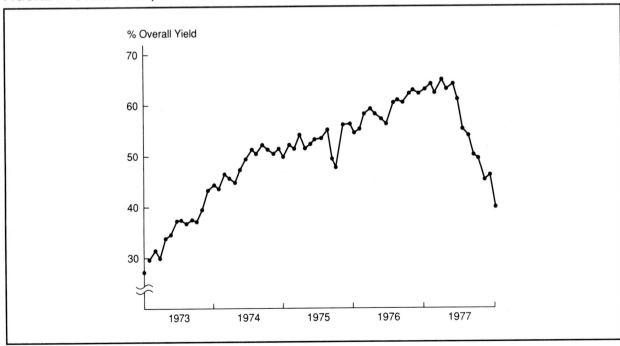

Since June of that year, yields on the Z-Glass process at the division's Harrisburg plant had declined sharply (see *Figure A.*) Substantial effort by the plant organization failed to change the downward plunge in yields and in October, Oliver Williams, director of manufacturing for Industrial Products, met with Leibson to establish an M&E project at Harrisburg.

Williams, a chemical engineer with an MBA from N.Y.U., had been named director of manufacturing in November 1976, after 18 years in various engineering and operations positions at Corning. He felt that the product's importance (corporate expectations for Z-Glass were great) coupled with the seriousness of the problem warranted strong measures. Williams and Leibson agreed that an M&E project team would work in the plant under the general supervision of a review board composed of Leibson, Williams, Martin Abramson, head of process engineering in the M&E Division, and Bill Chenevert, head of M&E's equipment development group (see *Figure B* for an organization chart). The team's charter was to

increase yields, define and document the process, and train the operating people (see *Exhibit 1*). A budget, the team's size, specific goals, and a timetable were to be developed in the first month of the team's operation.

Although the plant manager and his staff had not participated in the decision to bring in the M&E team, Williams and Leibson agreed that their involvement and support were essential. A decision was made to allocate all M&E charges to the Industrial Products Division to relieve the plant of the extra overhead. Moreover, M&E specialists assigned to the project would be at the plant full-time.

Since this was M&E's first turnaround project, Leibson personally selected the team leader and key project engineers. He easily found people willing to work on the project. Everyone in the M&E group realized that turnarounds were the next major activity for the group and that those working on the first team would be breaking new ground. Leibson chose Eric Davidson to lead the Harrisburg project. He was 32 years old with a

FIGURE B Organization Chart

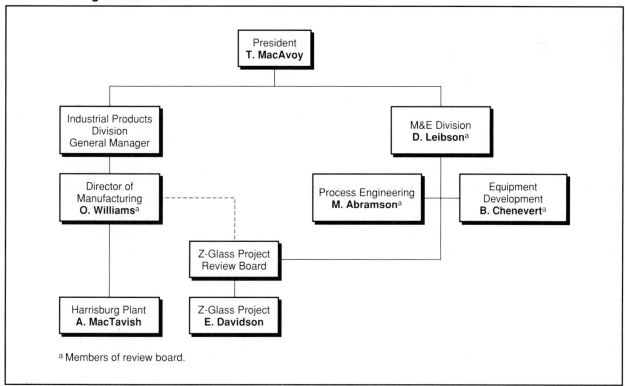

a Members of review board.

EXHIBIT 1 Memorandum on Team Charter

To: Harrisburg Project Team
From: E. Davidson
Date November 24, 1977
Re: Team Charter

The charter of the project team is yield improvement as a top priority, definition and documentation of the process, and operator training. Enclosed is a copy of the proposed Process Definition and Documentation Program; it will serve as the framework for process diagnosis and control. Its main elements are as follows:

Priority

1	Define best known *operating setpoint* for each major variable.
2	Establish auditing system to track variables daily with built-in feedback loop.
3	Develop and implement *process troubleshooting* guides.
4	Write and implement *Operating Procedures.*
5	*Train* operating personnel in procedure usage.
6	*Audit* operating procedures on random frequency.
7	Write and implement *Machine Specification Procedures.*

Your comments on the program are encouraged.

master's degree in mechanical engineering from Cornell and six years of experience at Corning. Davidson had completed several projects in the M&E Division, including one in France, and had also worked as an assistant plant manager. A close friend and colleague commented on Davidson's reputation: "To say that Eric is on the fast track is a bit of an understatement. He has been given one challenging assignment after another and has been very successful. The word around M&E is that if you have a tough problem you want solved, just give it to Eric and get out of the way."

Working under Leibson's direction, Davidson spent the first two weeks meeting with the plant management and selecting members of the M&E team. At the outset, he chose four specialists to work on the first phase of the project—data collection and problem definition:

Richard Grebwell: 35 years old, an expert in statistical process analysis with 10 years at Corning. Although Grebwell was considered a bit eccentric by some, his characteristically brillant use of statistical analysis was vital to the project.

Jennifer Rigby: 28 years old, with a master's

degree in industrial engineering from the University of Texas. She had worked in the Harrisburg plant for six months on her first assignment at Corning.

Arthur Hopkins: 40 years old, a mechanical engineer with 12 years at Corning. Hopkins had worked with Davidson on the French project and was, in Davidson's words, "a wizard with equipment."

Frank Arnoldus: 37 years old, a chemist with Corning for six years, he also had worked on the French project and had earned Davidson's admiration for his ability to solve processing problems.

For the first two or three weeks Davidson planned to use the small group to identify problems and then expand the team as specific tasks and subprojects were established. Focusing his objectives on the long term, he explained:

I'm after increases in yields as soon as we can get them, but what I'm really shooting for is permanent improvements in the process. To do that we've got to define the process and document its operation. My whole approach is based on the idea of *receivership:* whatever solutions we come up with have to be received, or accepted, by the plant organization. And I mean really accepted;

they have to *own* the changes. That's why I will be taking a team approach—each project we do will have two coleaders, one from M&E (the transferrer) and one from the plant (the receiver).

After a brief period to get acquainted and develop a plan, Davidson and his M&E team began working in the plant on December 10, 1977.

Z-Glass: Product and Process

Z-Glass was Corning's code name for a multilayered, compression-molded glass product that was exceptionally strong and impact-resistant for its weight. Its durability and hardness, combined with its low weight and competitive cost, made it an attractive substitute for ceramic and plastic products used in the construction and auto industries. Introduced in 1973, Z-Glass products were an immediate success. From 1973 to 1977 production capacity grew 35% to 40% annually yet failed to meet demand (see *Exhibit 2*.) Many people thought that the array of products was only the beginning of Z-Glass applications.

To Corning's knowledge, no other company in the world had yet developed the capability to make a product like Z-Glass and if one did, presumably it would have to license the technology from Corning. In fact, much of this technology was still an art form because numerous characteristics of most Z-Glass products were not completely explainable in known glass technology: people knew what it could do and roughly why it could do it, but were still utilizing trial-and-error methods to perfect existing products and develop new ones.

Blackburn and his staff developed Z-Glass during the early 1970s. The product was literally Blackburn's baby. He not only conceived the idea but, typical of the way Corning operated before the M&E Division was created, he and his staff solved numerous technical problems, built all the machinery and equipment needed for prototype production, and even worked in the plant during start-up. Futhermore, Blackburn had championed the product in discussions with top management. Several times when the project faltered, his reputation and skills of persuasion obtained the necessary funding. When yields began to fall in 1977, engineers at Harrisburg had consulted Blackburn when necessary; he still felt responsible for the product and intimately knew its nuances and subtleties.

The Process

Making Z-Glass products consisted of three main steps: melting, molding, and finishing, which were linked and had to be carried out in a fixed time sequence. The process required precise control over the composition and thicknesses of the various glass layers, as well as careful timing and monitoring during the molding and finishing operations. Maintaining this precision in a high-volume environment required continuous, tight controls as well as a feel for the process.

MELTING. The first step was the preparation of the different types of molten glass that composed the various layers. These mixtures were prepared in separate electrically heated vats, designed and built by Corning. Each vat was carefully monitored to insure that the ingredients of the glass were in correct proportion, evenly distributed throughout the vat, and at the appropriate temperature.

The base layer was poured continuously onto a narrow (2 to 3 feet) moving strip. The other layers were poured on top of each other at precisely controlled intervals so that when the layered strip arrived at the molding stage each layer of the multilayered glass sandwich was at the proper temperature and thickness for molding. Minor (and, at the beginning of process development, almost unmeasurable) deviations from the recipe could lead to major problems, often requiring ad hoc solutions utilizing the unprogrammable skill of the operators and technicians.

Some problems were clearly identifiable with the melting operation. For example, the existence of *blisters* (tiny bubbles in one or more of the glass layers), *stones* (unmelted bits of sand), and *streaks* (imperfectly melted or mixed ingredients) were visible and obvious indicators of problems. Separation of the different layers, either after the molding or after the finishing operations, often could also be traced to improper execution during melting. But when the glass sandwich did not mold properly, there was usually some question as to which operation was at fault.

EXHIBIT 2 Harrisburg Plant—Sales by Product Line, 1973–1978 (numbers in thousands)

	Z1		Z4[a]		Z10		Z35		Z12[b]		Total	
	Pieces	$	Pieces	$	Pieces	$	Pieces	$	Pieces	$	Pieces	$
1973	–	–	–	–	119	$2,220.1	495	$5,217.8	–	–	614	$7,437.9
1974	–	–	–	–	232	4,315.2	549	6,313.5	–	–	781	10,628.7
1975	384	$5,161.5	–	–	239	4,983.2	552	6,513.6	–	–	1,175	16,658.3
1976	784	11,514.2	45	$552.3	268	5,831.9	591	7,541.7	82	$1,213.2	1,770	26,653.3
1977	803	12,005.0	407	5,372.4	264	6,087.6	671	8,689.5	534	8,410.5	2,679	40,565.0
1978[c]	171	2,565.1	35	493.5	145	1,957.5	250	2,975.2	61	988.3	662	8,979.6

[a] Introduced in early 1975.

[b] Introduced in late 1976.

[c] Data for 1978 cover reporting periods 1–3 (i.e., first 12 weeks of 1978). Note that because of seasonal factors it is not possible to arrive at an accurate indication of annual output of a particular product by multiplying the 1978 (1–3) results by $1\tfrac{3}{3}$.

A process engineer explained the difficulty of melting control:

> The secret to avoiding problems at the melting state is maintaining its stability. Sometimes it's easy to tell when something has gone wrong there, but more often you don't find out until something goes wrong at a later stage. And usually it takes a long time to determine whether you've really solved the problem or are simply treating a symptom of a larger problem. It's tough to keep on top of what is going on in each of those melting vats because it's largely a chemical operation.

Despite the difficulty of maintaining control over the melting operation and of correcting it when problems developed, Corning had been able to achieve yields as high as 95% at this stage of the process.

MOLDING. In contrast to melting, molding was basically a physical operation: rectangles of the soft glass sandwich were cut off the moving strip and moved onto a series of separated conveyor belts. Each slab was inserted between the jaws of a compression-molding device that contained several molds for the particular parts being produced. After the parts were stamped out, they continued down the conveyor line while the glass trim was discarded. Depending on the product mix, several conveyors might pool their contents before the parts entered the finishing stage.

Despite the apparent simplicity of this process (problems could be detected quickly and usually corrected quickly), so many different problems arose and so many different variables could be manipulated that it was generally considered to be even more difficult to control this stage than the melting stage. Typical problems included the basic dimensional specifications of the product, its edge configuration, and buckling and flattening after molding. These problems, together with machine downtime associated both with correcting problems and changing the product mix, made it difficult to achieve more than 80% efficiency (good output to rated machine capacity) during this stage.

FINISHING. The finishing operation consisted of heat treating the molded objects, then applying one of several possible coatings. Heat treating stabilized the internal tensions generated by the molding operation and appeared to improve the lamination between the various layers of the glass sandwich. Since it required a precise sequence of temperatures and their duration, this operation occurred as the objects passed on conveyor belts through long ovens. Cracks or layer separation occurred infrequently, sometimes caused by the heat-treating operation.

The application of coatings, however, was more of a job-shop operation and could be done off-line. There were numerous coatings that could be applied, from the practical (improving the reflective, insulating, or electrical conducting properties of the surface) to the ornamental. Sometimes decals were also applied either in place of or in addition to a coating. The selection of coatings was steadily increasing, and one process engineer characterized the operation as "a continual bother: lots of new processes and equipment, lots of short runs but a necessity to maintain high speeds." The seldom-attained target yield was 95%.

The unique characteristics of the three stages made overall control and fine-tuning of the total process quite difficult. The backgrounds and skills of the hot-end workers varied considerably from those at the cold end, and involved entirely separate branches of engineering. When problems arose, many went undetected for some time, and often only appeared during destructive testing of parts after they had completed the process. Then it was often difficult to isolate which part of the process was at fault, because there appeared to be a high degree of interrelation among them. And, finally, once a problem and its cause were identified, it sometimes took a long period of trial-and-error fiddling until people could be convinced that it was indeed corrected.

The Harrisburg Plant

The decision to put Z-Glass into the Harrisburg plant had been based on its availability. Built in 1958 and long devoted to the production of headlights and other auto products, the plant had operated at excess capacity for several years in the late 1960s. In 1972 headlight production was consolidated in the Farwell, Ohio, plant while Harrisburg was set up for Z-Glass production. Several of the production foremen and manufacturing staff members were transferred to Farwell and replaced by individuals who had been involved in Z-Glass prototype production. (*Table A* contains a profit and loss statement for the Harrisburg plant in 1975–1976.)

The Harrisburg plant manager was Andrew MacTavish, a 54-year-old Scotsman. He came to the United States shortly after World War II and began working at Corning as a helper on a shipping crew at the old main plant. Over the years, MacTavish had worked his way up through various supervisory positions to production superintendent and finally to plant manager. He was a large man with a ruddy complexion and a booming voice. Although his temper was notorious, most people who had worked with him felt that some of his tirades were more than a little calculated. Whatever peoples' perceptions of his personality might be, there was no question who was in charge at Harrisburg.

In mid-1977 MacTavish had been at Harrisburg for six years. From the beginning he had developed a reputation as a champion of the little people as he called them. He wore what the workers wore, and spent two to three hours each day on the factory floor talking with foremen, supervisors, and production workers. If he had a philosophy of plant operations, it was to keep management as close to the people as possible and to rely on the experience, judgment, and skill of his workers in solving problems.

The Harrisburg plant was organized along department lines, with a production superintendent responsible for three general foremen who managed the melting, forming, and finishing departments. Ron Lewis, production superintendent, had come to the plant in 1975 after eight years at Corning. He was quietly efficient and had a good rapport with the foremen and supervisors. Besides Lewis, three other managers reported to MacTavish: Al Midgely, director of maintenance and engineering, Arnie Haggstrom, director of production planning and inventory control, and Royce Ferguson, head of personnel.

By June 1977 the management group at the Harrisburg plant had worked together for two years and had established what MacTavish thought was a solid organization. He commented to a visitor in May 1977:

> I've seen a lot of plant organizations in my time, but this one has worked better than any of them. When we sit down in staff meetings every morning everyone is on top of their situation and we've learned to get to the heart of our problems quickly. With the different personalities around here you'd think it would be a dog fight, but these people really work together.

Of all the managers on his staff, MacTavish worked most closely with Midgely. Midgely, 46 years old, came to the plant with MacTavish, had a B.S. in mechanical engineering, and was regarded as a genius when it came to equipment. "He can build or fix anything," MacTavish claimed. Midgely was devoted to MacTavish: "Ten years ago, Andy MacTavish saved my life. I had some family problems after I lost my job at Bausch and Lomb, but Andy gave me a chance and helped me pick up the pieces. Everything I have I owe to him." Several people in the Harrisburg plant gratefully acknowledged MacTavish's willingness to help his people.

M&E Project at Harrisburg

Davidson's top priority in the first two weeks of the project was to define the problem. Overall yields had declined, but no one had analyzed available information to identify the major causes. The M&E group believed that the plant organization had spent its time on fire fighting during the past six months with little overall direction. Grebwell analyzed the historical data collected by the production control department. Other team members spent this time familiarizing themselves with the process, meeting with their counterparts in the plant organization, and meeting together to compare notes and develop hypotheses about what was going on.

One problem surfaced immediately: the relative inexperience of the department supervisors. As MacTavish explained to them, four of the six supervisors had been in the plant less than nine months. The people they replaced had been with the Z-Glass process since its prototype days. MacTavish felt that part of the explanation for the decline in yields was the departure of experts. He expressed confidence in the new people and indicated that they were rapidly becoming quite knowledgeable.

TABLE A Harrisburg Plant—Profit and Loss Statement, 1976–1977 ($ thousands)

	1976	1977
Sales[a]	$26,653.3	$40,565.0
Direct expenses		
Materials	9,947.2	16,214.2
Labor	3,714.3	6,194.7
Gross profit	12,991.8	18,156.1
Manufacturing overhead		
Fixed[b]	6,582.6	11,106.9
Variable[c]	1,429.3	2,114.4
Plant administrative expenses	1,784.5	2,715.2
Plant profit	3,195.4	2,219.6

[a] Capacity utilization (on a nominal sales basis) was 92% in 1976 and 84% in 1977.

[b] Included depreciation, insurance, taxes, maintenance, utilities, and supervision.

[c] Included fringe benefits, indirect labor, tools, and supplies.

Grebwell's preliminary statistical work (see *Exhibit 3*) pointed to the molding department as the primary source of defects, with melting the second major source. The team identified four areas for immediate attention: overall downtime, trim settings, glass adhesion, and layer separation. As Grebwell's work proceeded, other projects in other departments were identified and staff members were added to the team. By mid-January it was evident that the overall project would have to encompass activities throughout the plant. It was decided that the only way to measure performance equitably was to use overall yield improvement. A timetable for improved yields was established and approved by the review board in late January 1978.

Davidson commented on the first six weeks of the project:

> Our initial reception in the plant was lukewarm. People were a little wary of us at first, but we did establish a pretty good relationship with Ron Lewis and some of the people in the production control group. I was confident that with time we could work together with MacTavish and people in other departments, but I wasn't as confident that the problems themselves could be solved. My objective was to obtain longterm improvements by defining and documenting the process, but when I arrived I found an inadequate data base and a process more complex than anyone had imagined.

Davidson encountered resistance to the very idea of process documentation. The view of MacTavish and others in the plant was aptly summarized by Blackburn, who appeared in Harrisburg off and on throughout the first three months of the M&E project. On one such visit he took Davidson into a conference room to converse:

Blackburn [after drawing on the blackboard]: Do you know what this is? This is a corral and inside the corral is a bucking bronco. Now what do you suppose this is?

Davidson: It looks like a cowboy with a book in his hand.

Blackburn: That's right, sonny, it's a greenhorn cowboy trying to learn how to ride a bucking bronco by reading a book. And that's just what you are trying to do with all your talk about documentation. And you'll end right where that greenhorn is going to end up—flat on your face.

EXHIBIT 3 Grebwell's Memorandum on Preliminary Statistics

To: M&E Project Team
From: R. Grebwell
Re: Yield Report for December 1977

Below are data on yields in period 13 (provided by the production control department) along with notes based on preliminary observations. Rejects are based on 100% inspection. Note that selecting a reason for rejection is based on the concept of "principal cause"; if more than one defect is present, the inspector must designate one as the primary reason for rejection.

Harrisburg Plant
Yield Report Period 13, 1977

I. Melting

	Good Output as a % of Scheduled Capacity[a]					Downtime[b] as a % of Total Scheduled Time
	Z1	Z4	Z10	Z35	Z12	
Glass	70.4	65.4	72.3	73.5	66.9	–
Equipment Downtime	–	–	–	–	–	10.3

II. Molding and Finishing

	% Rejected by Product, Reason, and Department[c]					Downtime as a % of Total Scheduled Time
	Z1	Z4	Z10	Z35	Z12	
A. Molding						
Trim[d]	6.4	12.8	4.1	3.4	10.2	–
Structural	3.7	6.2	1.7	2.8	5.7	–
Adhesion	4.5	8.3	2.5	3.1	8.5	–
Downtime	–	–	–	–	–	15.2
					24.4	
B. Finishing						
Cracks	0.8	4.2	0.3	1.2	3.6	
Separation	2.6	3.8	1.5	2.2	4.4	
Coatings	1.9	2.4	0.6	1.7	2.1	
Downtime						12.6

(continued on next page)

Conflict Emerges

Following the review board's acceptance of the proposed timetable, Davidson intended to create subproject terms, with an M&E specialist and a plant representative as coleaders. Despite Blackburn's lecture, Davidson pressed ahead with plans for process definition and documentation. A key element of the program was the development of instrumentation to collect information on the critical operating variables (glass temperature, machine speeds, timing, and so forth). Beginning in early January, Arnoldus had spent three weeks quietly observing the process, asking questions of the operators, and working on the development of instruments. He had decided to debug and confirm the systems on one production line (there were five separate lines in the plant) before transferring the instruments to other lines.

The instrumentation project was scheduled to begin on February 1, with the installation of sensors to monitor glass temperature in the molding process. No plant representative for the project had been designated by that time, however, and Davidson postponed the installation. A series of meetings between Davidson and MacTavish followed, but not until two days before the next

EXHIBIT 3 (Continued)

III. Summary[e]

	Z1	Z4	Z10	Z35	Z12	Total
			Good Output as a % of Scheduled Capacity			
Melting	70.4	65.4	72.3	73.5	66.9	—
Molding	72.4	61.6	77.8	76.9	64.1	—
Finishing	82.8	78.3	85.3	82.9	78.6	—
Overall	42.2	31.5	48.0	46.9	33.7	40.7

[a] This is overall yield and includes the effect of glass defects as well as downtime.

[b] No data are available on equipment downtime by product; the overall figure is applied to each product.

[c] The data are presented by department. They indicate the percentage of *department* output rejected and the principal reason for rejection. Total overall process yield (good output as a % of rated capacity) depends on both product defects and downtime.

[d] The reasons for rejection break down as follows:

Molding

Trim: This is basically two things—dimensions and edge configuration. It looks to me like the biggest problem is with the edges. The most commoon cause of defects in the runs I have watched is that the settings drift out of line. Apparently this depends on where the settings are established, how they are adjusted and the quality of the glass.

Structural: Pieces are rejected if they buckle or if the surface has indentations. This one is a real mystery—it could be a problem with the equipment (not right specs) or the operating procedures. Without some testing it's hard to tell. One possibility we need to check is whether the temperature of the incoming glass is a factor.

Adhesion: If compression ratios are too low or if the glass temperature is not "just right" or the glass has stones, then the glass adheres to the surface of the molds. The operators check the ratios, but the ideal range is marked on the gauges with little bits of tape, and I suspect the margin of error is pretty large.

Finishing

Cracks: Pieces sometimes develop cracks after heat treating. The principal suspect is consistency of temperature and flame zone. It is very hard to tell whether this is due to poor initial settings or changes in flames once the process starts. Inconsistencies in the material may be another source of cracks.

Layer

Separation: Layer separation seems to be caused by same factors as cracks.

Coatings: This is almost entirely a problem of operator error—handling damage, poor settings on the equipment, inattention to equipment going out of spec, and so forth.

e. There are four steps to calculating overall yield.
1. For a given product in a given department, add up reject rates by reason and subtract from 1;
2. Then multiply by (1 − % downtime) to get department yield for that product (e.g., molding yield for Z12 = (1 − .244) (1 − .152) = .641)
3. Multiply department yields to get overall yield by product (e.g., yield for Z12 = .669 × .641 × .786 = .337);
4. To get overall yield, take a weighted average of product yields, with share in total output (on a total pieces basis) as weights; in period 13 these weights were Z1 = .3, Z4 = .15, Z10 = .10, Z35 = .25, and Z12 = .2.

review board meeting on February 23 were plant representatives for each subproject chosen. Even then, things did not go smoothly. Arnoldus described his experience:

I didn't want to impose the instrumentation program on the people; I wanted them to understand that it was a tool to help them do their jobs better. But I had a terrible time getting Hank Gordel (the coleader of the project team) to even talk to me. He claimed he was swamped with other things. The thing of it is, he *was* busy. The plant engineering group had several projects of their own going, and those people were working 15 hours a day. But I knew there was more to it than that when I started hearing people refer to the M&E team as *spies*. After a while, people stopped talking to me and even avoided me in elevators and the cafeteria.

24. Corning Glass Works: The Z-Glass Project

The other subprojects suffered a similar fate. The only team to make any progress was the group working on materials control. Ron Lewis thought the program was a good one and supported it; he had appointed one of his better supervisors to be coleader. In the other areas of the plant, however, little was accomplished. Attempts to deal informally (lunch, drinks after work) with people in the plant organization failed, and Davidson's meetings with MacTavish and his requests for support were fruitless. Indeed, MacTavish viewed the M&E team as part of the problem. He forcefully expressed himself in a meeting with Davidson in late March 1978:

> I've said right from the beginning that this yield problem is basically a people problem. My experienced production people were promoted out from under me, and it has taken a few months for the new people to get up to speed. But this kind of thing is not going to happen again. I've been working on a supervisor backup training program that will give me some bench strength.
>
> I'm not saying we don't have problems. I know there are problems with the process, but the way to solve them is to get good people and

FIGURE C Yields and Downtime, 1976–1978

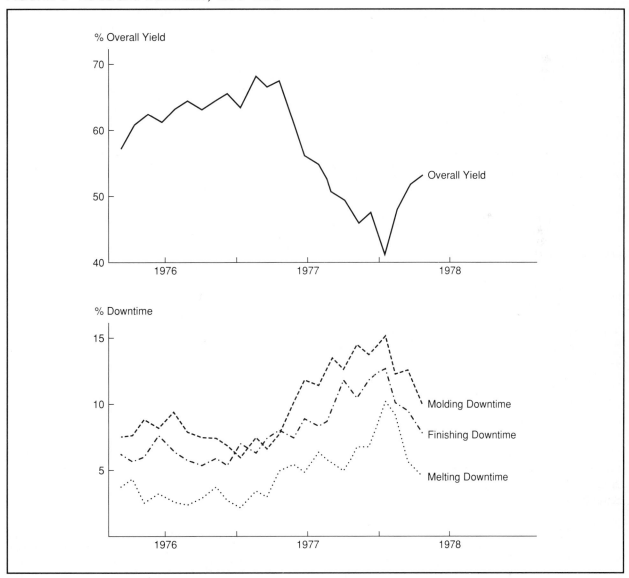

TABLE B Harrisburg Plant—Summary of Yields, Period 3, 1978

Department	Z1	Z4	Z10	Z35	Z12	Total
			Product Lines			
Melting	74.6	69.3	76.6	77.9	70.9	—
Molding	79.7	71.3	83.5	83.8	72.4	—
Finishing	85.8	83.7	88.7	87.6	84.9	—
Overall	51.0	41.4	56.7	57.2	43.6	53.4

give them some room. What this process needs now is some stability. Last year two new products were introduced, and this year I've got you and your engineers out there with your experiments and your projects, fiddling around with my equipment and bothering my people.

And then there's Blackburn. He blows in here with some crazy idea and goes right out there on the floor, and gets the operators to let him try out his latest scheme. The best thing for this plant right now would be for all of you to just get out and let us get this place turned around.

I am convinced we can do it. In fact, we've already been doing it. You've seen the data for the last 12 weeks. Yields have been increasing steadily and we're now above the average for last year. While you people have been making plans and writing memos, we've been solving the problem. [Data from the preliminary yield report are presented in *Figure C* and *Table B*.]

Resolving the Crisis

Davidson sat at his desk in the Harrisburg plant on March 24, 1978, and reviewed the events of the last three months. He realized that he also had been guilty of excessive fire fighting, and had not taken the time to step back from the situation and plot out a course of action. The situation demanded careful thought.

He was genuinely puzzled by the recent improvement in yield performance; since the M&E team had done very little beyond data analysis the improvement must have come from elsewhere. All his training and experience supported the concept of definition and documentation, but he had never encountered such a complex process. Perhaps MacTavish was right, but he just couldn't bring himself to believe that.

Several options came to mind as he thought of ways to resolve the crisis; none of them were appealing. He could go to Leibson and Williams and ask, perhaps demand, that MacTavish be replaced with someone more supportive. He could continue to try to build alliances with supporters in the plant (there were a few such people) and get a foothold in the organization. Or he could develop a new approach to the problem (perhaps new people) and attempt to win over MacTavish. Davidson knew that his handling of this situation could have important consequences for the M&E Division, for the company, and for the careers of several people, his included.

Module 4
Competing on New Products and Processes*

New products and processes pose special problems for managers because they seldom mesh perfectly with the existing organization. Their defining characteristic, after all, is that they are unfamiliar and demand creative responses. Old routines must usually be revised, and new approaches developed. Information and measurement systems may require readjustment. Even deeply rooted cultures and decision-making styles may need to be redefined.

Is it any wonder, then, that the track record in this area is so poor? New products, for example, fail with distressing regularity. Studies of consumer goods have shown that new offerings fail as much as fifty to sixty percent of the time, often because they are imitative or "me-too" products.[1] Other studies, based on a broad range of industries, have routinely found failure rates of thirty to forty percent.[2]

Nor are new processes normally introduced without disruption. Few reach their expected efficiencies within planned startup periods, or within budget. A study of continuous casters in steel mills, for example, found that managers expected startup periods (the "time from production of the first acceptable product until the plant is operating regularly at full capacity") to last less than a year; the actual duration was, on average, two and one-half times longer.[3] Costs are usually impacted as well, and in equally unfavorable ways. One recent study of the determinants of factory productivity concluded that "[i]n most cases the additional costs . . . of adding new equipment (in terms of lost labor productivity, increased waste, equipment idle time, and so forth) appeared to be greater than the cost of the equipment itself."[4]

Despite these problems, companies continue to research, study, plan, and develop new products and processes. Most have little choice. Whatever the industry, markets are usually evolving, new competitors are emerging, and customer preferences are subject to change. Even long-established companies are vulnerable. During the 1900s, for example, there was considerable turnover among the 100 largest U.S. corporations. Many declined in size, and several disappeared completely as new patterns of demand emerged. In recent years, however, the rate of turnover has decreased. Managers have become more willing to diversify and introduce new product lines, showing that adaptability is closely linked to long-term survival.[5]

What, then, is the likely impact of new products and processes? The preceding discussion suggests two rules of thumb:

* Excerpt from *Operations Strategy Module Overview: Competing on New Products and Processes*, Harvard Business School Teaching Note 5-690-058. Copyright © 1990 by the President and Fellows of Harvard College.

1. Most innovations fail.
2. Firms that do not innovate die.

There is something unsettling and paradoxical about these observations. Faced with the first rule, risk-averse managers might well conclude that new products and processes are to be avoided: They have uncertain payoffs, and are likely to impose heavy financial burdens. But faced with the second rule, most managers would reach a far different conclusion: New products and processes are essential because, without them, their organizations are likely to have no future at all.

For such reasons, new products and processes are of great strategic interest. Successful efforts both enhance a company's existing competitive position and create capabilities for the future. Yet surprisingly, many companies still view product and process development in technical, rather than business, terms.[6] A primary goal of the module is therefore to sketch out these business and financial impacts more clearly, and to explore the differences between strategic and technical approaches to development.

At the same time, operational issues cannot be ignored. Even products and processes that fully meet strategic needs will fail if they are not organized and implemented with care. Managers must be sensitive to a range of practical concerns. What, for example, are the required steps in moving a new product from laboratory experiments to field tests, and then to full-scale production? How are new manufacturing processes best upgraded from low yielding, dimly understood "art" to well-grounded proceduralized "science"? How are the risks of product and process development kept limited or controlled? What are the elements of successful project management?

Together, these strategic and operational issues suggest the need for a new set of manufacturing skills. New products and processes put a premium on flexibility and responsiveness. Fine tuning the status quo is no longer enough to ensure success. As a recent report on U.S. manufacturing has observed:

> The changes needed can be described broadly as a shift from the traditional management goal of maximizing stability, productivity, and return on investment in the short term to the new goal of maximizing adaptability to a rapidly changing market, with long-term competitiveness as the first priority ... [M]anagers must learn to manage change.[7]

Major Themes

This module is organized around five major themes. They range from broad conceptual issues, such as the importance of learning, to narrow operating questions, such as the best way to transfer new products from the laboratory to the production line. All, however, focus in some way on the management of technology.

LEARNING AND EXPERIMENTATION

New products and processes typically arise from a concerted effort to create and apply knowledge. Their success or failure is often determined by the degree to which a company has mastered these activities and is able to transfer knowledge quickly and efficiently from one part of the organization to another. Learning is thus an essential element—perhaps, *the* essential element—in successful product and process development. As the chairman of a leading semiconductor manufacturer has observed, in a world of rapid change "the rate at which individuals and organizations learn may become the only sustainable competitive advantage." [8]

But what exactly is a learning organization? [9] And how does it avoid becoming stagnant and fossilized? The core requirement is an attentiveness and willingness to improve, coupled with explicit strategies for achieving that end. Learning organizations constantly seek to expand their knowledge bases, to learn from their own past experiences and the experiences of others. They actively experiment with new approaches and strive to capture the knowledge in forms that are readily transferable to other parts of the company. And, perhaps most important, they never assume that the status quo is good enough, or that they have a complete understanding of their products, processes, markets, or customers. For such companies, there is always more to learn.

Every case in the module deals with an organization that is actively learning. Four critical activities are described. The first is experimentation: the systematic search for new data, new approaches, and new ways of operating. In Corning Z-Glass, for example, the M&E team is pursuing a formal program of instrumentation, documentation, and statistical analysis to improve its understanding of the critical setpoints and parameters of the Z-Glass production process. In Boeing design engineers have developed programs to assess the performance of new materials, such as composites, by subjecting them to in-flight tests. Both of these cases involve relatively narrow, focused experiments. Allstate and Project Nantucket, on the other hand, raise larger issues of experimental design. At Allstate, chemists have been asked to experiment with a wholly new approach to developing products. In the past they created molecules with little attention to market needs; now they are engaged in targeted experiments. Because the desired goals have been clearly specified, the results are likely to better match user requirements. This new approach to experimentation has helped institutionalize a new development philosophy. Project Nantucket involves equally broad questions about how, and where, to conduct experiments, especially those involving new processes. What, for example, are the desired characteristics of the test bed for a new process technology? What constitutes a good process experiment, and what makes for a bad one?

The second critical aspect of a learning organization is its ability to learn from its own past experience, and especially from its failures. All too often, companies sweep failures under the rug. At best, they give them a cursory review; at worst, they ignore them completely. Yet failures are an invaluable source of insight, because they contain such rich data. Analyzed carefully, they can help companies distinguish workable from unworkable approaches and salvage potentially promising ideas for future use. A study of 158 new products, for example, uncovered a common pattern of evolution, where "the knowledge gained from failures was often instrumental in achieving subsequent successes." [10] In a learning organization, such knowledge is pursued actively and systematically. The best example is Boeing's Project Homework, a several year effort to derive lessons from comparisons of the company's experiences with the 707 and 727 programs, which were profitable and highly successful, and the 737 and 747 programs, which nearly resulted in bankruptcy. One result of these comparisons has been a set of design, manufacturing, and purchasing policies that guided the launch of the 767, making it the most successful, error-free startup in Boeing's history.

Of course, companies can learn from external as well as internal sources. Improvement comes not only from self-assessment, but also from reviewing the experiences of other organizations. Here, it is especially important to identify best practices and see if they can be adapted for use in one's own industry or operations. Xerox has pioneered this approach, called "benchmarking," and has made it the core of its competitive strategy. At heart, it is simply another way of encouraging learning and ensuring continual improvement:

> Benchmarking is the search for industry best practices that will lead to superior performance ... In the formal sense, [it] is an ongoing investigation and learning experience that ensures that best industry practices are uncovered, analyzed, adopted, and implemented.[11]

Of the cases in the module, Allstate's attempt to use Du Pont's market-driven approach to R&D best exemplifies benchmarking.

Finally, learning organizations are characterized by their skill at transferring knowledge internally. Typically, two approaches are used: embedding the knowledge in people, or in manuals and procedures. Rogers, Lehrer McGovern, and Boeing all illustrate the first approach. Each relies heavily on project teams and shifting work assignments to spread learning. Together, the cases provide several lessons: the need for early involvement by key departments, such as manufacturing and purchasing, to lay the groundwork for transfers out of the laboratory; the need for co-location of key individuals, to ensure that emerging problems are dealt with in real time and critical details are not overlooked because of poor communication; and the need for shared standards and accountabilities, to keep team members aligned and focused on the same scorecard. Corning and Allstate rely more on the second approach for transferring learning. Both favor codified knowledge over informal communication and personal contact. Written instructions are the desired end, and manuals and procedures are common. At Corning these instructions take the form of rules for operating the production process, while at Allstate they take the form of guidelines for new product development.

Eventually, as learning increases and products and processes become better understood, companies progress to higher stages of knowledge.[12] They may begin by assuming that a new manufacturing process is an "art," controllable only by feel and the judgment of skilled operators; later, after experiments have been conducted and operating parameters have been set, they may conclude that "science" is a more accurate description. Progressions of this sort—from ignorance to understanding, and from knowing how a process works to knowing why it performs as it does—are critical to successful new product introductions, for they translate directly into higher yields, improved productivity, and fewer rejects. Both Corning and Rogers describe attempts to make processes more scientific by shifting from lower to higher stages of knowledge.

PRODUCT AND PROCESS DEVELOPMENT PATHS

Development is a dynamic process, with a well-defined sequence of steps. Knowledge accumulates, and, in most cases, an orderly evolution is followed. Activities are not random; instead, they proceed in expected, preestablished patterns. An awareness of these patterns and how they combine to form product and process development paths is an essential part of understanding and managing technology.

New products, for example, usually progress through three stages.[13] First comes *product research*: basic R&D, the creation of new knowledge, and the development of a product concept. Next comes *product development*: the construction of prototypes, field testing and market research, and agreement on preliminary specifications. Last comes *final design*: the development and approval of complete technical specifications, working drawings, and bills of materials. Each of these steps has its own logic and supporting activities, and its own requirements for success. They are examined in detail in several cases, including Allstate, Rogers, Boeing, and Lehrer McGovern.

Like products, processes progress through several stages of development. But here the required steps vary by industry. For businesses like chemicals and glass-making, where continuous processes are the norm, product and process are difficult to separate. The two are usually developed simultaneously in the laboratory. Scale up then becomes critical, with three distinct stages: the initial bench or laboratory work, an intermediate-sized pilot plant or semiworks, and full scale production.[14] Each involves a step up in cost and verisimilitude, and each requires the use of more cumbersome, factory-like equipment. As Corning and Rogers illustrate, scale ups are often problematic. What works in the laboratory does not always work in pilot plants or on production lines. The latter are run at higher volumes, involve more complex operating conditions, and are harder to control.

Fabrication and assembly processes follow a different sequence of steps because they permit the decoupling of product and process development. In such settings product planning can, and often does, proceed independently of process planning. Process development then reduces to those activities that convert technical specifications—the output of product planning—into a precise description of manufacturing requirements. Among the most critical activities are the development of routing sheets, showing the path that parts and materials must follow through the production process; lists of required tooling, equipment, and personnel; and instructions for materials handling and operations to be performed.[15] Both Project Nantucket and Boeing include detailed process plans that are representative of fabrication and assembly businesses.

An understanding of product and process development paths is important for three reasons. First, both managerial and technical tasks differ at key points along the paths. Without a clear sense of these tasks and how they unfold over time, errors are inevitable. The wrong perspective may be assumed at a critical juncture, or the wrong person may be assigned to a project. For example, in the early stages of product research, the dominant mode is speculative. Experimentation is a key activity, and premature closure is to be avoided. The goal is to generate a wide range of potential product concepts. Soon, however, the tasks become more applied. Attention shifts to design and testing, and there is continual interaction among engineers and potential customers. Economic and technical feasibility are now the critical objectives. Finally, in the last stage of development, commercial goals become paramount, and skill at managing the ramp up to volume production and the provision of marketing support are essential. It should be clear from the above description that each period requires a shift in orientation and focus, as well as a new mix of talents and competencies.[16] The needed changes are examined in Allstate, Boeing, and Lehrer McGovern, which include detailed chronological descriptions of the emergence and development of three diverse products: a specialty chemical, a wide-bodied jet, and several innovative office buildings.

A second reason for studying product and process development paths is the help they provide in troubleshooting new technologies. Frequently, problems arise at the transition points between activities, especially the shift from open-ended R&D to more focused development and the jump from laboratory scale to higher volume processes. Even under the best of circumstances, it is difficult for companies to transfer information from one group to another. But here, the changing nature of the required tasks adds greatly to the challenge. For example, as processes move from bench to pilot scale and from pilot scale to full-blown factory, companies often find that they have grasped the basics of the process but have not yet mastered its repeatability. A working process that establishes feasibility is quite different from one that is fully characterized, with known setpoints and operating rules that guarantee the same results every time. Yet even companies that recognize this distinction find the transition difficult to manage, because new perspectives and skills are required. Both Corning and Rogers illustrate the problems of scaling up and characterizing new processes.

New products often lead to similar conflicts, especially when exploratory R&D gives way to market development, application engineering, and field testing. Again, a wholly new way of thinking is required, and decisions are guided by different rules of thumb. Allstate and Boeing explore the difficulties of this transition.

A third reason for studying product and process development paths is their link to a critical competitive variable: time to market. Time to market is heavily affected by the sequencing of product and process activities, and the amount of overlap.[17] At one extreme is *linear* or *phased development*. Product planning is fully completed before process planning begins, and each activity proceeds independently and in isolation. Project Nantucket best illustrates this approach. At the other extreme is *simultaneous development*, in which product and process planning overlap completely. The two are so closely linked that they proceed together, often under the direction of a single individual or project team. This approach is most common in continuous process industries, where the dividing line between product and process technology is difficult to draw. Corning and Rogers provide vivid examples. Finally, an intermediate approach is *overlapping development*, in which some, but not all, downstream activities begin while upstream work is still incomplete. Product and process planning are neither fully separate nor totally simultaneous. Instead, they overlap partially, to ensure a speedier development process. Lehrer McGovern, an advocate of "fast track" construction, begins site work before complete architectural plans are in hand; Boeing, to compress a decade-long development cycle, begins parts fabrication before designs are fully locked in, as long as twenty-five percent of structural engineering drawings are complete. Clearly, companies pursuing simultaneous or overlapping development require close cooperation between product and process planners, as well as the rapid and continuous exchange of information. Both are also necessary for successful technology transfer.

TECHNOLOGY TRANSFER

Whatever the sequencing of product and process development, a handoff from R&D to manufacturing is required. The task is surprisingly complex, and often the problems seem insurmountable. Yet they can usually be reduced to manageable proportions by dividing the transfer process into four distinct, but interrelated, decisions.

The first decision involves *timing*. When is a new product or process ready to be handed off? How much laboratory work is enough? When should a division insist on further development? Here, several competing concerns must be weighed: the need for products that match customer requirements; the need for specifications and operating parameters that are detailed enough to ensure efficient, repeatable manufacturing; and the need for short development cycles to preempt competitors. The latter need is especially important today. A study by McKinsey & Company found that, in the 1980s, if a high technology company was even six months late in bringing a product to market, its profits could fall by as much as a third.[18] Yet somehow this need must be contained if premature release is to be avoided, and workable products and processes are to emerge. The timing of technology transfer is thus something of a judgment call, and a delicate balancing act. To smooth the process, formal guidelines, documentation requirements, and clear cut policies, such as procedures for statistical verification and rules specifying the amount of engineering work to be completed before handoffs are permitted, help enormously. They provide consistency and stability, and serve as a rallying point for managers. Allstate, Rogers, and Boeing all include descriptions of handoffs and raise questions about their timing and procedures.

The second decision about technology transfer involves *location*. Where should a new product or process be housed? Should it be sent to an existing division, a new division, or a hybrid organization, such as a commercial development group, whose primary purpose is the nurturing of new ventures? Again, several competing needs must be weighed: the divisions' closeness to R&D, suppliers, and customers; their marketing and technical skills; their match with product and process requirements; their desire to accept unproven ventures; and their promise as sites for stimulating wider organizational learning. Here, a common difficulty is the reluctance of existing divisions to accept untested technologies because they might depress short-term profits. One response has been the creation of "halfway houses," specially designed to cultivate and protect risky projects. They go by various names—new venture divisions, commercial development groups, producibility laboratories—but share a willingness to experiment and an often freewheeling, entrepreneurial culture.[19] Allstate discusses the role of such groups explicitly, while both Rogers and Project Nantucket raise related questions about the best place to start up new products and processes.

The third decision about technology transfer involves *people*. Who should be involved in the transfer process? Which individuals should play a direct role, and which should be responsible for oversight and control? Here, the experts are in wide agreement: Project teams, composed of developers and receivers of the technology, are most effective in ensuring smooth transfers, and top managers must actively monitor the process if business, rather than technical, goals are to dominate.[20] Occasionally, special review boards or audit procedures are needed for complex, sophisticated projects. Project teams are discussed in Corning, Allstate, Rogers, Boeing, and Lehrer McGovern, while review boards and audit procedures are examined in Corning, Allstate, and Boeing.

The fourth decision about technology transfer involves *communication*. How is knowledge best transferred from R&D to manufacturing? What methods are most effective in bridging the cultural, informational, and geographical gaps that often separate the two groups? Typically, one of three approaches is used: multi-functional teams with responsibility throughout the entire project, the direct transfer of personnel, and formal documentation. Boeing and Lehrer McGovern best illustrate the first approach. Both form teams early, insist on broad functional representation, and keep teams intact and meeting regularly until projects are complete. Allstate and Rogers best illustrate the second approach. Both transfer R&D personnel to manufacturing divisions when scaling up processes to higher volumes. Corning, with its Manufacturing and Engineering Division and heavy reliance on instrumentation and data collection, best illustrates the third approach. Rogers Total Quality Concept is similar in philosophy, but less developed.

In combination, these decisions about timing, location, people, and communication constitute the core of technology transfer. The four areas are, of course, strongly interrelated. But a disaggregated approach, focusing on a question at a time, provides both clarity and simplicity, and the likelihood of wiser decisions.

PROJECT MANAGEMENT

Because they fall outside the daily operating tasks of business, new products and processes are normally managed as discrete projects. Over time, project management has developed into a field with its own distinctive tools, techniques, and specialized activities. For convenience, they can be divided into two categories: planning, and control.[21]

Formal approaches to project planning have long been a staple of the management literature. The best known are scheduling techniques, such as the Critical Path Method (CPM) and Program Evaluation and Review Techniques (PERT). Both link individual activity times to the time required for overall project completion. Other methods for planning projects include learning curves and value analysis. These methods focus on cost rather than time. Learning curves use historical data to predict the relationship between new product costs and cumulative production volumes, while value analysis uses a multi-step process to redesign products and reduce their costs, but without compromising customer satisfaction. Boeing employs learning curves to predict the costs of new airplanes. Lehrer McGovern, a construction manager specializing in difficult and innovative projects, has built its reputation on creative value analysis. Both companies also rely heavily on sophisticated scheduling systems, such as CPM and PERT.

Once projects have been planned, they must be monitored and controlled to ensure that milestones are met and unexpected problems do not impede performance or inflate costs. Careful tracking is essential, as is the early surfacing of problems.[22] Boeing, for example, has developed an "early warning system" to flush out problems before they escalate and become more serious. Discipline is also needed, whether the source is peer pressure, compensation schemes, procedural guidelines, or audits by senior management. Such methods are discussed in several cases, including Corning, Allstate, Rogers, Boeing, and Lehrer McGovern.

Yet even with these tools, project management remains difficult, and failures are common. The problem, according to experts, is largely one of perspective:

> . . . the tendency of senior managers to treat development efforts solely as technical projects. As important as technical competence is, . . . development projects are business projects and should be managed as such.[23]

> . . . the conventional wisdom in new product development and technology suffers from a key underlying problem: these two issues are seen in tactical rather than strategic terms.[24]

Managers must never forget that new products and processes are being pursued for business reasons. They need to link development efforts with strategic plans, continually canvas customers for new ideas, and keep a close eye on competitors. But even with this perspective, operational issues must still be addressed. Successful projects are not only strategically driven; they also share a clearly defined mission, top management support, detailed schedules, active communication and consultation with clients, trained and skilled personnel, timely monitoring and control, an effective information and communication network, and the ability to handle unexpected crises.[25] Allstate, Boeing, and Lehrer McGovern all show effective approaches in these areas, while Corning and Rogers illustrate the problems that arise when one or more elements are missing.

MANAGING RISK

Because they involve so many unknowns, new products and processes are accompanied by substantial risk. Typically, the risks of a project increase with the level of uncertainty, the probability of failure, and the required financial commitment.[26] Understanding and controlling these risks is vital to the successful introduction of new technologies.

The first step for managers is distinguishing among different kinds of risk. *Market risks*, for example, involve uncertainties on the demand side. They raise the question: Will customers actually purchase a new product, and if so, in what volumes? *Competitive risks* reflect the difficulty of predicting other companies' responses. *Technological risks* reflect the unknowns of newly developed materials and methods: What are their properties and how will they perform? *Organizational risks* arise because traditional structures, staffing, and reporting relationships are often unable to accommodate radically new technologies. *Production risks* reflect the difficulties of start up and implementation: Will full-scale production lead to problems that did not appear in prototypes or bench work? And *financial risks* arise because large dollars are often at stake, with uncertain payoffs.

Distinguishing among these risks is important, for each imposes its own demands on managers. Companies may well find some types of risk more palatable than others, and better matched to their culture. A further complexity is introduced by the fact that the risks are interrelated, and actions to reduce one type may simultaneously increase others. Boeing, for example, now relies extensively on risk-sharing partners and subcontractors to reduce the massive market and financial risks of new plane programs. A new airplane requires an up front commitment of several billion dollars; with shared development, Boeing's outlay is sharply reduced. But at the same time, organizational and production risks are larger because more players are involved, greater coordination is required, and less work is done internally. Allstate, Rogers, and Project Nantucket describe other types of risk and their interrelationships.

Once the types of risk have been identified and the desired "risk profile" selected, the next step is risk reduction. One approach that works particularly well for market, technological, and production risks is formal programs of experimentation and field testing. Allstate and Rogers work with customers throughout the development process to see how their products perform in selected applications; before adopting new materials, Boeing first conducts in-service tests with airlines. A system of checks and balances is equally effective in limiting risks and ensuring that no single view dominates. Allstate uses a management review board to keep research efforts on track; Boeing employs audit teams reporting directly to the chairman; and Lehrer McGovern, a construction manager, positions itself midway between architects and contractors, using value engineering to ensure that design and cost goals are kept in balance. Redundancies and overlaps are an additional tool for risk management. To avoid the possibility of premature closure, companies will sometimes pursue parallel development projects, as Boeing did with the two- and three-engine versions of the

767. Such efforts reduce risk because they provide additional information and a sounder basis for decisions.

Perhaps the best way of reducing risk is the simplest: limiting the difference between the old and the new. As one expert has observed:

> Risk can be thought of as resulting from movements away from the existing state of affairs in any of three dimensions: technology, product, and market ... The farther along each dimension that a development is situated, the greater the risk. Movement out on two dimensions at once *greatly* increases the risk. The locus of greatest risk is movement along all three.[27]

Allstate clearly raises this issue. Dynarim, its latest offering, is a new product (a speciality rather than commodity chemical), aimed at a new market (automobile manufacturers), using a new technology (reaction injection molding). Not surprisingly, it has met a cool reception from Allstate's existing divisions. Boeing, by contrast, proceeds incrementally with new developments. Composites, a new technology, were first introduced on existing planes, and even then only on noncritical parts. Ford is facing a similar decision in Project Nantucket: whether to introduce its new automation process on a recently redesigned product, or to test it first on a stable, known design.

Of course, incremental improvement is not without risk. Because it is an inherently conservative approach, it leaves companies vulnerable to competitive leap-frogging. Market and technological risks may fall, but competitive risks are correspondingly higher. Here, as elsewhere in the course, the final decision for managers involves the juggling of tradeoffs.

NOTES

1. J. Hugh Davidson, "Why Most New Consumer Brands Fail," *Harvard Business Review*, March–April 1976, pp. 117–122, and Glen L. Urban and John R. Hauser, *Design and Marketing of New Products* (Englewood Cliffs, NJ: Prentice-Hall, 1980), pp. 2–3.
2. Harry S. Abrikian, "New Product Innovation: Empirical Findings and Marketing Applications," Technical Report No. 67, Graduate School of Business, Stanford University, mimeographed, June 1981, pp. 36–38.
3. Michiel R. Leenders and Ross Henderson, "Startup Research Presents Purchasing Problems and Opportunities (I)," *International Journal of Operations & Production Management* 1, 2 (1980), pp. 84–87.
4. Robert H. Hayes and Kim B. Clark, "Exploring the Sources of Productivity Differences at the Factory Level," in Kim B. Clark, Robert H. Hayes, and Christopher Lorenz, eds., *The Uneasy Alliance: Managing the Productivity-Technology Dilemma* (Boston: Harvard Business School Press, 1985), p. 184.
5. F.M. Scherer, *Industrial Market Structure and Economic Performance* (Chicago: Rand McNally, 1970), pp. 47–50.
6. Robert H. Hayes, Steven C. Wheelwright, and Kim B. Clark, *Dynamic Manufacturing* (New York: Free Press, 1988), ch. 10–11.
7. Manufacturing Studies Board, *Towards a New Era in U.S. Manufacturing* (Washington, D.C.: National Academy Press, 1986), p. 22.
8. Ray Stata, "Organizational Learning—The Key to Management Innovation," *Sloan Management Review*, Spring 1989, p. 64. The head of planning at Royal Dutch/Shell holds a similar view. See Arie P. de Geus, "Planning as Learning," *Harvard Business Review*, March–April 1988, p. 71.
9. There is considerable academic debate about what constitutes individual and organizational

learning. For a brief summary of the literature, see C. Marlene Fiol and Marjorie A. Lyles, "Organizational Learning," *Academy of Management Review,* vol. 10, no. 4 (1985), pp. 803–813.

10. Modesto A. Maidique and Billie Jo Zerger, "The New Product Learning Cycle," *Research Policy* no. 14 (1985), p. 229.

11. Robert C. Camp, "Benchmarking: The Search for Best Practices that Lead to Superior Performance," *Quality Progress,* January 1989, pp. 67–68.

12. For a detailed discussion of the stages of knowledge, see Ramchandran Jaikumar and Roger E. Bohn, "The Development of Intelligent Systems for Industrial Use: A Conceptual Framework," in Richard S. Rosenbloom, ed., *Research on Technological Innovation, Management and Policy,* vol. 3 (Greenwich, Conn.: JAI Press, 1986), pp. 179–188.

13. The description here follows Howard L. Timms, *The Production Function in Business* (Homewood, Ill.: Richard D. Irwin, 1966), pp. 180–187, and Edwin A. Gee and Chaplin Tyler, *Managing Innovation* (New York: John Wiley & Sons, 1976), pp. 87–90.

14. Gee and Tyler, *Managing Innovation,* pp. 80–87.

15. Timms, *The Production Function in Business,* pp. 285–325, and Evan D. Scheele, William L. Westerman, and Robert J. Wimmert, *Principles and Design of Production Control Systems* (Englewood Cliffs, NJ: Prentice-Hall, 1960), pp. 79–89.

16. Richard S. Rosenbloom, "Managing Technology for the Longer Term: A Managerial Perspective," in Clark, Hayes, and Lorenz, *The Uneasy Alliance,* pp. 302–311.

17. For comparisons of these approaches and their links to development cycle times, see Joseph L. Bower and Thomas M. Hout, "Fast-Cycle Capability for Competitive Power," *Harvard Business Review,* November–December 1988, pp. 110–118; Kim B. Clark and Takahiro Fujimoto, "Overlapping Problem Solving in Product Development," in Kasra Ferdows, ed., *Managing International Manufacturing* (Amsterdam: Elsevier Science, North Holland, 1989), pp. 127–152; and Hirotaka Takeuchi and Ikujiro Nonaka, "The New New Product Development Game," *Harvard Business Review,* January–February 1986, pp. 137–146.

18. "Silicon Valley's Design Renaissance," *The New York Times,* August 6, 1989, section 3, p. 6.

19. For discussions of new venture divisions and commercial development groups, see Christopher K. Bart, "New Venture Units: Use Them Wisely to Manage Innovation," *Sloan Management Review,* Summer 1988, pp. 35–43; Robert A. Burgelman, "Managing the New Venture Division: Research Findings and Implications for Strategic Management," *Strategic Management Journal,* vol. 6 (1985), pp. 39–54; and Norman D. Fast, "The Future of Industrial New Venture Departments," *Industrial Marketing Management,* vol. 8 (1979), pp. 264–273. For a discussion of producibility laboratories, see *Aviation Week & Space Technology,* October 10, 1988, p. 91.

20. See, for example, Paul S. Adler, Henry E. Riggs, and Steven C. Wheelwright, "Product Development Know-How: Trading Tactics for Strategy," *Sloan Management Review,* Fall 1989, pp. 7–17; Richard T. Hise and Stephen W. McDaniel, "What Is the CEO's Role in New Product Efforts?", *Management Review,* February 1989, pp. 44–48; and Dorothy Leonard-Barton and William A. Kravis, "Implementing New Technology," *Harvard Business Review,* November–December 1985, pp. 102–110.

21. Lowell W. Steele, *Managing Technology* (New York: McGraw-Hill, 1989), pp. 135–156.

22. Hayes, Wheelwright, and Clark, *Dynamic Manufacturing,* p. 317.

23. Ibid, p. 274.

24. Adler, Riggs, and Wheelwright, "Product Development Know-How," p. 8.

25. Dennis P. Slevin and Jeffrey K. Pinto, "Balancing Strategy and Tactics in Project Implementation," *Sloan Management Review,* Fall 1987, p. 34.

26. While they are often used interchangeably, the words "risk" and "uncertainty" are technical terms with different meanings. One classic work defines risk as "measurable uncertainty," with a known probability of outcome, and uncertainty as "unmeasurable or unknowable," with a probability of outcome that cannot be determined. See Frank H. Knight, *Risk, Uncertainty, and Profit* (Chicago: University of Chicago Press, 1971), p. 233.

27. Steele, *Managing Technology,* pp. 122–3.

25. Allstate Chemical Company: The Commercialization of Dynarim

In February 1986, Pete Kennedy, director of the Dynarim project, and his boss, Eric Reinhalter, sat down with Jack Cousins, president of Allstate Chemical Company, to discuss the future of the new Dynarim product. Dynarim, a liquid resin fabricated into structural parts by a new molding technology, now had repeat orders approaching $1 million. The project had been housed in an incubator group called Commercial Development for the past two years, but it could not remain there indefinitely. Cousins therefore wanted to review its status and future location, even though a move was not yet imminent.

The Company

ALLSTATE CHEMICAL IN THE 1970S. Allstate Chemical Company (ACC) produced commodity and specialty chemicals, and distributed commodity chemicals for virtually every major chemical producer in the United States. Its distribution philosophy, supported by the largest distribution network in the country, was "Tell us what you want, and we will get it to you." ACC itself supplied about 15–20% of the product sold through its network. Distribution accounted for about half of total revenues. Another 15% of sales came from the production of diverse specialty chemicals such as adhesives, foundry products, and electronics chemicals, most of which ACC had acquired during the last decade. Like Allstate's existing divisions, these additions operated with considerable autonomy and possessed the full range of functions needed for P&L accountability. (See *Exhibit 1*.)

This case was prepared by Artemis March under the direction of David A. Garvin.

RELATIONSHIP WITH THE CORPORATION. Allstate Chemical was a wholly owned subsidiary of the $8 billion Allstate Oil Corp. (AOC). During most of the 1970s, according to Jack Cousins, who became president of ACC in mid-1983,

> Chemicals were not perceived as a significant growth or investment area. It was tacitly understood that our mission was to provide a positive cash flow to the corporation for use in other areas.

Refinery closings and divestment of some oil-producing properties in the late 1970s reduced the pressure on ACC to be a cash provider, and generated funds for reinvestment in businesses other than oil. For the first time, chemical distribution and specialty chemicals were targeted for reinvestment and growth. Corporate expected a high return from the chemical business—12–13% ROI—as well as long-term growth. This sometimes produced conflicts: $4 million per year for a development project, for example, translated into ½% less ROI.

STRATEGIC SHIFT TOWARD SPECIALTY CHEMICALS IN THE 1980S. Such pressures from AOC were one of several factors leading ACC management to decide that its future lay in specialty chemicals (coupled with a continued focus on distribution) rather than commodities. Because of differences between the two types of chemicals, major organizational and policy changes were required to support the shift.

Customers bought commodity chemicals to meet a specification and because the price was right. Products were generic, and the market determined their price. Purchasing departments made the buying decisions, largely on the basis

EXHIBIT 1 Selected Financial Data

<table>
<tr><td colspan="6" align="center">(numbers are in millions of dollars)</td></tr>
<tr><td></td><td>1985</td><td>1984</td><td>1983</td><td>1982</td><td>1981</td></tr>
<tr><td>Sales and Operating Revenues</td><td>$1,500</td><td>$1,500</td><td>$1,200</td><td>$1,200</td><td>$1,300</td></tr>
<tr><td>Operating Income</td><td>70</td><td>55</td><td>0</td><td>30</td><td>40</td></tr>
<tr><td>Identifiable Assets</td><td>500</td><td>500</td><td>420</td><td>400</td><td>460</td></tr>
<tr><td>Funds Provided from Operations</td><td>60</td><td>50</td><td>20</td><td>45</td><td>50</td></tr>
<tr><td>Additions to Plant, Property and Equipment</td><td>40</td><td>20</td><td>20</td><td>30</td><td>35</td></tr>
<tr><td>Depreciation, Depletion and Amortization</td><td>25</td><td>25</td><td>20</td><td>20</td><td>15</td></tr>
</table>

All figures have been rounded
Source: 1985 Annual Report.

of price, quality, and delivery. Commodities were sold to end users and fabricators. Because the cost of the chemical was a key part of these customers' costs, a supplier that was 1–2¢ high usually lost the business. This emphasis on cost led to in-house manufacturing, in which, one manager noted, "Life revolves around the plant because low cost wins the game." Although high volume had brought ACC healthy profits, margins were less than for specialties, where performance set the price.

In specialties, the approach was usually to start from the customer's use and work backward. Applications were critical. Specialty chemicals were usually a small part of the price of the customer's product; as long as products performed as needed, business was not lost over pennies. Purchasing played a largely administrative role because decisions to buy or specify critical ingredients were made by design engineers and plant people. These demands increased the need for marketing and technical staff. Because specialties were sold in the tens of millions of pounds per year rather than in billions, they were more likely to be made in batches than by continuous processes. This enormously reduced the scope and cost of capital investment—from hundreds of millions of dollars to tens of millions. But commodity plants could not be converted to specialty production. Specialties, however, allowed a company to forego

in-house manufacturing, particularly in the early, risky stages of a product's life. Cousins explained:

> With an uncertain new product, why own a plant when you can rent a reactor? You would only want to bring manufacturing in-house if you had a well-established, high-volume product, or if you couldn't protect the technology, or if the manufacturing sequence was very complex and an outside company couldn't do it right or very consistently.

In specialties, ACC management felt it was important to be a leader rather than a follower. An early entrant could not only gain market share, set the price and ground rules, and gain lead time; it could also dictate the performance parameters a competitor would need to exceed to displace it. Later entrants had to provide significantly better performance, because their products were seldom "drop-ins" for the customer's equipment and process. Switching costs might include new molds, or repiping, and, most significantly, requalification testing, which could take years and cost millions of dollars. Second entrants also had to overcome reluctance to change from the known to the unknown.

Between 1980 and 1985, Allstate closed and sold several commodity businesses, including plants, and added specialties by acquiring and building facilities and using outside processors. Specialties doubled from 15% of Allstate's business to 30%, while distribution of commodities continued to account for about half of the company's sales. George Prince, general manager of the Polyesters Division, which now derived most of its profits from specialties, commented on what the changes had meant for his division.

> You have much more exposure in the corporation when you're identified as a division that needs to be grown. We have made timely acquisitions that fit our technological and customer base, and we intend to make more since the corporation is now willing to fund them. Our staff has increased dramatically. Two years ago, we did no market development. But now, for example, we are trying to get engineers to design in our resins for the Pontiac Firebird, and that requires marketing.
>
> Specialties are also more quality-oriented, and there's been more emphasis on how we control processes and how we report data to customers. For that reason, we do all of our own specialty manufacturing, and are investing in things like computer control of reactors. Our productivity has gone up because we're not making off-spec product.

Research, 1977–1986

FORMATION OF VENTURE RESEARCH. Until 1977, Allstate Chemical had no significant central research organization. Small research groups in each division focused on short-term technical service to customers. Under the impetus of Cousins, who was then administrative vice president for research, engineering and finance, 25% of the company's research budget and people were pulled from the divisions to form Venture Research (VR).

VR's charter was to develop projects that would lead to major new businesses, with "major" defined as at least several hundred million dollars in annual sales. The group was to look for home runs outside existing division interests. Initially, Cousins and other senior managers wanted VR to focus on breakthrough process changes for producing high-volume, commodity chemicals. To head VR, Allstate recruited Dick Winthrop, whose process work at a competitor had won several industry awards.

RESEARCH STRATEGY: FROM PROCESS/COMMODITY FOCUS TO PRODUCT/SPECIALTY. Process research required a broad range of chemical and engineering skills, a large commitment of people for long periods, and heavy investments in capital equipment. During the research stage, for example, this might mean building a series of reactors of increasing size, each of which could study a larger number of process variables. If the researchers succeeded in creating a commercially viable reaction, engineers would then have to create the equipment to make it. Process research typically started with petrochemicals that could be refined from crude oil (such as benzene), and sought cheaper ways to produce derivative monomers (such as styrene) or polymers (such as polystyrene), by significantly reducing the costs of raw materials, of capital, or both.[1]

VR's initial strategy aimed to replicate what Winthrop had accomplished at Noroil. Process changes had so dramatically lowered Noroil's price for a high-volume monomer that they had "knocked the bottom out of the market," as one manager put it. Although Allstate did develop two new processes, neither achieved commercial success. In one case, the cost advantage was not large enough; in the other, ACC had to compete with potential customers' captive monomer production. The 1981–83 industry recession and the domestic industry's shift to offshore production dealt the final blows to ACC's process/commodity research strategy. Cousins ruefully acknowledged: "It took us five years and $50 million to see that this was the wrong way to go."

As process research was cut back, VR slowly gravitated toward product/specialty research. By 1984, its charter had shifted to supporting and strengthening the divisions. Prince described Polyesters' changing relationship to VR:

> We used to do almost no new-product development; what we did was handholding, firefighting and low-level product improvement to satisfy specific customer needs. Now we are identifying market opportunities and developing new chemistries for which we want VR's expertise. We want them to do original chemistry, to invent new polymers that we develop for the market. Therefore, we need close contact to see that they

---

[1] Monomers are small molecules (i.e., molecules having low molecular weight), usually in liquid form. Also called resins or prepolymers, they are an intermediate product that needs further processing (polymerization plus molding into a part) to make a final product. Monomers are the bricks and mortar for constructing the polymer "house." Polymers are large molecules that have been put together to create a solid material that, when molded, has desired properties such as stiffness or strength.

25. Allstate Chemical Company: The Commercialization of Dynarim

are on track—we don't want them doing any blue-sky stuff. So when we see an opportunity for expanding our product line, I lobby Jack and the others, and they go to Dr. Winthrop and tell him to work on it.

Less capital intensive than process research, polymer research normally involved working with a certain type of chemistry (such as esters, urethanes, or alcohols) to produce either an entirely new molecule or improvements in the performance of existing molecules. Results were typically the product of years of studying such basic phenomena as what made adhesives work. According to Cousins, the shift in research strategy was brought about by a combination of "SEP oversight, reviews of projects, yelling, and handholding."

STRATEGIC EXPANSION PROJECT (SEP) BOARD. Shortly after becoming president, Cousins established the Strategic Expansion Project Board to oversee research. Its members were Cousins and five group vice presidents; and its charter was to identify and fund those research projects that had significant strategic and commercial potential. The board looked for projects that fit Allstate's strength in technology or markets, and could open up new businesses. Such projects had to be more than mere line extensions, which remained the responsibility of divisions. VR could still fund projects at a relatively low level from its own budget, but continued funding or significant expansions of the work required board approval. SEP-approved projects were funded from "Jack's budget" until they broke even.

With this mechanism, the company's chief operating officers supported the start-up costs of new businesses from company rather than division profits, and exercised control over funding. If necessary, the board could kill a project that was not showing significant progress or whose commercial potential had waned. Cousins was satisfied that commercial considerations now guided Allstate's research in new areas. He noted, however, that "Dick Winthrop doesn't totally approve of this approach. There are areas he would like to expand that don't have a chance of succeeding commercially. But he knows that I will not approve a test-tube project." Winthrop conceded that "they have shelved a few projects I would like to have continued," but pointed out the board's usefulness in giving VR direction:

They advise us of areas to keep away from, and give me guidance on time frames and capital expenditures so that I, in turn, can provide better guidance to the projects. The cross-play between divisions is valuable, and they may see areas we don't know about. But I would like them to do more in the way of suggesting areas of R&D that would be good for Venture Research.

One of VR's earliest polymer projects—and one that did gain SEP approval—was eventually commercialized as Dynarim. In the beginning, however, Dynarim was a molecule without a purpose or a home.

The RIM Polymer Project

V110: A NEAT MOLECULE WITH NO USE, 1976–1980. Originally, the project had sought to plug a hole in the high end of Allstate's ester product line. In 1976, Hank Benoit and Joe Finnigan, both research chemists, were asked to create a molecule that would outperform competitors' vinyl esters. Benoit and Finnigan invented a family of low molecular weight, liquid resins. During the next few years, they explored innumerable variations in the family's chemistry and spatial configuration; eventually, they narrowed the field to four molecules. By 1980, Winthrop had selected one of the four, V110, as clearly superior. Yet despite agreement among the co-inventors, their section head, Ron Church, and Winthrop that they had a "neat molecule," and despite efforts to involve the divisions, no one was interested in or could find applications for V110.

The polymer had excellent properties when molded: strength, stiffness, and resistance to high temperatures. But it was too brittle for commercial use without the addition of other materials. Fiberglass reinforcement eliminated the brittleness, but processing difficulties with the fiberglass resin sometimes created consistency problems with the product. These problems disappeared if a new molding technique, reaction injection molding (RIM) was used instead of conventional compression molding. But fabricators were resistant to the different type of fiberglass handling required to make large RIM parts.

ADDING RIM TECHNOLOGY. RIM technology and equipment were first developed in Europe. By

1980, approximately 500 machines had been installed in the United States, with ownership distributed about equally between multiple independent molders and a few captive producers, mostly in the auto industry. By contrast, compression (or press) molding equipment was owned primarily by 20 major end users, six of whom dominated the business. The differences in equipment distribution reflected the technologies' cost differences. Press molding required enormous heat and pressure, and thus enormous equipment and energy, to make parts. RIM, on the other hand, could fabricate large parts using smaller, cheaper equipment. For a part 8 inches by 5 feet (such as an automobile bumper), the contrast was between a 750-ton, $400,000 machine and a 25-ton, $200,000 machine. RIM's energy costs, molding costs, and tooling costs were much lower as well.[2] The major reason for these differences was that RIM polymerized the liquid monomers (the reaction), and formed them into a solid part (injection molding) in one step, rather than the two required by compression molding.

Not all monomers, however, were suitable for use in this process. Because the reaction occurred very quickly, RIM required liquid materials, such as urethane, that flowed easily at room temperature and reacted quickly with an isocyanate. The Allstate V110 team realized that its molecules so reacted, and thus made the link to RIM. Moreover, the result was a rigid product that could be used for structural parts, unlike the usually floppy, urethane-based products. Winthrop commented:

> Once we recognized the technological opportunity, it took six months to get the project redirected and the chemists working on tailoring a molecule for RIM use. We also needed someone who knew plastics markets to head the commercial development of the RIM project [the new name of the V110 project].

MARKET AND APPLICATIONS DEVELOPMENT, 1980–1983. Pete Kennedy was recruited from Du Pont in August 1980 to identify market opportunities for V110, to reorient Allstate's chemists to those markets, and to develop a business strategy. Cousins commented:

> We knew we had a neat molecule in one of our VR projects, but we didn't know how to talk to the market. We had always made interesting molecules and then tried to figure out how to use them. Now, instead of working in a vacuum, we needed to bring information from the market into the lab. But we weren't set up to do that. So we hired Pete Kennedy, a hybrid, a Ph.D. chemist with street experience, who understood pricing and marketing, and who knew the auto market.

Initially, there was some uncertainty about whom Kennedy should work for. As a first step, Cousins decided to place him within the VR organization, reporting to Winthrop.

Kennedy began visiting design engineers and materials people in the automotive and aerospace industries to identify their needs for V110-based materials, to generate and validate industry interest, and to develop market pull. He encouraged customers to test Allstate's materials, and worked with molders to make prototypes. He also began to create an applications laboratory, noting that it "is one of the first things you add when you want to commercialize a product." Such a laboratory duplicated customers' facilities, running parts on the same kinds of equipment and then testing them. For this reason, within a few months of his arrival Kennedy got approval to buy a RIM machine for $80,000. A VR project manager pointed out the importance of an applications laboratory, which was a new concept for Allstate:

> You need both a pilot plant and an applications laboratory for product development. The applications or field support staff provide know-how to the customer and to the molder. They show him how to make the part, and demonstrate that it won't tear up his equipment. They give customers the comfort of knowing their parts can in fact be made.

Kennedy identified a wide range of materials that could be of use to customers. The project broadened from V110 to a larger category of potential products: high-performance engineering materials that could be RIMed.[3] A few of these would

---

[2] RIM had even greater cost advantages over injection molding, the third major molding technique. Huge clamping forces were required for injection molding, making it inappropriate for large parts. For most purposes, the primary comparison was therefore between RIM and compression molding.

[3] Polymers could be divided into three groups on the basis of broad performance capabilities. At the low end were plastics used in applications such as packaging, toys, and housewares. Engineering materials were higher-performance polymers that

displace existing urethane and thermoplastic materials, but most would try to displace metal. Kennedy commented:

> I am not committed to V110, but to a market with opportunities for new chemistries. I have an open strategy on materials. I want to create engineering-type RIM polymers that customers want. If my product becomes obsolete, I want to be the one to obsolete it.

Despite his charter to tailor V110 to the market, Kennedy initially lacked both staff and authority. The four research chemists still reported to Ron Church. Friction between the two slowed the project. Benoit recalled:

> When Kennedy joined us, there was a period of severe adjustment. I resisted him for six months before I saw the light. Then I began to see that we needed to work toward performance requirements to commercialize a product. Before, we had just varied things willy-nilly: "Gee, what happens if we do this?" But when Kennedy talked to customers, they would say, "We need X, can you formulate it to do that?" Of course, they don't give you clear specifications. They are more likely to say, "If I can bang it against the side of my desk and it doesn't crack, it's good," rather than tell you what tensile strength they want. So you need to translate such comments into something concrete. Pete Kennedy can do that.

By stimulating market interest, Kennedy built internal credibility for the project. And by building relationships with individual chemists and helping them solve technical problems, he began reorienting RIM research toward market needs.

PRODUCT AND PROCESS DEVELOPMENT, 1980–1983. Because molders resisted using fiberglass reinforcement, Kennedy wanted to begin work on a new resin that did not require it. Top management soon wanted the RIM team to cut back pilot runs for V110 process specification so it could devote most of its energy to creating such a molecule. But, because Kennedy also felt Allstate had "to have a product we could make and a way we could make it," he thought it was just as imperative to do extensive applications development on V110 materials and define a manufac-

---

stood up to certain temperatures, were chemically resistant, and had desirable characteristics for particular work applications. Structural polymers were a subset of engineering materials. Usually reinforced, they could substitute for metal and be designed into structures where they performed load-bearing functions. V110 was a structural engineering polymer.

turing process for that molecule as it was to start work on a new molecule. He therefore went down two tracks: initiating work on a molecule that did not require fiberglass reinforcement while doing as much applications work and as many pilot runs as he could get through. He summarized his approach: "No one said 'no,' and I didn't ask." In the words of his eventual boss, Eric Reinhalter, Kennedy

> went from using "springs and mirrors" to "officially condoned bootlegging." He began operating, perhaps subconsciously, as the general manager of a business that did not yet exist, talking to customers, making prototypes, and looking into manufacturing possibilities.

Process development entailed two major tasks: specifying the process variables, and getting a manufacturing organization in place. Allstate's pilot plant, which was run by VR, could make virtually any chemical Allstate made or was likely to. Batches of V110 made in the pilot plant were studied to identify key variables and their interactions, or used for prototypes and customer evaluations. By the end of 1983, Kennedy felt that Allstate still needed to understand much more about these interactions to define "the window within which we could safely operate" the V110 process, which included a very flammable reactant.

Eventually, commercial-scale manufacturing of V110 would be necessary. Since Allstate had no reactor available with the right capabilities, Kennedy opted for toll processing—manufacture of the chemical by an outside processor under contract. Allstate management often used toll processors, and Kennedy found it appropriate at this stage of V110 development: "Before we make any dedicated capital investment that could become obsolete, I want to be sure that the product has a stable position and its chemistry is the final one."

A Market-Driven Technology Strategy

Guiding product development toward market-based performance targets was a new approach to research at Allstate. Through presentations and one-to-one meetings with chemists, Kennedy advocated this approach in the 1980–1983 period.

He recalled:

> I was saying, "Make me a molecule that does these things." This was scary to chemists because they didn't have a basic molecule to work from. Instead, they had all of nature to deal with, so they didn't even know where to begin. Most were impressed with the elegance of the analysis, but found it hard to use. Even today, it hasn't become part of our working environment; when Venture Research designs a new molecule, it still does it the old way.

The method articulated by Kennedy provided a starting point for structuring the approach to polymer design. It established product performance targets and then identified process parameters that immediately eliminated much chemistry from consideration. The researchers then concentrated their search within those classes of polymers whose spatial relationships made them likely to meet the desired performance and process parameters. (See *Exhibit 2*.)

One of Kennedy's tools for communicating this approach was a positioning chart for RIM resins. (See *Exhibit 3*.) For each of seven key attributes, such as stiffness, he compared the performance ranges covered by existing thermoplastics and RIM materials with those that were currently unserved. For example, thermoplastics covered almost the entire range of stiffness, but existing RIM materials showed major gaps in this area. Such gaps, which could be met by engineering-type RIM resins, would become the focus of Allstate's research, and the basis for refining and varying the V110 family of molecules.

The Formation of Commercial Development

After setting up the SEP Board and clarifying Venture Research's role, Cousins considered other ways to link research more closely with marketing. One was to push the specialty divisions to become more market-sensitive. A second was to let Venture Research develop its own marketing efforts, an option he rejected because "they tend to be naive about marketing, and research management might not listen." The third option, which was eventually adopted, was to create a high-level group with the commercialization of new businesses as its main charter, and the spread of marketing as a secondary goal.

CD LEADERSHIP AND ORGANIZATION. To head this new group, called Commercial Development (CD), Cousins wanted

> a marketing animal with on-the-ground success in markets and technologies similar to ours. He had to know enough technology to talk with Research. His personal makeup had to be consistent with our culture—laid back and informal.

In Eric Reinhalter, he found someone who had developed, marketed and sold applications for polymer materials to large end users for over 20 years. Originally he was slated to report to the SEP Board; but after insisting that he have one formal boss, Reinhalter was assigned to report directly to Cousins, and joined the company in January 1984. He commented:

> I felt that a clear reporting relationship to one senior manager was essential. Jack's choice that it be him sent a signal that CD would be an important new effort, and it has worked well for both of us. I keep Jack informed, but he manages me by exception rather than on a day-to-day basis. I also defer to the SEP board—of which I am a member—and it treats me as an unequal equal.

TRANSFER OF RIM TO CD. Reinhalter was offered three projects; he accepted them all. Of these, RIM was the most mature and the only one with a product. The CD group began quite small; it consisted of the technical people Reinhalter inherited from the three projects, plus three business analysts. Kennedy was immediately appointed sole project manager for RIM. He observed:

> I now had a boss who understood business and marketing. Eric validated my feelings about what I had been doing—that markets were key. The project now had a place in the organization and it fit the new strategic direction.

One of Reinhalter's early initiatives was a contest to name V110 to give it a new, commercial identity and team mentality. The winner was "Dynarim." Dynarim referred to the entire family of RIM resins, and Dynarim 1100 referred to V110 specifically.

If RIM had not been housed within Commercial Development, it would have been sent to a division. That option, however, had little support. There was no obvious fit with any existing

EXHIBIT 2 Key Steps in Market-Driven Technology Strategy for Engineering RIM Resins

1. *PRODUCT PERFORMANCE TARGETS:*

Establish performance characteristics the product must meet.

For Engineering RIM polymers, seven such characteristics and their ranges were established, including:

flexural modulus (stiffness)	250,000–500,000 psi
tensile strength	8,000 psi (minimum)
etc.	

A resin had to meet all seven characteristics within the target range, giving considerable latitude for trade-offs, experimentation, and judgment, resulting in multiple resins with a different balance of properties.

2. *PROCESS PARAMETERS:*

Establish boundaries within which the resins must fall in order to be processed on equipment chosen.

RIM processing equipment required:

a. Materials must be liquid (low viscosity) at operating temperatures in order to flow properly.
b. Individual components must be transportable as liquids at temperatures less than 300°F.
c. There must be no by-products because all reactions will take place very quickly in the mold.

This eliminated many materials from consideration.

3. *POLYMER ARCHITECTURE:*

Because broad classes of spatial relationships are associated with certain performance features, it is possible to eliminate whole classes of polymers from consideration and concentrate on those most likely to meet targets.

With regard to RIM materials:

a. Linear polymers tended to be stiff, have high viscosity, and high melting points, features that made them prime candidates for RIM resins. Branched linear polymers, being less stiff, lower in viscosity, and having lower melting points than unbranched, were easily eliminated from consideration, whatever their chemistry.
b. Higher molecular weight polymers were always tougher, and longer molecules had higher molecular weight. However, getting the molecular weight up required more cycle time, thereby increasing manufacturing costs. Was it possible to design a molecule that acted like longer/higher weight molecules but in fact required less molecular weight? Yes, if one constructed it to take advantage of certain kinds of bonding between molecules whose effect took the place of single, large molecules.

CONCLUSION:

It is possible and efficient to design polymers to fit market-determined performance features and hardware requirements by concentrating one's research in areas most likely to pay off according to a structural analysis linking polymer morphology with performance tendencies.

EXHIBIT 3 RIM Resin Positioning

A shows that IM materials cover the whole performance spectrum for this feature.
B shows major holes in the performance spectrum being met by existing RIM materials, c. 1980–1981.
C shows how Allstate proposes to fill those gaps in areas most important to market (300–1,500 range).

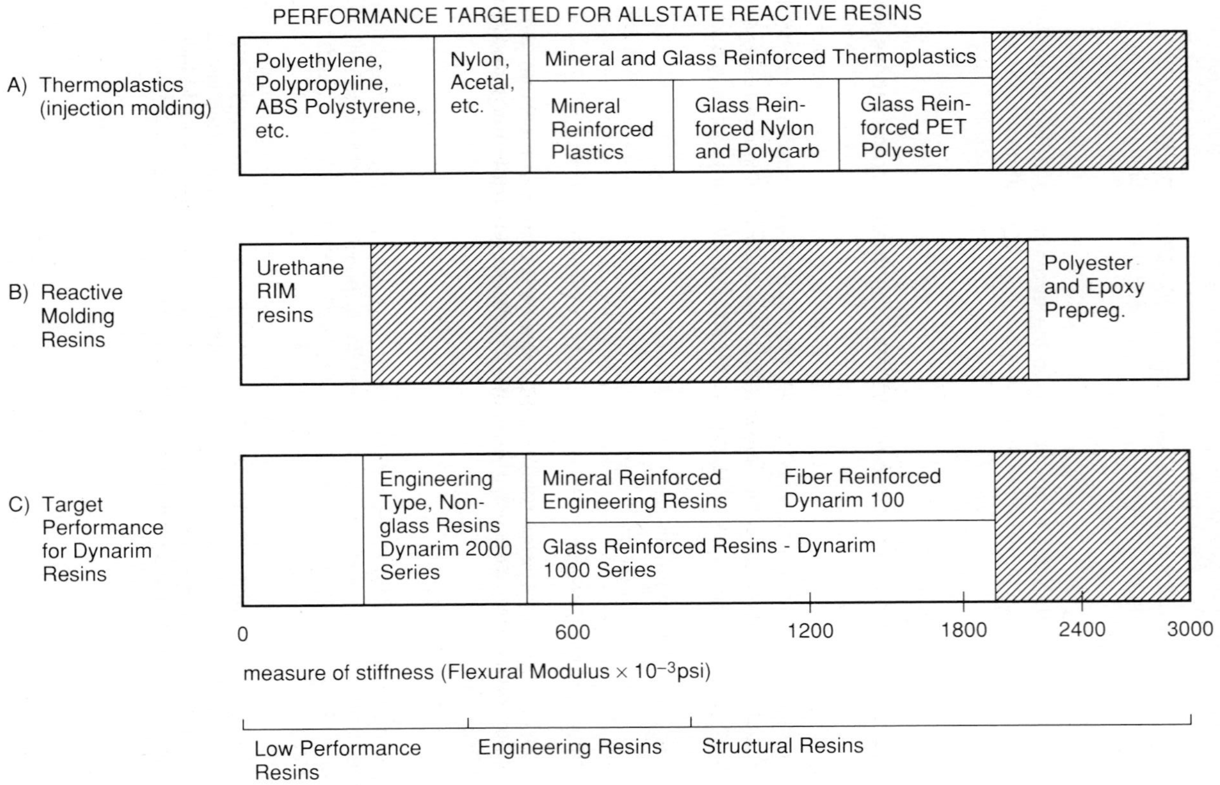

PERFORMANCE TARGETED FOR ALLSTATE REACTIVE RESINS

measure of stiffness (Flexural Modulus × 10⁻³psi)

| 0 | 600 | 1200 | 1800 | 2400 | 3000 |

Low Performance Resins   Engineering Resins   Structural Resins division; and RIM would have had to compete with more established profitable products for funds and attention.

The Role of CD

Cousins had given CD a deliberately broad charter. He wanted it to manage two or three projects at a time ($2–4 million per year per project meant more were too expensive), to guide research, and to bring more of a marketing perspective to the company. But he had only rough guidelines for deciding when projects should be transferred into and out of CD. He did not want to saddle a division with foreign technologies, products, or markets. He was also inclined to put a project in CD if a division lacked critical skills to make the project successful; he commented, "With RIM, for example, we put it in CD because we didn't have market development skills in the divisions." Once projects were assigned to CD, Cousins wanted it to be a portfolio manager, providing research and marketing direction, functioning as an intermediary between VR and the divisions. Most of all, Cousins wanted to avoid redundancy:

> If a division already has a certain capability, we shouldn't set up anything in CD that duplicates it. I don't want CD to worry about process development or manufacturing—that's a distraction. I don't want a self-contained business unit; I want them to develop a product that can be handed off to a division. For example, why should we recreate a custom manufacturing facility for Dynarim when we already have six or eight divisions set up to manufacture?

George Prince summarized his view of CD's role:

> CD should work with chemistries we in the divisions don't practice but which are akin to our markets. Process development should take place before a project goes too far: is there a known process? Do we have the equipment? The expertise? This should be coordinated—the marketing by CD, the chemistry by VR, and the engineering and manufacturing by a division. CD should do very little manufacturing, but they need to be able to scope out what's required.

Before a product was handed off to a division, Prince thought that its commercial feasibility needed to have been demonstrated:

> First you need a commercial process, and the demonstration that it is economically feasible.

Then a division can take it and commercialize it. But if it's still hard to meet specifications consistently on scaled-up production, then we shouldn't take it.

While he thought it was possible in some cases for a product to be handed off directly from Venture Research to a division, Prince felt that CD, with greater resources for product and market development, could generally take a project earlier than a division. He commented: "If Venture Research can take a product from A to H, then CD might need to get it to L or M before a division takes it."

According to CD's own mission statement, its goal was to identify, develop, and commercialize profitable new business opportunities. In Reinhalter's view, this meant CD had to be active in four areas:

> We have to develop the product, get it made, develop the market, and have applications people who go to the customer. Applications development is the norm in specialties; you have to work with the customer to make the part. Marketing includes everything needed to sell the product: creating demand from the end user, calling on molders who fabricate it—whatever it takes. We must also demonstrate the ability to sell the product and to make it. But it can actually be made anywhere; we just need someone on the team who is responsible for getting it made right and who can deal with any problems.

The growth in staff for the RIM project reflected these priorities. Between 1984 and 1986, applications development expanded to 9 people, research (renamed product development) to 8, and marketing to 5. The marketing and sales people both developed markets and handled accounts. One manufacturing engineer served as liaison with the toll processor.

Reinhalter distinguished between three key manufacturing activities: demonstrating manufacturability, process development, and production responsibility. Demonstrating the manufacturability of a new product was, in his view, the responsibility of the seller. Thus, Winthrop had to convince Reinhalter a product could be made, and he in turn had to convince the SEP Board and Cousins. Both paper exercises and physical demonstrations were usually required. Process development then followed. Reinhalter believed it should be done by whomever had the most expertise, but in practice, it usually fell to the group with the greatest interest. Reinhalter commented:

> CD should not be manufacturing-intensive; it needs only enough process development expertise to get a particular job done. With Dynarim, I would have been happy to have an existing division handle it, but none stepped forward—they all had jobs already. So we developed the process and transferred it to production.

Kennedy supported this approach, with qualifications. He too wanted to minimize CD's work-in-process development, but at the same time wanted to be certain the product fit tight parameters. He commented:

> I have no product until I can make it. You must tie down the interface between manufacturing and product performance, so you can't turn it over to someone who doesn't know that a 700 viscosity gives you a different product from 600. But I will do the minimum necessary to assure myself that I have the product I want. If I can get this from a division, fine; if I have to go outside, I will; and if I have to do it myself, I will.

Finally, once it became clear that a potential new business had emerged, full-scale manufacturing was necessary. Reinhalter wanted clear responsibility for manufacturing lodged somewhere in the company. But he cared less about where it was lodged than that there was someone who could be held accountable.

Although Reinhalter agreed with CD's original charter, he felt the mission had become less clear over time. "We have to decide if the plate is full enough already. Should we keep adding more? Do we really want to move things in and out?" He also pointed to a possible conflict between CD's original charter and the recruitment and motivation of staff. Reinhalter argued that operating people who had a personal stake (which he called "psychological ownership") in a program would do a better job than "pass-through people," but recognized they would probably have trouble letting go of projects.

The Dynarim Project, 1984–1986

Kennedy developed a strategic plan in 1984 with the goal of becoming the worldwide leader in engineering-type RIM materials. He argued that RIM hardware had opened up new opportunities for high-performance materials, that a large, unserved market for such materials already existed, and that Allstate was far ahead in grasping this opportunity and developing the required products. Accordingly, applications development on the Dynarim 1100 series expanded; by 1985, heavy product development was under way on the Dynarim 2000 series as well. Molecules in the 1100 series were iterations based on the original V110 chemistry, and were targeted for large, structural, nonappearance parts used in transportation equipment. Dynarim 2000 was based on a new chemistry that could be used with or without reinforcement; it would eventually take RIM resins into such markets as cabinetry for business and medical equipment.

During 1984–1985, interest in Dynarim picked up at General Motors for use as tire covers (the platform covering the well in which spare tires were placed, which became the floor of the trunk). Covers for several models were tested, and the first order, for use in selected Cadillacs, Oldsmobiles, and Buicks, came in April 1985. A year later repeat orders had generated $1.4 million in sales. Kennedy was confident that business would soon expand, both to other auto models, and to additional parts. In both areas, testing and evaluation were well under way.

Toll processing continued to be the manufacturing method of choice, despite the cost premium of 10 cents per pound and the need to share proprietary information. Patents on Dynarim reduced anxiety about sharing such information. Toll processing was also consistent with Cousins' desire to reduce capital intensity, and his view that manufacturing was not a competitive key, at least at that time.

Managing a toll processor required skills similar to those needed to manage an in-house manufacturing operation; these included getting raw materials to the processor, paying bills, and handling off-spec production. It also required the ability to identify appropriate processors in the first place, and then to negotiate and administer contracts. Because the manufacturing engineer assigned to the RIM project was only 24 years old and had little experience in these areas, an engineer from Polyesters acted as a consultant.

Allstate managers thought they might want to bring Dynarim manufacturing in-house within three to five years. Some of the factors that would shape the decision would be the size of the required investment (about $2.5 million to convert an existing plant, $5 million to build a new one), the company's willingness and ability to make the investment, whether Allstate had a plant with the right equipment that was underused at the time, EPA regulations, and projected volume.

Future Dynarim Decisions

Eventually, decisions would have to be made about moving Dynarim out of Commercial Development. Issues involved timing, location, and the size of the group to be moved. But no one felt decisions were needed soon. Reinhalter, for example, observed:

> It's not important to me to define the future if the trend is right. I am not preoccupied with whether or not Dynarim goes to a division, although I would prefer to leave it where it is until it's obvious that it's time to change. When there's a compelling reason to move, it should be obvious—for example, if we need a sales force. But if you change, don't screw up what made it work before.

Cousins also felt no urgent need to move Dynarim to a division. But he cautioned:

> Leaving it forever in CD is not an option, although I'm perfectly comfortable with it in CD this year and next. Polyesters probably wouldn't even want it right now because they are profit-oriented and Dynarim is still losing money. But I don't want CD to spend all its time on RIM, either.

Reinhalter's primary concern was keeping the project team intact, or at least allowing whoever wanted to move with the product to be able to do so.

> I don't want to lose the momentum that's been built by having critical mass. I worry about culture change. Pete Kennedy built an environment here—I just added to it—where we do more than we think we can. The "can do" attitude has generated extremely rapid progress, and that could get lost if the team was broken up.

Although Polyesters remained the division most likely to receive Dynarim, an alternative was for it to go to a new division. The choice was complicated because Dynarim had already spun off a new product, Dynatech, that was being developed in Polyesters. In the long run, there were three possibilities: Dynarim could join its sister product in the Polyesters division; the two products could form the basis of a new division; or Dynatech could remain in Polyesters while Dynarim became the core of a new business unit.

Dynatech's chemistry was identical to Dynarim 1100's for the V110 molecule was the foundation of both products. Dynarim, however, was then RIMed, forming a polymer and a part in a single operation, while Dynatech was to be used in compression molding. Once the Dynatech project had a marketable product, press-molding fabricators would buy V110 resin, combine it with a fiberglass resin to form a sheet-molding compound (SMC), and then mold a part. The resulting parts would be similar in performance to Dynarim,[4] and thus superior to vinyl ester's performance. Compared with other SMCs, Dynatech's fumes would be much less noxious, an advantage in dealing with environmental regulations. Finnigan thought the use of compression molding gave Dynatech a financial advantage as well:

> If a fabricator were starting from scratch, it would make sense to buy RIM equipment for large parts. But few of them have RIM equipment yet, while lots of them have heavily depreciated press-molding equipment. With both products, we can cover all the bases.

Dynatech had emerged from an SEP-funded project in 1984 that focused on polyester fabrication processes. The project had been instigated by Finnigan, who saw an opportunity for Polyesters to do something with the V110 chemistry. The year's work convinced Prince that Dynatech was a commercially feasible product, and Polyesters then picked up its funding. Prince described the difference between his division's acceptance of Dynatech in 1985 and its resistance to Dynarim in 1984:

---

[4] Kennedy disputed this in part, pointing out that the vertical walls of large press-molded parts were weaker than the walls of similar parts that had been RIMed. These differences resulted from the rates at which resins flowed in the two processes. In Kennedy's view, the consequence was that Dynarim could cross over more easily into Dynatech markets than the reverse. Prince disagreed; he believed that RIM products were restricted to nonappearance applications, while Dynatech could be used in appearance applications such as car fenders.

Both Dynatech and Dynarim will concentrate on the transportation industry, with automotive being our initial target. We already market our speciality polyesters to domestic auto producers, and work with the press molders that fabricate auto parts. While we have lots of expertise in compression molding, we know little about RIM and have no relationships with RIM molders. So Dynatech fit our customers' business and equipment without our having to fiddle, while Dynarim would have required our hiring several people we couldn't afford.

Markets for Dynatech and Dynarim 1100 overlapped—although just how, and to what extent, was still unclear. Currently, both products were expected to replace metal in nonappearance structural applications in transportation and other equipment. Estimates of potential crossover in each direction varied. Most Allstate managers viewed the overlap as broadening Allstate's market coverage, rather than as a source of competitive problems. In fact, both Dynatech and Dynarim had based applications engineers in the same Detroit office. These people talked to one another constantly, exchanged leads, and, according to Reinhalter, seldom fought over applications. In most cases, the line dividing the two products was obvious: the size, shape, and volume of a part usually dictated whether RIM or compression molding should be used. If product choice was not resolved at this level, customers were likely to make the decision. Reinhalter pointed out, "Our customers are very sophisticated, so they know which method is better for their application. They also have preferred molders or fabricators that they want to use."

While end-user applications were similar for the two products, there were subtle, but in Kennedy's view, critical, distinctions between the required marketing processes. RIM was strongly end-user driven, while Polyester's SMCs were more processor-driven. Kennedy observed:

> The SMC community is relatively small and composed of big, influential processors who create a creditable supply for, say, a General Motors. GM determines only the performance specs, and leaves it to the processor to choose particular materials from particular vendors. Quality is controlled by the processors' skill. We, on the other hand, want the end user to specify a particular material; the specifications are for a particular formulation, not just for performance. Quality would then be controlled by the materials.

While Prince acknowledged that, in the past, Polyesters had tried to sell against performance specifications, Allstate's new emphasis on specialties was affecting the division's marketing approach:

> We now spend time with end users, talking with their engineers to try and get our resins designed into products. We want them to tell fabricators to make the parts from our resins; then we work with molders to make it easy for them to do so.

These considerations affected the eventual location of the two new products. Cousins, for example, thought the organizational separation of the two was "fine for now"; but he noted that eventually they were "likely to become the same business." Because of the similarity of product and end-user markets, Cousins indicated he "would have no hesitation putting the two products together."

Prince, on the other hand, believed that the size of the eventual Dynarim market was a key consideration in deciding where it should go. If it appeared that that market would be $50–100 million, then Dynarim had grounds for becoming a new division. But if it looked more like a market of $5–15 million, Prince believed it made more sense to "graft Dynarim onto an existing division," most likely Polyesters because "our ultimate customers are similar."

Reinhalter and Kennedy both favored continued separation of the two products. Surface similarities, they argued, were less important than differences in how the two were marketed, sold, distributed and used. Therefore, Dynatech was best handled by Polyesters, while Dynarim would be better off as the core of a new division. RIM technology, they added, did not fit within the existing corporate structure, and was properly the basis of a new business unit. If a division like Polyesters were to absorb Dynarim, it would then have to add a significant number of RIM specialists—possibly absorbing most of Kennedy's group in the process.

Although Kennedy and Reinhalter felt the immediate issue was achieving commercial success with Dynarim, they knew such success would reopen the location issue. To create a new division, they would have to develop strong arguments favoring the separation of the two products.

26. The Rogers Corporation: Electroluminescent Lamps (A)

In June 1984, Norman (Norm) Greenman, president of the Rogers Corporation, was preparing to announce the division in which a new product, electroluminescent (EL) lamps, would be built. EL lamps were flat, greenish panels used for area lighting that could be cut to shape for different applications. The location of EL manufacturing was but one of several, closely related decisions then facing Greenman. He also had to decide whether EL should be sold only as finished lamps or also as semifinished material, and when EL products should be introduced to the market.

Company Background

Founded as a paper mill in Connecticut in 1832, Rogers soon began experimenting with paper-making methods. Product and process innovation continued over the next century. By the 1930s, the company was seeking diversification beyond paperboard, and found it in the new field of polymer materials. In the next two decades, its labs created many unique materials by combining fibers, polymers and chemicals. Rogers then began seeking opportunities for forward integration, devising components that were based upon its proprietary materials. Continued product development and two small acquisitions brought the company's sales to $137 million in 1984. Over two-thirds of these sales involved components, and 76% were to electronics markets. A typical product line sold in the $5–10 million range.

Technology, Markets and Strategy

Rogers made high-quality, high-reliability polymer materials and components. Often price competitive, it also sold many products at a premium. The company sought to dominate narrow niches which demanded, and would pay for, highly engineered products. It preferred situations in which it could secure its position over time with strong patents. But the company had learned to patent only what was enforceable, and to maintain other proprietary knowledge as trade secrets. Because it was hard to enforce patents on processes, Rogers no longer tried to patent them.

Rogers viewed its broad knowledge of polymer materials as a major competitive strength. Greenman, a former chemical engineer and president since 1966, stated:

> Materials are our fundamental competency; they are the base upon which we build. When we look at a project, we first decide if we can add something special—something unique and new based on our materials competency. We try to come up with products where we have protection against low-cost producers; this is very important in international competition. Technology is our defense.

Rogers proprietary knowledge encompassed both materials and processes. Its product engineers needed to know not only the characteristics of materials, but also how they were likely to behave during operations such as extrusion, molding and grinding. This dual knowledge was critical because in the materials business, product and process were tightly linked. One division manager observed:

> You can't separate the product from the process. Your process determines your design standards and guidelines. It shows you *how* to get there, not just *where* you want to go.

The design of a Rogers product therefore did not end with the specifications that it had to meet,

This case was prepared by Artemis March under the direction of David A. Garvin.

for the specifications would be met only if materials were first processed in a particular way. Product development usually started from the properties desired in the end product and worked backwards to the process and starting materials. For example, if a product had problems with moisture penetration, engineers would select materials that had lower transmission rates and thus would be slower to conduct the moisture.

While the development of process and product were thus inseparable, reverse engineering of products did not immediately reveal the details or steps in the process used in manufacturing. While one could determine that a product had been laminated, for example, neither inspection nor analysis of the product would tell the temperatures, pounds of pressure, or length of time required for different processing steps. In this respect, the real product was the process.

Materials vs. Components

Rogers was in both the materials and components businesses. Frequently, it had to decide in what form it would sell its products: as sheets, rolls, or rods for fabrication by another company, or in finished form for end users. In either case, Rogers rarely made the basic raw materials (such as base resins); it left commodity production to giants such as Du Pont. The company focused instead on laminates and substrates—intermediate materials in which one material was bonded to another (laminates) or in which one material acted as a base on which other materials set (substrates). Using one or more of these proprietary materials, Rogers also made components that were small, highly engineered, and often critical to the functioning of the industrial products of which they were a part—usually unseen by the end user.

Many of the requirements for success in materials and components businesses were similar. A good product was needed out of R&D; this involved close working relationships with both vendors and customers, and often a fairly long development cycle. For example, Rogers had worked closely with the Ford Motor Company to develop certain molding materials; Ford then chose the molder, and Rogers sales engineers worked closely with it as well. Materials required tight process controls in manufacturing; otherwise, they would not mold or fabricate properly when made into components. Components also required tight controls that fit the demands of the customer's application.

There were differences between the businesses, however. Product life cycles of materials were generally longer than those of components, although the life cycles of all products were getting shorter. Shorter life cycles meant faster development times were required of R&D, plus more judgment about what the market needed and when. New components also necessitated more design and development resources than new materials. While Rogers normally tried to develop semistandard products in the materials area, component customers, particularly in electronics, usually wanted their own variations on a product.

Decisions about whether new products should be sold as materials or components were made on a case-by-case basis. Greenman described some of the criteria he used:

> We don't want to do something anyone can do; we look for things that are complex to make and which require sophisticated manufacturing methods. Sometimes we have a proprietary material that we don't want to send out, so we decide to make the final component ourselves. Also, we look for component markets where there is either enough volume—such as gas carburetor floats—or high enough margins—such as military nose cones—for us to make money.

> We tend not to go into components if the process technology is a type we're not good at, if we can't protect our position as well as we would like to, or if analysis of customer requirements shows that components are not a good fit for us.

Company Organization

Product Groups and Divisions

In its early life, a new Rogers product was likely to be part of the division whose major product line(s) had spawned it. Eventually, if sales grew large enough, the product might be spun off to become a free-standing division. There were no rules for when this change took place, but it typically occurred when a business had grown to the point where it needed concentrated management attention.

In 1984, Rogers had 11 divisions organized into two groups: Interconnection Products and Polymer Products. While all Rogers products were based on polymer materials, interconnection products shared an additional common function: they distributed, transmitted or controlled electrical signals in electronic equipment. The interconnection group focused on components that were sold to a wide range of electronics manufacturers, making everything from disk drives to satellites. Most of the group's plants were in the west, and concentrated in Arizona. The four polymer divisions were more materials-oriented, and sold primarily to the automotive, printing, office equipment, footwear, and electronic component industries. Most of their plants were in Connecticut.

R&D

Rogers R&D laboratory, which housed 75–80 scientists and technicians in 1984, was located across the street from company headquarters in Rogers, Connecticut. While large chemical companies were primarily involved with the chemistry of making basic materials, Rogers was more concerned with their physics. It focused on qualities such as strength, durability, melting points, and flexibility, as well as other mechanical and surface properties critical to product performance. Richard (Dick) Berry, senior vice president for technology, commented on the company's approach to R&D:

> We have a lot of informality, some projects just evolve. We also interact a lot with Norm. In choosing projects, we look at the size of the opportunity, R&D's ability to address it, marketing's capacity to assimilate it, the level of competition, and the need to balance long- and short-run projects.

R&D had extensive contact with marketing and with customers. In fact, close communication and coordination with marketing was taken for granted, and extended into the rank-and-file. R&D managers and engineers also visited customers (always with representatives of sales and marketing) to determine their needs. These self-initiated visits, which took place on an as-needed basis, elicited such useful information as what customers wanted a product to do, how they planned to use it in manufacturing, and how they expected to test it. R&D personnel also obtained or developed product information for customers and created new products or prototypes responsive to their needs. Although these customer interac-

tions were not the only form of market intelligence, they were considered to be a key competitive advantage.

TECHNOLOGY TRANSFER. R&D's primary contact with manufacturing came when technology was transferred from the R&D laboratory to the divisions. To facilitate this process, two preferred methods were the direct transfer of people and project teams. In direct transfer, someone from the division receiving the product spent time at R&D, learning firsthand both the product and the process. Alternatively, someone from R&D went with the product to the division; in some cases, a two-way exchange was involved. Although people had been sent from R&D to the divisions several times in the past, there was still no budgetary mechanism to support the move. An R&D manager had to give up one of his budgeted positions if he followed this route.

Project teams, whose initial members were chosen by Berry and the division manager, came from R&D and division marketing. They developed objectives for the new product, as well as a reporting framework, milestones and timetables. Later on, division operations and engineering became more heavily involved and representatives from these groups joined the project team. Attention then shifted to getting stable process specifications and working out how the laboratory project would be scaled-up for volume manufacturing.

Process specifications included precise, quantitative documentation of the purity and grade of materials vendors had to supply, how the process operated, the tests to be used during the process to verify its performance, the characteristics of the product itself, and the statistical analysis required to monitor the process over time. Developing specifications was a complex task, made even more difficult by the scale-up from laboratory to manufacturing. Typically, scale-ups entailed moving from smaller, more precise equipment to larger, less refined equipment. The implications of this shift could be subtle: for example, it meant a change in the surface-to-volume ratio of equipment and a need to adjust the settings of production equipment to take such factors into account. In addition, while research and development was the responsibility of technicians, production runs were carried out by less skilled operators, requiring more explicit instructions and training.

The need for a complete set of specifications was a major factor affecting the timing of transfers out of the laboratory. Usually product specifications had been established and process documentation was in some stage of development when pressure mounted to move products to the divisions. Berry described R&D's preferences:

> We try to move products out as soon as possible, because there are a lot of other things we'd like to be working on; the divisions want that too. Before we move products out, though, we want their specifications to be established, and we want controls on the process. Manufacturing generally agrees with this. It's those with a marketing bent, including Norm, who want the transfer earlier.

In fact, Berry observed that market pressure was frequently so strong that "we seldom have a fully specified process when we turn it over to manufacturing." As a result, processes tended to evolve both during and after transfers. Sometimes they were still being fine-tuned by R&D even though manufacturing was already trying to produce a saleable product.

Frequently, R&D employed pilot lines to smooth the transfer process. These were manufacturing lines, housed at the laboratory, whose size, equipment type, and output more closely approximated full-scale production than did bench methods in which samples were made by hand. Pilot lines gave engineers and technicians a chance to see how the real production process would work and to discover problems before products reached the divisions. For example, when working at full scale, they might discover that an ink that had worked in a bench test was now drying too quickly and was clogging the equipment, requiring a change in solvents. While it was sometimes possible to start immediately with a pilot line, more often work started on the bench and moved later to the pilot stage.

Despite these mechanisms for smoothing the transfer of technology, divisions were not altogether satisfied with the results. One division manager commented:

> It's hard to get R&D to say they've finished; you have to *pull* product. The R&D mentality wants to keep on creating, but that's not a disciplined process. They are very responsive to prototyping for customers, but less to developing and finishing products.

Other division managers echoed these sentiments while adding other concerns. Many felt that R&D's charges to the divisions were too high; others wanted more control over the choice of R&D projects and thus over how R&D spent their money. There was also a feeling that more development work should take place in the divisions. In fact, there had already been some shift in this direction over the past decade. Several development engineers had been moved to divisions to work on short-term product and process improvement; meanwhile, R&D was encouraged to focus on more advanced, long-term projects.

Marketing

Division marketing had primary responsibility for the day-to-day marketing of products. Key tasks included product planning and the hosting of regular meetings that served as forums for discussion among top management, marketing and R&D about new and ongoing products. Corporate marketing handled advertising, and the new functions of market research and market development. The latter, which included visiting customers with representatives from R&D, spending time at the laboratory, and providing marketing support, focused on areas that were new to the company and had no division home. There was as yet no set method by which market development handed off new products to division marketing.

Manufacturing

Rogers had 17 small plants, most of which made either materials or components for one or two divisions. Materials manufacturing included poron (a material developed initially for the inner-soles of shoes), electrical insulation, and molding materials made in New England plants, as well as flexible circuit and microwave materials made in Arizona. Traditional materials operations involved mixing batches of materials, extrusion, casting, laminating, and milling. Critical process variables were time, pressure and temperature. The manufacture of mechanical components involved many of the same key process variables as did materials, and required control of their density, uniformity, and finish. Electrical components were quite different. Typical operations were blanking, bending, etching and drilling. Materials, mechanical, and electrical components, however,

26. The Rogers Corporation: Electroluminescent Lamps (A)

all required tight controls. The realization that controls were neither as complete nor as precise as had been thought led to the first phase of a corporatewide quality effort.

Rogers Quality Program

Beginning in 1981, Rogers introduced a major initiative in quality called TQC, or "total quality concept." ("Concept" pointed to something larger than a program—to quality as a way of life for the company.) TQC had two guiding principles: to build an environment in which everyone participated and to encourage decision making based on facts and statistics rather than emotions.

The first phase of TQC was aimed at improving the company's manufacturing skills so that they reached a par with marketing and R&D. Divisions developed quality programs that emphasized the use of analytical techniques by problem-solving teams. Workers learned basic statistics—frequency distributions, probability, measures of central tendency and dispersion—as a basis for tracking manufacturing processes, for deciding whether they were in control,[1] and for learning when adjustments were called for. These methods had already produced dramatic savings in the costs of rework and scrap.

As divisions gained experience with the tools of statistical process control, they began to look differently at R&D's work and to question the manufacturing focus of the TQC program. One division manager commented:

> We're much more demanding today about what comes out of R&D in terms of their database, and the statistical soundness of their data. In the divisions we're doing some very sophisticated experiments; now, we're ahead of them. They should come here!

Another division manager observed:

> Five years ago, we were not very disciplined in manufacturing. R&D was right: manufacturing

was out of control. During the last five years—pushed by division managers and the TQC program—manufacturing has gained the ability to solve many of its problems. Now engineering can spend more time on the future. But if we don't bring staff functions like R&D into the TQC program, they may be left behind.

R&D was pleased with the increased sophistication in the divisions. According to Berry:

> The main effect of TQC on R&D has been that is has provided a much more controlled environment in which products can be introduced. The divisions have gained an understanding of how products can vary while still under control and how one can form false impressions from inadequate experimentation. Their sophistication will result in our doing a better job because we will provide a more complete package; before, they wouldn't have been able to absorb it.

Greenman acknowledged the legitimacy of divisions asking that technology transfer be governed by the principle of TQC. He commented:

> When R&D delivers a product to a division, they will have to do it with a much deeper understanding of material specifications and process controls. We are just starting with this. We thought we had it before, but we didn't.

Both Greenman and Berry recognized that TQC would be different in functions outside of manufacturing, but acknowledged that they didn't know what form it would take. Much R&D work, for example, was nonrepetitive. It was therefore not well-suited to the application of statistical controls in the same way that they were used in manufacturing.

The EL Project

Rogers became interested in improving EL in 1981 as a way to enhance the military keyboards made by its new acquisition, the Flex-Key Corporation. At the time, EL was used to backlight keyboards. But market research soon revealed a broader opportunity, and in mid-1982 a project team was formed. (See *Exhibit 1* for a description of EL technologies, competitors, and products.) Marketing and R&D were represented on the team, but not manufacturing or a division, since EL did not fit with any existing division. The team first

[1] To be "in control," a process had to perform consistently within upper and lower limits that were statistically determined. Because of differences in raw materials, machine settings, and operator skills, variation was endemic to all manufacturing processes. However, acceptable variation (that due to statistical chance) could be distinguished from variation that indicated trouble (and that fell outside of the range established by statistical probability). To meet customer specifications, outputs also had to fall within the tolerance ranges specified by customers.

EXHIBIT 1 EL Technologies, Competitors and Products (based on research during the 1983–1984 period)

	EL Products	Luminescent Systems, Inc.	Grimes Division Midland-Ross Corp.	Ball Engineering	Timex	Rogers
Technology	Aclar	Aclar	Aclar	Silkscreen	Micro-Encapsulation	Silkscreen
Half-Life (hrs.)	800–1,500	800–1,500	800–1,500	Very Short	?	1,200–1,500 (if cover film used)
Brightness (ftL)	16–20	16–20	16–20	5–10	8–12?	16–20
Edge Lighting	No	No	No	No	Yes	Yes
Leads Durability	Poor	Poor	Poor	Excellent	Fair	Good
Thickness (mils.)	15–30	15–30	15–30	10–15	10	10 (without cover film)
Flexibility	Good	Poor	Poor	Good	None	Good
Price	High	High	High	Low	Low	Medium-High
Power Consumption	Medium	Medium	Medium	Medium	High	Medium
Moisture Resistance	Poor	Poor	Poor	?	Poor	Fair
Heat Generation	–	–	–	–	High	–
Target Markets	Military and aircraft	Auto copiers, LCD	Military and aircraft	High volume	High volume	Military
Estimated EL Sales	$2–$3 Million	$3 + Million	$6 + Million	–	–	–
Vulnerabilities	Compete with own customers Quality and delivery complaints		Compete with own customers Buy coated substrate from GE (dependent) Long delivery	Trouble with brightness	No market	?
Resources/Strengths	Good relations with military Have only product that works in switches	Doubled EL production space	Midland-Ross has poured $2 million in, but wants rapid payoff	Ball is innovative Young, creative, energetic people Mounting serious effort	Large capacity	Materials expertise Edge lighting Better leads Phosphor research

selected a screening process, similar to the silk-screening of T-shirts or art prints, as the best approach to manufacturing. The person within Rogers with the greatest screening expertise was Bill Harper, an experienced manufacturing engineer then in Arizona. Jeff Otto, an R&D product development manager and head of the team, brought Harper to R&D to head up the EL work.

Otto recalled:

I admired Bill Harper. He's a very creative person, though not really a trained scientist. I don't know of anyone who dislikes organization as much as he does, but he makes things happen. He'd talk to people, play with the old equipment he trucked here to start his lab. He started getting ideas for improving EL performance, for modifying the materials, and for modifying the process.

EXHIBIT 2A Estimated Market for EL

	1983	1984	1985	1986	1987
Total Estimated Market for Lamps (millions of $)	$10.1	$13.6	$17.0	$21.1	$28.5
Rogers Estimated Share of Lamps					
(in millions of $)	0.0	0.0	1.0	2.9	6.2
(in %)	0.0%	0.0%	6.0%	14%	22%
Lamp Segments (Rogers estimated % in parentheses)					
Aircraft Cockpits	.5	.6	1.1 (22)	1.6 (30)	1.8 (35)
Other Military	1.0	1.5	1.8 (7)	2.5 (15)	3.8 (25)
Other Aircraft	0.0	0.0	.3 (–)	.5 (25)	.8 (25)
Auto	5.7	6.1	6.7 (5)	7.2 (10)	9.1 (25)
Copiers	.5	.6	.6 (17)	.7 (25)	.7 (25)
LCD Backlighting	.5	.8	1.2 (–)	1.5 (25)	1.9 (25)
Keyboards (nonmilitary)	.6	1.0	1.3 (8)	1.6 (25)	3.0 (25)
Other	1.3	3.0	4.0 (3)	5.5 (5)	7.4 (10)
	10.1	13.6	17.0 (6)	21.1 (14)	28.5 (22)

Assumptions:
Growth rate of segments varies.
Competition is among already known players.

EXHIBIT 2B Production Needs for EL (derived from sales and price projections)

	1985	1986	1987
Average Price/Square Inch ($)	$ 1.05	$ 1.00	$ .93
Gross Sales (millions of $)	1.0	2.9	6.2
Unit Sales (M square inch) [gross sales ÷ price/sq. in.]	.95	2.90	6.67
Lamps Sold (in 000s) [unit sales in sq. in. ÷ 21 sq. in.]	45.2	138.1	317.6
Panels Sold (in 000s) [lamps sold ÷ 14]	3.2	3.9	22.7
Total Panels Made (in 000s) [panels sold ÷ 75% yield factor]	4.3	13.2	30.3
	c. 4K	c. 13K	c. 30K

Assumptions:
Weighted average selling price declines yearly.
Average lamp size is 21 square inches (based on weighted average of 1986 segments).
14 lamps per panel.
Panel size is 18 inches by 18 inches.
75% yield (cumulative yield figure for substrate, based on multiplying projected yields at each step of substrate production).
Good panels made are sold—i.e., no inventory.

EXHIBIT 2C Estimated Equipment, Material and Labor Costs

	1985	1986	1987
Equipment Needs:			
Panels to be made (in 000s) [from Exhibit 2B]	4	13	30
Machine Capacities: [capacity ÷ # panels = # new machines]			
Screening (28,000 panels/year)	1	0	1
Drying (1 for every 2 screeners)	1	0	0
Pressing (14,000 panels/year)	1	0	2
Die Cutting (100,000 panels/year)	1	0	0
Equipment Costs: [cost × # new machines needed]			
Screen Printer ($40k)	40	—	40
Oven ($40k)	40	—	—
Press ($50k)	50	—	100
Clicker ($20k)	20	—	—
Test Equipment	60	60	90
Photometric Equipment	110	30	—
Material Handling Equipment	10	10	20
Prototype Lab	60	—	45
Clean Room	80	40	120
Other	80	80	80
	550	220	495
Material Costs:			
Materials Cost/Panel = $25.92			
Material Costs/Year (nearest 5,000) [$25.92 × # panels made]	105	340	780
Labor Costs:			
Direct labor (# people)	7	11	18
(@ 15k)	105	165	270
Indirect Labor (# people)	5	11	21
(@ $15k)	75	165	315

Over the next few years the team broadened its goal to the establishment of a new business, and asked Steve Etzel, who had become EL product planner, to draw up a business plan in the spring of 1984. (See *Exhibits 2A–D*.)

Product and Process Development, 1982–84

The broad design of Harper's lamp was not unlike those of competitors. (See *Exhibit 3A*.) But Rogers departed from the competition in choosing screening rather than another manufacturing process, and in not using an aclar film to cover and protect its lamp from the environment.

The critical proprietary materials in the lamp were the three "inks" (or binder systems) that were screened onto the substrate. (See *Exhibit 3B*.) They were also the key link between the starting materials and the manufacturing process. Binder systems were not created as free-standing materials, but as materials appropriate for use in a particular process; inks appropriate for screening, for example, were not appropriate for other coating methods. The most salient quality of inks was their rheology: how evenly they squeezed through the screen, or, in Harper's words, "how it squoshes when you shove it." He continued:

26. The Rogers Corporation: Electroluminescent Lamps (A)

EXHIBIT 2D Profit and Loss Projections for EL (000s of $)

	1985	1986	1987
Gross Sales (total estimated market × Rogers estimated share of market)	$1,000	$2,900	$6,200
Less Returns and Allowances	50	150	300
Net Sales	$ 950	$2,750	$5,900
Cost of Sales:			
Direct Labor	105	165	270
Materials	105	340	780
Variable Overhead	300	550	950
Fixed Overhead	775	1,115	1,510
	$1,285	$2,170	$3,510
Manufacturing Profit	(335)	580	2,390
Commercials			
R&D	550	550	450
Sales, Marketing, Administrative	500	700	1,000
PBIT	(1,385)	(670)	940

The better you understand the rheology of the inks, the less you have to worry about compensating in the screening stage. So we need to do the best possible job in characterizing the starting materials so that we depend less on the skills of the operators.[2]

Ink rheology was but one of some 50 process variables that affected the final product. Others included the mesh of the screen, its condition (screens became less taut with use), the speed at which inks were laid down, the tension of the upper and lower printer plates, and as it later turned out, the temperature and humidity in the room. Using a pilot line, Harper and his technicians constantly adjusted these variables, as well as such things as the ratio of binder to filler and the amount of solvent used, and then observed changes in the resulting lamp qualities.

Early in the project, there was as much uncertainty about desired product characteristics as there was about key process parameters. Otto described the situation:

We would love to have had a few key properties to shoot for, but the market was unclear about what it wanted. There were more parameters than a company our size could handle. And because we didn't have the resources, we couldn't study them all.

For example, Rogers knew that brightness was important, but it was not clear just how bright was bright enough. Nor were the physical char-

EXHIBIT 3A Lamp Design

Lamp Layers:
- Indium Oxide (capacitor/electrode)
- Phosphor (light emission)
- Barium Titanate (increase electric field)
- Aluminum Foil (electrode)

[2] "Characterization" refers to a detailed, scientifically precise description of the performance characteristics and capabilities of a material. By running physical tests, for example, one might specify how many times a key could be pushed before it was likely to fail, or the temperature ranges within which certain performance could be expected.

EXHIBIT 3B EL Production

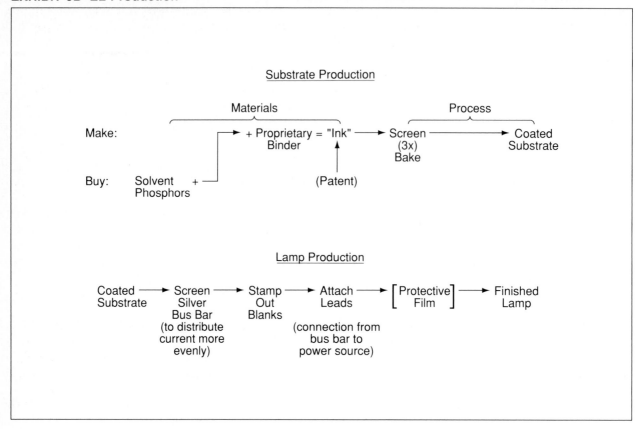

acteristics required to produce a bright-enough lamp well understood. When R&D realized that excess moisture quickly killed brightness, it then narrowed its search to binders whose transmission rates (of moisture) were low.

Using such an iterative process—cycling between process variables and product characterization—Harper's team of three worked toward making a superior product that would overcome the problems plaguing other EL lamps. These problems included a short half-life (the time it took to lose half of the lamp's brightness), poor reliability, fragile leads, poor moisture resistance, inadequate brightness, and lamps that were unlighted along their edges. These problems were interrelated. Moisture, for example, was the greatest enemy of both the phosphors and indium oxide; it caused these materials, and thus the lamp's brightness, to degrade. Moisture frequently seeped into lamps through the area around the lead attachments, for the aclar used to seal lamps did not adhere well to the copper leads. The seal also

left an unlit ⅛″ margin around the lamp's edges, imposing a design constraint that was especially significant in such applications as automobile dashboards.

Etzel's research, plus regular sharing of prototypes with customers, soon showed that increased brightness and half-life were the features of greatest importance to every market segment. This meant that the moisture problem had to be solved. As a long-term solution, Rogers had in 1983 begun basic research in phosphors. The expected payoff from this research, however, was still several years away.

By mid-1984, neither the moisture, brightness nor half-life problems had been solved. In these areas, Rogers lamps were neither significantly better nor worse than those of its competitors. However, R&D reported considerable progress on several secondary problems. It had developed leads that were strongly attached, solderable, and resistant to breaking during routine handling. Because there was no aclar seal, the lamps also lit to the edge, a feature noted favorably by customers.

By mid-1984 the laboratory had produced what one manager called a "first-generation lamp" with improved secondary characteristics. Because of its materials expertise, Rogers had been able to create proprietary binder systems for which patents had been applied. Known competitors, managers believed, lacked the ability to reverse-engineer the product, even if they had been so inclined.

Key Decisions Concerning EL

By June 1984, three decisions had to be made: whether to sell EL as lamps, as substrates, or both; when to move the product out of R&D to a division; and in which division manufacturing should be located.

Lamps or Substrates?

Greenman was uncertain about whether EL was best sold as a material, as lamps, or as some combination of the two. Three major options had evolved:

SELL COATED SUBSTRATE TO EL COMPETITORS, AS WELL AS LAMPS TO END USERS. In this scenario, Rogers new technology—in materials, processes, and lamp characteristics—would become the industry standard. It would be seen as *the* innovative company. This, it was argued, would also help Rogers sell lamps. Selling both intermediate materials and final products could increase total sales; although margins would be lower for substrate, they would be high enough to keep competitors' final lamp prices in line with Rogers. Those who wanted to see the product located in Connecticut, where wages were higher, argued for this option because much of the direct labor costs were in lamp finishing. Others argued against selling substrate; they felt that supplying multiple lamp fabricators compounded the risks of using an as yet imperfect, not fully standardized, substrate.

SELL COATED SUBSTRATE TO FLEX-KEY AND SELECTED LICENSEES, AS WELL AS LAMPS TO END USERS. Under this option, substrate production would be to stock, decoupled from lamp production

that was to order. Reliance on Flex-Key and other licensees would relieve Rogers of the need to customize small orders; in effect, these companies would become value-added distributors. Rogers had been exploring such a relationship with Hoffman Engineering, a manufacturer of small precision parts that had had close ties to military customers, for over a year. Why not let Hoffman, and Flex-Key as well, handle the military, for whom it was used to customizing orders in batches of tens and twenties? To start, Rogers could license Hoffman to produce lamps for a single market segment, aircraft panel manufacturers.

SELL LAMPS TO END USERS ONLY. Under this option, labor costs would be higher, but so would margins. Supporters argued that since Rogers did not yet know enough about the production process to tell others how to finish lamps, the preceding options, which involved multiple fabricators, were likely to complicate marketing by creating unforeseen problems. For example, there might be a large number of field failures. Supporters therefore believed it made more sense to control the final product until Rogers itself was sure how to make it.

Timing of Commercialization

According to the business plan, EL would be moved from the laboratory to a division in a staged transfer process. The chosen division would first learn the lamp finishing process, but would continue to use R&D's substrate, without making any of its own, well into 1985. Pressure was mounting, however, to transfer EL to a division and to move to an earlier commercialization. The two divisions most often named in connection with EL—Poron/Composites and Keyboard—were both described as "bleeding at the time" and "crying for new products." Moreover, since EL had no assigned division, it also had no division champion for its R&D budget, making it a prime candidate for being cut back if it stayed in R&D.

Pressure for earlier commercialization also arose because of a window in the largest market segment, automobiles. American automobile manufacturers were considering changes in dashboard and lighting displays; it was critical to get EL considered before the preliminary design work on these changes was completed. The process of evaluating new materials and products usually began two years before a model was introduced. Because Buick, on whom Rogers had concentrated its efforts, wanted to incorporate EL (if approved) into a few 1986 models, samples were needed by the end of 1984.

R&D, however, remained concerned about the unsolved moisture and brightness problems. It felt that going to market was premature and could give the product a permanent, or hard-to-live-down, black eye. In June 1984, new test results deepened R&D's concern. Under high humidity conditions, the lamps decayed rapidly, resulting in a half-life longer than one competitor's, and shorter than three competitors' aclar-covered lamps. The news was a surprise. While some life tests had been conducted during the winter, none had involved high humidity conditions.

Where to Locate the EL Product

There were four possibilities for the location of EL production: keep it in R&D, transfer it to the Poron/Composites or Keyboard divisions, or transfer it to the Flex-Key Corporation.

RUN EL OUT OF R&D FOR AN INDEFINITE PERIOD. Because the problem of maintaining lamps' brightness was still unresolved—and in many ways, was only partially understood—some managers felt that it was necessary to keep EL in R&D. The original pilot line could be used to manufacture low volumes of product for prototyping or outside sales. In fact, there were a number of precedents for running products out of R&D when production processes and specifications were still in flux. Proponents claimed that this option also allowed R&D to focus its attention on the problem of maintaining brightness; it was therefore more likely to achieve a breakthrough than if R&D resources were split between problem-solving and technology transfer. Reporting by technical people was also likely to result in more precise information. The Connecticut union, however, argued that if production were run out of R&D, the pilot line should be manned by union people rather than technicians.

PORON/COMPOSITES DIVISION-ROGERS, CONNECTICUT. Most members of the project team preferred to put EL in the Poron/Composites Division. A key reason was the proximity of the composites plant to R&D—a five-minute walk. In the past, Rogers had experienced problems with some of its long-distance hand-offs, and engineers had sometimes made dozens of trips to the plants. Berry described R&D's view:

> The R&D guys like to be there at the start-up and after to be sure the product is running okay. Typically, problems will arise a few weeks out; things you don't expect turn out to be important. Also, the scale-up changes the physical parameters. R&D has already gotten a feel for the process and is likely to have a sense of what adjustments need to be made on the new equipment.

The project team also had strong confidence in the Poron/Composites people, including its engineers, managers and hourly workers. As one member described the situation:

> Poron has some pretty sharp people who now have time available because of their mature product line. Most of Rogers is overbooked, but here are good people with not enough to do.

Poron/Composites also needed new products. Once Rogers largest division, it now lacked the volume to cover its overhead. Moreover, enthusiasm for EL had already been built because of the involvement of Poron's new general manager, Ron Robinson, and two of his managers on the EL project team. The mid-1983 invitation of the division onto the project team hinted at EL's permanent placement; later in the year, Robinson had told his people that EL would be coming to the division. In January 1984, Poron/Composites began to be charged for EL's R&D expenses.

On the downside, labor costs were higher in Connecticut (around $9 an hour on the average) than in Gloucester ($5.50 an hour) or Arizona ($6 an hour). More immediate labor problems were posed by the union in Connecticut. Should EL be located there, and should the union press its seniority provisions, EL manufacturing might continually have to use people who had been bumped from other divisions or product lines.

KEYBOARD DIVISION-CHANDLER, ARIZONA. Those who wished to locate EL in the Keyboard Division pointed out that Chandler was the only Rogers plant that practiced screening. The division therefore had process expertise as well as the necessary equipment (although no individual pieces of equipment had as yet been identified as appropriate for EL, it was assumed that something at Chandler would be suitable). Chandler was also capable of high-volume production. But in the past Chandler had had considerable problems with screening far less sophisticated than EL, and did not inspire great confidence among project team members or at headquarters. Problems included the uniformity of the screened layer and its being the right thickness throughout.

Chandler was also somewhat suspect in Connecticut because its history raised questions about the amount of attention that EL would get were it to be manufactured there. Before Keyboard became a separate division in mid-1983, its only product line, membrane keyboards, had been overshadowed by another product line manufactured in the same factory. During that period, membrane's market share shrank drastically; it received only limited attention because the market for the dominant line had suddenly exploded. Even after becoming a division, Keyboard had for several months lacked a full-time manager.

The management situation at Keyboard was about to change, however. Greenman had told Mike Zinck in January 1984 that by July he would be going back to Arizona to head the Keyboard Division full time. Zinck had recently turned around the company's Atlanta Division—taking it from a substantial loss to a solid profit (of 13%)—in two years. He wanted the challenge of EL for his new and troubled division, and, like Robinson, needed a new product. Greenman had earlier told Zinck that he thought Rogers should get out of the membrane keyboard business entirely; at a minimum, Zinck knew that he would be cutting back on his only product. And because he had been vocal about the need to improve technology transfer, Zinck wanted the opportunity to manage the process himself. He saw R&D proximity as potentially crippling and Chandler as the right place to build manufacturing skills. Yet Zinck was also aware of the risks: the need to rebuild management and technical strength at the division, as well as Chandler's past problems with screening.

FLEX-KEY CORPORATION/GLOUCESTER, MASSACHUSETTS. When Rogers purchased the Flex-Key Corporation (FKC) in 1981, it had been a small struggling firm known for its strength in design. Over time, Flex-Key had moved from the low to the high end of the market, from predominantly commercial customers to a focus on the military. It specialized in highly reliable, complex, low-volume keyboards. These required moderate screening expertise, plus sophisticated mechanical and electronic skills.

Locating EL at Flex-Key had certain advantages. FKC already had strong relationships with the military, which had been targeted by Rogers as the first market for its new product. Flex-Key's position in high-end, high value-added, low-volume segments of the keyboard market fit with several projected EL niches. And FKC was also relatively close to Rogers—about 100 miles away— which would simplify the transfer of technology. Unlike Connecticut, it had no union, and wage levels were about half as high. Its employees had a reputation for being energetic and hard working.

On the other hand, although FKC did some screening, it had less experience and equipment than Chandler. Nor were its electronic, mechanical engineering, and fabrication skills well-matched to EL's production needs. FKC's strengths were in engineering and prototyping rather than volume production. Should the new product take off, EL would no doubt have to be transferred again to a facility better suited for high volume.

27. Project Nantucket

In mid-February 1973, Bernie Muench, Ford Motor Company manager of Light Trucks, called his secretary to bring him the production facilities file. The time had come for him to decide whether he should accept or reject the proposal to automate the Ohio Truck Plant—a proposal that would add almost $10 million to the cost of Project Nantucket.

Nantucket was the code name for the $200-million project that would introduce a new model Econoline van and Club Wagon to the market in March 1975. The "blue letter," a formal intercompany proposal prepared for projects that require approval at corporate committee level, had been approved in November 1972, four months after Muench had taken his job. The approval provided for extensive product development and expanded production capacity at the Ohio Truck Plant. It would raise the capacity for Econolines to 45 per hour by early 1975, in contrast to the 1972 capacity of 25 per hour. Bodies would be produced with minimum automation and light tooling; however, it was understood that extensive automation of body production would be considered in time for 1975 models.

Since November 1972, the Automotive Assembly Division (*Exhibit 1*), and particularly the assembly manufacturing team headed by Ray K. Doty, had been developing the automation plan. Body shop operations would be the most extensively automated in the United States and probably in the world. The incremental investment in tooling and other equipment would be $9.9 million over that for the nonautomated process. The automated process was expected to minimize rat-

tling and improve strength, endurance, weld reliability, and dimensional tolerances for mating body parts.

It was the automation proposal that Muench now had to review. Funding approval for Project Nantucket had required the unqualified support of the entire Truck Operations management group. There was every indication that additional funding for automation would also be strongly supported. Muench was not directly responsible for production or manufacturing engineering;[1] however, as manager of Light Trucks, he had the power to veto the proposal. It was imperative that he carefully review the proposal and any other aspect of the project with product-line implications. Would it involve any traps for him as a product-line manager, responsible for performance and profit?

Econoline Background

Muench had worked in Truck Operations since 1970, two years after joining Ford and five years after receiving his MBA from Columbia in finance. Truck Operations had proved an interesting challenge, because the market for vans and buses had both changed and grown rapidly (from 190,000 U.S. registrations in 1966 to a projected 450,000 in 1974). Decisions in this product line seemed to be more susceptible to objective analysis than in automobiles, where the basis for buyer product preference was relatively subjective.

This case was prepared by William J. Abernathy.

Copyright © 1975 by the President and Fellows of Harvard College. Harvard Business School case 676-043.

[1] Since the early 1960s, U.S. automobile and truck production at Ford had been centrally controlled by Automotive Assembly Operations. Thus product managers only had advisory responsibilities for decisions about manufacturing methods.

The light-economy-truck concept had emerged from the product-development organization in 1959. At that time, Ford had held about 35% of the U.S. truck market and was particularly strong in pickups and medium trucks. Marketing research in late 1959 had showed that an inexpensive enclosed vehicle that could be locked to prevent theft of contents was a promising concept. In 1961, Ford introduced its economy line, "Econoline," including a light pickup truck and a van on a 90-inch wheelbase. The standard van was rated at ¼ ton with a payload capacity of just over 900 pounds. It used a Falcon drive-train package based on a six-cylinder engine, under an economical unit construction body.

Unit construction eliminated the separate frame. The body served the purpose of volume containment, as well as carrying the structural load and the power train that would otherwise be carried by the frame. Unit construction had been introduced in Ford cars in 1958;[2] the Econoline had been the first application to trucks. The design offered manufacturing economies. Vehicle weight could be reduced, and the entire vehicle could be bulit as one unit, a design better suited to the use of automated welding.

In 1972, other trucks and most Ford cars used frame construction (*Exhibit 2*). The power train, brakes, engine, wheels, and radiator were built up to form a nearly complete chassis. The body, constructed separately, was added to the chassis in final assembly. The final assembly line

[2] The Lincoln Zephyr, introduced in 1936, had a streamlined unit construction body that was larger than, but similar to, the VW Bug in many respects. This earlier body, however, had been designed and produced for Ford by suppliers.

EXHIBIT 1 Organization Chart

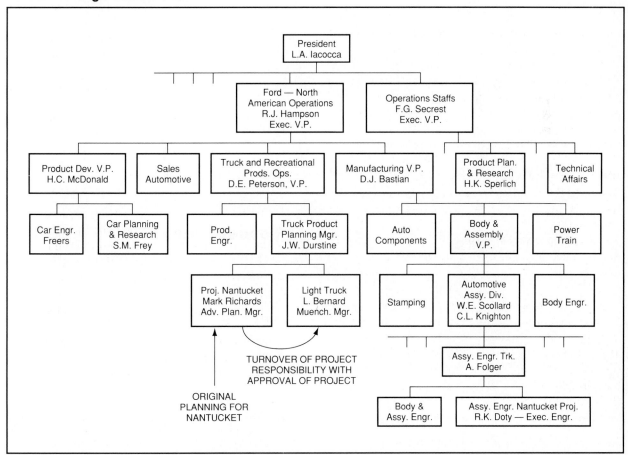

EXHIBIT 2 Frame Construction

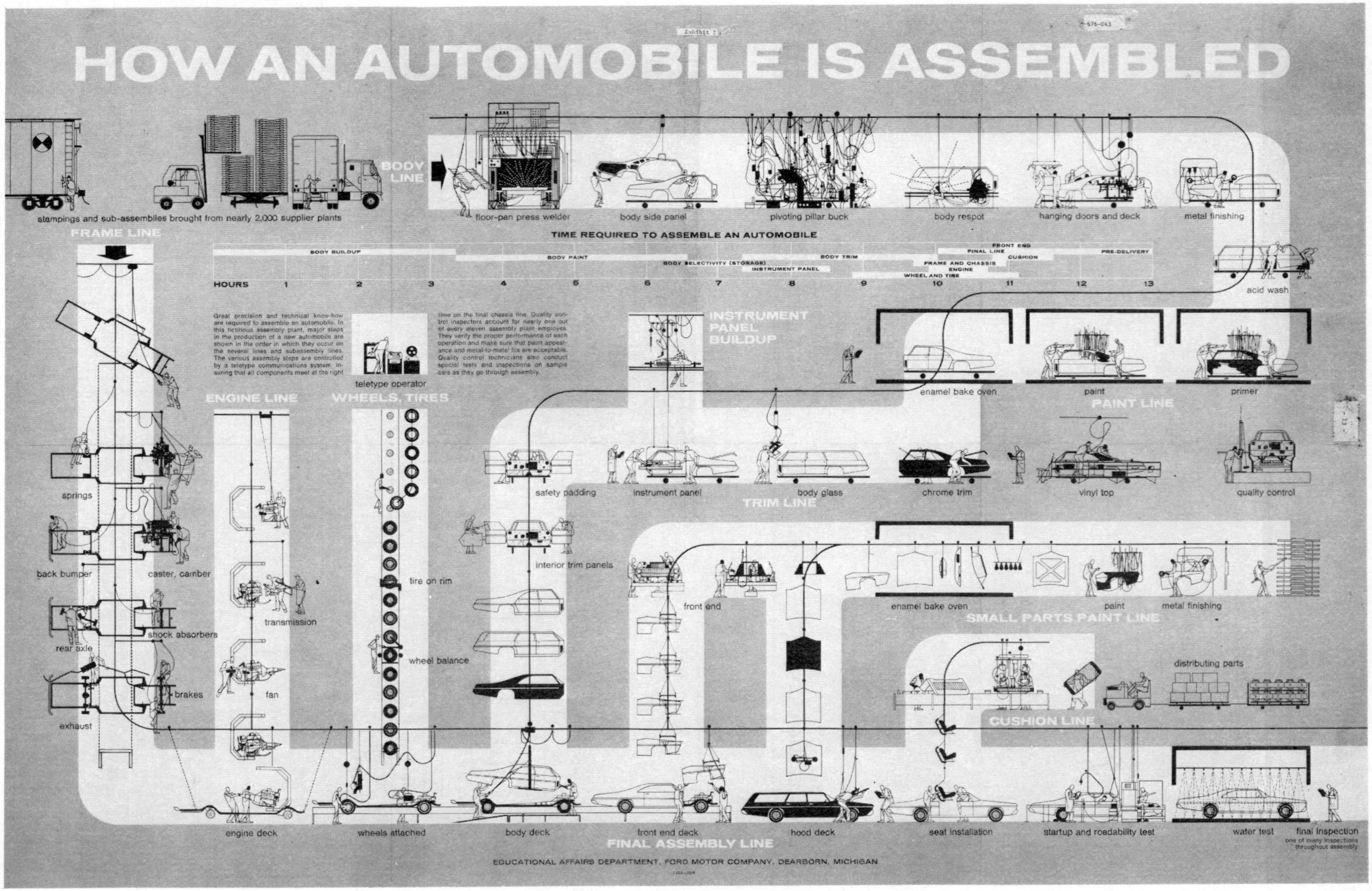

HOW AN AUTOMOBILE IS ASSEMBLED

was paced by the movement of the chassis, which began with the buildup of the frame. Frame construction made it easier to isolate the passenger compartment from road noises, since the body could be mounted on rubber isolators. With frame construction also, modifications were less costly to introduce, since the body and the frame could be altered somewhat independently.

Unit construction required several changes in assembly plant operation. More space and a higher line speed were required for the same output rate because each car took up more space on the line. (Separate frames were considerably shorter than entire bodies and could be spaced closer on the line.) Power-train components, brakes, springs, etc., had to be assembled directly to the body with unit construction, rather than to the more open chassis. This meant that assembly work was more awkward, with more "pit work" underneath the car.

The introduction of the Econoline in 1961 had revealed that the traditional pickup market (rural users, construction firms, etc.) did not want an "economy" pickup. But a strong new market had developed for closed vans and buses in a ratio of roughly five to one. The van had attracted an urban commercial market, including some of the pickup market. The bus (with windows, seats, and passenger appointments) which Ford called the Club Wagon, had attracted both commercial and consumer markets as a shuttle bus, a recreational vehicle, and a basic vehicle that small, specialized "body builders" could fit with special bodies, such as campers, for subsequent resale.

General Motors had entered the market with a similar idea using the Corvair power train in 1963. Dodge had entered with a larger vehicle; in 1965, Dodge had offered a more powerful V-8 engine and, in 1967, had extended the wheelbase, offering more cubic and gross weight carrying capacity. Chevrolet had also increased capacities during this period. *Exhibits 3* and *4* show the changes in market share which accompanied these alterations.

Ford had introduced its second-generation Econoline midyear in 1968, offering a larger forward engine and three gross vehicle weight (GVW)[3]

---

[3] The gross vehicle weight is the overall allowable weight of the vehicle when fully loaded. This is a generally accepted measure of the vehicle's weight class. Prior to 1968, the Econoline model had offered GVW ratings of 4500 and 5000 pounds.

options, up to 7,000 pounds. These had wheelbases of 105 ½ inches and 123 ½ inches. The package had offered greater cubic and gross weight carrying capacity and new unit construction bodies. Market reaction had been strong and favorable. Ford had regained 55% market share by 1970 in the larger van market and ten additional percentage points of market share in the bus (i.e., Club Wagon) market. Halfway through the 1970 model year Dodge and Chevrolet had reacted to the new Econoline model with second-generation van and bus designs. The changes had provided them a clear edge in the large V-8 engines and GVW capacity, and Dodge had offered an extended length optional package by welding a sheet metal "bustle" extension forward of the rear door. These competitors' advantages in power, weight, and carrying volume had affected the "people carrying" and consumer markets as reflected in Club Wagon market share (*Exhibit 3*). For the van market, which was more sensitive to cubic load capacity, the effect had been even stronger (*Exhibit 4*).

The new challenge to Ford's position in the market in 1970 had led to Project Nantucket. Extensive market research indicated that there were chances for improvement other than greater GVW and volume capacity: more convenient access to the engine for maintenance, better isolation of road noise for recreational vehicle converters, better handling in parking maneuvers, and several others.

Emerging Plans for the New Model

As product development plans were laid for the 1975 Econoline, Ford decided to drop unit construction in favor of a design with separate frame and body. The new design would offer wheelbase options of 124 and 138 inches. For cutaway versions, the wheelbase would be 158 inches with GVW ratings ranging up to 11,000 pounds and payloads to 5,975 pounds with dual rear wheels. This compared to the maximum of 7,000 GVW and 4,250-lb. payload for the current Econoline. Tentative prices for 1975 models would be 11% more than 1974 models. The product development effort included extensive testing to reduce service labor time by 10%; improved energy absorption during collision through crush zones in the frame; body mounts and tuning to reduce vibration; an

EXHIBIT 3 Comparative U.S. Vehicle Registration Statistics for Club Wagons (Calendar Years)

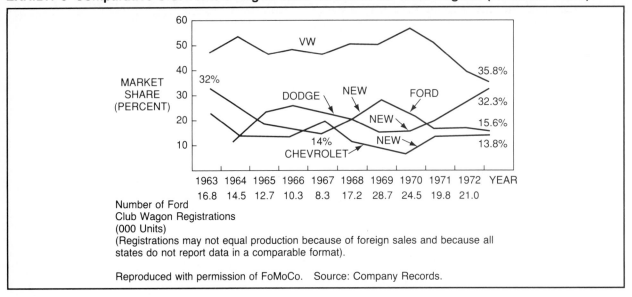

	1963	1964	1965	1966	1967	1968	1969	1970	1971	1972
	16.8	14.5	12.7	10.3	8.3	17.2	28.7	24.5	19.8	21.0

Number of Ford
Club Wagon Registrations
(000 Units)
(Registrations may not equal production because of foreign sales and because all
states do not report data in a comparable format).

Reproduced with permission of FoMoCo.   Source: Company Records.

EXHIBIT 5 Proposed Econoline III Features and Model Illustration

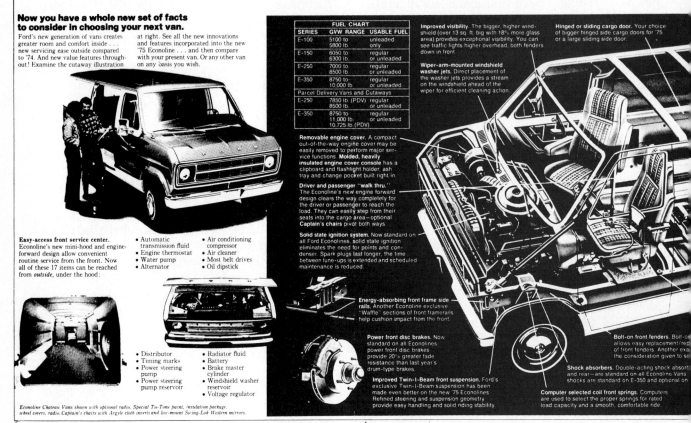

EXHIBIT 4 Comparative U.S. Vehicle Registration Statistics For Economy Vans (Calendar Year)

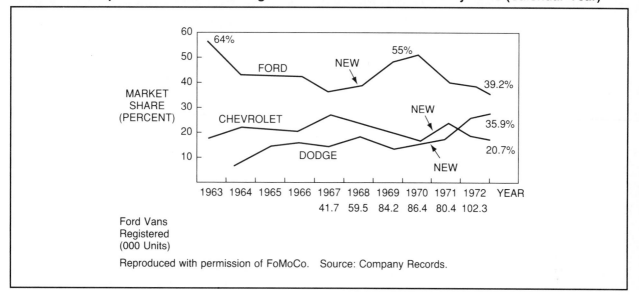

Ford Vans
Registered
(000 Units)

Reproduced with permission of FoMoCo.   Source: Company Records.

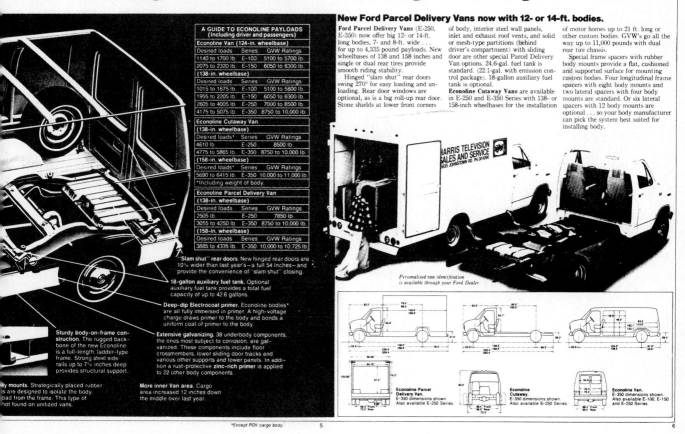

27. Project Nantucket

EXHIBIT 6 Projected Competitive Product Comparisons

	1975 Econoline	1974 Dodge	1974 Chevrolet
Products	Cargo Van Display Van Cutaway Club Wagon (5 to 12 passengers)	Tradesman Van (merchandised with optional window packages) Cutaway Sportsman (5 to 15 passengers)	Chevy Van (merchandised with optional window packages) Cutaway Sportsvan (5 to 12 passengers)
Wheelbases	124″ 138″ 158″	109″ 127″ 145″	110″ 125″
Gross Vehicle Weights	5,100–11,000	4,600–8,200	4,500–8,300
Engine Mix (cubic inch displacement of engine [CID])	300–460 CID	225–360 CID	250–350 CID
Unique superior features offered by each company	54″ rear cargo door, largest windshield and side-glass area	Only van with extended length	54.5″ rear cargo door, coolant recovery system

underbody heat shield to reduce the transmission of heat through floor to body compartments; and other programs to improve the vehicle (*Exhibit 5*). *Exhibit 6* compares planned 1975 Econoline features with those of projected 1974 features of Chevrolet and Dodge products.

The 1974 model and its specifications are shown in *Exhibit 7*. Projected 1974 retail prices and tentative prices for Econoline III were:[4]

Club Wagon *(5 Passenger)*		*Van*	
105″ wheelbase	$3,868	$3,175	projected 1974 price
123″ wheelbase	3,995	3,297	projected 1974 price
124″ wheelbase	4,446	3,683	tentative 1975 price

Econoline III would offer 548 different body

[4] The dealer's margin would be around 17% of this retail price.

permutations compared with 153 for Econoline II. Through extensive market research with mock-ups, the Econoline III had been compared with Econoline II, competing models and (where possible) projected characteristics of competitive models. Field tests with these models showed that users strongly preferred the new designs, by two to one in many instances. The superiority of features, the extensive breadth of new line, and the flexibility of frame construction in accommodating modifications (in contrast to the relatively extensive cost of change with unit construction) provided a package that Ford believed would nail down the market and sustain high-volume economic production for many years without further major model development.[5] The strength of the

[5] The only change that could be foreseen was for an extended van/passenger derivative to offer extended length. Dodge offered this as an option. This option had been cut from the 1975 Econoline package as now being proposed and was rescheduled for possible later introduction.

27. Project Nantucket

EXHIBIT 7 1974 Econoline Van

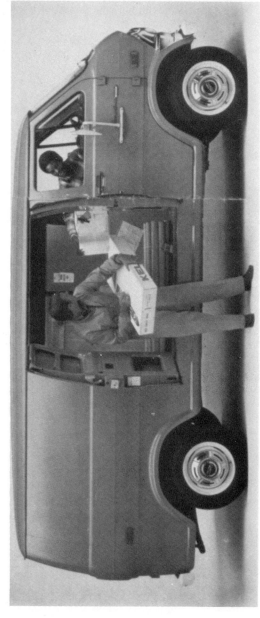

Display Van has windows in right side and rear
Two-tone paint and mirrors shown are optional

Window Van has glass all around
Custom trim, bright mirrors and whitewall tires are optional

Regular Van   SuperVan

SuperVan has a range of GVW's up to 8,300 pounds; mirrors, bright grille and hub caps are optional

YOU MADE IT THE FIRST CHOICE VAN BECAUSE WE MAKE IT THE WAY YOU WANT IT!

- Choice of gliding or swinging side cargo doors—same price
- Big loads, capacities up to 4,250 pounds
- Exclusive Twin-I-Beam independent front suspension for a smooth ride
- Wide-track axles for excellent stability, little wind wander, small turning circles
- Choice of two body lengths in many payload capacities
- Choice of Parcel Delivery or Camper Special Chassis
- Choice of 10- or 12-ft. parcel delivery bodies
- Choice of Six or V-8 engine
- Power brakes available on all models
- Power steering available on all models
- Handy, timesaving front service center

Ford Econolines are the best-selling vans year after year. And for the best of reasons. Ford comes up with better ideas. Better ideas to get around in traffic. Better ideas to make the ride and handling easy. Better ideas designed to cut service time and expense. Better ideas in complete parcel-type vans and chassis-cabs (floor and front-end section only; both types shown on page 5). Better ideas to make vans last long, and do an excellent job.

Only Ford has Twin-I-Beam front suspension. The independent suspension that smooths and stabilizes the ride—toughens up the van. And Ford gives you a choice of gliding or swinging side cargo doors at no extra charge. Whichever door you select, you get Ford's tight, sturdy construction and simple, sure operation.

When it comes to loadspace, only Econolines give you so much usable loadspace in so little roadspace. The engine is up front so it's out of the cargo area. But not so far forward that it overextends vehicle length or interferes with maneuverability. And Ford pays off its large cargo area with plenty of payload

capacity. The Econoline E-300 Series allows you to tote over two tons—up to 4,250 pounds. Ford's combination of smooth toughness, serviceability, big loadspace and payload keeps Econoline first in better ideas and value.

Econoline Vans are offered in three job-tailored series with the following GVW ranges: E-100—4,325 lb. to 4,800 lb., E-200—5,250 lb. to 6,000 lb., and E-300—6,050 lb. to 8,300 lb. This choice allows you to select a model with the capacity just right for your job. You may choose either a 105.5-in. or 123.5-in. wheelbase for the proper body length and weight distribution.

The Econoline Van is a handy, compact unit with 105.5-in. wheelbase. Overall length is two feet less than a conventional short wheelbase pickup, yet the load length on the floor from rear doors to the instrument panel is 11½ feet. You get 8½ feet of clear floor length behind the driver's seat and engine cover. Width between the rear wheelhousings is 53.5 inches. Ford's standard Econoline Van will carry 4' x 8' sheets of building materials flat on the floor.

The SuperVan with its 123.5-in. wheelbase is a really big load carrier. You get over 10 feet of clear floor length behind the engine plus 13 feet on the floor to the right of the engine. All this in less than 16 feet overall. No other van offers so much usable space for your loads in such a short overall length.

Both the Van and SuperVan allow you to order shelving, cabinets or racks and still have plenty of open cargo area to handle appliances or other bulky cargo. Attractive Custom Equipment Package is also available for all models. Custom trim includes:chrome front and rear bumpers (front only on Parcel Delivery Van) • bright-metal grille, hub caps, taillights and side marker light bezels • bright-metal windshield and vent window moldings • deluxe pleated vinyl seat trim, front door armrest (RH w/adjustable passenger seat) and left-side floor mat, all color-keyed • horn ring • cigar lighter • glove box door with lock (not available with radio).

Econoline Vans are available in your choice of four-teen standard colors, and two-tone combinations are optional (see back cover).

market would be important to the economic success of the automation program. A rough idea of stability over time in external body design may be obtained by comparing the original Econoline (*Exhibit 8*) with the 1974 model (*Exhibit 7*).

The Production Picture

In January 1972, Econoline produciton was concentrated in the Lorain assembly plant; 6,000 hourly workers were employed on two final assembly lines, one for the Econoline at a maximum output rate of 25.5 vehicles per hour and the second for Ford passenger vehicles. The fact sheet given to plant visitors listed the characteristics of the plant in 1971 as follows:

Employees: Hourly, 6,220; salary, 714 – total, 6,934

Daily production: Passenger, 57/hour; Econoline, 25.5/hour

Sole source for Montego, Econoline; also produce Torinos

Total payroll for 1970, $66,261,000

Average weekly earnings of hourly employees, $192.00

Parts:		
	Number unique to Torino	1,217
	Number unique to Montego	627
	Number unique to Econoline	2,288
	Number common to all models	5,998
		10,130

EXHIBIT 8 Original Econoline Model

Source: *Ford Automotive Highlights 1896–1971*, Published by North American Automotive Operations, Ford Motor Company, Dearborn Michigan. June, 1971

27. Project Nantucket

With overtime and two-shift operations, 138,387 Econolines had been produced in 1970; 104,450 in 1971; around 140,000 in 1972—considerably in excess of planned capacity. It appeared that 145,000 could be produced in 1973, but the plant would be pushing its capacity. Furthermore, 7,000 employees at one facility was near the upper limit that Ford considered manageable in an assembly plant. The capacity situation had contributed to the erosion of market share. Action was essential.

In the fall of 1972, intending to expand production of the Econoline, Ford had bought an 860,000-square-foot trailer plant from the Fruehauf Corporation. It had been rumored that Fruehauf was eager to sell because of labor difficulties in the area. The plant was nineteen miles from the Lorain Assembly Plant. Ford's relationship with the local union was businesslike and workable. By following a pragmatic pattern of working out difficulties at the local level, as Ford had in other areas, an outstanding production record had been achieved in Lorain. Local plant management expected to operate both plants from Lorain. Consequently, when Project Nantucket had been approved, in November Ford had decided to purchase the Fruehauf plant at a net cost of around $15 million (much less than the cost of current construction). It was redesignated the Ohio Truck Plant.

Since the mid-1950s, assembly plants, particularly those producing bodies, had become increasingly specialized, employing automated fixtures and welding presses that saved labor but could produce only one body type. By 1972, few Ford vehicles were produced in more than two plants. The concept of a lightly tooled assembly plant that afforded shipping economies no longer applied. Ford's Econoline production had been different, however, for the Budd Company produced the Econoline II body components. Budd made individual parts in its own stamping plant, fabricated them into major body subassemblies, and shipped them to the Lorain plant. As a consequence, Econoline II body shop operations at Lorain consisted largely of body framing and subsequent operations such as painting and trimming. (See *Exhibit 2*.)

In introducing the new Econoline, Ford planned to integrate backwards into body component manufacturing. Budd would still make

stamped parts and some components such as doors; however, these parts would be fabricated into major subassemblies, such as body sides, pillars, or underbodies, at the new Ohio Truck Plant. This increased integration, and other changes related to the new model introduction, would reduce the variable cost of a Club Wagon by $37,[6] compared to projected costs of carrying over the 1974 van without new model change. The automation proposal, if adopted, would reduce variable costs still further.

The plans for the intermediate future called for the new Ohio Truck Plant to accommodate component buildup, body framing, door mounting, metal-surface finishing, phosphate treatment, electrocoating, painting, and baking. Then five bodies at a time would be transported nineteen miles in special vans to the Lorain Assembly Plant where the chassis would be built up and the bodies merged in final assembly. Later, if market conditions warranted, a final assembly capability might be added to the Ohio Truck Plant.

In the more immediate future, before the new body facilities were added, the new plant was to provide incremental capacity for the Lorain plant. Starting in the fall of 1973, bodies that were framed at Lorain were to be trucked round trip to the Ohio Truck Plant for painting. This expedient was expected to permit a production rate of 175,000 Econoline units per year.

In this environment of capacity bottlenecks, lost sales, and expensive expedients, the management of Truck Operations had to decide on the facilities' plan for the new Ohio Truck Plant.

Proposed Manufacturing Methods

The proposed automation plan was a radical departure from conventional methods. The recommendation to automate was based on an operation-by-operation analysis of each production stage, comparing the best manual method with the best automated method.

For example, in the best manual method of manufacturing for the left-hand body side assembly of the van (*Exhibit 9*), operators positioned

---

[6] Estimated direct variable cost of the 1975 Econoline Club Wagon, including variable overhead, was $2,500.

EXHIBIT 9 Major Body Component Divisions for Automated Lines

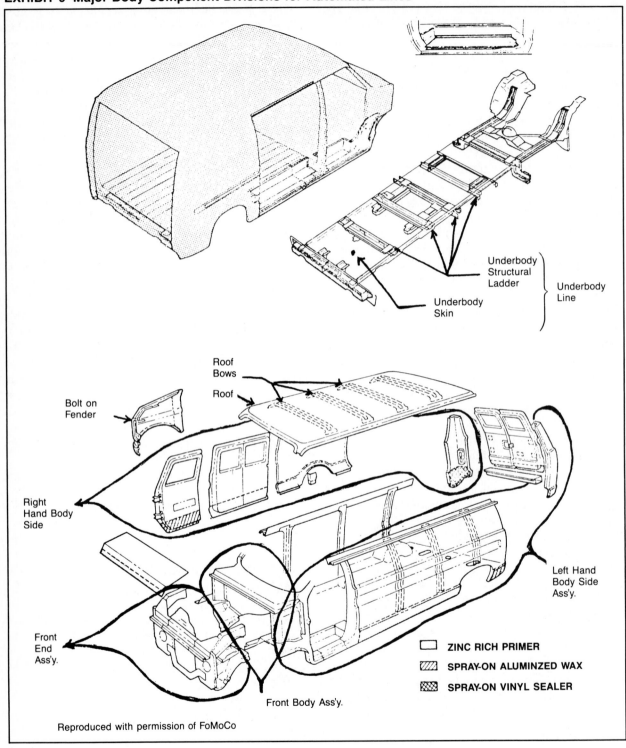

Underbody Structural Ladder

Underbody Line

Underbody Skin

Roof Bows

Roof

Bolt on Fender

Right Hand Body Side

Left Hand Body Side Ass'y.

Front End Ass'y.

☐ ZINC RICH PRIMER

▨ SPRAY-ON ALUMINZED WAX

▩ SPRAY-ON VINYL SEALER

Front Body Ass'y.

Reproduced with permission of FoMoCo

parts on a series of fixtures, manually clamped them in place, and welded them with guns. A typical fixture used was a metal frame with guides to align sheet metal parts as they were added to the body side assembly, and more clamps to hold parts in place until they could be welded. After several sheet-metal parts had been added, the partially completed subassembly was moved to another fixture. The assembly was eventually respotted (that is, additional welds would be made, usually with a hand gun) to give the necessary structural strength. About 55 operators and 30 stations were required per shift for each body side, including the feeder lines that built up the pillars at the front and back of the body. The work involved many manual operations and much parts handling, with the risk that critical welds might be missed.

With the automated method, the alignment of parts, the clamping, welding, and unclamping, and the movement of the partially completed assembly to the next station, would be automatic (*Exhibits 10 and 11*). The presses, clamps, spot-welding guns and overhead transfer mechanisms on this body side line would be operated by automatic pneumatic or hydraulic devices. The proposed approach would involve automatic welding stations with automatic transfer to build up each of the four pillars for each side of the body. These would feed into a main side body assembly line that had seven active welding press stations, all automatically operated, with automatic transfer. Following this, the body side would be transferred through three more press stations for automated respotting. This line would involve transfer through more than eleven active automatic stations.

The operations recommended in the plan, such as those in the body side assembly line, combined the best manual and automated approaches. They offered improvements in production management, product quality, and a minimum

EXHIBIT 10 Illustration of Transfer Line Integration with Automated Welding Presses

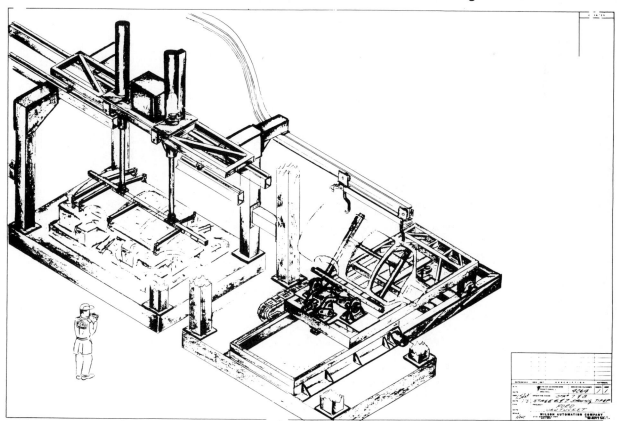

EXHIBIT 11 Process Flow Schematic for Body Buildup

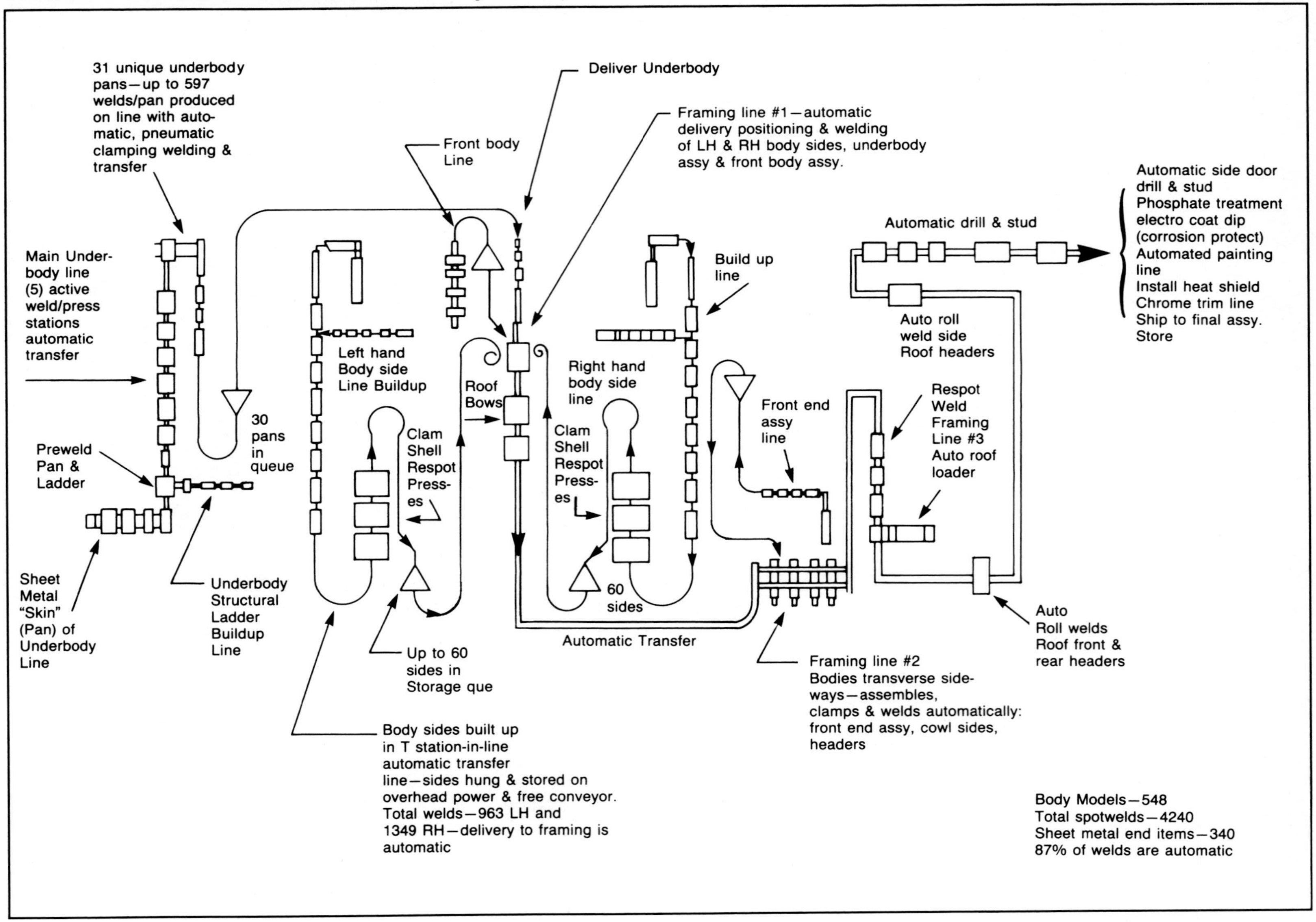

Automatic side door
drill & stud
Phosphate treatment
electro coat dip
(corrosion protect)
Automated painting
line
Install heat shield
Chrome trim line
Ship to final assy.
Store

Auto
Roll welds
Roof front &
rear headers

Body Models—548
Total spotwelds—4240
Sheet metal end items—340
87% of welds are automatic

Automatic drill & stud

Auto roll
weld side
Roof headers

Respot
Weld
Framing
Line #3
Auto roof
loader

Framing line #2
Bodies transverse side-
ways – assembles,
clamps & welds automatically:
front end assy, cowl sides,
headers

Front end
assy
line

Deliver Underbody

Framing line #1 – automatic
delivery positioning & welding
of LH & RH body sides, underbody
assy & front body assy.

Build up
line

Right hand
body side
line

Clam
Shell
Respot
Press-
es

60
sides

Automatic Transfer

Front body
Line

Roof
Bows

Clam
Shell
Respot
Press-
es

Up to 60
sides in
Storage que

Body sides built up
in T station-in-line
automatic transfer
line—sides hung &
stored on
overhead power & free conveyor.
Total welds—963 LH and
1349 RH—delivery to framing is
automatic

Left hand
Body side
Line Buildup

30
pans in
queue

Underbody
Structural
Ladder
Buildup
Line

31 unique underbody
pans—up to 597
welds/pan produced
on line with auto-
matic, pneumatic
clamping welding &
transfer

Main Under-
body line
(5) active
weld/press
stations
automatic
transfer

Preweld
Pan &
Ladder

Sheet
Metal
"Skin"
(Pan) of
Underbody
Line

30% ROI saving during a seven-year economic life with a two-shift operation.

The resulting composite plan would integrate five subsidiary lines, each involving extensive in-line transfer and automated welding, into a single automated transfer line. The five lines would be for the five major body components (*Exhibit 9*):

1. The underbody line, which included the underbody structural ladder and the sheet-metal "skin" over the ladders.
2. Separate left-hand and right-hand body side assembly build-up lines.
3. The front body assembly line.
4. The front end assembly line.
5. The body framing line which integrated the other component lines.

Automated in-line transfer, as proposed, differed from the robotics approach to automation that General Motors had used at Lordstown in 1971 and that Ford had also used to a lesser extent at its Pinto factory.[7] The U.S. auto industry had pioneered in the use of robots, but its early experience with robots had been widely interpreted in the industry as a failure to demonstrate their much-touted flexibility. It was true that minor year-to-year variations had been accommodated by simply reprogramming the robots but conventional presses could also be designed to accommodate some variation and minor degrees of change. Major model changes had continued to be carried out as before. When the entire manufacturing process had been changed the robots were pulled out and refitted and reinstalled just the way conventional equipment was.

At Ford major process work was done by a contractor, for the company did not employ enough skilled labor for periodic jobs of this type. Moreover, it was considered good practice to begin a multiyear model run with equipment that was either new or completely overhauled. This idea extended to robots. Outside contracting for overhaul took equipment out of use and lengthened the changeover period. When prevailing practice

meant that process change required a major investment in time and money anyway, robots seemed to offer little advantage.

The new proposed automated approach employed automated presses and transfer lines. In contrast to other methods of automation in which a part remained at one station for a complex set of operations, the parts moved from one process operation to the next by means of an automatic transfer mechanism, forming a continuous-process flow line. At each automated transfer station, the mechanism stopped the part, automatically indexed or positioned it for the work that was to be performed and then moved it to the next station. In extensive applications of this approach, both the movement and the welding presses at each station were automatic; no operator intervention was necessary.

In Ford's proposed plan, 87% of the 4240 spot welds on a typical model would be automatic. The main functions of the worker in the automated portions of the line would be to position pieces to be added to the main component, to monitor and adjust machines, and to load and unload at points where automated transfer was not complete. The operator would indicate with push buttons which model was to be produced at the input station for the major line: welding presses would automatically set up for this model, sense the parts to confirm correspondence between parts and instructions, perform the required welding operations, and electronically pass model identification to the next automated station as the component was transferred. In this way, models could be mixed on the line. While the five major lines could accommodate any body option, within the specified cycle time, the tasks on many feeder lines varied with the body option so that the entire facility had to be balanced for the mix of options. A manual method of manufacturing was typically proposed for tasks such as those that varied by model option. *Exhibit 11* shows the proposed layout and process flow.

UNDERBODY LINE: The underbody would receive around 525 spot welds depending upon which of the 31 unique floor plans was involved. The main underbody line would be fed by a feeder line using four welding presses and automatic transfer to build up the structural ladder. This would merge

---

[7] At Lordstown, the car moved along a line. Eleven programmable "Unimate" robots on each side made about twenty welds each and could be reprogrammed to weld different locations.

EXHIBIT 12 Comparisons of Methods of Assembly

	Proposed Method	Best Manual Method
Underbody line		
Workers per shift	11	46
Investment in tooling	$5,500,000	$3,500,000
Body side lines		
Workers per shift	33	110
Investment in tooling	$13,500,000	$8,700,000
Front body assembly		
Workers per shift	7	14–15
Investment in tooling	$1,300,000	$ 850,000
Front-end assembly		
Workers per shift	7	14
Investment in tooling	$1,500,000	$1,100,000
Body framing		
Workers per shift	5–6	40
Investment in tooling	$8,700,000	$6,500,000

with the sheet-metal skin flow. The entire underbody structure would then be transferred through five or more automatic welding presses to an inspection station and then to a final station where skids would be installed. Next, the complete underbody would be transported by roller conveyor to a buffer storage of 31 pans and later to the body framing line. (*Exhibit 12* compares labor and investment requirements for the proposed and the best manual methods.)

BODY SIDE LINES: Each body side line could produce any of twenty-one unique versions in any sequence as set up by the operator at the input station. It would also be sequenced with the body framing line. More than 250 welds would be performed during a sequence of stages involving in-line automated transfer. Nine stages (seven active) would be involved in the main line, including three respot stations to add additional welds. This line would be fed by a series of feeder lines to build up pillars and other components. Upon completion, each body side would be automatically transported overhead into a first in, first

out buffer storage and then transferred to the main framing line.

FRONT BODY ASSEMBLY: This line would be composed of four automatic assembly fixtures, manually loaded and unloaded, and four in-line automatic assembly fixtures with adjoining idle stations. The completed assembly would be manually loaded on an overhead conveyor and transported to the framing line.

FRONT END ASSEMBLY: Four automatic assembly fixtures and five in-line automatic assembly fixtures were proposed. Once loaded into the in-line sequence of five fixtures, the transfer of the front end and the operations would be automatic. Power transport to body framing would be manually loaded.

BODY FRAMING: The body framing line would be composed of three subsidiary transfer groups: framing lines 1, 2 and 3. The line would assemble the body shell from five major subassemblies and parts, performing 490 spot welds in 11 different fixtures. Transfer would be automatic between each station and the major groups of stations in the line. In framing line one, the underbody, body sides, and front end components would be automatically loaded, clamped in position to close tolerances in large presses, and welded automatically. The framed body would be automatically turned and travel sideways to framing line two. Here the front end and other parts would be added and welded. Transfer would be automatic to framing line three for additional welds. Next, the roof would be loaded and welded. Finally, the body would be transferred for additional operations at another station.

OTHER FEATURES: In addition to these improvements, the proposal sought $2.4 million of incremental investment in an advanced painting facility with glass-enclosed spray booths that promised a better work environment, closer supervision, and a paint recovery system to reduce pollution. Other automation features were sought in other aspects of body production, but these steps were not so radical as the five main body building lines.

Evaluating the Proposal

A number of important arguments were advanced in favor of the proposed automation plan, chief among them advantages in product quality and direct manufacturing cost. Significant problems were involved in achieving close dimensional tolerance, consistency in individual weld placement and quality, and overall structural integrity for a mass-produced mechanical structure as large and complex as a body. The use of large welding presses and mechanical positioners to clamp and hold the body parts in close alignment and to weld them in place promised very high consistency and close tolerance body assembly. To ensure repeatable production, individual welds would be exactly specified and located. As for labor productivity, wage rates for 1975 were projected in the $7.50 to $7.75 per hour range; fringe benefits might increase out-of-pocket employment costs by 50%; overtime would probably be required in peak periods. These trends, plus the persistent 5% inflation rate, which might rise even higher, made it even more important to improve labor produc-

tivity. (See *Exhibit 13* for other operating statistics.)

Even though significant advances in automation were proposed, no jobs would be lost at the Ohio facilities. To the contrary, several hundred new jobs would be created at both the new Ohio Truck Plant and the Lorain plant. Econoline production alone would employ some 3,300 workers when two shifts were in operation; of these, around 1,100 would be at the new Ohio Truck Plant, including about sixty maintenance personnel.

Many thought the impact of Project Nantucket would be decidedly favorable on working conditions. Shorter work cycles resulted from the higher output rate, but these were still longer than the typical rate of one per minute in most car plants. In addition, the switch from unit to frame construction eliminated most of the pit jobs which required less desirable overhead work. From twenty to sixty pit work stations might be required in an assembly plant producing unit construction vehicles. With separate frame construction as now proposed, the entire chassis could be assembled from above. The proposed automation would shift worker functions from performing tasks to controlling machines, performing light tasks, monitoring, and, of course, reacting to system failures. The body building shop in conventional plants produced the highest frequency of worker complaints and the approach would eliminate most sources of problems.

Although he was aware of the major benefits the proposal had in store, Bernie Muench also knew that there were possible disadvantages to the proposal. The main concerns that had been raised by some groups at Ford centered on equipment reliability and overall process flow configuration. When Ford had pioneered in the application of transfer line to engine plants twenty years before, it had taken years to work out the problems involved in the process change. The Cleveland Engine Plant, opened in 1952, for instance, had introduced a single automated synchronous transfer line[8] integrating the equivalent of 150 stations, each equivalent to a single-purpose machine center. The experience with this and subsequent

---

[8] The term "synchronous" refers to the interlocking of transfer so that all transfers at all stations occur at the same time. Thus the failure of one station stops all stations.

EXHIBIT 13 Selected Operating Statistics: FoMoCo

	1972	1971	1970	1969	1968
Ford World Wide Operations					
Sales ($000,000)	20,194.4	16,433.0	14,979.9	14,755.6	14,075.1
Total Operating Costs	18,576.5	15,165.6	13,965.1	13,695.6	12,796.2
Net Income (after tax)	870.0	656.7	515.7	546.5	626.6
Depreciation & Amortization of Special Tools	931.3	823.6	823.5	803.7	748.2
Stockholders Equity	5,961.3	5,547.2	5,467.9	5,222.0	4,946.6
Purchases (% of Sales)	56.9	56.3	57.4	58.0	56.7
Unit Sales Cars & Trucks (000)	5,698	5,024	4,861	4,944	4,744
North American Operations					
Unit Sales Cars & Trucks (000)	3,848	3,351	3,214	3,363	3,448
US Hourly Employees Avg.	158,723	151,749	155,448		
Avg. Hourly Labor Cost	7.83	7.21	6.40	5.78	5.46
Consumer Price Index (1958 = 100)	145.9	141.6	135.2	128.2	122.3

engine plants showed that equipment downtime in such long transfer lines was a serious problem, making maintenance critical.

The use of automation for body assembly as presently proposed raised some of the issues afresh. On one hand, the lines were much shorter, and a few buffer inventories were placed at strategic locations so that if major lines were down, they could be temporarily bypassed, except for the main framing line. On the other hand, the equipment was new, and because of the special challenges involved in handling large sheet-metal pieces, much more complex. Some 22,000 relays would have to operate repeatedly if the system were to function without failure, and 100,000 or more switches, pneumatic clamps, or welding-gun controls would have to work as a unit. Seven major subcontractors would participate in the automation plan under Ford's overall control. This would be the first time their separate equipment would have to function together in so complex an application.

A margin of safety was built into the proposed equipment plan. While the equipment would be designed for a maximum operating cycle of sixty bodies per hour, the operating design capacity of the facility was for only forty-five units per hour. At capacity the equipment would operate at only 75% of its rated design speed.

There was also the question of product change. Minor changes in the contour or surface of individual body parts could be accommodated. Individual pieces could be changed as long as major interfaces with other parts were not involved. But any significant change in the height of a body side, for example, would mean that essentially all presses would have to be modified, entailing a shutdown of six weeks. Each press cost around $250,000, including controls and tooling. The cost of a major modification would approximate the purchase price of the unit. Costs associated with changing the more manual method would only be two-thirds to one-half of those with the automated system. The proposed plan incorporated an option to add a bustle (extended length van) at a cost of $800,000 in initial tooling cost. This meant that such a provision could be added without a six-week shutdown of the plant. It was not clear whether this was the only change the market might demand or not.

Bernie Muench knew that the need to go ahead of competition in manufacturing capability was a factor in the decision as far as senior management was concerned. General Motor's Lordstown plant had gone further than any other major U.S. manufacturer in reducing labor content in assembly through automation. Volkswagen and other European small car producers were still further ahead in mechanized assembly. The Japanese producers seemed likely to carry automation farthest of all, and there were strong signals that they would try to penetrate the U.S. market in light trucks as well as cars. In this case, Ford would likely find itself in head-on price competition where manufacturing cost would be critical. Project Nantucket could provide a base of skills and experience which would allow Ford to leapfrog competition.

28. The Boeing 767: From Concept to Production (A)

In August 1981, eleven months before the first scheduled delivery of Boeing's new airplane, the 767, Dean Thornton, the program's vice president-general manager, faced a critical decision. For several years, Boeing had lobbied the Federal Aviation Administration (FAA) for permission to build wide-bodied aircraft with two-, rather than three-person cockpits. Permission had been granted late in July. Unfortunately, the 767 had originally been designed with a three-person cockpit, and 30 of those planes were already in various stages of production.

Thornton knew that the planes had to be converted to models with two person cockpits. But what was the best way to proceed? Should the changes be made in-line, inserting new cockpits into the 30 planes without removing them from the flow of production, or off-line, building the 30 planes with three-person cockpits as originally planned and then retrofitting them with two-person cockpits in a separate rework area? Either way, Thornton knew that a decision had to be made quickly. Promised delivery dates were sacred at Boeing, and the changes in cockpit design might well impose substantial delays.

The Airframe[1] Industry

Commercial aircraft manufacturing was an industry of vast scale and complexity. A typical 767 contained 3.1 million individual parts; federal regulations required that many be documented and traceable. There were 85 miles of wiring

[1] An airframe is an airplane without engines. Technically, Boeing competed in the airframe industry. In this case, however, the terms airframe, airplane, and aircraft are used interchangeably.

This case was prepared by David A. Garvin, Lee J. Field, and Janet Simpson.

alone. Manufacturers employed thousands of scientists and engineers to develop new technologies and production systems, and also to attack design problems. Facilities were on a similarly grand scale. Boeing assembled the 747, its largest commercial airplane, in the world's largest building—62 acres under a single roof—with a work force of 28,600 people.

Few companies were able to marshal such massive resources. In 1981 the industry had only three major players: the American manufacturers, Boeing and McDonnell Douglas, and the European consortium, Airbus. A fourth manufacturer, Lockheed, left the commercial airplane industry in 1981 after its wide-bodied jet, the L-1011, had incurred losses of $2.5 billion. Boeing and McDonnell Douglas were competitors of longstanding; Airbus, on the other hand, made its commercial debut in May 1974. It was not generally regarded as a serious competitive threat until 1978, the date of its first large sale to a U.S. airline. By 1981, Airbus has sold 300 planes to 41 airlines, and had options for 200 more. It received direct financing and subsidies from the French, Spanish, German, and British governments.

Airframe manufacturing was a business of enormous risks, for in no other industry was so much capital deployed with so much uncertainty. Launching a new plane meant up-front development costs of $1.5–2 billion, lead times of up to four years from Go-ahead to first delivery, and the qualification and management of thousands of subcontractors.

Projects of this scale could put a company's entire net worth on the line. For that reason, industry executives were sometimes characterized as "gamblers," sporting participants in a high-stakes game. Side bets—actual wagers between manufacturers and airlines regarding airplane performance, features, or delivery dates—occasionally accompanied purchase negotiations. The odds against a successful new product were large. According to one industry expert, in the past thirty years only two new plane programs, the Boeing 707 and 727, actually made money.[2] (According to Boeing, the 737 and 747 programs have also been profitable.) If a new program were successful, however, the potential returns were enormous. A successful new plane could lock up its chosen market segment for as long as 20 years, producing sales of $25–45 billion and huge profits. It was also likely to bring great prestige, power, and influence to the company and managers that created it.

Success required a long-term view. Competitive pricing was essential. Pricing practices, however, contributed risks of their own. New plane prices were based not on the cost of producing the first airplane, but on the average cost of 300 to 400 planes, when required labor hours had declined because of learning. This effect, the so-called learning curve, was hardly unique to airframe manufacturing. But small annual volumes and long manufacturing cycles—even during peak periods Boeing planned to build only eight 767s per month—meant that break-even points stretched further into the future in airframe manufacturing than was typical of most other industries, where mass production was the norm.

Manufacturers were therefore anxious to build orders for new planes as quickly as possible. Buyers—primarily the 50 leading airlines around the world—used that knowledge to enhance their bargaining positions, often delaying orders until the last possible moment. Negotiations on price, design modifications, and after-sales parts and service became especially aggressive in the 1970s, when airlines that had been making steady profits began losing large sums of money. Cost savings became a dominant concern. As Richard Ferris, the CEO of United Airlines, remarked: "Don't bug me about interior design or customer preference, just guarantee the seat-mile performance."[3]

[2] John Newhouse, *The Sporty Game* (New York: Alfred A. Knopf, 1982), p. 4.
[3] Ibid., page 84. Seat-mile performance is the cost of operating a plane divided by the product of miles flown and the number of seats available.

The Boeing Company

Boeing was the sales leader of the airframe industry, as well as one of America's leading exporters. It had built more commercial airplanes than any other company in the world. Sales in 1981 were $9.2 billion; of the total, $5.1 billion were ascribed to the Boeing Commercial Airplane Company, the firm's aircraft manufacturing division. Other divisions produced missiles, rockets, helicopters, space equipment, computers and electronics.

HISTORY. The Boeing Company was founded in 1916 by William E. Boeing, the son of a wealthy timber man who had studied engineering at Yale. In its earliest days, the company built military aircraft for use in World War I. It began to prosper in the 1920s and 1930s, when the civil aviation market expanded, primarily because of the demand for mail carrying. At about that time, William Boeing issued a challenge that has remained the company's credo:

> Our job is to keep everlastingly at research and experimentation, to adapt our laboratories to production as soon as possible, and to let no new improvement in flying and flying equipment pass us by.

To meet this challenge, Boeing originally relied on extensive vertical integration. It not only manufactured entire planes itself, but also provided engines through its Pratt & Whitney subsidiary, and bought and flew planes through its United Air Lines subsidiary. A government mandate separated the three entities in 1934. As the costs of developing and producing new aircraft grew ever larger, the company became even more focused. By the late 1970s and early 1980s, Boeing no longer assumed all development costs itself, nor did it fabricate entire airplanes. Instead, it carefully selected partners, some of whom participated on a risk sharing basis, who were then subcontracted portions of each plane and developed and built parts and subassemblies that Boeing later assembled. The primary exceptions were the nose section and wings, which Boeing continued to build in-house. One manager summarized the situation in the 1970s by saying: "Today Boeing is an assembler who makes wings."

In part, such efforts to limit up-front investment and reduce risks were prompted by Boeing's near disastrous experiences with its first wide-bodied jet, the 747. In 1969, when the company was introducing the 737 as well as the 747, management problems, declining productivity, steep development costs and unanticipated problems with the engine, plus cutbacks in commercial and government orders, produced a severe cash crunch. Boeing was close to bankruptcy. In the next three years, the company's work force fell from 150,000 to 50,000; unemployment in Seattle, Boeing's home base, rose to 14 percent. Eventually, such belt tightening, plus efforts to resolve problems with the 737 and 747 programs, carried the day, and Boeing emerged from the crisis leaner and stronger, but with a renewed sense of the inherent risks of major development programs.

STRATEGY. Ever since the 707 was introduced in 1955, Boeing had competed by selling families of planes. Each new generation of aircraft was created with several variations in mind, drawing on the same base airframe concept. By 1987 the 747, for example, was being offered in eleven varieties, including the 747-100B (standard), 747-200B (long range), 747F (freighter), and 747C (convertible to either passenger or cargo configurations). Flexible designs with inherent growth potential were essential to this approach. Modifications such as a stretched fuselage to increase capacity had to be accommodated without wholesale revisions in design or the need to startup entirely separate development programs.

A more efficient design and development process was only one benefit of the family of planes concept. There were manufacturing benefits as well. A common family of planes, produced on a common assembly line, ensured that learning was not lost as new models were added. Experience accumulated rapidly, as Thornton observed:

> We're good partly because we build lots of airplanes. And each new plane absorbs everything we have learned from earlier models.

One result of this approach was break-even points that were reached far earlier than they would have been without shared designs.

Other cornerstones of Boeing's strategy were expertise in global marketing, technological leadership, customer support, and production skills. Large centralized facilities were coupled with sophisticated manufacturing systems and tools for project management. The result, according to informed observers, was the industry's low cost producer. Or as one aerospace analyst summarized the company's reputation: "If someone hired me to rebuild the Great Pyramid, I'd ask ... Boeing to assemble it." [4]

CULTURE. Boeing managers believed that the company had a distinct corporate identity. Teamwork was especially valued, as was interfunctional cooperation. According to Dexter Haas, a manager in corporate planning:

> At Boeing, employees are expected to be both competent and capable of working as members of a team. We feel that technically brilliant but uncooperative individuals can do as much harm to a program as cooperative but mediocre team members.

Such concerns were especially acute on new plane programs, which were a prime vehicle for management development. Programs required close cooperation among managers for five to ten years, often under intense time pressures and 60–70 hour work weeks. To make these programs work, Thornton commented, "You don't necessarily select the best people; you select the best team."

Once selected, teams were granted considerable autonomy. But a disciplined decision-making process was expected, as was detailed planning. Both were viewed by managers as characteristic Boeing traits. According to Fred Cerf, director of systems and equipment:

> A part of Boeing's culture is absolute dedication to commitments—from individuals within the company and from suppliers. We expect people to honor their commitments and adhere to plans. We don't regard plans as exercises, but as forecasted events.

Meeting schedules was an especially high priority for managers. A variety of tools, several of them unique to Boeing, were used to develop realistic schedules and monitor them over time. Among them were a Master Phasing Plan, which mapped out the entire development cycle, including critical milestones, for each new plane program; parametric estimating techniques, which estimated costs and established relationships be-

[4] Ibid., p. 139.

tween critical sections of a schedule, such as the time at which engineering drawings were released and the start-up of production, by using historical data drawn from earlier plane programs; and a management visibility system, which was designed to surface problems before they became serious enough to cause delays. Regular communication was encouraged, even if it meant bringing bad news. According to John Schmick, director of planning:

> Early exposure of problems is not a sin at Boeing. We tend not to kill our managers for taking that approach. Here, it's much worse if you bury the problem.

The 767 Program

In 1969, Boeing assembled a New Airplane Program (NAP) study group. Its goal was not to develop a new plane, but to review the company's past experiences with each of its major programs—the 707, 727, 737, and 747—so that problems, such as those incurred by the 737 and 747 programs, would not be repeated. As Neil Standal, a member of the NAP group who later became the 767 program manager, observed:

> We knew that we were going to have another commercial airplane. But we didn't know what, or when, it was going to be. Our objective was to provide lessons for the future, to look at our history and decide what we had done right and what we had done wrong.

This process, called Project Homework, took three years and produced a long list of "lessons learned", as well as a reasonable idea of the costs of developing the next generation airplane.

Meanwhile, pressures were beginning to mount within Boeing to launch a new airplane program. Salespeople were especially insistent, as T.A. ("T") Wilson, Boeing's chairman, recalled:

> Our salespeople kept saying, "We need a new product." They didn't really care what it was, as long as it was new.

Because the company's last new plane, the 747, had been launched in 1966, there was also concern among the board of directors that Boeing's next generation of leaders was not being trained in the best way possible: by developing a new plane of their own.

In 1973, at Wilson's behest, Boeing initiated a new airplane study, naming it the 7X7 (X stood for development model). Key team members, including J.F. Sutter, the program's first leader, and Dean Thornton, who replaced Sutter after he was promoted to vice president of operations and development, were handpicked by Wilson. The team was given a broad charter: to define and, if approved, to develop, Boeing's next generation airplane.

Program Definition

The first stage of the process, called program definition, extended from May 1973 to December 1977 (see *Exhibit 1*). During this period, Boeing worked the puzzle of market, technology, and cost. Team members projected airline needs into the future to see if there were holes in the market not met by existing planes; considered alternative plane configurations; examined new technologies to see what might be available within the next few years; and estimated, in a preliminary fashion, likely development and production costs.

MARKET ASSESSMENT. Forecasting the airframe market for the 1980s and 1990s was a complex and challenging task. Market analysts began by talking directly with the major airlines to get their estimates of future needs. That information was then combined with econometric models to generate three forecasts—optimistic, conservative, and expected—for each market segment. Segments were defined by range of travel—short (less than 1,500 nautical miles), medium (1,500–3,000 nautical miles), and long (greater than 3,000 nautical miles)—and all forecasts were based on the following assumptions: continued regulation of the airline industry; continued airline preferences for routes that directly linked pairs of major cities; steadily rising fuel prices; and no new competition from other airframe manufacturers in the medium range market. Complete forecasts were run annually and readjusted quarterly.

Boeing's expected forecast for 1990 was a total market of $100 billion. The critical medium range segment—the expected target of the new airplane—was estimated at $19 billion. In that segment, Boeing expected to capture 100 percent of domestic sales. Continued production of the 727 would meet most replacement needs, and the 7X7 would be positioned for market growth.

EXHIBIT 1 Critical Program Decisions & Reviews

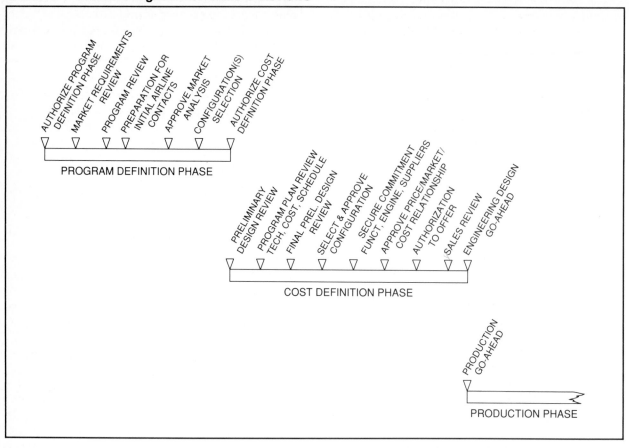

CONFIGURATION. While these forecasts were being developed, another group was working on design specifications. After a year or two of study, the basics were decided. Market research indicated that the new plane should carry approximately 200 passengers; have a one-stop, U.S. transcontinental range; and offer minimal fuel burn. The last requirement was regarded as especially important. With the rise in oil prices that followed the 1973 Arab oil embargo, fuel costs had become an ever larger portion of airlines' operating expenses. Moreover, airline preferences were changing, as Frank Shrontz, president and CEO, observed:

> In the old days, airlines were infatuated with technology for its own sake. Today the rationale for purchasing a new plane is cost savings and profitability.

Market needs were thus reasonably clear, at least within broad outlines. Designers, however, still faced a number of critical choices. All involved some aspect of the plane's basic shape.

The most vexing question was whether to design the 7X7 with two or three engines. A two engine version would be lighter and more fuel efficient; a three engine version would offer greater range. But exactly what were the tradeoffs? And how far was engine technology likely to advance in the next few years? Boeing, after all, did not build its own engines, but bought them from one of three manufacturers: General Electric, Pratt & Whitney, and Rolls Royce. Airlines paid separately for airframes and engines; however, they could only choose engines that were offered for the airplane. (This was necessary because Boeing guaranteed the performance of every plane it sold.) Early in the 7X7 program, managers chose to offer engines from both General Electric and Pratt & Whitney, despite the additional time and expense that Boeing would incur. This decision was a direct outgrowth of the company's experi-

28. The Boeing 767: From Concept to Production (A)

ences with the 747. Managers felt that continued competition among engine manufacturers was essential to moderate costs. Equally important, competition was expected to provide a steady stream of improvements in engine technology.

The certification decision proved to be far easier than the choice between a two and three engine plane. In fact, for most of the program definition phase, the 7X7 team worked simultaneously on two and three engine models. Eventually, fuel efficiency won out—as one manager put it, "in those days, an engineer would shoot his mother-in-law for a tenth of a percent improvement in fuel savings"—and the two engine version was selected.

Other key configuration decisions involved the wings and tail. Both decisions showed the family of planes concept in action, and the need for designs that were adaptable to future needs. The 7X7 was conceived originally as a medium-range aircraft; however, later additions to the 7X7 family were expected to target longer-range flights. Engineers therefore selected a wing size—3,000 square feet—that was larger than necessary for short and medium-range flights. It added weight to the basic design, with some loss of fuel efficiency. But the design was highly adaptable: it could be used, without modification, on longer-range versions and stretched models with greater carrying capacity.

Because they were so complex, configuration decisions required the close coordination of marketing, engineering, and production personnel. The airlines were also intimately involved. After a new configuration was developed, Boeing's marketing managers brought it to the airlines, who reviewed, among other things, its flight characteristics, range, cruising speed, interior, cockpit, systems, and operating costs. Their reactions were then fed back to designers, and the process was repeated. Haas observed:

> Designing airplanes to best meet the unique requirements of customers is a difficult process. Each airline would prefer that it was designed a bit differently—a little longer, a little shorter, a few more people, a few less. Therefore, the configuration changes constantly.

TECHNOLOGY. Configuration decisions could not be made without assessing the technology that was then available. What was desired by the market might not be possible or economical given the current state of knowledge.

Technology development was an on-going process at Boeing, and included such areas as structures, flight systems, aircraft systems (hydraulic and electrical), and aerodynamics. Each area had its own chief engineer, who was responsible for overseeing research, development, and application of the technology. The last requirement was regarded as especially critical, as David Norton, chief of technology, pointed out:

> There is nothing that brings me up quicker than thinking of how long we have to live with our decisions. At Boeing, applying a new technology is as important as developing it. We had better be right.

When a new plane was proposed, engineers first reviewed all existing technology projects to see if any were appropriate. They asked three questions of every project: (1) What is its ultimate value to the customer? (2) Is it an acceptable technological risk? and (3) Can it be incorporated within schedule and cost? Responsibility for answering these questions was divided among the chief engineers of each technology and a chief engineer in charge of the plane program. Line engineers therefore reported through a matrix, and were accountable to two bosses: the chief engineer of their technology and the chief engineer of the program. The former was more concerned with technical questions (e.g., What is the most efficient approach? Will we have a technologically superior product?), while the latter had more practical concerns (e.g., What will the airlines think of the new technology? How will its initial costs compare with the reduced maintenance costs expected over the plane's lifetime? What will be the program's cost and schedule?).

A number of the "new" technologies considered for the 7X7 had, in fact, already been employed elsewhere, primarily on space vehicles. They were therefore regarded as proven, with few technological risks. For example, digital avionics prototype systems in the cockpit, which replaced the traditional analog systems, had originally been developed for the SST program in 1969. Because it offered improved reliability, more accurate flight paths, lower maintenance costs, and the potential for a two-person cockpit, it was incorporated into the 7X7 with little debate.

Decisions involving unproven technologies were considerably more difficult. As Everette Webb, the 7X7's chief engineer, pointed out: "In such cases, deciding what is an acceptable risk is largely a judgment call." Composites provide an example of Boeing's approach.

Composites are complex materials, formed by combining two or more complementary substances. They appeal to airframe manufacturers because they combine great strength with light weight. In the 1960s and 1970s, Boeing engineers conducted a number of laboratory tests on large, composite panels; eventually, they found a promising material, a mixture of graphite and kevlar. Laboratory tests, however, were not regarded as representative of the "real world airline environment." To gather such data, Boeing worked with a small number of airlines and conducted limited, in-service tests. Boeing fabricated structural parts, such as wing control surfaces or spoiler panels, using composites; had them installed on a plane then in production; and monitored the material's performance as the plane underwent normal airline use. These tests soon indicated a problem with water absorption in environments of high heat and humidity, such as Brazil. A layer of fiberglass was added to the composite panels to solve the problem, and tests continued through the early 1970s. Yet, despite the tests, engineers decided against using composites for the 7X7's primary structure, and recommended instead that they be used only for secondary parts, where the safety risks were lower. Norton explained, "We push technology very hard, but we're conservative about implementation."

AUDIT TEAMS. Audit teams were also active during the program definition phase, starting in September 1976. Teams were staffed by experienced Boeing managers, and were assigned to review every significant element of the 7X7 program, including technology, finance, manufacturing, and management. Teams acted as "devil's advocates," and a typical audit took three months. According to Standal:

> In the past, we occasionally used outside consultants as auditors. But we found that, for the most part, we do a better job with our own people. We isolate them organizationally and give them a separate reporting line straight to T. Wilson.

Cost Definition

In September 1977, the 7X7 program was renamed the 767, and in January 1978, the cost definition phase began (see *Exhibit 1*). This shift was a major step: it indicated escalating program commitment and required the authorization of the president of the Boeing Commercial Airplane Company. Approximately $100 million had already been spent on the 7X7; most of it, however, was regarded as part of ongoing research and development. Now the critical decision was at hand: Would Boeing commit to building a new plane and, in the process, incur up-front costs of several billion dollars?

Only the board of directors could make such a decision. First, however, detailed cost estimates were necessary; they, in turn, had to be based on a single configuration. Cost definition forced engineers and marketing managers to stand up and say, "We want to offer *this* airplane." The 767's basic design, including the long-delayed choice between two and three engines, was finally frozen in place in May 1978 (see *Exhibit 2*).

PARAMETRIC ESTIMATES. Once the basic design was established, costs could be estimated using a parametric estimating technique. This method, adapted by Boeing, had been developed by the New Airplane Program study group from comparisons of the 707, 727, 737, and 747. It predicted the costs of a new plane from design characteristics, such as weight, speed, and length, and historical relationships, such as the number of parts per airplane, that were known well in advance of production.

The critical calculation involved assembly labor hours. Managers began with data from a benchmark (and profitable) program, the 727, and noted, for every major section of the plane, the number of labor hours per pound required to build the first unit. That number was then multiplied by the expected weight of the same section of the 767; this result, in turn, was multiplied by a factor that reflected Boeing's historical experience in improving the relationship between labor hours and weight as it moved to the next generation airplane. Totaling the results for all plane sections provided an estimate of the labor hours required to build the first 767. A learning curve was then

EXHIBIT 2 Airplane Configuration

BOEING 767

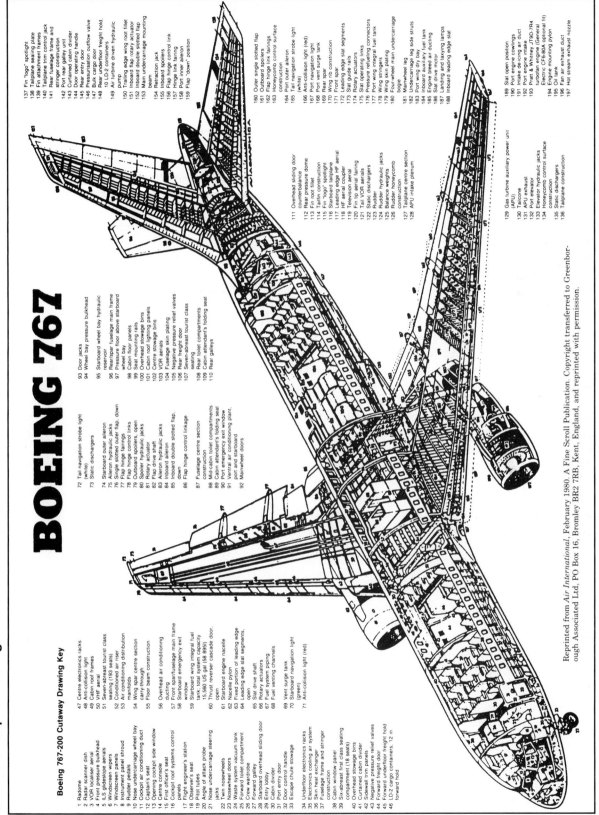

Boeing 767-200 Cutaway Drawing Key

1 Radome
2 Radar scanner dish
3 VOR localiser aerial
4 Front pressure bulkhead
5 ILS glideslope aerials
6 Windscreen wipers
7 Windscreen panels
8 Instrument panel shroud
9 Rudder pedals
10 Nose undercarriage wheel bay
11 Cockpit air conditioning duct
12 Captain's seat
13 Opening cockpit side window
14 Centre console
15 First officer's seat
16 Cockpit roof systems control panels
17 Flight engineer's station
18 Observer's seat
19 Pitot tubes
20 Angle of attack probe
21 Nose undercarriage steering jacks
22 Twin nosewheels
23 Nosewheel doors
24 Waste system vacuum tank
25 Forward toilet compartment
26 Crew wardrobe
27 Forward galley
28 Starboard overhead sliding door
29 Entry lobby
30 Cabin divider
31 Port entry door
32 Door control handle
33 Escape chute stowage
34 Underfloor electronics racks
35 Electronics cooling air system
36 Skin heat exchanger
37 Fuselage frame and stringer construction
38 Cabin window panel
39 Six-abreast first class seating compartment (18 seats)
40 Overhead stowage bins
41 Curtained cabin divider
42 Forward freight door
43 Sidewall trim panels
44 Negative pressure relief valves
45 Forward freight hold
46 LD2 cargo containers, 12 in forward hold

47 Centre electronics racks
48 Anti-collision light
49 Cabin roof frames
50 VHF aerial
51 Seven-abreast tourist class seating (193 seats)
52 Conditioned air riser
53 Air conditioning distribution manifolds
54 Wing spar centre section carry-through
55 Floor beam construction
56 Overhead air conditioning ducting
57 Front spar/fuselage main frame
58 Starboard emergency exit
59 Starboard wing integral fuel tank, total system capacity 15,560 US gal (58 895l)
60 Thrust reverser cascade door, open
61 Starboard engine nacelle
62 Nacelle pylon
63 Fixed portion of leading edge
64 Leading edge slat segments, open
65 Slat drive shaft
66 Rotary actuators
67 Fuel system piping
68 Fuel venting channels
69 Vent surge tank
70 Starboard navigation light (green)
71 Anti-collision light (red)

72 Tail navigation strobe light (white)
73 Static dischargers
74 Starboard outer aileron
75 Aileron hydraulic jacks
76 Single slotted outer flap, down
77 Flap hinge fairings
78 Flap hinge control links
79 Outboard spoilers, open
80 Spoiler hydraulic jacks
81 Rotary actuator
82 Flap drive shaft
83 Aileron hydraulic jacks
84 Inboard aileron
85 Inboard double slotted flap, down
86 Flap hinge control linkage
87 Fuselage centre section construction
88 Mid-cabin toilet compartments
89 Cabin attendant's folding seat
90 Port emergency exit window
91 Ventral air conditioning plant, port and starboard
92 Mainwheel doors

93 Door jacks
94 Wheel bay pressure bulkhead
95 Starboard wheel bay hydraulic reservoir
96 Rear/spar fuselage main frame
97 Pressure floor above starboard wheel bay
98 Cabin floor panels
99 Seat mounting rails
100 Overhead stowage bins
101 Cabin roof lighting panels
102 Centre stowage bins
103 VOR aerials
104 Fuselage skin plating
105 Negative pressure relief valves
106 Rear freight door
107 Seven-abreast tourist class seating
108 Rear toilet compartments
109 Cabin attendant's folding seat
110 Rear galleys

111 Overhead sliding door counterbalance
112 Rear pressure dome
113 Fin root fillet
114 Tailfin construction
115 Starboard tailplane
116 Starboard elevator
117 "Logo" spotlight
118 Leading edge HF aerial
119 HF aerial coupler
120 Television aerial
121 Fin tip aerial fairing
122 Tail VOR aerials
123 Rudder
124 Rudder hydraulic jacks
125 Balance weights
126 Rudder honeycomb construction
127 Tailplane centre section
128 APU intake plenum
129 Gas turbine auxiliary power unit (APU)
130 Tailcone
131 APU exhaust
132 Port elevator
133 Elevator hydraulic jacks
134 Honeycomb control surface construction
135 Static dischargers
136 Tailplane construction

137 Fin "logo" spotlight
138 Tailplane sealing plate
139 Fin attachment frames
140 Tailplane trim control jack
141 Rear fuselage frame and stringer construction
142 Port rear galley unit
143 Curtained cabin divider
144 Door operating handle
145 Rear entry door
146 Pressurisation outflow valve
147 Bulk cargo door
148 Rear underfloor freight hold.
149 10 LD-2 containers
150 Trailing edge wing root fillet
151 Inboard flap rotary actuator
152 Inboard double slotted flap
153 Main undercarriage mounting beam
154 Retraction jack
155 Inboard spoilers
156 Flap hinge control link
157 Hinge link fairing
158 Port inner aileron
159 Flap "down" position

160 Outer single slotted flap
161 Outboard spoilers
162 Flap hinge link fairings
163 Honeycomb control surface
164 Port outer aileron
165 Tail navigation strobe light (white)
166 Anti-collision light (red)
167 Port navigation light
168 Port vent surge tank
169 Rear spar
170 Wing rib construction
171 Front spar
172 Leading edge slat segments
173 Slat guide rails
174 Rotary actuators
175 Slat operating links
176 Pressure refuelling connectors
177 Port wing integral fuel tank
178 Wing stringers
179 Wing skin plating
180 Four-wheel main undercarriage bogie
181 Mainwheel leg
182 Undercarriage leg side struts
183 Port wing dry bay
184 Inboard auxiliary fuel tank
185 Engine bleed air ducting
186 Slat drive motor
187 Landing and taxiying lamps
188 Inboard leading edge slat

189 Slat open position
190 Port engine cowlings
191 Intake de-icing air duct
192 Port engine intake
193 Pratt & Whitney JT9D-7R4 turbofan engine (General Electric CF6-80A optional fit)
194 Engine mounting pylon
195 Oil tank
196 Fan air exhaust duct
197 Hot stream exhaust nozzle

Reprinted from *Air International*, February 1980. A Fine Scroll Publication. Copyright transferred to Greenborough Associated Ltd, PO Box 16, Bromley BR2 7RB, Kent, England, and reprinted with permission.

applied to estimate the number of labor hours required to build subsequent planes.

Engineers believed that the historical relationships underlying these calculations remained valid for long periods. According to Dennis Wilson, manager of scheduling for the 767:

> Unless we drastically change the way we do business, we will be able to use the same parametrics to compare programs. After all, an airplane is an airplane.

Parametric estimates were, however, carefully fine-tuned to account for differences in plane programs. Adjustments could go in either direction. Improved equipment and management control systems, an enforced reduction in engineering change orders, and heavy use of Computer Aided Design and Computer Aided Manufacturing (CAD/CAM) suggested that the 767 would require fewer hours than predicted by parametrics derived from the 727; increased product complexity and a larger variety of customers suggested that more hours would be required. These factors were combined to form a final, adjusted estimate of total assembly hours.

A similar process was used to develop the Master Phasing Plan, which established the program schedule and identified major milestones (see *Exhibit 3*). The critical task was linking the schedules of interdependent groups, such as engineering and production, to avoid schedule compression or delays. Parametrics were used for that purpose. For example, comparisons of the 727 and 747 programs suggested that, if problems were to be avoided, fabrication should not begin until 25 percent of structural engineering drawings were complete, and that major assembly should not begin until 90 percent of engineering drawings were complete. Such values became the baseline for the 767's Master Phasing Plan. The initial plan was completed in October 1977, and was revised repeatedly as more up-to-date information became available.

THE GO/NO-GO DECISION. In February 1978, Boeing's board of directors was asked to commit to the 767. Prior to that time, Wilson and the 767 team had briefed them, reviewing all aspects of the program. The board agreed to authorize the new plane, but only if two conditions were met: commitments to purchase were received from one foreign and two domestic airlines, and pre-production orders totaled at least 100 planes.

On July 14, 1978, United Airlines placed a $1 billion order for 30 767s, making it Boeing's first customer. Being the first customer had certain risks—the offer to sell was conditional, and could be cancelled at a later date—but offered advantages as well. Prices were lower, and the first buyer had an opportunity to help shape the plane's final configuration. By November 1978, American and Delta Airlines had also placed orders, bringing the total to 80 planes, with an additional 79 on option. The board then committed Boeing to full production of the 767. The cost definition phase had ended in July 1978; meanwhile, teams began to flesh out the details of supplier and production management.

Supplier Management

A complete 767 consisted of 3.1 million parts, which were supplied by 1,300 vendors. Of these, the most important were the two program participants and four major subcontractors, who built such critical parts as body structures, tail sections, and landing gear. Program participants were, in effect, risk-sharing partners who bore a portion of the costs of design, development, and tooling; major subcontractors were similar, but took on a smaller share of the work. Both were necessary because new airplane programs had become too big for Boeing, or any other single company, to handle alone. On the 767, Aeritalia, the Italian aircraft manufacturer, and the Japan Aircraft Development Company (JADC), a consortium made up of Mitsubishi, Kawasaki, and Fuji Industries, were the two program participants. Both were contracted with in September 1978.

In the late 1960s and 1970s, Aeritalia had worked with Boeing on several proposed airplane designs, including one plane with short field takeoff and landing capacity. Based on that experience, Aeritalia asked to participate in future work with Boeing. Cerf recalled:

> Boeing honored Aeritalia's request. We decided tht they would produce the 767's wing control surfaces and tail, parts which were considered to be significant but which were less critical than body panels to the final assembly line. As it turned out, materials technology advanced in the meantime, and most of the control surface parts were changed from aluminum struc-

EXHIBIT 3 Program Schedule and Major Milestones

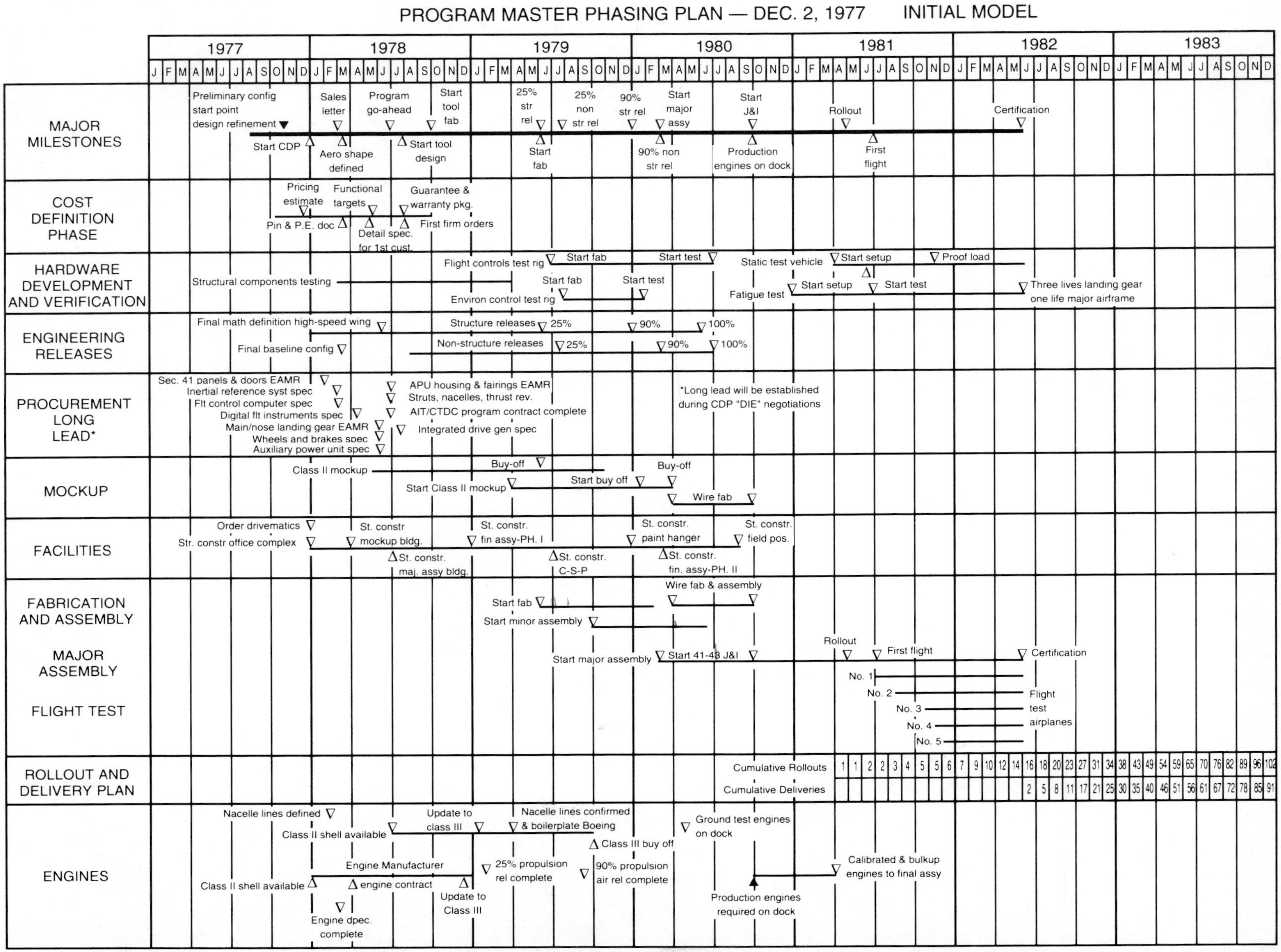

PROGRAM MASTER PHASING PLAN — DEC. 2, 1977   INITIAL MODEL

Row categories (left side):

- MAJOR MILESTONES
- COST DEFINITION PHASE
- HARDWARE DEVELOPMENT AND VERIFICATION
- ENGINEERING RELEASES
- PROCUREMENT LONG LEAD*
- MOCKUP
- FACILITIES
- FABRICATION AND ASSEMBLY
- MAJOR ASSEMBLY
- FLIGHT TEST
- ROLLOUT AND DELIVERY PLAN
- ENGINES

Years: 1977, 1978, 1979, 1980, 1981, 1982, 1983

MAJOR MILESTONES: Preliminary config start point design refinement ▼; Sales letter; Program go-ahead △; Start tool fab; Rollout ▽; Certification ▽

COST DEFINITION PHASE: Start CDP △; Aero shape defined △; Start tool design △; Pricing △; Functional targets △; Guarantee & warranty pkg. ▽; First firm orders △; Pin & P.E. doc △; Detail spec. for 1st cust. △

HARDWARE DEVELOPMENT AND VERIFICATION: Structural components testing; Flight controls test rig ▽; Start fab ▽; Start test ▽; Environ control test rig ▽; Static test vehicle ▽; Fatigue test ▽; Start test ▽; Proof load ▽; Three lives landing gear one life major airframe ▼

ENGINEERING RELEASES: Final math definition high-speed wing ▽; Final baseline config ▽; Structure releases ▽ 25% ▽ 90% ▽ 100%; Non-structure releases ▽ 25% ▽ 90% ▽ 100%; 25% str rel; 25% non str rel; 90% str rel; 90% non str rel

PROCUREMENT LONG LEAD*: Sec. 41 panels & doors EAMR ▽; Inertial reference syst spec ▽; Flt control computer spec ▽; Digital flt instruments spec ▽; Main/nose landing gear EAMR ▽; Wheels and brakes spec ▽; Auxiliary power unit spec ▽; APU housing & fairings EAMR ▽; Struts, nacelles, thrust rev. ▽; AIT/CTDC program contract complete ▽; Integrated drive gen spec ▽; *Long lead will be established during CDP "DIE" negotiations

MOCKUP: Class II mockup ▽; Start Class II mockup ▽; Buy-off ▽; Start buy off ▽; Buy-off ▽

FACILITIES: Str constr office complex ▽; Order drivematics ▽; St. constr ▽; St. constr maj. assy bldg. ▽; St. constr fin assy-PH. I ▽; St. constr mockup bldg. ▽; St. constr C-S-P △; St. constr paint hanger ▽; St. constr field pos. ▽; fin. assy-PH. II

FABRICATION AND ASSEMBLY: Start fab ▽; Start minor assembly ▽; Wire fab & assembly ▽; Wire fab ▽

MAJOR ASSEMBLY: Start minor assembly ▽; Start major assembly ▽; Start 41-43 J&I ▽; Rollout ▽

FLIGHT TEST: Rollout ▽; First flight ▽; Certification ▽; No. 1, No. 2, No. 3, No. 4, No. 5; Flight test airplanes

ROLLOUT AND DELIVERY PLAN: Cumulative Rollouts; Cumulative Deliveries

ENGINES: Nacelle lines defined ▽; Class II shell available ▽; Class II shell available △; Engine dpec. complete △; Engine Manufacturer △; engine contract △; Update to Class III △; Nacelle lines defined ▽; 25% propulsion rel complete ▽; Update to class III ▽; Nacelle lines confirmed & boilerplate Boeing ▽; Class III buy off ▽; 90% propulsion air rel complete ▽; Ground test engines on dock ▽; Calibrated & bulkup engines to final assy ▽; Production engines required on dock ▼

28. The Boeing 767: From Concept to Production (A)

ture to graphite composites. That helped to make them one of the more complex jobs on the airplane.

JADC, on the other hand, was responsible for the several large body sections. The Japanese participants had been interested in working with Boeing for years and had done progressively more important work on other aircraft. Now, their workmanship was considered exacting enough to meet Boeing standards for the production of major sections of structure.

TECHNOLOGY TRANSFER. Boeing worked closely with all of its subcontractors, from initial planning to final delivery. Cerf observed:

> Generally, at Boeing we do not contract with suppliers and then walk away. We feel responsible for them and *have* to make it work. This was especially true of the 767 program participants. Because the content of their work was so significant, a failure would have precluded our ability to salvage an industrial operation of this size.

To begin, the Italian and Japanese participants were asked to work together with Boeing engineers. Engineering management helped to select the Italian and Japanese engineers who would participate in the 767 program, and rated them according to their skill levels. The Italian and Japanese engineers then worked alongside Boeing engineers in Seattle. At the 25 percent structures release point (a critical milestone, at which point stress analyses had been completed), they returned to their home companies, accompanied by their Boeing engineering counterparts, who were then integrated into the Italian and Japanese engineering organizations. At the same time, in mid-1978, Boeing established residence teams in Italy and Japan, consisting of some of Boeing's best operations people. The operations teams evaluated and helped to establish participants' facilities, training, and manufacturing processes, and also certified their quality assurance processes. If problems arose, rapid communication with Seattle was often necessary; this was assured by a private telephone network connecting Boeing to each participant.

AN EXAMPLE OF SUPPLIER MANAGEMENT: THE JAPANESE TRANSPORTATION PLAN. Initially, JADC had argued that transporting body sections from its factories in Japan to Boeing's assembly plant near Seattle would present few problems. Boeing, to be absolutely certain, had insisted that scale models of all sections be built and carried along the proposed route. The parts proved to be too large for Japan's narrow, rural roads; as a result, an old steel factory, located closer to shipping facilities, was converted by one Japanese company to assemble major sections. Another company constructed a final assembly plant located directly on the water. As insurance, Boeing also requested that the body sections be air transportable, and their designs were sized accordingly.

Boeing then put one of its transportation specialists to work with his Japanese counterparts to develop a transportation plan. This effort took several months, as Cerf recalled:

> We went through a major exercise to prove that all of the Japanese companies could support our assembly schedule in Seattle. We brought their representatives to see the complete plan, which covered the walls of a huge meeting room, and worked with them carefully to plan what would be on their shipping docks, what would be on the high seas, and what would be in our plants at any one time.
>
> The level of detail was quite astounding. We kept asking them representative questions, such as "Do you have the right permits and who will get them? What does the transportation container look like and has it been stressed properly for transport by sea?" Surprisingly, the Japanese didn't object to this process at all. They weren't just cooperative; they were used to working at this level of detail and wanted to learn all we knew.
>
> All of this was a good thing because there was no backup once the decision was made to build the major body sections in Japan. We were committed because our plants at Boeing were working at capacity.

Production Management

Part fabrication began in July 1979, minor (subsection) assembly in April 1980, and major assembly in July 1980. Such long lead times were necessary to meet the planned rollout of the first 767 in August 1981. Flight tests began immediately after rollout, and FAA certification was expected in July 1982.

All 767s were assembled in Everett, Washington, in the same facility used for 747s. Half of the building was devoted to assembly of major subsections; the other half to final assembly. In the final stages of assembly, a line flow process was used, with seven major work stations (see *Exhibit 4* for a rough sequence of manufacturing operations). Every four days, partially completed planes were moved, using large overhead cranes, from one work station to the next. At each work station, teams of skilled employees positioned a single plane in massive tools and fixtures, and then riveted, wired, and connected parts and pieces.

During the assembly stage, mangers faced two critical tasks: maintaining schedule, and ensuring that learning curve goals were met. Both were complicated by a key difference between airframe manufacturing and other industries: the difficulty of managing a large number of engineering change orders. Haas observed:

An airplane is not something you design, turn over to manufacturing, and then forget. The configuration is constantly changing. So you commit to a schedule, and then incorporate changes and improvements as they come.

This task was especially critical because cost estimates assumed that assembly labor hours would decline predictably over time, following a preset learning curve. Managers therefore had to ensure that learning goals were met at the same time that they were accommodating unanticipated changes.

SCHEDULING AND CHANGE CONTROL. Requests for changes came from internal and external sources. Some, such as the color of carpeting or seating arrangements, were negotiated by airline

EXHIBIT 4 767-200 Manufacturing Sequence

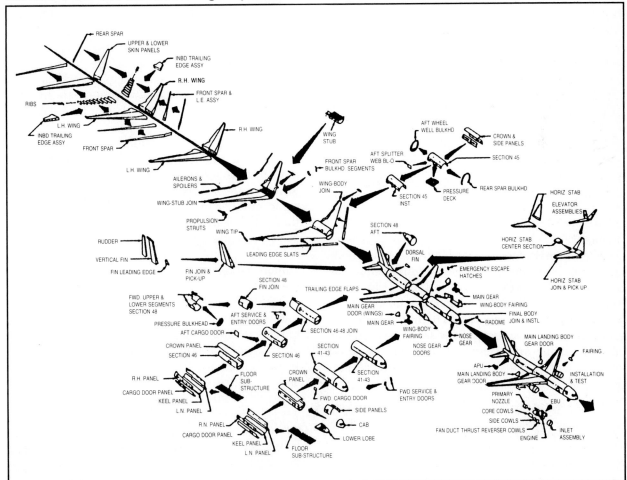

customers; others, such as parts or wiring changes, were proposed by engineers. In total, the two sources generated 12,000 changes on the first 767.

Managers tracked these changes carefully. Even before the plane's basic design was frozen, all major changes had to be filed using the same formal procedure. This was done to ensure that specifications remained accurate. Once assembly began, a Production Change Board, chaired by the operations department, reviewed all engineering change requests and assessed their likely impact on schedule and cost. If the changes were approved, an implementation plan was then developed. Three general approaches were used: incorporating changes into the normal flow of production; installing old parts as originally planned and then retrofitting new parts off-line, outside the normal flow of production; and expediting changes by assigning additional workers, a process known as "blue streak."

In all cases, a primary concern was maintaining schedule. Boeing faced substantial penalties if a plane was delivered even one day late, because airlines planned their schedules around promised delivery dates and expected a new plane to be flying immediately. According to Haas:

> For a long time, we have stressed the importance of schedule performance. The airplane *will* move [from one work station to the next] on the day that it is supposed to move. Management will get in a lot more trouble for not moving an airplane, assembly, or part on schedule than for a budget overrun. Over the years, budgets have gained significantly in importance, but not at the expense of schedules.

To ensure that schedules were maintained, Boeing employed a management visibility system. Schedules were prominently posted, and marathon status meetings, which were attended by representatives of all affected departments, were held weekly to review slippages and highlight potential problems. Every manager discussed what he or she was doing and what he or she was owed by others. The emphasis was on early notification, as Dennis Wilson observed:

> If I'm at a status meeting and I find that someone has missed a critical milestone, the first question I ask is, "Why didn't you tell me about the problem last week?", not, "Why did you miss the milestone?"

In June 1981, as assembly of the first 767 moved into its final stages, a First Flight Committee was established. The committee reported directly to Dean Thornton and met daily during the six weeks before the plane's first test flight. At that point, the test pilot had final say in setting priorities and selecting the tasks to be completed.

LEARNING CURVES. Learning curves were also used to manage the assembly process. Based on historical experience, Boeing had developed learning curves for every major work center. Machining, assembly, and sheet metal fabrication had curves of their own, each with a different slope. However, curves were used in the same way at all centers.

To begin, an optimum crew size was defined for the operation, based on available work space, engineering guidelines, and tooling to be employed. For example, the optimum crew size for forward body section assembly was eight people. A parametric estimate was then made of the number of labor hours needed to assemble that section of the very first 767. The total (in this case, 6,000 hours) was then divided by the number of labor hours available each day (in this case, 128 hours, equal to eight people working eight hours per shift, two shifts per day) to give the number of days to complete the very first assembly (47 days).

At this point, a learning curve was invoked. The next assembly would be scheduled not for 47 days but for a lesser number, to reflect the historical rate of learning on that operation. The same number of people would be employed, but they would work faster and more efficiently. (When precise calculations were impossible, Boeing varied staffing levels within minimum and maximum values, rather than sticking to a single, optimum crew size.)

Learning curves were also applied to change management. Work centers were initially staffed to reflect a large number of changes. For example, of the eight people assigned to forward body section assembly, three might initially be responsible for incorporating changes. But because the number of changes fell sharply as more planes were produced—the first 767 had 12,000 changes, while the seventieth 767 had only 500—fewer people would be needed for the activity as time passed, and staffing would be reduced over time.

Such improvements did not come automatically. Three tools were used to ensure that targets were met: specific work station goals; stand-up meetings with first-line supervisors; and the management visibility system discussed earlier. Hourly goals were set for every employee and displayed prominently on bar charts by their work stations. The game, as one manager put it, then became "worker versus bar chart." Stand-up meetings were held only if targets were not met. First-line supervisors had to stand up at these meetings and identify what was impeding their ability to meet learning curve goals. Managers were then responsible for solving the problems.

Three-Crew to Two-Crew Conversion

In the late 1970s, airframe manufacturers, led by Boeing, proposed a switch from three- to two-person cockpits. Advanced technology, they argued, had made a three-person crew unnecessary. The Air Line Pilots Association (ALPA) objected strongly to these arguments, claiming that safety levels were certain to fall if the number of crew members was reduced. To resolve the debate, a presidential task force was convened; both parties agreed to accept its findings. In July 1981, the task force concluced that two-person cockpits presented no unusual safety problems, and that manufacturers could offer them on all planes.

Airlines, including those that had already ordered 767s, soon expressed an interest in having their planes delivered with two-person cockpits. Boeing had anticipated such a response and, years earlier, had conducted preliminary studies to determine how best to convert the 767 from its original, three-person cockpit design to a two-person model (see *Exhibit 5* for a comparison of the two cockpits). Further studies were immediately begun; their goal was to identify the number of planes then in process that would require rework or modification to become two-crew models, and the likely impact of these changes on cost and schedule. Engineers concluded that the thirty-first 767 was still far enough from completion that it, and all subsequent planes, could be built with two-person cockpits without modification. Thirty planes, however, were in relatively advanced stages of production. Some were nearly ready to be rolled out and flown; others had complete cockpits but

were not yet tested; others had bare cockpits without any electronics installed. But since all thirty were being built according to the plane's original, three-person cockpit design, all would require some modification.

Customers were notified of the additional cost and delivery delay they could expect on these thirty planes. The impact was not large: a small percentage increase in costs and an average delay of one month from promised delivery dates. All but one airline chose to have their planes built with two-person cockpits.

In August 1981 a special task force, reporting directly to Thornton, was formed to determine the best way of modifying these planes. It soon narrowed the choice to two alternatives: (1) building the thirty airplanes as they had originally been designed, with three-person cockpits, and then converting them to two-person cockpits after they had left the production floor (but before delivery to customers), and (2) modifying the production plans for the thirty airplanes so that conversion would take place during production and no parts would be installed only to be removed later (which meant leaving some cockpits temporarily unfinished while drawings and parts for two-person cockpits were being developed).

COMPLETION OF PRODUCTION AND SUBSEQUENT MODIFICATION. In this approach, production would continue as planned, without delay. Neither learning curves nor schedules would be disrupted by attempts to modify airplanes during the assembly process. The modification program would be managed as a separate, tightly-controlled activity, apart from the normal flow of production, and special teams of "modification experts," skilled at parts removal, modification, and repair, would be assigned to it. Approximately one million additional labor hours were thought to be required if this method was used.

The primary advantage of this approach was that flaps, ailerons, landing gear, hydraulics, and other airplane systems would be functionally tested during the final assembly process, as originally planned. Problems would be identified and corrected on the spot, rather than hidden or disguised by subsequent assembly activities. And because the airplane that rolled out of production would be fully tested and functional, any problems iden-

FLIGHT DECK ARRANGEMENTS

2 CREW MEMBERS

CLOSET/ SUITCASES

2ND OBSERVER (OPTION)

SUITCASES

FIRST OFFICER

FLT KIT

FLT KIT

CAPTAIN

1ST OBSERVER (BASIC)

3 CREW MEMBERS

FLIGHT ENGINEER

CLOSET/ SUITCASES

2ND OBS (OPTION)

FIRST OFFICER

FLT KIT

FLT KIT

CAPTAIN

1ST OBSERVER (BASIC)

SUITCASES

tified after installation of the two-person cockpit could be isolated, with some assurance, to the cockpit area.

The risk of this approach was the potential "loss of configuration" (i.e., when the plane was actually built, the integrity of the overall design might be compromised). Parts required for three-person cockpits would be installed firmly in place, only to be removed and replaced later by modification experts. (Because these parts had been ordered months before and were already on-hand and paid for, this option did not impose greater scrap costs than the other option.) If the modification was not done carefully, many of the plane's operating systems might be disrupted. Boeing experts, however, believed that the management controls used for modification would prevent this from occurring. To minimize the risk, additional functional testing would be required after modification.

Space was also a problem. There was not enough room within the factory to modify all thirty planes. Work would therefore have to be done outside, but even then space was limited. A special parking plan would have to be developed, and the planes being modified would have to be parked extremely close together. The required arrangement would violate fire regulations, so special fire control plans and waivers would be necessary.

Several managers had reservations about this approach, for they objected to its underlying philosophy. The end result would be an airplane that had been modified, after the fact, to accommodate a two-person cockpit. As Standal put it: "It goes against our grain and better judgment to roll out an aircraft and then tear the guts out."

MODIFICATION DURING PRODUCTION. In this approach, all modification of the thirty planes would be done during production, rather than after the fact. No parts would be installed only to be removed later. Instead, all panels, instruments, and switches that were associated with three-person cockpits would be identified and their installation halted. Meanwhile, production would continue on other sections of the plane. Once plans and parts were available for two-person cockpits, they would be incorporated within the flow of production.

This was the traditional method of making engineering and design changes. It was used routinely for the thousands of configuration changes on every new airplane. The primary advantage of this approach was that all parts were installed only once. Because there would be no installation and subsequent removal, the configuration was more likely to remain secure. Moreover, because modification would occur during production, all activities would be controlled by normal management procedures, rather than by a separate program.

The primary disadvantage of this approach was that the original production plan would be disrupted. Separate plans would have to be developed for the first thirty airplanes, which required modification, and all subsequent planes. Learning curves would be disrupted as well, because a large number of additional workers would have to be added temporarily, at selected work stations, to complete the modification of the first thirty planes. If this method was used, modification was expected to require approximately two million additional labor hours.

Because all cockpit work would be deferred until engineering drawings and parts were available for two-crew models, test procedures would also have to change. Traditionally, functional testing was done sequentially, with each system (flaps, ailerons, etc.) tested as it became operational. That approach would be impossible here because all cockpit work would be deferred until complete plans and drawings were available. Functional testing would therefore have to be done after the two-person cockpit was fully installed. Problems might not be detected and corrected immediately and might well be hidden by systems that were installed later, making problem diagnosis much more difficult.

*   *   *   *

Thornton knew that it was time to make a choice between the two approaches so that production could continue. The risks, however, were great; as his staff kept telling him, the decision was a potential "show-stopper." He wondered: "Should I authorize after-the-fact conversion of planes or modification during production? And for what reasons?"

29. Lehrer McGovern Bovis, Inc.

In November 1986, Peter Lehrer and Gene Mc-Govern, co-founders of Lehrer McGovern Bovis, Inc. (LMB), one of the fastest growing firms in the construction industry, were on their way to the monthly senior management meeting. Two issues were on the agenda:

1. The impact of a changing client mix on the firm's resources.
2. The equitable allocation of bonuses among profit centers.

LMB provided construction management services to investment builders and corporate clients. Hired for their construction expertise, they offered clients a range of project management services, including construction supervision. Their key management challenge was to continue to grow while maintaining quality. Peter Lehrer explained:

> When we started the business, we didn't have a grand design. We wanted challenging projects and the ability to enjoy what we do. We didn't set out to be the largest construction management firm in the industry, but the best. The critical issue for us now is, how big do we become?

The Construction Industry

For many years, the construction industry has been the largest industry and imployer in the United States. In 1985, total new construction plans were valued at $206.6 billion, nearly 10% of the Gross National Product. More than four million construction workers and three million people in related construction services depended on the core industry for their livelihood.

Despite its importance in the U.S. economy, the industry has been slow to invest in innovative methods, materials, and processes. In 1985, industry R&D expenditures averaged just 0.01% of sales, a figure comparable to the research dollars spent on razor blades. Only 3% of the firms in the industry owned computer-aided design systems, and there was no market demand for industrial robots. By contrast, the Japanese construction industry spent 3% of sales on R&D and was experimenting with robots for quality improvements.

There were three significant barriers to innovation in the U.S. construction industry: the industry's structure, the litigious nature of the business, and the traditional separation of design from construction. The fragmented structure of the industry (over 80,000 domestic contractors) and the absence of significant foreign competition were responsible, in part, for the continued use of traditional construction methods. Low margins and fierce domestic competition precluded the kind of investment needed to develop new methods or materials. Liability concerns further exacerbated an industry preference for proven construction methods, increasing the risk of working with new materials or processes. The traditional separation of contractors, who built the buildings, from architects, who designed them, also added to construction inefficiencies. Constructability (how easily a building could be assembled) was virtually ignored until designs were complete, making changes both costly and time-consuming.

Rising construction costs, schedule delays, and quality problems led clients to demand im-

This case was prepared by Janet Simpson under the direction of David A. Garvin.

provements in traditional building practices. A new service called construction management had emerged to meet these needs, promising to manage construction costs, not just monitor them.

Construction Methods

Clients with construction needs typically chose one of three building methods for construction projects: (1) the *traditional method of construction,* in which the client hired an architect to develop the building design and a general contractor to manage the physical construction; (2) the *design-build method of construction,* in which one firm took total responsibility for both design and construction; and (3) the *phased, or "fast-track" method of construction,* in which the client hired an architect and a construction manager concurrently so that the building was constructed as it was being designed. In most cases, the choice of building methods was determined by the complexity of the project, the client's resources and past experiences, and the client's corporate policies regarding construction contracts.

General Contracting and the Traditional Method of Construction

Historically, general contractors and the traditional method of construction were used for almost all large buildings. (*Exhibit 1.*) General contractors were firms hired to plan and supervise the physical construction of a building. They typically provided 20% of the field staff, including superintendents and general foremen, from their permanent organization and hired subcontractors for the rest of the work. General contracting was used with the traditional method of construction, a sequential process with three distinct phases: the design phase, the bid phase, and the construction phase. Facilities were designed by architects and their engineers under negotiated contracts. Construction was performed by general contractors selected through competitively bid, fixed-priced contracts.

THE DESIGN PHASE. A client retained the services of an architect and engineering firm to develop the plans and specifications for the building. The architect was responsible for preparing a design which met the client's objectives in such areas as

aesthetics, cost and functionality. Engineers were responsible for determining the specifications of the building's systems. Here, specialization was the rule. An electrical engineer selected the building's electrical systems, a civil engineer selected the sewage and water systems, and so forth. Between them, the architect and engineers determined which equipment, methods, and materials were most suitable for the project.

THE BID PHASE. After drawings and specifications were completed, the entire package was given to several general contractors for competitive bidding. Each general contractor solicited bids from subcontractors who would construct the building's components. The general contractors then collected these bids and submitted their own, all-inclusive bids to the client. The contract was awarded to the general contractor submitting the lowest bid.

THE CONSTRUCTION PHASE. Construction started after the client and general contractor signed a fixed-price contract. Costs and schedule were monitored by the general contractor who provided on-site supervision of construction. The general contractor assumed the financial risks of the project, being liable for contracts negotiated with the subcontractors. Labor problems, material handling problems, and the complete logistics of the job were managed by the general contractor.

In the traditional approach, the activities of the architect, engineers and general contractor were coordinated by either the architect or a project manager hired by the client for that purpose. Building construction was coordinated by the general contractor whose experience with construction methods and materials enabled him to sequence predictably the tasks of subcontractors. In fact, the skillful management of construction logistics was essential to the on-time completion of projects.

Despite its wide use, some clients were unhappy with this arrangement. Lehrer explained:

> On the surface, general contracting seems straightforward. Construction does not start until general contractors promise to deliver everything shown on the plans and specifications for a fixed price. In practice, however, companies frequently found that the general contracting process fell apart. Once the contract was signed, the general contractors' incentives were to maximize profits

EXHIBIT 1 Traditional Versus Phased Construction

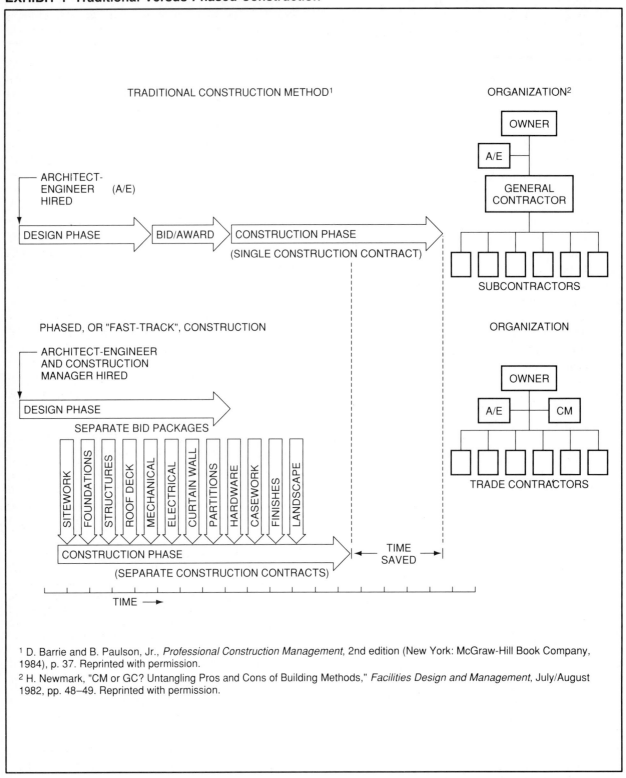

TRADITIONAL CONSTRUCTION METHOD[1]

ORGANIZATION[2]

PHASED, OR "FAST-TRACK", CONSTRUCTION

ORGANIZATION

[1] D. Barrie and B. Paulson, Jr., *Professional Construction Management*, 2nd edition (New York: McGraw-Hill Book Company, 1984), p. 37. Reprinted with permission.

[2] H. Newmark, "CM or GC? Untangling Pros and Cons of Building Methods," *Facilities Design and Management*, July/August 1982, pp. 48–49. Reprinted with permission.

and minimize costs. They would do nothing to enhance the project that cost money; quality was often compromised to keep to schedule and budget. Clients, who usually had limited construction expertise, wound up just paying the bills.

The Design-Build Method of Construction

An alternate to the traditional method of construction had emerged when large general contractors began offering design services. The design-build method of construction offered clients an easier way to manage construction projects because it kept total responsibility for both design and construction in one firm. This method became the preferred approach for identical or related repeat projects because it saved time over the traditional method and often had a lower first cost. In 1985, design-build contracts totaled $26.1 billion; 25 of the top 40 general contractors reported that they acted as design-build agents.

The design-build method had some disadvantages, particularly for an inexperienced client. The normal checks and balances between architect and general contractor were missing. In many cases, the firm used standard rather than customized designs to improve profit margins. And cost-cutting methods, such as value engineering, were often ignored.

Construction Management and the Phased Construction Method

The third construction method, phased or "fast-track" construction, arose because of a new player in the industry, the contruction manager. Fast-track was a scheduling process that overlapped the traditionally sequential stages of design and construction. Its basic premise was that there was no reason to wait until all details of a building had been specified before starting construction. By overlapping the design and construction phases, the time period between concept and tenant occupancy was dramatically reduced.

Construction management emerged in response to clients' need for an agent with construction expertise to represent them in all phases of project execution. The construction manager pro-

vided a broad range of project management services, including procurement and logistics planning and proven cost-cutting methods, such as value engineering. The construction manager typically was hired early in the design phase to assure constructability and to identify opportunities for cost reduction or schedule improvement. As the design progressed, the construction manager procured materials, negotiated the client's contracts with subcontractors, and managed construction. From design through construction, the construction manager's objective was to keep the project on time and within budget.

THE DESIGN PHASE. During the design phase, the construction manager, client and architect formed a team to develop the building design. The construction manager evaluated the proposed design's cost and time implications, rather than its aesthetics. This information was given to the architect early in the design process, allowing the architect to maintain design integrity at least cost. Occasionally, the construction manager's input resulted in major design changes. Mike Holloway, an assistant vice president at LMB, described one of the early projects he had managed:

> We were hired as the construction manager for a $21 million ABC-TV studio project on New York's West End Avenue. The client was under pressure to complete the project in nine months.
> Because of zoning restrictions on the overall building height, the initial design decision was to drop the building 20 feet into the ground. As part of our evaluation, we took site borings and discovered that the site was solid rock dotted with concrete caves. To complicate matters, the site had once been a railyard and tracks ran along the sides of the lot and underground. We determined the location of the rock and caves; we also located the old drawings of the railyard in Penn Central's files. From this information, we were able to quantify the cost of lowering the building 20 feet.
> I brought the numbers to a meeting with the architect and engineers. Seeing how prohibitive the excavation costs would be, the architect came up with a pyramid design which met the zoning requirements but only required excavating 10 feet of rock.

Holloway explained how the process would have differed if a general contractor had been used on the project:

A general contractor would likely have gone through the same exercise once he received the bid documents from the architect. The difference would have been that at that point, perhaps four months into the project, the design would already have been fixed. The decision for the client would then have been either to pay the extra million dollars to do the excavation or go back to the drawing board and revise the design. In all likelihood the client would have missed the nine-month deadline.

THE BID PHASE. Using the fast-track method, the architect prepared the design documents in stages, so that the construction manager could solicit bids from subcontractors as quickly as possible. The construction manager was responsible for recommending subcontractors and negotiating final contracts for the client.

The construction manager's responsibilities also included the procurement of materials for construction. By knowing early in the design process what materials were required, the construction manager could take advantage of market conditions to negotiate favorable prices. Early purchasing of items with long lead times, such as high-speed elevators which could take as long as 10 months to deliver, reduced delays during construction. And each day saved meant lower costs for the client.

THE CONSTRUCTION PHASE. Construction managers enabled a new way of building: "fast-track," or phased construction. With fast-track construction, the building was designed in stages, bid in stages, and constructed in stages. Site clearing and grading, foundations and structure were bid and under construction within a few months after the start of the basic design. Mechanical, electrical and plumbing designs and contracts followed quickly, with details of architectural finishes decided, designed and bid while the core of the building was under construction.

One Seaport Plaza, a 34-story office tower, was a typical fast-track project managed by LMB. To speed construction, the firm had shifted as much work as possible away from the site. Slabs of Canadian granite were shipped from Quebec to Totowa, New Jersey, and assembled into panels of four to five pieces each. By working at the site with panels rather than individual slabs, the construction crew erected the building facade in 6 rather than 10 months. Twelve months after

the first piece of steel went up, the tenants moved in. "In the past," said McGovern, "that project would have taken at least 18 months, maybe 2 years."[1]

Critics argued that fast-track construction was risky. Because construction was completed as the design evolved, decisions and commitments were made based on incomplete drawings. Specifications for early items were loose, and substitutions frequent. The architect also had less design flexibility as the building progressed. Despite these concerns, rising construction costs increased the popularity of construction management among clients. As a result, many general contractors and design firms began offering construction management services.

Fees

Fee structures for construction projects fell along a continuum. At one extreme was the general contractor, who guaranteed a fixed-price contract and assumed the financial risks associated with subcontractor payments. At the other extreme was the construction manager, who provided project management services for a fixed *fee*. Along the continuum were combinations of fees and players; some construction managers assumed full liability exposure for projects and some general contractors offered construction management services on a fee-only basis. The kind of fee structure used for a construction project depended on the policies of the contractor or construction manager, the client, and the banks.

LMB worked on a fee-only basis. They charged a fee equal to a project's expenses plus a percentage of the total cost of the project. Fees typically ranged from 2% to 5% of project costs. One senior manager described the impact that fee structures had on client relationships:

> Because we work for a fixed fee, our interests are aligned with those of our clients. There is no incentive to increase project costs. The clients get what they are willing to pay for. If clients want changes, we tell them what their options are and what the cost implications will be. If clients want to proceed with a change, we negotiate a fair and reasonable price in the marketplace. Our clients therefore have more control over costs and quality.

[1]Albert Scardino, "Project Managers in a Hurry," *New York Times*, April 28, 1986, p. D5.

29. Lehrer McGovern Bovis, Inc.

Unlike general contractors, construction managers did not guarantee budget or schedule. Slipped schedules and budget overruns were paid by the client but at a major cost to the construction manager's reputation. Lehrer observed:

> We compete on the basis of three items: reputation, first, qualifications, second, and fees, third. If construction managers can't deliver the job on time and on budget, they'll soon be out of business.

Competition for Construction Management Projects

In 1985, the top 400 U.S. contractors recorded $136.1 billion in foreign and domestic contracts. Of these contracts, $81.7 billion were for traditional general contractor projects, $36.4 billion were for construction management projects and $18.0 billion for design-build contracts. The top construction managers were full-service firms who

EXHIBIT 2 The 1985 Top 20 Construction Management (CM) Firms (in $ millions)

		CM Contract Value[a]	Total Contract Value[a]
1.	The Parsons Group	$5,223.2	$8,620.0
2.	Morrison Knudsen Corp.	4,581.0	5,887.7
3.	CRSS Constructors Inc.	2,977.8	3,381.7
4.	Fluor Corp.	2,875.0	5,127.5
5.	Bechtel Group Inc.	1,797.0	7,364.0
6.	HRH Construction Corp.	1,716.2	1,716.2
7.	Gilbane Building Co.	1,606.6	1,676.5
8.	Tishman Realty & Construction	1,043.6	1,043.6
9.	Ebasco Services Inc.	983.6	2,751.9
10.	Kaiser Engineers Inc.	943.2	1,587.5
11.	Huber, Hunt & Nichols Inc.	907.0	1,009.3
12.	Morse Diesel Inc.	893.0	893.0
13.	Kitchell Corp.	871.5	876.8
14.	Barton-Marlow Co.	805.8	875.8
15.	Day & Zimmerman Inc.	777.0	913.1
16.	Devon Construction	777.0	869.0
17.	Lehrer McGovern Bovis	590.0	590.0
18.	Rust International Inc.	509.8	5,097.9
19.	Turner Corp.	483.9	2,924.7
20.	Raymond International Inc.	455.3	721.5

[a] These figures represent the erected value of construction projects. Revenues earned from those projects were not reported.

Source: Roger J. Hannan, "The Top 400 Contractors," *Engineering News Record*, April 17, 1986, pp. 61–70, 92.

offered construction management services in all industry segments. (*Exhibit 2.*) The Parsons Corp., the nation's largest general contractor, ranked first with new construction management projects of $5.2 billion. Morrison-Knudsen, the nation's largest design firm, ranked second with $4.6 billion in construction management projects. "With both designers and general contractors offering construction management services," said one observer, "it's hard to pin down your competition."

The Company

In 1985, Lehrer McGovern Bovis ranked 17th among construction management firms. By mid-1986, the company employed 465 people in nine offices, eight in the U.S. and one in London.

(*Exhibit 3.*) Total 1985 revenues were $36.4 million; 1986 revenues were projected to exceed $55 million (*Exhibit 4*).

Early Strategy

In June 1979, Peter Lehrer and Gene McGovern left their senior-level positions at Morse-Diesel, the nation's 12th largest construction management firm to start a company of their own. Three days later, they formed Lehrer/McGovern, Inc.,[2] armed with only their personal reputations and 32 years of construction expertise. Within two

---

[2] In 1986, Lehrer/McGovern, Inc. merged with Bovis International, Ltd. to become Lehrer McGovern Bovis, Inc. (LMB).

EXHIBIT 3 Organizational Chart

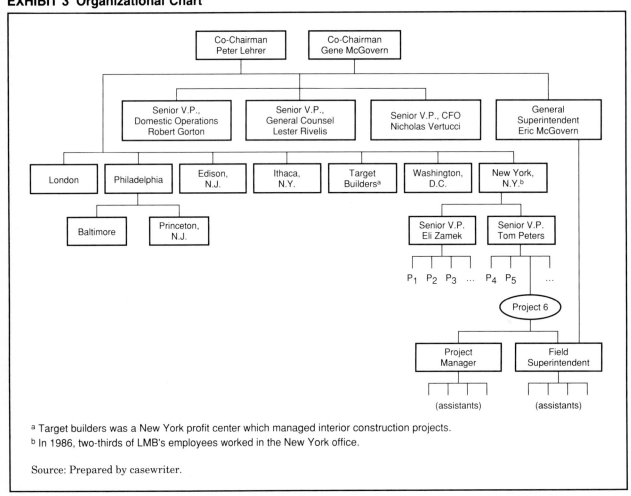

[a] Target builders was a New York profit center which managed interior construction projects.
[b] In 1986, two-thirds of LMB's employees worked in the New York office.

Source: Prepared by casewriter.

EXHIBIT 4 LMB's Construction Management (CM) Fee Revenue by Market (in $ thousands)

	1984		1985		1986 (Est.)	
Total Revenues	$27,000		$36,400		$55,900	
Net CM Fee Revenues[a] (Market Mix)	$	%	$	%	$	%
Developers	$ 5,514	84%	$ 4,598	67%	$ 6,794	57%
Corporate Clients	707	11	922	14	2,451	20
Institutions	200	3	231	3	988	8
Restoration	163	2	1,068	16	1,822	15
Total Net CM Fee Revenues	$ 6,584	100%	$ 6,819	100%	$12,055	100%
Other fees[b]	$ 1,600		$ 3,561		$ 4,777	
Total Net Fee Revenues	$ 8,184		$10,380		$16,832	

[a] Revenues less project-reimbursable expenses.
[b] Includes consulting fees for special projects and mortgage monitoring.

Source: Lehrer McGovern Bovis, Inc.

weeks, they had secured a contract to build a factory and office building for Colorforms Corporation in northern New Jersey.

The firm's early strategy was to select jobs that would attract immediate attention. In 1981, they accepted the challenge of removing a 10-ton, 24-foot-high statue from atop the old AT&T headquarters in Manhattan. The gold-leafed, bronze statue, nicknamed Golden Boy, had crowned the building for 64 years; some experts believed that it could not be moved from its 30-story perch. LMB's crew started work on a Sunday afternoon; Monday morning, Golden Boy was down.

This unusual job brought the firm wide attention among builders and developers seeking construction management services. New projects came quickly, and the offices of LMB were shortly moved from their homes to a modern suite on Park Avenue South.

The firm's reputation was solidly established two years later when LMB won the 30-month contract to restore the Statue of Liberty. More than 25 firms submitted proposals to coordinate the activities of some 500 engineers, architects, contractors, and craftsmen. After an exhaustive screening process, LMB was awarded the job.

The project's objective was to restore the statue before its centennial celebration on July 4, 1986. Weather, pollution and normal wear-and-tear had damaged the 151-foot statue's torch, flame, right arm and inner structure. The statue's iron framework had corroded; extensive structural problems required renovation.

As the construction manager, LMB selected the subcontractors and supervised the rebuilding of the statue. "It was one big R&D project," a senior manager explained. "No one was sure what to expect." The statue's location on Liberty Island in New York Harbor further complicated the work. All materials and workers had to be taken to and from the island by boat, while winds and tides threatened worker safety and the project's tight time schedule. Yet, despite these challenges, the statue was ready for her 100th birthday celebration.

Both Lehrer and McGovern pointed to the Statue of Liberty project as a watershed in the company's history. But they were quick to add that its visibility was a double-edged sword. With worldwide attention focused on the restoration, the firm's reputation was clearly at risk. As one manager noted, "We couldn't reschedule the centennial celebration to August 16th."

Client Mix

DEVELOPERS. The growth of LMB coincided with one of the most spectacular bull markets in the city's real-estate history. As construction flourished, developers demanded that buildings be erected quickly for early tenant occupancy. Fast-track construction met that need.

Lehrer and McGovern's project management expertise and experience with fast-track construction placed their firm in contention for many of the new development projects in Manhattan. Jack Resnick & Sons, Dan Brodsky, The William Kaufman Organization, Fred Wilpon of Sterling Equities, and other New York developers hired LMB for office and residential construction. Satisfied with their performance, they then rehired the firm for additional work. As a result, most of LMB's early clients were speculative developers with fast-track projects.

CORPORATE CLIENTS. In the early years, Lehrer and McGovern also looked for opportunities to work for corporate clients. In 1981, they secured their first corporate project: a new General Foods headquarters in Rye, New York. General Foods had intended to use a general contractor to build their 1.1 million-square-foot corporate headquarters. When all bids came in way over budget, they sought out the services of a construction manager. LMB was awarded the contract.

Because of its complexity, the General Foods project received considerable publicity in the industry. The architect had recommended using aluminum siding as the enclosure wall for the seven-story building, even though it was rarely used on commercial structures. LMB was involved early on to assure constructibility and to help locate a contractor experienced enough to install 260,000 square-feet of aluminum siding. Months of testing were required to make sure that the siding would be secure against wind and water. The architect later won the coveted Pritzker Prize in architecture, and LMB greatly enhanced their standing among potential corporate clients. In fact, by 1986, projects for corporate clients and developers comprised 77% of LMB's market mix. (*Exhibit 4.*)

Project Management

Through such efforts as the Golden Boy project, the Statue of Liberty, and the General Foods headquarters, LMB had earned a reputation for completing challenging projects on time and within budget. Managers claimed that a major reason for these successes was their team approach to project management.

Construction projects at LMB were managed by project teams formed when the firm first received a request for a building proposal. The team was responsible for responding to the proposal, winning the contract, and then managing all facets of the construction project. At LMB, project managers, with support from the rest of the team, were totally responsible for the successful completion of their building.

Conceptually, project management at LMB could be divided into three stages: *winning the proposal,* when the team responded to a request for proposal; *preconstruction activities,* when value engineering was done, bid packages were prepared, and construction logistics were planned; and *construction,* when the foundation was dug and the building was erected.

WINNING THE PROPOSAL. A dedicated project team was first assembled to respond to a building request. A typical team included Lehrer and McGovern; a project executive, who supervised several projects simultaneously; a project manager, who was dedicated to one project; an estimator; and a mechanical/electrical manager, who provided specific technical support concerning the building's mechanical and electrical systems. The team worked through the proposal to evaluate the client's requirements and to identify opportunities for cost savings. The time investment at this stage was large, as Nicholas Vertucci, the firm's chief financial officer explained:

> Before we respond to a proposal, we're already starting to formulate ideas for time and cost savings. This is done to differentiate us from our competitors. And it seems to work. After one client got our written proposal, he said, "You've sent us a book; your competitors sent us three pieces of paper."

Once the written proposal was reviewed by the client, the project team prepared a client presentation. A typical presentation included a description of LMB's services and how they would approach the building's construction. Bob Borton, the Edison, New Jersey profit center manager, described how they won a recent contract to build a new corporate headquarters:

> The project came out of an existing relationship with the architect. The client wanted to hire a construction manager for the project; we were included on the list of potential candidates. About seven or eight of our people worked on the proposal. More than anything else, the key to winning the contract was the chemistry between our project team and the client. They were very comfortable with us.

PRECONSTRUCTION ACTIVITIES. Once hired, a project team had to complete several tasks before construction could begin. The design was value engineered to reduce costs; bid packages were prepared and subcontractors hired; and construction logistics were planned.

Value Engineering. The project team's first task was to scrutinize the design, as it was being completed, to identify opportunities for cost reduction. Value engineering was used to systematically evaluate alternatives in order to reduce costs without compromising quality or performance. (*Exhibits 5a and 5b.*) Using value engineering techniques, the project manager isolated each building component looking for ways to use new or alternate construction materials and methods. The amount of time devoted to value engineering depended on the complexity of the project and its timetable. For example, Borton's team spent four months value engineering the new headquarters facility. Their recommended changes saved the client $6.6 million in construction costs, nearly 10% of the project cost.

Before value-engineered changes were implemented, the LMB project team met with the client and architect to secure approval. These recommendations were not always welcomed by architects, whose concern for aesthetics sometimes clashed with the team's concern for cost and efficiency. "It's a polite, professional battle," said one senior manager, "and one from which the client ultimately benefits."

After the client, architect and project team agreed on the design changes, the LMB team developed a final budget and construction schedule.

Bid Packages. Among other items, the construction schedule included the dates when the architect would forward completed design documents to LMB. If the project was being constructed by fast-track methods, the architect would prepare the documents in stages, so that the project team could solicit bids from subcontractors as quickly as possible. LMB's project manager would then break the completed design documents into bid packages, which were sent to subcontractors for pricing. Each bid package contained drawings, component specifications and a detailed scope of work for services the subcontractor was expected to provide. In most cases, a large number of bids were solicited for each subcontract. These were then reviewed by the project manager; usually, the lowest bidders were recommended to the clients.

Once the client approved these recommendations, the project manager negotiated contracts with subcontractors. Earlier discussions smoothed the negotiation process. One project manager observed, "To avoid change orders after construction starts our bid documents are very detailed. They don't give a lot of room for negotiation."

EXHIBIT 5a Value Engineering in The Construction Industry[a]

Value engineering is a technique used to reduce the costs associated with a product without compromising quality or performance. Historically, there was little incentive for architects and contractors to use value engineering to reduce construction costs. Obsolete building codes often bound them to past construction practices. Moreover, architects and contractors seldom wanted to take the financial risks associated with new materials or methods.

The architect's objective was to produce a competitive design from available materials at minimum design cost. Value engineering meant additional time and expense searching for and testing new materials, communicating proposed changes to clients, and finding contractors with the equipment and skills needed to use the new approaches in construction. Because fees were usually a percentage of project costs, the resulting cost savings meant that the architect also made less money. To architects, then, value engineering meant more work, more uncertainty, and a lower fee—hardly incentives to search for, test, and promote new materials or methods.

Similarly, contractors normally relied on past experience in quoting fixed prices for projects. To control costs, contractors wanted to use familiar construction methods and materials in order to sequence subcontractors predictably during construction. Different materials meant different fabrication techniques, unforeseen problems, and perhaps costly delays and repairs. Contractors, naturally, were reluctant to bid for projects requiring new materials or practices without adding contingency costs to their bids. Such costs often counter-balanced the savings from value-engineering.

Nonetheless, some contractors successfully employed value engineering. However, they applied the technique to already completed designs, where both resistance to, and the costs of, change were high. For this reason, construction managers claimed that their use of value engineering yielded greater savings, since it occurred earlier in the design process and was thus more likely to result in significant changes in materials and techniques.

Value Engineering Methodology. A five-step approach was normally used. First, the construction manager quantified the cost of each building component. Design specifications were reviewed on a system-by-system basis, with the foundation and structural components evaluated first, and then the curtain wall, mechanical and electrical systems, plumbing, and so forth. Those components which appeared to be out-of-line with historical costs or the construction manager's experience were isolated for further study.

The construction management team then defined the primary function of the component, that is, what the component **did**. The team brainstormed alternate materials that could provide the same function for lower cost. Consideration was given to new materials or process technology, modification of the client's needs, and feedback from field experience. The most promising alternatives were then evaluated on the basis of cost and how well they met the project's requirements. Because a design change might improve initial construction costs while increasing the long term maintenance costs of a building, the impact of a component change on the total cost of designing, building, operating and maintaining the facility (the life-cycle costs) was also determined.

Finally, recommendations for change were documented and presented to the architect and client for approval.

---

[a] For a complete description of the value engineering technique, see the *Note on Value Analysis*, HBS Case Services 9-687-066.

EXHIBIT 5b Value Engineering in the Construction Industry: An Example

The following example illustrates a value engineering exercise completed for one of LMB's construction projects.

LMB was awarded a contract for a new corporate headquarters. The building complex had three low-rise buildings connected by atriums, bridges and tunnels. Most building space was devoted to offices, but there were a number of highly finished common areas including a cafeteria, executive dining rooms, a large auditorium, a multi-media center, a health club and medical facilities.

LMB's initial cost estimate was $89.50/sq.ft. for the 690,000 square-foot facility. Value engineered changes reduced construction costs to $79.89/sq.ft., a $6.63 million savings. Changes in four major systems contributed most of the cost savings:

System	Components	Savings
1. Structural	Structural Steel for the Roof and Office Bays	$1,586,761

(Evaluated 4 roof and 20 office bay designs. Selected designs which satisfied customer requirements for least cost.)

System	Components	Savings
2. Sitework	Roadway and Parking Paving, Exterior Lighting	$ 868,952

(Modified paving materials; reduced number of light poles; changed lamps.)

System	Components	Savings
3. Curtain Wall	Exterior and Interior Walls of the Building	$ 430,000

(Reviewed suggestions for cost savings from seven curtain wall contractors. Successful bidder met design intent with cost savings.)

System	Components	Savings
4. Finishes	Partitions, Ceilings, Flooring, Doors	$1,967,035

(Evaluated and revised materials used for partitions, acoustical ceilings, flooring and door finishes.)

	Total Savings	$4,852,748

Construction Planning. While the project manager worked on the bid packages, the field staff prepared the construction site logistics plan. This plan described how the construction equipment and materials should be arranged on-site so that construction was as efficient as possible. Issues such as permits, power, water, sanitation facilities, and site conditions were addressed at this time. Through such planning, construction would be able to start as soon as the first subcontractors were hired.

CONSTRUCTION. During a building's construction phase, the project manager remained in-house, negotiating subcontractor contracts for the client and purchasing any additional materials needed for the job. The physical construction of the project was managed by a field superintendent and assistants, under the supervision of Eric McGovern, the general superintendent.

Construction started as soon as the foundation subcontractor had been hired. While the foundation was being dug, the field superintendent completed the site logistics plan. He prepared and posted the equipment time and work schedules, determined how the construction crews would be sequenced, and scheduled material deliveries.

When the foundation was partially completed, the field superintendent held the first of many coordination meetings with subcontractors. Jim Abadie, a field superintendent, described these meetings:

> We don't wait for the architect and engineers to initiate meetings with subcontractors. Before the first floor is poured, I pull the subcontractors into a coordinating meeting, lock the door, and don't let them leave until they map out the first floor. We work off of the drawings and try to make it all fit. We decide where everything goes and how the work should be coordinated. These meetings are repeated for every floor.

During the contruction phase, the field superintendent, his first assistant, and Eric McGovern held weekly status meetings with the project executive and project manager. The project manager, in turn, scheduled weekly meetings with the client and architect to keep them informed of progress. Construction costs and schedule were monitored by the project manager.

Site Management. The proper sequencing of men, materials and equipment was essential to meeting tight construction schedules. Work crews had to be closely scheduled so that they did not interfere with one another, but had a minimum of idle time. Equally important, the hoists had to be strategically positioned to place materials and equipment efficiently and in their proper location. A hoist book, often called "the superintendents' Bible," was used to record the movement of all materials on the job site.

The proper placement of materials and machines could sharply reduce unnecessary delays and wasted motion. Great skill was required to do this effectively. For example, a senior manager at LMB described one field superintendent as a "master chess player":

> He's always several moves ahead. He'll tell them to put the steel in the southwest corner of the building on the second floor, because several days later the hoists will be there and the steel won't have to be moved again. And sure enough, the hoists will be there.

The project team controlled the schedule through material and equipment purchases, ordering such items as sinks, tubs, refrigerators, and electric fixtures directly. When the schedule called for those items to be installed, the project team had the materials delivered to the job site where subcontractors simply completed the installation. LMB also provided the scaffolding for some projects, rather than purchasing it from each subcontractor. By moving the scaffolding up on schedule, the project team put pressure on subcontractors to finish their work quickly on the lower floors.

Overall, LMB's managers attributed much of their firm's success to their team approach to construction management. According to one project manager:

> The difference is just getting people involved in the project. Here we say, "It's your project, so get it done." Other companies have more corporate levels; you could be a shining star and no one would know. But, here, decisions are made by the project team. You're in charge of your own destiny. As a result, everyone becomes an innovator, an entrepreneur.

Many of LMB's larger competitors had a more departmentalized approach to construction management. They might have a separate proposal team, which sold projects to clients; a preconstruction department, which performed value engineering; a purchasing department, which ordered all construction materials; and a construction department, which managed all fieldwork. Although competitors gained some economies of scale by providing such services across projects, LMB project managers felt that their team approach provided better client service and tighter project control. One manager explained:

> The advantage of having me do the buying is that I'm responsible for the project's success. I know the job; I know what I want when. If I need a brick, I get it; I don't have to knock on doors. I also end up with a different relationship with subcontractors. They know that I recommended them for the job. In a way, they owe me one. And I have control over that favor.

Project Support

People. All of LMB's project teams were staffed with experienced construction managers. They also drew informally on the expertise of Lehrer, McGovern and other senior managers. For example, Phil Kleiner, a vice president, was a structural steel expert with over 30 years in the business. On complicated projects, he was part of the project team. More frequently, he worked as an internal consultant, answering questions about the nuances of steel fabrication or visiting job sites to offer advice.

Recruiting. In the early years, Lehrer and McGovern had hired experienced project managers and field staff, often people with whom they had previously done business. Once the supply of experienced people was exhausted, they began actively recruiting young engineering talent on college campuses. All engineering applicants were interviewed by Gene McGovern. McGovern described how he evaluated them:

> I listen to how they answer questions, how confident they are talking to "the boss." I find out where they want to be in a few years, whether or not they have worked their way through school. I look for confidence, ambition, a strong work ethic . . . the right attitude. No matter how well someone does in school, the real world starts when you're standing 40 stories high. I'd rather hire someone with the right attitude and bolt on the technical experience than try to do it the other way around.

In 1986, all hiring decisions were approved by either Lehrer or McGovern. "We don't have a personnel department," explained McGovern, "because personnel people tend to hire people like themselves."

Training. Most training at LMB was done informally—"hands-on"—under the guidance of project teams. A training program for new college graduates, however, was being formalized in 1986. During their first two years with LMB, all new hires would split their time between the field and the office, working as assistants to either field superintendents or project managers. During the third year and beyond, assignments would be based on project needs and employees' preferences for field or project management work. Assignments would be made by the general superintendent and the appropriate senior vice president.

Appraisals/Rewards. In their first two years, new employees were reviewed every six months and annually thereafter. One of the rewards for a job well done was the satisfaction of seeing a project completed and the opportunity for another challenge. In a firm with only three senior managers over 40 years of age, it was not uncommon to find young engineers managing major projects. For example, one project manager, in his late 20s, was responsible for an $80 million apartment building. According to Eric McGovern, "You won't see that at other firms."

Additional incentives came in 1984, with the creation of regional profit centers. These centers gave experienced managers an opportunity to be entrepreneurial. A bonus system was established to reward profit centers for strong performance, with the bonus pool based on a formula that included the profit center's profitability goal, set during the budgeting process, plus its increase in profitability over the past year. Bonuses were awarded annually; the size of an individual's bonus was left to the discretion of his or her manager.

SUPPORT SERVICES. Project teams at LMB were backed by support services in marketing, estimating, scheduling and accounting. The New York headquarters had a full complement of support groups, including legal and computer services. The regional profit centers formed support staffs as soon as their size warranted;[3] until then, they used the resources available from New York.

[3] In 1986, all profit centers had a project accounting staff. Ithaca had an estimating staff; Washington and Philadelphia had estimating and marketing staffs.

CONTROL SYSTEMS. Project managers were responsible for monitoring costs and schedules for clients. Initial budgets, prepared with estimators, were the basic mechanisms for project control. These budgets segregated work by trades so that actual costs could be easily monitored during construction. In 1986, budgets were prepared manually, although a computerized project management system was in the process of being implemented. Scheduling software, such as *Prima Vera* or *Network,* were also available for project managers. But many preferred to prepare schedules manually and have them enhanced by the scheduling department before client presentations.

PLANNING. Lehrer, McGovern and the profit center managers met monthly to discuss strategic and operations issues. "When Gene and I started the company," said Lehrer, "a lot of decisions were driven by the kind of work the two of us wanted to do." In 1986, senior managers had more input into strategic decisions. "We're a close-knit group," continued Lehrer. "We have the same philosophical viewpoint about work, the desire to succeed, an entrepreneurial spirit. We don't have a business plan on paper; it's in our heads."

Growth Issues

In 1986, LMB's senior management had made two key strategic decisions. The first was to merge the company with Bovis International, Ltd., a London-based construction management firm. The second, prompted by changing market conditions, was to shift from the firm's traditional markets of commercial and restoration projects to the construction of corporate facilities and institutions, such as hospitals, colleges and universities.

The merger with Bovis was not expected to significantly affect operations at LMB. The motivation was primarily financial and included better access to projects in the New York area that were financed by foreign sources. The shift in client mix, however, was expected to have more of an impact on operations because of the size of corporate projects and clients' reporting needs. One project manager explained:

> The technical skills required are the same for all clients. But corporate clients are more bureaucratic than developers. You have to work through the hierarchy to get changes approved. Corporate procedures must be followed and reports filed. Corporate project managers want support when they report to their superiors; that requires the creation of an audit trail.

Changing market conditions also meant that other construction firms would be pursuing these same clients. Competition was expected to be intense. "Fee structures might be hurt," said Bob Borton, "but it's important to keep our people busy. We don't want to lose them."

Systems. The anticipated increase in corporate clients had implications for systems at LMB. Ken Colyer, a project manager, who had come to LMB from a corporate construction department, commented:

> The first thing I noticed at the company was the absence of support systems comparable with those commonly found in the corporate environment. Until now, each project team has relied on its own resources, which has both strengths and weaknesses. One weakness is that whatever the team lacks, it has no place to draw from. Because the company has been very project-focused, people don't interrelate with others on other projects. It's a vertical, not a horizontal, organization.

Colyer identified three items that he thought were necessary to support growth: systems for scheduling, cost control, and document control; technical support, such as mechanical and electrical experts; and strong project control, i.e., experienced project managers. In 1986, LMB was addressing each of these needs. One senior manager commented, "The question that we're wrestling with is, do we build an infrastructure for growth and then go after more business, or do we get the business first and then add internal resources? Right now, we're trying to do both at once."

STAFFING. Growth at LMB was linked to the firm's ability to staff projects with the right people. During 1986, LMB increased its staff by 160 employees, 40 project managers and 120 support staff (*Exhibit 6*). One senior manager noted that employee turnover was an issue for LMB, and the industry as a whole:

> On average, people in this industry change jobs every two to four years. Our challenge is to provide an incentive package and work environ-

EXHIBIT 6 LMB's Management and Staff

	1984	1985	1986	Salary Range
Project Executives and Project Managers	32	60	100	$40K–150K
Project Support Staff (includes estimators, accountants, assistants)	80	170	290	$15K–95K
Nonproject-related Support (includes legal, data processing, general accounting)	30	75	75	$10K–120K
Total	142	305	465	

Source: Lehrer McGovern Bovis records.

ment that defeats the tendency of construction personnel to move from job to job.

BONUSES. Toward the end of 1986, the performance of the Edison, New Jersey profit center raised an immediate question about how to reward profit centers equitably. The Edison, New Jersey profit center had an extremely profitable year; net revenues leaped from $100 thousand in 1985 to $1.56 million in 1986. The profitability formula could not be used to determine their bonus pool.

One project credited to the New Jersey office was a new office building in Queens, New York. Although the building fell geographically within the jurisdiction of the New York profit center, the client had specifically requested that Bob Borton manage the project. Borton was given the assignment and the full-time support of six members of the New York staff. For bonus purposes, the staff's time was charged directly to the project; all project revenues were credited to the New Jersey profit center.

McGovern explained that the situation was part of the growth process. "Borton's case is a rough spot," he said. "We'll have to work it out. Right now, the profit centers are new; if this happend five years from now I'd be much more concerned."

The issues surrounding systems, staffing and bonuses were all created by LMB's rapid growth. As he looked toward the future, McGovern saw the firm's ability to manage growth without compromising quality as a key management challenge. He was equally concerned with keeping the firm energized:

> When you look at other companies in this business, you see a lot of lethargy and stale thinking. There are few companies our size, and few companies where the principals are deeply involved in the firm's operations. We continually have to prove ourselves; I hope that it stays that way.

30. A Note on Value Analysis:[1] Its History and Methodology

Value analysis is a technique used to reduce the costs associated with a product without compromising quality or performance. Many cost-cutting methods simply reduce a product's material or labor content; the result is often inferior products and dissatisfied customers. By contrast, value analysis aims at improving a product's value through design simplification and the elimination of unnecessary costs. Originally, the technique was used to find ways of producing the same product for lower cost; today, it is equally concerned with developing better ways of meeting customer needs.

History

Value analysis was developed by Lawrence Miles of General Electric during World War II. Miles' assignment was to procure vital materials for GE's skyrocketing production of military hardware. Because of the war, certain materials were not available; others were prohibitively expensive. Expanding production needs and overextended suppliers forced Miles to seek out substitutes for materials that would provide the same function as his original need. Freed from all restrictions associated with the original material, his only concern was what the material did (i.e., it's function) and what else could do the same job.

Miles' functional approach was so successful that his staff later systematized the process,

calling it value analysis. In the next 17 years, GE saved more than $200 million using the technique. Because of GE's success, value analysis was gradually adopted by other industries.

Methodology[2]

The task of analyzing value follows the general pattern of the scientific method, incorporating problem solving techniques and teamwork. A team of employees is assembled to evaluate a product or process. Ideally, the value team should possess a balanced combination of skills crossing functional lines. For example, representatives from design, manufacturing, procurement, production planning and marketing could comprise a value team. But more frequently, a few key individuals with intimate product knowledge will spearhead the value analysis effort, drawing upon other functional resources as needed.

Value analysis is best practiced by following a specific job plan of five phases: the information phase, the analytic phase, the creative phase, the evaluation phase, and the implementation phase. An example of the process appears in *Exhibits 1–5.*

THE INFORMATION PHASE. The value team gathers product information in order to isolate those components of the product with the greatest potential for improving value. Before organizing the search, the team defines how much time and how many people can be devoted to this task. The team collects information regarding:

---

[1] Value analysis is often called value engineering. But because the technique is used to evaluate services as well as products, the former term is used in this note.

This note was prepared by Janet Simpson under the direction of David A. Garvin.

[2] This discussion draws heavily on C. Fallon, *Value Analysis to Improve Productivity,* (New York: Wiley Interscience, 1971), Chapters 5–9.

EXHIBIT 1 The Information Phase

A value team was assembled to evaluate the design of a proposed water distribution system of a communications facility. To get started, the team first listed the components of the system, defined their function, and determined their cost. They prepared the exhibit shown below.

Column 4 lists an estimate of each component's worth. Worth is defined as the lowest cost to perform the basic function of the component with current technology. For example, for item #1, the least expensive way to "supply water" is to use garden hoses which cost $2,000. Thus the worth of the more complicated $21,000 lawn sprinkler system is only $2,000. The component with the highest cost-to-worth (C/W) ratio, in this case the lawn sprinkler system, is isolated for further study.

Item: Water Distribution System
Basic Function: Supply Water

Component	Function	Original Cost	Worth
1. Lawn sprinkler	Supply Water	$21,000. C/W = 21/2 = 10.5	$ 2,000.
2. Fire protection system	Supply Water	$18,400. C/W = 18.4/8 = 2.3	$ 8,000.
3. Domestic water supply	Supply Water	$15,000. C/W = 15/8 = 1.9	$ 8,000.
4. Sanitary waste removal	Remove Water	$27,000. C/W = 27/17.5 = 1.5	$17,500.
5. Storm drainage system	Remove Water	$15,000. C/W = 15/2 = 7.5	$ 2,000.

EXHIBIT 2 The Analytic Phase

The value team then defined the primary function of the lawn sprinkler system and each component's function and cost.

System: Water Distribution
Subsystem: Lawn Sprinkler System
Basic Function: Water Vegetation

Component	Function	Cost
Pipe and Fittings	Carry Water	$ 9,000.
Valves and Controls	Control Flow	4,350.
Nozzles	Spread Water	6,850.
Bubblers	Spread Water	700.
Backflow preventer	Prevent Contamination	100.
Water	Sustain Growth	0.
Total		$21,000.

EXHIBIT 3 The Creative Phase

The value team brainstormed alternate methods for providing the sprinkler's primary function: to "water vegetation". Criticism was withheld until a number and variety of ideas were generated. A few of those ideas are presented below with the team's assessment of the advantages and disadvantages. Ideas #3 and # 4 were selected as the most promising changes.

System: Water Distribution
Subsystem: Lawn Sprinkler System
Basic Function: Water Vegetation

Ideas	Advantages	Disadvantages
1. Garden Hose	Cheaper. Portable. Easily Replaced. Concentrate water.	Needs Replacing. Requires more manpower hours. Safety hazard.
2. Natural Rainfall	No cost. No labor. No maintenance.	Limits amount of vegetation. High risk of losing plants. Limits type of vegetation.
3. Reduce amount of vegetation	Less time required for maintenance. Requires less initial cost.	Employees would object.
4. Change type and head pattern.	Less initial cost. Less maintenance.	Possible dry areas.

EXHIBIT 4 The Evaluation Phase

The most promising ideas generated during the creative phase were compared on the basis of initial and life-cycle costs. Alternate #2, changing the type and pattern of the sprinkler heads and reducing the quantity of heads and bubblers, required the lower initial cost and incurred lower maintenance costs over the 40 year life-cycle estimate.

System: Water Distribution
Subsystem: Lawn Sprinkler System
Basic Function: Water Vegetation

	Unit		
	Quantity	Cost	Total Cost
Original Design	1	$21,000.	$21,000.
Alternate 1 (Idea 3)			
Reduce amount of vegetation	88	$ 100.	($ 8,800.)
Reduce quantity of heads	heads		
Eliminate drain box	deleted		
		Total Savings:	($ 8,800.)
		Total Cost:	$12,200.
Alternate 2 (Idea 4)			
Change type and head pattern	lump sum		($ 8,500.)
Reduce quantity of heads			
Reduce quantity of bubblers	35	$ 100.	($ 3,500.)
		Total Savings:	($12,000.)
		Total Cost:	$ 9,000.

30. A Note on Value Analysis: Its History and Methodology

EXHIBIT 5 The Implementation Phase

Based on this value analysis, the team recommended revising the number and type of sprinkler heads in the lawn sprinkling system. They also recommended removing a planting area in the parking lot. A schematic of their implemented changes appears below. These changes saved $10,700, or 51 percent of the original cost.

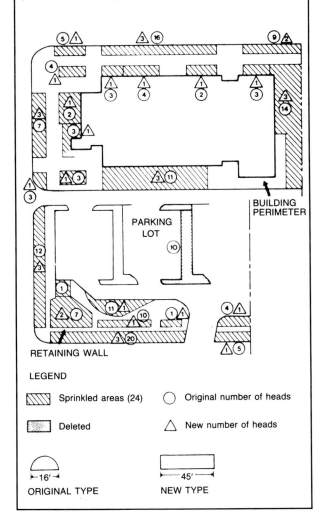

BUILDING PERIMETER

PARKING LOT

RETAINING WALL

LEGEND

▧	Sprinkled areas (24)	○	Original number of heads
▨	Deleted	△	New number of heads

⌒ ←16'→ ORIGINAL TYPE

▭ ←45'→ NEW TYPE

- Customer Requirements
  What contributes most to sales: safety, reliability, performance, appearance, easy maintenance, low cost, . . .
- Cost Information
  What are the costs of tooling, raw materials, purchased parts and components, manufactur-

ing costs, engineering support, warranty service, customer's cost of operation, maintenance, repair, downtime, . . .

- Current Specifications
  What are the special requirements of the product, how is it made, what materials are used, how many parts does it have, what are the allowed tolerances, . . .

An effective search will determine whether the current product is taking full advantage of state-of-the-art technology, new materials, new markets, new manufacturing methods, and new capital equipment. Equally important, the team will assess future customer needs and desires. In these areas, vendors and customers are useful sources of information.

The information collected in this phase is used to select a few product components for further study, based on the following criteria: potential gain for effort expended, technical feasibility, availability of information, availability of skills, timeliness, and probability of implementation.

THE ANALYTIC PHASE. Once a component or product has been selected for study, the task group asks, "What does it do?" The answer to this simple question helps the team define the function or functions of the product. The phrase "primary function" is used to designate the main reason why a product works or sells; it is also the reason why the customer buys the product.

The team describes the primary function of the product in two words, an active verb and a measurable noun. For example, the primary function of a pencil could be to "make marks." The eraser's function would be to "remove marks"; the paint, to "protect wood" or "provide beauty", and so on. The value team analyzes the functions of the product and ranks the benefits the product provides in order of relative importance to the customer. For example, the primary function of an automobile is to "transport people." However, buying criteria vary among consumer groups. Speed and appearance may be top priorities for the sports car buyer, but the economy car buyer wants a low purchase price and good operating economy. Understanding what the customer wants helps the value team concentrate its efforts on the areas which promise the greatest return.

Once the functions have been described, the team answers three questions: what does the function cost? what should it cost? what should it do?

If a product is selling well, the last question might not be considered. However, if customers are no longer buying the product or if a competitor can produce and sell the product at less than the value team's manufacturing cost, it is time to ask, "what should it do?" Value analysis then becomes an aid to new product development.

THE CREATIVE PHASE. The creative phase moves the value team from matters of fact to matters of value—from what **is** to what **should be.** After the product's functions have been defined, the value team brainstorms ideas for developing better methods for performing these functions. New methods, new materials, and new customer requirements are considered. Variations of time (sequencing), matter (weight), space (size), and energy (sources of power) are considered. Absurd or "way out" ideas are entertained as catalysts for less traditional thinking. Criticism is withheld until a large number and variety of ideas have been generated.

The functional analysis completed during the previous phase frees the task force from a major barrier to innovation: the constraint imposed by the product's original design. Suspending critical judgment during brainstorming stimulates the flow of ideas; only later are these ideas refined and evaluated in light of the firm's resources and customers' desired benefits.

THE EVALUATION PHASE. The most promising ideas generated during the creative phase are compared on the basis of cost and ability to meet customer needs. The latter requires that the value team review marketing information on customer buying criteria, resources, and intended use of the product. The team then determines which of the available choices best satisfies customer requirements and the firm's business objectives with respect to time, money and risk.

THE IMPLEMENTATION PHASE. As a final step, the value team prepares a presentation to gain management approval for its recommendations. The presentation typically includes the gains, costs and risks of the project, as well as an implementation work schedule. Once approved, the value team monitors implementation of the proposal using Gantt charts or comparable scheduling techniques.

Benefits

Value analysis can significantly reduce product costs in three ways. First, identifying the cost of each of a product's components can usually save 5% by highlighting simple opportunities for cost reduction, such as reducing material costs by volume price discounts. Second, improvements in the choice of materials and fabrication methods can often save an additional 10%. For example, a furniture manufacturer replaced a computer table's 10 machined-steel gears with injection-molded plastic gears. Labor and materials savings amounted to $40 of the original $400 unit cost. Finally, redesigning the expensive components of a product can save 30 percent or more. A value team studying the penthouse structure of a medical building recommended replacing concrete supports with a steel frame. That plus other structural changes saved $34,700 (41%) of the $85,340 original design cost.[3]

[3]A. Dell'Isola, *Value-Engineering in the Construction Industry* (New York: Construction Publishing Company, 1974), p. 95. This edition is out of print. Third edition (1991) available through Value Management Division, Smith, Hinchman, & Grylls, 1050 17th Street, N.W., Suite 800, Washington, DC 20036.

PART THREE

Planning and Implementing Operations Strategies Over Time

Module 5
Planning and Implementing Operations Strategies Over Time*

The literature on operations strategy is now over twenty years old.[1] It has already made its mark. Books and articles on the subject have proliferated, and it is no longer unusual to hear a chairman or chief executive officer assert that manufacturing is his or her first priority. The era of operations has finally arrived.

Bold pronouncements, however, are one thing; tangible results quite another. As one manufacturing expert has put it: "[S]trategy . . . is easier said than done."[2] Long-term success requires a sound strategy, to be sure, but also thoughtful planning and careful execution. Edicts alone are seldom sufficient. Instead, effective implementation rests on management's ability to create, control, and orchestrate a process for realizing strategic goals.[3] Persistence is important too, because early successes do not always translate into lasting gains. For sustained success, renewal and recommitment must be designed into the process. Other requirements include specific goals, policies and procedures that are formalized rather than ad hoc, and the diffusion of innovations throughout the organization to ensure a broad base of support.[4]

These requirements are difficult enough in a stable environment. But for most companies, the challenge is compounded by disruptions and unfolding events. Such events—at times predictable, at times unexpected—can undermine even the best planned strategies. In operations common challenges include rapid growth, shifts in customer requirements, the rise of aggressive competitors, and unforeseen implementation problems. Mid-course corrections then become necessary, and sometimes entire strategies must be revised. In fact, several scholars have observed that operations strategy usually becomes important to companies for precisely these reasons. When the corporate strategy changes, a shift occurs in the company's business environment, a new product or facility is contemplated, or the performance of an existing facility lags, manufacturing becomes a much greater strategic concern.[5]

Here again, the critical task is managing change, especially over extended periods of time. The job is complex and multi-faceted. Managers must create a demand for change within their organizations, overcome employee resistance, nurture innovative programs, gain support and commitment at all levels, respond to unfolding events, and ensure that new approaches are embedded in the company's culture and systems.[6] Because employees often fear change—believing that, in personal terms, the costs will exceed the benefits—resistance can run deep. Traditional approaches will then be difficult to dislodge, and implementation decisions may suffer from "errors of ritual": courses of action that are followed simply because "we've always done things that way."[7]

In such circumstances, forceful leadership is required. Both a clear vision and an attentiveness to implementation are necessary; the two complement one another, like the blades of a scissors. Such leadership demands a new type of manufacturing manager:

> These are special times for manufacturing. The dependable old fundamental rules . . . are gone . . . [P]roduction management is rapidly becoming a whole new game . . . call[ing] for leaders who are architects of change, not housekeepers.[8]

Major Themes

This module is built around five major themes. Each focuses on manufacturing excellence and the tools, activities, and policies required to achieve it.

WORLD CLASS MANUFACTURING

Because superior manufacturing has, in many industries, become a competitive necessity, companies today are steadily upgrading their operations. While such efforts are admirable, they frequently lack clear direction. Before projects are selected and new programs are initiated, a clear set of goals is required. All too often the desired endpoint, "world class manufacturing," remains vague and ill-defined. Part of the problem is the term itself: It can be interpreted in at least three different ways.

To some analysts, world class manufacturing requires the achievement of specific quantitative targets: inventory turns of 80 to 100 times per year, defect rates of 200 parts per million or less, value-added lead times that are at least fifty percent of total manufacturing times.[9] Such targets are generally derived from best-in-class competitors, who set the standard for an industry or class of products. They are invaluable for dramatizing the vast gulf that separates the leaders in manufacturing from the followers, and for forcing the development of new policies and behaviors. Both Digital and Signetics cases illustrate the use of this approach. Digital, in its Endpoint Model, has set precise quantitative targets for cycle time reduction (from forty weeks to fifteen days), while Signetics is considering a contract that would require it to produce semiconductors at defect rates of 200 parts-per-million.

Other experts interpret world class manufacturing as more of a mindset or philosophy. They cite a few core principles: continuous improvement, simplification, streamlined processes, reduced variability, and the elimination of waste.[10] Each requires changes in people, technology, and systems, and each is likely to lead to improved quality, cost, responsiveness, and customer satisfaction. But because attention focuses on the means of improvement rather than the ends, practices and philosophies are viewed as the truest test of a company's status. Lehrer McGovern's use of "fast track" methods to overlap design and construction activities is representative of this approach, as is Copeland's reduction of complexity at its Sidney plant through the use of separate plants-within-a-plant.

Finally, some analysts view world class manufacturing in strategic terms.[11] For them, the critical question is the extent to which manufacturing contributes to the business strategy and ensures competitive superiority. Does it, for example, provide capabilities such as customization, tight tolerances, or quick turnaround times that are desired by customers? Are these capabilities unique or superior enough to create a sustainable competitive edge? If so, world class status has been obtained, because manufacturing has become "externally supportive."[12] Boeing's skill at project management—its ability to design and assemble enormously complex products, containing thousands of engineering changes and the latest technology, while still meeting scheduled delivery dates—fits this definition, as does Copeland's use of focused factories to serve the needs of particular products and markets.

Together, these three definitions sketch out the full extent of world class manufacturing. Demanding goals must be met, common practices and philosophies must be in place, and strategic needs must be served. All of the cases in the module describe companies pursuing such ends. Their methods differ, and they may have chosen to emphasize one of the three elements over the others, but in the breadth of their visions and the dominant role they have accorded manufacturing, each is well on its way to world class status.

DEMONSTRATION PROJECTS

In most cases, world class manufacturing requires fundamental changes in a company's policies, procedures, and modes of operation. New ways of thinking must be internalized, and new methods must be devised and implemented. Changes of this sort are difficult to introduce, especially if models are lacking. For this reason, demonstration projects—focused examples of the desired behaviors, undertaken at the plant or divisional level, with the explicit goal of expanding organizational capabilities—are often essential for effective implementation. They serve an important symbolic role as well:

> . . . some executives purposely undertake highly visible actions which wordlessly convey complex messages that could never be communicated as well—or as credibly—in verbal terms . . . Organizations often need such symbolic moves—or decisions they regard as symbolic—to build credibility behind a new strategy.[13]

The paced start-up of Copeland's Hartselle plant fits this description, as does the decision of GM's Wilmington plant manager to accept the opinion of an employee about whether an expensive, problem-plagued machine should be repaired or replaced. The former changed permanently the relationship between Copeland's marketing and manufacturing managers, while the latter helped redefine the roles of Wilmington's plant management and work force.

Demonstration projects share a number of other characteristics. Typically, they are the first projects to embody principles and approaches that a company hopes to adopt on a larger scale. As such, they are more transitional efforts than endpoints. Learning by doing is usually involved, and mid-course corrections are common. Few demonstration projects can be fully specified in advance; most are best classified as ongoing experiments. Yet at the same time, managers cannot run such projects without some understanding of the changes they hope to effect. Demonstration projects, after all, set vital precedents: They establish decision rules and policy guidelines that will shape initiatives to come. Managers must therefore be especially attentive to projects that change the "rules of the game." Then, employees will be looking continually for guidance and will often create tests of commitment to see if the rules truly have changed. In such circumstances success normally requires strong signals from senior management, a respected multifunctional team to oversee implementation, open channels of communication, and explicit strategies for transferring a project's lessons to other parts of the organization.

Several cases have already described demonstration projects. Vought's Flexible Machining Cell (FMC) is representative. By providing experience with flexible automation and the associated changes in vendor management, team composition, software requirements, and start-up procedures, it paved the way for the company's next generation projects, the Integrated Machining System (IMS) and Flexible Composites Center (FCC). Allstate used its Dynarim project for similar purposes: to demonstrate to employees long familiar with commodity chemicals that specialty products required new approaches to research, development, marketing, and manufacturing.

Demonstration projects figure prominently in this module, appearing in four cases: General Motors, Digital, Signetics, and Copeland. The modernization of General Motors' Wilmington plant is, in its entirety, a massive demonstration project. The investment is huge—over $300 million—and there have been fundamental changes in policies and procedures. Manufacturing is now an active partner in the design process, working side by side with engineering; quality goals have become as important as cost and efficiency targets; employee involvement is now cultivated and backed by extensive training programs; automation is state-of-the-art and carefully debugged before installation; and an atmosphere of open communication has been encouraged through meetings with senior management and the sharing of once-privileged competitive information. Digital's demonstration project is less expensive, although equally fundamental: It involves the installation of a Manufacturing Resource Planning (MRPII) system at a components factory and its impact on the other DEC divisions who are its customers. The (B) and (C) cases vividly illustrate the difficulty such projects encounter when they attempt to alter the rules of the game—in this case, changing an environment based on expediting to one requiring precise forecasts, fixed schedules, and formal planning—and the steps management must take to overcome resistance. At Signetics there are two demonstration projects; both involve quality. One, however, is complete, while the other is anticipated. A successful quality program is already in place at the company's Orem, Utah plant; at the same time, a parts-per-million contract is being considered for a major customer. The (B) case allows several months to pass and raises questions about the actions to take, precedents to set, and decision rules to use as the quality program unfolds over time. Copeland, another multi-part case series, begins by describing the planning, construction, and start-up of a new factory at Hartselle, Alabama that fundamentally altered the company's approach to manufacturing. Hartselle was Copeland's first focused factory. As such, it provided lessons about the role and functioning of project teams, the phasing of product and process development, the desired balance of power between marketing and manufacturing, and the importance of limiting a factory to a narrow, compatible set of demands.

Because they chart new territory, most demonstration projects are risky, uncertain ventures. The four examples in this module are no exception. Each shows the need to first establish credibility—for new concepts, methods, and policies—if broad acceptance is to be obtained. Often, the surest route to success is starting small:

> The best medicine for malaise is a few small success stories ... A small success can also be beneficial when a company enters a new area, when it may be used to build consensus for the new policy. Arranging for a small success at an early stage will lessen resistance to the new enterprise and will show the organization that this strategic direction is appropriate. With greater acceptance, momentum will build faster.[14]

GM, Digital, Signetics, and Copeland all show managers using this approach to gain a foothold for their demonstration projects.

CONFUSION, CONTROL, AND CONTINUOUS IMPROVEMENT

Just as marketing has its four P's—the core concepts of price, product, place, and promotion—operations strategy has its three C's: confusion, control, and continuous improvement. Here, however, the terms represent stages in a sequence rather than complementary parts. Together, they trace out an evolution and advancement over time.

The initial phase of a new manufacturing strategy, and a common trigger for change, is confusion on the shop floor. In most cases the problems are obvious, at least to outsiders: high inventories, jumbled product flows, extensive rework, poor communication, and a lack of priorities or long-term plans. Expediting is frequently driving the system, and product proliferation has often resulted in unmanageable levels of complexity. The former problem is clearly evident at Digital's Augusta plant prior to MRPII; the latter problem is seen at Copeland's Sidney plant before focused factories and the offloading of products. Such problems reflect a general sloppiness in operations that one scholar has called, only partly in jest, the "seven deadly sins of manufacturing":

> In the medieval church, there came to be known seven sins that were . . . viewed as so heinous, they were termed 'deadly' sins, punishable by hellfire.
>
> The medieval church is now history to us but, with the resurgence of manufacturing's importance, it is intriguing to ponder what could send a manufacturing plant straight to hell. My candidates . . . [are] . . . inconsistency, complication, waste, meandering, impatience, permissiveness, and sloth.[15]

All seven sins fall neatly under the umbrella of confusion.

To remedy these problems, better control is required. Communication must be improved; customer needs must be clarified; processes must be better understood; and standards must be established. Tighter discipline is essential; without it, improvement is unlikely because benchmarks will be unavailable and cause-and-effect relationships will be difficult to untangle. The needed discipline can come from diverse sources, including formal systems, new reporting requirements, and rules that replace ad hoc procedures. Here, Lehrer McGovern and Boeing provide an instructive contrast. Both companies consider project management to be a core skill, yet only Boeing has the formal systems—parametric estimating techniques, master phasing plans, and detailed tracking systems—to ensure that implementation remains disciplined and controlled. At Lehrer McGovern the process is more loosely managed and heavily dependent on individual initiative, with a far greater potential for error.

Once control has been established, companies can move to the next stage: continuous improvement. They can strive to better their operations in such key areas as quality (e.g. General Motors, Signetics, Copeland), cost (e.g. General Motors, Boeing, Copeland), and delivery (e.g. Digital). Two routes are available: incremental progress and strategic leaps.[16] The former requires small, steady steps that together produce great gains; the latter involves infrequent breakthroughs that individually yield substantial benefits. Of the two, incremental progress is clearly closer in spirit to the original concept of continuous improvement, with its Japanese roots.[17] But both approaches are valuable, and both appear in the module. Digital, with its Endpoint Plan, has chosen an incremental approach; Copeland, with the focusing of its Hartselle plant, and GM, with the modernizing of its Wilmington plant, have chosen strategic leaps; and Signetics, with the option of continuing its existing quality programs or accepting a new parts-per-million contract, is currently choosing between the two.

Continuous improvement marks the third and final step in the progression. Each step builds on its predecessors; in fact, it is difficult to advance without marching through the entire sequence. For example, an operation that is confused and out of control can seldom be improved without first imposing strong discipline. Otherwise, there would be no foundation or direction for change. The Japanese have long understood this principle, especially as it applies to automation:

> . . . a basic principle of Japanese factory management [is that] automation should follow, rather than lead, quality improvement. First, production processes [are] to be brought under control; only then [are] robots or automated devices to be introduced. Otherwise, quality problems [are] inevitable . . .[18]

Control is necessary for another reason as well: It provides better information. A confused environment yields little learning. Problem-solving is usually ad hoc; firefighting is rampant; and backsliding is common. Tighter discipline—through improved measurement systems, perhaps, or clearer specifications—ensures that the necessary information is generated to trace problems to their source and solve them permanently. Such "root-cause analysis" is at the heart of continuous improvement.

This progression suggests a subtle paradox. Tighter control is an essential step on the road to continuous improvement, yet the two are, to a surprising degree, at odds philosophically. The former concept is static, while the latter is dynamic. Shifting between the two is thus a difficult task. For example, improved quality requires that production processes first be brought into statistical control, yet for many years the same statistical techniques were used to justify static and unvarying Acceptable Quality Levels (AQLs).[19] Only when Japanese manufacturers entered the fray did the perspective change. The same dilemma is visible when improved responsivnesss is the goal, leading to what one scholar has called the "paradox of flexibility":

> . . . the extent and nature of discipline you are willing to impose on the factory will, in fact, decide the kinds of flexibilities you will be able to enjoy. Being permissive will only cause the factory to gum up, to lose the flexibility that permissiveness seeks in the first place.[20]

In this analysis, control is a waystation or midpoint, of interest primarily because of its eventual contribution to continuous improvement. Digital's plan to reduce cycle times and improve responsiveness by first introducing an MRPII system that freezes the production schedule thirteen weeks in advance is a classic example of this approach.

SPONSORS, CHAMPIONS, AND IMPLEMENTERS

World class manufacturing requires an organization-wide commitment. It is seldom achieved without the enthusiasm and involvement of employees at all levels. Yet successful implementation requires more than broad participation, especially if demonstration projects are used and companies are making the transition from control to continuous improvement. Three specific roles must also be filled. There must be a sponsor, who supports the effort and provides the necessary resources; a champion, who spearheads the project and shapes its design; and an implementer, who oversees daily operations and ensures that changes are introduced as planned.[21]

Sponsors usually come from high in the organization and are typically senior managers with considerable visibility. They provide political support, run interference, deflect challenges, and protect projects from outside influences. They are especially critical in securing resources and sustaining funding over time. Sponsors are seldom involved in the daily management of change efforts, but they are absolutely essential for success:

> Any new strategy, no matter how brilliant or responsive, no matter how much agreement the formulators have about it, will stand a good chance of not being implemented fully—or sometimes, at all—without someone with power pushing it.[22]

Lewis Campbell, a manufacturing manager in charge of six GM plants, plays this role in the Wilmington modernization; Paul Stevens, a group manufacturing manager, plays it in Digital's Endpoint Plan; and Chuck Harwood, the CEO, plays it in Signetics' quality improvement program.

Champions are more directly involved in the change process. Often, they lead it personally, serving as change agents, challenging the status quo, and participating in program design. Equally important is their role as cheerleaders, at times to the point of obsessiveness. Champions can—and often must—be singleminded in pursuit of their goals in order to overcome opposition. For this reason, they are frequently viewed as unreasonable or uncompromising by others in the organization. Jerry Evans, who created the Industrial Modernization (IMOD) group at Vought and led its development of the Flexible Machining Cell, had this reputation, as did Pete Kennedy, who spearheaded Allstate's Dynarim project. In this module champions include Donald Mitchell, manager of GM's Wilmington plant; Carl Porter, manager of Digital's Augusta plant; and D. C. McKenzie, director of quality control at Signetics.

Finally, *implementers* are required to translate lofty visions into reality and ensure that change programs are enacted. They are intimately involved in daily operations, where one of their primary responsibilities is to gain the cooperation of the work force. Typically, implementers operate at the plant or project level; often, they are organized into teams. John Washington, union shop steward of GM's Wilmington plant, and Dick Peltier and Wes Granville, managers of Copeland's Hartselle and Sidney plants, represent individuals playing this role. The MRPII project team at Digital's Augusta plant, with members drawn from finance, engineering services, personnel, MIS, manufacturing, and materials, is representative of the team approach.

Successful implementation requires that all three of these roles be filled. Three separate individuals, however, are not always necessary, because one person may serve in more than one role. Matt Diggs, president and CEO of Copeland, is a dramatic example. During Copeland's earliest experiments with focused factories, he was simultaneously a sponsor (providing resources and high level support), a champion (providing vision and critical inputs to design), and an implementer (providing direction to plant managers on the pacing of each plant start-up).

TOOLS OF THE OPERATING MANAGER

To achieve their goals, operating managers have a number of tools at their disposal. These tools have been on display throughout the course; they are especially visible in this module because the subject is implementation. For convenience, the tools can be grouped into six broad areas: measurement systems, technology, organizational structure, people, leadership signals, and culture.

Measurement systems are necesary for tracking, reporting, and evaluating manufacturing performance. Virtually any category of performance can be assessed, and in recent years a range of new approaches have been developed.[23] Most, however, devote some attention to the traditional goals of quality, cost, and schedule. Quality measurement is discussed in Signetics, where the focus is on the costs of poor quality, and GM, where the focus is on warranty repairs and customer satisfaction. Cost measurement is discussed in Boeing, where the focus is on learning curves and parametric estimates of the cost of the company's next generation plane programs. Schedule measurement is discussed in Boeing and Lehrer McGovern, where the focus is on critical path methods and master phasing plans, and Digital, where the focus is on cycle time reduction.

Technology is a second tool available to operating managers. It offers several advantages: improved productivity, superior quality, greater precision and replicability, and, when some of the newer technologies are used, increased flexibility. Implementation can be difficult, however, because automation and advanced processes normally require changes in operating rules and procedures. GM examines the retrofitting of a conventional automobile assembly plant with robots and automated guided vehicles (AGVs), while Digital examines the installation of a state-of-the-art information system to connect suppliers, customers, and designers directly with the shop floor.

Organization, the third tool available to operating managers, is softer and less tangible than measurement systems or technology. But it is of profound importance. How a company configures its facilities, allocates products to plants, and manages the resulting network is a major part of its operations strategy. The same is true of companies' approaches to new manufacturing initiatives: whether they are led by teams or individuals, what reporting relationships are specified, and how responsibility is divided among line and staff managers. Multi-plant networks and the configuration of facilities are discussed in Lehrer McGovern, Signetics, Digital, and Copeland. Project teams and their role in large-scale development projects are discussed in every case in the module.

People would hardly seem to qualify as a tool of the operating manager, yet they are invaluable in making an operations strategy work. Having the right people in the right positions at the right time is often the key to long-term success. The roles of sponsor, champion, and implementer must be filled, and diverse activities must be performed. All cases in the module—in fact, every case in the course—examine the contributions that people make to operations strategy from such varied positions as president and CEO; vice president or director of R&D, manufacturing, quality, or productivity; plant manager; and line worker.

Even with the best people, clear direction is required. Employees need to know the relative importance of a company's initiatives so that they can focus their energies. Here, the most effective tool is *leadership signals:* the messages that managers send, and employees receive, about the organization's goals and priorities. Such signals take a variety of forms, including written directives, changes in management style, and precedent-setting decisions. At GM's Wilmington plant a powerful message about employee participation came from the plant manager, who allowed a mechanic to overturn his decision to junk an expensive piece of automated equipment; at Copeland the balance of power between manufacturing and marketing shifted dramatically when the CEO rebuffed marketing's request to speed the ramp-up of a new plant. Both examples show the importance of backing words with deeds. According to the chairman of Signetics:

> We realized that if we were going to prove that we meant it when we said quality, we were going to have to put time into it. We knew about the 'managers' apparent interest index,' which says, in effect, 'people watch your feet, not your lips.' If the boss does a lot of preaching, but doesn't invest a lot of hours himself, people see through it.[24]

The sixth tool available to operating managers, which considerably impacts behavior, is *culture*. Culture is part of the fabric of an organization: It reflects tradition, past practice, and the accumulated weight of events. But managers can shift their organization's culture to some degree, or at least partially reshape it. Boeing, for example, has a strong measurement and control culture, while Lehrer McGovern's culture is entrepreneurial and risk-taking. Both would benefit from the other's strengths, and both are moving slowly in that direction. Copeland, through the efforts of its CEO, Matt Diggs, has built a culture committed to focused factories and manufacturing excellence; Chuck Harwood, the CEO of Signetics, is hoping to do the same thing with quality improvement. In both cases culture change was essential because of its pervasive, but often unseen, role in shaping employees' norms, values, and behavior.

Together, these six tools form a powerful arsenal for operating managers. Yet they must be applied thoughtfully and sensitively if the desired ends are to be achieved. Choices must be made about which tools to use, in what sequence, and with what degree of emphasis. These are surprisingly difficult decisions, especially as manufacturing becomes more strategic:

> What is wrong with our factories is that markets and machines have changed while our management routines have not.[25]

The challenge, as never before, is to develop managers who have mastered manufacturing.

NOTES

1. The seminal article is Wickham Skinner, "Manufacturing—Missing Link in Corporate Strategy," *Harvard Business Review,* May–June 1969, pp. 136–145.
2. Wickham Skinner, "What Matters to Manufacturing," *Harvard Business Review,* January–February 1988, p. 16.
3. Paul C. Nutt, "Identifying and Appraising How Managers Install Strategy," *Strategic Management Journal* 8 (1979), p. 9.
4. Paul S. Goodman, "Why Productivity Programs Fail: Reasons and Solutions," *National Productivity Review,* Autumn 1982, pp. 369, 379–380.
5. Jeffrey G. Miller and Margaret B. W. Graham, "Production/Operations Management: Agenda for the '80s," *Decision Sciences,* October 1981, p. 551.
6. For discussions of how to manage change, see Michael Beer, "Managing Change: Beyond Quick Programs," Harvard Business School Working Paper 9-786-016, rev. 1/86, mimeographed; Rosabeth Moss Kanter, "Change Masters and the Intricate Architecture of Corporate Culture Change," *Management Review,* October 1983, pp. 18–28; John P. Kotter and Leonard A. Schlesinger, "Choosing Strategies for Change," *Harvard Business Review,* March–April 1979, pp. 106–114; Paul R. Lawrence, "How to Deal with Resistance to Change," *Harvard Business Review,* January–February 1969, pp. 4–13; and Jay W. Lorsch, "Managing Change," Harvard Business School Case Services 9-474-187, 1974, mimeographed.

7. Thomas V. Bonoma and Victoria C. Crittenden, "Managing Marketing Implementation," *Sloan Management Review*, Winter 1988, p. 13.

8. Kasra Ferdows and Wickham Skinner, "The Sweeping Revolution in Manufacturing," *Journal of Business Strategy*, Fall 1987, p. 69.

9. Thomas G. Gunn, *Manufacturing for Competitive Advantage* (Cambridge, MA: Ballinger, 1987), p. 26. For examples of benchmarks in a single industry, textile manufacturing, see "World Class Manufacturers Cut Labor Needs in Half," *Textile World*, October 1989, pp. 71–72, 75–76.

10. Richard J. Schonberger, *World Class Manufacturing* (New York: Free Press, 1986), p. 2, and Michael J. Stickler, "Going for the Globe, Part I—Assessment," *Target: The Magazine of Manufacturing Performance*, October 1989, pp. S6, S8, S10.

11. Steven C. Wheelwright and Robert H. Hayes, "Competing Through Manufacturing," *Harvard Business Review*, January–February 1985, pp. 99–109, and Elizabeth A. Haas, "Breakthrough Manufacturing," *Harvard Business Review*, March–April 1987, pp. 75–81.

12. Wheelwright and Hayes, "Competing Through Manufacturing," p. 103. See also Kim B. Clark, Robert H. Hayes, and Steven C. Wheelwright, *Dynamic Manufacturing* (New York: Free Press, 1988), pp. 349–355.

13. James Brian Quinn, "Managing Strategic Change," *Sloan Management Review*, Summer 1980, p. 6.

14. Hiroyuki Itami, *Mobilizing Invisible Assets* (Cambridge: Harvard University Press, 1987), p. 151.

15. Roger W. Schmenner, "The Seven Deadly Sins of Manufacturing," in Patricia E. Moody, ed., *Strategic Manufacturing* (Homewood, Illinois: Dow-Jones Irwin, 1990), p. 277.

16. Robert H. Hayes and Steven C. Wheelwright, *Restoring Our Competitive Edge* (New York: John Wiley & Sons, 1984), pp. 382–388.

17. On the links between continuous improvement and incremental progress, see Masaaki Imai, *Kaizen* (New York: Random House, 1986), esp. ch. 1–2, and Kiyoshi Suzaki, *The New Manufacturing Challenge* (New York: Free Press, 1987).

18. David A. Garvin, *Managing Quality* (New York: Free Press, 1988), p. 211.

19. Ibid., pp. 6–12, 25–26, and Richard J. Schonberger, *Japanese Manufacturing Techniques* (New York: Free Press, 1982), pp. 52–53.

20. Schmenner, "The Seven Deadly Sins of Manufacturing," p. 297.

21. Dorothy Leonard-Barton and William A. Kraus, "Implementing New Technology," *Harvard Business Review*, November–December 1985, pp. 102–110, and Thomas J. Peters and Robert H. Waterman, *In Search of Excellence* (New York: Harper & Row, 1982), pp. 208–209. Leonard-Barton and Kraus actually suggest that four roles are necessary, rather than three: sponsors, champions, project managers, and integrators. But because the latter two categories frequently overlap, they have been grouped here under the single term, implementers.

22. Kanter, "Change Masters and the Intricate Architecture of Corporate Culture Change," p. 23.

23. Robert S. Kaplan, ed., *Measures for Manufacturing Excellence* (Boston: Harvard Business School Press, 1990).

24. Charles C. Harwood, "The View from the Top," *Quality Progress*, October 1984, p. 28.

25. Skinner, "What Matters to Manufacturing," p. 16.

31. Building on the Past

For a half-century, General Motors Corporation hardly modernized its Baltimore manufacturing plant. In 1983, the facility's nine-millionth vehicle rolled off the same sort of assembly line that had produced its first in 1935. Almost every bolt, weld and paint stroke was applied manually by people who, in many cases, were descendants of the plant's original work force.

For GM, the benefits of automation never seemed worth the costly closing needed for a retrofit, says Herbert Leitz, regional manager of six GM truck and bus plants. After all, he reasons, an assembly line is like a printing press churning out currency: "If you don't print money, you don't make money."

Last year, continued pressure from highly automated Japanese competitors finally persuaded GM to modernize the plant. But the automaker's $270 million game plan presented engineers and technologists with a confounding challenge: to rebuild, retool and rethink the manufacturing process, but keep the aging assembly line moving.

To complete the task, GM retained hundreds of imaginative and technologically proficient outside contractors, known as industry cowboys, to supervise the redesign and reconstruction of the plant. As the plant was being rebuilt around them, workers kept the assembly line running for all but four months of the 23-month retrofit. And

when the resulting "factory of the future" began turning out GM's new Safari and Chevrolet Astro minivans in September, it was crowned GM's ideal of retrofit ingenuity.

The massive project runs counter to the conventional wisdom that to truly reap the benefits of technology, manufacturers must build new plants from scratch. It also proves that an auto plant can operate despite the intrusion of a 1,500-person retrofit team. And though it may take years to discern all the benefits and drawbacks, the project could prove to be an industry bench mark. Competing manufacturers have made pilgrimages here—joining public tours of the plant—as they struggle with their own decisions to revitalize or scrap old plants.

Meanwhile, the plant remains fraught with unsettling problems. Engineers grapple with the logistics of keeping robots, computers and human hands in sync. Some workers claim that GM may have over-automated, giving robots some jobs that people can do better. And production often is slowed by workers' unfamiliarity with new equipment, a sign of insufficient training.

"GM can afford to buy all the new technology on earth, but the problem is putting people together with the process," says Steven Miller, a Carnegie-Mellon University professor who has monitored the project. "This takes expertise and experience that they can only acquire a day at a time with lots of mistakes."

GM agrees that a robot is only as good as the worker standing next to it. That is why the reputation of a potential work force was a prime consideration in 1982 when GM scouted 17 sites for its minivan modernization project. "There are places where the labor climate is such that even if you could save $500 million, you wouldn't go there," says Mr. Leitz.

Built in 1935, the Baltimore plant prospered for decades by turning out Oldsmobiles, Pontiacs, and Chevrolet cars and trucks and during World War II, military parts. Recognized by GM for quality, workmanship and efficiency, the plant's employees also were noted for having few work stoppages. Their last strike was in 1970.

At its peak in 1976, the plant turned out about 1,000 cars and 400 trucks a day and employed 7,000 people. But by the early 1980s, demand for its products—the mid-sized Pontiac Bonneville and Grand Prix, and the Chevy Monte Carlo and Malibu—had softened with the recession and rising gasoline prices.

By 1982, about 4,000 of the plant's workers were laid off, several models of the mid-sized cars were set to be phased out, and GM was considering closing the entire facility. "Some of our people are the third generation working here," says Walter Gregonis, the plant manager. "How could we walk away from a plant like this after 50 years?"

Desperate for a product, the Baltimore plant's joint union-management task force, backed by city and state officials, went to GM's top brass to bid for the minivan project. The task force knew that some within the company favored building the modern minivan plant from the ground up, known as the green-field approach. "In a green-field, you aren't dictated by building constraints, so you can create efficiency," says Earl Shiflett, the plant's engineering administrator.

But the Baltimore plant sold itself on its workers' reliability—which couldn't be assured by a green-field project in a new community—and its vow to keep the assembly line moving during a retrofit. GM gave the outdated plant the nod.

Chrysler Corporation, Toyota Motor Corporation, and Volkswagen of America, Inc., already had beaten GM into the booming market for minivans, which offer passengers the space of station wagons and the cargo capacity of larger vans. But after spending $330 million for research and development, GM was convinced that the minivan was no short-lived fad. "In the year 2000, we'll still be building these vans," predicts Ernest

Vahala, director of manufacturing engineering for GM's truck and bus group.

Retrofitting Baltimore for minivan production began in September 1982. One problem: originally designed for manual assembly of 1935 cars, some of the plant's ceilings weren't high enough to fit automated equipment and had to be lifted, sometimes by helicopters. As autoworkers rubbed elbows with the retrofit team, GM built temporary ceilings and safety walls around the assembly line.

Had the plant been designed in green-field style, it would have been built in a long, one-story rectangular shape with high ceilings so the assembly lines could be efficient straight-aways. But to accommodate the boxy two-story Baltimore plant, designers had to fashion winding, roller-coaster-like assembly lines. Still GM says that the retrofit was cheaper and faster than building a green-field plant, and that it avoided such tasks as installing sewer and power systems.

Throughout the retrofit, the auto maker depended on outside contractors because GM engineers are often too busy keeping outdated facilities running to stay abreast of new technology. "GM is a multi-billion-dollar operation, but it still needs little guys like me to get through these projects," says Clifton Schmult, president of CS Systems & Design, Inc., Rogers City, Michigan. "As an independent contractor, I've been involved in many different plants and I've kept up with changing technology."

In Baltimore, Mr. Schmult helped oversee installation of the electronic communication system connecting robots, automated equipment and a host computer. There were well over 500 electricians on the job. "For every minute you're inspecting something, 100 men are creating something new to be inspected," he says.

Some GM engineers were reluctant to implement outsiders' ideas. Mr. Schmult says he had to convince GM that the plant didn't need a mechanical backup plan for certain computer systems. "They had little faith in the new electronics, because in their infancy stage these things weren't reliable," he says. "But products evolve. They get better."

In March 1984, GM closed the assembly line for four months of round-the-clock construction by an expanded 2,600-person retrofit team. GM's autoworkers, meanwhile, attended retraining classes to learn work processes, 90% of which were totally new. The classes were also geared to win acceptance of automation. "Our (seat) cushion room had 60 people who had been together for 20 or 30 years," says Mr. Gregonis, the plant manager. "Now they'd be scattered around the plant. It was traumatic."

GM acknowledges that it should have provided more hands-on-training, but some aspects of automation were untrainable. "You can't simulate top-line speed," says Thomas Schneck, the plant's controller. Indeed, when the assembly line started up the following September, test minivans crawled from station to station. Automated equipment and 48 robots handled 95% of the 3,019 welds on each van, once a totally manual process.

But there were glitches: like the gang that couldn't shoot straight, the robot arms bashed into steel where they expected windows and "welded in places where there wasn't even material," says Arden McConnell, director of plant engineering.

Many workers had trouble adjusting to robots. "In the manual system, if material was slightly off, guys on the line could push and bang and keep it moving," says Mr. Miller of Carnegie-Mellon. "In the automated system, if parts aren't exactly right, the machines jam. And workers can't talk to machines like they would their buddies. The only way to communicate is through computer terminals."

Richard Andrews, an electrician, found that making mistakes was the only way to learn. "I wrecked a lot of jobs," he says. He also discovered the hazards of keeping workers exactly in tune with tireless robots. "If a guy yawns, you lose a second of cycle time," which could disrupt the whole system, he explains.

GM admits that its start-up was slower than it had expected. Though the plant now produces 700 vans a day, it turned out just 40 vans in its first three months. Equipment downtime has plagued the plant, but GM says it can weather "hiccups" in productivity until its current work force of 4,200 masters the technology.

A few welding chores were returned to humans after GM couldn't get the bugs out of its robot welders. But mostly, GM says, it has found the plant's technology to be startling in its efficiency. A computerized system, for example, for the first time bends exhaust pipes right on the assembly line. This allows each pipe to be $1\frac{3}{4}$ inches shorter than it was by traditional methods, saving $1 million a year in material alone, GM says.

To cut carpeting for the vans, GM compresses water and speeds it through a tube the width of a needle, making it a razor-sharp cutting tool. Before, the plant couldn't handle its own cutting and bore the expense of storing 50 combinations of cut carpets to accommodate various seating and stick-shift arrangement. Also, by hooking up outside suppliers to its computers, GM receives car seats or dashboards to exact color and options specifications just hours before they will be installed in vans. This "just in time" shipping, pioneered in Japan, keeps storage costs down and allows defective parts to be replaced quickly.

GM is proudest of what it calls "the world's first 100% robotic paint shop." Seven robots can spray the inside and outside of a van in 3.6 minutes. Programmed for any of 65 different "paint dances" for various van models, the robots win praise for their consistently high quality. "Regardless of how conscientious a man is, when he sprays a door opening all day long, his back and wrist get tired and he doesn't paint as well," says Mr. McConnell, the plant engineer.

United Auto Workers Local 239, which represents the plant's hourly workers, says it approved of robots replacing employees in such "undesirable" jobs as the paint shop, where workers had to wear protective hoods and masks. The union also appreciates that the vans ride through the cleaner, quieter plant at eye level, so workers no longer have to stand in trenches to work on the underside of vehicles.

Although robots do the work of 500 to 1,000 people, the union recognizes that the modernization project literally saved the plant. And because the minivan is more complicated to build than cars, GM actually called back about 700 laid-off workers.

But David Wolff, the local's president, warns, "You can only go so far with high technology, or there won't be enough people earning money to buy cars. At some point, you have to slow down on automation to preserve jobs." But he adds that if automation turns out a better product and increases GM's sales, the auto maker could increase its output and "that's job security for us."

Indeed, GM says customer-comment cards on the new minivans are among the most favorable the auto maker has ever received. Jack Summers, the plant's personnel director, recalls one card that he particularly appreciated:

"One buyer wrote back and asked, 'Are you sure this van wasn't made in Japan?'"

32. Digital Equipment Corporation: The Endpoint Model (A)

In October 1986, Paul Stevens, the Distributed Systems Manufacturing (DSM) Group manufacturing manager at Digital Equipment Corporation, reflected on the activities of the past 18 months:

> It's difficult to manage change in a successful company. Doing things differently is not natural behavior. Old habits die hard. And most employees want to see results indicating that change is "the right thing to do" before offering their full commitment.

In April 1985, Stevens had been assigned responsibility for the DSM group, including support engineering, value engineering, purchasing, and all manufacturing activities across three plants. Within months his staff had developed a new manufacturing strategy—called the EndPoint model—and had launched a wave of new programs to implement the strategy. Now that the programs were well underway, Stevens wanted to review the group's progress and identify the challenges that remained.

The Company: Its History and Product Strategy

In 1986, Digital Equipment Corporation (DEC) was the world's second largest manufacturer of computer systems, with revenues of $7.6 billion and 94,700 employees. Founded in 1957 by Kenneth Olsen, an MIT engineer, DEC had changed the way that people computed by introducing the first inexpensive minicomputer, the PDP-8. Before DEC, all computers were mainframes, housed in special centers, and used to process large batches of data. DEC's small, rugged machines allowed scientists and engineers to computerize a variety of routine tasks such as machining, typesetting, and medical scanning. The widespread use of minicomputing helped lay the groundwork for the personal computer revolution.

In 1979, Digital's chief engineers won approval to develop a new generation of superminicomputers, based on a single computer architecture called VAX. Ranging from small desk-top machines to computer clusters that could compete with mainframes, the proposed VAX-based machines would be fully compatible, use uniform operating system software, and communicate across shared networks. This product strategy differed from the then standard industry practice of developing different computer architectures and software systems for different sizes and classes of computers. According to DEC's engineers, the new VAX-based computers would enable customers to build computer networks of almost any size and scope, from a few desk-top systems linked by a single cable within the same room, to ones involving hundreds of large, powerful computers spread throughout a global organization. "The concept was very simple," said Olsen, "but there were billions of dollars involved in doing it."[1]

This case was prepared by Janet Simpson under the direction of David A. Garvin.

[1] P. Fuhrman, "Brickbats into Roses," *Forbes,* September 22, 1986, p. 160.

Networks soon became a cornerstone of Digital's corporate mission. According to Olsen:

> Our goal is to connect all parts of an organization—the office, the factory floor, the laboratory, the engineering department—from the desk-top to the data center. We can connect everything within a building; we can connect a group of buildings on the same site or at remote sites; we can connect an entire organization around the world. We propose to connect a company from top to bottom with a single network that includes the shipping clerk, the secretary, the manager, the vice president, even the president.[2]

In Digital's pursuit of this vision, the Distributed Systems Manufacturing group, which made DEC's network products, was a key player.

The Manufacturing Organization

In 1986, Digital's manufacturing function employed 28,800 people in 108 sites worldwide. DEC's products were manufactured by one of six groups: Computer Systems Manufacturing (CSM) produced mid-range and large VAX-based systems; Small Systems Manufacturing (SSM) made microVAX systems, work stations, and personal computers; Storage Systems Manufacturing (STORAGE), produced tapes, disks, and diskdrives; Low End Systems and Technologies (LEST) made printed circuit boards, terminals and printers; and GIA and EUROPE produced a combination of systems and options for European and other markets.

DISTRIBUTED SYSTEMS MANUFACTURING (DSM). DSM, part of the Computer Systems Manufacturing Group, manufactured 500 line items including local area network[3] and communications products, modems, expander cabs, and power controllers. DSM employed 1100 people in four design centers, one central business organization, and three manufacturing plants located in Maine, Ireland, and Puerto Rico.

[2] Digital Equipment Corporation, 1986 Annual Report, p. 3.

[3] A local area network (LAN) is a data communications link over an inexpensive carrier (generally coaxial cable or twisted pair wire) that acts as an intra- or inter-premise electronic highway to transport information among communication devices such as office automation equipment, microcomputers, and peripherals. Digital's LAN is called DECnet Ethernet.

Historically, DSM was not a significant part of Digital's revenue stream; its traditional products were shipped to 6 DEC plants in an arrangement that one manager likened to "supplying transmissions for cars." But by 1986, DSM's network products were also being sold directly to original equipment manufacturers (OEMs), end users and distributors. The growth of internal and independent demand for DSM's products boosted 1986 revenues by 32%, to several hundred million dollars. DSM's revenues were projected to grow 60% more in 1987, and double again by 1989.

DSM's Manufacturing Strategy

In April 1985, Stevens and Jeff Lockwood, the business planning manager, met to discuss DSM's five-year business plan. At the time, DSM's charter was to become the high-quality, low-cost supplier of network and communications products worldwide. DSM had also been given ambitious business goals: to double ROA and improve margins by 10 percentage points over the next five years. "Such goals," said Stevens, "could not be achieved through incremental changes." He continued:

> We were not currently under competitive pressure to make changes in our manufacturing strategy. But we recognized that we had a leadership position in networks and a two- to three-year window of opportunity before IBM and others entered the market. We wanted to capitalize on that advantage.

To develop their manufacturing strategy, DSM managers assessed future customer requirements, the activities of competitors, and advances in manufacturing process technology and business systems.

CUSTOMER REQUIREMENTS. Over the next five years, DSM's customers were expected to become more demanding in the areas of quality and product performance. Equally important, they were expected to require DSM to respond quickly and predictably to changing product needs. Stevens explained:

> A *minimum* requirement for future success was the ability to supply high quality products that met customers' performance requirements.

Customers were also likely to demand responsiveness from suppliers in the form of just-in-time purchasing. "Ease of doing business" was expected to become increasingly important in vendor selection.

DSM managers realized that future customer demands could not be met without reducing their manufacturing cycle time—the time from vendor shipment of parts and materials to customer delivery of finished products. In 1985, DSM's cycle time averaged 40 weeks.

COMPETITIVE ANALYSIS. DSM staff reviewed what other manufacturers were doing to reduce cycle time through co-location of vendors or more sophisticated process technologies. They identified three approaches:

(a) the "GM model": large centralized production facilities with vendors required to locate nearby;
(b) the "generic industry" model: decentralized production facilities co-located near suppliers; and
(c) the "IBM model": a centralized, highly automated, vertically integrated facility in which computer-aided manufacturing methods were employed.

According to Stevens:

> To remain competitive, we knew that DSM had to link closely all elements of supply, manufacturing, and sales without centralizing operations. But none of the models we identified was a good fit with our three geographically dispersed plants and 2,000 suppliers. So, we came up with the idea of "virtual integration," in which our plants, vendors, engineering staff, and customers would remain geographically dispersed, but would be "virtually integrated" through networked systems.

This "virtually integrated" model—a multiplant computer-integrated manufacturing system connected by networks to vendors and customers—represented DSM's vision of its future. Within the DSM plants, networked systems would gather, track, and route information among members of the purchasing, marketing, finance, design, and manufacturing departments. New or updated product designs would be transferred automatically from engineering to production planning,

EXHIBIT 1 DSM EndPoint Model–Virtual Integrated Manufacturing

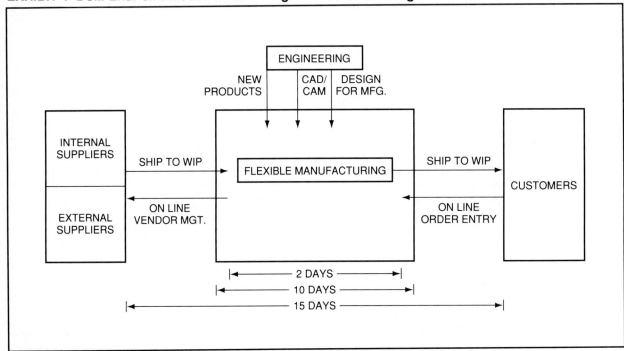

while flexible manufacturing systems[4] on the factory floor would automate manufacturing processes and material handling. Externally, customers and vendors would be connected on-line with the plants, exchanging order information and, in some cases, production schedules and plans. DSM managers called this "virtually integrated" system the EndPoint model. (*Exhibit 1.*)

The EndPoint Model

Instituting and operationalizing the EndPoint model became the goal of DSM's five-year business plan. The planning staff also reviewed DSM's manufacturing process to establish a cycle time target for the EndPoint model.

THE MANUFACTURING PROCESS. In 1985, DSM's manufacturing cycle had four major stages: component test and burn-in (6-8 weeks), module assembly (20 weeks), systems integration (6-8 weeks), and distribution (6 weeks).

Component Test and Burn-In. Components from vendors were not shipped directly to DSM's plants. Instead, they were first delivered to a centralized testing facility for 100% inspection. A stress test, called burn-in, was used to screen out key components that would fail in the field. Inventory and test time totaled 6 to 8 weeks.

Module Assembly. After passing the test and burn-in process, components were shipped to one of three DSM plants for printed circuit board assembly. Inventory and in-process assembly at the plants accounted for 20 weeks of cycle time.

Systems Integration. The printed circuit boards not incorporated into stand-alone units were shipped to one of two facilities for systems test with a CPU system. Systems integration added 6 to 8 weeks to cycle time.

Distribution. Customer orders were consolidated at one of three distribution warehouses. In 1985, these warehouses contained 6 weeks of inventory.

CYCLE TIME TARGET. Through inventory reductions, automation, and computer integration of functional tasks, DSM planners estimated that cycle time could be reduced to 15 days by 1990.

[4] Flexible manufacturing systems (FMS) are often considered to be the building blocks of total factory automation. An FMS may include robotics, numerically controlled machines, tool-changing systems, and material handling systems.

(*Exhibit 2.*) The 15-day total included two days for receipt of raw materials; 10 days to build the product in-plant (of which only 2 days was work-in-process); and three days for systems integration and shipment to customers.

DSM's managers believed that the key to achieving the 15-day target was improving information accuracy and velocity—the care and speed with which information was exchanged. One manager explained:

> An internal study found that 75% of the transactions done in manufacturing were information transactions, such as compiling numbers from different reports; the remaining 25% were material transactions. It was clear that in the long run, information velocity, not material velocity, would determine how close we could get vendors and customers to lie within the same "box" in the EndPoint model.

In this area, senior managers felt that DSM had a strong competitive advantage. One of them explained:

> There are two pieces to the integration of a manufacturing system. The first piece is the hardware—the computer equipment and networks. Unlike many of our competitors, DSM is already very integrated from a hardware perspective. Because of this, we can focus on the second piece of systems integration: integrating the data and information that flows over the network.

The EndPoint Plan

The DSM planning group developed a five year timeline of programs and activities to achieve the EndPoint model and reduce cycle time to 15 days. (*Exhibit 3.*) The plan focused on integrating four elements:

(a) *systems information and management tools,* including software and computer-aided design;

(b) *control,* measured by progress toward achieving build-to-order capabilities;

(c) *physical manufacturing processes,* such as automated material handling systems and local area networks, which impacted both the material and information flow on the factory floor; and

(d) *programs and philosophies,* such as customer/vendor partnerships and work force reskilling.

EXHIBIT 2 Cycle Time Reduction Model

	Test and Burn-In	Board Assembly	Systems Integration	Distribution Warehouses	Total Cycle Time
ORIGINAL MANUFACTURING CYCLE TIME	6–8 weeks	20 weeks	6–8 weeks	6 weeks	40 weeks
STEP 1. • Move warehouse inventory from all distribution points and field offices to manufacturing location				(5 weeks)	35 weeks
STEP 2. • Develop Ethernet set of products which do not require systems integration • Develop quality certification at board level to eliminated need to test at systems level • Eliminate inventory holdings as hedges for delivery performance	(5 weeks)		(6–8 weeks)		23 weeks
STEP 3. • Eliminate component test of incoming materials • Eliminate kitting; pull to WIP • Achieve Class A, MRPII; reduce safety stock, WIP FGI; eliminate receiving inspection	(8 days)	(10 weeks)		(2 days)	11 weeks
STEP 4. • Eliminate safety stock • Reduce cycle time through automation		(5 weeks)			6 weeks
STEP 5. • Eliminate finished goods inventory; build to order		(3 weeks)			3 weeks
ENDPOINT	2 days	10 days	0 days	3 days	15 days

Note: A step does not have to be fully completed before the following step is begun.

32. Digital Equipment Corporation: The Endpoint Model (A)

EXHIBIT 3 The EndPoint Plan

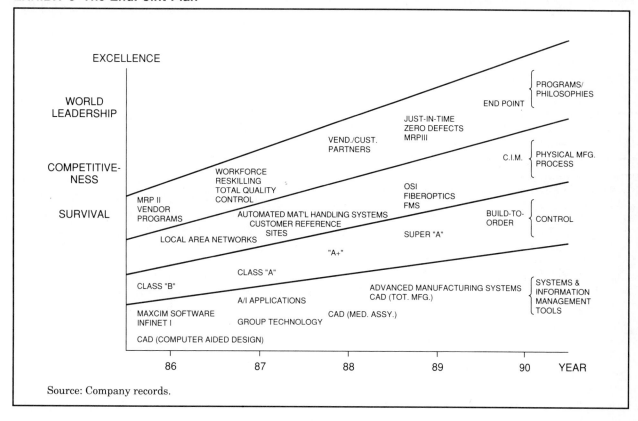

Source: Company records.

The EndPoint plan sequenced the programs required, at both the plant and group levels, to systematically reduce cycle time. Vendor partnerships, managed at the group level, would address raw material procurement time and cost. Programs at the plant level, such as Manufacturing Resource Planning (MRPII), Just-in-Time (JIT), and Total Quality Control (TQC) would reduce product-in-process time. And pilot studies regarding information velocity would be conducted by the group staff, supported by corporate manufacturing development funds.

Many of these programs were not new to DSM's plants. In fact, the plants had been working on a variety of projects to reduce manufacturing cycle time. But, according to Stevens:

> We had islands of automation in the factories—tactical solutions, not strategic solutions. We didn't understand how facilities, process technology and people could work together synergistically. The EndPoint plan pulled these efforts together.

Manufacturing Resource Planning (MRPII)

Several programs in the EndPoint plan were launched or underway in 1985; the first milestone was for DSM to become certified as a Class A, MRPII manufacturer.[5] MRPII, a computer-supported planning and scheduling system that links a firm's business, operating, and financial systems, was thought to be a necessary first step because of the tight integration it imposed. MRPII requires that all departments use the same set of numbers; it therefore provides management with a tool for monitoring performance throughout the manufacturing process. Users of MRPII systems are rated from "Class A" to "Class D." Class A

[5] For a more complete explanation of MRPII, see *A Note on Manufacturing Resource Planning (MRPII)*, HBS Case Services 9-687-097.

firms use MRPII as a companywide game plan for sales, finance, manufacturing, purchasing, and engineering; Class D companies have the system working only at the data processing level.

To achieve Class A status, discipline in decision-making is required. MRPII integrates a firm's financial and sales plans with the constraints imposed by delivery or design lead times and plant capacity. An effective MRPII system therefore requires accountability in demand forecasts by product line, accurate inventory records, and careful planning and schedule maintenance. At DSM, MRPII was considered essential for just these reasons. Stevens explained:

> DEC's dramatic growth had historically depended on and rewarded those behaviors tied to informal systems such as expediting. MRPII forces functional executives to come together monthly to develop the production plan. It's a tough discussion. But management discipline is essential if the EndPoint model is to be achieved.

In June 1985, seven plant managers in the Computer Systems Manufacturing (CSM) Group signed a statement in which they agreed to achieve a Class A rating by June 1986. DSM's plant in Augusta, Maine was one of the seven plants. Carl Porter, Augusta's plant manager, recalled, "If there was one goal that we were determined to reach in 1986, it was Class A status."

MRPII: The Augusta Plant

By June 1985, the Augusta plant had been working on manufacturing systems and software integration for two years. The plant had a variety of computer-supported systems in place, including a shop floor control system, called Infinet, used to schedule and track orders released to the production floor, and a material requirements planning system, called MC-10, used to schedule and order materials. Each of these systems was a discrete entity, using software tailored to the needs of a single functional area. The result, according to one materials manager, was a disjointed information flow:

> We had sophisticated systems that never talked to one another. As a result, most of the time the functional organizations were trying to

second guess what others were doing. For example, suppose there was a need to build 1000 units. Production control (PC) might decide to order 1100 units, because they didn't always get what they wanted from material control. Material control might think, "PC never gets their forecasts straight; I know they'll ask for more." So, they might add 20% to the PC request. Purchasing would then receive a request to order material for 1300 units, 300 more than required. Such "just-in-case" scenarios were common because the original need was never visible at the back-end of the system.

Systems differences were as significant among the CSM plants. One manager noted, for example, that although all CSM materials organizations used the MC-10 software, "each system had been customized to the point that no two looked alike." Thus an MRPII system, based on uniform software, would not only allow all functional areas within a plant to work with a common set of numbers, but would also, if required, allow all seven plants to share information.

MRPII Implementation

Porter selected an experienced materials manager, Jerry Sabel, to spearhead the MRPII implementation. At Porter's request, Sabel became a regular participant in Augusta's senior management staff meetings. Sabel's MRPII project team included representatives from finance, engineering services, personnel, MIS, manufacturing, and materials.

PERFORMANCE METRICS. Sabel and the six MRPII program managers (one from each plant) established 13 performance metrics to measure progress toward meeting Class A requirements. (*Exhibit 4.*) Each metric was a measure of business, scheduling, planning, or record accuracy. For example, the sales plan was evaluated by measuring the accuracy of forecasts by product line; the master schedule, by comparing scheduled units to units completed; and purchasing, by the on-time delivery record of vendors. An average total score of 90% for two consecutive months was required to become certified as a Class A manufacturer.

SOFTWARE SELECTION. The software selected for the MRPII system was called MAXCIM, a

EXHIBIT 4 MRPII: DMS's 13 Performance Metrics

Measurement of:	MRPII Component:	Performance Metrics:
Top Management Planning	1. Business Planning 2. Sales Plan 3. Production Plan	Return on Assets Sales Plan Accuracy Validity of Production Plan
Plant Performance	4. Master Schedule 5. Material Plan 6. Capacity Plan	Master Schedule Planning Reschedule Reliability Plan Capacity Properly
Database Accuracy	7. Bills of Material 8. Inventory Control 9. Routings	Accurate Bills of Material Inventory Record Accuracy Routings Accuracy
Plant Execution	10. Material Acquisition 11. Shop Floor Control 12. Schedule Performance 13. Order Execution	Schedule Performance Schedule Performance Customer Satisfaction Executable Orders

Source: Company records.

closed-loop manufacturing system which has production planning and master scheduling capabilities as well as the elements required to generate financial figures, marketing forecasts and engineering plans. MAXCIM also provides management with tools to monitor schedules and plans.

At Augusta, the conversion to MAXCIM was targeted for January 1986. During the summer of 1985, 22 individuals were trained on the MAXCIM system. These employees, in turn, conducted MAXCIM training sessions in each functional area. By 1986, the 600 Augusta plant employees had received 68,000 hours of training. But one manager recalled:

> Some people didn't take the training to heart. It was difficult getting them to see that this was more than a materials system—that they, and their jobs, were part of a plantwide system rather than an isolated entity.

In January 1986, the MAXCIM system was installed. The plant had prepared for the conversion by stockpiling two weeks of finished goods inventory and creating manual back-up systems for each functional area's computer-supported activities. One team member explained the scope of the task:

> To change an operating system means that you essentially rip out the guts of the plant and replace it. All of the knowledge accumulated over the years ceases to exist. Despite our best efforts, we underestimated the magnitude of the task.

One crisis arose over unfilled purchase orders. MAXCIM required a purchase order format that was not compatible with Augusta's old system. Thus, all outstanding purchase orders had to be reentered into the MAXCIM system. Buyers were moved to the receiving floor to help manage receiving. Temporary clerical help was hired to input the new data. "We almost buckled under the strain of the data input alone," one team member recalled.

When plant performance was evaluated at the end of January, the Augusta plant's metrics averaged 80%, up from 65% the prior year. To further focus attention on achieving Class A requirements, a 4' × 8' board was installed in the Augusta cafeteria, listing the name of the plant staff member responsible for each of the 13 performance metrics, and an updated weekly score. Porter's name appeared next to the business performance metric.

MRPII: DSM Group Materials Management

In addition to the activities at the Augusta plant, DSM's group materials staff focused on developing accurate sales projections for each of DSM's product lines. David Chandler, the group materials manager, explained:

> We could not attain a Class A rating or performance without accurate product forecasts. It is these forecasts that drive manufacturing to allocate resources, order material, and have labor available to produce and ship to plan.

> Because DEC is a systems company, sales were projected by computer systems, not units of network products. To obtain the level of detail required for MRPII, we had to broaden our role in manufacturing and develop a detailed sales plan for DSM's network products.

In 1985, most of DSM's products were sold internally to 6 DEC systems plants. Because network products were a small portion of the total cost of computer systems, these plants maintained high inventory levels of DSM's products and often ordered more than needed to meet systems production requirements. In 1985, DSM took back all of its products inventoried at the systems plants. Chandler recalled:

> The plants were assured that they would get products when they ordered them. They were only too happy to give up their inventory—in some cases they had as much as several years' supply. Stevens and Porter took the hit in their numbers.

According to DSM managers, this action gave DSM more control over internal demands for its products. But it also put additional pressure on the group materials department to improve product forecast accuracy. As one manager explained, "You can't hold up the sale of a computer system because you've run out of a relatively inexpensive network component."

Chandler's staff thus turned to the more difficult problem of translating corporate sales projections in dollars to units of network products by product line. Unpredictable sales growth and new product introductions made the task challenging. To clarify sales demand, the group materials staff held frequent meetings with customers and attended a weekly forum with product management, marketing, and manufacturing. Chandler commented:

> We had to do a lot of education within DEC to overcome the perception that we were the "poor cousin," the Class "C" component supplier. In the past, that attitude had created situations where Porter and the plant frequently had to respond to last-minute requests for network products. With MRPII, the sales plan had to be frozen 13 weeks prior to the beginning of each quarter.

From these meetings, the group materials staff developed a sales plan by product family type. This unit sales plan was then converted to a production plan for the three DSM plants. The group materials staff met formally with the plants on a monthly basis and reviewed the numbers weekly. Changes were made as needed, usually once per week.

According to Chandler, MRPII changed the focus of DSM's group materials management:

> Historically, we focused on obsolescence and inventory. Now we're concerned with sales, marketing, product planning and pipeline planning.

But the formality of the MRPII system changed Chandler's normal operating style. He observed:

> In the past, if sales exceeded plan, I could call Porter and ask him to expedite 20,000 more units. With MRPII, I lose two to three weeks of time working through the formal system. Initially, MRPII looked like it was there to get in the way. But the informal system didn't show the trauma that people at the plant went through. And from a business perspective, my request actually might have hurt the company, causing us to lose a sale from another customer. With MRPII, you make the trade-offs explicitly.

Chandler also noted that MRPII added accountability to the sales planning process:

> MRPII took informality and finger-pointing and formalized it. If the manufacturing facility builds to plan and the plan is not accurate, it's not the plant manager's fault. With MRPII, you understand the boundaries. Still, no one liked the discipline.

In May 1986, the Augusta metrics averaged 90% for the first time. In June, the plant achieved its Class A rating. Porter observed:

> Implementing MRPII is like trying to run a four-minute mile. You start at 5.5 minutes, then 5.4, 5.3, and so on. Each step gets harder and harder to achieve. We consider Class A to be our first step. There are many more beyond it.

Other DSM Programs

By the fall of 1986, several additional programs had been launched to move DSM toward the EndPoint model.

INFORMATION VELOCITY. In 1986, the DSM group staff received corporate manufacturing development funds to conduct pilot studies for improving information velocity. While some of these studies focused on the mechanics of data integration, such as developing a data highway, others were concerned with improving information flow. One project, for example, aimed to reduce inefficiencies in DSM's production planning process. Two industrial engineers were assigned to evaluate the process from product forecast through order generation to identify inefficient methods, meetings or procedures, and make recommendations for corrective action. The staff intended to apply the methodology and lessons learned from this pilot project to all information-intensive processes at DSM.

THE PARTNERSHIP PROGRAM. The DSM group staff also launched a partnership program with several key vendors/customers. Ellen Phillips, DSM's external ventures business manager, explained the purpose of the partnership program:

> Our goal is to work together to implement programs that achieve excellence in manufacturing performance—thereby reducing cycle times and improving the quality of our business.

By the fall of 1986, DSM staff had approached five firms with the intention of creating a partnership arrangement. These firms had been selected from DSM's vendors and customer base after an exhaustive screening process. All potential candidates were rated using two lists of selection criteria: *descriptive criteria,* including geographic location, relationship with DSM (vendor, OEM or customer), and use of diverse computer equipment; and *evaluative criteria,* which were weighted more heavily, including Class A MRPII status, advanced product manufacturing (i.e., a producer of high-tech products), and excellence in human resource management. Information came from DEC's customer account managers, purchasing managers, and published sources such as annual reports and the trade press.

After narrowing the list to five candidates, DSM staff worked with DEC's account managers to customize programs for each firm. During initial meetings with the firms, the staff shared DSM's EndPoint plan and the objectives of the partnership program. Phillips explained:

> We knew that vendors almost could not say "No" to DEC, because of our leverage with them. However, our intent was to work on issues that would be mutually beneficial. In the past, we gave vendors a performance report; now we wanted them to give us one.

To lend credibility to the program, DSM agreed to give the vendors product forecasts on a monthly basis so that they could plan their production runs accordingly. DSM further agreed to finance a review of its specifications, at a cost of $250,000. In return, vendors were expected over the long term to improve delivery time while working with DSM to reduce total cost.

The partnership program was not without risk. Phillips explained:

> These firms are also five of DSM's top ten customers, so our credibility is at risk if we don't follow through. Short term, we are also asking our people to expose themselves while implementing changes in our manufacturing practices; the partners will see us making mistakes. But the risks are worthwhile. Without a strong partnership program, we will not meet the goals of the EndPoint model. In the short run, the issue is survival. In the long run, it is world class performance.

TOWARD THE ENDPOINT. Once MRPII was in place, DSM launched three complementary programs to reduce manufacturing cycle times: *CIM* (Computer-Integrated Manufacturing), which focused on information collection and control; *TQC* (Total Quality Control), which had as its goal zero defects in both product and information quality; and *JIT* (Just-In-Time), which focused on eliminating waste and reducing inventories to zero.

CIM. In the spring of 1986, while group staff members studied data integration among DSM's plants, a CIM project team was assembled in Augusta to focus on data and information integration within the plant. The MAXCIM software gave each functional area a common tool for planning and scheduling, but it was not able to collect data, such as direct labor hours or machine output, on a real-time basis. That capability would be required to support a just-in-time manufacturing process. The CIM team's goal was to develop a communication vehicle consisting of networks, standards, and a common database, that would allow managers to collect data in real-time and would provide all functional areas with access to the data in the format required.

TQC. In the fall of 1986, a Total Quality Control (TQC) program, which focused on improving both product and data quality, was also on the launching pad. Historically, DSM's product quality was monitored by macro-measures such as AQLs (acceptable quality levels), and reliability (mean time between failures). Vendor quality was assessed by incoming inspection. The TQC program's objectives were to attain zero defects in products and information, and establish a "ship to WIP" relationship with vendors.

JIT. Reducing lot sizes, shortening lead times, and eliminating safety stock were essential if DSM was going to meet its 15-day cycle time target. In the fall of 1986, the Augusta plant staff was involved in a fact-finding and educational

EXHIBIT 5 DSM's Performance

	FY84	FY85	EndPoint Model		
			FY86 (ytd)	FY87 (forecast)	FY88
Revenue Growth (%/yr.)	NA	26%	32%	54%	70%
Revenue/Person Growth (%/yr.)	NA	28%	19%	26%	68%
Revenue/Square Foot Growth (%/yr.)	NA	26%	31%	56%	59%
Inventory/Revenue Dollar	$0.28	$0.33	$0.15	$0.15	$0.07
New Products Shipped	6	6	3	11	25

NA = not applicable.

Source: Company records.

32. Digital Equipment Corporation: The Endpoint Model (A)

process aimed at understanding the JIT concept. At DSM, MRPII was envisioned as the vehicle for moving toward a just-in-time production process. Stevens explained:

> MRPII provides the complete information needed to run a quality manufacturing operation. But the system does not question manufacturing lead times, lot sizes, queues, or safety stocks. By tightening the requirements for MRPII performance metrics while making physical changes in our manufacturing processes, we can set goals for continuous improvement. For example, today we consider a vendor delivery to be on time if it is shipped within three days of schedule. In 1987, on-time delivery will mean within one day of due date. In 1988, Class A vendor delivery will mean within one day of the due date with zero defects. Through such a process, MRPII can be used to focus attention on those areas that contribute most significantly to cycle time.

THE RESULTS. By October 1986, the impact of these programs were evident in DSM's financial and performance statistics (*Exhibit 5*). Cycle time had already dropped 10 percent; an ambitious schedule of programs was expected to reduce it another 50 percent by 1988. DSM managers were encouraged by their success. However, one manager questioned the pace of change:

> How quickly can people assimilate these programs? MRPII was a backbreaker. It required dramatic changes in behavior . . . a lot of stress. JIT and TQC are much more difficult. MRPII just works on basic manufacturing discipline; JIT and TQC actually change the way you manufacture products.
>
> Today, the plants also have to deal with a changing product mix and 30% to 40% projected growth. It is wise to divert management's attention away from growth to implement these programs?

33. A Note on Manufacturing Resource Planning (MRPII)

Manufacturing Resource Planning (MRPII) is a computer-based planning and scheduling system designed to improve management's control of manufacturing and its support functions. MRPII translates a firm's business, sales and production plans into specific day-to-day tasks through such well-defined techniques as master scheduling, materials planning, capacity planning, shop floor control and vendor scheduling. The system enables management to set priorities, anticipate crises, and measure performance to schedules and plans.

MRPII evolved from Material Requirements Planning (MRP), a computerized tool for scheduling and ordering materials. MRP is a technique for exploding bills of material to calculate net materials requirements and plan future production. Early MRP systems used four pieces of information to determine what materials should be ordered and when: the master production schedule, which describes when each product is scheduled to be manufactured; bills of material, which list exactly the parts or materials required to make each product; production cycle times and materials needs at each stage of the production cycle; and supplier lead times. The master schedule and bills of material indicate what materials should be ordered; the master schedule, production cycle times and supplier lead times then jointly determine when orders should be placed. Over time, such features as capacity planning,

vendor scheduling, and work-in-process tracking were added to MRP systems, so that management could also monitor operating performance.

MRP is only one element of a complete MRPII system. Technically, MRPII marries an MRP operating system to the firm's financial system, allowing all departments to work from a single, visible set of numbers. Equally important, MRPII provides a management process for integrating financial planning, marketing, engineering, and purchasing with manufacturing. As one user has observed: "To work well, MRPII has to cut across business disciplines. These disciplines are driven by differing motivations; normally no one is rewarded for integrating them."[1]

Components of MRPII

An MRPII system has three components: Top Management Planning, Operations Management Planning, and Operations Management Execution. (*Exhibit 1.*)

TOP MANAGEMENT PLANNING. In a fully integrated MRPII system, a firm's business, sales and production plans are fed into the MRPII execution model and updated monthly.

> **Business Planning** sets specific goals for margins, return on assets (ROA), and other business objectives. These goals are drawn from the firm's strategic plan for markets, products and profits.

This note was prepared by Janet Simpson under the direction of David A. Garvin.

[1] John Teresko, "MRPII: A Strategic Tool for Survival," *Industry Week*, September 30, 1985, p. 42.

EXHIBIT 1 Manufacturing Resource Planning (MRPII)

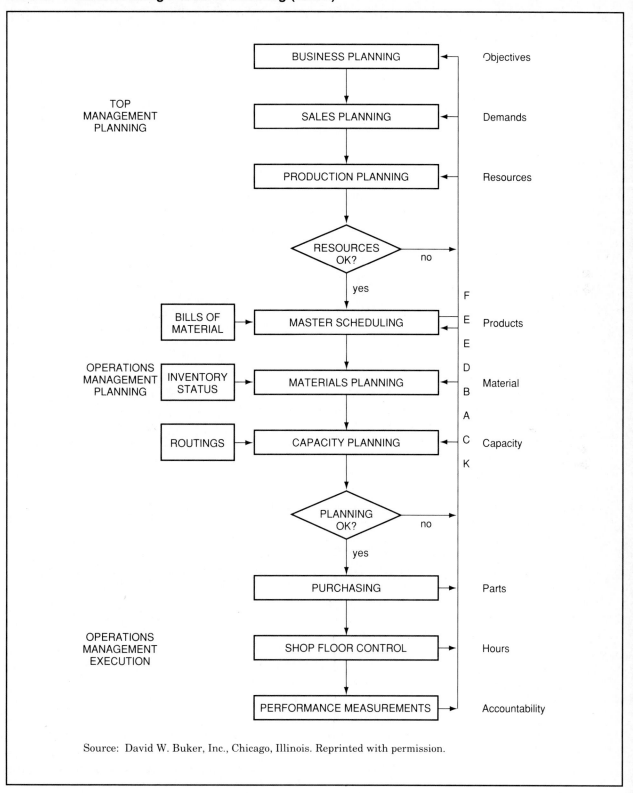

Source: David W. Buker, Inc., Chicago, Illinois. Reprinted with permission.

Sales Planning provides product projections—rather than dollar forecasts—based on anticipated market demand.

Production Planning balances the sales plan with available capacity and constraints derived from engineering (time to release new designs), vendors (lead times), and manufacturing (facilities, equipment and people). Resource allocation decisions based on capacity, inventory levels, and the desired level of customer service are then incorporated into the production plan.

OPERATIONS MANAGEMENT PLANNING. The master scheduler converts the production plan into a *Master Production Schedule,* a specific statement of what products are to be built, in what quantities, and when. The master production schedule then drives the ordering and scheduling of all material (*Materials Planning*) and provides direction for optimal use of labor and machine capacity (*Capacity Planning*). These plans are evaluated weekly; proper execution requires accurate bills of material, inventory records and routings.

OPERATIONS MANAGEMENT EXECUTION. Operations management plans are communicated, in the form of daily schedules, to engineering, tooling shops, purchasing, and the production floor. The material plan provides *Purchasing* with schedules for material acquisition that specify parts, quantities, and dates. The capacity plan and master schedule generate daily work center schedules to assist shop supervisors in setting priorities and assigning work to people or machines. *Shop Floor Control* encompasses all of these daily lists, plus work-in-process tracking, shop order delivery, and scheduling and rescheduling controls. On-time vendor delivery and shop floor performance are essential if master schedule targets are to be met.

Classification of Users

A checklist and an ABCD rating scheme are widely used to measure how well a firm is operating its MRP or MRPII system. Using the checklist, independent consultants evaluate technical considerations (such as the mechanics of capacity planning), data integrity, ongoing employee education, and performance to plans and schedules.

Firms are then rated from "Class A" to "Class D," based on the following generally accepted industry criteria:[2]

CLASS A. A Class A MRP company has material requirements planning, capacity planning, shop floor dispatching, and vendor scheduling systems in place and being used. Management participates in production planning and constantly monitors the accuracy of inventory records, bills of material, and routings, as well as the attainment of master schedules, and capacity plans.

A Class A MRPII user has tied its financial system to its MRP system. Simulation capabilities have been developed so that "what if" questions can be answered. Management uses MRPII to run the business and monitor performance. In a Class A firm, the system provides a companywide game plan for sales, finance, manufacturing, purchasing, and engineering. Each of these functions uses the formal system; there is no attempt to override schedules through expediting or shortage lists.

CLASS B. A Class B firm uses components of an MRP or MRPII system for production and inventory control. The Class B company typically has materials requirements planning, capacity planning and shop floor control systems in place, but has done little with purchasing. Top management does not use the system to run the business directly and shortage lists tend to override shop schedules.

CLASS C. A Class C company uses MRP/MRPII primarily as an inventory ordering technique rather than a scheduling tool. Shop scheduling is still done from a shortage list, and the master schedule is typically inaccurate.

CLASS D. A Class D company has MRP/MRPII working only in its data processing department. Typically, inventory records are poor. If the company has a defined master schedule, it is usually grossly mismanaged.

In 1985, a survey of 1,123 American MRP/MRPII users found that fewer than 200 plants

---

[2] The description of rating criteria was adapted from O. Wight, *The Executive's Guide to Successful MRPII*, (NH: O. Wight Publications, 1984) pp. 107–108.

met Class A criteria.[3] Those that did reported a 28% improvement in customer service, a 25% reduction in inventory levels, a 16% increase in productivity, and an 11% reduction in purchase costs. These improvements produced significant costs savings. For example, 40% of the Class A users reported annual savings exceeding $1 million, while only 2% reported savings of less than $100 thousand annually. Other classes of users also reported improvements in customer service, productivity, and inventory reduction, but their cost savings were markedly lower (*Exhibit 3*).

MRPII Implementation

In practice, MRPII users employ a series of performance metrics to monitor progress toward achieving a Class A rating. These metrics typically address the accuracy of each key component in the MRPII model. For example, the sales plan may be evaluated by measuring the accuracy of

[3] The Oliver Wight Companies 1985 Newsletter: *Control of the Business* (Newbury, NH: 1985).

forecasts by product line; the master schedule, by comparing scheduled units to units completed; and purchasing, by on-time vendor delivery. Systems are said to be operating at a Class A level when the average accuracy of these metrics reaches 90 percent. A sample list of metrics appears in *Exhibit 2*.

While the proper use of these metrics can highlight problem areas during implementation of MRPII, they may also be used to improve performance once the Class A rating is achieved. For example, vendor delivery may initially be considered "on-time" if deliveries arrive within one week of the due date. Once that target is achieved, on-time delivery may be redefined to mean deliveries arriving within one day of the due date. Through such practices, a firm can use MRPII to gain continuous improvement in its manufacturing performance.

According to the 1985 survey cited above, companies spent an average of $907,000 to implement MRP/MRPII systems. Class A users spent $1,181,000. Surprisingly, Class D users spent nearly the same amount, $1,002,000. However, sharp

EXHIBIT 2 MRPII: Representative Performance Metrics

MRPII Component	Performance Metric
Top Management Planning	
Business Planning	Return On Assets
Sales Planning	Product Forecast Accuracy
Production Planning	Production Planning Accuracy
Plant Performance	
Master Scheduling	Scheduling Accuracy
Materials Planning	Accurate Material Priority Planning
Capacity Planning	Accurate Work Center Scheduling
Database Accuracy	
Bills of Material	Accurate Bills of Material
Inventory Control	Accurate Inventory Records
Routings	Routings Accuracy
Plant Execution	
Purchasing	On-Time Vendor Delivery
Shop Floor Control	On-Time Shop Order Completion

EXHIBIT 3 1985 O. Wight Survey of MPR/MRPII Users

1. What is the approximate dollar volume (in millions) of your plant or division?

	All MRP Companies	Class A Companies
Under $10 million	10%	4%
$10–24 million	20	12
$25–49 million	22	31
$50–99 million	18	19
Over $100 million	30	34

2. What were your approximate costs in implementing MRP/MRPII?

	All MRP Companies	Class A Companies
	(000s)	
Computer Hardware	$ 257	$ 394
Computer Software	176	175
Inventory Record Accuracy	52	108
Bill of Material Accuracy	43	52
Routing Accuracy	29	39
Education	66	97
Consulting	45	48
Other Costs	239	268
Total	$ 907	$1,181

3. What would you estimate to be your yearly benefits from MRP/MRPII?

	All MRP Companies	Class A Companies
Under $100 thousand	25%	2%
$100–249 thousand	19	11
$250–499 thousand	16	26
$500–749 thousand	12	14
$750–999 thousand	5	7
$1.0–1.4 million	10	14
$1.5–1.9 million	3	9
$2.0–2.9 million	5	6
$3.0–3.9 million	1	—
$4.0–4.9 million	1	1
$5.0–5.9 million	—	1
Over $6 million	3	9

(continued on next page)

33. A Note on Manufacturing Resource Planning (MRPII)

EXHIBIT 3 *(Continued)*

4. In implementing MRP/MRPII, which of the following did your plant or division do?

	All MRP Companies	Class A Companies	Class D Companies
Top Management Education	64%	82%	50%
Formal Cost/Benefit	46	66	36
Full-Time Project Leader	68	83	49
Proven Implementation Plan	43	60	24
MRP Consultant	51	73	44
Key Mgrs. Educated Outside Classes	69	86	58
Video-Assisted Education	62	70	55
Ongoing Education-Classes	47	73	32
Ongoing Education-Video	32	49	24

5. What would you have done differently in implementing MRP/MRPII?

	All MRP Companies	Class A Companies
More Education	55%	35%
Better Software	28	23
Top Management Commitment	48	20
Other, Not Listed	21	18
Would Do Nothing Differently	11	39

Source: The Oliver Wight Companies 1985 Newsletter: *Control of the Business* (1985): Newbury, NH). Reprinted with permission.

differences between the groups were reported in two areas: top management commitment, and education. Only 20% of Class A users felt they had not received enough top management support; by contrast, 78% of the Class D users reported a lack of management commitment. In addition, while more than half the companies surveyed reported they should have done a better job educating their employees, Class A companies had been far more active. For example, 82% of the A users had educated their top management at outside classes against only 50% of the D users. A summary of these survey results appears in *Exhibit 3*.

34. Signetics Corporation: Implementing a Quality Improvement Program (A)

In 1979, as part of a four-year planning process at Signetics, Mr. D. C. McKenzie, Director of Corporate Quality Control, was asked to forecast his department's growth through 1984. McKenzie believed that "quality" would become the battleground of the future. However, his management and budget forecasts—showing exponential increases in inspectors and QC activities—convinced him that if Signetics were to compete successfully against other U.S. and Japanese manufacturers, it would require the complete reorganization of the quality control function. A new philosophy would have to be implemented—one that would hold every employee accountable for quality and that would have zero defects as its goal.

During the fall of 1979, McKenzie held several meetings with his staff to define a major program for implementing this new philosophy. That program also incorporated quality as a measure in all Signetics' managers' semiannual performance reviews.

By the spring of 1980, substantial progress had been made in defining a redirected quality improvement program at Signetics, getting top management support, and taking initial steps toward its implementation. However, in April McKenzie decided there was a need to assess just what had and had not been accomplished, and to evaluate several possible next steps. In particular, McKenzie and his quality managers had come up with three different types of projects, each of which would require a significant commitment on the part of his organization. One option emphasized working with vendors, another working with customers, while a third focused on internal operations. McKenzie felt that this next step would be an important one; it had to keep the momentum growing while guarding against a major setback in the overall program or a dilution of effort from trying to do too much at once.

The remainder of this case describes the company background, the circumstances that led to the redirecting of its quality philosophy in late 1979, and a review of some of the specific actions taken as part of that redirection program. In addition, the three types of projects under consideration in April 1980 are described and data on their resource requirements and other issues in their evaluation are provided.

Company Background

Signetics Corporation was founded in Sunnyvale, California, in 1961. It was the first company in the world established for the sole purpose of designing, manufacturing, and selling integrated circuits (ICs). By 1980 Signetics had become the sixth largest U.S. semiconductor company and it offered one of the broadest lines of integrated circuits in the industry. Since 1972, the company had experienced a compound annual growth rate of 26 percent. In 1980 gross sales were expected to exceed $360 million.

From 1962 to 1975 Signetics was owned by Corning Glass Works. In 1975 Signetics was purchased by the U.S. Philips Corporation, a subsidiary of N. V. Philips of the Netherlands. With worldwide sales in 1979 in excess of 33 billion guilders (approximately $16 billion 1979 U.S. dollars), N. V. Philips was a diversified manufacturing firm participating in industries ranging from lighting products to consumer electronics to scientific instruments and semi-conductors.

Although operated independently of N. V. Philips, by 1980 Signetics' relationship with the Netherlands firm had become very important. Philips bought and sold products under the Signetics name and provided its subsidiary access to its worldwide research and development capability, advanced manufacturing process know-how, and technology.

Company Products and Markets

Signetics had developed several thousand different circuits for such diverse markets as data processing, industrial controls, instrumentation, consumer product, telecommunications, automotive, and defense. Product lines included PROMs (Programmable Read Only Memory), Fuse Programmable Logic Arrays, LSI (Large Scale Integration), logic and analog circuits. (*Exhibit 1* provides a glossary of semiconductor terminology and *Exhibit 2* summarizes generic product categories offered by Signetics.)

Signetic's major U.S. competitors were: Texas Instruments, National Semiconductor, Motorola, Intel, and Fairchild Camera. *Table 1* provides comparative sales data for 1979.

TABLE 1 1979 Integrated Circuit Sales by U.S. Manufacturers

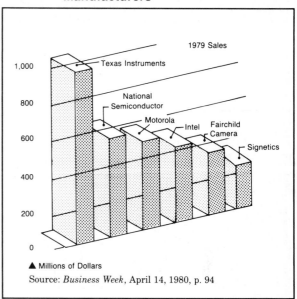

▲ Millions of Dollars

Source: *Business Week*, April 14, 1980, p. 94

EXHIBIT 1 Glossary of Technical Terms

Semiconductor: A solid material (i.e., silicon or germanium) with properties of both a conductor and an insulator.

Transistor: A small chip of semiconductor material that amplifies or switches electrical current. Known as discrete (single-function) semiconductors, transistors replaced vacuum tubes and started the solid-state revolution.

Integrated circuit (ICs): Many transistors and other circuit elements "integrated" on a single silicon chip.

LSI: Large Scale Integration, where more transistors are put on a chip than on an IC, enabling the chip to perform several functions rather than one. LSIs are then interconnected on a circuit board to make up entire computers.

Microprocessor: Called the "computer-on-a-chip" because the arithmetic and logic functions of a computer are placed on a single silicon chip.

Microcomputer: A microprocessor with memory chips, for storing software (e.g. operating instructions), and communication chips, for "talking" to the outside world.

MOS: Metal-oxide-silicon, one of two basic IC designs, is the fastest growing because it is cheaper and easier to use.

Bipolar: The second fundamental design for ICs. Bipolar chips are faster but more costly to manufacture.

Wafer: A three- or four-inch thin disc of silicon on which up to 500 separate chips can be printed and then cut into individual ICs.

Logic: The part of the computer that does the arithmetic or makes decisions.

Memory: Stores needed facts, along with instructions on what to do with them and when. Each memory component stores a number of bits of binary data normally denoted in multiples of kilobits where one kilobit equals 1,024 bits.

RAM: Random Access Memory, which stores digital information temporarily and can be changed by the user. It constitutes the basic storage element in computer terminals and is replacing magnetic core memories in main-frame computers.

ROM: Read Only Memory, which stores information used repeatedly such as tables of data, characters for electronic displays, etc. Unlike RAM, ROM cannot be altered.

E/PROM: Erasable Programmable Read Only Memories are similar to ROMs but enable the user to erase stored information and replace it with new information at the end of a normal operation.— K.K.W.

Source: "How to Talk High Tech," *Forbes*, November 26, 1979, p. 54.

Memory components accounted for at least 40% of the semiconductor industry's global sales, which were projected to reach some $13 billion in 1980 and had been rising at the impressive rate of 18% annually. By 1979, U.S. manufacturers were doing about two-thirds of that volume. By 1988, semiconductor output in the United States was expected to increase to $30 billion, about 55% of the world total.

Semiconductors had been dubbed "the crude oil of the 1980s," partly because of the size and growth anticipated in the semiconductor industry

EXHIBIT 2 Generic Product Categories Offered by Signetics

LOGIC

Arithmetic Units/
    Microprocessor CPUs
Decoder/Drivers
Parity Generators
Encoders
Latches
Comparators
Counters
Data Selector/Multiplexer
Decoders/Multiplexers
Flip-Flops
Registers
Seven Segment Decoder/
    Drivers With Zero
    Suppression and Lamp Test
Line Receivers
Line Drivers
Buffers/Inverters
Special Functions
Bus Transceiver
Semi-custom LSI Design
    (T^2L compatible)
    Gate Arrays
Composite Cell Logic (CCL)

MOS MICROPROCESSOR

Microprocessors and
    Microcomputers
I/O Peripheral Interface
Training
Development Hardware
LSI Support Devices
Development Systems

BIPOLAR MEMORY

CAMS
RAMSs
FPLAs
FPGAs
FPLSs
PROMs

ANALOG

TV Circuits
Audio Circuits
Radio Circuits
Interface
Video Amplifiers
MOSFET-Analog/
    Digital Switches (D-MOS)
Microminiature Packages
MOSFET-RF (D-MOS)
Op Amps
Data Acquisition
Timers
Phase Locked Loops
Transistor Arrays
Display Drivers
Power Control Circuits
Comparators

MOS MEMORY

ROMs

BIPOLAR LSI

Microprocessors
Sequencers
I/O Interface
Special-purpose Circuits
Memories (PROMs and ROMs)
Memories (RAMS)
Support Circuits
Field Programmable
    Logic Arrays
Development Hardware
    and Kits
Development Software
8X300 Software
    Training Materials

Source: Company brochure

and partly because of the pervasiveness of the applications of ICs. Many other manufacturers were expanding their commitment and capabilities in the field, most notably the Japanese, who, owing in part to their product quality record, were making significant inroads in world markets.

	1978	1979
WORLD IC PRODUCTION (MILLIONS OF DOLLARS)		
Producing Region	1978	1979
U.S.		
IC Merchant	3,238	4,071
IC Captive	1,344	2,010
IC Total U.S.	4,582	6,081
Western Europe		
IC Total	453	600
Japan		
IC Total	1,195	1,750
Rest of World		
IC Total	782	675
Total ICs	7,012	9,106

Source: Company estimates

In early 1980, to take advantage of the fast growth anticipated for MOS (metal-oxide-silicon) technology, Signetics began a four-year program to invest in new manufacturing facilities and equipment. A new 250,000-square-foot plant was built in Albuquerque, New Mexico, primarily for MOS manufacturing. It was the company's objective to become a major supplier in the mainstream of MOS technology by 1984.

In addition to an extensive program to develop its own new products, Signetics had joined with Motorola, Inc., to manufacture that company's family of 16-bit microprocessors. Through this agreement, Signetics was able to offer one of the most sophisticated 16-bit microprocessors available. In keeping with the company's family-of-products philosophy, Signetics had begun to offer a line of high-performance peripheral input/output and communication chips as well.

On the research side, Signetics and Philips had organized a team of scientists and engineers to explore complex IC technologies and processes

of the future, and to advance Signetics' capabilities in both Bipolar and MOS technology. Planning was underway for a 120,000-square-foot Signetics Advanced Technology Center to be located in Sunnyvale. When completed, the Center was expected to be one of the most sophisticated research and development facilities in the industry, providing space for more than 100 scientists and engineers.

Internal Organization and Operations

Signetics was organized into eight divisions, as shown below. Six designed, manufactured, and marketed ICs. The remaining two finished and tested these products for conformance to the rigid specifications demanded by the military and automotive/telecommunication markets. The eight divisions reported to one of two major technology groups: Bipolar Digital and MOS/Analog. (See *Exhibit 3*.)

Divisions in the *MOS/Analog Group* designed and manufactured MOS microprocessors (the so-called "computers on a chip") and their peripheral circuits. Applications included those that transmitted computer data over telephone

SIGNETICS ORGANIZATION—1980	
Groups	Divisions
	Analog
MOS/Analog Products Group	MOS Microprocessor
	MOS Memory
	Logic
	Bipolar LS1
Bipolar Digital Products Group	Bipolar Memory ⎫
	Military ⎬ Market Segment Divisions
	Auto/Telecom ⎭

EXHIBIT 3 1980 Organization Chart

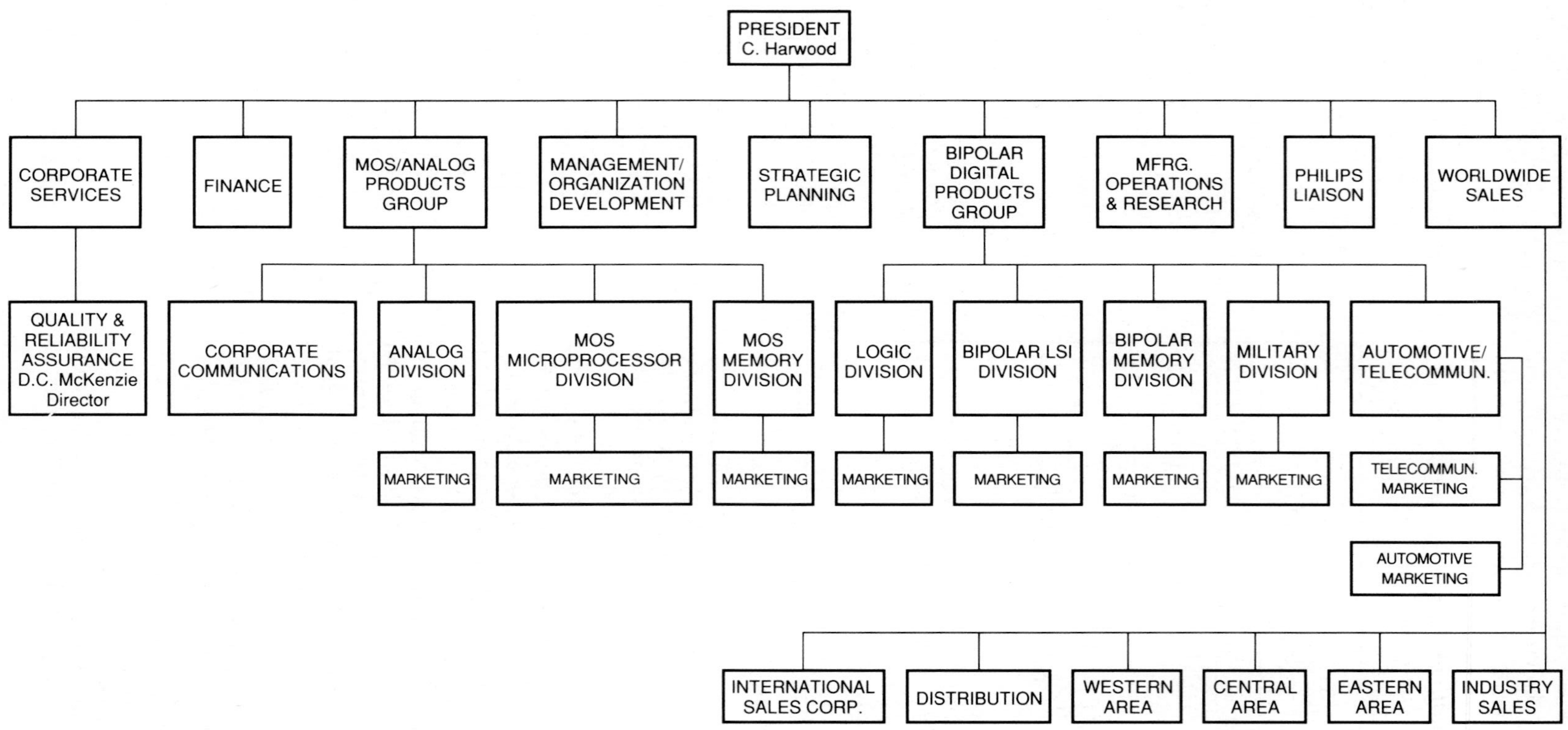

Source: Company document

lines, MOS Memory circuits, and Analog IC's used in computer products, industrial products, and consumer products such as radios, TVs, and electronic games.

The divisions in the *Bipolar Digital Group* made high-speed memory circuits, and families of complex logic microprocessors and control ICs for computers and their peripheral equipment, as well as a variety of industrial, telecommunications, and consumer control systems.

Most of Signetics' facilities were located in Sunnyvale. The corporate offices were nearby in Santa Clara, California; Wafer Fabrication and Test Operations were split between Orem, Utah, and Sunnyvale, and the company's three Assembly and Test facilities were in Seoul, Korea; Bangkok, Thailand; and Manila, the Philippines.

Making semiconductor devices involved more than 150 steps and required extremely intricate manufacturing processes. A silicon ingot was sliced into thin wafers. Through miniaturization involving photographic reduction and photolithography, some 200 to 3,000 elaborate chips were created on each wafer. Following the proper buildup of layers of metals and chemicals, each wafer was cut into individual dies (or chips), gold leads were attached, and each die was packaged on a frame with electrical connectors to become a final unit.

Development of the Quality Improvement Program

Before the fall of 1979, the Quality and Reliability (Q&R) philosophy at Signetics had functioned as though Q&R staff had full responsibility for quality, while production was responsible only for output. D. C. McKenzie expressed a firm conviction as to why the quality control concept within the company had to be revamped:

> My feelings about the inappropriateness of our philosophy came to a head in the fall of '79 when I began to prepare my part of a long-range corporate growth plan. I concluded that the number of Q&R personnel operating as "police people" would have to expand exponentially to keep pace with Signetics' forecasted growth in volume. Q&R had been concentrating on establishing test procedures and setting specifications (commonly thought of as appraisal and gating/screening activities) and then trying to make sure that everyone adhered to our specs. It was just hopeless to

continue down that path. The requirements of the future clearly called for quality performance levels possible only through more sophisticated prevention programs.

McKenzie's Q&R staff had met to examine two options—continue past practices or initiate change. During the spring of 1979 alternatives to past practices were discussed. Determined to explore those further, McKenzie organized an off-site three-day planning meeting in September 1979 for all the corporate Q&R managers. He enlisted the help of one of Signetics' Organization Development staff, who opened the meeting with an introduction to a problem-solving technique called A-B-C. As McKenzie explained it:

> ABC stands for Assumptions, Behavior, and Consequences. The idea is that by looking at the current state for each of those three areas, and then looking at what is desired, it's possible to concentrate on problem solving without having to point blame.

McKenzie then presented the problem he wanted his staff to focus upon—that the philosophy that Q&R should act as a police force in Signetics operations needed to be changed radically.

> I was nervous when I got through writing it on the board and turned back to get my staff's response; but right off the bat four of the six agreed with me 100 percent and the other two agreed as soon as they understood more about it. The two who weren't right with me at first don't work directly in the police force role.
>
> We spent the rest of the meeting outlining the before-and-after contrast of a quality philosophy and the details of the transition plan. (see *Exhibits 4a* and *4b.*)

Initial Q&R Program Actions

As a skeletal framework for the new Q&R philosophy, McKenzie introduced a fourteen-point program based on the book, *Quality Is Free*, by Philip B. Crosby.[1]

While the group viewed Crosby's program, originally developed for ITT, as not totally complete, it felt the need to have an anchor and a method of instruction—one that had been articulated and would be recognized by other compa-

[1] A summary of that program is provided in Signetics Corporation (D)—Overview *Quality Is Free* (S-MM-3D)

nies and in some published works. In addition, the initial success was based on the humanistic aspects of the program, and not its technical content.

Throughout the fall of 1979, the Q&R managers held a series of meetings to develop the methods required to implement the program. A division was chosen for a pilot program, the training that would be required was defined, the people who could do the training were identified, and the changes in responsibilities that would result from the new philosophy were examined.

In early 1980 the Q&R staff met with Signetics president Chuck Harwood to ask his approval and support for the detailed pilot program. It proposed that all the basic elements be in place by late 1980: throughout the company the Q&R police role would be replaced by individual accountability with a goal of zero defects. In describing their program to Harwood, the Q&R staff even made rough comparisons of how each manager's Responsibility, Measures, and Objectives (RMO) goals (a management by objectives type system in place throughout Signetics) would change after the pilot program. Harwood was asked to communicate his personal support by presenting the program to employees and key customers and by chairing a corporate quality committee that would meet monthly to review the program's progress.

Harwood agreed to the program, but one of the group vice-presidents had serious concerns, typical of the conventional wisdom, about the quality department abdicating its role, of keeping the people honest with regard to quality. Since the manager of the division chosen to serve as the pilot site was anxious to get going on the program, approval to begin was given with the understanding that such questions would be answered to corporate satisfaction before the program was adopted company-wide.

Reorganization of the Quality Department

The first of two organizational steps was taken in early 1980. This step included a series of organization changes that decentralized the quality functions into the operating groups. Starting in the Analog Division, the plan was to proceed throughout the other product divisions and manufacturing operations so that by the end of 1980 the transition would be completed. As McKenzie explained:

The essence of the reorganization consisted of consolidating the various quality activities—Wafer Fabrication Quality Control (QC), Product Assurance, Electrical Sort Quality Control, Quality Engineering, and Reliability Engineering—

EXHIBIT 4a Before and After Contrast of Quality—Fall 1979

Before	After
Screen for quality	Plan for quality
Quality is Q&R's responsibility	Quality is everybody's responsibility
Some mistakes are inevitable	Zero defects is possible
Quality means inspection	Quality means conformance to requirements
Scrap and rework are the major costs of poor quality	Scrap and rework are only a small part of the costs of nonconformance
Quality is a tactical issue	Quality is a strategic imperative
Production units are where quality should be measured	Individual accountability is where quality should be measured

EXHIBIT 4b Rough Outline of a Four-Year Quality Improvement Program

1980–1981
  Raise the quality consciousness level of all personnel
  Division and Plant Managers begin active leadership roles
  Quality tied to everyone's performance review

1981–1982
  Utilization of the cost of nonconformance as an improvement planning tool
  Zero defects a part of the culture—ppm is standard notation
  Greater emphasis on technical planning
  Major quality improvements made through the quality improvement teams

1983–1984
  Logistics and technical data systems working
  Cooperating routinely with key customers on special programs

under the Divisional Quality/Reliability Assurance (QRA) managers. The QRA managers became direct members of the Division Vice Presidents staffs; the previous structure had them reporting to Corporate Q&R. In the manufacturing/operations groups, a similar transition was accomplished with Assembly and Incoming QC. The Assembly QC functions became part of the Sunnyvale Manufacturing operation and Incoming QC was transferred to Material Control (Purchasing). (See *Exhibit 5*.)

The fundamental reason behind this organizational change was to put the control tools into the hands of the responsible parties. We hoped this would generate a team atmosphere and a sense of ownership. By eliminating the check-and-balance system which had existed, it was hoped that there would be an intensification in the involvement with quality at the earliest possible time and lowest possible level. The greatest benefit was expected to come from stressing prevention, instead of inspection and corrective action after the fact.

By the end of 1980, Corporate Q&R would consist of the five functional activities it had prior to the transition, but with different objectives. Elimination of the inspection function would make it possible for Corporate Q&R to improve planning and overview activities. In addition to previous activities—such as qualification programs, corrective action, and monitors/audits—anticipated new corporate responsibilities included data compilation/trend analysis, corporate quality systems standards/procedures, training, quality improvement, and prevention programs.

Status of the Quality Improvement Program (April 1980)

While the pilot program had been set up to run from early 1980 through November of 1980, by April, McKenzie and his Q&R management people felt a need to reassess their progress to date and decide just which avenues should be pursued, and how fast, over the next several months. While external (competitor and customer) pressures were adding support to the types of ideas incorporated in the quality improvement program, McKenzie and his people were concerned that they not confuse their own enthusiasm for and agreement on the program with that in the rest of the organization. Thus, in late March, McKenzie asked his group to provide him with information on the progress they thought Signetics had made over the preceding several months and to identify some of the major options that might be pursued as further steps in Signetics' quality improvement efforts.

EXHIBIT 5 Q&R Organizational Evolution

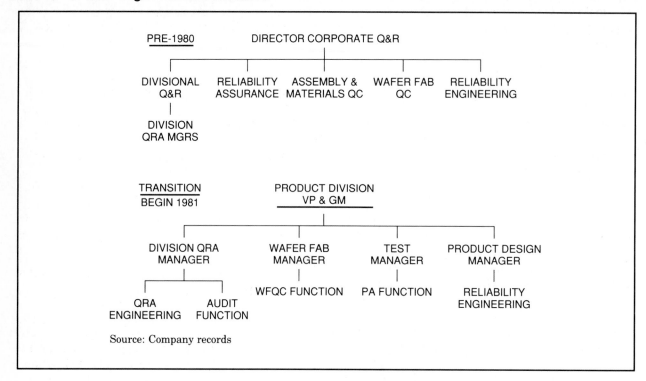

Source: Company records

As McKenzie reviewed these reports, he concluded that significant progress had been made among his own quality and reliability management people with regard to terminology and definitions. Some things that seemed to be clearly in place included:

1. The Q&R managers generally understood the philosophy change represented by the decentralization of the Q&R function (illustrated in *Exhibit 5*). While that decentralization was still in progress, at least those managers whose reporting relationships would be directly affected seemed to have a good understanding of what those organizational changes hoped to accomplish.

2. "Quality" had been redefined as "conformance to specification." Q&R people seemed to be in general agreement that everyone should "perform exactly like the stated requirements or cause those requirements to be officially changed to what the process could produce and what the customers really needed."

3. The Q&R group agreed that the major thrust of the improvement program was to stress prevention rather than correction. The notions that "it is better to plan for quality than to screen for it" and that "mistakes are not a way of life" seemed to be tying in nicely with the belief that a zero defects philosophy could be developed.

While McKenzie felt confident that a strong consensus had formed within his own Q&R group, it was clear that others within the company still had a long way to go. One aspect of this was that of measurement and reporting. As part of the quality improvement program, McKenzie and his group had decided that the cost of nonconformance should be used as the performance measure for quality. Working with the financial controller, they proposed measurement procedures aimed at identifying the cost of "not doing things right the first time." As shown in *Exhibit 6*, this approach required data gathering and reporting on a variety of dimensions. While those procedures were not yet functioning, it was clear that there was already some growing opposition to this whole notion of the cost of poor quality. For some in accounting, this looked like a lot of work and they were already under pressure as an "overhead group" to keep the costs of accounting under control. A number of line managers had voiced considerable doubt, both as to the likelihood of ever getting and maintaining accurate data on the factors in *Exhibit 6* and the negative motivational impact of telling manufacturing that their poor quality was the source of 15–20% (the preliminary number cited by Q&R) of total costs.

A second aspect of measurement and reporting that was still in the early stages of implementation was the inclusion of quality both in each manager's job specifications and in his or her Responsibility, Measures, and Objectives statement. While those involved in the pilot program seemed to be making good progress on this, it had been hoped that the entire organization would adopt it in 1980. However, the results seemed to be mixed, depending on the division and the level of support coming from division senior management. For many managers it looked like another "procedure" that kept them from their real task of producing product to meet customer needs at a profit (that is, emphasis on volume, delivery and profit).

McKenzie and his people also had been able to gather some information about the attitudes of managers throughout the company. As McKenzie had anticipated, the behavior and response varied from extremely negative to extremely positive. At the former end of the spectrum was the whole notion of the quality improvement program of keeping people honest and quality having to compete with productivity, which was already lower than it should have been. Clearly, they hadn't made much progress in areas where such a view prevailed.

At the other end were the results achieved to date in the Orem, Utah, plant, which was part of the pilot program. The plant manager, Dennis Peasenell, was extremely enthusiastic about the program and performance statistics already indicated that:

> Wafer lines were running at rates consistently higher than both the U.S. industry average and the plant's own 1979 performance.

> The number of defective circuits uncovered in destructive physical analysis performed in Sunnyvale on Orem-made products had plummeted from 12% to something down in the 1 to 2% range.

> One fab line seemed well on its way to doubling the number of good dies per wafer and expected to reach that goal in another three months.

EXHIBIT 6 Cost of Nonconformance

INTERNAL
- REWORK
- SCRAP
- YIELD LOSS—STANDARD IS 100%
- SCREENS
- CORRECTIVE ACTIONS

EXTERNAL
- CUSTOMER RETURNS
- FAILURE ANALYSIS (FIELD FAILURES)

APPRAISAL
- QUALITY COSTS (QA/QC—INSPECTIONS)
- PRODUCTION—TEST/INSPECTION
- RELIABILITY ENGINEERING MONITORS (SURE)

PREVENTION
- TRAINING
- RELIABILITY (TESTING/QUALIFICATIONS)
- QUALITY ACTIVITIES—QUALITY CIRCLES/QUALIFICATION ENGINEERING
- PREVENTATIVE MAINTENANCE/CALIBRATIONS
- DESIGN REVIEWS AND PROCESS RELEASE REVIEWS

Reworks had declined from 20% in 1979 to what the plant manager projected would be 2% by the end of 1980 if the current trend continued.

McKenzie and his people were extremely pleased with the results at the Orem plant. The plant manager was highly committed, as was his boss; several other people were also playing key roles, including the workforce, which seemed to be particularly receptive to the whole idea. The results had come not from simply following a 14-step program, but from broad-based support and commitment to the entire philosophy.

Major Options for Future Quality Improvement Actions

McKenzie had also asked his managers to think about what additional projects might support Signetics' quality improvement activities. Based on his discussions with several of his managers, as well as many of the other managers throughout Signetics, he saw three major areas that might be pursued at various activity levels or in various sequences during coming months. These grouped roughly into internal activities (aimed at Signetics' own employees and managers), external activities involving materials suppliers and vendors, and activities involving customers. The commitment to each of these three areas could range from very low to that required for a significant change in direction.

Possible Vendor-Related Activities

One type of purchasing and supplier-related activity that had already received some discussion within Signetics was what McKenzie viewed as an educational program for suppliers. While not yet completely defined, it would include discussing specifications with suppliers, giving them exposure to the terminology and framework being used within Signetics and gradually trying to improve their adherence to specifications. Given the range of suppliers, their sizes, current levels of quality, and various orientations, even such an educational program could take a significant amount of time and resources (on the order of 3 or 4 man-years) on Signetics' part.

Another option that McKenzie was considering amounted to a shock treatment for Signetics' suppliers. The Signetics purchasing manager, who had been with the firm eighteen years, prided himself on never shutting down a production line because of a lack of components. Although that was an admirable record, Q&R had found that many incoming materials did not meet Signetics' stated specifications (specs). Incoming materials were being put into one of three categories when they arrived at the plant: Acceptable, because they met specs; Returned to the Vendor, because they were totally unacceptable; or Set Aside, because even though they did not fully meet specs they probably could be used with some modification to keep production lines running. As Q&R had examined Signetics' behavior with regard to these three categories, they found that those items traditionally set aside (about 15% of all incoming materials) eventually got "waived" into production because they were needed immediately. It was then Production's job to make them usable.

A radical approach to dealing with vendor quality would require convincing the purchasing and production managers to eliminate the "waived" category so that there would be only two categories in which materials could be placed upon receipt—either they would meet specs and move into production or they would not meet specs and would be returned immediately. McKenzie knew that Purchasing would view an immediate shift to such a policy as disastrous to the company's reputation among its vendors. Production, too, would view such a policy as disastrous to its productivity and shipment schedules. Thus, if such a program were to be undertaken, Q&R would have to convince Signetics' own purchasing department that it made sense, and also to convince vendors of the need to change their behavior. Moreover, they would need the cooperation of the plant, so that materials would be rejected when they didn't meet specifications, no matter how badly they were needed.

Although there were several drawbacks to such an approach (and considerable risks if it was adopted and failed), McKenzie also thought it had many attractions. One of these was that if it could be done and adhered to, he felt certain that most vendors would get very involved in figuring out either how to meet Signetics' specs or convincing the company as to why a different and more appropriate set of specs should be adopted. This source of ideas for quality improvements might be very helpful throughout the Signetics organization and lead to higher-quality products going to customers. He also felt that such a radical change in policy would provide a clear signal, not only to vendors but to everybody within Signetics, that the company was serious about quality and was making a major reorientation in its position.

Internal Signetics Projects

When the pilot program was adopted in 1980, the plan had been to work with a single part of the Signetics organization to get it to assimilate the Crosby Fourteen-Point framework for quality, to incorporate a quality objective in each person's RMO, and to establish procedures for timely data collection and feedback to management on the cost of nonconformance. It was hoped, in addition, that some significant improvements in the quality performance in that pilot organization would take place, but the pilot program was viewed primarily as establishing the groundwork for a subsequent significant improvement in Signetics' quality efforts. Debugging the measurement of the cost of nonconformance, making sure that the other management procedures required to support the RMO program and the new philosophy were in place, and beginning the decentralization of the Q&R organization were the pilot program's primary goals.

One option available to McKenzie with regard to Signetics' internal quality improvement efforts was to continue the pilot program and simply to extend it to the rest of the organization by the end of 1980. That had been the original plan; this option was simply to stick with it for the next several months, at least as far as the internal quality improvement efforts were concerned.

A very different kind of option had been triggered by the significant progess that had already been made in the wafer fabrication and test operations in Orem, Utah. It now appeared feasible to think about taking something like the Orem operation and using it not only as a pilot program for procedural and groundwork-type changes, but also to demonstrate what might be possible in other parts of the organization. This would involve going well beyond the pilot program stage for Orem and setting some very significant targets for the remainder of 1980. As those targets were met, Orem might well become the "model" within the company. If this were done, the types of activities that might be adopted included quality circles, increased commitment to process changes that produced more reliable products, and revising product designs to improve quality. (In a sense, this would amount to giving the Orem operation first priority on resources that were generally shared across multiple facilities.)

While McKenzie was sure that Dennis Peasenell, the plant manager in Orem, would be pleased to take on this challenge (and in fact, was already taking a lot of initiative in this direction), he also saw potential problems in taking resources from other operations—which might be able to show a better payback and greater need—and giving them to Orem. In addition, if the Orem operation set its goals too high and didn't make them, it might be a major setback for the overall program.

Customer-Linked Quality Improvement Activities

As part of the original proposal for the quality improvement program, McKenzie and his Q&R group had anticipated the development of an atmosphere of open communication with customers. At a minimum, this included presentations to each of the company's major customers explaining Signetics' commitment to quality. From preliminary discussions with selected customers, it was anticipated that those like the military, who had always emphasized high reliability, would simply respond by congratulating Signetics on finally "getting with it." Other industrial customers who viewed quality as a particularly important aspect of their business were also likely to have high praise for Signetics' efforts. However, those firms who viewed quality in their own organization as a "police function" would probably be unimpressed by such a presentation. Even among those customers who would applaud Signetics' efforts, it was unclear whether such presentations would have any significant impact on Signetics' ability to attract new business. Thus, the results were likely to be a gradual change in Signetics' image as a supplier. This would become a factor in customer decisions only as Signetics' actual performance improved relative to that of competitors.

An alternative project linking Signetics' efforts directly with customer efforts had recently surfaced in the Automotive Division and was referred to as the Parts-Per-Million program. This program represented a radical departure from what had been Signetics' traditional relationship with its customers. In fact, it was a type of approach that Signetics had rejected, at least implicitly, a few years earlier.

During the last half of the seventies, Signetics, like many other American semiconductor manufacturers, had been approached by Japanese firms looking for additional suppliers. However, Japanese quality requirements appeared formidable and unfamiliar to most potential American suppliers, including Signetics. Since World War II, American manufacturers had largely utilized the AQL (acceptable quality level) criterion. AQLs that allowed more than one percent defects were common in U.S. industry.

In the late 1970s, potential Japanese semiconductor customers required much lower levels, stating quality requirements in terms of PPM (parts-per-million). These firms were perceived as asking for legal guarantees on the level of commitment that a firm like Signetics would make to improve quality and specifying targets of performance that would change over time. Under such a PPM program, defect levels less than 0.1 percent were not uncommon goals. Because of the liability issue and the difficulty of working with an entirely new type of customer under such stringent specifications, Signetics had chosen not to negotiate contracts with Japanese firms.

In late 1979, Signetics was approached by a U.S. automotive parts manufacturer which required extremely high IC quality levels to assure reliability through a five-year, 50,000-mile auto warranty period. In a presentation to Signetics management, the manufacturer spelled out its quality requirements for the coming years, which included a failure rate of no more than 200 parts-per-million, a level significantly lower than that achieved by most U.S. IC manufacturers.

Military contracts had required similar low defect rates for years, but the semiconductor industry had traditionally filled those contracts through 100% testing. While this tended to weed out any defective parts before delivery to the customer, such testing was applied to normal production runs, significantly increasing the cost per unit shipped. Generally, military contracts for high reliability (hi-rel) products had been priced at levels that covered the additional testing and screening costs incurred by the semiconductor manufacturers, and still made the business very attractive.

With a major prospective automotive customer wanting a parts-per-million program, there was a sudden interest on the part of Signetics in considering such an agreement. In addition, with increasing pressure for improved quality coming from international competitors, it was clear that this particular proposal might be a good learning experience for the company. This prospect made Signetics somewhat nervous, however, since it required not just higher testing levels but a commitment to eliminate the causes of poor quality, that is, potential problems in engineering/design, manufacturing processes, workforce procedures, material defects, etc.

Tom Endicott, PPM program manager in the Automotive Division, felt that this appeared to be a business where Signetics could achieve a substantial market share if it moved quickly. However, accepting the contract meant making a significant—and relatively open-ended—commitment. Not only would Signetics have to commit resources to set up a new manufacturing line (at a cost of more than fifteen million dollars) but, since the automotive division was basically a marketing operation, pursuing this particular program would require bringing together people from wafer fabrication, assembly production, and design into a much closer working arrangement than currently existed. Endicott felt that they couldn't really separate those functions if a true PPM program were to be successful, because what one function did might well put others beyond the limits of their own technical capabilities.

Signetics management recognized that the proposed PPM automotive relationship would be unique. As part of the contract, the customer was prepared to supply capital for development and testing, to negotiate lead times acceptable to both parties, and to specify minimum order values, with penalty payments in the event of future

EXHIBIT 7 PPM Assembly/Test Operations—Feedback Requirements

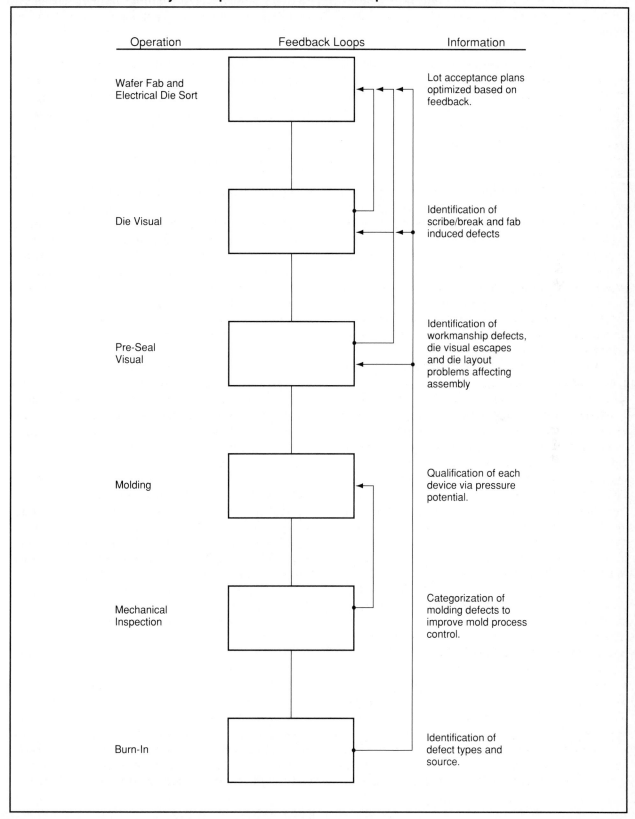

Operation	Feedback Loops	Information
Wafer Fab and Electrical Die Sort		Lot acceptance plans optimized based on feedback.
Die Visual		Identification of scribe/break and fab induced defects
Pre-Seal Visual		Identification of workmanship defects, die visual escapes and die layout problems affecting assembly
Molding		Qualification of each device via pressure potential.
Mechanical Inspection		Categorization of molding defects to improve mold process control.
Burn-In		Identification of defect types and source.

contact cancellations. While this was fairly standard for large supply contracts, the arrangement would also involve both the customer and Signetics in identifying types of defects and their sources. This represented an unusual relationship between customer and supplier and required a high level of teamwork: "our product problems" would be solved jointly. If the PPM program were to be truly successful, the automotive parts manufacturer would have to participate in Signetics' decision-making process, systems would have to be agreed to, and a technical interchange would have to be established. (Q&R's preliminary estimates of the internal feedback activities required to support the PPM effort are summarized in *Exhibit 7, p. 459.*)

McKenzie felt that this option had perhaps the greatest leverage of any being considered, but also held some of the greatest risks. On the positive side, the parts-per-million concept complemented the zero defects philosophy that Signetics was already introducing internally. Both approaches defined quality as "performance to specification." PPM, however, was both a concept and a precise measurement of defects arrived at through statistical analysis, testing, materials, and assemblies. If pursued, it was intended to reduce the level of unacceptable product being produced by at least an order of magnitude. Zero defects, on the other hand, offered an overall philosophy but did not necessarily include such precise and significant targets.

Such a PPM program would clearly demonstrate commitment to those within Signetics' own organization, as well as to customers. There was the possibility, however, that in order to solve some problems within the PPM framework, Signetics would have to commit significantly more resources than was currently envisioned. That is, until the contract was undertaken and the feedback loops started to operate, Signetics would not know just what kinds of resources and what level of resource commitments would be required. Thus, it could find itself having to choose between not living up to its part of the contract and committing resources that would cause the contract to be unprofitable.

Worse, this might prevent Signetics from committing resources to other potentially more profitable projects and products. Thus, if this approach were to have any hope of being successful, Signetics would have to commit itself philosophically and then follow through, even if, operationally, it became uncomfortable to do so. McKenzie wasn't sure the company was far enough along in its own internal quality improvement efforts to make such an ironclad commitment.

A Time for Decision

As McKenzie reviewed these alternatives and thought about comments he'd received from his colleagues in the past few weeks, he knew that the PPM proposal required an immediate decision. While Signetics might currently have the leading edge in getting that contract, there were certain to be other suppliers who would take over if Signetics chose not to accept the offer within the next week or two. The other alternatives did not present any pressing need for decision—they could simply continue with the pilot program and gradually educate vendors as originally planned. However, McKenzie felt he should consider the full set of options as he made this PPM decision.

35. Signetics Corporation (D): Quality Is Free—Overview[1]

Step One: Management Commitment

Purpose: To make clear where management stands on quality.

It is necessary that we consistently produce conforming products and services at the optimum price. The device to accomplish this is the use of defect prevention techniques in our operating departments: engineering, manufacturing, quality control, purchasing, sales, and others. No one is exempt.

It is much less expensive to prevent errors than to rework, scrap, or service them. The expense of waste can run as much as 15 to 25 percent of sales, and does in some companies.

The first action that must take place in improvement is that the management of the company must understand what is needed, and make the decision themselves that they indeed want to improve. This decision is made when they decide to adopt the attitude of defect prevention as their personal standard.

The reason that this is important is obvious but bears repeating. It is a matter of the quality policy.

The quality policy of an organization is too important to be left to those responsible for the acceptance of the product. The quality manager, or the inspector, asked to judge continuously whether the product is good enough or not, will bias the product or service according to his or her own background and personal attitudes.

What Is The Quality Policy?

It is the state of mind held by the company personnel concerning how well they must do their jobs. It is this policy, whether it has been stated or not, that determines in advance how successfully the next job will be done.

If a formal policy is not established by the management of the organization, then the personnel will select their own—individually. This policy must be stated and established by the top executives of the organization, much in the same manner as the financial policy. To delegate this function to the quality manager, or other vertically oriented executives, is dangerous. . . .

The policy statement recommended is: *Perform exactly like the requirement . . . or cause the requirement to be officially changed to what we and our customers really need.*

COMMENT: It is vital that each member of operating management understand and agree with this policy, and more important—implement it.

Step Two: The Quality Improvement Team

Purpose: To run the quality improvement program.

Since every function of an operation is a contributor to defect levels, every portion must participate in the quality improvement effort. The degree of participation is best determined by the particular situation that exists. However, everyone has the opportunity to improve.

The quality improvement team is strictly a

[1] Crosby, Philip B., *Quality Is Free: The Art of Making Quality Certain*, New York: McGraw-Hill, 1979. Used by permission.

part-time job for the members except the chairperson, who will become rather deeply involved. Therefore, the selection of the chairpersons is an important step. There are really only two requirements.

1. The chairperson should be a mature member of management who understands the need to improve and agrees with the concept of Zero Defects and defect prevention.
2. The general manager and the manager's staff must have confidence in the person chosen.

No special skills are involved. Some companies have selected their quality manager, and some have used executives from industrial relations, manufacturing, engineering, or finance.

The chairperson should assemble a team representing each department, and together they should examine the purpose of the program and the concepts involved. Then this group runs the program.

The responsibilities of the members are:

1. Lay out the entire quality improvement program.
2. Represent their department on the team.
3. Represent the team to their department.
4. Cause the decisions of the team to be executed in their department.
5. Contribute creatively to the implementation of the improvement activity.

COMMENT: The establishment of this team and the organization of the improvement program does not represent an additional expense for the operation. It is really pulling together and organizing things that are happening in one form or another at the present time. By formalizing it and centralizing the effort, it is possible to eliminate duplication of effort.

Step Three: Quality Measurement

Purpose: To provide a display of current and potential nonconformance problems in a manner that permits objective evaluation and corrective action.

Manufacturing Measurement

General Operation

Basic quality measurement data come from the inspection and test reports, which are broken down by operating areas of the plant. By comparing the rejection data with the input data, it is possible to know the rejection rates. Since most companies have such systems, it is not necessary to go into them in detail. It should be mentioned that unless these data are reported properly they are useless. After all, their only purpose is to warn management of serious situations. They should be used to identify specific problems needing corrective action, and they should be reported by the quality department.

Quality measurement is only effective when it is done in a manner that produces information people can understand and use. Therefore, the operating and reporting methods should be straightforward and expressed in terms such as "defects per unit," "percent defective," and so forth. In addition, defects singled out for their frequency, or problem potential, should be classified as to seriousness, cause, and responsibility. This eliminates the necessity of spending time on less significant items while more important worlds are waiting to be conquered.

Step Four: The Cost of Quality

Purpose: To define the ingredients of the cost of quality, and explain its use as a management tool.

General Operation

1. The cost of quality is composed of the following:
   Scrap
   Rework
   Warranty
   Service (except regular maintenance)
   Inspection labor
   Quality control labor
   Test labor
   Acceptance equipment costs
   Engineering changes
   Purchase order changes
   Software correction
   Consumer affairs

Audit

Other costs of doing things wrong

2. This total expense should represent no more than 2.5 percent of your sales dollar.

3. If your cost of quality is more than 2.5 percent, you have a direct opportunity to increase your return on sales by the exact amount you can reduce this expense. This reduction is most efficiently and quickly taken by concentrating on preventing the defects rather than on reducing the amount of acceptance operations, since it constitutes only a small part of the cost.

Step Five: Quality Awareness

Purpose: To provide a method of raising the personal concern felt by all personnel in the company toward the conformance of the product or service and the quality reputation of the company.

General Operation

1. By the time you are ready for the quality awareness step, you should have a good idea of the types and expense of the problems you face. These will have been revealed by the quality measurement and cost of quality steps.

2. The idea of quality awareness is to show everyone the need for improvement and prepare them for eventual commitment to the Zero Defects program.

3. The quality awareness activity has two essential ingredients:

   a. Regular meetings must be held between management and employees to discuss specific nonconformance problems and to attempt to arrive at some steps that can be taken to remove these problems. These meetings should not only be between workers and their supervisors but also between the supervisors and their managers. Meetings should be short, positive, and to the point. They must take place on a regular basis, and promises made must be kept.

   b. Information about the quality program must be communicated through posters, articles in the house organ, and special events. The purpose of this is to provide reassurance that the company is serious about the emphasis on quality and to keep the message constantly in front of the people. The material necessary is quite inexpensive and can even be homemade. Some companies run quality poster contests for the employees and their families, giving small prizes for the winners while at the same time amassing a huge supply of free posters.

The quality awareness portion of the program should be planned by the improvement team. However, they should lean heavily on public relations, personnel, and similarly skilled functions.

Step Six: Corrective Action

Purpose: To provide a systematic method of resolving forever the problems that are identified through previous action steps.

General Operation

1. Problems that are identified during the acceptance operation, or by some other means, must be documented and then resolved formally. The most direct method is to establish four levels of constant activity.

   a. Hold daily meetings between the area supervisor and a quality engineer or supervisor to examine the problems detected. Determine methods of correcting the present situations while preventing their recurrence in the future. These meetings should be documented on an item-by-item action chart that states the problem, the seriousness of the problem, and its cause, as well as who is going to do what when.

   b. Hold weekly meetings between the production general supervision and senior quality management to attack problems that cannot be, or were not, solved at the lower level. They should invite to their meetings the other department personnel involved. The meetings should be documented on the same type of action chart mentioned above.

   c. Monthly or special meetings should be held by the general manager and staff to review the unresolved problems. Items reaching this level should be specific; those requiring complex or long-range action should be assigned to a task team.

d. Task teams should consist of responsible members of each affected organization with one person appointed as chairperson. The jobs of the task team should be carefully spelled out, and their completion time specified. The team may have to meet daily until the problem is resolved. At the time the problem is judged to be eliminated, the team should be dissolved.

Step Seven: Zero Defects Planning

Purpose: To examine the various activities that must be conducted in preparation for formally launching the Zero Defects program.

General Operation

The quality improvement task team should list all the individual action steps that build up to ZD day in order to make the most meaningful presentation of the concept and action plan to personnel of the company. These steps, placed on a schedule and assigned to members of the team for execution, will provide a clean energy flow into an organization-wide ZD commitment. Since it is a natural step, it is not difficult, but because of the significance of it, management must make sure that it is conducted properly.

SPECIFIC POINTS: The main portions of ZD planning are:

1. Explaining the concept and program to all supervisory personnel. Preparing supervisors to explain it to their people.
2. Determining what material will be necessary and ensuring its preparation.
3. Deciding what method of launching the program will best suit the cultural environment of your particular operation.
4. Spelling out the functions that will be accomplished.
5. Examining the recognition policy of the company and determining what type of recognition should be used in praising improved performance.
6. Setting up the time schedule and rehearsing those who will take part.
7. Identifying the error-cause-removal program and making the plans for its execution. (step 11).

Step Eight: Supervisor Training

Purpose: To define the type of training that supervisors need in order to actively carry out their part of the quality improvement program.

General Operation

The supervisor, from the board chairman down, is the key to achieving improvement goals. The supervisor gives the individual employees their attitudes and work standards, whether in engineering, sales, computer programming, or wherever. Therefore, the supervisor must be given primary consideration when laying out the program. The departmental representatives on the task team will be able to communicate much of the planning and concepts to the supervisors, but individual classes are essential to make sure that they properly understand and can implement the program.

Supervisory training is divided into areas to be conducted at different times:

1. At the time that quality awareness is started the supervisors should be given at least six hours of instruction covering the Quality Measuring system, the cost of quality numbers, the corrective actions sytem, and the purpose of the quality awareness action. This instruction should be well planned, and should be conducted as much as possible by significant levels of management. Everyone must attend.
2. At least four weeks before the planned Zero Defects day, the supervisors should receive complete briefing on the ZD program and the error-cause-removal system that is to follow in a few weeks. It is very important that they be able to answer the questions of their subordinates. Many companies prepare a handbook

for supervisors which describes the program in detail.

3. Do it over again.

Step Nine: ZD Day

Purpose: To create an event that will let all employees realize, through a personal experience, that there has been a change.

General Operation

Zero Defects is a revelation to all involved that they are embarking on a new way to corporate life. Working under this discipline requires personal commitments and understanding. Therefore it is necessary that all members of the company participate in an experience that will make them aware of this change.

SPECIFIC POINTS: If possible, all employees should be oriented at the same time by people who are significant to the employees. Some companies have taken their personnel to the local stadium; or have brought everyone together out in front of the plant. A few have used closed-circuit television.

Face to face is best. Don't be afraid to use a little show business in the meeting. There is nothing wrong with fun and celebration on such a grand day.

Step Ten: Goal Setting

Purpose: To turn pledges and commitments into action by encouraging individuals to establish improvement goals for themselves and their groups.

General Operation

About a week after ZD day, the individual supervisors should ask their people what kind of goals they should set for themselves. Try to get two goals from each area. These goals should be specific and measurable. For example, two possibilities are:

- Reduce defects per unit 20 percent in one month.
- Win the good housekeeping award next week.

Stay away from schedule improvement goals in association with ZD; the schedule will automatically improve as the defects reduce. (Zero delinquences.)

SPECIFIC POINTS: Goal setting is most effective when it is done by the personnel themselves rather than established by the supervisor. However, the supervisor should have some idea of what he or she wants before talking to the people.

COMMENT: Don't let people settle for easy tasks. Post the goals in a conspicuous place. Make a big fuss over any group that improves—progress is a start.

Step Eleven: Error-Cause Removal

Purpose: To give the individual employee a method of communicating to management the situations that make it difficult for the employee to meet the pledge to improve.

General Operation

One of the most difficult problems employees face is their inability to communicate problems to management. Sometimes they just put up with problems because they do not consider them important enough to bother the supervisor. Sometimes supervisors just don't listen anyway. Suggestion programs are some help, but in a suggestion program the worker is required to know the problem and also propose a solution. Error-cause-removal (ECR) is set up on the basis that the worker has stated the problem, the proper department in the plant can look into it. Studies of ECR programs show that over 90 percent of the items submitted are acted upon, and fully 75 percent can be handled at the first level of supervision. The number of ECRs that save money is extremely high, since the worker generates savings every time the job is done better or quicker. . . .

There are always people who are afraid that doing a program like ECR will cause a lot of internal trouble because people might write abusive things when they have the chance to address notes to management. Yet it hasn't happened that way. It is like the fear of union reaction. Unions always support ZD programs because if nothing else the programs focus attention on the workers.

Step Twelve: Recognition

Purpose: To appreciate those who participate.

General Operation

People really don't work for money. They go to work for it, but once the salary has been established, their concern is appreciation. Recognize their contribution publicly and noisily, but don't demean them by applying a price tag to everything.

Supervisors are very concerned about getting people to work better. By this they mean that they want their employees to put forth a little extra—particularly in the areas of output, quality, and efficiency. Recognition must be given for achieving specific goals worked out in advance, and the employees must have the opportunity to help select the goals.

The Quality Management Maturity Grid

QUALITY MANAGEMENT MATURITY GRID

Rater _____   Unit _____

Measurement Categories	Stage I: Uncertainty	Stage II: Awakening	Stage III: Enlightenment	Stage IV: Wisdom	Stage V: Certainty
Management understanding and attitude	No comprehension of quality as a management tool. Tend to blame quality department for "quality problems."	Recognizing that quality management may be of value but not willing to provide money or time to make it all happen.	While going through quality improvement program learn more about quality management; becoming supportive and helpful.	Participating. Understand absolutes of quality management. Recognize their personal role in continuing emphasis.	Consider quality management an essential part of company system.
Quality organization status	Quality is hidden in manufacturing or engineering departments. Inspection probably not part of organization. Emphasis on appraisal and sorting.	A stronger quality leader is appointed but main emphasis is still on appraisal and moving the product. Still part of manufacturing or other.	Quality department reports to top management, all appraisal is incorporated and manager has role in management of company.	Quality manager is an officer of company; effective status reporting and preventive action. Involved with consumer affairs and special assignments.	Quality manager on board of directors. Prevention is main concern. Quality is a thought leader.
Problem handling	Problems are fought as they occur; no resolution; inadequate definition; lots of yelling and accusations.	Teams are set up to attack major problems. Long-range solutions are not solicited.	Corrective action communication established. Problems are faced openly and resolved in an orderly way.	Problems are identified early in their development. All functions are open to suggestion and improvement.	Except in the most unusual cases, problems are prevented.
Cost of quality as % of sales	Reported: unknown Actual: 20%	Reported: 3% Actual: 18%	Reported: 8% Actual: 12%	Reported: 6.5% Actual: 8%	Reported: 2.5% Actual: 2.5%
Quality improvement actions	No organized activities. No understanding of such activities.	Trying obvious "motivational" short-range efforts.	Implementation of the 14-step program with thorough understanding and establishment of each step.	Continuing the 14-step program and starting Make Certain.	Quality improvement is a normal and continued activity.
Summation of company quality posture	"We don't know why we have problems with quality."	"Is it absolutely necessary to always have problems with quality?"	"Through management commitment and quality improvement we are identifying and resolving our problems."	"Defect prevention is a routine part of our operation."	"We know why we do not have problems with quality."

The contest and the measurement are the key. The prize is not significant. It only matters that all of an individual's contemporaries know that he or she has fought the good fight and won.

Above all, individuals must know that management seriously needs their help and sincerely appreciates it.

Step Thirteen: Quality Councils

Purpose: To bring together the professional quality people for planned communication on a regular basis.

General Operation

It is vital for the professional quality people of an organization to meet regularly just to share their problems, feelings, and experiences with each other. Primarily concerned with measurement and reporting, isolated even in the midst of many fellow workers, it is easy for them to become influenced by the urgency of activity in their work areas.

Consistency of attitude and purpose is the essential personal characteristic of one who evaluates another's work. This is not only because of the importance of the work itself but because those who submit work unconsciously draw a great deal of their performance standard from the professional evaluator.

So bring the quality control people together regularly. Let them ask their own questions, and expose them to other members of management. Do everything in a formal manner.

In multiplant operations the worth of interchange becomes even more apparent. Councils should select their own chairmen, create their own agenda, and determine their own meeting times. Free exchange brings growth. Membership should not be restricted by the organizational rank of the professional.

Step Fourteen: Do It Over Again

Purpose: To emphasize that the quality improvement program never ends.

General Operation

There is always a great sigh of relief when goals are reached. If you are not careful, the entire program will end at that moment. It is necessary to construct a new team, and to let them begin again and create their own communications.

36. Copeland Corporation: Evolution of a Manufacturing Strategy, 1975–1982 (A)

In February 1982, senior managers of the Copeland Corporation were struggling to decide how the company's home plant in Sidney, Ohio, should be reorganized. During the previous five years, Copeland had built three new state-of-the-art plants and had transferred products from Sidney to the new facilities. Each of these plants was a "focused factory," confined to a limited product line or production process. (For more on the concept of focused factories, see *Exhibit 1*.) Each had enjoyed immediate success. But because of this strategy, the Sidney plant now seemed a confused jumble, consisting of 13 product lines, as well as diverse production processes and equipment.

One obvious solution—moving the remaining products out of Sidney to newly constructed facilities—was not possible. Costs were prohibitive, and management wanted to avoid shutting the Sidney plant. Two options were therefore under consideration; both involved separating the existing factory into distinct parts, or "plants within a plant." In one case the split would be by process—a separation of machining and assembly activities; in the other, by product—hermetic versus semi-hermetic compressors. Either way, a successful reorganization would require skills and approaches different from those used in the other focused factories. As Matthew (Matt) Diggs, Jr., Copeland's president and CEO, observed:

This case was prepared by Artemis March under the direction of David A. Garvin.

Copyright © 1986 by the President and Fellows of Harvard College. Harvard Business School case 686-088.

Unlike our three previous projects, it's been very hard to get an engineering handle on Sidney. The issues have been softer, more interpersonal, and have called for artistry and precision investment rather than bold strokes.

History, Products, and Markets

Since 1937, the Copeland Corporation had made compressor and condenser units for commercial refrigeration. Compressors were the most costly component of a refrigeration system; they soon became and remained about 90% of the company's outside sales.

Semi-hermetic Compressors

In the 1940s, Copeland achieved a major breakthrough in compressor design. It encased both motor and pump within the same cast-iron housing, so that it was "hermetic," or sealed. But the interior was still accessible because the head, gaskets, and other parts were bolted together; the entire unit could be either assembled or taken apart with wrenches or air guns. Such accessibility meant that the compressor was field-serviceable and that a parts business was viable. Because the compressor was both accessible and sealed, it was called "*semi*-hermetic." Copeland referred to these compressors as "Copelametics." (See *Exhibit* 2.)

The company developed two primary refrigeration markets for its semi-hermetic compressors: original equipment manufacturers (OEMs),

EXHIBIT 1 Focused Factories and Manufacturing Strategy

1. *Manufacturing should be a strategic, not simply a technical, activity.*
   a. The objectives, structure, and infrastructure of the manufacturing system should derive from and support the strategic objectives of the business.
   b. Manufacturing's structure (capacity, facilities, technology, and degree of vertical integration) and infrastructure (work force, organization, and systems) need to be internally consistent with each other as well as with the company's decisions on how to compete.

2. *Typically, this link between competitive strategy and manufacturing is missing.*
   a. Top management's discomfort with technical and nuts-and-bolts issues frequently leads it to delegate not merely these tactical decisions, but also the de facto manufacturing policies that result from myriad—and often conflicting—operating decisions made by technical specialists.
   b. Top management is often unaware that all production systems involve trade-offs. No one system can do everything well, but conflicting demands placed on manufacturing frequently assume that it can.

3. *Management must recast its thinking. Instead of asking, "How do we cut costs/increase productivity?", it must ask, "How can we compete?"*
   a. Different competitive choices impose different demands on the manufacturing system.
   b. The question management must ask is: "What must we be good at in manufacturing in order to enhance our competitive position?"
   c. The answer to this question defines the key manufacturing tasks of the business: the critical objectives that manufacturing must achieve in order to support the strategy.

4. *The manufacturing task provides the basis for focusing manufacturing.*
   a. A focused factory limits the number of process technologies, market demands, product volumes, and quality levels that the plant attempts to handle.
   b. A focused factory thus has a limited, concise, manageable set of tasks.
   c. A focused factory accepts the reality that no one plant can be all things to all people and consciously accepts the trade-offs inherent in any production system.

5. *Implementation of a focused factory approach does not necessarily entail building new plants. A practical alternative is a "plant within a plant" (PWP) approach.*
   a. An existing facility can be divided physically and organizationally into two or more plants.
   b. Each PWP has its own manufacturing task, its own work force, production systems, quality standards, production volumes, equipment, and support services.

Note: This summary draws upon the following articles: Wickham Skinner, "Manufacturing—Missing Link in Corporate Strategy," *Harvard Business Review*, May–June 1969; Wickham Skinner, "The Anachronistic Factory," *Harvard Business Review*, January–February 1971; Wickham Skinner, "The Decline, Fall, and Renewal of Manufacturing Plants," *Industrial Engineering*, October 1974; and Wickham Skinner, "The Focused Factory," *Harvard Business Review*, May–June 1974.

EXHIBIT 2 Semi-Hermetic and Hermetic Compressors

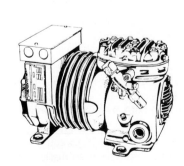

Copelametic®
Semi-Hermetic Compressor

Copelaweld®
Hermetic Compressor

such as Hussmann and Friedrich, and wholesalers. The advanced design and high reliability of these tough, cast-iron "workhorses" enabled Copeland to develop a significant lead in supermarket refrigeration and gain a strong position in all related segments of the market. Because the refrigeration industry was highly fragmented and many OEMs specialized in narrow product lines, Copeland rapidly expanded its offerings. Refrigeration applications came to include produce and meat cases for grocery stores and supermarkets, ice cream and frozen-food cases, back-room cabinets and racks for sequenced defrosting of different types of food, walk-in coolers, milk tanks, and vending machines.

Copeland leveraged its sales to OEMs by strength in after-sales service. The company's national network of 450 independent refrigeration wholesalers, developed during the 1940s and 1950s, guaranteed four-hour replacement should a supermarket case fail. Such service was, according to Diggs, "a powerful incentive to OEMs to use

EXHIBIT 3 Remanufacturing

What is Remanufacturing?

"Remanufacturing is an industrial process in which worn-out products (called 'cores') are restored to like-new condition. In a typical remanufacturing process, identical cores are grouped into production batches, completely disassembled, and thoroughly cleaned. Component parts are replaced at least back to the level of the product when new. The product is assembled, finished, tested, packaged, and distributed in the same manner as new products. Even the warranty on a remanufactured product is usually similar or identical to the OEM new product warranty."

How Is Remanufacturing Different from Original Manufacturing?

"The major differences between manufacturing and remanufacturing arise as a consequence of using worn-out, discarded, or defective products as the primary materials source. This factor affects not only the production process employed but also the contractual relationship with customers, who are also suppliers. . . . The incoming material—the core—is known to be defective in some way. . . . The production of reliable products from parts of unknown quality is one of the greatest tests of a remanufacturer's skills. . . .

"Because a very high percentage of parts are recovered during remanufacture, there is little or no need for large investments in parts-making capital equipment. The major machinery investments are in cleaning, refurbishing, assembly, and testing equipment. Remanufacturing tends to be labor intensive rather than capital intensive."

What Are the Criteria that Distinguish Products that Lend Themselves to Remanufacturing?

a) The product technology is stable;
b) the process technology is stable;
c) the product is one that fails functionally rather than by dissolution or dissipation;
d) the product has a "core" that can be the basis of the restored product;
e) a continuing supply of such cores is available (such as through a service agency or wholesaler network);
f) the core is capable of being disassembled and of being restored to its original condition;
g) the product is one that is factory-built rather than field-assembled;
h) the recoverable value added in the core is high relative to both its market value and to its original cost.

Note: The quotations and description are taken with permission from Robert T. Lund, *Guidelines for an Original Equipment Manufacturer Starting a Remanufacturing Operation* (Massachusetts Institute of Technology, Center for Policy Alternatives, 1983).

our compressors. If the case fails, the supermarket doesn't call us, it doesn't call the OEM, it calls the local Copeland wholesaler."

The compressors sold by Copeland's wholesalers could be new, but since 1960 were more likely to have been rebuilt or remanufactured. Rebuilds were factory-repaired compressors. Bad parts were replaced or repaired; since there was little or no regauging of functioning parts, rebuilt products retained their "used" identity. By contrast, remanufactured products were completely disassembled and cleaned; parts were then replaced or brought back to their original condition and reassembled from inventories of new and regauged parts. The original product thus lost its identity, and the final compressor was virtually as good as new. (See *Exhibit 3* for a fuller description of remanufacturing.) The primary competition faced by Copeland wholesalers carrying its rebuilt or remanufactured compressors consisted of 200 independent rebuilders who competed on price. Copeland's primary selling point in this market was the reliability and quality of its products.

Hermetic Compressors

During the 1950s, Copeland moved into three segments of the growing air-conditioning market: commercial, residential central, and room (or window) units. While semi-hermetic compressors could be used in larger commercial air-conditioning applications, they were too powerful and costly for smaller commercial and most residential use. For these new businesses, the company, as Diggs later put it, "blundered into hermetics," but brought with it a "semi-hermetic mentality: rugged, overdesigned, customized, and low volume." Hermetic compressors were so named because they were totally sealed within a welded shell and thus were not field-serviceable. For this reason, hermetics were also called "welded" compressors, and Copeland referred to its own products in this category as Copelawelds. (See *Exhibits 2* and *4*.)

From the 1950s on, Copeland faced much tougher competition in the three air-conditioning markets than in refrigeration. In each segment, it faced Tecumseh Products, a high-volume, low-cost producer that sold *its* bills of materials to customers and refused to customize its products;

it also faced captive producers. Moreover, air-conditioning OEMs had thinner margins than their refrigeration counterparts and bought compressors on price. Wholesalers as well as OEMs usually bought new compressors; at $80–$120 (contrasted with $500–$1,200 for semi-hermetics), field repairs were seldom cost-effective, and rebuilds were neither essential nor widely available.

Compressor Manufacturing

From their inception, both Copelametics and Copelawelds were manufactured at the Sidney plant. The company purchased raw castings, which would become the bodies of its compressors, as well as most other components such as valve plates, pistons, and rods. Copeland's skilled machinists then milled, bored, and drilled the many openings, surfaces, and parts, first to rough dimensions, and then, on finish lines, reamed and honed to precise tolerances (.0001 inch). After machining, parts were brought by miles of overhead conveyors to the assemblers at carousels. These slowly rotating lines had 20–25 workstations, at which fixtures, sized for a particular model, held partially assembled compressors in place. Each assembler added a component or a subassembly that had been put together elsewhere. The compressor was then dried out in the dehydration department, final components were added, it was tested for leaks, painted to retard rust, packed and shipped. All the steps following the machining of components were loosely referred to as "assembly."

Matt Diggs Arrives

Matt Diggs's first contact with Copeland came in 1969 as a member of a Booz, Allen & Hamilton consulting team called in to investigate Copeland's cost and quality problems. The team recommended management changes and marketing reorganization, leading the board to hire a new president, Carl Moeller, a General Electric executive who had run the company's air-conditioning business. Moeller concentrated on putting in tight financial controls and other complex systems; these changes sensitized managers to quality and impressed on them the need for more than words or slogans. In 1972, Moeller hired Diggs as vice president of marketing.

Diggs shifted the company's marketing ap-

EXHIBIT 4 Timeline

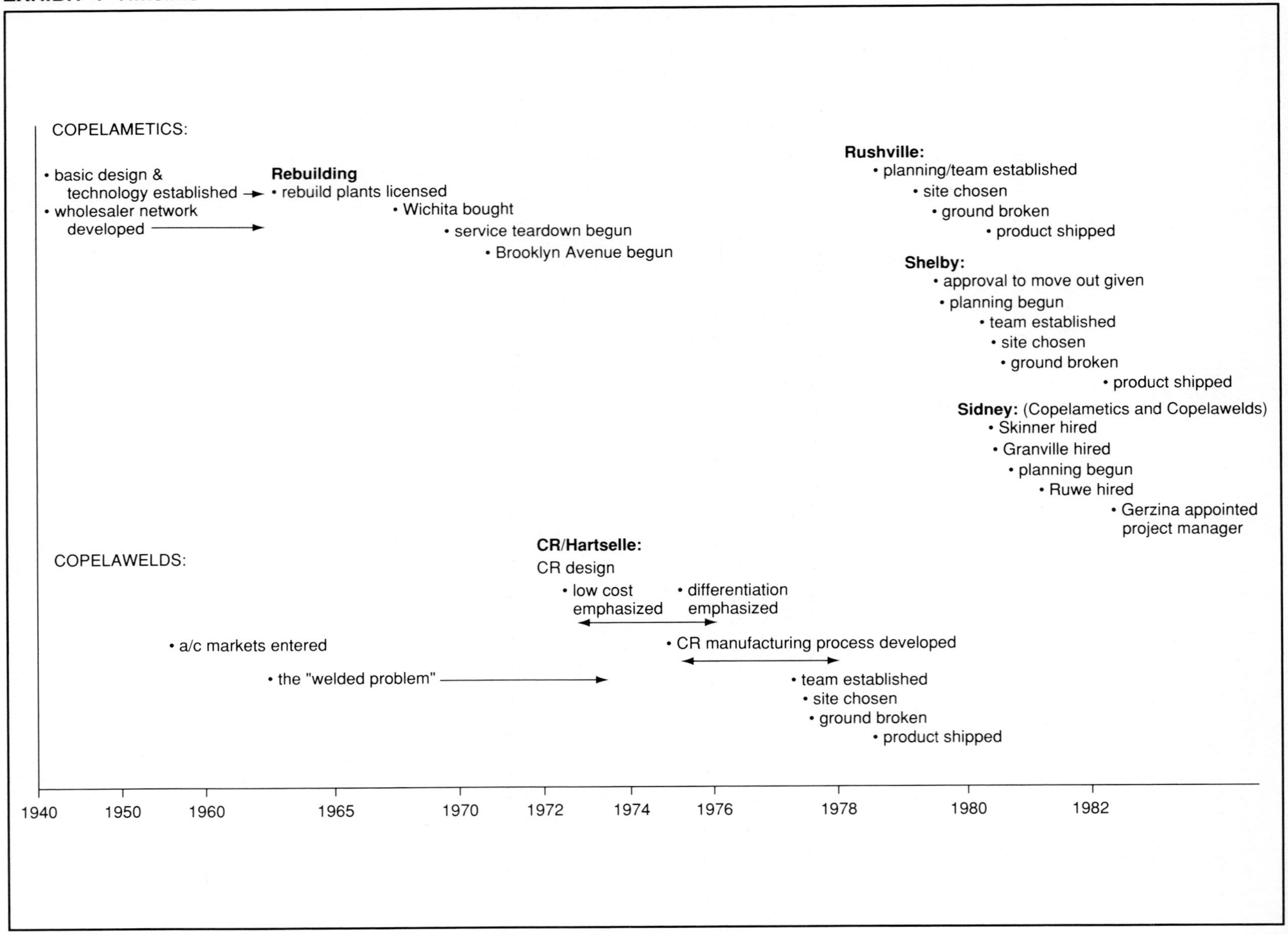

COPELAMETICS:

Rebuilding

- basic design &
  technology established → • rebuild plants licensed
- wholesaler network   • Wichita bought
  developed   • service teardown begun
                                        • Brooklyn Avenue begun

Rushville:
- planning/team established
  • site chosen
    • ground broken
      • product shipped

Shelby:
- approval to move out given
  • planning begun
    • team established
      • site chosen
        • ground broken
          • product shipped

Sidney: (Copelametics and Copelawelds)
- Skinner hired
  • Granville hired
    • planning begun
      • Ruwe hired
        • Gerzina appointed
          project manager

CR/Hartselle:
CR design
- low cost   • differentiation
  emphasized   emphasized
              • CR manufacturing process developed
                  • team established
                    • site chosen
                      • ground broken
                        • product shipped

COPELAWELDS:
- a/c markets entered
  • the "welded problem"

| 1940 | 1950 | 1960 | 1965 | 1970 | 1972 | 1974 | 1976 | 1978 | 1980 | 1982 |

36. Copeland Corporation: Evolution of a Manufacturing Strategy, 1975–1982 (A)

proach to one of defining and serving distinct markets. Previously, he observed,

> We had customers and sold to them. But we did not differentiate between them as parts of different markets. We were customer-oriented—very flexible, very accommodating—but not market-oriented.

Diggs also set up a Product Services group within marketing to focus on after-market sales to refrigeration wholesalers.

Evolution of the CR Product

The "Welded Problem"

During the 1960s and early 1970s, the company invested major resources in its hermetic compressors. Yet their contribution remained small, their costs high, and their failure rates just marginally acceptable. Management referred to these difficulties as the "welded problem." Moeller thought the high costs resulted from an absence of vertical integration and proposed that the company become more integrated. He also initiated work on a new hermetic design called the CR line, a product whose vertically integrated production would cut costs by 20% and which would be aimed at the heart of the unitary residential market.

Diggs, however, viewed the situation differently. He saw the 1973 energy crisis as a once-in-a-lifetime opportunity to differentiate Copeland's hermetic products, normally considered commodities, by their energy efficiency. Moreover, Diggs reasoned that Tecumseh, which was no more vertically integrated than Copeland, actually derived its cost advantage from skill in high-volume, repetitive manufacturing. He concluded that vertical integration was not the answer to Copeland's welded problem.

Product and Process Design

After Carl Moeller's retirement in 1975, Diggs assumed the presidency of Copeland. Immediately, he pressed for a CR design that was highly energy efficient rather than inexpensive; indeed, his insistence on improved reliability ultimately led to cost increases. The number of parts was reduced, all major components were standardized across models, and the number of models became few and standardized.

The design process for the CR differed from past design efforts in several ways. For example, Diggs wanted a quantum change in quality; to get it, he insisted on three stages of reliability testing: accelerated performance and life testing during development to predict field performance; field testing to verify that performance; and qualification testing to determine whether the compressor was visually, dimensionally, and functionally within specifications. Improved reliability was also sought by bringing engineering and manufacturing together before, rather than after, designs were ready for tooling, initiating a practice that would be used in the future for all new products.

The design group began by considering such problems as how to reduce defects and scrap. Its constraint was an assumed total investment in the CR project of $10 million–$12 million. But when members of the group would propose a new idea, Diggs would say, "It's not good enough. Let's do it right," and would send it back for revision. Eventually, "right" would come to include $500,000 for an automated air gap station, which ensured that the rotor (which was pressed on one end of the crankshaft) was absolutely centered relative to the stator, as well as automated body and piston lines, which had solid-state programmable controllers and automatic tool adjustment. As one observer summarized the process:

> The vision came from Matt. If the team had been left to its own devices, the results would have been fairly pedestrian. Matt pushed and encouraged, and that's what led to the bold stroke.

In its final form, the bold stroke was a $30 million investment in a new design and a new manufacturing process, to be located in a new plant, adding one million units of capacity to the industry. To make an investment of this size pay off, Copeland, whose net worth was then $50 million, would have to take at least 10 market share points.

Location of Manufacturing

Until mid-1976, it had been assumed that the CR would be made at Sidney, replacing existing Sidney Copelawelds. But a bitter three-month strike and customer concerns about potential disruption of supply changed Diggs's perspective. Moreover, the prevailing manufacturing mindset at Sidney also pointed toward a new location. An outside consulting firm was called in for advice; it concluded that Copeland would surely fail if it tried a new product, a new plant, a new process, and new management all at once. Nevertheless, Diggs decided to proceed with the new plant.

To coordinate all aspects of the project, Diggs created a project management team reporting directly to him. Assistant Project Manager Michael (Mike) O'Keeffe summarized the team's role by saying, "We forced people to communicate and to put their cards on the table."

HARTSELLE. The team's mission was to find a site for the factory, supervise its construction, and begin the hiring process. After considering several southern sites, it settled on Hartselle, Alabama. To manage the factory, Diggs wanted someone who was progressive, ambitious, strongly oriented to quality, and who knew the compressor business. In April 1978, he hired Richard (Dick) Peltier, who had spent 10 years building hermetic compressors at General Electric, as plant manager. Peltier recalled:

> Matt said to me, "You need to be good at precision machining and assembly; anything else—like trying to lower costs through vertical integration—is peripheral. Your mission is to make a high-volume, narrow product line in long runs at low costs. There will be lots of drive on the part of this organization to proliferate the product; you resist, and I'll back you."

Key Manufacturing Tasks

To achieve high volume at low costs, Diggs believed quality was essential. He had therefore steered the engineers toward machines and processes that would consistently hold precise tolerances, making assemblers' jobs simpler and final products more likely to work. For these reasons, planning and investment had focused on the machine shop. In the same spirit, Peltier chose process control in machining as his key task and developed systems to make it a reality. He concentrated on statistical quality control because of its fit with the quality-through-automation approach to equipment. To support this approach,

the quality manager became the number-two man at Hartselle—"a very unusual situation," according to O'Keeffe.

Manufacturing-Marketing Relationships

Hartselle opened its doors in record time. The first products were made in October 1978. To get from start-up to full production, however, Diggs insisted on a more moderate pace. He told Peltier: "Tell me how rapidly you can come up and still keep things under control, and that's how many orders we'll take." This directive was quickly tested during Hartselle's second winter, when demand for the CR escalated rapidly. At that time, Diggs accepted orders only for what Hartselle could machine, temporarily shifting additional CR assembly to Sidney (because Hartselle could machine more than it could assemble, this shift left the two activities in balance). But many customer requests still went unfilled; as Diggs recalled, "Some of our customers were furious." The effects of such a paced start-up were felt throughout the organization. According to O'Keeffe, "Marketing had always run the company, so they just couldn't believe it. The change was visible at the highest levels, and it went down hard."

But manufacturing at Hartselle was still driven by the market, as Diggs noted in retrospect:

> We were working with a narrow conception of manufacturing strategy: What does it take to serve *this* market? It was really a marketing strategy, with manufacturing the key to achieving our marketing objectives. We knew that our product-design features could be matched in a few years, but we wanted to make our competitive advantage endure. We did that through the reliability provided by our manufacturing process.

Manufacturing's support of marketing was given visibility by Hartselle's use as a showplace for customers. To convince customers that Hartselle's quality could not be beaten, plant tours were frequently arranged.

Results and Learning

Rewards for the paced start-up came almost immediately. High-volume production was attained without a hitch—something that had never before happened in the air-conditioning industry. Previously, all new products had experienced call-backs, field failures, or other quality problems. Industry veterans were amazed; as one observer noted, "word spread like wildfire." The CR took a respectable share of the hermetic market in 1980 and held a quarter of the entire unitary market the following year. Subsequent to Hartselle, none of the captive producers expanded their hermetic production. Diggs summarized the impact that Hartselle had on Copeland:

> Our present management team began to come together around Hartselle. We learned we had to excel, not just be good. We found we could break some barriers on quality and on process. And we saw from our market results that we could differentiate a black metal device in the minds of our customers.

The term "focused factory" was used for the first time at Copeland to refer to the Hartselle plant. After having seen the word "focus" in another company's annual report, Diggs described Hartselle, in his own 1978 annual report, as a "focused plant, where the organization, manufacturing processes, and facilities are all concentrated on a single product—the CR compressor." Hartselle had begun as an opportunity to "step out" and create an enduring competitive advantage in a single product line; over time, its impact was far greater. According to Diggs:

> Before Hartselle, our plants made stuff. But after Hartselle, our orchestra had a new section in it, and we had a new weapon—a tank. For the first time, we realized that manufacturing could be a competitive weapon.

Rebuilding and Remanufacturing

Copeland's Early Rebuild Efforts, 1960–71

During the 1960s, Copeland licensed three independent firms to rebuild its semi-hermetic compressors, bought a fourth, and began rebuilding at Sidney. The latter activity, called "service teardown," was located in the midst of original manufacturing. Control was loose, and remachined parts often intermingled with new ones, becoming incorporated in new compressors. Separate accounting procedures, materials systems,

and qualification areas were therefore developed, and rebuilds were assigned to the new Product Services group, which brought together all aftermarket activities.

Brooklyn Avenue, 1972–76

Service teardown was next moved to an old wooden structure on Brooklyn Avenue, about three miles from the main Sidney plant. Because of their proximity, the two plants were governed by the same union and same seniority rules on bumping. Diggs began to appreciate the need for a separate work force to perform rebuilding because of the specialized knowledge and skills required. Rebuild workers not only had to recognize, by sight, the enormous number of parts contained in current models, but also had to recognize compressor parts going back 20 or 30 years. In addition, they had to be able to spot defective parts, know how to test for defects, when to throw parts away, and how to salvage what could be rebuilt.

While the move to Brooklyn Avenue had reduced rebuild problems and improved aftermarket delivery, problems of materials control, layout, and capacity remained. To Diggs, these issues were secondary to the potential threat posed to Copeland by the poor quality of its rebuilt compressors. He commented:

> Our failure rates were upsetting. But because wholesalers provided rapid replacement, our refrigeration customers had not yet perceived a problem. Even so, I felt our rebuilds were making us vulnerable at the heart of our core business. By then, I perceived the quality problem as inherent in the rebuild process itself. I wanted new processes in a real factory and a dedicated work force.

Diggs devised a two-pronged attack: moving rebuilds out of Brooklyn Avenue and establishing clearly in the minds of customers the superiority of Copeland's rebuilt products. The term "remanufactured" would be used to herald the change and to distinguish the new products. In order to escape the work-force disruption caused by bumping between original manufacturing and rebuilding, Diggs concluded that semi-hermetic remanufacturing would have to be located outside of Sidney. The site chosen was Rushville, Indiana.

Remanufacturing at Rushville

The world-class remanufacturing plant envisioned by Diggs had several objectives. Like Hartselle, it was expected to differentiate Copeland products through manufacturing excellence. The production process would therefore be state-of-the-art, especially when compared with rebuilding. The latter was typically a labor-intensive, cash-cow business in which equipment investment rarely exceeded $200,000. By contrast, Copeland expected to spend $6 million on plant and equipment at Rushville in order to "do it right."

To begin, Diggs set up a project team headed by Bruce Oelschlager, who had run the rebuild plant bought by Copeland; its aim was "to rely on the process to control itself." The team designed a layout and materials handling system that ensured the product was never off the line. Flexibility became a primary goal, since Rushville had to handle all 10 semi-hermetic bodies. Dedicated fixtures, designed for one or two body sizes (as in original manufacturing), were therefore ruled out. At each disassembly step, broken or obsolete parts were thrown into scrap bins and segregated by metal type, as were all running parts, such as rod-and-piston assemblies, which were routinely replaced. Rotors, stators, and bodies were remachined and requalified in separate routings that fed back to the assembly area. Other salvageable parts were remachined and regauged, with each station in the machine shop reworking a particular part to precise tolerances. Fine-tuning was the heart of the operation, in contrast to the more substantial work, using large machine tools, that typified original compressor manufacturing. After machining and gauging, requalified parts returned to the assembly area, where they were put together in sequence, reversing the steps that had been used to take them apart.

Quality was sought through investment in one-of-a-kind equipment (such as the derust washer designed to clean all body cavities and all iron and steel parts); through special gauges that were themselves requalified every six months (a desk full of small gauges for measuring crankshafts to .0001 inch cost $50,000); and through efforts to ensure operator responsibility. Operators were trained to both perform and inspect work activities, including their own setups; they were also held responsible for the quality of parts that left their areas.

Once Rushville was up and running in 1980, reporting relationships were reorganized. Remanufacturing was pulled from Product Services to become part of operations, even though other after-market functions stayed in marketing. The shift in technology was the major reason for regrouping. Now that remanufacturing relied upon sophisticated production and quality-control methods, manufacturing expertise was deemed essential for proper control.

Large Cope Focused Factory: Shelby

Stimulus for Change

Once Hartselle was operational and Rushville planning was underway, Diggs turned to the remaining products at Sidney. In particular, he was concerned about large Copelametics, the 20–40 horsepower models that were the heart of the refrigeration market. These could be distinguished from other Copelametics by their manufacturing requirements and by their markets. Tooling, fixtures, and body lines, for example, were all heavier and more costly than for smaller models.

Several factors triggered the decision to move "large Copes" out of Sidney. Two were technical. Copeland had recently devised a new type of valve that was 15% more energy efficient and thus particularly cost-effective for large compressors. Use of this valve, however, would put more stress on other components. For this reason, and because large Copes already had higher failure rates than desired, Diggs saw the new valve as an opportunity to upgrade the entire product design. Second, the high failure rates of large rebuilt compressors were due not only to the rebuild process used prior to Rushville, but also to marginal tolerances established during the products' original manufacture. Therefore, retooling the machine shop for large Copes would enhance Rushville's long-term success while also improving the reliability of new products. But making these product and process investments in Sidney seemed unwise to Diggs, particularly after a 1979 strike rekindled the question of continuity of supply. After pickets blocked the company's directors from entering the building for a board meeting, Diggs recommended and received approval to move large Copelametics out of Sidney. He observed, "We had a very high market share and customers who were very dependent on us. I could no longer take the risk of being held hostage by the labor situation."

Large Cope Focused Factory (LCFF) Project

Diggs asked product engineering to upgrade the large Cope designs to improve their performance and reliability, and advanced manufacturing engineering to size the plant, plan the investment, develop a layout, and order equipment. But when offered several early investment proposals, he rejected them, because of their high costs. O'Keeffe, who by then was Diggs's assistant, recalled, "The engineers were frustrated because they could not make it perfect." Once a more realistic budget of $20 million was established, Diggs withdrew from active project management. The project team reported to the vice president of manufacturing, whose greatest strengths lay in technical problem solving.

SELECTIVE INVESTMENT. With limits now established on Shelby spending, the engineers quickly became more selective about investment, looking for ways, as one member put it, "to get the biggest bang for the buck." Assembly was given top billing because the cost of completely new assembly equipment, which was desirable because of the complexity of Copelametics, was only $3 million. Engineers then developed a method for investing selectively in the machine shop. Because ease of assembly required certain tolerances to be achieved consistently, manufacturing engineers asked product engineers, What are the dimensions critical to Copelametic performance? These were then color-coded by degree of importance. Next, quality control was asked, What tolerances can you hold? These responses were also ranked and color-coded. When the two sets of color-coded drawings were placed side-by-side, major deficiencies were immediately visible, indicating areas of needed investment. This procedure led to a $6 million body line, which had precision boring, drilling, and honing machines that created absolute perpendicularity between cylinder bores and crankshafts, and a $5 million crankshaft line with programmable controllers.

NEW ASSEMBLY. That Shelby emphasized assembly to a greater degree than Hartselle reflected a basic difference between semi-hermetic and hermetic compressors. Because of their design, the former had many more parts per unit; because of product proliferation they also had many more parts overall. According to one expert:

> Copeland's semi-hermetic compressors were designed in the 1940s and 1950s, so they are much more likely to fail if they are not put together right. There's also a wider distribution of dimensions, so you get more variability among parts. For example, if you've got a "big" cylinder, you're going to need a "big" piston—even though we're talking tenths of thousandths of an inch, it makes a difference in ensuring that parts fit together and function. Assemblers of semi-hermetics will therefore do a lot more sorting of parts and more fitting and fussing.

Semi-hermetic assembly was therefore heavily operator-dependent. By contrast, welded products like the CR were easier to put together; if their parts were precisely machined, they were also guaranteed to function properly. The implication, according to Peltier, was that:

> At Hartselle, we needed to control the process, so we paid a lot of attention to the machine shop. But at Shelby we needed to control the product, so assembly was critical. Where Copelametics are concerned, operators must look at every product they're working on to ensure that they have the right parts, that they're putting them together correctly, and that the right product is shipped.

For these reasons, an intelligent, well-educated work force was a prime factor in site selection. Shelby had a good school system, and half of the hourly workers had some college education. Virtually all were trained for several operations. Innovations in individual workstation design were also made to ensure that compressors were assembled correctly.

What to Do About Sidney

By mid-1980, Copeland had focused factories operating at Hartselle and Rushville, and was planning a third at Shelby. Sidney's collection of diverse product lines had been greatly reduced. But even after large Copes were moved out, the factory would still be home to eight Copelametic and five Copelaweld families. Diggs described the situation:

> We had initiated three bold strokes and now were left with a mediocre plant. There was no marketing imperative, no external force driving change, no complaints about quality. But I could see that Sidney's products were not going to be adequate in the future; there would be cost and quality problems somewhere down the road. So what should be done with this plant?

Closing Sidney was an option that management preferred not to take. Copeland had been headquartered there for many years, and Diggs felt responsible for the work force and the local community. Moreover, if products were moved to another site, all Copelametic blueprints would have to be redrawn, since manufacturing methods had evolved at Sidney through years of shop practice. Copelametic manufacturing was now run by "managing the gaps" between blueprints and actual products; these gaps were spanned by years of experience carried in operators' heads. It would take enormous work to redraw the blueprints and develop test programs for each one, a necessity if the factory were moved. Because of the time and cost involved, and because of the age of Sidney's products, a move could not be justified.

In September 1980, Copeland hired a new plant manager, Wesley (Wes) Granville. Diggs recalled his expectations:

> I wanted someone who could manage people. I hoped we could get the labor situation stabilized and could run the plant better, but I didn't think the labor problem was solvable. We still had no idea of restructuring Sidney; we just wanted to do it better.

Granville was experienced in machining and in statistical quality control. He considered his prime task to be the development of people who could run their own plant, and he quickly got to know his hourly workers on a first-name basis. Granville recalled:

> We had to get the corporate guys out of Sidney. At the time, you'd walk into the plant and they were everywhere. The plant people were dependent on them. That kind of dependence can only be changed by growing people so that they not only learn their own roles, but also how to work as a unit.

Early Discussions About Change

A few weeks after he was hired, Granville began talking with other Sidney managers about changes in the machine shop that could be made without major capital investments. A prime goal was the reduction of Copelaweld costs. Diggs called in Wickham (Wick) Skinner, who had developed the focused factory concept, to consult with them about how to modernize Sidney's "white elephant." In January 1981, he hired Dean Ruwe as vice president of operations.

Ruwe spent his first few months on the job trying to understand Sidney better. The process was immensely frustrating, as he later acknowledged:

> Nothing I had ever encountered had the complexity and problems I found at Sidney. At first I thought maybe we could try harder, but then I saw that they had been trying harder for a long time and just couldn't get it any better. More basic change was needed.

Throughout 1981, Ruwe orchestrated an educational process based on Skinner's work on manufacturing strategy. Diggs later acknowledged that he had been frustrated at the time by the slowness of the process, but felt that "we needed the kind of consensus that Dean built. He had to create a manufacturing management team that functioned in a different way." O'Keefe also cited Ruwe's contribution:

> We had floundered for months talking about Sidney and really didn't make any progress until Dean had been here for awhile. He understood what Matt was asking for, saw Wick as a resource, and knew how to involve people.

The year-long dialogue produced four strategic goals for Sidney: a quantum improvement in Copelametic quality, a quantum improvement in Copelaweld costs, a quantum improvement in systems, and simplification of certain design specifications. These goals were refined, and in some cases, quantified. The idea that Sidney had to be focused through the use of "plants within a plant" began to take hold, although there was some resistance at first. Several managers felt that if Sidney were split in this way, costs could only go up because two of everything—for example, management teams, engineering groups, and materials systems—would be required. Ruwe, however, with support from Diggs and Skinner, proceeded "on faith." Eventually, the experience of wrestling with these problems brought home the real meaning of focused factories, as Granville recalled:

> When *most* plants are built, they're expected to concentrate on a particular product. That's not peculiar to focused factories. But when you get an old plant like Sidney and try to split it up, then you really begin to understand what's involved in focus. For us, that's when the concept finally sunk in.

Over time, many terms were applied to the project; the one that stuck was "Sidney Revitalization."

Sidney Revitalization

In early 1982, Ruwe replaced Sidney's large planning group with a much smaller one consisting of Granville, O'Keeffe, who was now manager of corporate advanced manufacturing engineering, Bud Gerzina, who had managed a number of Copeland's smaller manufacturing improvement projects, and himself. The group had two options for separating the plant: a process split, as at Rushville; or a product split, as at Hartselle and Shelby. In either case, Sidney's existing layout and union agreements would serve as points of departure.

Existing Layout

All machining was done in one half of the plant; the other half, consisting of large, enclosed, air-conditioned rooms, was devoted to assembly. (See *Exhibit 5*.) Both areas were organized by departments, and each department contained functionally similar lines. In machining, for example, all Copelametic and Copelaweld body lines were grouped together; each, however, had separate departments and foremen because of the many people and machines involved. The Copelaweld and Copelametic piston departments were similarly organized, although a single foreman oversaw both. Assembly followed much the same pattern. Copelametic carousels were interspersed with Copelaweld carousels and together formed a single department with two foremen. Both product lines went through the same dehydration, paint-

ing and finishing, and inspection and packing departments. A single foreman oversaw each of these departments.

Work-Force Seniority Rules

While most equipment was dedicated to particular product lines, workers were not. In machining, for example, layoffs or transfers were made solely by component line. Each worker could bump into any other line within his or her job classification; thus, a drill press operator could work on any line requiring that job classification, whether it involved Copelametics or Copelawelds. As a last resort, bumping was even permitted between machining and assembly. Under this system, the greater seasonality of welded products caused considerable movement. Management therefore wanted to increase work-force continuity, whether a product or process focus was chosen, and viewed modification of the union contract—for example, the creation of separate work forces governed by their own bumping rules—as a top priority. Because labor relations had improved considerably since Granville's arrival, management was optimistic that it would gain labor-force cooperation in making the necessary contract changes.

Process Focus: Machining versus Assembly

Under this option, Sidney would be split to reflect the differing technological, cultural, and skill requirements of machining and assembly. Most investment, for example, was concentrated in machining. Many managers considered Copeland's core competence to be its ability to machine cast iron and steel to precise tolerances. And in this area, the focus was on equipment. Even though machining foremen had to manage people and materials as well as equipment, when asked to cite their biggest problems, they almost always talked about machines. Because process control, setup times, equipment maintenance, and downtime were such key concerns, the machine shop also required the bulk of Sidney's engineering and maintenance support.

Assembly, by contrast, employed less sensitive equipment; as Granville noted, "If the parts are there, you make standard." When asked about their biggest problems, assembly foremen usually

EXHIBIT 5 Sidney Plant Layout in 1981: Process

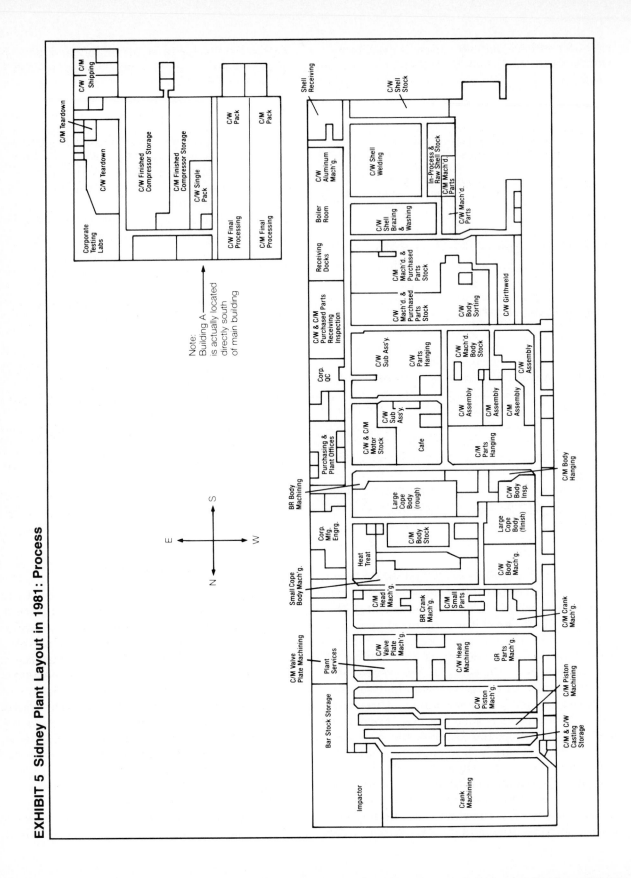

36. Copeland Corporation: Evolution of a Manufacturing Strategy, 1975–1982 (A)

talked about people. John Vordemark, assembly manager, commented on his priorities:

> In assembly, you want to concentrate on maximum efficiency of people—that's where you spend your time. And then you guard quality. In machining, it's the other way around: you do everything to get a good part. You never jeopardize that for efficiency or cost.

These differences resulted in distinct machining and assembly cultures. Granville described the differences:

> In machining you get dirty. Your days have more variety, you set up your machines, there are breakdowns, you move around more, there's greater freedom. In assembly, you're putting the same type of components together over and over. Breakdowns are rare. It's cleaner, quieter, and you take breaks with a whole group of people. It's almost like a family.

These cultural differences extended into the component lines and were reinforced by the process of job bidding, which allowed people to gravitate toward the line cultures of their choice.

Emerging global competition also made the process focus option more attractive. International markets were rapidly becoming more important, and Copeland already had several overseas plants. Early thinking about a global strategy suggested that not all plants should be involved in both machining and assembly. The two processes were likely to be decoupled, with machining of particular components or bodies concentrated in different plants and assembly assigned to plants closer to markets. To inaugurate this global manufacturing organization, several managers argued, why not start with Sidney?

WHAT WOULD BE REQUIRED. While machining and assembly could be split without moving any equipment, a first-rate layout would require more substantial moves. Interwoven product lines would have to be separated so that within the machining plant, Copelametics and Copelawelds had their own separate areas. A more rational production flow would also require changes in layout; at the moment, after rough machining on several body lines, compressor bodies were placed on skids and moved to another set of rough machining operations, then stacked and moved to the finish machining lines. Rearranging these lines would achieve significant improvements in throughput, materials flow, inventory, and labor utilization, while also bringing operators performing related tasks within shouting distance of one another.

These changes would not, however, require relocation of Sidney's "monuments." The monuments were large pieces of equipment whose foundations were linked to the building's infrastructure; for this reason, some managers feared that they would crumble if moved. Among the monuments were a five-stage washer, a heat-treating furnace, and the dehydration line. But the monument arousing greatest concern was a 17-station transfer line that machined bodies for small Copelametics and accounted for 100,000 units per year. Not only were its foundations sunk into the floor, but it had also taken 18 years to fine-tune the machine's alignment so that it consistently held tolerances for the critical center line of small compressors. The transfer line would not be moved if Sidney were focused by process; a product/market focus, on the other hand, might require the line to be relocated.

Although splitting Sidney by machining and assembly would not require major work-force reassignments, they were nevertheless viewed as desirable. To pursue this route—changing bumping rules, for example, to reduce the volatility of the work force—management would have to obtain modification of the union contract.

Product Focus: Copelametic versus Copelaweld

Under this option, Sidney would be split to reflect the product and market differences of Copelametics and Copelawelds. Semi-hermetic growth, for example, was predicted to be very small. Copeland aimed to hold onto these markets through superior quality, reliability, delivery, and replacement, while continuing to proliferate its products. Almost half of all Copelametic orders were for five or fewer units; 80% were for ten units or less. The maturity of the basic product design, the flat, stable market, and the already large investments in Rushville and Shelby suggested that future investments in Copelametics would be incremental, aimed at preserving and extending Copeland's leadership position.

Copelawelds, by contrast, were sold to customers whose requirements often changed quickly and dramatically. These sales fluctuations imposed special delivery demands. Peltier observed:

> In commercial refrigeration, you need *reliable* delivery. The customer says, "I want three." You tell him when *you* can deliver; then he sets up his production. But you had better have them there on time because he has set his runs to conform to what you promised. In residential air conditioning, you need *clockwork* delivery. The customer orders 2,000 units and needs them by a certain date; you have to get the orders there on the day *he* wants them.

The welded compressors faced intensified competition from new Japanese rotary technology and from Tecumseh; in contrast to the CR, whose market share continued to climb, the share of some Sidney Copelawelds had already begun to fall. For these reasons, welded products would demand a continuing infusion of engineering resources, new products, new technology, and upgraded facilities if they were to remain competitive and secure a position of cost leadership.

WHAT WOULD BE REQUIRED. To split Sidney by Copelawelds and Copelametics would require a reorganization of the plant, since the two product lines were now scattered throughout the factory. (See *Exhibit 6*.) Both the amount of equipment to be moved and the scope of the moves would be significantly greater under this option than under a process split. For example, equipment would have to be regrouped so that Copelametic machining was next to Copelametic assembly; the entire Copelamatic plant would then have to be separated from the Copelaweld plant by a brick wall. Other physical changes would be needed to reinforce these efforts, ensuring that workers identified with products and their customers rather than with crankshafts and pistons, or machining and assembly, as in the current culture. Likely changes included separate parking lots, entrances, and cafeterias for Copelametic and Copelaweld employees. As a critical step, labor policies would need to be changed to prevent employees associated with one product line from bumping or transferring into the other.

Despite these complications, separating Copelametics from Copelawelds had strong intuitive appeal. It acknowledged long-standing differences in the manufacturing demands imposed by the two products. Copelametic production, for example, was fairly stable over the year; its turnover was lower and workers more senior. And because Copelametic machinists used general-purpose equipment that performed but a single operation at a time, the pace was slower, with 100 rather than 1,000 pieces being turned out per shift. Quality was operator-dependent. Copelaweld machining, by contrast, involved higher volume, higher speed, and dial index dedicated equipment that performed several operations at each station. Machines were more complex to set up and maintain, but required little of operators while they were being run. The result, as Granville noted, was that different kinds of people had gravitated to the two products:

> In Copelametics, you have older people, the graybeards, the artists who massage the equipment, while in Copelawelds, you have the young bucks, people who are resilient, who can deal with layoffs and recalls and the faster pace, and who enjoy riding the ragged edge.

The two also had different scheduling problems in assembly. The greater part of Copelametic scheduling could be done by model and horsepower (the "mechanicals"), while extensive proliferation came in the final stages: "electricals," valves, labels, and such. Copelaweld scheduling, on the other hand, had to take account of proliferation from the beginning, creating two schedules—one for the compressor and the second for its shell—so that compressor and shell would meet at the right point.

* * * *

On February 8, 1982, O'Keeffe, Gerzina, Granville, and Ruwe met for a final time to decide how Sidney should be focused. They knew that a decision had to be made by the end of the meeting, and recommendations prepared for Diggs, so that attention could shift to problems of implementation.

EXHIBIT 6 Sidney Plant Layout in 1981: Product

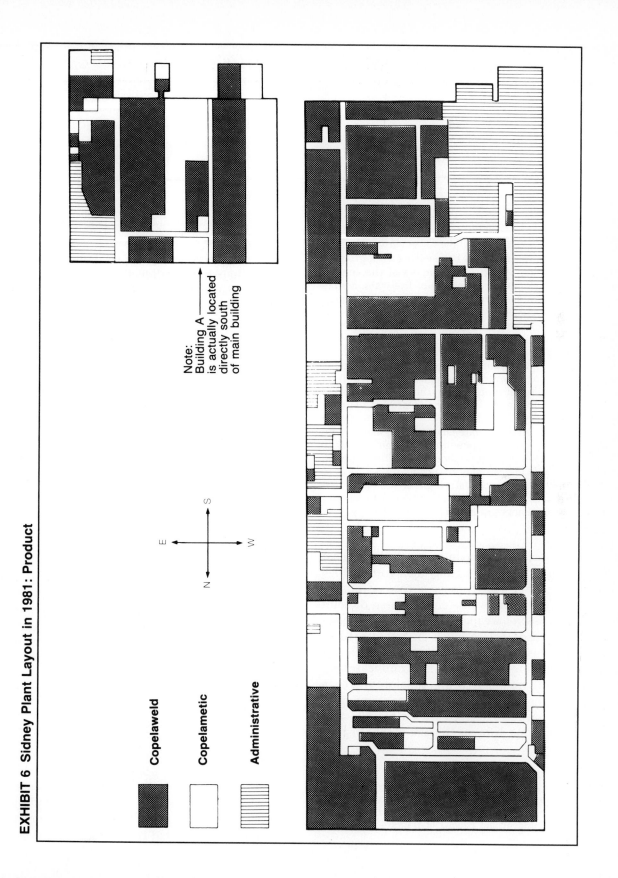

Note:
Building A
is actually located
directly south
of main building

Copelaweld

Copelametic

Administrative

37. Competing through Manufacturing

The past several years have witnessed a growing awareness among American managers of the central importance to competitive success of first-rate competence in the work of production. At the top of many corporate agendas now rests the determination to boost productivity, product quality, and new product innovation. This is all to the good. What managers still lack, however, is a powerful descriptive framework for understanding how their manufacturing organizations are contributing to overall strategic goals, as well as the other kinds of contribution those organizations could be asked to make. This article provides such a framework.

Drawing on their extensive field research, the authors outline a developmental continuum of four stages that, taken together, identify the different roles that manufacturing can play in a company's efforts to formulate and achieve its strategic objectives. Even more important, they make clear the key choices and managerial challenges at each of these stages.

Manufacturing companies, particularly those in the United States, are today facing intensified competition. For many, it is a case of simple survival. What makes this challenge so difficult is that the "secret weapon" of their fiercest competitors is based not so much on better product design, marketing ingenuity, or financial strength as on something much harder to duplicate: superior overall manufacturing capability. For a long time, however, many of these companies have systematically neglected their manufacturing organizations. Now, as the cost of that neglect

grows ever clearer, they are not finding it easy to rebuild their lost excellence in production.

In most of these companies, the bulk of their labor force and assets are tied to the manufacturing function. The attitudes, expectations, and traditions that have developed over time in and around that function will be difficult to change. Companies cannot atone for years of neglect simply by throwing large chunks of investment dollars at the problem. Indeed, it normally takes several years of disciplined effort to transform manufacturing weakness into strength. In fact, it can take several years for a company to break the habit of "working around" the limitations of a manufacturing operation and to look on it as a source of competitive advantage.

In practice, of course, the challenge for managers is far more complex than is suggested by the simple dichotomy between "weakness" and "strength." There is no single end that every manufacturing function must serve—and serve well. There are, instead, several generic kinds of roles that the function can play in a company and—as *Exhibit 1* suggests—these roles can be viewed as stages of development along a continuum. At one extreme, production can offer little contribution to a company's market success; at the other, it provides a major source of competitive advantage.

Understanding the possibilities along this continuum can help managers identify both their company's current position and the transformations in attitude and approach that will be necessary if it is to advance to a higher stage of competitive effectiveness. Such understanding is also useful in judging how quickly a company may reasonably be expected to progress from stage to

EXHIBIT 1 Stages in Manufacturing's Strategic Role

Stage 1	Minimize manufacturing's negative potential: "internally neutral"	Outside experts are called in to make decisions about strategic manufacturing issues
		Internal, detailed, management control systems are the primary means for monitoring manufacturing performance.
		Manufacturing is kept flexible and reactive
Stage 2	Achieve parity with competitors: "externally neutral"	"Industry practice" is followed
		The planning horizon for manufacturing investment decisions is extended to incorporate a single-business cycle
		Capital investment is the primary means for catching up with competition or achieving a competitive edge
Stage 3	Provide credible support to the business strategy: "internally supportive"	Manufacturing investments are screened for consistency with the business strategy
		A manufacturing strategy is formulated and pursued
		Longer-term manufacturing developments and trends are addressed systematically
Stage 4	Pursue a manufacturing-base competitive advantage: "externally supportive"	Efforts are made to anticipate the potential of new manufacturing practices and technologies
		Manufacturing is involved "up front" in major marketing and engineering decisions (and vice versa)
		Long-range programs are pusued in order to acquire capabilities in advance of needs.

stage. It is useful, too, in pointing out the changes that must be made in other parts of the company in order to sustain each higher level of manufacturing's contribution.

Stages of Manufacturing Effectiveness

Before describing each of these generic roles (or stages) in detail and outlining the problems that can arise when trying to move from one to the next, we must say a few things about the kind of framework we are proposing. First, the stages are not mutually exclusive. Every manufacturing operation embodies a set of important choices about such factors as capacity, vertical integration, human resource policies, and the like. (See *Exhibit 2* for a listing of these.) A given operation may be—and often is—composed of factors that are themselves at different levels of development. What determines the overall level of the operation is where the balance among these factors falls— that is, where in the developmental scheme the operation's center of gravity rests.

Second, it is difficult, if not impossible, for a company to skip a stage. A new business can, of course, attempt to begin operations at any level it chooses, but a manufacturing function that is already up and running has far less freedom of choice. Attitudes and established modes of doing things are well entrenched, and it takes a tremendous effort just to move things along from one level to the next. Hence, the organizational strain imposed by an effort to leapfrog a stage makes the probability of failure uncomfortably high. In addition, it is the mastery of activities at one stage that usually provides the underpinnings for a successful transition to the next.

It is possible, however, for a given operation to contain factors of the sort already mentioned that are well separated on the developmental continuum. But here, too, the forces of organizational gravity are remorselessly at work. Over time, the less advanced part of the operation will tend to draw the more advanced part back to its own level. The production group responsible for Apple's Macintosh computer has, for example, tried to push its capability in materials handling and test processes well ahead of the rest of its capabilities. The resulting strain has made it hard for the group to maintain a stable organization. By contrast, Hewlett-Packard's personal computer manufacturing group has tried to push ahead at a slower and steadier pace—but along a very broad front.

EXHIBIT 2 Major Types of Manufacturing Choices

Capacity	Amount, timing, type
Facilities	Size, location, specialization
Equipment and process technologies	Scale, flexibility, interconnectedness
Vertical integration	Direction, extent, balance
Vendors	Number, structure, relationship
New products	Hand-off, start-up, modification
Human resources	Selection and training, compensation, security
Quality	Definition, role, responsibility
Systems	Organization, schedules, control.

Third, although it is appealing in theory for companies to move as a single entity through these stages, the real work of development occurs at the business unit level. Certainly, it is nice to have backing from a central corporate office so that several business units can evolve together and help each other, but it is at the business unit, not corporate, level that the critical nuts-and-bolts coordination among factors and across functions takes place.

With these three points in mind, we now turn to a consideration of the stages themselves. We will give special attention to the shift from Stage 3 to Stage 4 because this transition is the most difficult of all and because reaching Stage 4 has the largest payoff in terms of competitive success. In fact, Stage 4 operations characterize all companies that have achieved the status of world class manufacturers.

Stage 1

This lowest stage represents an "internally neutral" orientation toward manufacturing: top managers regard the function as neutral—incapable of influencing competitive success. Consequently, they seek only to minimize any negative impact it may have. They do not expect manufacturing (indeed, they tend to discourage it from trying) to make a positive contribution.

Stage 1 organizations typically view manufacturing capability as the direct result of a few structural decisions about capacity, facilities, technology, and vertical integration. Managers attach little or no strategic importance to such infrastructure issues as work force policies, planning and measurement systems, and incremental process improvements. When strategic issues involving manufacturing do arise, management usually calls in outside experts in the belief that their own production organization lacks the necessary expertise (a self-fulfilling prophecy).

When faced with the need to make a change in facilities, location, or process technology, their production managers run into top-level insistence to remain flexible and reactive so as not get locked into the wrong decisions. Similarly, they are expected to source all manufacturing equipment from outside suppliers and rely on these suppliers for most of their information about manufacturing technology and new technological developments.

On balance, Stage 1 organizations think of production as a low-tech operation that can be staffed with low-skilled workers and managers. They employ detailed measurements and controls of operating performance, oriented to near-term performance, to ensure that manufacturing does not get too far off-track before corrective action can be taken. The aim is not to maximize the function's competitive value but to guard against competitively damaging problems.

Not surprisingly, the top managers of such companies try to minimize their involvement with, and thus their perceived dependence on, manufacturing. They concern themselves primarily with major investment decisions, as viewed through the prism of their capital budgeting process. As a result, they tend to regard their company's production facilities and processes as the embodiment of a series of once-and-for-all decisions. They are uneasy with the notion that manufacturing is a *learning* process that can create and expand its own capabilities—and may therefore not be totally controllable. Hence, they will agree to add capacity only when the need becomes obvious, and, when they do, prefer to build large general-purpose facilities employing known—that is, "safe"—technologies purchased from outside vendors. Eager to keep the manufacturing function as simple as possible, they feel justified in thinking that "anybody ought to be able to manage manufacturing," an attitude reflected in their assignment of people to that department.

This Stage 1 view occurs both in companies whose managers see the manufacturing process as simple and straightforward and in those whose managers do not think it likely to have much impact on overall competitive position. Many consumer products and service companies fall into this category. So, too, do a number of sophisticated high-technology companies, which regard *product* technology as the key to competitive success and *process* technology as, at best, neutral.

Experience shows, however, that the competitive difficulties encountered by many U.S. consumer electronics and electrical equipment manufacturers have their roots in the attitude that manufacturing's role is simply to assemble and test products built from purchased components. Even in these high-tech companies, the manufacturing operation can appear clumsy and unprepared when confronted with such straightforward tasks as providing adequate production capacity, helping suppliers solve problems, and keeping equipment and systems up-to-date. With a self-limiting view of what manufacturing can do, managers find it difficult to upgrade their labor-intensive, low-technology processes when products involving a new generation of technology appear. Nor can their unfocused, general purpose facilities compete effectively with the highly focused, specialized plants of world-class competitors.

Stage 2

The second stage in our progression also represents a form of manufacturing "neutrality," but Stage 2 companies seek a competitive or "external" neutrality (parity with major competitors) on the manufacturing dimension rather than the internal ("don't upset the apple cart") neutrality of Stage 1. Typified by—but not restricted to—companies in traditional, manufacturing-intensive industries like steel, autos, and heavy equipment, Stage 2 organizations seek competitive neutrality by:

- Following industry practice in matters regarding the work force (industrywide bargaining agreements with national unions, for example), equipment purchases, and the timing and scale of capacity additions

- Avoiding, where possible, the introduction of major, discontinuous changes in product or process. In fact, such changes tend to come—if at all—from competitors well outside the mainstream of an industry.

- Treating capital investments in new equipment and facilities as the most effective means for gaining a temporary competitive advantage.

- Viewing economies of scale related to the production rate as the most important source of manufacturing efficiency.

As noted, this approach to manufacturing is quite common in America's smokestack industries, most of which have an oligopolistic market structure and a well-defined set of competitors who share a vested interest in maintaining the status quo. It is also common in many companies engaged in electronic instrument assembly and pharmaceutical production, which consider manufacturing to be largely standardized and unsophisticated and which assume product development people can be entrusted with designing process changes whenever they are needed. Like those in Stage 1, Stage 2 companies—when they make an improvement in their process technology—rely on sources outside of manufacturing; unlike companies in Stage 1, however, they often turn to their own (largely product-oriented) R&D labs as well as to outside suppliers.

Top managers of Stage 2 companies regard resource allocation decisions as the most effective means of addressing the major strategic issues in manufacturing. Offensive investments to gain competitive advantage are usually linked to new products; manufacturing investments (other than those for additional capacity to match increases in the demand for existing products) are primarily defensive and cost-cutting in nature. They are usually undertaken only when manufacturing's shortcomings have become obvious.

Stage 3

Stage 3 organizations expect manufacturing actively to support and strengthen the company's competitive position. As noted in *Exhibit 1*, these organizations view manufacturing as "internally supportive" in that its contribution derives from and is dictated by overall business strategy. That contribution includes:

- Screening decisions to be sure that they are consistent with the organization's competitive strategy.
- Translating that strategy into terms meaningful to manufacturing personnel.
- Seeking consistency within manufacturing through a carefully thought-out sequence of investments and systems changes over time.
- Being on the lookout for longer term developments and trends that may have a significant effect on manufacturing's ability to respond to the needs of other parts of the organization.
- Formulating a manufacturing strategy, complete with plant charters and mission statements, to guide manufacturing activities over an extended period of time.

Companies often arrive at Stage 3 as a natural consequence of both their success in developing an effective business strategy, based on formal planning processes, and their wish to support that strategy in all functional areas. They want manufacturing to be creative and to take a long-term view in managing itself. When push comes to shove, however, the majority of them act as if such creativity is best expressed by making one or two bold moves—the introduction of robots, just-in-time, or CAD/CAM, for example—while they continue to run most of the function as a Stage 2 activity. The beer industry is a good case in point: after building a number of new, large-scale facilities in the 1970s and rationalizing their existing operations, they began to drift back into a "business as usual" attitude toward the manufacturing function.

While Stage 2 companies at times also pursue advances in manufacturing practice, they tend to regard these in strictly defensive terms: as a means of keeping up with their industry. Stage 3 companies, however, view technological progress as a natural response to changes in business strategy and competitive position.

Another characteristic of Stage 3 organizations is that their manufacturing managers take a broad view of their role by seeking to understand their company's business strategy and the kind of competitive advantage it is pursuing. Some of these managers even follow career paths that lead to general management. Notwithstanding the potential for advancement or the greater equality of titles and pay across all functions in Stage 3 companies, manufacturing managers are expected only to support the company's business strategy, not to become actively involved in helping to formulate it.

Stage 4

The fourth and most progressive stage of manufacturing development arises when competitive strategy rests to a significant degree on a company's manufacturing capability. By this we do not mean that manufacturing dictates strategy to the rest of the company but only that strategy derives from a coordinated effort among functional peers—manufacturing very much among them.

As noted in *Exhibit 1*, the role of manufacturing in Stage 4 companies is "externally supportive," in that it is expected to make an important contribution to the competitive success of the organization. The leading companies in process-intensive industries, for example, usually give manufacturing a Stage 4 role, for here the evolution of product and process technologies is so intertwined that a company virtually must be in Stage 4 to gain a sustainable product advantage.

What then is special about Stage 4 companies?

- They anticipate the potential of new manufacturing practices and technologies and seek to acquire expertise in them long before their implications are fully apparent.
- They give sufficient credibility and influence to manufacturing for it to extract the full potential from production-based opportunities.
- They place equal emphasis on structural (buildings and equipment) and infrastructural (management policies) activities as potential sources of continual improvement and competitive advantage.
- They develop long-range business plans in which manufacturing capabilities are expected to play a meaningful role in securing the company's strategic objectives. By treating the manufac-

turing function as a strategic resource—that is, as a source of strength by itself as well as a means for enhancing the interactive development of business, manufacturing, and other functional strategies.

Stage 4 organizations are generally of two types. The first includes those companies like Emerson Electric, Texas Instruments, Mars (candy), and Blue Bell, whose business strategies place primary emphasis on a manufacturing-based competitive advantage such as low cost. In fact, these companies sometimes regard their manufacturing functions as so important a source of competitive advantage that they relegate other functions to a secondary or derivative role—an action which can be just as dysfunctional as relegating manufacturing to a reactive role. The other type of Stage 4 company seeks a balance of excellence in all its functions and pursues "externally supportive" Stage 4 roles for each of its integrated functions. We describe in detail two such organizations in a later section of this article.

In both types of organization, manufacturing complements its traditional involvement in the capital budgeting process with a considerable amount of qualitative analysis to compensate for the blind spots and biases inherent in financial data. In addition, there are extensive formal and informal horizontal interactions between manufacturing and other functions that greatly facilitate such activities as product design, field service, and sales training. Manufacturing's direct participation in formulating overall business strategy further enhances this functional interaction. Finally, equally with the other functions, manufacturing is a valued source of general management talent for the entire organization.

Managing the Transition

Because the four stages just outlined fall along a continuum, they suggest the path that a company might follow as it seeks to enhance the contribution of its manufacturing function. They suggest, too, the speed with which a company might follow that path. The inertia of most large organizations—their entrenched attitudes and prac-

tices—favors a gradual, systematic, and cumulative movement from one developmental stage to the next, not an effort to skip a stage by throwing more resources at problems. Getting from here to there is not simply a question of applying endless resources. Indeed, managing the transition between stages represents a significant and often dramatic challenge for most organizations.

At the least, successfully negotiating such a transition requires leadership from within the manufacturing function. Managing change in an established operation is always difficult, but here that difficulty is compounded by the need to bring all manufacturing personnel to a new view of things long familiar. Consider, for example, the kinds of production choices mentioned in *Exhibit 2*.

As a company or business unit moves along the continuum, dealing with vendors or making facilities choices requires many changes: cost-minimization goals give way to a concern for enlisting vendors' critical capabilities, and planning for general-purpose facilities gives way to an appreciation of focused factories. Said another way, managing these transitions requires a special kind of leadership because the task at hand is to change how people think, not merely how they can be instructed to act.

Nowhere is this deep shift in viewpoint more important than in attitudes toward a company's human resources. As *Exhibit 3* (courtesy of our colleague, Earl Sasser) suggests, Stages 1, 2, and 3 adhere fairly closely to the traditional "command and control" style of human resource management. Now, to be sure, moving from Stage 1 to Stage 2 and then on to Stage 3 requires an ever more polished execution of that style, with enhanced management development efforts and more thoughtful analysis of underlying commands. But there is no radical shift within these stages in the way managers think of the work force's contribution to overall competitive performance. In Stage 4, however, the dominant approach to the work force must be in terms of teamwork and problem solving, not command-and-control. In the earlier stages the key leadership task is the management of controlled effort, but getting to Stage 4—and prospering there—demands instead the management of creative experimentation and organizational learning.

EXHIBIT 3 Alternate Views of Work Force Management

Stages 1, 2, and 3 traditional, static	Stage 4 broad potential, dynamic
Command and control	Learning
Management of effort	Management of attention
Coordinating information	Problem-solving information
Direct (supervisory) control	Indirect (systems and values) control
Process stabilty/ worker independence	Process evolution/worker dependence

Why Move At All?

Most young companies assign either Stage 1 or Stage 2 roles to manufacturing, to some extent because these roles require little attention and specific knowledge on the part of senior managers. In the United States, companies tend to start out with a unique product or with the identification of an unexploited niche in a market. As a result, they place primary emphasis on marketing, product design, or other nonmanufacturing functions. Top management does not see the need to become smart about—or give close attention to—the work of production.

Companies are likely to remain at their initial stage until external pressures force a move. As long as no direct competitor successfully develops Stage 3 or Stage 4 manufacturing capabilities, they will find Stages 1 and 2 comfortable, secure, and apparently effective. The post-World War II experience of many U.S. industries convinced a generation of managers that a policy of stability can remain satisfactory for decades, a view reinforced by the stable economic growth associated with the 1960s. What they first saw as common practice they came to see as *good* practice.

In general the transition from Stage 1 to Stage 2 comes when problems arise in the manufacturing function that can be solved by the "safe" application of an already proven practice. It can also occur if managers decide that the leading companies in their industry owe at least part of their success to their manufacturing process. The transition to Stage 3, however, usually begins when managers come to doubt the effectiveness of their traditional approaches or to wonder about the implications of new manufacturing technologies. A direct threat from a major competitor that has moved to a higher stage or a recognition of the competitive advantages of moving to Stage 3 (or the potential perils of not doing so) may also trigger action.

During the early 1980s all these factors came together to encourage literally hundreds of companies to shift toward Stage 3. In many industries, long dominated by a few large companies following stable competitive ground rules, the sudden appearance of foreign competition and globalized markets jolted laggards into action. With no end to such competitive pressures in sight, many more companies are likely to attempt transitions to Stage 3 over the next several years.

Unfortunately many, if not most, of these companies are unlikely to achieve a full, lasting move to Stage 3 before they revert to Stage 2. The reasons for such a retreat are subtle, yet powerful. Moving from Stage 2 to Stage 3 often occurs in a crisis atmosphere when—as with U.S. producers of steel, autos, and machine tools—managers and workers alike see their real objective as regaining competitive parity with their attackers. The changes that are required to adapt fully to Stage 3 require such sustained effort and broad-based support, however, that these companies may not be able to cement them in place before improved business conditions relieve some of the competitive pressure. The natural tendency, of course, is to return to a "business as usual" Stage 2 mentality as soon as the crisis appears to have passed.

The great irony here is that too quick success often spells doom for permanent change. If, as often happens, the managers responsible for building manufacturing to Stage 3 levels are quickly promoted into other responsibilities and other, lesser managers are left to be the caretakers of recent changes, the necessary follow-up activities may not occur.

The Big Jump to Stage 4

However difficult it is to get from Stage 2 to Stage 3, our experience sugests that the shift from Stage 3 to Stage 4 demands an effort substantially greater both in kind and in degree. Earlier transitions, which take place largely within the manufacturing function, are a form of "manufacturing fixing itself." Moving to Stage 4, however, involves changing the way that the rest of the organization thinks about manufacturing and interacts with it. Because coordination among functions is crucial, manufacturing must first have its own house in order. Entering Stage 4 is not something an organization simply chooses to do. It must first pay its dues by having done all the appropriate groundwork.

The differences between Stages 3 and 4 should not be underestimated. In Stage 3, manufacturing considerations feed into business strategy, but the function itself is still seen as reactive (in that its role is a derived one), not as a source of potential competitive advantage. Stage 4 implies a deep shift in manufacturing's role, in its self-image, and in the view of it held by managers in other functions. It is, at last, regarded as an equal partner and is therefore expected to play a major role in strengthening a company's market position. Equally important, it helps the rest of the organization see the world in a new way. Stage 3 companies will, for example, treat automation as essentially a cost-cutting and labor-saving activity. A Stage 4 manufacturing operation will bring automation into focus as a means of boosting process precision and product quality.

There is an expectation in Stage 4 that all levels of management will possess a high degree of technical competence and will be aware of how their actions may affect manufacturing activities. Further, they are expected to have a general understanding of the way products, markets, and processes interact and to manage actively these interactions across functions. Traditional approaches to improving performance—providing flexibility through excess capacity, for example, or raising delivery dependability through holding finished-goods inventory, or reducing costs through improvements in labor productivity—no longer are considered as the only way to proceed. Tighter integration of product design and process capabilities can also lead to increased flexibility, as well as to faster deliveries (through shorter production cycle times) and to lower costs (through improved product quality and reliability).

Most American top managers, in our experience, regard the transition from Stage 1 to Stage 2, and then on to Stage 3, as a desirable course to pursue. Yet few view achieving Stage 4 capabilities as an obvious goal or strengthen their companies' manufacturing functions with the clear intent of moving there.

In fact, most companies that reach Stage 3 do not perceive a move to Stage 4 as either essential or natural. Their managers, believing that Stage 3 provides 90% of the benefits attainable, resist spending the extra effort to advance further. Many prefer to play it safe by remaining in Stage 3 for a sustained period before deciding how and whether to move on. A sizable number doubt the value of Stage 4—some because they think it extremely risky in organizational terms; others because they feel threatened by the kind of initiatives manufacturing might take when unleashed. One company, in fact, ruled out a move to Stage 4 as being potentially destabilizing to its R&D group, which historically had played the key role in establishing the company's competitive advantage.

Although the benefits of operating in Stage 4 will vary from company to company and will often be invisible to managers until they are just on the edge of Stage 4 operations, four variables can serve as a sort of litmus test for a company's real attitude toward the competitive role its manufacturing organization can—and should—play and thus indicate its placement in Stage 3 or Stage 4.

THE AMOUNT OF ONGOING IN-HOUSE INNOVATION. Stage 4 organizations continually invest in process improvements, not only because they benefit existing products but also because they will benefit future products. This is not to say these companies are uninterested in big-step improvements, but that they place great importance on the cumulative value of continual enhancements in process technology.

THE EXTENT TO WHICH A COMPANY DEVELOPS ITS OWN MANUFACTURING EQUIPMENT. The typical Stage 3 operation continues to rely on outside suppliers for equipment development. A Stage 4 company wants to know more than its suppliers about everything that is critical to its business. It may continue to buy much of its equipment, but it will also produce enough internally to ensure that it is close to the state-of-the-art in equipment technology.

Our experience with Stage 4 German and Japanese manufacturers is that they follow this practice much more than most of their American counterparts. Yet even in Germany, where leading companies develop their own equipment, suppliers such as those making machine tools remain strong and innovative. Reducing their market does not cripple their competitive viability. Instead, the increased competition and the greater technical sophistication among equipment users have made the interactions between manufacturers and suppliers more innovative for both.

THE ATTENTION PAID TO MANUFACTURING INFRASTRUCTURE. Stage 4 managers take care to integrate measurement systems, manufacturing planning and control procedures, and work force policies in their structural decisions on capacity, vertical integration, and the like. They do not necessarily give infrastructure and structural elements equal weight, but they look on both as important, and complementary, sources of competitive strength.

THE LINK BETWEEN PRODUCT DESIGN AND MANUFACTURING PROCESS DESIGN. Stage 3 companies focus on improving the hand-offs from product design to manufacturing; in Stage 4 the emphasis is on the parallel and interactive development of both products and processes.

If managers choose not to attempt the transition to Stage 4, that choice should be made intentionally, not by default or through a failure to understand the kind of benefits that new stage could offer. Rather, it should reflect a reasoned judgement that the risks were too great or the rewards insufficient.

Getting There from Here

Two examples of organizations that, in the early 1980s, chose to attempt the transition to Stage 4 are General Electric's dishwasher operation (at the business unit level) and IBM (at the corporate level). Taking a closer look at these two experiences may help bring into focus the benefits of, and the obstacles to, a successfully managed transition.

General Electric Dishwasher

Dishwashers are one of several major consumer appliances that GE has produced for decades. In the late 1970s GE's dishwasher strategic business unit (SBU) did a careful self-analysis and concluded that it had dated and aging resources: a 20-year-old product design, a 10- to 20-year-old manufacturing process, and an aging work force (average seniority of 15 to 16 years) represented by a strong, traditional union. Its manufacturing operations were primarily located, together with five other major appliance plants, at GE's Appliance Park in Lousiville, Kentucky. A single labor relations group dealt with all of the site's 14,000 hourly workers, whose relations with management were neutral at best.

Nevertheless, it was a very successful business, holding the leading position in the U.S. dishwasher market and turning out about one-third of the units sold. In late 1977, as part of its normal planning for product redesign, the SBU proposed to corporate management that it invest $18 million in the incremental improvement of the product and its manufacturing process. With dishwasher manufacturing more or less at Stage 2 (it was essentially following "GE Appliance Park manufacturing practice"), those involved saw the request as a proposed foray into Stage 3, and expected the unit to return to Stage 2 once the improvements in products and processes began to age.

GE's senior managers normally would have approved such an investment and allowed the SBU to carry on with its traditional approach. In this case, however, they asked a number of tough questions about the long-term prospects for the business and encouraged SBU managers to think about pursuing a more innovative and aggressive course. The idea of making a fundamental change in the SBU's strategy gained rapid support from some key middle managers, who saw major opportunities if GE could break out of its traditional thinking. They began laying the groundwork for a solid move to Stage 3.

37. Competing through Manufacturing

Over the next several months, as this reformulated proposal to upgrade product design and manufacturing processes began to take shape, the nature of the dishwasher business suggested possible benefits from moving on through Stage 3 to Stage 4:

- GE product designers had developed a top-of-the-line product with a plastic tub and plastic door liner. Although currently more expensive than the standard steel model, it offered significantly improved operating performance and used proprietary GE materials.
- More disciplined product design could increase component standardization because little of the product was visible after installation.
- Since only 55% of U.S. households owned dishwashers, there was considerable growth potential in the primary market as well as a sizable replacement market.

In combination with GE's strong competitive position, these factors led management to conclude that if the "right" product were introduced at the "right" price and with the "right" quality, GE could greatly expand both industry demand and its own market share, particularly in the private label business.

Accordingly, SBU managers decided not just to fix current problems but to do it right. They jettisoned their modest proposal for incremental product and process improvement and developed much bolder proposals requiring an investment of more than $38 million.

This revised plan rested on a major commitment to improve the factory's working environment through better communication with the work force as well as to encourage its involvement in redesigning the manufacturing process. Laying the groundwork for this new relationship took almost two years, but the time was well spent. Once established, this relationship markedly enhanced the contribution manufacturing could make to the overall business of the SBU.

The new plan also called for a complete redesign of the product around a central core consisting of a single-piece plastic tub and a single-piece plastic door. To ensure that the product would meet quality standards, management established stringent specifications for GE and for its vendors and demanded that both internal and external suppliers reduce their incidence of defects to one-twentieth of the levels formerly allowed. To meet the new specifications and the new cost targets, managers now had to carry out process and product development in tandem, not separate them as they had done in the past.

The revised proposal addressed, as well, the design of the production process. Automation was essential—not just to reduce costs but also to improve quality. Thus, modifications in product design had to reflect the capabilities and constraints of the new process. In addition, that process had to accommodate more worker control and shorter manufacturing cycle times, along with other nontraditional approaches to improve flexibility, quality, delivery dependability, and the integration of product testing with manufacturing.

By late 1980, there was general agreement on the major building blocks of this new strategy. Each of the functions—product design, marketing, and manufacturing—was to move aggressively toward defining its contribution in Stage 4 terms. To manufacturing management also fell the task of helping to develop performance measures that, if tracked over subsequent years, would indicate how well the function was carrying out its responsibilities.

As *Exhibit 4* shows, by the end of 1983 there was pronounced improvement in such important areas as service call rates, unit costs, materials handling, inventory turns, reject rates, and productivity—with a promise of still further improvements in 1984. Nor was this all. Other benefits included a 70% reduction in the number of parts, the elimination of 20 pounds of weight in the finished product (and thus reduced freight costs), and much more positive worker attitudes. Perhaps most important of all was the large jump in market share that GE won in the 12 months following the new product's introduction. Indeed, during the summer of 1983, *Consumer Reports* rated it as offering the best value among U.S. dishwashers.

Although these results were impressive, SBU managers also gained a much better understanding of the effort needed to secure fully a Stage 4 position for manufacturing. Their experience underlined the need to treat product and process design in a more iterative and interactive fashion

EXHIBIT 4 General Electric Dishwasher SBU redesign

Performance measure	1980–1981	1983	1984 Goal
Service call rate (index)*	100	70	55
Unit cost (index)	100	90	88
Number of times tub or door is handled	27 + 27	1 + 3	1 + 3
Inventory turns	13	25	28
Reject rates (mechanical/electrical test)	10%	3%	2.5%
Output per employee (index)	100	133	142

*Lower is better.

and the importance of involving the work force in solving problems.

Of late, a rebounding economy with increased consumer demand has turned up pressure on the SBU to revert to its traditional view that output is paramount, no matter the compromises. Hence, even though the SBU's manufacturing function is now in Stage 4, it must doggedly fight to stay there and to help the rest of the organization complete the transition rather than allow itself to drift back toward Stage 3.

IBM Corporation

In the early 1980s, IBM viewed its worldwide activities as comprising 13 major businesses including, for example, typewriters and large computer systems. Like its competitors in each of these product markets, IBM faced rapidly changing environments and so had to be especially careful in designing and coordinating strategies. Hence, in each, the manufacturing organization was expected to play a role equal to that of the other major functions in developing and executing overall business strategy. Unlike its competitors, most of whom still assigned Stage 2 or Stage 3 roles to manufacturing, IBM recognized that pro-

duction—responsible for 49% of IBM's assets, 110,000 of its employees, and 40% of its final product costs—had much to contribute to the competitive advantage of each business.

IBM's worldwide strategy for moving the manufacturing operations of each business into Stage 4 required those businesses to address seven areas of concern in a manner consistent with a Stage 4 approach to production. These areas were:

LOW COST. IBM firmly believed that to be successful it must be the low-cost producer in each of its businesses, success being defined as having the best product quality, growing as fast or faster than the market, and being profitable. Reaching this low-cost position required stabilizing the manufacturing environment (reducing uncertainty wherever possible) and linking manufacturing more effectively to marketing and distribution. To this end, marketing had "ownership" of finished-goods inventory, and factory production rates were to be smoothed out by the adoption of a 90-day shipping horizon. In addition, IBM decided to design products around certain standard modules and, although it produced different configurations of these standard modules to customer order, it would not manufacture customized modules.

INVENTORIES. IBM's goal was to reduce inventories significantly, first by measuring stock carefully and frequently and then by reducing "order churn" (the fluctuation in mix and volume that occurs before an order actually gets into the final production schedule). Lower in-process inventories, derived in part from the adoption of a just-in-time philosophy and from the standardization of components, helped IBM cut its inventory costs by hundreds of millions of dollars within 18 months while supporting ever-increasing sales.

QUALITY. IBM estimated that 30% of its products' manufacturing cost—the *total* cost of quality prevention, detection, and appraisal—arose directly from not doing it right the first time. Significant improvements in the quality and manufacturability of design, the pursuit of zero defects, and the systematic stress testing of products during design and manufacturing all contributed to the lowering of these costs.

AUTOMATION. Automation in a Stage 4 orientation is of value in that it leads to higher product quality, encourages interaction between product design and process design, and cuts overhead. This, in turn, means managing the evolution of the manufacturing process according to a long-term plan, just as with product evolution.

ORGANIZATION. To provide the product design and marketing functions with a better linkage with manufacturing, IBM defined an additional level of line manufacturing management, a "production management center," which was responsible for all plants manufacturing a product line. For example, the three large system plants (located in France, Japan, and the United States) were all under a single production management center that served as the primary linkage with marketing for that product line, as well as with R&D's efforts to design new products. Such centers were intended not only to create effective functional interfaces but also to be responsible for planning manufacturing processes, defining plant charters, measuring plant performance, and ensuring that the processes and systems employed by different facilities were uniformly excellent.

MANUFACTURING SYSTEMS. The purpose here was to develop integrated systems that provided information, linked directly to strategic business variables, for both general and functional managers. Such systems had to be compatible with each other yet flexible enough for each business to be able to select the modules it needed. As part of this systems effort, IBM rethought its entire manufacturing measurement system with the intent of reducing its historical focus on direct labor and giving more emphasis to materials, overhead, energy, and indirect labor. IBM believed that its manufacturing systems, like its product lines, should be made up of standard modules based on a common architecture. Each business could then assemble its own customized configuration yet still communicate effectively with other IBM businesses.

AFFORDABILITY. By making external competitiveness, not internal rules of thumb, the basis for evaluating manufacturing performance, IBM no longer evaluated manufacturing against its own history but rather against its competitors. As part of this concern with affordability, IBM also sought to reduce its overhead, which exceeded 25% of total manufacturing costs.

Out of these seven areas of concern emerged a set of three management principles fully in harmony with the move to a Stage 4 appreciation of the competitive contribution that manufacturing can make. The first—emphasizing activities that facilitate, encourage, and reward effective interaction between manufacturing and both marketing and engineering—requires people able to regard each other as equals and to make significant contributions to areas other than their own. Information, influence, and support should—and must—flow in both directions.

The second principle recognizes that product and process technologies must interact. Process evolution (including automation) and product evolution must proceed in tandem. Indeed, IBM uses the terms "process windows" and "product windows" to describe these parallel paths and the opportunities they offer to exploit state-of-the-art processes in meeting customer needs and competitive realities.

The third principle is a focus of attention and resources on only those factors—manufacturing, quality, and overhead reduction, for example—that are essential to the long-term success of the business.

Getting Things Moving in Your Company

Our experience suggests that building manufacturing excellence requires that managers do more than simply understand the nature of the current role that manufacturing plays in their organizations and develop a plan for enhancing its competitive contribution. They must also communicate their vision to their organizations and prepare the ground for the changes that have to be made.

In virtually all the Stage 4 companies we have seen, at least one senior manager has been a key catalyst for the transition. Such leaders spring from all functional backgrounds and are concerned not to elevate manufacturing at the expense of other functions but to see their companies "firing on all cylinders." Seeking ways to integrate all functions into an effective whole, they must be strong enough, persuasive enough, and tough enough to push beyond conventional management thinking and to force their organizations to grapple with the deeper challenges prevailing in the increasingly competitive world of industry.

Today, there is considerable pessimism in some quarters about the long-term prospects for U.S. manufacturing. We are neither pessimistic nor optimistic; the answer "lies not in our stars but in ourselves." We have seen many organizations focus their efforts on achieving Stage 4 and make incredible improvements in short periods of time. Unfortunately, we have also seen many of them subsequently lose that commitment. After making tremendous strides, they begin to get comfortable and fall behind again.

Manufacturing can contribute significantly to the competitive success of any business. But it takes managers with determination, vision, and the ability to sustain focused effort over a long period of time and often in the face of stiff organizational resistance. The industrial race is no longer decided (if it ever was) by a fast and furious last-minute cavalry charge. It is a long, patient, persistent process of working together to clear the land, cultivate the fields, and continually extend the frontiers of an organization's capabilities.

INDEX

installation of its anodising plant, 10–11
key competitive variable at, 3
late 1977 decisions facing, 18–21
marketing strategy at, 17–18
multiple priorities of, 3
process description, 12–17
quality issues at, 4
sales force of, 17–18
technical tradeoffs at, 4
workforce of, 16–17
Industrial engineering, 213
Industrial modernization, 283–290
Industry cowboys, 424
Information systems, 196, 428–439
Infrastructure, 492
Intercon International, 60–72
company background of, 60–61
delivery issues at, 4
European operations of, 64–65
international division of, 62–63, 67
international manufacturing of, 63
PIC program of, 69–72
quality issues at, 4
United Kingdom plant of, 65–72
International Business Machines Corporation (IBM), 49, 430, 494–495
computers of, 63
International Telephone & Telegraph (ITT), 279–282
International Union of Electrical Workers, 176
Interplant competition
encouragement of, 5
Inventories, 62–67, 494
Irwin, Richard D., 331

J

Jaikumar, Ramchandran, 331
Japan
aerospace industry, 384
automobile industry, 375, 424–427
electronics industry, 62
piano industry, 165–167
quality management of, 130, 165–167, 179, 191–194
steel industry, 276
turn-around of a factory, 173–179
Japan Aircraft Development Company, 384
Japanese quality control (QC) style
American vs., 191–200
Joint ventures, 172
Jordan, Peter, 290
Judson, Arnold S., 211
Juran, Joseph, 180, 184–187
breakthrough sequence of, 187

K

Kaiser Aluminum, 8
Kantrow, Alan W., xvii
Kaplan, Robert S., 423

Kawai (company), 158, 165–167, 171
Kendrick, John W., 211
Kerr, John, 290
Kimball International, 163–165
Klein, Janice A., 211
Knight, Frank H., 331
Knogo Corporation, 53, 56
Kotter, John P., 422
Krauss, William A., 423
Kravis, William A., 331
Kroger Supermarkets, 49
Kucera, Randolph, 290
Kufel, Joyce, 290
Kyj, Myroslow J., 7

L

Labor force, 484
    See also Employees
Labor relations, 120–121
Law of bureaucratic behavior, 80
Lawrence, Paul R., 422
Laws of organization, 78, 80
Layoffs, 92
Learning
curves, 388–389
process, 486–487
value of, 237–238
Leasing, 287
Leenders, Michiel R., 330
Lehn, Lloyd, 290
Lehrer McGovern Bovis, Inc. (LMB), 392–407
client mix of, 400
company profile of, 398
construction fees, 396–397
construction industry, background, 392–393
construction methods, 392–396
early strategy of, 398–400
growth issues at, 406
    bonuses, 407
    merger with Bovis International, Ltd., 406
    staffing, 406–407
project management at, 400
    construction, 404
    preconstruction activities, 401, 404
    winning the proposal, 401
project support at, 405
    control systems, 406
    people, 405
    planning, 406
    services, 405
Lehrer, Peter, 392, 393, 397, 398, 400, 401, 405, 406
Leitz, Herbert, 424, 425
Leonard-Barton, Dorothy, 331, 423
Life cycles, 82, 84, 324–326, 346
Line managers, 208–209
as decision-making leaders, 6
at work, 6
contrasted with staff managers, 60–72, 73–80, 97–109, 212–219, 308–320

Production operations
  implications of interrelationship with corporate
      strategy, 24–25
Productivity
  barriers to improvement of, 207–208
  competing on, 204–210
  defense industry, in, 283–290
  director of, 212
  factories in general, comparisons, of, 232–241
  improvement, 207–208, 234–235
  measurement of, 192–193, 205–207, 215, 232
  organizing for improvement of, 208–209
  performance, 213
  portfolios of, 209–210
  programs, 204–211, 212–219
  quality and, 192–193
  route to superior, 209
  strategic approaches to, 210
Program Evaluation and Review Techniques (PERT),
      328
Programs (task-oriented), 273
Project Management, 328
  at Allstate, 332–343
  at Boeing, 376–391
  at Lehrer McGovern Bovis, Inc., 400–404
Project Nantucket (of Ford Motor Company), 358–375
Purchasing, 132–148, 172–199, 442

Q

Quality, 126–131
  analysis of, 191–203
  assessment of, 182
  awareness, 188, 463
  classifying plants by performance, 200–203
  closing U.S.-Japanese gap in, 200
  competitive advantage, 127
  competitive priority, 3
  control, 131, 438
  costs of, 128, 185–186, 188–189, 193–194, 462–463
  definition of, 127–128, 187–188
  dimensions of, 126–131
  five states of awareness, 188
  future of, 157
  improvement, 126–127, 150–152, 188–190, 200,
      446, 457, 461, 463, 478
  information systems, 130, 196
  Japanese management of, 130, 184
      See also Japan
  management, 126–127, 130–131, 188–189, 466
  measuring, 126, 128–129, 191–194, 454–455
  on the line, 191–203
  phases of, 411–412
  product design and, 196–198
  product stability and, 198
  production and work force policies and, 198–199
  productivity and, 192–193
  programs, policies, attitudes, and, 185, 194–196
  research methods in determining, 197

  sources of, 129–130, 194–200
  standards of, 150–151, 172–175
  strategic management of, 130–131
  total quality concept (TQC), 349
  various elements of, 4
  vendor management, 199–200
  views on, 180–190
Quality assurance (QA)
  at American Food and Grains, 135, 139–141
Quality Is Free, 451
    See also Quality
Quality planning, 126, 186 (chart), 452

R

Reich, Robert B., xvii
Release-ease. See Applichem
Remanufacturing, 470–471, 475–476
Research, 214, 225–231, 265, 274–275
  focus of, 335
  product, 325
Research and development, xiv, 53–54, 60, 137–139,
      158, 284–285, 309, 347
Research methods, 191, 197
Retail industry, 149–157
Return on investment, 193, 288, 297, 371
Reynolds Aluminum, 8
Richardson, Peter R., xvii
Riggs, Henry E., 331
RIM polymer project. See Allstate
Risks, 329–330
  at Boeing, 376–391
  at Lehrer McGovern Bovis, Inc., 392–407
  at Vought, 291–295
Robertson, Arthur L., xvii
Rogers Corporation, The, 345–357
  company background of, 345
  company organization of
    manufacturing, 348–349
    marketing, 348
    product groups and divisions, 346–347
    research and development (R&D), 347–348
  electroluminescent lamps (EL) project background,
      349–352
    key decisions concerning, 355–357
    market for, 351 (chart)
    product and process development from 1982–1984,
      352–355
    production needs for, 351 (chart)
    profit and loss projections for, 353 (chart)
  Flex-Key Corporation division of, 349, 355–357
  technology, markets, and strategy of, 345–346
  "total quality concept" (TQC) of, 349
Roosevelt, Franklin, 80
Rosenbloom, Richard S., 331
Ruch, William A., 211

organizational changes, 301
  IMOD, 301
  manufacturing development and support, 301
productivity improvement, 207

W

Wages, 54, 64, 125
Warranty costs, 193–194
Warwick Electronics Corporation, 172, 173
Wasserman, Neil H., xvii
Waste reduction, 235–236
Waterman, Robert H., 423
Weapons systems, 283–285
  development of, 285
Werther, William B., 211
Westerman, William L., 331
Wheelwright, Steven C., xvii, 6–7, 110, 330, 331,
        423, 484
White House Conference on Productivity (1983), 127
Wiersema, Frederick D., 193
Wight, O., 442
Wimmert, Robert J., 331
Women's Wear Daily (periodical), 153
Work in process (WIP), 66, 236
Workforce, 16–17, 37, 92, 198–199, 251–253, 489–490
  See also Employees
World class manufacturing, ix–xvi, 2–6, 414–415,
        428–439

X

Xerox Corporation, 49

Y

Yamaha (company), 130, 158, 165–167, 171

Z

Z-Glass project. *See* Corning Glass Works
Zerger, Billie Jo, 331
Zero defects, 494
  Crosby, Philip B., 188
  planning, 464–465